≫ A NORTON CRITICAL EDITION ≪

SAMUEL LANGHORNE CLEMENS

ADVENTURES OF
HUCKLEBERRY FINN

AN ANNOTATED TEXT
BACKGROUNDS AND SOURCES
ESSAYS IN CRITICISM

≫ ≪

Edited by

SCULLEY BRADLEY
UNIVERSITY OF PENNSYLVANIA

RICHMOND CROOM BEATTY
LATE OF VANDERBILT UNIVERSITY

E. HUDSON LONG
BAYLOR UNIVERSITY

≫ ≪

W · W · NORTON & COMPANY · INC · *New York*

➤➤➤ W. W. Norton & Company, Inc. is also the publisher of
The Norton Anthology of English Literature, edited by M. H.
Abrams, Robert M. Adams, David Daiches, E. Talbot Donaldson,
George H. Ford, Samuel Holt Monk, and Hallett Smith; *The
American Tradition in Literature*, edited by Sculley Bradley, Rich-
mond Croom Beatty, and E. Hudson Long; *World Masterpieces*,
edited by Maynard Mack, Kenneth Douglas, Howard E. Hugo,
Bernard M. W. Knox, John C. McGalliard, P. M. Pasinetti,
and René Wellek; and *The Norton Reader*, edited by Arthur M.
Eastman, Caesar R. Blake, Hubert M. English, Jr., Alan B. Howes,
Robert T. Lenaghan, Leo F. McNamara, and James Rosier.

SBN 393 05324 5   Cloth Edition
SBN 393 09506 1   Paper Edition

PRINTED IN THE UNITED STATES OF AMERICA

456789

Contents

Essays in Criticism

Introduction

Several generations of Americans have read this, Mark Twain's masterpiece, with undiminished affection, because for each generation increasingly it has recaptured a lost world of childhood and an earlier reality of their country which it is valuable to keep in memory. But in the largest sense, "only adults will read it," as its author less aptly remarked of *Tom Sawyer.* On the adult level this is a complex work of art, sometimes approaching profundity in its psychological perceptions, its moral judgments, and its social criticism. It is precisely located in place and time; yet by its power and its truth it has attained universal recognition as a classic.

In structure, *Adventures of Huckleberry Finn* resembles the earliest and simplest form of the novel. In the novella known to Chaucer, just as in the earliest British novels shaped by Defoe or Fielding, the form was episodic; so was the frontier narrative that first influenced Mark Twain. In its most popular examples this literature always dealt with the roguish adventures of characters ranging from fantastic pranksters to genuine badmen. This "picaresque" element was prominent in the burlesque romances, such as *Don Quixote* and *Gil Blas,* which inspired Mark Twain, in this book and elsewhere, in making his attack on the shams of romantic chivalry.

Huckleberry Finn was a literary creation from materials which were traditional in the sense that the humor, folkways, legends, and speech of a country are a common inheritance. Such characters as the duke, the king, Widow Douglas, and Colonels Grangerford and Sherburn, however much Twain individualized them, were recognizably derived from frontier legend and its literature. Mark Twain's accretions for this novel came first from his boyhood experience many years before, and second from a process not unusual in the literary shaping of traditional sources. He once said that he wrote on a plan of "spontaneous combustion," but in this case the spontaneity was only sporadically sustained. The book, like its legendary sources, had to grow up; the eight years' lapse between the beginning and the conclusion of this composition were necessary to let the book "make up its mind," as Twain said. He began in 1876 what he called then "another boy's book * * * more to be at work than for anything else," and he carried it through the first sixteen chapters, when the raft has missed the mouth of the Ohio and gone below freedom-land. In two spurts during 1879 and 1880 he added five chapters, bringing the narrative through the Grangerford feud and the Sherburn-Boggs incident at Bricksville. He then abandoned it. Huck somewhere remarks, "Providence always did put the right words in my mouth, if I left it alone"; and two years later, this happened to the author as the result of a long summer visit among the old scenes on the Mississippi. In a burst of inspiration he finished the book in the next eighteen months.

His inspiration fulfilled again the exuberant demands of a literary genre long neglected. Twain's novel is, as Fielding called his early work, a "comic epic in prose": comic, because it employs great strokes of wit and humor—and the scourge of laughter—to attack the evils of mankind and the consequent sins of society; epic, because its moving force, the great River, is also a stream in time and in history, bearing its raft of argonauts to various shores where lie the relics, wrecks, and hopes of a civilization in transition. As his narrator, Twain chose Huck; this was a clear act of genius. Huck "had known and suffered all" that was on the River, and he could speak expertly, in the speech of the author's boyhood Hannibal. In the speech of Huck Finn Twain fashioned a new literary language in colloquial American, seen at its best in the descriptions of the River, where the cadences and vigor of the spoken language are expressed by a great artist with such authority that a whole generation of realistic authors, from Sherwood Anderson to Hemingway and Faulkner, were influenced. As Eliot remarked, "like Dryden and Swift," he brought the language "up to date."

The River is a fundamental element in the structure of this novel, but it is also the central symbol to which other symbolic elements are referred. "It's lovely to live on a raft," says Huck, and "sometimes we'd have that whole river to ourselves for the longest time." The literary discovery of the River, which we owe to Mark Twain, made it part of a continental myth somewhat similar to those of the Ganges, the Nile, and the Amazon, rivers which were also gods. In this story the River accorded with Huck's loneliness; and whether it ravened the land or was at peace, it was a clean and trustworthy reality for Jim, a fugitive from slavery, and Huck, fleeing from all the brutality of "civilization" epitomized in his father. The Pokesvilles and Bricksvilles along the shore were not all bad, nor were the people, yet their pollution was always sufficiently evident to make the return to the raft a repeated experience of regeneration. Even though they were driven by the storm beyond the mouth of the Ohio, which was the gateway to legal freedom for the slave, the River and the raft still offered the best freedom of all. The intrusion of the king and the duke upon this sanctuary, although it brought such evil as only the community of man could foster, was not disastrous, so long as they all remained on the raft, where, as

Huck says, it is necessary "for everybody to * * * feel right and kind toward the others." This is the epitome of this novel's social criticism. Whatever evil appeared in society was the evil of men, and Twain here used Huck to carry on his relentless excoriation of "the damned human race," and to condemn stereotypes of right and wrong with which the rulers of society justified their own selfish interests. In this novel the representative stereotype was slavery. Huck had to battle with his conscience continuously, because according to the morality of society and church, he should report as a runaway slave this Jim whom he had come to love as a brother. His final decision in Jim's favor was concluded with his famous reflection, "All right, then, I'll go to hell!" Yet when Aunt Sally asked whether the steamboat explosion hurt anyone, he automatically responded, "No'm. Killed a nigger."

The English edition of *Huckleberry Finn* appeared on December 4, 1884, some time before the first American copies, dated 1885, were officially received for copyright. The present text follows a photographic reproduction of the first American edition, first issue, 1885, with the annotated correction of typographical errors.

In deciding to include with the text a collection of criticism, the editors had in mind their own experience with groups of students primarily interested in studying the book itself as a work of literature. We rejected principles of selection and organization which might have been given preference had it been our object to represent the history of the scholarship or the varieties of critical method that have been motivated by the problems of *Huckleberry Finn*. Within the limits of the space available the editors have preferred to assemble critical writings, excellent in themselves, which have suffused with insight the intrinsic characteristics of this work of art, its evocation of values inherent in the culture of a people, its power to extend itself into the continuous experience of successive generations of readers.

Yet in selecting such works and arranging them in the order of their appearance, certain patterns were automatically revealed. Beginning in the year of the novel's publication, four of the first five critics, two British and two American, show concern for the supposed crudity of the psychological and social experience of the American West which the book somehow transcended. About 1950 such authors as Lionel Trilling and T. S. Eliot memorably praised the novel's symbolic power and spiritual insight; Leo Marx represented a group who in opposition noted the novel's flaws of structure, sensibility, or sociological rectitude—five articles, pro and con, represent this critical debate. The Contents page shows four of those who participated in another debate, about five years later, which arose when Lauriat Lane wrote that *Huckleberry Finn* was a

great world novel and William Van O'Connor replied that it was not
even the great American novel. The concluding essays represent the
increasing sophistication and complexity of recent criticism, and a
tendency to project the experience of Huck and Jim into universal
aspects of the human experience.

The first group of selections following the text of the novel
represents some Backgrounds and Sources; brief notes included there
may explain the connection of these primitive materials with the
personal and American experience which formed the matrix of this
novel. The foreground of this fiction was the Mid-American continental culture during the early life of Mark Twain; nevertheless,
even a few illustrations may show the gulf between the epic artist
and his sources. The bibliography at the end of the volume, listing
writings concerning Mark Twain and *Huck Finn*, is intended as a
judicious selection.

S. B., R. C. B., E. H. L.

A Note on the
Texts and Documentation

Since the editors share the concern for the teaching of scholarly
fidelity in the documentation of research work, we list here the
editorial principles we have followed in reproducing the source
materials and critical essays included in this Critical Edition. The
text for each selection is printed from a photographic facsimile of
the original publication, and, in each case, the footnote numbers
are those of the original. The first footnote for each title is a bibli-
ographical record of the item, giving its source and the original page
numbers. Occasional additional footnotes supplied by the editors are
indicated by a dagger (†) and the bracketed word "[Editors]." Titles
of selections not original with their authors have been enclosed in
brackets.

The majority of the articles have been printed in their entirety.
Where matter irrelevant to this book has been excluded, the deletion
is indicated by three asterisks; where a deletion is extensive, we have
usually noted the general subject of the deleted material.

The editors have not, in this Critical Edition, followed the
practice of indicating the pagination of each original document
within the texts as here printed. In our opinion, the principle to be
taught is the scrupulous documentation of the present source of
reference, whether it be the first or later edition or a transcript.
The citation of the original source, if possible, should also be included for the benefit of others who may be able to consult it.
In the use of this Critical Edition for documented themes, the
researcher could be advised, in his first reference to any article
in the collection, to give the location, the date, and the pagination
of the original as shown in our first footnote, followed by the number of the page in the Critical Edition on which the quoted or
designated matter appears. A second reference to the same article
could be abbreviated to the author's name, with or without a short
title, followed by the page number in the Critical Edition.

Adventures of Huckleberry Finn

(TOM SAWYER'S COMRADE)
SCENE: THE MISSISSIPPI
TIME: FORTY TO FIFTY YEARS AGO

NOTICE

Persons attempting to find a motive in this narrative will be prosecuted; persons attempting to find a moral in it will be banished; persons attempting to find a plot in it will be shot.

BY ORDER OF THE AUTHOR
PER G. G., CHIEF OF ORDNANCE.

EXPLANATORY

In this book a number of dialects are used, to wit: the Missouri negro dialect; the extremest form of the backwoods South-Western dialect; the ordinary "Pike-County" dialect; and four modified varieties of this last. The shadings have not been done in a hap-hazard fashion, or by guess-work; but pains-takingly, and with the trustworthy guidance and support of personal familiarity with these several forms of speech.

I make this explanation for the reason that without it many readers would suppose that all these characters were trying to talk alike and not succeeding.

THE AUTHOR

Contents

Chapter I

You don't know about me, without you have read a book by the name of "The Adventures of Tom Sawyer,"[1] but that ain't no matter. That book was made by Mr. Mark Twain, and he told the truth, mainly. There was things which he stretched, but mainly he told the truth. That is nothing. I never seen anybody but lied, one time or another, without it was Aunt Polly, or the widow, or maybe Mary. Aunt Polly—Tom's Aunt Polly, she is—and Mary, and the Widow Douglas, is all told about in that book—which is mostly a true book; with some stretchers, as I said before.

Now the way that the book winds up, is this: Tom and me found the money that the robbers hid in the cave, and it made us rich. We got six thousand dollars apiece—all gold. It was an awful sight of money when it was piled up. Well, Judge Thatcher, he took it and put it out at interest, and it fetched us a dollar a day apiece, all the year round—more than a body could tell what to do with. The Widow Douglas, she took me for her son, and allowed she would sivilize me; but it was rough living in the house all the time, considering how dismal regular and decent the widow was in all her ways; and so when I couldn't stand it no longer, I lit out. I got into my old rags, and my sugar-hogshead[2] again, and was free and satisfied. But Tom Sawyer, he hunted me up and said he was going to start a band of robbers, and I might join if I would go back to the widow and be respectable. So I went back.

The widow she cried over me, and called me a poor lost lamb, and she called me a lot of other names, too, but she never meant no harm by it. She put me in them new clothes again, and I couldn't do nothing but sweat and sweat, and feel all cramped up. Well, then, the old thing commenced again. The widow rung a bell for supper, and you had to come to time. When you got to the table you couldn't go right to eating, but you had to wait for the widow to tuck down her head and grumble a little over the victuals, though there warn't really anything the matter with them. That is, nothing only everything was cooked by itself. In a barrel of odds and ends it is different; things get mixed up, and the juice kind of swaps around, and the things go better.

After supper she got out her book and learned me about Moses and the Bulrushers;[3] and I was in a sweat to find out all about him; but by-and-by she let it out that Moses had been dead a considerable long time; so then I didn't care no more about him; because I don't take stock in dead people.

Pretty soon I wanted to smoke, and asked the widow to let me. But she wouldn't. She said it was a mean practice and wasn't clean, and I must try to not do it any more. That is just the way with

1. Published nine years earlier, in 1876.
2. A large barrel, emptied of its shipment of sugar, Huck's place of refuge
behind the abandoned slaughterhouse. *Cf. Tom Sawyer*, Chapter XXXV.
3. *Cf.* Exodus ii: 1–10.

some people. They get down on a thing when they don't know nothing about it. Here she was a bothering about Moses, which was no kin to her, and no use to anybody, being gone, you see, yet finding a power of fault with me for doing a thing that had some good in it. And she took snuff too; of course that was all right, because she done it herself.

Her sister, Miss Watson, a tolerable slim old maid, with goggles on, had just come to live with her, and took a set at me now, with a spelling-book. She worked me middling hard for about an hour, and then the widow made her ease up. I couldn't stood it much longer. Then for an hour it was deadly dull, and I was fidgety. Miss Watson would say, "Dont put your feet up there, Huckleberry;" and "dont scrunch up like that, Huckleberry—set up straight;" and pretty soon she would say, "Don't gap and stretch like that, Huckleberry—why don't you try to behave?" Then she told me all about the bad place, and I said I wished I was there. She got mad, then, but I didn't mean no harm. All I wanted was to go somewheres; all I wanted was a change, I warn't particular. She said it was wicked to say what I said; said she wouldn't say it for the whole world; *she* was going to live so as to go to the good place. Well, I couldn't see no advantage in going where she was going, so I made up my mind I wouldn't try for it. But I never said so, because it would only make trouble, and wouldn't do no good.

Now she had got a start, and she went on and told me all about the good place. She said all a body would have to do there was to go around all day long with a harp and sing, forever and ever.[4] So I didn't think much of it. But I never said so. I asked her if she reckoned Tom Sawyer would go there, and, she said, not by a considerable sight. I was glad about that, because I wanted him and me to be together.

Miss Watson she kept pecking at me, and it got tiresome and lonesome. By-and-by they fetched the niggers[5] in and had prayers, and then everybody was off to bed. I went up to my room with a piece of candle and put it on the table. Then I set down in a chair by the window and tried to think of something cheerful, but it warn't no use. I felt so lonesome I most wished I was dead.[6] The stars was shining, and the leaves rustled in the woods ever so mournful; and I heard an owl, away off, who-whooing about somebody that was dead, and a whippowill and a dog crying about somebody that was going to die; and the wind was trying to whisper

---

4. The traditional pearly-gate concept of heaven was again ridiculed by Twain in *Extract from Captain Stormfield's Visit to Heaven* (1907).
5. In slave states, "nigger" was not necessarily an abusive word, but merely the ordinary colloquial term for a slave.
6. The essential loneliness of the individual, a recurrent theme in Twain's work, is best symbolized in the boy, Huck, confronted, as in the following passage, by the vast wilderness of forests and waters. His superstitious fancies, although common to all boyhood, are an emotional verification of an American frontier experience.

something to me and I couldn't make out what it was, and so it made the cold shivers run over me. Then away out in the woods I heard that kind of a sound that a ghost makes when it wants to tell about something that's on its mind and can't make itself understood, and so can't rest easy in its grave and has to go about that way every night grieving. I got so down-hearted and scared, I did wish I had some company. Pretty soon a spider went crawling up my shoulder, and I flipped it off and it lit in the candle; and before I could budge it was all shriveled up. I didn't need anybody to tell me that that was an awful bad sign and would fetch me some bad luck, so I was scared and most shook the clothes off of me. I got up and turned around in my tracks three times and crossed my breast every time; and then I tied up a little lock of my hair with a thread to keep witches away. But I hadn't no confidence. You do that when you've lost a horse-shoe that you've found, instead of nailing it up over the door, but I hadn't ever heard anybody say it was any way to keep off bad luck when you'd killed a spider.

I set down again, a shaking all over, and got out my pipe for a smoke; for the house was all as still as death, now, and so the widow wouldn't know. Well, after a long time I heard the clock away off in the town go boom—boom—boom—twelve licks—and all still again—stiller than ever. Pretty soon I heard a twig snap, down in the dark amongst the trees—something was a stirring. I set still and listened. Directly I could just barely hear a *"me-yow! me-yow!"* down there. That was good! Says I, *"me-yow! me-yow!"* as soft as I could, and then I put out the light and scrambled out of the window onto the shed. Then I slipped down to the ground and crawled in amongst the trees, and sure enough there was Tom Sawyer waiting for me.

Chapter II

We went tip-toeing along a path amongst the trees back towards the end of the widow's garden, stooping down so as the branches wouldn't scrape our heads. When we was passing by the kitchen I fell over a root and made a noise. We scrouched down and laid still. Miss Watson's big nigger, named Jim, was setting in the kitchen door; we could see him pretty clear, because there was a light behind him. He got up and stretched his neck out about a minute, listening. Then he says,

"Who dah?"

He listened some more; then he come tip-toeing down and stood right between us; we could a touched him, nearly. Well, likely it was minutes and minutes that there warn't a sound, and we all there so close together. There was a place on my ankle that got to itching; but I dasn't scratch it; and then my ear begun to itch; and next my back, right between my shoulders. Seemed like

I'd die if I couldn't scratch. Well, I've noticed that thing plenty of times since. If you are with the quality, or at a funeral, or trying to go to sleep when you ain't sleepy—if you are anywhere where it won't do for you to scratch, why you will itch all over in upwards of a thousand places. Pretty soon Jim says:

"Say—who is you? Whar is you? Dog my cats ef I didn' hear sumf'n. Well, I knows what I's gwyne to do. I's gwyne to set down here and listen tell I hears it agin."

So he set down on the ground betwixt me and Tom. He leaned his back up against a tree, and stretched his legs out till one of them most touched one of mine. My nose begun to itch. It itched till the tears come into my eyes. But I dasn't scratch. Then it begun to itch on the inside. Next I got to itching underneath. I didn't know how I was going to set still. This miserableness went on as much as six or seven minutes; but it seemed a sight longer than that. I was itching in eleven different places now. I reckoned I couldn't stand it more'n a minute longer, but I set my teeth hard and got ready to try. Just then Jim begun to breathe heavy; next he begun to snore—and then I was pretty soon comfortable again.

Tom he made a sign to me—kind of a little noise with his mouth—and we went creeping away on our hands and knees. When we was ten foot off, Tom whispered to me and wanted to tie Jim to the tree for fun; but I said no; he might wake and make a disturbance, and then they'd find out I warn't in. Then Tom said he hadn't got candles enough, and he would slip in the kitchen and get some more. I didn't want him to try. I said Jim might wake up and come. But Tom wanted to resk it; so we slid in there and got three candles, and Tom laid five cents on the table for pay. Then we got out, and I was in a sweat to get away; but nothing would do Tom but he must crawl to where Jim was, on his hands and knees, and play something on him. I waited, and it seemed a good while, everything was so still and lonesome.

As soon as Tom was back, we cut along the path, around the garden fence, and by-and-by fetched up on the steep top of the hill the other side of the house. Tom said he slipped Jim's hat off of his head and hung it on a limb right over him, and Jim stirred a little, but he didn't wake. Afterwards Jim said the witches bewitched him and put him in a trance, and rode him all over the State, and then set him under the trees again and hung his hat on a limb to show who done it. And next time Jim told it he said they rode him down to New Orleans; and after that, every time he told it he spread it more and more, till by-and-by he said they rode him all over the world, and tired him most to death, and his back was all over saddle-boils. Jim was monstrous proud about it, and he got so he wouldn't hardly notice the other niggers. Niggers would come miles to hear Jim tell about it, and he was more looked up to than any nigger in that country. Strange niggers would stand with their mouths open and look him all over, same as if he was a wonder. Niggers is always talking about witches in the dark by the kitchen fire; but whenever one was talking and letting on to know all about such things, Jim would happen in and say, "Hm! What you know 'bout witches?" and that nigger was corked up and had to take a back seat. Jim always kept that five-center piece around his neck with a string and said it was a charm the devil give to him with his own hands and told him he could cure anybody with it and fetch witches whenever he wanted to, just by saying something to it; but he never told what it was he said to it. Niggers would come from all around there and give Jim anything they had, just for a sight of that five-center piece; but they wouldn't touch it, because the devil had had his hands on it. Jim was most ruined, for a servant, because he got so stuck up on account of having seen the devil and been rode by witches.

Well, when Tom and me got to the edge of the hill-top, we looked away down into the village[7] and could see three or four lights twinkling, where there was sick folks, may be; and the stars over us was sparkling ever so fine; and down by the village was the river, a whole mile broad, and awful still and grand. We went down the hill and found Jo Harper, and Ben Rogers, and two or three more of the boys, hid in the old tanyard. So we unhitched a skiff and pulled down the river two mile and a half, to the big scar on the hillside, and went ashore.

We went to a clump of bushes, and Tom made everybody swear to keep the secret, and then showed them a hole in the hill, right in the thickest part of the bushes. Then we lit the candles and crawled in on our hands and knees. We went about two hundred yards, and then the cave opened up. Tom poked about amongst the passages and pretty soon ducked under a wall where you wouldn't a noticed that there was a hole. We went along a narrow place and got into a kind of room, all damp and sweaty and cold, and there we stopped. Tom says:

"Now we'll start this band of robbers and call it Tom Sawyer's Gang. Everybody that wants to join has got to take an oath, and write his name in blood."

Everybody was willing. So Tom got out a sheet of paper that he had wrote the oath on, and read it. It swore every boy to stick to the band, and never tell any of its secrets; and if anybody done anything to any boy in the band, whichever boy was ordered to kill

7. Hannibal, Missouri; other frontier river towns described in this book really portray various aspects of Hannibal.

that person and his family must do it, and he mustn't eat and he mustn't sleep till he had killed them and hacked a cross in their breasts, which was the sign of the band. And nobody that didn't belong to the band could use that mark, and if he did he must be sued; and if he done it again he must be killed. And if anybody that belonged to the band told the secrets, he must have his throat cut, and then have his carcass burnt up and the ashes scattered all around, and his name blotted off of the list with blood and never mentioned again by the gang, but have a curse put on it and be forgot, forever.

Everybody said it was a real beautiful oath, and asked Tom if he got it out of his own head. He said, some of it, but the rest was out of pirate books, and robber books, and every gang that was high-toned had it.[8]

Some thought it would be good to kill the *families* of boys that told the secrets. Tom said it was a good idea, so he took a pencil and wrote it in. Then Ben Rogers says:

"Here's Huck Finn, he hain't got no family—what you going to do 'bout him?"

"Well, hain't he got a father?" says Tom Sawyer.

"Yes, he's got a father, but you can't never find him, these days. He used to lay drunk with the hogs in the tanyard, but he hain't been seen in these parts for a year or more."

They talked it over, and they was going to rule me out, because they said every boy must have a family or somebody to kill, or else it wouldn't be fair and square for the others. Well, nobody could think of anything to do—everybody was stumped, and set still. I was most ready to cry; but all at once I thought of a way, and so I offered them Miss Watson—they could kill her. Everybody said:

"Oh, she'll do, she'll do. That's all right. Huck can come in."

Then they all stuck a pin in their fingers to get blood to sign with, and I made my mark on the paper.

"Now," says Ben Rogers, "what's the line of business of this Gang?"

"Nothing only robbery and murder," Tom said.

"But who are we going to rob? houses—or cattle—or—"

"Stuff! stealing cattle and such things ain't robbery, it's burglary," says Tom Sawyer. "We ain't burglars. That ain't no sort of style. We are highwaymen. We stop stages and carriages on the road, with masks on, and kill the people and take their watches and money."

"Must we always kill the people?"

8. Twain's comic portrayal of the boy's world of make-believe is consistent with his ridicule of romantic fiction and its writers.

"Oh, certainly. It's best. Some authorities think different, but mostly it's considered best to kill them. Except some that you bring to the cave here and keep them till they're ransomed."

"Ransomed? What's that?"

"I don't know. But that's what they do. I've seen it in books; and so of course that's what we've got to do."

"But how can we do it if we don't know what it is?"

"Why blame it all, we've *got* to do it. Don't I tell you it's in the books? Do you want to go to doing different from what's in the books, and get things all muddled up?"

"Oh, that's all very fine to *say*, Tom Sawyer, but how in the nation[9] are these fellows going to be ransomed if we don't know how to do it to them? that's the thing I want to get at. Now what do you *reckon* it is?"

"Well I don't know. But per'aps if we keep them till they're ransomed, it means that we keep them till they're dead."

"Now, that's something *like*. That'll answer. Why couldn't you said that before? We'll keep them till they're ransomed to death —and a bothersome lot they'll be, too, eating up everything and always trying to get loose."

"How you talk, Ben Rogers. How can they get loose when there's a guard over them, ready to shoot them down if they move a peg?"

"A guard. Well, that *is* good. So somebody's got to set up all night and never get any sleep, just so as to watch them. I think that's foolishness. Why can't a body take a club and ransom them as soon as they get here?"

"Because it ain't in the books so—that's why. Now Ben Rogers, do you want to do things regular, or don't you?—that's the idea. Don't you reckon that the people that made the books knows what's the correct thing to do? Do you reckon *you* can learn 'em anything? Not by a good deal. No, sir, we'll just go on and ransom them in the regular way."

"All right. I don't mind; but I say it's a fool way, anyhow. Say —do we kill the women, too?"

"Well, Ben Rogers, if I was as ignorant as you I wouldn't let on. Kill the women? No—nobody ever saw anything in the books like that. You fetch them to the cave, and you're always as polite as pie to them; and by-and-by they fall in love with you and never want to go home any more."

"Well, if that's the way, I'm agreed, but I don't take no stock in it. Mighty soon we'll have the cave so cluttered up with women, and fellows waiting to be ransomed, that there won't be no place for the robbers. But go ahead, I ain't got nothing to say."

9. Euphemism for "damnation."

Little Tommy Barnes was asleep, now, and when they waked him up he was scared, and cried, and said he wanted to go home to his ma, and didn't want to be a robber any more.

So they all made fun of him, and called him cry-baby, and that made him mad, and he said he would go straight and tell all the secrets. But Tom give him five cents to keep quiet, and said we would all go home and meet next week and rob somebody and kill some people.

Ben Rogers said he couldn't get out much, only Sundays, and so he wanted to begin next Sunday; but all the boys said it would be wicked to do it on Sunday, and that settled the thing. They agreed to get together and fix a day as soon as they could, and then we elected Tom Sawyer first captain and Jo Harper second captain of the Gang, and so started home.

I clumb up the shed and crept into my window just before day was breaking. My new clothes was all greased up and clayey, and I was dog-tired.

Chapter III

Well, I got a good going-over in the morning, from old Miss Watson, on account of my clothes; but the widow she didn't scold, but only cleaned off the grease and clay and looked so sorry that I thought I would behave a while if I could. Then Miss Watson she took me in the closet and prayed, but nothing come of it. She told me to pray every day, and whatever I asked for I would get it. But it warn't so. I tried it. Once I got a fish-line, but no hooks. It warn't any good to me without hooks. I tried for the hooks three or four times, but somehow I couldn't make it work. By-and-by, one day, I asked Miss Watson to try for me, but she said I was a fool. She never told me why, and I couldn't make it out no way.

I set down, one time, back in the woods, and had a long think about it. I says to myself, if a body can get anything they pray for, why don't Deacon Winn get back the money he lost on pork? Why can't the widow get back her silver snuff-box that was stole? Why can't Miss Watson fat up? No, says I to myself, there ain't nothing in it. I went and told the widow about it, and she said the thing a body could get by praying for it was "spiritual gifts." This was too many for me, but she told me what she meant—I must help other people, and do everything I could for other people, and look out for them all the time, and never think about myself. This was including Miss Watson, as I took it. I went out in the woods and turned it over in my mind a long time, but I couldn't see no advantage about it—except for the other people—so at last I reckoned I wouldn't worry about it any more, but just let it go.

Sometimes the widow would take me one side and talk about Providence in a way to make a boy's mouth water; but maybe next day Miss Watson would take hold and knock it all down again. I judged I could see that there was two Providences, and a poor chap would stand considerable show with the widow's Providence, but if Miss Watson's got him there warn't no help for him any more. I thought it all out, and reckoned I would belong to the widow's, if he wanted me, though I couldn't make out how he was agoing to be any better off then than what he was before, seeing I was so ignorant and so kind of low-down and ornery.[1]

Pap he hadn't been seen for more than a year, and that was comfortable for me; I didn't want to see him no more. He used to always whale me when he was sober and could get his hands on me; though I used to take to the woods most of the time when he was around. Well, about this time he was found in the river drowned, about twelve miles above town, so people said. They judged it was him, anyway; said this drowned man was just his size, and was ragged, and had uncommon long hair—which was all like pap—but they couldn't make nothing out of the face, because it had been in the water so long it warn't much like a face at all. They said he was floating on his back in the water. They took him and buried him on the bank. But I warn't comfortable long, because I happened to think of something. I knowed mighty well that a drownded man don't float on his back, but on his face. So I knowed, then, that this warn't pap, but a woman dressed up in a man's clothes. So I was uncomfortable again. I judged the old man would turn up again by-and-by, though I wished he wouldn't.

We played robber now and then about a month, and then I resigned. All the boys did. We hadn't robbed nobody, we hadn't killed any people, but only just pretended. We used to hop out of the woods and go charging down on hog-drovers and women in carts taking garden stuff to market, but we never hived any of them. Tom Sawyer called the hogs "ingots," and he called the turnips and stuff "julery" and we would go to the cave and pow-wow over what we had done and how many people we had killed and marked. But I couldn't see no profit in it. One time Tom sent a boy to run about town with a blazing stick, which he called a slogan (which was the sign for the Gang to get together), and then he said he had got secret news by his spies that the next day a whole parcel of Spanish merchants and rich A-rabs was going to camp in Cave Hollow with two hundred elephants, and six hundred camels, and over a thousand "sumter" mules, all loaded with di'monds, and they didn't have only a guard of four hundred sol-

1. Like Huck, the author pondered religious faith. Of the many instances in his writings, the massive example is *The Mysterious Stranger*. His comic criticism is largely of sentimentality and cant.

diers, and so we would lay in ambuscade, as he called it, and kill the lot and scoop the things. He said we must slick up our swords and guns, and get ready. He never could go after even a turnip-cart but he must have the swords and guns all scoured up for it; though they was only lath and broom-sticks, and you might scour at them till you rotted and then they warn't worth a mouthful of ashes more than what they was before. I didn't believe we could lick such a crowd of Spaniards and A-rabs, but I wanted to see the camels and elephants, so I was on hand next day, Saturday, in the ambuscade; and when we got the word, we rushed out of the woods and down the hill. But there warn't no Spaniards and A-rabs, and there warn't no camels nor no elephants. It warn't anything but a Sunday-school picnic, and only a primer-class at that. We busted it up, and chased the children up the hollow; but we never got anything but some doughnuts and jam, though Ben Rogers got a rag doll, and Jo Harper got a hymn-book and a tract; and then the teacher charged in and made us drop everything and cut. I didn't see no di'monds, and I told Tom Sawyer so. He said there was loads of them there, anyway; and he said there was A-rabs there, too, and elephants and things. I said, why couldn't we see them, then? He said if I warn't so ignorant, but had read a book called "Don Quixote," I would know without asking. He said it was all done by enchantment. He said there was hundreds of soldiers there, and elephants and treasure, and so on, but we had enemies which he called magicians, and they had turned the whole thing into an infant Sunday school, just for spite. I said, all right, then the thing for us to do was to go for the magicians. Tom Sawyer said I was a numskull.

"Why," says he, "a magician could call up a lot of genies, and they would hash you up like nothing before you could say Jack Robinson. They are as tall as a tree and as big around as a church."

"Well," I says, "s'pose we got some genies to help *us*—can't we lick the other crowd then?"

"How are you going to get them?"

"I don't know. How do *they* get them?"

"Why they rub an old tin lamp or an iron ring, and then the genies come tearing in, with the thunder and lightning a-ripping around and the smoke a-rolling, and everything they're told to do they up and do it. They don't think nothing of pulling a shot tower up by the roots, and belting a Sunday-school superintendent over the head with it—or any other man."[2]

---

2. The foregoing medley of events drawn from the ancient *Arabian Nights* (Aladdin's lamp) and Cervantes' seventeenth-century *Don Quixote* represents a cross-section of Tom's mind and Twain's memory of his childhood reading. More importantly, these make-believe adventures provide the background for the real experience of Huck and Jim in the escape down the river.

"Who makes them tear around so?"

"Why, whoever rubs the lamp or the ring. They belong to whoever rubs the lamp or the ring, and they've got to do whatever he says. If he tells them to build a palace forty miles long, out of di'monds, and fill it full of chewing gum, or whatever you want, and fetch an emperor's daughter from China for you to marry, they've got to do it—and they've got to do it before sun-up next morning, too. And more—they've got to waltz that palace around over the country wherever you want it, you understand."

"Well," says I, "I think they are a pack of fatheads for not keeping the palace themselves 'stead of fooling them away like that. And what's more—if I was one of them I would see a man in Jericho before I would drop my business and come to him for the rubbing of an old tin lamp."

"How you talk, Huck Finn. Why, you'd *have* to come when he rubbed it, whether you wanted to or not."

"What, and I as high as a tree and as big as a church? All right, then; I *would* come; but I lay I'd make that man climb the highest tree there was in the country."

"Shucks, it ain't no use to talk to you, Huck Finn. You don't seem to know anything, somehow—perfect sap-head."

I thought all this over for two or three days, and then I reckoned I would see if there was anything in it. I got an old tin lamp and an iron ring and went out in the woods and rubbed and rubbed till I sweat like an Injun, calculating to build a palace and sell it; but it warn't no use, none of the genies came. So then I judged that all that stuff was only just one of Tom Sawyer's lies. I reckoned he believed in the A-rabs and the elephants, but as for me I think different. It had all the marks of a Sunday school.[3]

Chapter IV

Well, three or four months run along, and it was well into the winter, now. I had been to school most all the time, and could spell, and read, and write just a little, and could say the multiplication table up to six times seven is thirty-five, and I don't reckon I could ever get any further than that if I was to live forever. I don't take no stock in mathematics, anyway.

At first I hated the school, but by-and-by I got so I could stand it. Whenever I got uncommon tired I played hookey, and the hiding I got next day done me good and cheered me up. So the longer I went to school the easier it got to be. I was getting sort of used to the widow's ways, too, and they warn't so raspy on me. Living in a

3. Huck identifies the fanciful elements of romance with the supernatural elements of religion.

house, and sleeping in a bed, pulled on me pretty tight, mostly, but before the cold weather I used to slide out and sleep in the woods, sometimes, and so that was a rest to me. I liked the old ways best, but I was getting so I liked the new ones, too, a little bit. The widow said I was coming along slow but sure, and doing very satisfactory. She said she warn't ashamed of me.

One morning I happened to turn over the salt-cellar at breakfast. I reached for some of it as quick as I could, to throw over my left shoulder and keep off the bad luck, but Miss Watson was in ahead of me, and crossed me off. She says, "Take your hands away, Huckleberry—what a mess you are always making." The widow put in a good word for me, but that warn't going to keep off the bad luck, I knowed that well enough. I started out, after breakfast, feeling worried and shaky, and wondering where it was going to fall on me, and what it was going to be. There is ways to keep off some kinds of bad luck, but this wasn't one of them kind; so I never tried to do anything, but just poked along low-spirited and on the watch-out.

I went down the front garden and clumb over the stile, where you go through the high board fence. There was an inch of new snow on the ground, and I seen somebody's tracks. They had come up from the quarry and stood around the stile a while, and then went on around the garden fence. It was funny they hadn't come in, after standing around so. I couldn't make it out. It was very curious, somehow. I was going to follow around, but I stooped down to look at the tracks first. I didn't notice anything at first, but next I did. There was a cross in the left boot-heel made with big nails, to keep off the devil.

I was up in a second and shinning down the hill. I looked over my shoulder every now and then, but I didn't see nobody. I was at Judge Thatcher's as quick as I could get there. He said:

"Why, my boy, you are all out of breath. Did you come for your interest?"

"No sir," I says; "is there some for me?"

"Oh, yes, a half-yearly is in, last night. Over a hundred and fifty dollars. Quite a fortune for you. You better let me invest it along with your six thousand, because if you take it you'll spend it."

"No sir," I says, "I don't want to spend it. I don't want it at all —nor the six thousand, nuther. I want you to take it; I want to give it to you—the six thousand and all."

He looked surprised. He couldn't seem to make it out. He says:

"Why, what can you mean, my boy?"

I says, "Don't you ask me no questions about it, please. You'll take it—won't you?"

He says:

"Well I'm puzzled. Is something the matter?"

"Please take it," says I, "and don't ask me nothing—then I won't have to tell no lies."

He studied a while, and then he says:

"Oho-o. I think I see. You want to *sell* all your property to me—not give it. That's the correct idea."

Then he wrote something on a paper and read it over, and says:

"There—you see it says 'for a consideration.' That means I have bought it of you and paid you for it. Here's a dollar for you. Now, you sign it."

So I signed it, and left.

Miss Watson's nigger, Jim, had a hair-ball as big as your fist, which had been took out of the fourth stomach of an ox, and he used to do magic with it.[4] He said there was a spirit inside of it, and it knowed everything. So I went to him that night and told him pap was here again, for I found his tracks in the snow. What I wanted to know, was, what he was going to do, and was he going to stay? Jim got out his hair-ball, and said something over it, and then he held it up and dropped it on the floor. It fell pretty solid, and only rolled about an inch. Jim tried it again, and then another time, and it acted just the same. Jim got down on his knees and put his ear against it and listened. But it warn't no use; he said it wouldn't talk. He said sometimes it wouldn't talk without money. I told him I had an old slick counterfeit quarter that warn't no good because the brass showed through the silver a little, and it wouldn't pass nohow, even if the brass didn't show, because it was so slick it felt greasy, and so that would tell on it every time. (I reckoned I wouldn't say nothing about the dollar I got from the judge.) I said it was pretty bad money, but maybe the hair-ball would take it, because maybe it wouldn't know the difference. Jim smelt it, and bit it, and rubbed it, and said he would manage so the hair-ball would think it was good. He said he would split open a raw Irish potato and stick the quarter in between and keep it there all night, and next morning you couldn't see no brass, and it wouldn't feel greasy no more, and so anybody in town would take it in a minute, let alone a hair-ball. Well, I knowed a potato would do that, before, but I had forgot it.

Jim put the quarter under the hair-ball and got down and listened again. This time he said the hair-ball was all right. He said it would tell my whole fortune if I wanted it to. I says, go on. So the hair-ball talked to Jim, and Jim told it to me. He says:

"Yo' ole father doan' know, yit, what he's a-gwyne to do. Some-

4. Visceral objects, like the hair-ball, have had ancient sooth-saying significance.

times he spec he'll go 'way, en den agin he spec he'll stay. De bes' way is to res' easy en let de ole man take his own way. Dey's two angels hoverin' roun' 'bout him. One uv 'em is white en shiny, en 'tother one is black. De white one gits him to go right, a little while, den de black one sail in en bust it all up. A body can't tell, yit, which one gwyne to fetch him at de las'. But you is all right. You gwyne to have considable trouble in yo' life, en considable joy. Sometimes you gwyne to git hurt, en sometimes you gwyne to git sick; but every time you's gwyne to git well agin. Dey's two gals flyin' 'bout you in yo' life. One uv 'em's light en 'tother one is dark. One is rich en 'tother is po'. You's gwyne to marry de po' one fust en de rich one by-en-by. You wants to keep 'way fum de water as much as you kin, en don't run no resk, 'kase it's down in de bills dat you's gwyne to git hung."

When I lit my candle and went up to my room that night, there set pap, his own self!

Chapter V

I had shut the door to. Then I turned around, and there he was. I used to be scared of him all the time, he tanned me so much. I reckoned I was scared now, too; but in a minute I see I was mistaken. That is, after the first jolt, as you may say, when my breath sort of hitched—he being so unexpected; but right away after, I see I warn't scared of him worth bothering about.

He was most fifty, and he looked it. His hair was long and tangled and greasy, and hung down, and you could see his eyes shining through like he was behind vines. It was all black, no gray; so was his long, mixed-up whiskers. There warn't no color in his face, where his face showed; it was white; not like another man's white, but a white to make a body sick, a white to make a body's flesh crawl—a tree-toad white, a fish-belly white. As for his clothes—just rags, that was all. He had one ankle resting on 'tother knee; the boot on that foot was busted, and two of his toes stuck through, and he worked them now and then. His hat was laying on the floor; an old black slouch with the top caved in, like a lid.

I stood a-looking at him; he set there a-looking at me, with his chair tilted back a little. I set the candle down. I noticed the window was up; so he had clumb in by the shed. He kept a-looking me all over. By-and-by he says:

"Starchy clothes—very. You think you're a good deal of a big-bug, *don't* you?"

"Maybe I am, maybe I ain't," I says.

"Don't you give me none o' your lip," says he. "You've put on considerble many frills since I been away. I'll take you down a peg before I get done with you. You're educated, too, they say; can read and write. You think you're better'n your father, now, don't you, because he can't? I'll take it out of you. Who told you you might meddle with such hifalut'n foolishness, hey?—who told you you could?"

"The widow. She told me."

"The widow, hey?—and who told the widow she could put in her shovel about a thing that ain't none of her business?"

"Nobody never told her."

"Well, I'll learn her how to meddle. And looky here—you drop that school, you hear? I'll learn people to bring up a boy to put on airs over his own father and let on to be better'n what *he* is. You lemme catch you fooling around that school again, you hear? Your mother couldn't read, and she couldn't write, nuther, before she died. None of the family couldn't, before *they* died. *I* can't; and here you're a-swelling yourself up like this. I ain't the man to stand it—you hear? Say—lemme hear you read."

I took up a book and begun something about General Washington and the wars. When I'd read about a half a minute, he fetched the book a whack with his hand and knocked it across the house. He says:

"It's so. You can do it. I had my doubts when you told me. Now looky here; you stop that putting on frills. I won't have it. I'll lay for you, my smarty; and if I catch you about that school I'll tan you good. First you know you'll get religion, too. I never see such a son."

He took up a little blue and yaller picture of some cows and a boy, and says:

"What's this?"

"It's something they give me for learning my lessons good."

He tore it up, and says—

"I'll give you something better—I'll give you a cowhide."

He set there a-mumbling and a-growling a minute, and then he says—

"*Ain't* you a sweet-scented dandy, though? A bed; and bedclothes; and a look'n-glass; and a piece of carpet on the floor—and your own father got to sleep with the hogs in the tanyard. I never see such a son. I bet I'll take some o' these frills out o' you before I'm done with you. Why there ain't no end to your airs—they say you're rich. Hey?—how's that?"

"They lie—that's how."

"Looky here—mind how you talk to me; I'm a-standing about all I can stand, now—so don't gimme no sass. I've been in town two days, and I hain't heard nothing but about you bein' rich. I heard about it away down the river, too. That's why I come. You git me that money to-morrow—I want it."

"I hain't got no money."

"It's a lie. Judge Thatcher's got it. You git it. I want it."

"I hain't got no money, I tell you. You ask Judge Thatcher; he'll tell you the same."

"All right. I'll ask him; and I'll make him pungle,[5] too, or I'll know the reason why. Say—how much you got in your pocket? I want it."

"I hain't got only a dollar, and I want that to—"

"It don't make no difference what you want it for—you just shell it out."

He took it and bit it to see if it was good, and then he said he was going down town to get some whisky; said he hadn't had a drink all day. When he had got out on the shed, he put his head in again, and cussed me for putting on frills and trying to be better than him; and when I reckoned he was gone, he come back and put his head in again, and told me to mind about that school, because he was going to lay for me and lick me if I didn't drop that.

Next day he was drunk, and he went to Judge Thatcher's and bullyragged him and tried to make him give up the money, but he couldn't, and then he swore he'd make the law force him.

The judge and the widow went to law to get the court to take me away from him and let one of them be my guardian; but it was a new judge that had just come, and he didn't know the old man; so he said courts mustn't interfere and separate families if they can help it; said he'd druther not take a child away from its father. So Judge Thatcher and the widow had to quit on the business.

That pleased the old man till he couldn't rest. He said he'd cowhide me till I was black and blue if I didn't raise some money for him. I borrowed three dollars from Judge Thatcher, and pap took it and got drunk and went a-blowing around and cussing and whooping and carrying on; and he kept it up all over town, with a tin pan, till most midnight; then they jailed him, and next day they had him before court, and jailed him again for a week. But he said *he* was satisfied; said he was boss of his son, and he'd make it warm for *him*.

When he got out the new judge said he was agoing to make a man of him. So he took him to his own house, and dressed him up clean and nice, and had him to breakfast and dinner and supper with the family, and was just old pie to him, so to speak. And after supper he talked to him about temperance and such things till the old man cried, and said he'd been a fool, and fooled away his life;

5. Pay, or give up. Pap is claiming his legal right to his son's possessions. That is why, in Chapter IV, as soon as Huck saw his father's footprints he made a nominal transfer of his money to Judge Thatcher.

but now he was agoing to turn over a new leaf and be a man nobody wouldn't be ashamed of, and he hoped the judge would help him and not look down on him. The judge said he could hug him for them words; so *he* cried, and his wife she cried again; pap said he'd been a man that had always been misunderstood before, and the judge said he believed it. The old man said that what a man wanted that was down, was sympathy; and the judge said it was so; so they cried again. And when it was bedtime, the old man rose up and held out his hand, and says:

"Look at it gentlemen, and ladies all; take ahold of it; shake it. There's a hand that was the hand of a hog; but it ain't so no more; it's the hand of a man that's started in on a new life, and 'll die before he'll go back. You mark them words—don't forget I said them. It's a clean hand now; shake it—don't be afeard."

So they shook it, one after the other, all around, and cried. The judge's wife she kissed it. Then the old man he signed a pledge—made his mark. The judge said it was the holiest time on record, or something like that. Then they tucked the old man into a beautiful room, which was the spare room, and in the night sometime he got powerful thirsty and clumb out onto the porch-roof and slid down a stanchion and traded his new coat for a jug of forty-rod,[6] and clumb back again and had a good old time; and towards daylight he crawled out again, drunk as a fiddler, and rolled off the porch and broke his left arm in two places and was most froze to death when somebody found him after sun-up. And when they come to look at that spare room, they had to take soundings before they could navigate it.

The judge he felt kind of sore. He said he reckoned a body could reform the ole man with a shot-gun, maybe, but he didn't know no other way.

Chapter VI

Well, pretty soon the old man was up and around again, and then he went for Judge Thatcher in the courts to make him give up that money, and he went for me, too, for not stopping school. He catched me a couple of times and thrashed me, but I went to school just the same, and dodged him or out-run him most of the time. I didn't want to go to school much, before, but I reckoned I'd go now to spite pap. That law trial was a slow business; appeared like they warn't ever going to get started on it; so every now and then I'd borrow two or three dollars off of the judge for him, to keep from getting a cowhiding. Every time he got money he got drunk; and every time he got drunk he raised Cain around town; and every time

6. Whiskey strong enough to knock a man forty rods.

he raised Cain he got jailed. He was just suited—this kind of thing was right in his line.

He got to hanging around the widow's too much, and so she told him at last, that if he didn't quit using around there she would make trouble for him. Well, *wasn't* he mad? He said he would show who was Huck Finn's boss. So he watched out for me one day in the spring, and catched me, and took me up the river about three mile, in a skiff, and crossed over to the Illinois shore where it was woody and there warn't no houses but an old log hut in a place where the timber was so thick you couldn't find it if you didn't know where it was.

He kept me with him all the time, and I never got a chance to run off. We lived in that old cabin, and he always locked the door and put the key under his head, nights. He had a gun which he had stole, I reckon, and we fished and hunted, and that was what we lived on. Every little while he locked me in and went down to the store, three miles, to the ferry, and traded fish and game for whisky and fetched it home and got drunk and had a good time, and licked me. The widow she found out where I was, by-and-by, and she sent a man over to try to get hold of me, but pap drove him off with the gun, and it warn't long after that till I was used to being where I was, and liked it, all but the cowhide part.

It was kind of lazy and jolly, laying off comfortable all day, smoking and fishing, and no books nor study. Two months or more run along, and my clothes got to be all rags and dirt, and I didn't see how I'd ever got to like it so well at the widow's, where you had to wash, and eat on a plate, and comb up, and go to bed and get up regular, and be forever bothering over a book and have old Miss Watson pecking at you all the time. I didn't want to go back no more. I had stopped cussing, because the widow didn't like it; but now I took to it again because pap hadn't no objections. It was pretty good times up in the woods there, take it all around.

But by-and-by pap got too handy with his hick'ry, and I couldn't stand it. I was all over welts. He got to going away so much, too, and locking me in. Once he locked me in and was gone three days. It was dreadful lonesome. I judged he had got drowned and I wasn't ever going to get out any more. I was scared. I made up my mind I would fix up some way to leave there. I had tried to get out of that cabin many a time, but I couldn't find no way. There warn't a window to it big enought for a dog to get through. I couldn't get up the chimbly, it was too narrow. The door was thick solid oak slabs. Pap was pretty careful not to leave a knife or anything in the cabin when he was away; I reckon I had hunted the place over as much as a hundred times; well, I was 'most all the time at it, because it was about the only way to put in the time. But this time

I found something at last; I found an old rusty wood-saw without any handle; it was laid in between a rafter and the clapboards of the roof. I greased it up and went to work. There was an old horse-blanket nailed against the logs at the far end of the cabin behind the table, to keep the wind from blowing through the chinks and putting the candle out. I got under the table and raised the blanket and went to work to saw a section of the big bottom log out, big enough to let me through. Well, it was a good long job, but I was getting towards the end of it when I heard pap's gun in the woods. I got rid of the signs of my work, and dropped the blanket and hid my saw, and pretty soon pap come in.

Pap warn't in a good humor—so he was his natural self. He said he was down to town, and everything was going wrong. His lawyer said he reckoned he would win his lawsuit and get the money, if they ever got started on the trial; but then there was ways to put it off a long time, and Judge Thatcher knowed how to do it. And he said people allowed there'd be another trial to get me away from him and give me to the widow for my guardian, and they guessed it would win, this time. This shook me up considerable, because I didn't want to go back to the widow's any more and be so cramped up and sivilized, as they called it. Then the old man got to cussing, and cussed everything and everybody he could think of, and then cussed them all over again to make sure he hadn't skipped any, and after that he polished off with a kind of a general cuss all round, including a considerable parcel of people which he didn't know the names of, and so called them what's-his-name, when he got to them, and went right along with his cussing.

He said he would like to see the widow get me. He said he would watch out, and if they tried to come any such game on him he knowed of a place six or seven mile off, to stow me in, where they might hunt till they dropped and they couldn't find me. That made me pretty uneasy again, but only for a minute; I reckoned I wouldn't stay on hand till he got that chance.[7]

The old man made me go to the skiff and fetch the things he had got. There was a fifty-pound sack of corn meal, and a side of bacon, ammunition, and a four-gallon jug of whisky, and an old book and two newspapers for wadding,[8] besides some tow.[9] I toted up a load, and went back and set down on the bow of the skiff to rest. I thought it all over, and I reckoned I would walk off with the gun and some lines, and take to the woods when I run away. I guessed I wouldn't stay in one place, but just tramp right across the country,

7. Preferring the freedom of the woods to the restrictions of town life, Huck does not make the final decision to escape until he has genuine fears for his own safety. This illustrates one factor of the concept of freedom which the novel defines.
8. Material employed in packing the load of the guns of the period.
9. Rope made from broken strands of flax or hemp.

mostly night times, and hunt and fish to keep alive, and so get so far away that the old man nor the widow couldn't ever find me any more. I judged I would saw out and leave that night if pap got drunk enough, and I reckoned he would. I got so full of it I didn't notice how long I was staying, till the old man hollered and asked me whether I was asleep or drownded.

I got the things all up to the cabin, and then it was about dark. While I was cooking supper the old man took a swig or two and got sort of warmed up, and went to ripping again. He had been drunk over in town, and laid in the gutter all night, and he was a sight to look at. A body would a thought he was Adam, he was just all mud. Whenever his liquor begun to work, he most always went for the govment. This time he says:

"Call this a govment! why, just look at it and see what it's like. Here's the law a-standing ready to take a man's son away from him —a man's own son, which he has had all the trouble and all the anxiety and all the expense of raising. Yes, just as that man has got that son raised at last, and ready to go to work and begin to do suthin' for *him* and give him a rest, the law up and goes for him. And they call *that* govment! That ain't all, nuther. The law backs that old Judge Thatcher up and helps him to keep me out o' my property. Here's what the law does. The law takes a man worth six thousand dollars and upards, and jams him into an old trap of a cabin like this, and lets him go round in clothes that ain't fitten for a hog. They call that govment! A man can't get his rights in a govment like this. Sometimes I've a mighty notion to just leave the country for good and all. Yes, and I *told* 'em so; I told old Thatcher so to his face. Lots of 'em heard me, and can tell what I said. Says I, for two cents I'd leave the blamed country and never come anear it agin. Them's the very words. I says, look at my hat—if you call it a hat—but the lid raises up and the rest of it goes down till it's below my chin, and then it ain't rightly a hat at all, but more like my head was shoved up through a jint o' stove-pipe. Look at it, says I—such a hat for me to wear—one of the wealthiest men in this town, if I could git my rights.

"Oh, yes, this is a wonderful govment, wonderful. Why, looky here. There was a free nigger there, from Ohio; a mulatter, most as white as a white man. He had the whitest shirt on you ever see, too, and the shiniest hat; and there ain't a man in that town that's got as fine clothes as what he had; and he had a gold watch and chain, and a silver-headed cane—the awfulest old gray-headed nabob in the State. And what do you think? they said he was a p'fessor in a college, and could talk all kinds of languages, and knowed everything. And that ain't the wust. They said he could *vote*, when he was at home. Well, that let me out. Thinks I, what is the country a-coming to? It was 'lection day, and I was just about to go and vote, myself, if I warn't too drunk to get there; but when they told me there was a State in this country where they'd let that nigger vote, I drawed out. I says I'll never vote again. Them's the very words I said; they all heard me; and the country may rot for all me —I'll never vote agin as long as I live. And to see the cool way of that nigger—why, he wouldn't a give me the road if I hadn't shoved him out o' the way. I says to the people, why ain't this nigger put up at auction and sold?—that's what I want to know. And what do you reckon they said? Why, they said he couldn't be sold till he'd been in the State six months, and he hadn't been there that long yet. There, now—that's a specimen. They call that a govment that can't sell a free nigger till he's been in the State six months. Here's a govment that calls itself a govment, and lets on to be a govment, and thinks it is a govment, and yet's got to set stock-still for six whole months before it can take ahold of a prowling, thieving, infernal, white-shirted free nigger, and—"[1]

Pap was agoing on so, he never noticed where his old limber legs was taking him to, so he went head over heels over the tub of salt pork, and barked both shins, and the rest of his speech was all the hottest kind of language—mostly hove at the nigger and the govment, though he give the tub some, too, all along, here and there. He hopped around the cabin considerable, first on one leg and then on the other, holding first one shin and then the other one, and at last he let out with his left foot all of a sudden and fetched the tub a rattling kick. But it warn't good judgment, because that was the boot that had a couple of his toes leaking out of the front end of it; so now he raised a howl that fairly made a body's hair raise, and down he went in the dirt, and rolled there, and held his toes; and the cussing he done then laid over anything he had ever done previous. He said so his own self, afterwards. He had heard old Sowberry Hagan in his best days, and he said it laid over him, too; but I reckon that was sort of piling it on, maybe.

After supper pap took the jug, and said he had enough whisky there for two drunks and one delirium tremens. That was always his word. I judged he would be blind drunk in about an hour, and then I would steal the key, or saw myself out, one or 'tother. He drank, and drank, and tumbled down on his blankets, by-and-by; but luck didn't run my way. He didn't go sound asleep, but was uneasy. He groaned, and moaned, and thrashed around this way and that, for a long time. At last I got so sleepy I couldn't keep my eyes open, all I could do, and so before I knowed what I was about I was sound asleep, and the candle burning.

1. According to Dixon Wecter, *Sam Clemens of Hannibal,* there were free Negroes in Hannibal in the 1840's.

I don't know how long I was asleep, but all of a sudden there was an awful scream and I was up. There was pap, looking wild and skipping around every which way and yelling about snakes. He said they was crawling up his legs; and then he would give a jump and scream, and say one had bit him on the cheek—but I couldn't see no snakes. He started and run round and round the cabin, hollering "take him off! take him off! he's biting me on the neck!" I never see a man look so wild in the eyes. Pretty soon he was all fagged out, and fell down panting; then he rolled over and over, wonderful fast, kicking things every which way, and striking and grabbing at the air with his hands, and screaming, and saying there was devils ahold of him. He wore out, by-and-by, and laid still a while, moaning. Then he laid stiller, and didn't make a sound. I could hear the owls and the wolves, away off in the woods, and it seemed terrible still. He was laying over by the corner. By-and-by he raised up, part way, and listened, with his head to one side. He says very low:

"Tramp—tramp—tramp; that's the dead; tramp—tramp—tramp; they're coming after me; but I won't go— Oh, they're here! don't touch me—don't! hands off—they're cold; let go— Oh, let a poor devil alone!"

Then he went down on all fours and crawled off begging them to let him alone, and he rolled himself up in his blanket and wallowed in under the old pine table, still a-begging; and then he went to crying. I could hear him through the blanket.

By-and-by he rolled out and jumped up on his feet looking wild, and he see me and went for me. He chased me round and round the place, with a clasp-knife, calling me the Angel of Death and saying he would kill me and then I couldn't come for him no more. I begged, and told him I was only Huck, but he laughed *such* a screechy laugh, and roared and cussed, and kept on chasing me up. Once when I turned short and dodged under his arm he made a grab and got me by the jacket between my shoulders, and I thought I was gone; but I slid out of the jacket quick as lightning, and saved myself. Pretty soon he was all tired out, and dropped down with his back against the door, and said he would rest a minute and then kill me. He put his knife under him, and said he would sleep and get strong, and then he would see who was who.

So he dozed off, pretty soon. By-and-by I got the old split-bottom[2] chair and clumb up, as easy as I could, not to make any noise, and got down the gun. I slipped the ramrod down it to make sure it was loaded, and then I laid it across the turnip barrel, pointing towards pap, and set down behind it to wait for him to stir. And how slow and still the time did drag along.

2. *I.e.*, splint-bottom.

Chapter VII

"Git up! what you 'bout!"

I opened my eyes and looked around, trying to make out where I was. It was after sun-up, and I had been sound asleep. Pap was standing over me, looking sour—and sick, too. He says—

"What you doin' with this gun?"

I judged he didn't know nothing about what he had been doing, so I says:

"Somebody tried to get in, so I was laying for him."

"Why didn't you roust me out?"

"Well I tried to, but I couldn't; I couldn't budge you."

"Well, all right. Don't stand there palavering all day, but out with you and see if there's a fish on the lines for breakfast. I'll be along in a minute."

He unlocked the door and I cleared out, up the river bank. I noticed some pieces of limbs and such things floating down, and a sprinkling of bark; so I knowed the river had begun to rise. I reckoned I would have great times, now, if I was over at the town. The June rise used to be always luck for me; because as soon as that rise begins, here comes cord-wood floating down, and pieces of log rafts —sometimes a dozen logs together; so all you have to do is to catch them and sell them to the wood yards and the sawmill.

I went along up the bank with one eye out for pap and 'tother one out for what the rise might fetch along. Well, all at once, here comes a canoe; just a beauty, too, about thirteen or fourteen foot long, riding high like a duck. I shot head first off the bank, like a frog, clothes and all on, and struck out for the canoe. I just expected there'd be somebody laying down in it, because people often done that to fool folks, and when a chap had pulled a skiff out most to it they'd raise up and laugh at him. But it warn't so this time. It was a drift-canoe, sure enough, and I clumb in and paddled her ashore. Thinks I, the old man will be glad when he sees this—she's worth ten dollars. But when I got to shore pap wasn't in sight yet, and as I was running her into a little creek like a gully, all hung over with vines and willows, I struck another idea; I judged I'd hide her good, and then, stead of taking to the woods when I run off, I'd go down the river about fifty mile and camp in one place for good, and not have such a rough time tramping on foot.

It was pretty close to the shanty, and I thought I heard the old man coming, all the time; but I got her hid; and then I out and looked around a bunch of willows, and there was the old man down the path apiece just drawing a bead on a bird with his gun. So he hadn't seen anything.

When he got along, I was hard at it taking up a "trot" line.[3] He abused me a little for being so slow, but I told him I fell in the river and that was what made me so long. I knowed he would see I was wet, and then he would be asking questions. We got five cat-fish off the lines and went home.

While we laid off, after breakfast, to sleep up, both of us being about wore out, I got to thinking that if I could fix up some way to keep pap and the widow from trying to follow me, it would be a certainer thing than trusting to luck to get far enough off before they missed me; you see, all kinds of things might happen. Well, I didn't see no way for a while, but by-and-by pap raised up a minute, to drink another barrel of water, and he says:

"Another time a man comes a-prowling round here, you roust me out, you hear? That man warn't here for no good. I'd a shot him. Next time, you roust me out, you hear?"

Then he dropped down and went to sleep again—but what he had been saying give me the very idea I wanted. I says to myself, I can fix it now so nobody won't think of following me.

About twelve o'clock we turned out and went along up the bank. The river was coming up pretty fast, and lots of drift-wood going by on the rise. By-and-by, along comes part of a log raft—nine logs fast together. We went out with the skiff and towed it ashore. Then we had dinner. Anybody but pap would a waited and seen the day through, so as to catch more stuff; but that warn't pap's style. Nine logs was enough for one time; he must shove right over to town and sell. So he locked me in and took the skiff and started off towing the raft about half-past three. I judged he wouldn't come back that night. I waited till I reckoned he had got a good start, then I out with my saw and went to work on that log again. Before he was 'tother side of the river I was out of the hole; him and his raft was just a speck on the water away off yonder.

I took the sack of corn meal and took it to where the canoe was hid, and shoved the vines and branches apart and put it in; then I done the same with the side of bacon; then the whisky jug; I took all the coffee and sugar there was, and all the ammunition; I took the wadding; I took the bucket and gourd, I took a dipper and a tin cup, and my own saw and two blankets, and the skillet and the coffee-pot. I took fish-lines and matches and other things—every-thing that was worth a cent. I cleaned out the place. I wanted an axe, but there wasn't any, only the one out at the wood pile, and I knowed why I was going to leave that. I fetched out the gun, and now I was done.

I had wore the ground a good deal, crawling out of the hole and

3. A line suspended across a stream holding at intervals single hooks hung by short lines.

dragging out so many things. So I fixed that as good as I could from the outside by scattering dust on the place, which covered up the smoothness and the sawdust. Then I fixed the piece of log back into its place, and put two rocks under it and one against it to hold it there,—for it was bent up at that place, and didn't quite touch ground. If you stood four or five foot away and didn't know it was sawed, you wouldn't ever notice it; and besides, this was the back of the cabin and it warn't likely anybody would go fooling around there.

It was all grass clear to the canoe; so I hadn't left a track. I followed around to see. I stood on the bank and looked out over the river. All safe. So I took the gun and went up a piece into the woods and was hunting around for some birds, when I see a wild pig; hogs soon went wild in them bottoms after they had got away from the prairie farms. I shot this fellow and took him into camp.

I took the axe and smashed in the door—I beat it and hacked it considerable, a-doing it. I fetched the pig in and took him back nearly to the table and hacked into his throat with the axe, and laid him down on the ground to bleed—I say ground, because it *was* ground—hard packed, and no boards. Well, next I took an old sack and put a lot of big rocks in it,—all I could drag—and I started it from the pig and dragged it to the door and through the woods down to the river and dumped it in, and down it sunk, out of sight. You could easy see that something had been dragged over the ground. I did wish Tom Sawyer was there, I knowed he would take an interest in this kind of business, and throw in the fancy touches. Nobody could spread himself like Tom Sawyer in such a thing as that.

Well, last I pulled out some of my hair, and bloodied the ax good, and stuck it on the back side, and slung the ax in the corner. Then I took up the pig and held him to my breast with my jacket (so he couldn't drip) till I got a good piece below the house and then dumped him into the river. Now I thought of something else. So I went and got the bag of meal and my old saw out of the canoe and fetched them to the house. I took the bag to where it used to stand, and ripped a hole in the bottom of it with the saw,[4] for there warn't no knives and forks on the place—pap done everything with his clasp-knife, about the cooking. Then I carried the sack about a hundred yards across the grass and through the willows east of the house, to a shallow lake that was five mile wide and full of rushes—and ducks too, you might say, in the season. There was a slough or a creek leading out of it on the other side, that went miles away, I don't know where, but it didn't go to the river. The meal sifted out and made a little track all the way to the lake. I dropped pap's whetstone there too, so as to look like it had been

4. Early issues of the first edition read "was."

done by accident. Then I tied up the rip in the meal sack with a string, so it wouldn't leak no more, and took it and my saw to the canoe again.

It was about dark, now; so I dropped the canoe down the river under some willows that hung over the bank, and waited for the moon to rise. I made fast to a willow; then I took a bite to eat, and by-and-by laid down in the canoe to smoke a pipe and lay out a plan. I says to myself, they'll follow the track of that sackful of rocks to the shore and then drag the river for me. And they'll follow that meal track to the lake and go browsing down the creek that leads out of it to find the robbers that killed me and took the things. They won't ever hunt the river for anything but my dead carcass. They'll soon get tired of that, and won't bother no more about me. All right; I can stop anywhere I want to. Jackson's Island[5] is good enough for me; I know that island pretty well, and nobody ever comes there. And then I can paddle over to town, nights, and slink around and pick up things I want. Jackson's Island's the place.

I was pretty tired, and the first thing I knowed, I was asleep. When I woke up I didn't know where I was, for a minute. I set up and looked around, a little scared. Then I remembered. The river looked miles and miles across. The moon was so bright I could a counted the drift logs that went a slipping along, black and still, hundred of yards out from shore. Everything was dead quiet, and it looked late, and *smelt* late. You know what I mean—I don't know the words to put it in.

I took a good gap and a stretch, and was just going to unhitch and start, when I heard a sound away over the water. I listened. Pretty soon I made it out. It was that dull kind of a regular sound that comes from oars working in rowlocks when it's a still night. I peeped out through the willow branches, and there it was—a skiff, away across the water. I couldn't tell how many was in it. It kept a-coming, and when it was abreast of me I see there warn't but one man in it. Thinks I, maybe it's pap, though I warn't expecting him. He dropped below me, with the current, and by-and-by he come a-swinging up shore in the easy water, and he went by so close I could a reached out the gun and touched him. Well, it *was* pap, sure enough—and sober, too, by the way he laid to his oars.

I didn't lose no time. The next minute I was a-spinning down stream soft but quick in the shade of the bank. I made two mile and a half, and then struck out a quarter of a mile or more towards the middle of the river, because pretty soon I would be passing the ferry landing and people might see me and hail me. I got out amongst the drift-wood and then laid down in the bottom of the

5. The island also famous in *Tom Sawyer;* actually Glasscock's Island, since eroded away by the Mississippi River.

canoe and let her float. I laid there and had a good rest and a
smoke out of my pipe, looking away into the sky, not a cloud in it.
The sky looks ever so deep when you lay down on your back in the
moonshine; I never knowed it before. And how far a body can hear
on the water such nights! I heard people talking at the ferry landing.
I heard what they said, too, every word of it. One man said it was
getting towards the long days and the short nights, now. 'Tother
one said *this* warn't one of the short ones, he reckoned—and then
they laughed, and he said it over again and they laughed again; then
they waked up another fellow and told him, and laughed, but he
didn't laugh; he ripped out something brisk and said let him alone.
The first fellow said he 'lowed to tell it to his old woman—she
would think it was pretty good; but he said that warn't nothing to
some things he had said in his time. I heard one man say it was
nearly three o'clock, and he hoped daylight wouldn't wait more
than about a week longer. After that, the talk got further and
further away, and I couldn't make out the words any more, but I
could hear the mumble; and now and then a laugh, too, but it
seemed a long ways off.

I was away below the ferry now. I rose up and there was Jackson's
Island, about two mile and a half down stream, heavy-timbered and
standing up out of the middle of the river, big and dark and solid,
like a steamboat without any lights. There warn't any signs of the
bar at the head—it was all under water, now.

It didn't take me long to get there. I shot past the head at a
ripping rate, the current was so swift, and then I got into the dead
water and landed on the side towards the Illinois shore. I run the
canoe into a deep dent in the bank that I knowed about; I had to
part the willow branches to get in; and when I made fast nobody
could a seen the canoe from the outside.

I went up and set down on a log at the head of the island and
looked out on the big river and the black driftwood, and away over
to the town, three mile away, where there was three or four lights
twinkling. A monstrous big lumber raft was about a mile up stream,
coming along down, with a lantern in the middle of it. I watched it
come creeping down, and when it was most abreast of where I
stood I heard a man say, "Stern oars, there! heave her head to
stabboard!" I heard that just as plain as if the man was by my side.

There was a little gray in the sky, now; so I stepped into the
woods and laid down for a nap before breakfast.

Chapter VIII

The sun was up so high when I waked, that I judged it was
after eight o'clock. I laid there in the grass and the cool shade, think-

ing about things and feeling rested and ruther comfortable and satisfied. I could see the sun out at one or two holes, but mostly it was
big trees all about, and gloomy in there amongst them. There was
freckled places on the ground where the light sifted down through
the leaves, and the freckled places swapped about a little, showing
there was a little breeze up there. A couple of squirrels set on a
limb and jabbered at me very friendly.

I was powerful lazy and comfortable—didn't want to get up and
cook breakfast. Well, I was dozing off again, when I thinks I hears
a deep sound of "boom!" away up the river. I rouses up and rests
on my elbow and listens; pretty soon I hears it again. I hopped up
and went and looked out at a hole in the leaves, and I see a bunch
of smoke laying on the water a long ways up—about abreast the
ferry. And there was the ferry-boat full of people, floating along
down. I knowed what was the matter, now. "Boom!" I see the white
smoke squirt out of the ferry-boat's side. You see, they was firing
cannon over the water, trying to make my carcass come to the top.

I was pretty hungry, but it warn't going to do for me to start a
fire, because they might see the smoke. So I set there and watched
the cannon-smoke and listened to the boom. The river was a mile
wide, there, and it always looks pretty on a summer morning—so I
was having a good enough time seeing them hunt for my remainders, if I only had a bite to eat. Well, then I happened to
think how they always put quicksilver in loaves of bread and float
them off because they always go right to the drownded carcass and
stop there. So says I, I'll keep a lookout, and if any of them's floating around after me, I'll give them a show. I changed to the Illinois
edge of the island to see what luck I could have, and I warn't disappointed. A big double loaf come along, and I most got it, with a
long stick, but my foot slipped and she floated out further. Of course
I was where the current set in the closest to the shore—I knowed
enough for that. But by-and-by along comes another one, and this
time I won. I took out the plug and shook out the little dab of
quicksilver, and set my teeth in. It was "baker's bread"—what the
quality eat—none of your low-down corn-pone.

I got a good place amongst the leaves, and set there on a log,
munching the bread and watching the ferry-boat, and very well
satisfied. And then something struck me. I says, now I reckon the
widow or the parson or somebody prayed that this bread would find
me, and here it has gone and done it. So there ain't no doubt but
there is something in that thing. That is, there's something in it
when a body like the widow or the parson prays, but it don't work
for me, and I reckon it don't work for only just the right kind.

I lit a pipe and had a good long smoke and went on watching.
The ferry-boat was floating with the current, and I allowed I'd

have a chance to see who was aboard when she come along, because she would come in close, where the bread did. When she'd got pretty well along down towards me, I put out my pipe and went to where I fished out the bread, and laid down behind a log on the bank in a little open place. Where the log forked I could peep through.

By-and-by she come along, and she drifted in so close that they could a run out a plank and walked ashore. Most everybody was on the boat. Pap, and Judge Thatcher, and Bessie Thatcher, and Jo Harper, and Tom Sawyer, and his old Aunt Polly, and Sid and Mary, and plenty more. Everybody was talking about the murder, but the captain broke in and says:

"Look sharp, now; the current sets in the closest here, and maybe he's washed ashore and got tangled amongst the brush at the water's edge. I hope so, anyway."

I didn't hope so. They all crowded up and leaned over the rails, nearly in my face, and kept still, watching with all their might. I could see them first-rate, but they couldn't see me. Then the captain sung out:

"Stand away!" and the cannon let off such a blast right before me that it made me deef with the noise and pretty near blind with the smoke, and I judged I was gone. If they'd a had some bullets in, I reckon they'd a got the corpse they was after. Well, I see I warn't hurt, thanks to goodness. The boat floated on and went out of sight around the shoulder of the island. I could hear the booming, now and then, further and further off, and by-and-by after an hour, I didn't hear it no more. The island was three mile long. I judged they had got to the foot, and was giving it up. But they didn't yet a while. They turned around the foot of the island and started up the channel on the Missouri side, under steam, and booming once in a while as they went. I crossed over to that side and watched them. When they got abreast the head of the island they quit shooting and dropped over to the Missouri shore and went home to the town.

I knowed I was all right now. Nobody else would come a-hunting after me. I got my traps out of the canoe and made me a nice camp in the thick woods. I made a kind of a tent out of my blankets to put my things under so the rain couldn't get at them. I catched a cat-fish and haggled him open with my saw, and towards sundown I started my camp fire and had supper. Then I set out a line to catch some fish for breakfast.

When it was dark I set by my camp fire smoking, and feeling pretty satisfied; but by-and-by it got sort of lonesome, and so I went and set on the bank and listened to the currents washing along, and counted the stars and drift-logs and rafts that come down, and then went to bed; there ain't no better way to put in time when you are lonesome; you can't stay so, you soon get over it.

And so for three days and nights. No difference—just the same thing. But the next day I went exploring around down through the island. I was boss of it; it all belonged to me, so to say, and I wanted to know all about it; but mainly I wanted to put in the time. I found plenty strawberries, ripe and prime; and green summer-grapes, and green razberries; and the green blackberries was just beginning to show. They would all come handy by-and-by, I judged.

Well, I went fooling along in the deep woods till I judged I warn't far from the foot of the island. I had my gun along, but I hadn't shot nothing; it was for protection; thought I would kill some game nigh home. About this time I mighty near stepped on a good sized snake, and it went sliding off through the grass and flowers, and I after it, trying to get a shot at it. I clipped along, and all of a sudden I bounded right on to the ashes of a camp fire that was still smoking.[6]

My heart jumped up amongst my lungs. I never waited for to look further, but uncocked my gun and went sneaking back on my tip-toes as fast as ever I could. Every now and then I stopped a second, amongst the thick leaves, and listened; but my breath come so hard I couldn't hear nothing else. I slunk along another piece further, then listened again; and so on, and so on; if I see a stump, I took it for a man; if I trod on a stick and broke it, it made me feel like a person had cut one of my breaths in two and I only got half, and the short half, too.

When I got to camp I warn't feeling very brash, there warn't much sand in my craw; but I says, this ain't no time to be fooling around. So I got all my traps into my canoe again so as to have them out of sight, and I put out the fire and scattered the ashes around to look like an old last year's camp, and then clumb a tree.

I reckon I was up in the tree two hours; but I didn't see nothing, I didn't hear nothing—I only *thought* I heard and seen as much as a thousand things. Well, I couldn't stay up there forever; so at last I got down, but I kept in the thick woods and on the lookout all the time. All I could get to eat was berries and what was left over from breakfast.

By the time it was night I was pretty hungry. So when it was good and dark, I slid out from shore before moonrise and paddled over to the Illinois bank—about a quarter of a mile. I went out in the woods and cooked a supper, and I had about made up my mind I would stay there all night, when I hear a *plunkety-plunk, plunkety-plunk*, and says to myself, horses coming; and next I hear people's

6. Huck's discovery of the ashes is a dramatic incident similar to Robinson Crusoe's discovery of the footprint on *his* island in Chapter XI of Daniel Defoe's novel.

voices. I got everything into the canoe as quick as I could, and then went creeping through the woods to see what I could find out. I hadn't got far when I hear a man say:

"We better camp here, if we can find a good place; the horses is about beat out. Let's look around."

I didn't wait, but shoved out and paddled away easy. I tied up in the old place, and reckoned I would sleep in the canoe.

I didn't sleep much. I couldn't, somehow, for thinking. And every time I waked up I thought somebody had me by the neck. So the sleep didn't do me no good. By-and-by I says to myself, I can't live this way; I'm agoing to find out who it is that's here on the island with me; I'll find it out or bust. Well, I felt better, right off.

So I took my paddle and slid out from shore just a step or two, and then let the canoe drop along down amongst the shadows. The moon was shining, and outside of the shadows it made it most as light as day. I poked along well onto an hour, everything still as rocks and sound asleep. Well by this time I was most down to the foot of the island. A little ripply, cool breeze begun to blow, and that was as good as saying the night was about done. I give her a turn with the paddle and brung her nose to shore; then I got my gun and slipped out and into the edge of the woods. I set down there on a log and looked out through the leaves. I see the moon go off watch and the darkness begin to blanket the river. But in a little while I see a pale streak over the tree-tops, and knowed the day was coming. So I took my gun and slipped off towards where I had run across that camp fire, stopping every minute or two to listen. But I hadn't no luck, somehow; I couldn't seem to find the place. But by-and-by, sure enough, I catched a glimpse of fire, away through the trees. I went for it, cautious and slow. By-and-by I was close enough to have a look, and there laid a man on the ground. It most give me the fan-tods. He had a blanket around his head, and his head was nearly in the fire. I set there behind a clump of bushes, in about six foot of him, and kept my eyes on him steady. It was getting gray daylight, now. Pretty soon he gapped, and stretched himself, and hove off the blanket, and it was Miss Watson's Jim! I bet I was glad to see him. I says:

"Hello, Jim!" and skipped out.

He bounced up and stared at me wild. Then he drops down on his knees, and puts his hands together and says:

"Doan' hurt me—don't! I hain't ever done no harm to a ghos'. I awluz liked dead people, en done all I could for 'em. You go en git in de river agin, whah you b'longs, en doan' do nuffn to Ole Jim, 'at 'uz awluz yo' fren'."

Well, I warn't long making him understand I warn't dead. I was ever so glad to see Jim. I warn't lonesome, now. I told him I warn't afraid of *him* telling the people where I was. I talked along, but he only set there and looked at me; never said nothing. Then I says:

"It's good daylight. Le's get breakfast. Make up your camp fire good."

"What's de use er makin' up de camp fire to cook strawbries en sich truck? But you got a gun, hain't you? Den we kin git sumfn better den strawbries."

"Strawberries and such truck," I says. "Is that what you live on?"

"I couldn' git nuffn else," he says.

"Why, how long you been on the island, Jim?"

"I come heah de night arter you's killed."

"What, all that time?"

"Yes-indeedy."

"And ain't you had nothing but that kind of rubbage to eat?"

"No, sah—nuffn else."

"Well, you must be most starved, ain't you?"

"I reck'n I could eat a hoss. I think I could. How long you ben on de islan'?"

"Since the night I got killed."

"No! W'y, what has you lived on? But you got a gun. Oh, yes, you got a gun. Dat's good. Now you kill sumfn en I'll make up de fire."

So we went over to where the canoe was, and while he built a fire in a grassy open place amongst the trees, I fetched meal and bacon and coffee, and coffee-pot and frying-pan, and sugar and tin cups, and the nigger was set back considerable, because he reckoned it was all done with witchcraft. I catched a good big cat-fish, too, and Jim cleaned him with his knife, and fried him.

When breakfast was ready, we lolled on the grass and eat it smoking hot. Jim laid it in with all his might, for he was most about starved. Then when we had got pretty well stuffed, we laid off and lazied.

By-and-by Jim says:

"But looky here, Huck, who wuz it dat 'uz killed in dat shanty, ef it warn't you?"

Then I told him the whole thing, and he said it was smart. He said Tom Sawyer couldn't get up no better plan than what I had. Then I says:

"How do you come to be here, Jim, and how'd you get here?"

He looked pretty uneasy, and didn't say nothing for a minute. Then he says:

"Maybe I better not tell."

"Why, Jim?"

"Well, dey's reasons. But you wouldn' tell on me ef I 'uz to tell you, would you, Huck?"

"Blamed if I would, Jim."

"Well, I b'lieve you, Huck. I—I *run off*."

"Jim!"

"But mind, you said you wouldn't tell—you know you said you wouldn't tell, Huck."

"Well, I did. I said I wouldn't, and I'll stick to it. Honest *injun* I will. People would call me a low down Abolitionist and despise me for keeping mum—but that don't make no difference. I ain't agoing to tell, and I ain't agoing back there anyways. So now, le's know all about it."

"Well, you see, it 'uz dis way. Ole Missus—dat's Miss Watson—she pecks on me all de time, en treats me pooty rough, but she awluz said she wouldn' sell me down to Orleans. But I noticed dey wuz a nigger trader roun' de place considable, lately, en I begin to git oneasy. Well, one night I creeps to de do', pooty late, en de do' warn't quite shet, en I hear ole missus tell de widder she gwyne to sell me down to Orleans, but she didn' want to, but she could git eight hund'd dollars for me, en it 'uz sich a big stack o' money she couldn' resis'. De widder she try to git her to say she wouldn' do it, but I never waited to hear de res'. I lit out mighty quick, I tell you.

"I tuck out en shin down de hill en 'spec to steal a skift 'long de sho' som'ers 'bove de town, but dey wuz people a-stirrin' yit, so I hid in de ole tumble-down cooper shop on de bank to wait for everybody to go 'way. Well, I wuz dah all night. Dey wuz somebody roun' all de time. 'Long 'bout six in de mawnin', skifts begin to go by, en 'bout eight er nine every skift dat went 'long wuz talkin' 'bout how yo' pap come over to de town en say you's killed. Dese las' skifts wuz full o' ladies en genlmen agoin' over for to see de place. Sometimes dey'd pull up at de sho' en take a res' b'fo' dey started acrost, so by de talk I got to know all 'bout de killin'. I 'uz powerful sorry you's killed, Huck, but I ain't no mo', now.

"I laid dah under de shavins all day. I 'uz hungry, but I warn't afeared; bekase I knowed ole missus en de widder wuz goin' to start to de camp-meetn' right arter breakfas' en be gone all day, en dey knows I goes off wid de cattle 'bout daylight, so dey wouldn' 'spec to see me roun' de place, en so dey wouldn' miss me tell arter dark in de evenin'. De yuther servants wouldn' miss me, kase dey'd shin out en take holiday, soon as de ole folks 'uz out'n de way.

"Well, when it come dark I tuck out up de river road, en went 'bout two mile er more to whah dey warn't no houses. I'd made up my mine 'bout what I's agwyne to do. You see ef I kep' on tryin' to git away afoot, de dogs 'ud track me; ef I stole a skift to cross over, dey'd miss dat skift, you see, en dey'd know 'bout whah I'd lan' on de yuther side en whah to pick up my track. So I says, a raff is what I's arter; it doan' *make* no track.

"I see a light a-comin' roun' de p'int, bymeby, so I wade' in en shove' a log ahead o' me, en swum more'n half-way acrost de river, en got in 'mongst de drift-wood, en kep' my head down low, en kinder swum agin de current tell de raff come along. Den I swum to de stern uv it, en tuck aholt. It clouded up en 'uz pooty dark for a little while. So I clumb up en laid down on de planks. De men 'uz all 'way yonder in de middle, whah de lantern wuz. De river wuz arisin' en dey wuz a good current; so I reck'n'd 'at by fo' in de mawnin' I'd be twenty-five mile down de river, en den I'd slip in, jis' b'fo' daylight, en swim asho' en take to de woods on de Illinoi side.[7]

"But I didn' have no luck. When we 'uz mos' down to de head er de islan', a man begin to come aft wid de lantern. I see it warn't no use fer to wait, so I slid overboad, en struck out fer de islan'. Well, I had a notion I could lan' mos' anywhers, but I couldn't— bank too bluff. I 'uz mos' to de foot er de islan' b'fo' I foun' a good place. I went into de woods en jedged I wouldn' fool wid raffs no mo' long as dey move de lantern roun' so. I had my pipe en a plug er dog-leg,[8] en some matches in my cap, en dey warn't wet, so I 'uz all right."

"And so you ain't had no meat nor bread to eat all this time? Why didn't you get mud-turkles?"

"How you gwyne to git'm? You can't slip up on um en grab um; en how's a body gwyne to hit um wid a rock? How could a body do it in de night? en I warn't gwyne to show myself on de bank in de daytime."

"Well, that's so. You've had to keep in the woods all the time, of course. Did you hear 'em shooting the cannon?"

"Oh, yes. I knowed dey was arter you. I see um go by heah; watched um thoo de bushes."

Some young birds come along, flying a yard or two at a time and lighting. Jim said it was a sign it was going to rain. He said it was a sign when young chickens flew that way, and so he reckoned it was the same way when young birds done it. I was going to catch some of them, but Jim wouldn't let me. He said it was death. He said his father laid mighty sick once, and some of them catched a bird, and his old granny said his father would die, and he did.

And Jim said you mustn't count the things you are going to cook for dinner, because that would bring bad luck. The same if you shook the table-cloth after sundown. And he said if a man owned

7. Illinois was legally free soil but was separated only by the Mississippi and Ohio Rivers from slave states. By state law, any Negro without freedom papers was subject to arrest and a system of indentured labor. Jim's most practical access to one of the northern states sympathetic to runaway slaves would be the Ohio River.

8. A cheap tobacco.

a bee-hive, and that man died, the bees must be told about it before sun-up next morning, or else the bees would all weaken down and quit work and die. Jim said bees wouldn't sting idiots; but I didn't believe that, because I had tried them lots of times myself, and they wouldn't sting me.

I had heard about some of these things before, but not all of them. Jim knowed all kinds of signs. He said he knowed most everything. I said it looked to me like all the signs was about bad luck, and so I asked him if there warn't any good-luck signs. He says:

"Mighty few—an' *dey* ain' no use to a body. What you want to know when good luck's a-comin' for? want to keep it off?" And he said: "Ef you's got hairy arms en a hairy breas', it's a sign dat you's agwyne to be rich. Well, dey's some use in a sign like dat, 'kase it's so fur ahead. You see, maybe you's got to be po' a long time fust, en so you might git discourage' en kill yo'sef 'f you didn' know by de sign dat you gwyne to be rich bymeby."

"Have you got hairy arms and a hairy breast, Jim?"

"What's de use to ax dat question? don' you see I has?"

"Well, are you rich?"

"No, but I ben rich wunst, and gwyne to be rich agin. Wunst I had foteen dollars, but I tuck to specalat'n', en got busted out."

"What did you speculate in, Jim?"

"Well, fust I tackled stock."

"What kind of stock?"

"Why, live stock. Cattle, you know. I put ten dollars in a cow. But I ain't gwyne to resk no mo' money in stock. De cow up 'n' died on my han's."

"So you lost the ten dollars."

"No, I didn' lose it all. I on'y los' 'bout nine of it. I sole de hide en taller for a dollar en ten cents."

"You had five dollars and ten cents left. Did you speculate any more?"

"Yes. You know dat one-laigged nigger dat b'longs to old Misto Bradish? well, he sot up a bank, en say anybody dat put in a dollar would git fo' dollars mo' at de en' er de year. Well, all de niggers went in, but dey didn' have much. I wuz de on'y one dat had much. So I stuck out for mo' dan fo' dollars, en I said 'f I didn' git it I'd start a bank myself. Well o' course dat nigger want' to keep me out er de business, bekase he say dey warn't business 'nough for two banks, so he say I could put in my five dollars en he pay me thirty-five at de en' er de year.

"So I done it. Den I reck'n'd I'd inves' de thirty-five dollars right off en keep things a-movin'. Dey wuz a nigger name' Bob, dat had ketched a wood-flat,[9] en his marster didn' know it; en I bought it off'n him en told him to take de thirty-five dollars when de en' er

9. A flat-bottomed boat for transporting timber.

de year come; but somebody stole de wood-flat dat night, en nex' day de one-laigged nigger say de bank 's busted. So dey didn' none uv us git no money."

"What did you do with the ten cents, Jim?"

"Well, I 'uz gwyne to spen' it, but I had a dream, en de dream tole me to give it to a nigger name' Balum—Balum's Ass[1] dey call him for short, he's one er dem chuckle-heads, you know. But he's lucky, dey say, en I see I warn't lucky. De dream say let Balum inves' de ten cents en he'd make a raise for me. Well, Balum he tuck de money, en when he wuz in church he hear de preacher say dat whoever give to de po' len' to de Lord, en boun' to git his money back a hund'd times. So Balum he tuck en give de ten cents to de po', en laid low to see what wuz gwyne to come of it."

"Well, what did come of it, Jim?"

"Nuffn' never come of it. I couldn' manage to k'leck dat money no way; en Balum he couldn'. I ain' gwyne to len' no mo' money 'dout I see de security. Boun' to git yo' money back a hund'd times, de preacher says! Ef I could git de ten *cents* back, I'd call it squah, en be glad er de chanst."

"Well, it's all right, anyway, Jim, long as you're going to be rich again some time or other."

"Yes—en I's rich now, come to look at it. I owns myself, en I's wuth eight hund'd dollars. I wisht I had de money, I wouldn' want no mo'."

Chapter IX

I wanted to go and look at a place right about the middle of the island, that I'd found when I was exploring; so we started, and soon got to it, because the island was only three miles long and a quarter of a mile wide.

This place was a tolerable long steep hill or ridge, about forty foot high. We had a rough time getting to the top, the sides was so steep and the bushes so thick. We tramped and clumb around all over it, and by-and-by found a good big cavern in the rock, most up to the top on the side towards Illinois. The cavern was as big as two or three rooms bunched together, and Jim could stand up straight in it. It was cool in there. Jim was for putting our traps in there, right away, but I said we didn't want to be climbing up and down there all the time.

Jim said if we had the canoe hid in a good place, and had all the traps in the cavern, we could rush there if anybody was to come to the island, and they would never find us without dogs. And besides, he said them little birds had said it was going to rain, and did I

1. The Biblical Balaam's ass, whose story is irrelevant here.

want the things to get wet?

So we went back and got the canoe and paddled up abreast the cavern, and lugged all the traps up there. Then we hunted up a place close by to hide the canoe in, amongst the thick willows. We took some fish off of the lines and set them again, and begun to get ready for dinner.

The door of the cavern was big enough to roll a hogshead in, and on one side of the door the floor stuck out a little bit and was flat and a good place to build a fire on. So we built it there and cooked dinner.

We spread the blankets inside for a carpet, and eat our dinner in there. We put all the other things handy at the back of the cavern. Pretty soon it darkened up and begun to thunder and lighten; so the birds was right about it. Directly it begun to rain, and it rained like all fury, too, and I never see the wind blow so. It was one of these regular summer storms. It would get so dark that it looked all blue-black outside, and lovely; and the rain would thrash along by so thick that the trees off a little ways looked dim and spider-webby; and here would come a blast of wind that would bend the trees down and turn up the pale underside of the leaves; and then a perfect ripper of a gust would follow along and set the branches to tossing their arms as if they was just wild; and next, when it was just about the bluest and blackest—*fst!* It was as bright as glory and you'd have a little glimpse of tree-tops a-plunging about, away off yonder in the storm, hundreds of yards further than you could see before; dark as sin again in a second, and now you'd hear the thunder let go with an awful crash and then go rumbling, grumbling, tumbling down the sky towards the under side of the world, like rolling empty barrels down stairs, where it's long stairs and they bounce a good deal, you know.

"Jim, this is nice," I says. "I wouldn't want to be nowhere else but here. Pass me along another hunk of fish and some hot cornbread."

"Well, you wouldn't a ben here, 'f it hadn't a ben for Jim. You'd a ben down dah in de woods widout any dinner, en gittn' mos' drownded, too, dat you would, honey. Chickens knows when its gwyne to rain, en so do de birds, chile."

The river went on raising and raising for ten or twelve days, till at last it was over the banks. The water was three or four foot deep on the island in the low places and on the Illinois bottom. On that side it was a good many miles wide; but on the Missouri side it was the same old distance across—a half a mile—because the Missouri shore was just a wall of high bluffs.

Daytimes we paddled all over the island in the canoe. It was mighty cool and shady in the deep woods even if the sun was blazing outside. We went winding in and out amongst the trees; and some-times the vines hung so thick we had to back away and go some other way. Well, on every old broken-down tree, you could see rabbits, and snakes, and such things; and when the island had been overflowed a day or two, they got so tame, on account of being hungry, that you could paddle right up and put your hand on them if you wanted to; but not the snakes and turtles—they would slide off in the water. The ridge our cavern was in, was full of them. We could a had pets enough if we'd wanted them.

One night we catched a little section of a lumber raft—nice pine planks. It was twelve foot wide and about fifteen or sixteen foot long, and the top stood above water six or seven inches, a solid level floor. We could see saw-logs go by in the daylight, sometimes, but we let them go; we didn't show ourselves in daylight.

Another night, when we was up at the head of the island, just before daylight, here comes a frame house down, on the west side. She was a two-story, and tilted over, considerable. We paddled out and got aboard—clumb in at an up-stairs window. But it was too dark to see yet, so we made the canoe fast and set in her to wait for daylight.

The light begun to come before we got to the foot of the island. Then we looked in at the window. We could make out a bed, and a table, and two old chairs, and lots of things around about on the floor; and there was clothes hanging against the wall. There was something laying on the floor in the far corner that looked like a man. So Jim says:

"Hello, you!"

But it didn't budge. So I hollered again, and then Jim says:

"De man ain't asleep—he's dead. You hold still—I'll go en see."

He went and bent down and looked, and says:

"It's a dead man. Yes, indeedy; naked, too. He's ben shot in de back. I reck'n he's ben dead two er three days. Come in, Huck, but doan' look at his face—it's too gashly."

I didn't look at him at all. Jim throwed some old rags over him, but he needn't done it; I didn't want to see him. There was heaps of old greasy cards scattered around over the floor, and old whisky bottles, and a couple of masks made out of black cloth; and all over the walls was the ignorantest kind of words and pictures, made with charcoal. There was two old dirty calico dresses, and a sun-bonnet, and some women's under-clothes, hanging against the wall, and some men's clothing, too. We put the lot into the canoe; it might come good. There was a boy's old speckled straw hat on the floor; I took that too. And there was a bottle that had had milk in it; and it had a rag stopper for a baby to suck. We would a took the bottle, but it was broke. There was a seedy old chest, and an old hair trunk with the hinges broke. They stood open, but there warn't nothing left in them that was any account. The way things was scattered about, we reckoned the people left in a hurry and warn't fixed so as to carry off most of their stuff.

We got an old tin lantern, and a butcher-knife without any handle, and a bran-new Barlow knife² worth two bits in any store, and a lot of tallow candles, and a tin candlestick, and a gourd, and a tin cup, and a ratty old bed-quilt off the bed, and a reticule with needles and pins and beeswax and buttons and thread and all such truck in it, and a hatchet and some nails, and a fish-line as thick as my little finger, with some monstrous hooks on it, and a roll of buckskin, and a leather dog-collar, and a horse-shoe, and some vials of medicine that didn't have no label on them; and just as we was leaving I found a tolerable good curry-comb, and Jim he found a ratty old fiddle-bow, and a wooden leg. The straps was broke off of it, but barring that, it was a good enough leg, though it was too long for me and not long enough for Jim, and we couldn't find the other one, though we hunted all around.

And so, take it all around, we made a good haul. When we was ready to shove off, we was a quarter of a mile below the island, and it was pretty broad day; so I made Jim lay down in the canoe and cover up with the quilt, because if he set up, people could tell he was a nigger a good ways off. I paddled over to the Illinois shore, and drifted down most a half a mile doing it. I crept up the dead water under the bank, and hadn't no accidents and didn't see nobody. We got home all safe.

Chapter X

After breakfast I wanted to talk about the dead man and guess out how he come to be killed, but Jim didn't want to. He said it would fetch bad luck; and besides, he said, he might come and ha'nt us; he said a man that warn't buried was more likely to go a-ha'nting around than one that was planted and comfortable. That sounded pretty reasonable, so I didn't say no more; but I couldn't keep from studying over it and wishing I knowed who shot the man, and what they done it for.

We rummaged the clothes we'd got, and found eight dollars in silver sewed up in the lining of an old blanket overcoat. Jim said he reckoned the people in that house stole the coat, because if they'd a knowed the money was there they wouldn't a left it. I said I reckoned they killed him, too; but Jim didn't want to talk about that. I says:

"Now you think it's bad luck; but what did you say when I

2. A one-bladed jackknife, named for the maker.

fetched in the snake-skin that I found on the top of the ridge day before yesterday? You said it was the worst bad luck in the world to touch a snake-skin with my hands. Well, here's your bad luck! We've raked in all this truck and eight dollars besides. I wish we could have some bad luck like this every day, Jim."

"Never you mind, honey, never you mind. Don't you git too peart. It's a-comin'. Mind I tell you, it's a-comin'."

It did come, too. It was a Tuesday that we had that talk. Well, after dinner Friday, we was laying around in the grass at the upper end of the ridge, and got out of tobacco. I went to the cavern to get some, and found a rattlesnake in there. I killed him, and curled him up on the foot of Jim's blanket, ever so natural, thinking there'd be some fun when Jim found him there. Well, by night I forgot all about the snake, and when Jim flung himself down on the blanket while I struck a light, the snake's mate was there, and bit him.

He jumped up yelling, and the first thing the light showed was the varmint curled up and ready for another spring. I laid him out in a second with a stick, and Jim grabbed pap's whisky jug and began to pour it down.

He was barefooted, and the snake bit him right on the heel. That all comes of my being such a fool as to not remember that wherever you leave a dead snake its mate always comes there and curls around it. Jim told me to chop off the snake's head and throw it away, and then skin the body and roast a piece of it. I done it, and he eat it and said it would help cure him. He made me take off the rattles and tie them around his wrist, too. He said that that would help. Then I slid out quiet and throwed the snakes clear away amongst the bushes; for I warn't going to let Jim find out it was all my fault, not if I could help it.

Jim sucked and sucked at the jug, and now and then he got out of his head and pitched around and yelled; but every time he come to himself he went to sucking at the jug again. His foot swelled up pretty big, and so did his leg; but by-and-by the drunk begun to come, and so I judged he was all right; but I'd druther been bit with a snake than pap's whisky.

Jim was laid up for four days and nights. Then the swelling was all gone and he was around again. I made up my mind I wouldn't ever take aholt of a snake-skin again with my hands, now that I see what had come of it. Jim said he reckoned I would believe him next time. And he said that handling a snake-skin was such awful bad luck that maybe we hadn't got to the end of it yet. He said he druther see the new moon over his left shoulder as much as a thousand times than take up a snake-skin in his hand. Well, I was getting to feel that way myself, though I've always reckoned that looking at the new moon over your left shoulder is one of the carelessest and foolishest things a body can do. Old Hank Bunker done it once, and bragged about it; and in less than two years he got drunk and fell off of the shot tower and spread himself out so that he was just a kind of layer, as you may say; and they slid him edgeways between two barn doors for a coffin, and buried him so, so they say, but I didn't see it. Pap told me. But anyway, it all come of looking at the moon that way, like a fool.

Well, the days went along, and the river went down between its banks again; and about the first thing we done was to bait one of the big hooks with a skinned rabbit and set it and catch a cat-fish that was as big as a man, being six foot two inches long, and weighed over two hundred pounds. We couldn't handle him, of course; he would a flung us into Illinois. We just set there and watched him rip and tear around till he drowned. We found a brass button in his stomach, and a round ball, and lots of rubbage. We split the ball open with the hatchet, and there was a spool in it. Jim said he'd had it there a long time, to coat it over so and make a ball of it. It was as big a fish as was ever catched in the Mississippi, I reckon. Jim said he hadn't ever seen a bigger one. He would a been worth a good deal over at the village. They peddle out such a fish as that by the pound in the market house there; everybody buys some of him; his meat's as white as snow and makes a good fry.

Next morning I said it was getting slow and dull, and I wanted to get a stirring up, some way. I said I reckoned I would slip over the river and find out what was going on. Jim liked that notion; but he said I must go in the dark and look sharp. Then he studied it over and said, couldn't I put on some of them old things and dress up like a girl? That was a good notion, too. So we shortened up one of the calico gowns and I turned up my trouser-legs to my knees and got into it. Jim hitched it behind with the hooks, and it was a fair fit. I put on the sun-bonnet and tied it under my chin, and then for a body to look in and see my face was like looking down a joint of stove-pipe. Jim said nobody would know me, even in the daytime, hardly. I practiced around all day to get the hang of the things, and by-and-by I could do pretty well in them, only Jim said I didn't walk like a girl; and he said I must quit pulling up my gown to get at my britches pocket. I took notice, and done better.

I started up the Illinois shore in the canoe just after dark.

I started across to the town from a little below the ferry landing, and the drift of the current fetched me in at the bottom of the town. I tied up and started along the bank. There was a light burning in a little shanty that hadn't been lived in for a long time, and I wondered who had took up quarters there. I slipped up and peeped in at the window. There was a woman about forty year old in there, knitting by a candle that was on a pine table. I didn't know her face; she was a stranger, for you couldn't start a face in that town that I didn't know. Now this was lucky, because I was weakening; I was getting afraid I had come; people might know my voice and find me out. But if this woman had been in such a little town two days she could tell me all I wanted to know; so I knocked at the door, and made up my mind I wouldn't forget I was a girl.

Chapter XI

"Come in," says the woman, and I did. She says:
"Take a cheer."
I done it. She looked me all over with her little shiny eyes, and says:
"What might your name be?"
"Sarah Williams."
"Where 'bouts do you live? In this neighborhood?"
"No'm. In Hookerville, seven mile below. I've walked all the way and I'm all tired out."
"Hungry, too, I reckon. I'll find you something."
"No'm, I ain't hungry. I was so hungry I had to stop two mile below here at a farm; so I ain't hungry no more. It's what makes me so late. My mother's down sick, and out of money and everything, and I come to tell my Uncle Abner Moore. He lives at the upper end of the town, she says. I hain't ever been here before. Do you know him?"
"No; but I don't know everybody yet. I haven't lived here quite two weeks. It's a considerable ways to the upper end of the town. You better stay here all night. Take off your bonnet."
"No," I says, "I'll rest a while, I reckon, and go on. I ain't afeard of the dark."
She said she wouldn't let me go by myself, but her husband would be in by-and-by, maybe in a hour and a half, and she'd send him along with me. Then she got to talking about her husband, and about her relations up the river, and her relations down the river, and about how much better off they used to was, and how they didn't know but they'd made a mistake coming to our town, instead of letting well alone—and so on and so on, till I was afeard *I* had made a mistake coming to her to find out what was going on in the town; but by-and-by she dropped onto pap and the murder, and then I was pretty willing to let her clatter right along. She told about me and Tom Sawyer finding the six thousand dollars

(only she got it ten) and all about pap and what a hard lot he was, and what a hard lot I was, and at last she got down to where I was murdered. I says:

"Who done it? We've heard considerable about these goings on, down in Hookerville, but we don't know who 'twas that killed Huck Finn."

"Well, I reckon there's a right smart chance of people *here* that'd like to know who killed him. Some thinks old Finn done it himself."

"No—is that so?"

"Most everybody thought it at first. He'll never know how nigh he come to getting lynched. But before night they changed around and judged it was done by a runaway nigger named Jim."

"Why *he*—"

I stopped. I reckoned I better keep still. She run on, and never noticed I had put in at all.

"The nigger run off the very night Huck Finn was killed. So there's a reward out for him—three hundred dollars. And there's a reward out for old Finn too—two hundred dollars. You see, he come to town the morning after the murder, and told about it, and was out with 'em on the ferry-boat hunt, and right away after he up and left. Before night they wanted to lynch him, but he was gone, you see. Well, next day they found out the nigger was gone; they found out he hadn't ben seen sence ten o'clock the night the murder was done. So then they put it on him, you see, and while they was full of it, next day back comes old Finn and went boo-hooing to Judge Thatcher to get money to hunt for the nigger all over Illinois with. The judge give him some, and that evening he got drunk and was around till after midnight with a couple of mighty hard looking strangers, and then went off with them. Well, he hain't come back sence, and they ain't looking for him back till this thing blows over a little, for people thinks now that he killed his boy and fixed things so folks would think robbers done it, and then he'd get Huck's money without having to bother a long time with a lawsuit. People do say he warn't any too good to do it. Oh, he's sly, I reckon. If he don't come back for a year, he'll be all right. You can't prove anything on him, you know; everything will be quieted down then, and he'll walk into Huck's money as easy as nothing."

"Yes, I reckon so, 'm. I don't see nothing in the way of it. Has everybody quit thinking the nigger done it?"

"Oh, no, not everybody. A good many thinks he done it. But they'll get the nigger pretty soon, now, and maybe they can scare it out of him."

"Why, are they after him yet?"

"Well, you're innocent, ain't you! Does three hundred dollars lay round every day for people to pick up? Some folks thinks the nigger ain't far from here. I'm one of them—but I hain't talked it around. A few days ago I was talking with an old couple that lives next door in the log shanty, and they happened to say hardly anybody ever goes to that island over yonder that they call Jackson's Island. Don't anybody live there? says I. No, nobody, says they. I didn't say any more, but I done some thinking. I was pretty near certain I'd seen smoke over there, about the head of the island, a day or two before that, so I says to myself, like as not that nigger's hiding over there; anyway, says I, it's worth the trouble to give the place a hunt. I hain't seen any smoke sence, so I reckon maybe he's gone, if it was him; but husband's going over to see—him and another man. He was gone up the river; but he got back to-day and I told him as soon as he got here two hours ago."

I had got so uneasy I couldn't set still. I had to do something with my hands; so I took up a needle off of the table and went to threading it. My hands shook, and I was making a bad job of it. When the woman stopped talking, I looked up, and she was looking at me pretty curious, and smiling a little. I put down the needle and thread and let on to be interested—and I was, too—and says:

"Three hundred dollars is a power of money. I wish my mother could get it. Is your husband going over there to-night?"

"Oh, yes. He went up town with the man I was telling you of, to get a boat and see if they could borrow another gun. They'll go over after midnight."

"Couldn't they see better if they was to wait till daytime?"

"Yes. And couldn't the nigger see better, too? After midnight he'll likely be asleep, and they can slip around through the woods and hunt up his camp fire all the better for the dark, if he's got one."

"I didn't think of that."

The woman kept looking at me pretty curious, and I didn't feel a bit comfortable. Pretty soon she says:

"What did you say your name was, honey?"

"M—Mary Williams."

Somehow it didn't seem to me that I said it was Mary before, so I didn't look up; seemed to me I said it was Sarah; so I felt sort of cornered, and was afeard maybe I was looking it, too. I wished the woman would say something more; the longer she set still, the uneasier I was. But now she says:

"Honey, I thought you said it was Sarah when you first come in?"

"Oh, yes'm, I did. Sarah Mary Williams. Sarah's my first name. Some calls me Sarah, some calls me Mary."

"Oh, that's the way of it?"

"Yes'm."

I was feeling better, then, but I wished I was out of there, any-way. I couldn't look up yet.

Well, the woman fell to talking about how hard times was, and how poor they had to live, and how the rats was as free as if they owned the place, and so forth, and so on, and then I got easy again. She was right about the rats. You'd see one stick his nose out of a hole in the corner every little while. She said she had to have things handy to throw at them when she was alone, or they wouldn't give her no peace. She showed me a bar of lead, twisted up into a knot, and said she was a good shot with it gen-erly, but she'd wrenched her arm a day or two ago, and didn't know whether she could throw true, now. But she watched for a chance, and directly she banged away at a rat, but she missed him wide, and said "Ouch!" it hurt her arm so. Then she told me to try for the next one. I wanted to be getting away before the old man got back, but of course I didn't let on. I got the thing, and the first rat that showed his nose I let drive, and if he'd a stayed where he was he'd a been a tolerable sick rat. She said that that was first-rate, and she reckoned I would hive the next one. She went and got the lump of lead and fetched it back and brought along a hank of yarn, which she wanted me to help her with. I held up my two hands and she put the hank over them and went on talking about her and her husband's matters. But she broke off to say:

"Keep your eye on the rats. You better have the lead in your lap, handy."

So she dropped the lump into my lap, just at that moment, and I clapped my legs together on it and she went on talking. But only about a minute. Then she took off the hank and looked me straight in the face, but very pleasant, and says:

"Come, now—what's your real name?"

"Wh-what, mum?"

"What's your real name? Is it Bill, or Tom, or Bob?—or what is it?"

I reckon I shook like a leaf, and I didn't know hardly what to do. But I says:

"Please to don't poke fun at a poor girl like me, mum. If I'm in the way, here, I'll—"

"No, you won't. Set down and stay where you are. I ain't going to hurt you, and I ain't going to tell on you, nuther. You just tell me your secret, and trust me. I'll keep it; and what's more, I'll help you. So'll my old man, if you want him to. You see, you're a run-away 'prentice—that's all. It ain't anything. There ain't any harm in it. You've been treated bad, and you made up your mind to cut. Bless you, child, I wouldn't tell on you. Tell me all about it, now

—that's a good boy."

So I said it wouldn't be no use to try to play it any longer, and I would just make a clean breast and tell her everything, but she mustn't go back on her promise. Then I told her my father and mother was dead, and the law had bound me out to a mean old farmer in the country thirty mile back from the river, and he treated me so bad I couldn't stand it no longer; he went away to be gone a couple of days, and so I took my chance and stole some of his daughter's old clothes, and cleared out, and I had been three nights coming the thirty miles; I traveled nights, and hid day-times and slept, and the bag of bread and meat I carried from home lasted me all the way and I had a plenty. I said I believed my uncle Abner Moore would take care of me, and so that was why I struck out for this town of Goshen."

"Goshen, child? This ain't Goshen. This is St. Petersburg.[3] Goshen's ten mile further up the river. Who told you this was Goshen?"

"Why, a man I met at day-break this morning, just as I was going to turn into the woods for my regular sleep. He told me when the roads forked I must take the right hand, and five mile would fetch me to Goshen."

"He was drunk I reckon. He told you just exactly wrong."

"Well, he did act like he was drunk, but it ain't no matter now. I got to be moving along. I'll fetch Goshen before day-light."

"Hold on a minute. I'll put you up a snack to eat. You might want it."

So she put me up a snack, and says:

"Say—when a cow's laying down, which end of her gets up first? Answer up prompt, now—don't stop to study over it. Which end gets up first?"

"The hind end, mum."

"Well, then, a horse?"

"The for'rard end, mum."

"Which side of a tree does the most moss grow on?"

"North side."

"If fifteen cows is browsing on a hillside, how many of them eats with their heads pointed the same direction?"

"The whole fifteen, mum."

"Well, I reckon you *have* lived in the country. I thought maybe you was trying to hocus me again. What's your real name, now?"

"George Peters, mum."

"Well, try to remember it, George. Don't forget and tell me it's Elexander before you go, and then get out by saying it's George-Elexander when I catch you. And don't go about women in that

3. Mark Twain's fictitious name for Hannibal.

old calico. You do a girl tolerable poor, but you might fool men, maybe. Bless you, child, when you set out to thread a needle, don't hold the thread still and fetch the needle up to it; hold the needle still and poke the thread at it—that's the way a woman most always does; but a man always does 'tother way. And when you throw at a rat or anything, hitch yourself up a tip-toe, and fetch your hand up over your head as awkward as you can, and miss your rat about six or seven foot. Throw stiff-armed from the shoulder, like there was a pivot there for it to turn on—like a girl; not from the wrist and elbow, with your arm out to one side, like a boy. And mind you, when a girl tries to catch anything in her lap, she throws her knees apart; she don't clap them together, the way you did when you catched the lump of lead. Why, I spotted you for a boy when you was threading the needle; and I contrived the other things just to make certain. Now trot along to your uncle, Sarah Mary Williams George Elexander Peters, and if you get into trouble you send word to Mrs. Judith Loftus, which is me, and I'll do what I can to get you out of it. Keep the river road, all the way, and next time you tramp, take shoes and socks with you. The river road's a rocky one, and your feet 'll be in a condition when you get to Goshen, I reckon."

I went up the bank about fifty yards, and then I doubled on my tracks and slipped back to where my canoe was, a good piece below the house. I jumped in and was off in a hurry. I went up stream far enough to make the head of the island, and then started across. I took off the sun-bonnet, for I didn't want no blinders on, then. When I was about the middle, I hear the clock begin to strike; so I stops and listens; the sound come faint over the water, but clear—eleven. When I struck the head of the island I never waited to blow, though I was most winded, but I shoved right into the timber where my old camp used to be, and started a good fire there on a high-and-dry spot.

Then I jumped in the canoe and dug out for our place a mile and a half below, as hard as I could go. I landed, and slopped through the timber and up the ridge and into the cavern. There Jim laid, sound asleep on the ground. I roused him out and says:

"Git up and hump yourself, Jim! There ain't a minute to lose. They're after us!"

Jim never asked no questions, he never said a word; but the way he worked for the next half an hour showed about how he was scared. By that time everything we had in the world was on our raft and she was ready to be shoved out from the willow cove where she was hid. We put out the camp fire at the cavern the first thing, and didn't show a candle outside after that.

I took the canoe out from shore a little piece and took a look, but if there was a boat around I couldn't see it, for stars and shadows ain't good to see by. Then we got out the raft and slipped along down in the shade, past the foot of the island dead still, never saying a word.

Chapter XII

Must a been close onto one o'clock when we got below the island at last, and the raft did seem to go mighty slow. If a boat was to come along, we was going to take to the canoe and break for the Illinois shore; and it was well a boat didn't come, for we hadn't ever thought to put the gun into the canoe, or a fishing-line or anything to eat. We was in ruther too much of a sweat to think of so many things. It warn't good judgment to put *everything* on the raft.

If the men went to the island, I just expect they found the camp fire I built, and watched it all night for Jim to come. Anyways, they stayed away from us, and if my building the fire never fooled them it warn't no fault of mine. I played it as low-down on them as I could.

When the first streak of day begun to show, we tied up to a tow-head in a big bend on the Illinois side, and hacked off cotton-wood branches with the hatchet and covered up the raft with them so she looked like there had been a cave-in in the bank there. A tow-head is a sand-bar that has cotton-woods on it as thick as harrow-teeth.

We had mountains on the Missouri shore and heavy timber on the Illinois side, and the channel was down the Missouri shore at that place, so we warn't afraid of anybody running across us. We laid there all day and watched the rafts and steamboats spin down the Missouri shore, and up-bound steamboats fight the big river in the middle. I told Jim all about the time I had jabbering with that woman; and Jim said she was a smart one, and if she was to start after us herself *she* wouldn't set down and watch a camp fire—no, sir, she'd fetch a dog. Well, then, I said, why couldn't she tell her husband to fetch a dog? Jim said he bet she did think of it by the time the men was ready to start, and he believed they must a gone up town to get a dog and so they lost all that time, or else we wouldn't be here on a tow-head sixteen or seventeen mile below the village—no, indeedy, we would be in that same old town again. So I said I didn't care what was the reason they didn't get us, as long as they didn't.

When it was beginning to come on dark, we poked our heads out of the cottonwood thicket and looked up, and down, and across; nothing in sight; so Jim took up some of the top planks of the raft and built a snug wigwam to get under in blazing weather and rainy, and to keep the things dry. Jim made a floor for the wigwam, and raised it a foot or more above the level of the raft, so now the blankets and all the traps was out of the reach of steamboat waves. Right in the middle of the wigwam we made a layer of dirt about five or six inches deep with a frame around it for to hold it to its place; this was to build a fire on in sloppy weather or chilly; the wigwam would keep it from being seen. We made an extra steering oar, too, because one of the others might get broke, on a snag or something. We fixed up a short forked stick to hang the old lantern on; because we must always light the lantern whenever we see a steamboat coming down stream, to keep from getting run over; but we wouldn't have to light it up for upstream boats unless we see we was in what they call a "crossing;" for the river was pretty high yet, very low banks being still a little under water; so up-bound boats didn't always run the channel, but hunted easy water.

This second night we run between seven and eight hours, with a current that was making over four mile an hour. We catched fish, and talked, and we took a swim now and then to keep off sleepiness. It was kind of solemn, drifting down the big still river, laying on our backs looking up at the stars, and we didn't ever feel like talking loud, and it warn't often that we laughed, only a little kind of a low chuckle. We had mighty good weather, as a general thing, and nothing ever happened to us at all, that night, nor the next, nor the next.

Every night we passed towns, some of them away up on black hillsides, nothing but just a shiny bed of lights, not a house could you see. The fifth night we passed St. Louis, and it was like the whole world lit up. In St. Petersburg they used to say there was twenty or thirty thousand people in St. Louis, but I never believed it till I see that wonderful spread of lights at two o'clock that still night. There warn't a sound there; everybody was asleep.

Every night, now, I used to slip ashore, towards ten o'clock, at some little village, and buy ten or fifteen cents' worth of meal or bacon or other stuff to eat; and sometimes I lifted a chicken that warn't roosting comfortable, and took him along. Pap always said, take a chicken when you get a chance, because if you don't want him yourself you can easy find somebody that does, and a good deed ain't ever forgot. I never see Pap when he didn't want the chicken himself, but that is what he used to say, anyway.

Mornings, before daylight, I slipped into corn fields and borrowed a watermelon, or a mushmelon, or a pumpkin, or some new corn, or things of that kind. Pap always said it warn't no harm to borrow things, if you was meaning to pay them back, sometime; but the widow said it warn't anything but a soft name for stealing, and no decent body would do it. Jim said he reckoned the widow was partly right and pap was partly right; so the best way would be for us to pick out two or three things from the list and say we wouldn't borrow them any more—then he reckoned it wouldn't be no harm to borrow the others. So we talked it over all one night, drifting along down the river, trying to make up our minds whether to drop the watermelons, or the cantelopes, or the mushmelons, or what. But towards daylight we got it all settled satisfactory, and concluded to drop crabapples and p'simmons. We warn't feeling just right, before that, but it was all comfortable now. I was glad the way it come out, too, because crabapples ain't ever good, and the p'simmons wouldn't be ripe for two or three months yet.

We shot a water-fowl, now and then, that got up too early in the morning or didn't go to bed early enough in the evening. Take it all around, we lived pretty high.

The fifth night below St. Louis we had a big storm after midnight, with a power of thunder and lightning, and the rain poured down in a solid sheet. We stayed in the wigwam and let the raft take care of itself. When the lightning glared out we could see a big straight river ahead, and high rocky bluffs on both sides. By-and-by says I, "Hel-*lo*, Jim, looky yonder!" It was a steamboat that had killed herself on a rock. We was drifting straight down for her. The lightning showed her very distinct. She was leaning over, with part of her upper deck above water, and you could see every little chimbly-guy clean and clear, and a chair by the big bell, with an old slouch hat hanging on the back of it when the flashes come.

Well, it being away in the night, and stormy, and all so mysterious-like, I felt just the way any other boy would a felt when I see that wreck laying there so mournful and lonesome in the middle of the river. I wanted to get aboard of her and slink around a little, and see what there was there. So I says:

"Le's land on her, Jim."

But Jim was dead against it, at first. He says:

"I doan' want to go fool'n 'long er no wrack. We's doin' blame' well, en we better let blame' well alone, as de good book says. Like as not dey's a watchman on dat wrack."

"Watchman your grandmother," I says; "there ain't nothing to watch but the texas and the pilot-house; and do you reckon anybody's going to resk his life for a texas[4] and a pilot-house such a night as this, when it's likely to break up and wash off down the river any minute?" Jim couldn't say nothing to that, so he didn't try. "And besides," I says, "we might borrow something worth having, out of the captain's stateroom. Seegars, *I* bet you—and cost

---

4. Officers' cabin (so called because it was the largest) on the upper deck of the steamboat, with the pilot house before or on top.

five cents apiece, solid cash. Steamboat captains is always rich, and
get sixty dollars a month, and *they* don't care a cent what a thing
costs, you know, long as they want it. Stick a candle in your pocket;
I can't rest, Jim, till we give her a rummaging. Do you reckon
Tom Sawyer would ever go by this thing? Not for pie, he wouldn't.
He'd call it an adventure—that's what he'd call it; and he'd land
on that wreck if it was his last act. And wouldn't he throw style
into it?—wouldn't he spread himself, nor nothing? Why, you'd
think it was Christopher C'lumbus discovering Kingdom-Come. I
wish Tom Sawyer *was* here."

Jim he grumbled a little, but give in. He said we mustn't talk
any more than we could help, and then talk mighty low. The
lightning showed us the wreck again, just in time, and we fetched
the starboard derrick, and made fast there.

The deck was high out, here. We went sneaking down the slope
of it to labboard, in the dark, towards the texas, feeling our way
slow with our feet, and spreading our hands out to fend off the
guys,[5] for it was so dark we couldn't see no sign of them. Pretty
soon we struck the forward end of the skylight, and clumb onto it;
and the next step fetched us in front of the captain's door, which
was open, and by Jimminy, away down through the texas-hall we see
a light! and all in the same second we seem to hear low voices in
yonder!

Jim whispered and said he was feeling powerful sick, and told me
to come along. I says, all right; and was going to start for the raft;
but just then I heard a voice wail out and say:

"Oh, please don't, boys; I swear I won't ever tell!"

Another voice said, pretty loud:

"It's a lie, Jim Turner. You've acted this way before. You always
want more'n your share of the truck, and you've always got it, too,
because you've swore 't if you didn't you'd tell. But this time you've
said it jest one time too many. You're the meanest, treacherousest
hound in this country."

By this time Jim was gone for the raft. I was just a-biling with
curiosity; and I says to myself, Tom Sawyer wouldn't back out now,
and so I won't either; I'm agoing to see what's going on here. So
I dropped on my hands and knees, in the little passage, and crept
aft in the dark, till there warn't but about one stateroom betwixt
me and the cross-hall of the texas. Then, in there I see a man
stretched on the floor and tied hand and foot, and two men standing over him, and one of them had a dim lantern in his hand, and
the other one had a pistol. This one kept pointing the pistol at the
man's head on the floor and saying—

"I'd *like* to! And I orter, too, a mean skunk!"

5. Ropes fastened aloft for hoisting or dropping cargo.

The man on the floor would shrivel up, and say: "Oh, please don't, Bill—I hain't ever goin' to tell."

And every time he said that, the man with the lantern would laugh, and say:

" 'Deed you *ain't!* You never said no truer thing 'n that, you bet you." And once he said: "Hear him beg! and yit if we hadn't got the best of him and tied him, he'd a killed us both. And what *for?* Jist for noth'n. Jist because we stood on our *rights*—that's what for. But I lay you ain't agoin' to threaten nobody any more, Jim Turner. Put *up* that pistol, Bill."

Bill says:

"I don't want to, Jake Packard. I'm for killin' him—and didn't he kill old Hatfield jist the same way—and don't he deserve it?"

"But I don't *want* him killed, and I've got my reasons for it."

"Bless yo' heart for them words, Jake Packard! I'll never forget you, long's I live!" says the man on the floor, sort of blubbering.

Packard didn't take no notice of that, but hung up his lantern on a nail, and started towards where I was, there in the dark, and motioned Bill to come. I crawfished[6] as fast as I could, about two yards, but the boat slanted so that I couldn't make very good time; so to keep from getting run over and catched I crawled into a stateroom on the upper side. The man come a-pawing along in the dark, and when Packard got to my stateroom, he says:

"Here—come in here."

And in he come, and Bill after him. But before they got in, I was up in the upper berth, cornered, and sorry I come. Then they stood there, with their hands on the ledge of the berth, and talked. I couldn't see them, but I could tell where they was, by the whisky they'd been having. I was glad I didn't drink whisky; but it wouldn't made much difference, anyway, because most of the time they couldn't a treed me because I didn't breathe. I was too scared. And besides, a body *couldn't* breathe, and hear such talk. They talked low and earnest. Bill wanted to kill Turner. He says:

"He's said he'll tell, and he will. If we was to give both our shares to him *now*, it wouldn't make no difference after the row, and the way we've served him. Shore's you're born, he'll turn State's evidence; now you hear *me*. I'm for putting him out of his troubles."

"So'm I," says Packard, very quiet.

"Blame it, I'd sorter begun to think you wasn't. Well, then, that's all right. Les' go and do it."

"Hold on a minute; I hain't had my say yit. You listen to me. Shooting's good, but there's quieter ways if the thing's *got* to be done. But what *I* say, is this; it ain't good sense to go court'n

6. Crawled backward.

around after a halter, if you can git at what you're up to in some way that's jist as good and at the same time don't bring you into no resks. Ain't that so?"

"You bet it is. But how you goin' to manage it this time?"

"Well, my idea is this: we'll rustle around and gether up whatever pickins we've overlooked in the staterooms, and shove for shore and hide the truck. Then we'll wait. Now I say it ain't agoin' to be more 'n two hours befo' this wrack breaks up and washes off down the river. See? He'll be drownded, and won't have nobody to blame for it but his own self. I reckon that's a considerable sight better'n killin' of him. I'm unfavorable to killin' a man as long as you can git around it; it ain't good sense, it ain't good morals. Ain't I right?"

"Yes—I reck'n you are. But s'pose she *don't* break up and wash off?"

"Well, we can wait the two hours, anyway, and see, can't we?"

"All right, then; come along."

So they started, and I lit out, all in a cold sweat, and scrambled forward. It was dark as pitch there; but I said in a kind of a coarse whisper, "Jim!" and he answered up, right at my elbow, with a sort of a moan, and I says:

"Quick, Jim, it ain't no time for fooling around and moaning; there's a gang of murderers in yonder, and if we don't hunt up their boat and set her drifting down the river so these fellows can't get away from the wreck, there's one of 'em going to be in a bad fix. But if we find their boat we can put *all* of 'em in a bad fix—for the Sheriff 'll get 'em. Quick—hurry! I'll hunt the labboard side, you hunt the stabboard. You start at the raft, and—"

"Oh, my lordy, lordy! *Raf'?* Dey ain' no raf' no mo', she done broke loose en gone!—'en here we is!"

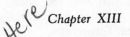 Chapter XIII

Well, I catched my breath and most fainted. Shut up on a wreck with such a gang as that! But it warn't no time to be sentimentering. We'd got to find that boat, now—had to have it for ourselves. So we went a-quaking and shaking down the stabboard side, and slow work it was, too—seemed a week before we got to the stern. No sign of a boat. Jim said he didn't believe he could go any further—so scared he hadn't hardly any strength left, he said. But I said come on, if we get left on this wreck, we are in a fix, sure. So on we prowled, again. We struck for the stern of the texas, and found it, and then scrabbled along forwards on the skylight, hanging on from shutter to shutter, for the edge of the skylight was in the water. When we got pretty close to the cross-hall door, there was the skiff, sure enough! I could just barely see her. I felt ever so thankful. In another second I would a been aboard of her; but just then the door opened. One of the men stuck his head out, only about a couple of foot from me, and I thought I was gone; but he jerked it in again, and says:

"Heave that blame lantern out o' sight, Bill!"

He flung a bag of something into the boat, and then got in himself, and set down. It was Packard. Then Bill *he* come out and got in. Packard says, in a low voice:

"All ready—shove off!"

I couldn't hardly hang onto the shutters, I was so weak. But Bill says:

"Hold on—'d you go through him?"

"No. Didn't you?"

"No. So he's got his share o' the cash, yet."

"Well, then, come along—no use to take truck and leave money."

"Say—won't he suspicion what we're up to?"

"Maybe he won't. But we got to have it anyway. Come along."

So they got out and went in.

The door slammed to, because it was on the careened side; and in a half second I was in the boat, and Jim come a tumbling after me. I out with my knife and cut the rope, and away we went!

We didn't touch an oar, and we didn' speak nor whisper, nor hardly even breathe. We went gliding swift along, dead silent, past the tip of the paddle-box, and past the stern; then in a second or two more we was a hundred yards below the wreck, and the darkness soaked her up, every last sign of her, and we was safe, and knowed it.

When we was three or four hundred yards down stream, we see the lantern show like a little spark at the texas door, for a second, and we knowed by that that the rascals had missed their boat, and was beginning to understand that they was in just as much trouble, now, as Jim Turner was.

Then Jim manned the oars, and we took out after our raft. Now was the first time that I begun to worry about the men—I reckon I hadn't had time to before. I begun to think how dreadful it was, even for murderers, to be in such a fix. I says to myself, there ain't no telling but I might come to be a murderer myself, yet, and then how would *I* like it? So says I to Jim:

"The first light we see, we'll land a hundred yards below it or above it, in a place where it's a good hiding-place for you and the skiff, and then I'll go and fix up some kind of a yarn, and get somebody to go for that gang and get them out of their scrape, so they can be hung when their time comes."

But that idea was a failure; for pretty soon it begun to storm again, and this time worse than ever. The rain poured down, and never a light showed; everybody in bed, I reckon. We boomed along down the river, watching for lights and watching for our raft. After a long time the rain let up, but the clouds staid, and the lightning kept whimpering, and by-and-by a flash showed us a black thing ahead, floating, and we made for it.

It was the raft, and mighty glad was we to get aboard of it again. We seen a light, now, away down to the right, on shore. So I said I would go for it. The skiff was half full of plunder which that gang had stole, there on the wreck. We hustled it onto the raft in a pile, and I told Jim to float along down, and show a light when he judged he had gone about two mile, and keep it burning till I come; then I manned my oars and shoved for the light. As I got down towards it, three or four more showed—up on a hillside. It was a village. I closed in above the shore-light, and laid on my oars and floated. As I went by, I see it was a lantern hanging on the jackstaff of a double-hull ferry-boat. I skimmed around for the watchman, a-wondering whereabouts he slept; and by-and-by I found him roosting on the bitts,[7] forward, with his head down between his knees. I give his shoulder two or three little shoves, and begun to cry.

He stirred up, in a kind of startlish way; but when he see it was only me, he took a good gap and stretch, and then he says:

"Hello, what's up? Don't cry, bub. What's the trouble?"

I says:

"Pap, and mam, and sis, and—"

Then I broke down. He says:

"Oh, dang it, now, *don't* take on so, we all has to have our troubles and this'n 'll come out all right. What's the matter with 'em?"

"They're—they're—are you the watchman of the boat?"

"Yes," he says, kind of pretty-well-satisfied like. "I'm the captain and the owner, and the mate, and the pilot, and watchman, and head deck-hand; and sometimes I'm the freight and passengers. I ain't as rich as old Jim Hornback, and I can't be so blame' generous and good to Tom, Dick and Harry as what he is, and slam around money the way he does; but I've told him a many a time 't I wouldn't trade places with him; for, says I, a sailor's life's the life for me, and I'm derned if I'd live two mile out o' town, where there ain't nothing ever goin' on, not for all his spondulicks and as much more on top of it. Says I—"

I broke in and says:

"They're in an awful peck of trouble, and—"

"*Who* is?"

"Why, pap, and mam, and sis, and Miss Hooker; and if you'd

7. Timbers above the deck to which cables or hawsers can be fastened.

take your ferry-boat and go up there—"

"Up where? Where are they?"

"On the wreck."

"What wreck?"

"Why, there ain't but one."

"What, you don't mean the **Walter Scott?**"[8]

"Yes."

"Good land! what are they doin' *there*, for gracious sakes?"

"Well, they didn't go there a-purpose."

"I bet they didn't! Why, great goodness, there ain't no chance for 'em if they don't git off mighty quick! Why, how in the nation did they ever git into such a scrape?"

"Easy enough. Miss Hooker was a-visiting, up there to the town—"

"Yes, Booth's Landing—go on."

"She was a-visiting, there at Booth's Landing, and just in the edge of the evening she started over with her nigger woman in the horse-ferry, to stay all night at her friend's house, Miss What-you-may-call-her, I disremember her name, and they lost their steering-oar, and swung around and went a-floating down, stern-first, about two mile, and saddle-baggsed on the wreck, and the ferry man and the nigger woman and the horses was all lost, but Miss Hooker she made a grab and got aboard the wreck. Well, about an hour after dark, we come along down in our trading-scow, and it was so dark we didn't notice the wreck till we was right on it; and so *we* saddle-baggsed; but all of us was saved but Bill Whipple—and oh, he *was* the best cretur!—I most wish't it had been me, I do."

"My George! It's the beatenest thing I ever struck. And *then* what did you all do?"

"Well, we hollered and took on, but it's so wide there, we couldn't make nobody hear. So pap said somebody got to get ashore and get help somehow. I was the only one that could swim, so I made a dash for it, and Miss Hooker she said if I didn't strike help sooner, come here and hunt up her uncle, and he'd fix the thing. I made the land about a mile below, and been fooling along ever since, trying to get people to do something, but they said, 'What, in such a night and such a current? there ain't no sense in it; go for the steam-ferry.' Now if you'll go, and—"

"By Jackson, I'd *like* to, and blame it I don't know but I will; but who in the dingnation's agoin' to *pay* for it? Do you reckon your pap—"

"Why *that's* all right. Miss Hooker she told me, *particular*, that

---

8. Twain comically names the steam-boat for the English author of ro- mances which, in his estimation, also foundered.

her uncle Hornback—"

"Great guns! is *he* her uncle? Looky here, you break for that light over yonder-way, and turn out west when you git there, and about a quarter of a mile out you'll come to the tavern; tell 'em to dart you out to Jim Hornback's and he'll foot the bill. And don't you fool around any, because he'll want to know the news. Tell him I'll have his niece all safe before he can get to town. Hump yourself, now; I'm agoing up around the corner here, to roust out my engineer."

I struck for the light, but as soon as he turned the corner I went back and got into my skiff and bailed her out and then pulled up shore in the easy water about six hundred yards, and tucked myself in among some woodboats; for I couldn't rest easy till I could see the ferry-boat start. But take it all around, I was feeling ruther comfortable on accounts of taking all this trouble for that gang, for not many would a done it. I wished the widow knowed about it. I judged she would be proud of me for helping these rapscallions, because rapscallions and dead beats is the kind the widow and good people takes the most interest in.

Well, before long, here comes the wreck, dim and dusky, sliding along down! A kind of cold shiver went through me, and then I struck out for her. She was very deep, and I see in a minute there warn't much chance for anybody being alive in her. I pulled all around her and hollered a little, but there wasn't any answer; all dead still. I felt a little bit heavy-hearted about the gang, but not much, for I reckoned if they could stand it, I could.

Then here comes the ferry-boat; so I shoved for the middle of the river on a long down-stream slant; and when I judged I was out of eye-reach, I laid on my oars, and looked back and see her go and smell around the wreck for Miss Hooker's remainders, because the captain would know her uncle Hornback would want them; and then pretty soon the ferry-boat give it up and went for shore, and I laid into my work and went a-booming down the river.

It did seem a powerful long time before Jim's light showed up; and when it did show, it looked like it was a thousand mile off. By the time I got there the sky was beginning to get a little gray in the east; so we struck for an island, and hid the raft, and sunk the skiff, and turned in and slept like dead people.

Here

Chapter XIV

By-and-by, when we got up, we turned over the truck the gang had stole off of the wreck, and found boots, and blankets, and clothes, and all sorts of other things, and a lot of books, and a spyglass, and three boxes of seegars. We hadn't ever been this rich before, in neither of our lives. The seegars was prime. We laid off all the afternoon in the woods talking, and me reading the books, and having a general good time. I told Jim all about what happened inside the wreck, and at the ferry-boat; and I said these kinds of things was adventures; but he said he didn't want no more adventures. He said that when I went in the texas and he crawled back to get on the raft and found her gone, he nearly died; because he judged it was all up with *him*, anyway it could be fixed; for if he didn't get saved he would get drownded; and if he did get saved, whoever saved him would send him back home so as to get the reward, and then Miss Watson would sell him South, sure. Well, he was right; he was most always right; he had an uncommon level head, for a nigger.

I read considerable to Jim about kings, and dukes, and earls, and such, and how gaudy they dressed, and how much style they put on, and called each other your majesty, and your grace, and your lordship, and so on, 'stead of mister; and Jim's eyes bugged out, and he was interested. He says:

"I didn' know dey was so many un um. I hain't hearn 'bout none un um, skasely, but ole King Sollermun, onless you counts dem kings dat's in a pack er k'yards. How much do a king git?"

"Get?" I says; "why, they get a thousand dollars a month if they want it; they can have just as much as they want; everything belongs to them."

"*Ain'* dat gay? En what they got to do, Huck?"

"*They* don't do nothing! Why how you talk. They just set around."

"No—is dat so?"

"Of course it is. They just set around. Except maybe when there 's a war; then they go to the war. But other times they just lazy around; or go hawking—just hawking and sp— Sh!—d' you hear a noise?"

We skipped out and looked; but it warn't nothing but the flutter of a steamboat's wheel, away down coming around the point; so we come back.

"Yes," says I, "and other times, when things is dull, they fuss with the parlyment; and if everybody don't go just so he whacks their heads off. But mostly they hang round the harem."

"Roun' de which?"

"Harem."

"What's de harem?"

"The place where he keep his wives. Don't you know about the harem? Solomon had one; he had about a million wives."

"Why, yes, dat's so; I—I'd done forgot it. A harem's a bo'd'n-house, I reck'n. Mos' likely dey has rackety times in de nussery. En

I reck'n de wives quarrels considable; en dat 'crease de racket. Yit
dey say Sollermun de wises' man dat ever live'. I doan' take no stock
in dat. Bekase why: would a wise man want to live in de mids' er
sich a blimblammin' all de time? No—'deed he wouldn't. A wise
man 'ud take en buil' a biler-factry; en den he could shet *down* de
biler-factry when he want to res'."

"Well, but he *was* the wisest man, anyway; because the widow
she told me so, her own self."

"I doan k'yer what de widder say, he *warn't* no wise man, nuther.
He had some er de dad-fetchedes' ways I ever see. Does you know
'bout dat chile dat he 'uz gwyne to chop in two?"[9]

"Yes, the widow told me all about it."

"*Well*, den! Warn' dat de beatenes' notion in de worl'? You jes'
take en look at it a minute. Dah's de stump, dah—dat's one er de
women; heah's you—dat's de yuther one; I's Sollermun; en dish-yer
dollar bill's de chile. Bofe un you claims it. What does I do? Does
I shin aroun' mongs' de neighbors en fine out which un you de bill
do b'long to, en han' it over to de right one, all safe en soun', de
way dat anybody dat had any gumption would? No—I take en
whack de bill in *two*, en give half un it to you, en de yuther half to
de yuther woman. Dat's de way Sollermun was gwyne to do wid de
chile. Now I want to ast you: what's de use er dat half a bill?—
can't buy noth'n wid it. En what use is a half a chile? I would'n give
a dern for a million un um."

"But hang it, Jim, you've clean missed the point—blame it,
you've missed it a thousand mile."

"Who? Me? Go 'long. Doan' talk to *me* 'bout yo' pints. I
reck'n I knows sense when I sees it; en dey ain' no sense in sich
doin's as dat. De 'spute warn't 'bout a half a chile, de 'spute was
'bout a whole chile; en de man dat think he kin settle a 'spute 'bout
a whole chile wid a half a chile, doan' know enough to come in out'n
de rain. Doan' talk to me 'bout Sollermun, Huck, I knows him by
de back."

"But I tell you you don't get the point."

"Blame de pint! I reck'n I knows what I knows. En mine you,
de *real* pint is down furder—it's down deeper. It lays in de way
Sollermun was raised. You take a man dat's got on'y one er two
chillen; is dat man gwyne to be waseful o' chillen? No, he ain't;
he can't 'ford it. *He* know how to value 'em. But you take a man
dat's got 'bout five million chillen runnin' roun' de house, en it's
diffunt. *He* as soon chop a chile in two as a cat. Dey's plenty mo'.
A chile er two, mo' er less, warn't no consekens to Sollermun, dad
fetch him!"

I never see such a nigger. If he got a notion in his head once,

9. *Cf.* I Kings iii: 16–27.

there warn't no getting it out again. He was the most down on Solomon of any nigger I ever see. So I went to talking about other kings, and let Solomon slide. I told about Louis Sixteenth that got his head cut off in France long time ago;[1] and about his little boy the dolphin,[2] that would a been a king, but they took and shut him up in jail, and some say he died there.

"Po' little chap."

"But some says he got out and got away, and come to America."

"Dat's good! But he'll be pooty lonesome—dey ain' no kings here, is dey, Huck?"

"No."

"Den he cain't git no situation. What he gwyne to do?"

"Well, I don't know. Some of them gets on the police, and some of them learns people how to talk French."

"Why, Huck, doan' de French people talk de same way we does?"

"No, Jim; you couldn't understand a word they said—not a single word."

"Well, now, I be ding-busted! How do dat come?"

"*I* don't know; but it's so. I got some of their jabber out of a book. Spose a man was to come to you and say *Polly-voo-franzy*— what would you think?"

"I wouldn' think nuff'n; I'd take en bust him over de head. Dat is, if he warn't white. I wouldn't 'low no nigger to call me dat."

"Shucks, it ain't calling you anything. It's only saying do you know how to talk French."

"Well, den, why couldn't he *say* it?"

"Why, he *is* a-saying it. That's a Frenchman's *way* of saying it."

"Well, it's a blame' ridicklous way, en I doan' want to hear no mo' 'bout it. Dey ain' no sense in it."

"Looky here, Jim; does a cat talk like we do?"

"No, a cat don't."

"Well, does a cow?"

"No, a cow don't, nuther."

"Does a cat talk like a cow, or a cow talk like a cat?"

"No, dey don't."

"It's natural and right for 'em to talk different from each other, ain't it?"

"'Course."

"And ain't it natural and right for a cat and a cow to talk different from *us*?"

---

1. In the first edition, erroneously printed "age."
2. The Dauphin, Louis Charles (1785– 1795?) survived the execution of his father, Louis XVI, in 1793, and died in prison. Huck alludes to one of the persistent legends of his escape and survival. *Cf.* the bogus pedigree of the "king" (and of the "duke") in Chapter XIX.

"Why, mos' sholy it is."

"Well, then, why ain't it natural and right for a *Frenchman* to talk different from us? You answer me that."

"Is a cat a man, Huck?"

"No."

"Well, den, dey ain't no sense in a cat talkin' like a man. Is a cow a man?—er is a cow a cat?"

"No, she ain't either of them."

"Well, den, she ain' got no business to talk like either one er the yuther of 'em. Is a Frenchman a man?"

"Yes."

"*Well*, den! Dad blame it, why doan' he *talk* like a man? You answer me *dat!*"

I see it warn't no use wasting words—you can't learn a nigger to argue. So I quit.

Chapter XV

We judged that three nights more would fetch us to Cairo,[3] at the bottom of Illinois, where the Ohio River comes in, and that was what we was after. We would sell the raft and get on a steamboat and go way up the Ohio amongst the free States, and then be out of trouble.[4]

Well, the second night a fog begun to come on, and we made for a tow-head to tie to, for it wouldn't do to try to run in fog; but when I paddled ahead in the canoe, with the line, to make fast, there warn't anything but little saplings to tie to. I passed the line around one of them right on the edge of the cut bank, but there was a stiff current, and the raft come booming down so lively she tore it out by the roots and away she went. I see the fog closing down, and it made me so sick and scared I couldn't budge for most a half a minute it seemed to me—and then there warn't no raft in sight; you couldn't see twenty yards. I jumped into the canoe and run back to the stern and grabbed the paddle and set her back a stroke. But she didn't come. I was in such a hurry I hadn't untied her. I got up and tried to untie her, but I was so excited my hands shook so I couldn't hardly do anything with them.

As soon as I got started I took out after the raft, hot and heavy, right down the tow-head. That was all right as far as it went, but the tow-head warn't sixty yards long, and the minute I flew by the

3. Pronounced locally as "Kay-ro."
4. Critical debates have centered on why the author did not carry out this plan for Jim's freedom. Reports on the manuscript indicate that Twain laid the book aside near the end of Chapter XVI for probably two years. When he took up the story again, it appears that he was enamored of the idea of the freedom of the River itself, a kind of time stream, in whose current there would be the escape from the cruelty and hypocrisy abroad on the land. *Cf.* Chapter VIII, note 7, and title note.

foot of it I shot out into the solid white fog, and hadn't no more idea which way I was going than a dead man.

Thinks I, it won't do to paddle; first I know I'll run into the bank or a tow-head or something; I got to set still and float, and yet it's mighty fidgety business to have to hold your hands still at such a time. I whooped and listened. Away down there, somewheres, I hears a small whoop, and up comes my spirits. I went tearing after it, listening sharp to hear it again. The next time it come, I see I warn't heading for it but heading away to the right of it. And the next time, I was heading away to the left of it—and not gaining on it much, either, for I was flying around, this way and that and 'tother, but it was going straight ahead all the time.

I did wish the fool would think to beat a tin pan, and beat it all the time, but he never did, and it was the still places between the whoops that was making the trouble for me. Well, I fought along, and directly I hears the whoop *behind* me. I was tangled good, now. That was somebody else's whoop, or else I was turned around.

I throwed the paddle down. I heard the whoop again; it was behind me yet, but in a different place; it kept coming, and kept changing its place, and I kept answering, till by-and-by it was in front of me again and I knowed the current had swung the canoe's head down stream and I was all right, if that was Jim and not some other raftsman hollering. I couldn't tell nothing about voices in a fog, for nothing don't look natural nor sound natural in a fog.

The whooping went on, and in about a minute I come a booming down on a cut bank with smoky ghosts of big trees on it, and the current throwed me off to the left and shot by, amongst a lot of snags that fairly roared, the current was tearing by them so swift.

In another second or two it was solid white and still again. I set perfectly still, then, listening to my heart thump, and I reckon I didn't draw a breath while it thumped a hundred.

I just give up, then. I knowed what the matter was. That cut bank was an island, and Jim had gone down 'tother side of it. It warn't no tow-head, that you could float by in ten minutes. It had the big timber of a regular island; it might be five or six mile long and more than a half a mile wide.

I kept quiet, with my ears cocked, about fifteen minutes, I reckon. I was floating along, of course, four or five mile an hour; but you don't ever think of that. No, you *feel* like you are laying dead still on the water; and if a little glimpse of a snag slips by, you don't think to yourself how fast *you're* going, but you catch your breath and think, my! how that snag's tearing along. If you think it ain't dismal and lonesome out in a fog that way, by yourself, in the night, you try it once—you'll see.

Next, for about half an hour, I whoops now and then; at last I hears the answer a long ways off, and tries to follow it, but I couldn't do it, and directly I judged I'd got into a nest of tow-heads, for I had little dim glimpses of them on both sides of me, sometimes just a narrow channel between; and some that I couldn't see, I knowed was there, because I'd hear the wash of the current against the old dead brush and trash that hung over the banks. Well, I warn't long losing the whoops, down amongst the tow-heads; and I only tried to chase them a little while, anyway, because it was worse than chasing a Jack-o-lantern. You never knowed a sound dodge around so, and swap places so quick and so much.

I had to claw away from the bank pretty lively, four or five times, to keep from knocking the islands out of the river; and so I judged the raft must be butting into the bank every now and then, or else it would get further ahead and clear out of hearing—it was floating a little faster than what I was.

Well, I seemed to be in the open river again, by-and-by, but I couldn't hear no sign of a whoop nowheres. I reckoned Jim had fetched up on a snag, maybe, and it was all up with him. I was good and tired, so I laid down in the canoe and said I wouldn't bother no more. I didn't want to go to sleep, of course; but I was so sleepy I couldn't help it; so I thought I would take just one little cat-nap.

But I reckon it was more than a cat-nap, for when I waked up the stars was shining bright, the fog was all gone, and I was spinning down a big bend stern first. First I didn't know where I was; I thought I was dreaming; and when things begun to come back to me, they seemed to come up dim out of last week.

It was a monstrous big river here, with the tallest and the thickest kind of timber on both banks; just a solid wall, as well as I could see, by the stars. I looked away down stream, and seen a black speck on the water. I took out after it; but when I got to it it warn't nothing but a couple of saw-logs made fast together. Then I see another speck, and chased that; then another, and this time I was right. It was the raft.

When I got to it Jim was setting there with his head down between his knees, asleep, with his right arm hanging over the steering oar. The other oar was smashed off, and the raft was littered up with leaves and branches and dirt. So she'd had a rough time.

I made fast and laid down under Jim's nose on the raft, and begun to gap, and stretch my fists out against Jim, and says:

"Hello, Jim, have I been asleep? Why didn't you stir me up?"

"Goodness gracious, is dat you, Huck? En you ain' dead—you ain' drowned—you's back agin? It's too good for true, honey, it's too good for true. Lemme look at you, chile, lemme feel o' you. No, you ain' dead! you's back agin, 'live en soun', jis de same ole Huck —de same ole Huck, thanks to goodness!"

"What's the matter with you, Jim? You been a drinking?"

"Drinkin'? Has I ben a drinkin'? Has I had a chance to be a drinkin'?"

"Well, then, what makes you talk so wild?"

"How does I talk wild?"

"*How?* why, hain't you been talking about my coming back, and all that stuff, as if I'd been gone away?"

"Huck—Huck Finn, you look me in de eye; look me in de eye. *Hain't* you ben gone away?"

"Gone away? Why, what in the nation do you mean? *I* hain't been gone anywheres. Where would I go to?"

"Well, looky here, boss, dey's sumf'n wrong, dey is. Is I *me*, or who *is* I? Is I heah, or whah *is* I? Now dat's what I wants to know?"

"Well, I think you're here, plain enough, but I think you're a tangle-headed old fool, Jim."

"I is, is I? Well you answer me dis. Didn't you tote out de line in de canoe, fer to make fas' to de tow-head?"

"No, I didn't. What tow-head? I hain't seen no tow-head."

"You hain't seen no tow-head? Looky here—didn't de line pull loose en de raf' go a hummin' down de river, en leave you en de canoe behine in de fog?"

"What fog?"

"Why *de* fog. De fog dat's ben aroun' all night. En didn't you whoop, en didn't I whoop, tell we got mix' up in de islands en one un us got los' en 'tother one was jis' as good as los', 'kase he didn' know whah he wuz? En didn't I bust up agin a lot er dem islands en have a turrible time en mos' git drownded? Now ain' dat so, boss —ain't it so? You answer me dat."

"Well, this is too many for me, Jim. I hain't seen no fog, nor no islands, nor no troubles, nor nothing. I been setting here talking with you all night till you went to sleep about ten minutes ago, and I reckon I done the same. You couldn't a got drunk in that time, so of course you've been dreaming."

"Dad fetch it, how is I gwyne to dream all dat in ten minutes?"

"Well, hang it all, you did dream it, because there didn't any of it happen."

"But Huck, it's all jis' as plain to me as—"

"It don't make no difference how plain it is, there ain't nothing in it. I know, because I've been here all the time."

Jim didn't say nothing for about five minutes, but set there studying over it. Then he says:

"Well, den, I reck'n I did dream it, Huck; but dog my cats ef it ain't de powerfullest dream I ever see. En I hain't ever had no dream b'fo' dat's tired me like dis one."

"Oh, well, that's all right, because a dream does tire a body like everything, sometimes. But this one was a staving[5] dream—tell me all about it, Jim."

So Jim went to work and told me the whole thing right through, just as it happened, only he painted it up considerable. Then he said he must start in and " 'terpret" it, because it was sent for a warning. He said the first tow-head stood for a man that would try to do us some good, but the current was another man that would get us away from him. The whoops was warnings that would come to us every now and then, and if we didn't try hard to make out to understand them they'd just take us into bad luck, 'stead of keeping us out of it. The lot of tow-heads was troubles we was going to get into with quarrelsome people and all kinds of mean folks, but if we minded our business and didn't talk back and aggravate them, we would pull through and get out of the fog and into the big clear river, which was the free States, and wouldn't have no more trouble.

It had clouded up pretty dark just after I got onto the raft, but it was clearing up again, now.

"Oh, well, that's all interpreted well enough, as far as it goes, Jim," I says; "but what does *these* things stand for?"

It was the leaves and rubbish on the raft, and the smashed oar. You could see them first rate, now.

Jim looked at the trash, and then looked at me, and back at the trash again. He had got the dream fixed so strong in his head that he couldn't seem to shake it loose and get the facts back into its place again, right away. But when he did get the thing straightened around, he looked at me steady, without ever smiling, and says:

"What do dey stan' for? I's gwyne to tell you. When I got all wore out wid work, en wid de callin' for you, en went to sleep, my heart wuz mos' broke bekase you wuz los', en I didn' k'yer no mo' what become er me en de raf'. En when I wake up en fine you back agin', all safe en soun', de tears come en I could a got down on my knees en kiss' yo' foot I's so thankful. En all you wuz thinkin' 'bout wuz how you could make a fool uv ole Jim wid a lie. Dat truck dah is *trash*; en trash is what people is dat puts dirt on de head er dey fren's en makes 'em ashamed."

Then he got up slow, and walked to the wigwam, and went in there, without saying anything but that. But that was enough. It made me feel so mean I could almost kissed *his* foot to get him to take it back.

It was fifteen minutes before I could work myself up to go and humble myself to a nigger—but I done it, and I warn't ever sorry

5. Fine, splendid.

for it afterwards, neither. I didn't do him no more mean tricks, and I wouldn't done that one if I'd a knowed it would make him feel that way.[6]

Chapter XVI

We slept most all day, and started out at night, a little ways behind a monstrous long raft that was as long going by as a procession. She had four long sweeps[7] at each end, so we judged she carried as many as thirty men, likely. She had five big wigwams aboard, wide apart, and an open camp fire in the middle, and a tall flagpole at each end. There was a power of style about her. It *amounted* to something being a raftsman on such a craft as that.

We went drifting down into a big bend, and the night clouded up and got hot. The river was very wide, and was walled with solid timber on both sides; you couldn't see a break in it hardly ever, or a light. We talked about Cairo, and wondered whether we would know it when we got to it. I said likely we wouldn't, because I had heard say there warn't but about a dozen houses there, and if they didn't happen to have them lit up, how was we going to know we was passing a town? Jim said if the two big rivers joined together there, that would show. But I said maybe we might think we was passing the foot of an island and coming into the same old river again. That disturbed Jim—and me too. So the question was, what to do? I said, paddle ashore the first time a light showed, and tell them pap was behind, coming along with a trading-scow, and was a green hand at the business, and wanted to know how far it was to Cairo. Jim thought it was a good idea, so we took a smoke on it and waited.[8]

There warn't nothing to do, now, but to look out sharp for the town, and not pass it without seeing it. He said he'd be mighty sure to see it, because he'd be a free man the minute he seen it, but if he missed it he'd be in the slave country again and no more show for freedom. Every little while he jumps up and says:

"Dah she is!"

But it warn't. It was Jack-o-lanterns, or lightning-bugs; so he set down again, and went to watching, same as before. Jim said it made him all over trembly and feverish to be so close to freedom. Well, I can tell you it made me all over trembly and feverish, too, to hear

6. The simple nobility of Jim's speech needs no comment. But this episode is the author's first fully developed example of the revelation of man and nature that, often through Jim's agency, gave scope for the natural innocence of Huck, which otherwise might have been lost in the deep knowledge of evil which marked his boyhood.

7. A long oar used to propel or steer.
8. *Life on the Mississippi* (1883) incorporated Twain's serial articles and the "Raft Passage" (which followed immediately after this paragraph in the unfinished *Huck* MS.), a famous description of early river life; *q.v.*, p. 229 above.

him, because I begun to get it through my head that he *was* most
free—and who was to blame for it? Why, *me.* I couldn't get that
out of my conscience, no how nor no way. It got to troubling me
so I couldn't rest; I couldn't stay still in one place. It hadn't ever
come home to me before, what this thing was that I was doing. But
now it did; and it staid with me, and scorched me more and more.
I tried to make out to myself that *I* warn't to blame, because I
didn't run Jim off from his rightful owner; but it warn't no use,
conscience up and says, every time, "But you knowed he was running for his freedom, and you could a paddled ashore and told
somebody." That was so—I couldn't get around that, noway. That
was where it pinched. Conscience says to me, "What had poor Miss
Watson done to you, that you could see her nigger go off right under
your eyes and never say one single word? What did that poor old
woman do to you, that you could treat her so mean? Why, she
tried to learn you your book, she tried to learn you your manners,
she tried to be good to you every way she knowed how. *That's* what
she done."

I got to feeling so mean and so miserable I most wished I was
dead. I fidgeted up and down the raft, abusing myself to myself,
and Jim was fidgeting up and down past me. We neither of us
could keep still. Every time he danced around and says, "Dah's
Cairo!" it went through me like a shot, and I thought if it *was*
Cairo I reckoned I would die of miserableness.[9]

Jim talked out loud all the time while I was talking to myself.
He was saying how the first thing he would do when he got to a
free State he would go to saving up money and never spend a single
cent, and when he got enough he would buy his wife, which was
owned on a farm close to where Miss Watson lived; and then they
would both work to buy the two children, and if their master
wouldn't sell them, they'd get an Ab'litionist to go and steal them.

It most froze me to hear such talk. He wouldn't ever dared to
talk such talk in his life before. Just see what a difference it made in
him the minute he judged he was about free. It was according to
the old saying, "give a nigger an inch and he'll take an ell." Thinks
I, this is what comes of my not thinking. Here was this nigger which
I had as good as helped to run away, coming right out flat-footed
and saying he would steal his children—children that belonged to
a man I didn't even know; a man that hadn't ever done me no harm.

I was sorry to hear Jim say that, it was such a lowering of him.
My conscience got to stirring me up hotter than ever, until at last

9. In the light of present attitudes toward slavery, one must remember that
in the South, at the time of this story,
slavery was supported by the social institutions of property and church. Huck
was a boy caught between conflicting
loyalties, and this conflict continues as
a principal motivation throughout the
book.

I says to it, "Let up on me—it ain't too late, yet—I'll paddle ashore at the first light, and tell." I felt easy, and happy, and light as a feather, right off. All my troubles was gone. I went to looking out sharp for a light, and sort of singing to myself. By-and-by one showed. Jim sings out:

"We's safe, Huck, we's safe! Jump up and crack yo' heels, dat's de good ole Cairo at las', I jis knows it!"

I says:

"I'll take the canoe and go see, Jim. It mightn't be, you know."

He jumped and got the canoe ready, and put his old coat in the bottom for me to set on, and give me the paddle; and as I shoved off, he says:

"Pooty soon I'll be a-shout'n for joy, en I'll say, it's all on accounts o' Huck; I's a free man, en I couldn't ever ben free ef it hadn' ben for Huck; Huck done it. Jim won't ever forgit you, Huck; you's de bes' fren' Jim's ever had; en you's de *only* fren' ole Jim's got now."

I was paddling off, all in a sweat to tell on him; but when he says this, it seemed to kind of take the tuck all out of me. I went along slow then, and I warn't right down certain whether I was glad I started or whether I warn't. When I was fifty yards off, Jim says:

"Dah you goes, de ole true Huck; de on'y white genlman dat ever kep' his promise to ole Jim."

Well, I just felt sick. But I says, I *got* to do it—I can't get *out* of it. Right then, along comes a skiff with two men in it, with guns, and they stopped and I stopped. One of them says:

"What's that, yonder?"

"A piece of a raft," I says.

"Do you belong on it?"

"Yes, sir."

"Any men on it?"

"Only one, sir."

"Well, there's five niggers run off to-night, up yonder above the head of the bend. Is your man white or black?"

I didn't answer up prompt. I tried to, but the words wouldn't come. I tried, for a second or two, to brace up and out with it, but I warn't man enough—hadn't the spunk of a rabbit. I see I was weakening; so I just give up trying, and up and says—

"He's white."

"I reckon we'll go and see for ourselves."

"I wish you would," says I, "because it's pap that's there, and maybe you'd help me tow the raft ashore where the light is. He's sick—and so is mam and Mary Ann."

"Oh, the devil! we're in a hurry, boy. But I s'pose we've got to. Come—buckle to your paddle, and let's get along."

I buckled to my paddle and they laid to their oars. When we had made a stroke or two, I says:

"Pap'll be mighty much obleeged to you, I can tell you. Everybody goes away when I want them to help me tow the raft ashore, and I can't do it by myself."

"Well, that's infernal mean. Odd, too. Say, boy, what's the matter with your father?"

"It's the—a—the—well, it ain't anything, much."

They stopped pulling. It warn't but a mighty little ways to the raft, now. One says:

"Boy, that's a lie. What *is* the matter with your pap? Answer up square, now, and it'll be the better for you."

"I will, sir, I will, honest—but don't leave us, please. It's the—the—gentlemen, if you'll only pull ahead, and let me heave you the head-line, you won't have to come a-near the raft—please do."

"Set her back, John, set her back!" says one. They backed water. "Keep away, boy—keep to looard. Confound it, I just expect the wind has blowed it to us. Your pap's got the small-pox, and you know it precious well. Why didn't you come out and say so? Do you want to spread it all over?"

"Well," says I, a-blubbering, "I've told everybody before, and then they just went away and left us."

"Poor devil, there's something in that. We are right down sorry for you, but we—well, hang it, we don't want the small-pox, you see. Look here, I'll tell you what to do. Don't you try to land by yourself, or you'll smash everything to pieces. You float along down about twenty miles and you'll come to a town on the left-hand side of the river. It will be long after sun-up, then, and when you ask for help, you tell them your folks are all down with chills and fever. Don't be a fool again, and let people guess what is the matter. Now we're trying to do you a kindness; so you just put twenty miles between us, that's a good boy. It wouldn't do any good to land yonder where the light is—it's only a wood-yard. Say—I reckon your father's poor, and I'm bound to say he's in pretty hard luck. Here —I'll put a twenty dollar gold piece on this board, and you get it when it floats by. I feel mighty mean to leave you, but my kingdom! it won't do to fool with small-pox, don't you see?"

"Hold on, Parker," says the other man, "here's a twenty to put on the board for me. Good-bye boy, you do as Mr. Parker told you, and you'll be all right."

"That's so, my boy—good-bye, good-bye. If you see any runaway niggers, you get help and nab them, and you can make some money by it."

"Good-bye, sir," says I, "I won't let no runaway niggers get by me if I can help it."

They went off, and I got aboard the raft, feeling bad and low, because I knowed very well I had done wrong, and I see it warn't no use for me to try to learn to do right; a body that don't get *started* right when he's little, ain't got no show—when the pinch comes there ain't nothing to back him up and keep him to his work, and so he gets beat. Then I thought a minute, and says to myself, hold on,—s'pose you'd a done right and give Jim up; would you felt better than what you do now? No, says I, I'd feel bad—I'd feel just the same way I do now. Well, then, says I, what's the use you learning to do right, when it's troublesome to do right and ain't no trouble to do wrong, and the wages is just the same? I was stuck. I couldn't answer that. So I reckoned I wouldn't bother no more about it, but after this always do whichever come handiest at the time.

I went into the wigwam; Jim warn't there. I looked all around; he warn't anywhere. I says:

"Jim!"

"Here I is, Huck. Is dey out o' sight yit? Don't talk loud."

He was in the river, under the stern oar, with just his nose out. I told him they was out of sight, so he come aboard. He says:

"I was a-listenin' to all de talk, en I slips into de river en was gwyne to shove for sho' if dey come aboard. Den I was gwyne to swim to de raf' agin when dey was gone. But lawsy, how you did fool 'em, Huck! Dat *wuz* de smartes' dodge! I tell you, chile, I 'speck it save' ole Jim—ole Jim ain't gwyne to forgit you for dat, honey."

Then we talked about the money. It was a pretty good raise, twenty dollars apiece. Jim said we could take deck passage on a steamboat now, and the money would last us as far as we wanted to go in the free States. He said twenty mile more warn't far for the raft to go, but he wished we was already there.

Towards daybreak we tied up, and Jim was mighty particular about hiding the raft good. Then he worked all day fixing things in bundles, and getting all ready to quit rafting.

That night about ten we hove in sight of the lights of a town away down in a left-hand bend.

I went off in the canoe, to ask about it. Pretty soon I found a man out in the river with a skiff, setting a trot-line. I ranged up and says:

"Mister, is that town Cairo?"

"Cairo? no. You must be a blame' fool."

"What town is it, mister?"

"If you want to know, go and find out. If you stay here botherin' around me for about a half a minute longer, you'll get something you won't want."

I paddled to the raft. Jim was awful disappointed, but I said never mind, Cairo would be the next place, I reckoned.

We passed another town before daylight, and I was going out again; but it was high ground, so I didn't go. No high ground about Cairo, Jim said. I had forgot it. We laid up for the day, on a towhead tolerable close to the left-hand bank. I begun to suspicion something. So did Jim. I says:

"Maybe we went by Cairo in the fog that night."

He says:

"Doan' less' talk about it, Huck. Po' niggers can't have no luck. I awluz 'spected dat rattle-snake skin warn't done wid it's work."

"I wish I'd never seen that snake-skin, Jim—I do wish I'd never laid eyes on it."

"It ain't yo' fault, Huck; you didn' know. Don't you blame yo'self 'bout it."

When it was daylight, here was the clear Ohio water in shore, sure enough, and outside was the old regular Muddy! So it was all up with Cairo.[1]

We talked it all over. It wouldn't do to take to the shore; we couldn't take the raft up the stream, of course. There warn't no way but to wait for dark, and start back in the canoe and take the chances. So we slept all day amongst the cotton-wood thicket, so as to be fresh for the work, and when we went back to the raft about dark the canoe was gone!

We didn't say a word for a good while. There warn't anything to say. We both knowed well enough it was some more work of the rattle-snake skin; so what was the use to talk about it? It would only look like we was finding fault, and that would be bound to fetch more bad luck—and keep on fetching it, too, till we knowed enough to keep still.

By-and-by we talked about what we better do, and found there warn't no way but just to go along down with the raft till we got a chance to buy a canoe to go back in. We warn't going to borrow it when there warn't anybody around, the way pap would do, for that might set people after us.

So we shoved out, after dark, on the raft.

Anybody that don't believe yet, that it's foolishness to handle a snake-skin, after all that that snake-skin done for us, will believe it now, if they read on and see what more it done for us.

The place to buy canoes is off of rafts laying up at shore. But we didn't see no rafts laying up; so we went along during three hours and more. Well, the night got gray, and ruther thick, which is the

---

1. Cairo lies at the confluence of the Ohio and Mississippi Rivers; hence they know they have passed the town in the fog when they see the clear water from the Ohio, still flowing along the east bank of the Mississippi, its waters not mingled with the Big Muddy. *Cf.* Chapter XV, note 4.

next meanest thing to fog. You can't tell the shape of the river, and you can't see no distance. It got to be very late and still, and then along comes a steamboat up the river. We lit the lantern, and judged she would see it. Up-stream boats didn't generly come close to us; they go out and follow the bars and hunt for easy water under the reefs; but nights like this they bull right up the channel against the whole river.

We could hear her pounding along, but we didn't see her good till she was close. She aimed right for us. Often they do that and try to see how close they can come without touching; sometimes the wheel bites off a sweep, and then the pilot sticks his head out and laughs, and thinks he's mighty smart. Well, here she comes, and we said she was going to try to shave us; but she didn't seem to be sheering off a bit. She was a big one, and she was coming in a hurry, too, looking like a black cloud with rows of glow-worms around it; but all of a sudden she bulged out, big and scary, with a long row of wide-open furnace doors shining like red-hot teeth, and her monstrous bows and guards hanging right over us. There was a yell at us, and a jingling of bells to stop the engines, a pow-wow of cussing, and whistling of steam—and as Jim went overboard on one side and I on the other, she come smashing straight through the raft.

I dived—and I aimed to find the bottom, too, for a thirty-foot wheel had got to go over me, and I wanted it to have plenty of room. I could always stay under water a minute; this time I reckon I staid under water a minute and a half. Then I bounced for the top in a hurry, for I was nearly busting. I popped out to my arm-pits and blowed the water out of my nose, and puffed a bit. Of course there was a booming current; and of course that boat started her engines again ten seconds after she stopped them, for they never cared much for raftsmen; so now she was churning along up the river, out of sight in the thick weather, though I could hear her.

I sung out for Jim about a dozen times, but I didn't get any answer; so I grabbed a plank that touched me while I was "treading water," and struck out for shore, shoving it ahead of me. But I made out to see that the drift of the current was towards the left-hand shore,[2] which meant that I was in a crossing; so I changed off and went that way.

It was one of these long, slanting, two-mile crossings; so I was a good long time in getting over. I made a safe landing, and clum up the bank. I couldn't see but a little ways, but I went poking along over rough ground for a quarter of a mile or more, and then I run across a big old-fashioned double log house before I noticed it. I was going to rush by and get away, but a log of dogs jumped

2. Kentucky, where the feud in the following chapters takes place.

out and went to howling and barking at me, and I knowed better
than to move another peg.

Chapter XVII

About half a minute somebody spoke out of a window, without
putting his head out, and says:

"Be done, boys! Who's there?"

I says:

"It's me."

"Who's me?"

"George Jackson, sir."

"What do you want?"

"I don't want nothing, sir. I only want to go along by, but the
dogs won't let me."

"What are you prowling around here this time of night, for—
hey?"

"I warn't prowling around, sir; I fell overboard off of the steamboat."

"Oh, you did, did you? Strike a light there, somebody. What did
you say your name was?"

"George Jackson, sir. I'm only a boy."

"Look here; if you're telling the truth, you needn't be afraid—
nobody'll hurt you. But don't try to budge; stand right where you
are. Rouse out Bob and Tom, some of you, and fetch the guns.
George Jackson, is there anybody with you?"

"No, sir, nobody."

I heard the people stirring around in the house, now, and see a
light. The man sung out:

"Snatch that light away, Betsy, you old fool—ain't you got any
sense? Put it on the floor behind the front door. Bob, if you and
Tom are ready, take your places."

"All ready."

"Now, George Jackson, do you know the Shepherdsons?"

"No, sir—I never heard of them."

"Well, that may be so, and it mayn't. Now, all ready. Step forward, George Jackson. And mind, don't you hurry—come mighty
slow. If there's anybody with you, let him keep back—if he shows
himself he'll be shot. Come along, now. Come slow; push the door
open, yourself—just enough to squeeze in, d' you hear?"

I didn't hurry, I couldn't if I'd a wanted to. I took one slow step
at a time, and there warn't a sound, only I thought I could hear
my heart. The dogs were as still as the humans, but they followed
a little behind me. When I got to the three log door-steps, I heard
them unlocking and unbarring and unbolting. I put my hand on

the door and pushed it a little and a little more, till somebody said, "There, that's enough—put your head in." I done it, but I judged they would take it off.

The candle was on the floor, and there they all was, looking at me, and me at them, for about a quarter of a minute. Three big men with guns pointed at me, which made me wince, I tell you; the oldest, gray and about sixty, the other two thirty or more—all of them fine and handsome—and the sweetest old gray-headed lady, and back of her two young women which I couldn't see right well. The old gentleman says:

"There—I reckon it's all right. Come in."

As soon as I was in, the old gentleman he locked the door and barred it and bolted it, and told the young men to come in with their guns, and they all went in a big parlor that had a new rag carpet on the floor, and got together in a corner that was out of range of the front windows—there warn't none on the side. They held the candle, and took a good look at me, and all said, "Why *he* ain't a Shepherdson—no, there ain't any Shepherdson about him." Then the old man said he hoped I wouldn't mind being searched for arms, because he didn't mean no harm by it—it was only to make sure. So he didn't pry into my pockets, but only felt outside with his hands, and said it was all right. He told me to make myself easy and at home, and tell all about myself; but the old lady says:

"Why bless you, Saul, the poor thing's as wet as he can be; and don't you reckon it may be he's hungry?"

"True for you, Rachel—I forgot."

So the old lady says:

"Betsy" (this was a nigger woman), "you fly around and get him something to eat, as quick as you can, poor thing; and one of you girls go and wake up Buck and tell him— Oh, here he is himself. Buck, take this little stranger and get the wet clothes off from him and dress him up in some of yours that's dry."

Buck looked about as old as me—thirteen or fourteen or along there,[3] though he was a little bigger than me. He hadn't on anything but a shirt, and he was very frowsy-headed. He come in gaping and digging one fist into his eyes, and he was dragging a gun along with the other one. He says:

"Ain't they no Shepherdsons around?"

They said, no, 'twas a false alarm.

"Well," he says, "if they'd a ben some, I reckon I'd a got one."

They all laughed, and Bob says:

"Why, Buck, they might have scalped us all, you've been so slow in coming."

"Well, nobody come after me, and it ain't right. I'm always kep'

3. In a notebook Twain definitely said that Huck was a "boy of 14" (Walter Blair, *Mark Twain and Huck Finn*, p. 143).

down; I don't get no show."

"Never mind, Buck, my boy," says the old man, "you'll have show enough, all in good time, don't you fret about that. Go 'long with you now, and do as your mother told you."

When we got up stairs to his room, he got me a coarse shirt and a roundabout[4] and pants of his, and I put them on. While I was at it he asked me what my name was, but before I could tell him, he started to telling me about a blue jay and a young rabbit he had catched in the woods day before yesterday, and he asked me where Moses was when the candle went out. I said I didn't know; I hadn't heard about it before, no way.

"Well, guess," he says.

"How'm I going to guess," says I, "when I never heard tell about it before?"

"But you can guess, can't you? It's just as easy."

"*Which* candle?" I says.

"Why, any candle," he says.

"I don't know where he was," says I; "where was he?"

"Why he was in the *dark!* That's where he was!"

"Well, if you knowed where he was, what did you ask me for?"

"Why, blame it, it's a riddle, don't you see? Say, how long are you going to stay here? You got to stay always. We can just have booming times—they don't have no school now. Do you own a dog? I've got a dog—and he'll go in the river and bring out chips that you throw in. Do you like to comb up, Sundays, and all that kind of foolishness? You bet I don't, but ma she makes me. Confound these ole britches, I reckon I'd better put 'em on, but I'd ruther not, it's so warm. Are you all ready? All right—come along, old hoss."

Cold corn-pone, cold corn-beef, butter and butter-milk—that is what they had for me down there, and there ain't nothing better that ever I've come across yet. Buck and his ma and all of them smoked cob pipes, except the nigger woman, which was gone, and the two young women. They all smoked and talked, and I eat and talked. The young women had quilts around them, and their hair down their backs. They all asked me questions, and I told them how pap and me and all the family was living on a little farm down at the bottom of Arkansaw, and my sister Mary Ann run off and got married and never was heard of no more, and Bill went to hunt them and he warn't heard of no more, and Tom and Mort died, and then there warn't nobody but just me and pap left, and he was just trimmed down to nothing, on account of his troubles; so when he died I took what there was left, because the farm didn't belong to us, and started up the river, deck passage, and fell overboard;

4. A short, close jacket.

and that was how I come to be here.[5] So they said I could have a home there as long as I wanted it. Then it was most daylight, and everybody went to bed, and I went to bed with Buck, and when I waked up in the morning, drat it all, I had forgot what my name was. So I laid there about an hour trying to think, and when Buck waked up, I says:

"Can you spell, Buck?"

"Yes," he says.

"I bet you can't spell my name," says I.

"I bet you what you dare I can," says he.

"All right," says I, "go ahead."

"G-o-r-g-e J-a-x-o-n—there now," he says.

"Well," says I, "you done it, but I didn't think you could. It ain't no slouch of a name to spell—right off without studying."

I set it down, private, because somebody might want *me* to spell it, next, and so I wanted to be handy with it and rattle it off like I was used to it.

It was a mighty nice family, and a mighty nice house, too. I hadn't seen no house out in the country before that was so nice and had so much style. It didn't have an iron latch on the front door, nor a wooden one with a buckskin string, but a brass knob to turn, the same as houses in a town. There warn't no bed in the parlor, not a sign of a bed; but heaps of parlors in towns has beds in them. There was a big fireplace that was bricked on the bottom, and the bricks was kept clean and red by pouring water on them and scrubbing them with another brick; sometimes they washed them over with red waterpaint that they call Spanish-brown, same as they do in town. They had big brass dog-irons that could hold up a saw-log. There was a clock on the middle of the mantel-piece, with a picture of a town painted on the bottom half of the glass front, and a round place in the middle of it for the sun, and you could see the pendulum swing behind it. It was beautiful to hear that clock tick; and sometimes when one of these peddlars had been along and scoured her up and got her in good shape, she would start in and strike a hundred and fifty before she got tuckered out. They wouldn't took any money for her.

Well, there was a big outlandish parrot on each side of the clock, made out of something like chalk, and painted up gaudy. By one of the parrots was a cat made of crockery, and a crockery dog by the other; and when you pressed down on them they squeaked, but didn't open their mouths nor look different nor interested. They squeaked through underneath. There was a couple of big wild-

5. Huck's autobiographical inventions are generally a commentary on the nature of his experience, compounded of sudden crisis, disaster, and death. Twain's use of these anecdotes is in the great tradition of the comic criticism of life.

turkey-wing fans spread out behind those things. On a table in the middle of the room was a kind of lovely crockery basket that had apples and oranges and peaches and grapes piled up in it which was much redder and yellower and prettier than real ones is, but they warn't real because you could see where pieces had got chipped off and showed the white chalk or whatever it was, underneath.

This table had a cover made out of beautiful oil-cloth, with a red and blue spread-eagle painted on it, and a painted border all around. It come all the way from Philadelphia, they said. There was some books too, piled up perfectly exact, on each corner of the table. One was a big family Bible, full of pictures. One was "Pilgrim's Progress," about a man that left his family it didn't say why. I read considerable in it now and then. The statements was interesting, but tough. Another was "Friendship's Offering,"[6] full of beautiful stuff and poetry; but I didn't read the poetry. Another was Henry Clay's Speeches, and another was Dr. Gunn's Family Medicine, which told you all about what to do if a body was sick or dead. There was a Hymn Book, and a lot of other books. And there was nice split-bottom chairs, and perfectly sound, too—not bagged down in the middle and busted, like an old basket.

They had pictures hung on the walls—mainly Washingtons and Lafayettes, and battles, and Highland Marys, and one called "Signing the Declaration." There was some that they called crayons, which one of the daughters which was dead made her own self when she was only fifteen years old. They was different from any pictures I ever see before; blacker, mostly, than is common. One was a woman in a slim black dress, belted small under the armpits, with bulges like a cabbage in the middle of the sleeves, and a large black scoop-shovel bonnet with a black veil, and white slim ankles crossed about with black tape, and very wee black slippers, like a chisel, and she was leaning pensive on a tombstone on her right elbow, under a weeping willow, and her other hand hanging down her side holding a white handkerchief and a reticule, and underneath the picture it said "Shall I Never See Thee More Alas." Another one was a young lady with her hair all combed up straight to the top of her head, and knotted there in front of a comb like a chair-back, and she was crying into a handkerchief and had a dead bird laying on its back in her other hand with its heels up, and underneath the picture it said "I Shall Never Hear Thy Sweet Chirrup More Alas." There was one where a young lady was at a window looking up at the moon, and tears running down her cheeks; and she had an open letter in one hand with black sealing-

6. One of many successful annual collections of poetry and prose, designed as gift books.

wax showing on one edge of it, and she was mashing a locket with a chain to it against her mouth, and underneath the picture it said "And Art Thou Gone Yes Thou Art Gone Alas." These was all nice pictures, I reckon, but I didn't somehow seem to take to them, because if ever I was down a little, they always give me the fan-tods. Everybody was sorry she died, because she had laid out a lot more of these pictures to do, and a body could see by what she had done what they had lost. But I reckoned, that with her disposition, she was having a better time in the graveyard. She was at work on what they said was her greatest picture when she took sick, and every day and every night it was her prayer to be allowed to live till she got it done, but she never got the chance. It was a picture of a young woman in a long white gown, standing on the rail of a bridge all ready to jump off, with her hair all down her back, and looking up to the moon, with the tears running down her face, and she had two arms folded across her breast, and two arms stretched out in front, and two more reaching up towards the moon—and the idea was, to see which pair would look best and then scratch out all the other arms; but, as I was saying, she died before she got her mind made up, and now they kept this picture over the head of the bed in her room, and every time her birthday come they hung flowers on it. Other times it was hid with a little curtain. The young woman in the picture had a kind of a nice sweet face, but there was so many arms it made her look too spidery, seemed to me.

This young girl kept a scrap-book when she was alive, and used to paste obituaries and accidents and cases of patient suffering in it out of the *Presbyterian Observer*, and write poetry after them out of her own head. It was very good poetry. This is what she wrote about a boy by the name of Stephen Dowling Bots that fell down a well and was drownded:

ODE TO STEPHEN DOWLING BOTS, DEC'D.[7]

And did young Stephen sicken,
   And did young Stephen die?
And did the sad hearts thicken,
   And did the mourners cry?

No; such was not the fate of
   Young Stephen Dowling Bots;
Though sad hearts round him thickened,
   'Twas not from sickness' shots.

7. Twain's parody of the lugubrious popular poetry of the time, such as the saccharine and atrocious verse of "The Sweet Singer of Michigan" (Julia A. Moore, 1847–1920), which so delighted Mark Twain. He also gleefully encouraged the effusions of Bloodgood Cutter (1819–1906), the "poet lariat" on board the *Quaker City* excursion in *Innocents Abroad* (1869).

No whooping-cough did rack his frame,
    Nor measles drear, with spots;
Not these impaired the sacred name
    Of Stephen Dowling Bots.

Despised love struck not with woe
    That head of curly knots,
Nor stomach troubles laid him low,
    Young Stephen Dowling Bots.

O no. Then list with tearful eye,
    Whilst I his fate do tell.
His soul did from this cold world fly,
    By falling down a well.

They got him out and emptied him;
    Alas it was too late;
His spirit was gone for to sport aloft
    In the realms of the good and great.

If Emmeline Grangerford could make poetry like that before she was fourteen, there ain't no telling what she could a done by-and-by. Buck said she could rattle off poetry like nothing. She didn't ever have to stop to think. He said she would slap down a line, and if she couldn't find anything to rhyme with it she would just scratch it out and slap down another one, and go ahead. She warn't particular, she could write about anything you choose to give her to write about, just so it was sadful. Every time a man died, or a woman died, or a child died, she would be on hand with her "trib-ute" before he was cold. She called them tributes. The neighbors said it was the doctor first, then Emmeline, then the undertaker— the undertaker never got in ahead of Emmeline but once, and then she hung fire on a rhyme for the dead person's name, which was Whistler. She warn't ever the same, after that; she never com-plained, but she kind of pined away and did not live long. Poor thing, many's the time I made myself go up to the little room that used to be hers and get out her poor old scrapbook and read in it when her pictures had been aggravating me and I had soured on her a little. I liked all that family, dead ones and all, and warn't going to let anything come between us. Poor Emmeline made poetry about all the dead people when she was alive, and it didn't seem right that there warn't nobody to make some about her, now she was gone; so I tried to sweat out a verse or two myself, but I couldn't seem to make it go, somehow. They kept Emmeline's room trim and nice and all the things fixed in it just the way she liked to have them when she was alive, and nobody ever slept there. The old lady took care of the room herself, though there was plenty of niggers, and she sewed there a good deal and read her Bible there, mostly.

Well, as I was saying about the parlor, there was beautiful curtains on the windows: white, with pictures painted on them, of castles with vines all down the walls, and cattle coming down to drink. There was a little old piano, too, that had tin pans in it, I reckon, and nothing was ever so lovely as to hear the young ladies sing, "The Last Link is Broken" and play "The Battle of Prague" on it. The walls of all the rooms was plastered, and most had carpets on the floors, and the whole house was whitewashed on the outside.

It was a double house, and the big open place betwixt them was roofed and floored, and sometimes the table was set there in the middle of the day, and it was a cool, comfortable place. Nothing couldn't be better. And warn't the cooking good, and just bushels of it too!

Chapter XVIII

Col. Grangerford was a gentleman, you see. He was a gentleman all over; and so was his family. He was well born, as the saying is, and that's worth as much in a man as it is in a horse, so the Widow Douglas[8] said, and nobody ever denied that she was of the first aristocracy in our town; and pap he always said it, too, though he warn't no more quality than a mudcat,[9] himself. Col. Grangerford was very tall and very slim, and had a darkish-paly complexion, not a sign of red in it anywheres; he was clean-shaved every morning, all over his thin face, and he had the thinnest kind of lips, and the thinnest kind of nostrils, and a high nose, and heavy eyebrows, and the blackest kind of eyes, sunk so deep back that they seemed like they was looking out of caverns at you, as you may say. His forehead was high, and his hair was black and straight, and hung to his shoulders. His hands was long and thin, and every day of his life he put on a clean shirt and a full suit from head to foot made out of linen so white it hurt your eyes to look at it; and on Sundays he wore a blue tail-coat with brass buttons on it. He carried a mahogany cane with a silver head to it. There warn't no frivolishness about him, not a bit, and he warn't ever loud. He was as kind as he could be—you could feel that, you know, and so you had confidence. Sometimes he smiled, and it was good to see; but when he straightened himself up like a liberty-pole, and the lightning begun to flicker out from under his eyebrows you wanted to climb a tree first, and find out what the matter was afterwards. He didn't ever have to tell anybody to mind their manners—everybody was always good

8. Erroneously printed "Douglass" in 1885.   9. A less-esteemed variety of catfish.

mannered where he was. Everybody loved to have him around, too; he was sunshine most always—I mean he made it seem like good weather. When he turned into a cloud-bank it was awful dark for a half a minute and that was enough; there wouldn't nothing go wrong again for a week.

When him and the old lady come down in the morning, all the family got up out of their chairs and give them good-day, and didn't set down again till they had set down. Then Tom and Bob went to the sideboard where the decanters was, and mixed a glass of bitters and handed it to him, and he held it in his hand and waited till Tom's and Bob's was mixed, and then they bowed and said "Our duty to you, sir, and madam;" and *they* bowed the least bit in the world and said thank you, and so they drank, all three, and Bob and Tom poured a spoonful of water on the sugar and the mite of whisky or apple brandy in the bottom of their tumblers, and give it to me and Buck, and we drank to the old people too.

Bob was the oldest, and Tom next. Tall, beautiful men with very broad shoulders and brown faces, and long black hair and black eyes. They dressed in white linen from head to foot, like the old gentleman, and wore broad Panama hats.

Then there was Miss Charlotte, she was twenty-five, and tall and proud and grand, but as good as she could be, when she warn't stirred up; but when she was, she had a look that would make you wilt in your tracks, like her father. She was beautiful.

So was her sister, Miss Sophia, but it was a different kind. She was gentle and sweet, like a dove, and she was only twenty.

Each person had their own nigger to wait on them—Buck, too. My nigger had a monstrous easy time, because I warn't used to having anybody do anything for me, but Buck's was on the jump most of the time.

This was all there was of the family, now; but there used to be more—three sons; they got killed; and Emmeline that died.

The old gentleman owned a lot of farms, and over a hundred niggers. Sometimes a stack of people would come there, horseback, from ten or fifteen mile around, and stay five or six days, and have such junketings round about and on the river, and dances and picnics in the woods, day-times, and balls at the house, nights. These people was mostly kin-folks of the family. The men brought their guns with them. It was a handsome lot of quality, I tell you.

There was another clan of aristocracy around there—five or six families—mostly of the name of Shepherdson. They was as high-toned, and well born, and rich and grand, as the tribe of Grangerfords. The Shepherdsons and the Grangerfords used the same steamboat landing, which was about two mile above our house; so sometimes when I went up there with a lot of our folks I used to see a lot of the Shepherdsons there, on their fine horses.

One day Buck and me was away out in the woods, hunting, and heard a horse coming. We was crossing the road. Buck says:

"Quick! Jump for the woods!"

We done it, and then peeped down the woods through the leaves. Pretty soon a splendid young man came galloping down the road, setting his horse easy and looking like a soldier. He had his gun across his pommel. I had seen him before. It was young Harney Shepherdson. I heard Buck's gun go off at my ear, and Harney's hat tumbled off from his head. He grabbed his gun and rode straight to the place where we was hid. But we didn't wait. We started through the woods on a run. The woods warn't thick, so I looked over my shoulder, to dodge the bullet, and twice I seen Harney cover Buck with his gun; and then he rode away the way he come—to get his hat, I reckon, but I couldn't see. We never stopped running till we got home. The old gentleman's eyes blazed a minute—'twas pleasure, mainly, I judged—then his face sort of smoothed down, and he says, kind of gentle:

"I don't like that shooting from behind a bush. Why didn't you step into the road, my boy?"

"The Shepherdsons don't, father. They always take advantage."

Miss Charlotte she held her head up like a queen while Buck was telling his tale, and her nostrils spread and her eyes snapped. The two young men looked dark, but never said nothing. Miss Sophia she turned pale, but the color come back when she found the man warn't hurt.

Soon as I could get Buck down by the corn-cribs under the trees by ourselves, I says:

"Did you want to kill him, Buck?"

"Well, I bet I did."

"What did he do to you?"

"Him? He never done nothing to me."

"Well, then, what did you want to kill him for?"

"Why nothing—only it's on account of the feud."

"What's a feud?"

"Why, where was you raised? Don't you know what a feud is?"

"Never heard of it before—tell me about it."

"Well," says Buck, "a feud is this way. A man has a quarrel with another man, and kills him; then that other man's brother kills *him*; then the other brothers, on both sides, goes for one another; then the *cousins* chip in—and by-and-by everybody's killed off, and there ain't no more feud. But it's kind of slow, and takes a long time."

"Has this one been going on long, Buck?"

"Well I should *reckon!* it started thirty year ago, or som'ers along there. There was trouble 'bout something and then a lawsuit to settle it; and the suit went agin one of the men, and so he up and shot the man that won the suit—which he would naturally do, of course. Anybody would."

"What was the trouble about, Buck?—land?"

"I reckon maybe—I don't know."

"Well, who done the shooting?—was it a Grangerford or a Shepherdson?"

"Laws, how do *I* know? it was so long ago."

"Don't anybody know?"

"Oh, yes, pa knows, I reckon, and some of the other old folks; but they don't know, now, what the row was about in the first place."

"Has there been many killed, Buck?"

"Yes—right smart chance of funerals. But they don't always kill. Pa's got a few buck-shot in him; but he don't mind it 'cuz he don't weigh much anyway. Bob's been carved up some with a bowie, and Tom's been hurt once or twice."

"Has anybody been killed this year, Buck?"

"Yes, we got one and they got one. 'Bout three months ago, my cousin Bud, fourteen year old, was riding through the woods, on t'other side of the river, and didn't have no weapon with him, which was blame' foolishness, and in a lonesome place he hears a horse a-coming behind him, and sees old Baldy Shepherdson a-linkin' after him with his gun in his hand and his white hair a-flying in the wind; and 'stead of jumping off and taking to the brush, Bud 'lowed he could outrun him; so they had it, nip and tuck, for five mile or more, the old man a-gaining all the time; so at last Bud seen it warn't any use, so he stopped and faced around so as to have the bullet holes in front, you know, and the old man he rode up and shot him down. But he didn't git much chance to enjoy his luck, for inside of a week our folks laid *him* out."

"I reckon that old man was a coward, Buck."

"I reckon he *warn't* a coward. Not by a blame' sight. There ain't a coward amongst them Shepherdsons—not a one. And there ain't no cowards amongst the Grangerfords, either. Why, that old man kep' up his end in a fight one day, for a half an hour, against three Grangerfords, and come out winner. They was all a-horseback; he lit off of his horse and got behind a little wood-pile, and kep' his horse before him to stop the bullets; but the Grangerfords staid on their horses and capered around the old man, and peppered away at him, and he peppered away at them. Him and his horse both went home pretty leaky and crippled, but the Grangerfords had to be *fetched* home—and one of 'em was dead, and another died the next day. No, sir, if a body's out hunting for cowards, he

don't want to fool away any time amongst them Shepherdsons, becuz they don't breed any of that *kind*."

Next Sunday we all went to church, about three mile, everybody a-hòrseback. The men took their guns along, so did Buck, and
kept them between their knees or stood them handy against the
wall. The Shepherdsons done the same. It was pretty ornery preaching—all about brotherly love, and such-like tiresomeness; but everybody said it was a good sermon, and they all talked it over going
home, and had such a powerful lot to say about faith, and good
works, and free grace, and preforeordestination,[1] and I don't know
what all, that it did seem to me to be one of the roughest Sundays
I had run across yet.

About an hour after dinner everybody was dozing around, some
in their chairs and some in their rooms, and it got to be pretty
dull. Buck and a dog was stretched out on the grass in the sun,
sound asleep. I went up to our room, and judged I would take a nap
myself. I found that sweet Miss Sophia standing in her door,
which was next to ours, and she took me in her room and shut the
door very soft, and asked me if I liked her, and I said I did; and
she asked me if I would do something for her and not tell anybody, and I said I would. Then she said she'd forgot her Testament,
and left it in the seat at church, between two other books and
would I slip out quiet and go there and fetch it to her, and not
say nothing to nobody. I said I would. So I slid out and slipped
off up the road, and there warn't anybody at the church, except
maybe a hog or two, for there warn't any lock on the door, and
hogs likes a puncheon floor[2] in summer-time because it's cool. If
you notice, most folks don't go to church only when they've got to;
but a hog is different.

Says I to myself something's up—it ain't natural for a girl to be
in such a sweat about a Testament; so I give it a shake, and out
drops a little piece of paper with *"Half-past two"* wrote on it with
a pencil. I ransacked it, but couldn't find anything else. I couldn't
make anything out of that, so I put the paper in the book again,
and when I got home and up stairs, there was Miss Sophia in her
door waiting for me. She pulled me in and shut the door; then she
looked in the Testament till she found the paper, and as soon as she
read it she looked glad; and before a body could think, she grabbed
me and give me a squeeze, and said I was the best boy in the world,
and not to tell anybody. She was mighty red in the face, for a
minute, and her eyes lighted up and it made her powerful pretty.
I was a good deal astonished, but when I got my breath I asked

1. Following the frontier's comic pattern of "made-up" words, Huck confuses two cardinal doctrines of Pres-
byterianism: predestination and fore-
ordination.
2. Made of the first slabs cut from logs,
with the rounded sides downward.

her what the paper was about, and she asked me if I had read it, and I said no, and she asked me if I could read writing, and I told her "no, only coarse-hand,"[3] and then she said the paper warn't anything but a book-mark to keep her place, and I might go and play now.

I went off down to the river, studying over this thing, and pretty soon I noticed that my nigger was following along behind. When we was out of sight of the house, he looked back and around a second, and then comes a-running, and says:

"Mars Jawge, if you'll come down into de swamp, I'll show you a whole stack o' water-moccasins."

Thinks I, that's mighty curious; he said that yesterday. He oughter know a body don't love water-moccasins enough to go around hunting for them. What is he up to anyway? So I says—

"All right, trot ahead."

I followed a half a mile, then he struck out over the swamp and waded ankle deep as much as another half mile. We come to a little flat piece of land which was dry and very thick with trees and bushes and vines, and he says—

"You shove right in dah, jist a few steps, Mars Jawge, dah's whah dey is. I's seed 'm befo', I don't k'yer to see 'em no mo'."

Then he slopped right along and went away, and pretty soon the trees hid him. I poked into the place a-ways, and come to a little open patch as big as a bedroom, all hung around with vines, and found a man laying there asleep—and by jings it was my old Jim!

I waked him up, and I reckoned it was going to be a grand surprise to him to see me again, but it warn't. He nearly cried, he was so glad, but he warn't surprised. Said he swum along behind me, that night, and heard me yell every time, but dasn't answer, because he didn't want nobody to pick *him* up, and take him into slavery again. Says he—

"I got hurt a little, en couldn't swim fas', so I wuz a considable ways behine you, towards de las'; when you landed I reck'ned I could ketch up wid you on de lan' 'dout havin' to shout at you, but when I see dat house I begin to go slow. I 'uz off too fur to hear what dey say to you—I wuz 'fraid o' de dogs—but when it 'uz all quiet agin, I knowed you's in de house, so I struck out for de woods to wait for day. Early in de mawnin' some er de niggers come along, gwyne to de fields, en dey tuck me en showed me dis place, whah de dogs can't track me on accounts o' de water, en dey brings me truck to eat every night, en tells me how you's a gitt'n along."

"Why didn't you tell my Jack to fetch me here sooner, Jim?"

"Well, 'twarn't no use to 'sturb you, Huck, tell we could do

3. Printing.

sumfn—but we's all right, now. I ben a-buyin' pots en pans en vittles, as I got a chanst, en a patchin' up de raf', nights, when—"

"*What* raft, Jim?"

"Our ole raf'."

"You mean to say our old raft warn't smashed all to flinders?"

"No, she warn't. She was tore up a good deal—one en' of her
was—but dey warn't no great harm done, on'y our traps was mos'
all los'. Ef we hadn' dive' so deep en swum so fur under water, en
de night hadn' ben so dark, en we warn't so sk'yerd, en ben sich
punkin-heads, as de sayin' is, we'd a seed de raf'. But it's jis' as well
we didn't, 'kase now she's all fixed up agin mos' as good as new,
en we's got a new lot o' stuff, too, in de place o' what 'uz los'."

"Why, how did you get hold of the raft again, Jim—did you
catch her?"

"How I gwyne to ketch her, en I out in de woods? No, some er
de niggers foun' her ketched on a snag, along heah in de ben', en
dey hid her in a crick, 'mongst de willows, en dey wuz so much
jawin' 'bout which un 'um she b'long to de mos', dat I come to
heah 'bout it pooty soon, so I ups en settles de trouble by tellin'
'um she don't b'long to none uv um, but to you en me; en I ast
'm if dey gwyne to grab a young white genlman's propaty, en git a
hid'n for it? Den I gin 'm ten cents apiece, en dey 'uz mighty well
satisfied, en wisht some mo' raf's 'ud come along en make 'm rich
agin. Dey's mighty good to me, dese niggers is, en whatever I wants
'm to do fur me, I doan' have to ast 'm twice, honey. Dat Jack's a
good nigger, en pooty smart."

"Yes, he is. He ain't ever told me you was here; told me to come,
and he'd show me a lot of water-moccasins. If anything happens,
he ain't mixed up in it. He can say he never seen us together, and
it'll be the truth."

I don't want to talk much about the next day. I reckon I'll cut
it pretty short. I waked up about dawn, and was agoing to turn over
and go to sleep again, when I noticed how still it was—didn't seem
to be anybody stirring. That warn't usual. Next I noticed that
Buck was up and gone. Well, I gets up, a-wondering, and goes down
stairs—nobody around; everything as still as a mouse. Just the
same outside; thinks I, what does it mean? Down by the wood-pile
I comes across my Jack, and says:

"What's it all about?"

Says he:

"Don't you know, Mars Jawge?"

"No," says I, "I don't."

"Well, den, Miss Sophia's run off! 'deed she has. She run off in
de night, sometime—nobody don't know jis' when—run off to git
married to dat young Harney Shepherdson, you know—leastways,

so dey 'spec. De fambly foun' it out, 'bout half an hour ago—maybe a little mo'—en' I *tell* you dey warn't no time los'. Sich another hurryin' up guns en hosses *you* never see! De women folks has gone for to stir up de relations, en ole Mars Saul en de boys tuck dey guns en rode up de river road for to try to ketch dat young man en kill him 'fo' he kin git acrost de river wid Miss Sophia. I reck'n dey's gwyne to be mighty rough times."

"Buck went off 'thout waking me up."

"Well I reck'n he *did!* Dey warn't gwyne to mix you up in it. Mars Buck he loaded up his gun en 'lowed he's gwyne to fetch home a Shepherdson or bust. Well, dey'll be plenty un 'm dah, I reck'n, en you bet you he'll fetch one ef he gits a chanst."

I took up the river road as hard as I could put. By-and-by I begin to hear guns a good ways off. When I come in sight of the log store and the wood-pile where the steamboats lands, I worked along under the trees and brush till I got to a good place, and then I clumb up into the forks of a cotton-wood that was out of reach, and watched. There was a wood-rank four foot high, a little ways in front of the tree, and first I was going to hide behind that; but maybe it was luckier I didn't.

There was four or five men cavorting around on their horses in the open place before the log store, cussing and yelling, and trying to get at a couple of young chaps that was behind the wood-rank alongside of the steamboat landing—but they couldn't come it. Every time one of them showed himself on the riverside of the wood-pile he got shot at. The two boys was squatting back to back behind the pile, so they could watch both ways.

By-and-by the men stopped cavorting around and yelling. They started riding towards the store; then up gets one of the boys, draws a steady bead over the wood-rank, and drops one of them out of his saddle. All the men jumped off of their horses and grabbed the hurt one and started to carry him to the store; and that minute the two boys started on the run. They got half-way to the tree I was in before the men noticed. Then the men see them, and jumped on their horses and took out after them. They gained on the boys, but it didn't do no good, the boys had too good a start; they got to the wood-pile that was in front of my tree, and slipped in behind it, and so they had the bulge on the men again. One of the boys was Buck, and the other was a slim young chap about nineteen years old.

The men ripped around awhile, and then rode away. As soon as they was out of sight, I sung out to Buck and told him. He didn't know what to make of my voice coming out of the tree, at first. He was awful surprised. He told me to watch out sharp and let him know when the men come in sight again; said they was up to some devilment or other—wouldn't be gone long. I wished I was out of that tree, but I dasn't come down. Buck begun to cry and rip, and 'lowed that him and his cousin Joe (that was the other young chap) would make up for this day, yet. He said his father and his two brothers was killed, and two or three of the enemy. Said the Shepherdsons laid for them, in ambush. Buck said his father and brothers ought to waited for their relations—the Shepherdsons was too strong for them. I asked him what was become of young Harney and Miss Sophia. He said they'd got across the river and was safe. I was glad of that; but the way Buck did take on because he didn't manage to kill Harney that day he shot at him—I hain't ever heard anything like it.

All of a sudden, bang! bang! bang! goes three or four guns—the men had slipped around through the woods and come in from behind without their horses! The boys jumped for the river—both of them hurt—and as they swum down the current the men run along the bank shooting at them and singing out, "Kill them, kill them!" It made me so sick I most fell out of the tree. I ain't agoing to tell *all* that happened—it would make me sick again if I was to do that. I wished I hadn't ever come ashore that night, to see such things. I ain't ever going to get shut of them—lots of times I dream about them.

I staid in the tree till it begun to get dark, afraid to come down. Sometimes I heard guns away off in the woods; and twice I seen little gangs of men gallop past the logstore with guns; so I reckoned the trouble was still agoing on. I was mighty down-hearted; so I made up my mind I wouldn't ever go anear that house again, because I reckoned I was to blame, somehow. I judged that that piece of paper meant that Miss Sophia was to meet Harney somewheres at half-past two and run off; and I judged I ought to told her father about that paper and the curious way she acted, and then maybe he would a locked her up and this awful mess wouldn't ever happened.

When I got down out of the tree, I crept along down the river bank a piece, and found the two bodies laying in the edge of the water, and tugged at them till I got them ashore; then I covered up their faces, and got away as quick as I could. I cried a little when I was covering up Buck's face, for he was mighty good to me.

It was just dark, now. I never went near the house, but struck through the woods and made for the swamp. Jim warn't on his island, so I tramped off in a hurry for the crick, and crowded through the willows, red-hot to jump aboard and get out of that awful country—the raft was gone! My souls, but I was scared! I couldn't get my breath for most a minute. Then I raised a yell. A voice not twenty-five foot from me, says—

"Good lan'! is dat you, honey? Doan' make no noise."

It was Jim's voice—nothing ever sounded so good before. I run along the bank a piece and got aboard, and Jim he grabbed me and hugged me, he was so glad to see me. He says—

"Laws bless you, chile, I 'uz right down sho' you's dead agin. Jack's been heah, he say he reck'n you's ben shot, kase you didn' come home no mo'; so I's jes' dis minute a startin' de raf' down towards de mouf er de crick, so's to be all ready for to shove out en leave soon as Jack comes agin en tells me for certain you *is* dead. Lawsy, I's mighty glad to git you back agin, honey."

I says—

"All right—that's mighty good; they won't find me, and they'll think I've been killed, and floated down the river—there's something up there that'll help them to think so—so don't you lose no time, Jim, but just shove off for the big water as fast as ever you can."

I never felt easy till the raft was two mile below there and out in the middle of the Mississippi. Then we hung up our signal lantern, and judged that we was free and safe once more. I hadn't had a bite to eat since yesterday; so Jim he got out some corn-dodgers and buttermilk, and pork and cabbage, and greens—there ain't nothing in the world so good, when it's cooked right—and whilst I eat my supper we talked, and had a good time. I was powerful glad to get away from the feuds, and so was Jim to get away from the swamp. We said there warn't no home like a raft, after all. Other places do seem so cramped up and smothery, but a raft don't. You feel mighty free and easy and comfortable on a raft.[4]

Chapter XIX

Two or three days and nights went by; I reckon I might say they swum by, they slid along so quiet and smooth and lovely. Here is the way we put in the time. It was a monstrous big river down there—sometimes a mile and a half wide; we run nights, and laid up and hid day-times; soon as night was most gone, we stopped navigating and tied up—nearly always in the dead water under a tow-head; and then cut young cottonwoods and willows and hid the raft with them. Then we set out the lines. Next we slid into the river and had a swim, so as to freshen up and cool off; then we set down on the sandy bottom where the water was about knee deep, and watched the daylight come. Not a sound, anywheres—perfectly still—just like the whole world was asleep, only some-

4. The two chapters devoted to the Grangerford episode contrast the idyllic and picturesque description of the family and their home with the hideous and vainglorious inhumanity of the feud, which even Huck's experience has not prepared him to stomach. In addition, there is the subtle realization of Twain's continuous contrast of the River with the shore and simple nature with human nature, epitomized here in Huck's final comment.

times the bull-frogs a-cluttering, maybe. The first thing to see, looking away over the water, was a kind of dull line—that was the woods on t'other side—you couldn't make nothing else out; then a pale place in the sky; then more paleness, spreading around; then the river softened up, away off, and warn't black any more, but gray; you could see little dark spots drifting along, ever so far away —trading scows, and such things; and long black streaks—rafts; sometimes you could hear a sweep screaking; or jumbled up voices, it was so still, and sounds come so far; and by-and-by you could see a streak on the water which you know by the look of the streak that there's a snag there in a swift current which breaks on it and makes that streak look that way; and you see the mist curl up off of the water, and the east reddens up, and the river, and you make out a log cabin in the edge of the woods, away on the bank on t'other side of the river, being a wood-yard, likely, and piled by them cheats so you can throw a dog through it anywheres; then the nice breeze springs up, and comes fanning you from over there, so cool and fresh, and sweet to smell, on account of the woods and the flowers; but sometimes not that way, because they've left dead fish laying around, gars, and such, and they do get pretty rank; and next you've got the full day, and everything smiling in the sun, and the song-birds just going it!

A little smoke couldn't be noticed, now, so we would take some fish off of the lines, and cook up a hot breakfast. And afterwards we would watch the lonesomeness of the river, and kind of lazy along, and by-and-by lazy off to sleep. Wake up, by-and-by, and look to see what done it, and maybe see a steamboat coughing along up stream, so far off towards the other side you couldn't tell nothing about her only whether she was stern-wheel or side-wheel; then for about an hour there wouldn't be nothing to hear nor nothing to see—just solid lonesomeness. Next you'd see a raft sliding by, away off yonder, and maybe a galoot on it chopping, because they're almost always doing it on a raft; you'd see the ax flash, and come down—you don't hear nothing; you see that ax go up again, and by the time it's above the man's head, then you hear the *k'chunk!*—it had took all that time to come over the water. So we would put in the day, lazying around, listening to the stillness. Once there was a thick fog, and the rafts and things that went by was beating tin pans so the steamboats wouldn't run over them. A scow or a raft went by so close we could hear them talking and cussing and laughing—heard them plain; but we couldn't see no sign of them; it made you feel crawly, it was like spirits carrying on that way in the air. Jim said he believed it was spirits; but I says:

"No, spirits wouldn't say, 'dern the dern fog.' "

Soon as it was night, out we shoved; when we got her out to about the middle, we let her alone, and let her float wherever the current wanted her to; then we lit the pipes, and dangled our legs in the water and talked about all kinds of things—we was always naked, day and night, whenever the mosquitoes would let us—the new clothes Buck's folks made for me was too good to be comfortable, and besides I didn't go much on clothes, nohow.

Sometimes we'd have that whole river all to ourselves for the longest time. Yonder was the banks and the islands, across the water; and maybe a spark—which was a candle in a cabin window—and sometimes on the water you could see a spark or two—on a raft or a scow, you know; and maybe you could hear a fiddle or a song coming over from one of them crafts. It's lovely to live on a raft. We had the sky, up there, all speckled with stars, and we used to lay on our backs and look up at them, and discuss about whether they was made, or only just happened—Jim he allowed they was made, but I allowed they happened; I judged it would have took too long to *make* so many. Jim said the moon could a *laid* them; well, that looked kind of reasonable, so I didn't say nothing against it, because I've seen a frog lay most as many, so of course it could be done. We used to watch the stars that fell, too, and see them streak down. Jim allowed they'd got spoiled and was hove out of the nest.

Once or twice of a night we would see a steamboat slipping along in the dark, and now and then she would belch a whole world of sparks up out of her chimbleys, and they would rain down in the river and look awful pretty; then she would turn a corner and her lights would wink out and her pow-wow shut off and leave the river still again; and by-and-by her waves would get to us, a long time after she was gone, and joggle the raft a bit, and after that you wouldn't hear nothing for you couldn't tell how long, except maybe frogs or something.

After midnight the people on shore went to bed, and then for two or three hours the shore was black—no more sparks in the cabin windows. These sparks was our clock—the first one that showed again meant morning was coming, so we hunted a place to hide and tie up, right away.[5]

One morning about day-break, I found a canoe and crossed over a chute[6] to the main shore—it was only two hundred yards—and paddled about a mile up a crick amongst the cypress woods, to see if I couldn't get some berries. Just as I was passing a place where a kind of a cow-path crossed the crick, here comes a couple of men tearing up the path as tight as they could foot it. I thought I was a goner, for whenever anybody was after anybody I judged it was

5. In this, one of Twain's famous descriptive passages, the return to the raft and the River provides another experience of nature, an idyllic interlude between two revelations of man's inhu-manity—tragic in the Grangerford feud and comic in the episodes to follow.
6. A narrow channel to the mainland, with swift-flowing water.

me—or maybe Jim. I was about to dig out from there in a hurry, but they was pretty close to me then, and sung out and begged me to save their lives—said they hadn't been doing nothing, and was being chased for it—said there was men and dogs a-coming. They wanted to jump right in, but I says—

"Don't you do it. I don't hear the dogs and horses yet; you've got time to crowd through the brush and get up the crick a little ways; then you take to the water and wade down to me and get in —that'll throw the dogs off the scent."

They done it, and soon as they was aboard I lit out for our tow-head, and in about five or ten minutes we heard the dogs and the men away off, shouting. We heard them come along towards the crick, but couldn't see them; they seemed to stop and fool around a while; then, as we got further and further away all the time, we couldn't hardly hear them at all; by the time we had left a mile of woods behind us and struck the river, everything was quiet, and we paddled over to the tow-head and hid in the cotton-woods and was safe.

One of these fellows was about seventy, or upwards, and had a bald head and very gray whiskers. He had an old battered-up slouch hat on, and a greasy blue woolen shirt, and ragged old blue jeans britches stuffed into his boot tops, and home-knit galluses—no, he only had one. He had an old long-tailed blue jeans coat with slick brass buttons, flung over his arm, and both of them had big fat ratty-looking carpet-bags.

The other fellow was about thirty and dressed about as ornery. After breakfast we all laid off and talked, and the first thing that come out was that these chaps didn't know one another.

"What got you into trouble?" says the baldhead to t'other chap.

"Well, I'd been selling an article to take the tartar off the teeth —and it does take it off, too, and generally the enamel along with it—but I staid about one night longer than I ought to, and was just in the act of sliding out when I ran across you on the trail this side of town, and you told me they were coming, and begged me to help you to get off. So I told you I was expecting trouble myself and would scatter out *with* you. That's the whole yarn—what's yourn?"

"Well, I'd ben a-runnin' a little temperance revival thar, 'bout a week, and was the pet of the women-folks, big and little, for I was makin' it mighty warm for the rummies, I *tell* you, and takin' as much as five or six dollars a night—ten cents a head, children and niggers free—and business a growin' all the time; when somehow or another a little report got around, last night, that I had a way of puttin' in my time with a private jug, on the sly. A nigger rousted me out this mornin', and told me the people was gatherin' on the quiet, with their dogs and horses, and they'd be along pretty soon and give me 'bout half an hour's start, and then run me down, if they could; and if they got me they'd tar and feather me and ride me on a rail, sure. I didn't wait for no breakfast—I warn't hungry."

"Old man," says the young one, "I reckon we might double-team it together; what do you think?"

"I ain't undisposed. What's your line—mainly?"

"Jour printer,[7] by trade; do a little in patent medicines; theatre-actor—tragedy, you know; take a turn at mesmerism and phrenology when there's a chance; teach singing-geography school for a change; sling a lecture, sometimes—oh, I do lots of things—most anything that comes handy, so it ain't work. What's your lay?"[8]

"I've done considerble in the doctoring way in my time. Layin' on o' hands is my best holt—for cancer, and paralysis, and sich things; and I k'n tell a fortune pretty good, when I've got somebody along to find out the facts for me. Preachin's my line, too; and workin' camp-meetin's; and missionaryin' around."

Nobody never said anything for a while; then the young man hove a sigh and says—

"Alas!"

"What 're you alassin' about?" says the baldhead.

"To think I should have lived to be leading such a life, and be degraded down into such company." And he begun to wipe the corner of his eye with a rag.

"Dern your skin, ain't the company good enough for you?" says the baldhead, pretty pert and uppish.

"Yes, it *is* good enough for me; it's as good as I deserve; for who fetched me so low, when I was so high? *I* did myself. I don't blame *you*, gentlemen—far from it; I don't blame anybody. I deserve it all. Let the cold world do its worst; one thing I know—there's a grave somewhere for me. The world may go on just as its always done, and take everything from me—loved ones, property, everything—but it can't take that. Some day I'll lie down in it and forget it all, and my poor broken heart will be at rest." He went on a-wiping.

"Drot your pore broken heart," says the baldhead; "what are you heaving your pore broken heart at *us* f'r? *We* hain't done nothing."

"No, I know you haven't. I ain't blaming you, gentlemen. I brought myself down—yes, I did it myself. It's right I should suffer—perfectly right—I don't make any moan."

"Brought you down from whar? Whar was you brought down from?"

"Ah, you would not believe me; the world never believes—let it pass—'tis no matter. The secret of my birth—"

"The secret of your birth? Do you mean to say—"

7. Journeyman printer: one who worked by the day, not yet a master printer.
8. The roving fraud was a stock comic character of frontier literature, but Twain turns his two specimens into real, fully drawn characters.

"Gentlemen," says the young man, very solemn, "I will reveal it to you, for I feel I may have confidence in you. By rights I am a duke!"

Jim's eyes bugged out when he heard that; and I reckon mine did, too. Then the baldhead says: "No! you can't mean it?"

"Yes. My great-grandfather, eldest son of the Duke of Bridge-water, fled to this country about the end of the last century, to breathe the pure air of freedom; married here, and died, leaving a son, his own father dying about the same time. The second son of the late duke seized the title and estates—the infant real duke was ignored. I am the lineal descendant of that infant—I am the right-ful Duke of Bridgewater; and here am I, forlorn, torn from my high estate, hunted of men, despised by the cold world, ragged, worn, heart-broken, and degraded to the companionship of felons on a raft!"

Jim pitied him ever so much ,and so did I. We tried to comfort him, but he said it warn't much use, he couldn't be much com-forted; said if we was a mind to acknowledge him, that would do him more good than most anything else; so we said we would, if he would tell us how. He said we ought to bow, when we spoke to him, and say "Your Grace," or "My Lord," or "Your Lordship"—and he wouldn't mind it if we called him plain "Bridgewater," which he said was a title, anyway, and not a name; and one of us ought to wait on him at dinner, and do any little thing for him he wanted done.

Well, that was all easy, so we done it. All through dinner Jim stood around and waited on him, and says, "Will yo' Grace have some o' dis, or some o' dat?" and so on, and a body could see it was mighty pleasing to him.

But the old man got pretty silent, by-and-by—didn't have much to say, and didn't look pretty comfortable over all that petting that was going on around that duke. He seemed to have something on his mind. So, along in the afternoon, he says:

"Looky here, Bilgewater," he says, "I'm nation sorry for you, but you ain't the only person that's had troubles like that."

"No?"

"No, you ain't. You ain't the only person that's ben snaked down wrongfully out'n a high place."

"Alas!"

"No, you ain't the only person that's had a secret of his birth." And by jings, *he* begins to cry.

"Hold! What do you mean?"

"Bilgewater, kin I trust you?" says the old man, still sort of sob-bing.

"To the bitter death!" He took the old man by the hand and squeezed it, and says, "The secret of your being: speak!"

"Bilgewater, I am the late Dauphin!"

You bet you Jim and me stared, this time. Then the duke says: "You are what?"

"Yes, my friend, it is too true—your eyes is lookin' at this very moment on the pore disappeared Dauphin, Looy the Seventeen, son of Looy the Sixteen and Marry Antonette."

"You! At your age![9] No! You mean you're the late Charlemagne; you must be six or seven hundred years old, at the very least."

"Trouble has done it, Bilgewater, trouble has done it; trouble has brung these gray hairs and this premature balditude. Yes, gentlemen, you see before you, in blue jeans and misery, the wanderin', exiled, trampled-on and sufferin' rightful King of France."

Well, he cried and took on so, that me and Jim didn't know hardly what to do, we was so sorry—and so glad and proud we'd got him with us, too. So we set in, like we done before with the duke, and tried to comfort *him*. But he said it warn't no use, nothing but to be dead and done with it all could do him any good; though he said it often made him feel easier and better for a while if people treated him according to his rights, and got down on one knee to speak to him, and always called him "Your Majesty," and waited on him first at meals, and didn't set down in his presence till he asked them. So Jim and me set to majestying him, and doing this and that and t'other for him, and standing up till he told us we might set down. This done him heaps of good, and so he got cheerful and comfortable. But the duke kind of soured on him, and didn't look a bit satisfied with the way things was going; still, the king acted real friendly towards him, and said the duke's great-grandfather and all the other Dukes of Bilgewater was a good deal thought of by *his* father and was allowed to come to the palace considerable; but the duke staid huffy a good while, till by-and-by the king says:

"Like as not we got to be together a blamed long time, on this h-yer raft, Bilgewater, and so what's the use o' your bein' sour? It'll only make things oncomfortable. It ain't my fault I warn't born a duke, it ain't your fault you warn't born a king—so what's the use to worry? Make the best o' things the way you find 'em, says I— that's my motto. This ain't no bad thing that we've struck here— plenty grub and an easy life—come, give us your hand, Duke, and less all be friends."

The duke done it, and Jim and me was pretty glad to see it. It took away all the uncomfortableness, and we felt mighty good over it, because it would a been a miserable business to have any unfriendliness on the raft; for what you want, above all things, on a raft, is for everybody to be satisfied, and feel right and kind to-

9. *Cf.* Chapter XIV, note 2. Had the Dauphin lived, he would have been in his mid-fifties.

wards the others.

It didn't take me long to make up my mind that these liars warn't no kings nor dukes, at all, but just low-down humbugs and frauds. But I never said nothing, never let on; kept it to myself; it's the best way; then you don't have no quarrels, and don't get into no trouble. If they wanted us to call them kings and dukes, I hadn't no objections, 'long as it would keep peace in the family; and it warn't no use to tell Jim, so I didn't tell him. If I never learnt nothing else out of pap, I learnt that the best way to get along with his kind of people is to let them have their own way.

Chapter XX

They asked us considerable many questions; wanted to know what we covered up the raft that way for, and laid by in the day-time instead of running—was Jim a runaway nigger? Says I—

"Goodness sakes, would a runaway nigger run *south?*"

No, they allowed he wouldn't. I had to account for things some way, so I says:

"My folks was living in Pike County, in Missouri, where I was born, and they all died off but me and pa and my brother Ike. Pa, he 'lowed he'd break up and go down and live with Uncle Ben, who's got a little one-horse place on the river, forty-four mile below Orleans. Pa was pretty poor, and had some debts; so when he'd squared up there warn't nothing left but sixteen dollars and our nigger, Jim. That warn't enough to take us fourteen hundred mile, deck passage nor no other way. Well, when the river rose, pa had a streak of luck one day; he ketched this piece of raft; so we reckoned we'd go down to Orleans on it. Pa's luck didn't hold out; a steamboat run over the forrard corner of the raft, one night, and we all went overboard and dove under the wheel; Jim and me come up, all right, but pa was drunk, and Ike was only four years old, so they never come up no more. Well, for the next day or two we had considerable trouble, because people was always coming out in skiffs and trying to take Jim away from me, saying they believed he was a runaway nigger. We don't run day-times no more, now; nights they don't bother us."

The duke says—

"Leave me alone to cipher out a way so we can run in the day-time if we want to. I'll think the thing over—I'll invent a plan that'll fix it. We'll let it alone for to-day, because of course we don't want to go by that town yonder in daylight—it mightn't be healthy."

Towards night it begun to darken up and look like rain; the heat lightning was squirting around, low down in the sky, and the leaves was beginning to shiver—it was going to be pretty ugly, it was easy to see that. So the duke and the king went to overhauling our wigwam, to see what the beds was like. My bed was a straw tick—better than Jim's, which was a corn-shuck tick; there's always cobs around about in a shuck tick, and they poke into you and hurt; and when you roll over, the dry shucks sound like you was rolling over in a pile of dead leaves; it makes such a rustling that you wake up. Well, the duke allowed he would take my bed; but the king allowed he wouldn't. He says—

"I should a reckoned the difference in rank would a sejested to you that a corn-shuck bed warn't just fitten for me to sleep on. Your Grace'll take the shuck bed yourself."

Jim and me was in a sweat agin, for a minute, being afraid there was going to be some more trouble amongst them; so we was pretty glad when the duke says—

" 'Tis my fate to be always ground into the mire under the iron heel of oppression. Misfortune has broken my once haughty spirit; I yield, I submit; 'tis my fate. I am alone in the world—let me suffer; I can bear it."

We got away as soon as it was good and dark. The king told us to stand well out towards the middle of the river, and not show a light till we got a long ways below the town. We come in sight of the little bunch of lights by-and-by—that was the town, you know —and slid by, about a half a mile out, all right. When we was three-quarters of a mile below, we hoisted up our signal lantern; and about ten o'clock it come on to rain and blow and thunder and lighten like everything; so the king told us to both stay on watch till the weather got better; then him and the duke crawled into the wigwam and turned in for the night. It was my watch below, till twelve, but I wouldn't a turned in, anyway, if I'd had a bed; because a body don't see such a storm as that every day in the week, not by a long sight. My souls, how the wind did scream along! And every second or two there'd come a glare that lit up the white-caps for a half a mile around, and you'd see the islands looking dusty through the rain, and the trees thrashing around in the wind; then comes a *h-wack!*—bum! bum! bumble-umble-um-bum-bum-bum-bum—and the thunder would go rumbling and grumbling away, and quit—and then *rip* comes another flash and another sockdolager. The waves most washed me off the raft, sometimes, but I hadn't any clothes on, and didn't mind. We didn't have no trouble about snags; the lightning was glaring and flittering around so constant that we could see them plenty soon enough to throw her head this way or that and miss them.

I had the middle watch, you know, but I was pretty sleepy by that time, so Jim he said he would stand the first half of it for me; he was always mighty good, that way, Jim was. I crawled into the wigwam, but the king and the duke had their legs sprawled around so there warn't no show for me; so I laid outside—I didn't

mind the rain, because it was warm, and the waves warn't running
so high, now. About two they come up again, though, and Jim
was going to call me, but he changed his mind because he reckoned
they warn't high enough yet to do any harm; but he was mistaken
about that, for pretty soon all of a sudden along comes a regular
ripper, and washed me overboard. It most killed Jim a-laughing. He
was the easiest nigger to laugh that ever was, anyway.

I took the watch, and Jim he laid down and snored away; and
by-and-by the storm let up for good and all; and the first cabin-
light that showed, I rousted him out and we slid the raft into
hiding-quarters for the day.

The king got out an old ratty deck of cards, after breakfast, and
him and the duke played seven-up a while, five cents a game. Then
they got tired of it, and allowed they would "lay out a campaign,"
as they called it. The duke went down into his carpet-bag and
fetched up a lot of little printed bills, and read them out loud. One
bill said "The celebrated Dr. Armand de Montalban of Paris,"
would "lecture on the Science of Phrenology" at such and such a
place, on the blank day of blank, at ten cents admission, and "furnish charts of character at twenty-five cents apiece." The duke said
that was *him*. In another bill he was the "world renowned
Shaksperean tragedian, Garrick the Younger,[1] of Drury Lane, London." In other bills he had a lot of other names and done other
wonderful things, like finding water and gold with a "divining
rod," "dissipating witch-spells," and so on. By-and-by he says—

"But the histrionic muse is the darling. Have you ever trod the
boards, Royalty?"

"No," says the king.

"You shall, then, before you're three days older, Fallen
Grandeur,"[2] says the duke. "The first good town we come to, we'll
hire a hall and do the sword-fight in Richard III. and the balcony
scene in Romeo and Juliet. How does that strike you?"

"I'm in, up to the hub, for anything that will pay, Bilgewater,
but you see I don't know nothing about play-actn', and hain't ever
seen much of it. I was too small when pap used to have 'em at the
palace. Do you reckon you can learn me?"

"Easy!"

"All right. I'm jist a-freezn' for something fresh, anyway. Less
commence, right away."

So the duke he told him all about who Romeo was, and who
Juliet was, and said he was used to being Romeo, so the king could
be Juliet.

1. *Cf.* the playbill and note 7 in Chapter XXI for the nonexistent David
Garrick the *Younger*.
2. The frontiersman's dexterity in the
coinage of ludicrous names as here in
"Bilgewater" and "Fallen Grandeur"
persists as one of Twain's comic devices
which assist him in individualizing
these two characters.

"But if Juliet's such a young gal, Duke, my peeled head and my white whiskers is goin' to look oncommon odd on her, maybe."

"No, don't you worry—these country jakes won't ever think of that.[3] Besides, you know, you'll be in costume, and that makes all the difference in the world; Juliet's in a balcony, enjoying the moonlight before she goes to bed, and she's got on her night-gown and her ruffled night-cap. Here are the costumes for the parts."

He got out two or three curtain-calico suits, which he said was meedyevil armor for Richard III. and t'other chap, and a long white cotton night-shirt and a ruffled night-cap to match. The king was satisfied; so the duke got out his book and read the parts over in the most splendid spread-eagle way, prancing around and acting at the same time, to show how it had got to be done; then he give the book to the king and told him to get his part by heart.

There was a little one-horse town about three mile down the bend, and after dinner the duke said he had ciphered out his idea about how to run in daylight without it being dangersome for Jim; so he allowed he would go down to the town and fix that thing. The king allowed he would go too, and see if he couldn't strike something. We was out of coffee, so Jim said I better go along with them in the canoe and get some.

When we got there, there warn't nobody stirring; streets empty, and perfectly dead and still, like Sunday. We found a sick nigger sunning himself in a back yard, and he said everybody that warn't too young or too sick or too old, was gone to camp-meeting, about two mile back in the woods. The king got the directions, and allowed he'd go and work that camp-meeting for all it was worth,[4] and I might go, too.

The duke said what he was after was a printing office. We found it; a little bit of a concern, up over a carpenter shop—carpenters and printers all gone to the meeting, and no doors locked. It was a dirty, littered-up place, and had ink marks, and handbills with pictures of horses and runaway niggers on them, all over the walls. The duke shed his coat and said he was all right, now. So me and the king lit out for the camp-meeting.

We got there in about a half an hour, fairly dripping, for it was a most awful hot day. There was as much as a thousand people there, from twenty mile around. The woods was full of teams and wagons, hitched everywheres, feeding out of the wagon troughs and stomping to keep off the flies. There was sheds made out of

3. The king's appearance as Juliet would disturb the audience more because of his age than because of his sex; Wecter in *Sam Clemens of Hannibal*, p. 186, says that in that time and place no lady could appear on the stage, and feminine roles were carried by men or boys, as in seventeenth-century England.

4. A stock situation of frontier humor was the pious fraud who got away with the collection basket at a camp-meeting. The classic example of this is "The Captain Attends a Camp-Meeting," an episode in the life of the legendary Suggs collected by Johnson J. Hooper in his *Some Adventures of Captain Simon Suggs*.

poles and roofed over with branches, where they had lemonade and gingerbread to sell, and piles of watermelons and green corn and such-like truck.

The preaching was going on under the same kinds of sheds, only they was bigger and held crowds of people. The benches was made out of outside slabs of logs, with holes bored in the round side to drive sticks into for legs. They didn't have no backs. The preachers had high platforms to stand on, at one end of the sheds. The women had on sunbonnets; and some had linsey-woolsey frocks, some gingham ones, and a few of the young ones had on calico. Some of the young men was barefooted, and some of the children didn't have on any clothes but just a tow-linen shirt. Some of the old women was knitting, and some of the young folks was courting on the sly.

The first shed we come to, the preacher was lining out a hymn. He lined out two lines, everybody sung it, and it was kind of grand to hear it, there was so many of them and they done it in such a rousing way; then he lined out two more for them to sing—and so on. The people woke up more and more, and sung louder and louder; and towards the end, some begun to groan, and some begun to shout. Then the preacher begun to preach; and begun in earnest, too; and went weaving first to one side of the platform and then the other, and then a leaning down over the front of it, with his arms and his body going all the time, and shouting his words out with all his might; and every now and then he would hold up his Bible and spread it open, and kind of pass it around this way and that, shouting, "It's the brazen serpent in the wilderness! Look upon it and live!" And people would shout out, "Glory! —A-a-*men!*" And so he went on, and the people groaning and crying and saying amen:

"Oh, come to the mourners' bench! come, black with sin! (*amen!*) come, sick and sore! (*amen!*) come, lame and halt, and blind! (*amen!*) come, pore and needy, sunk in shame! (*a-a-men!*) come all that's worn, and soiled, and suffering!—come with a broken spirit! come with a contrite heart! come in your rags and sin and dirt! the waters that cleanse is free, the door of heaven stands open—oh, enter in and be at rest!" (*a-a-men! glory, glory hallelujah!*)

And so on. You couldn't make out what the preacher said, any more, on account of the shouting and crying. Folks got up, everywheres in the crowd, and worked their way, just by main strength, to the mourners' bench, with the tears running down their faces; and when all the mourners had got up there to the front benches in a crowd, they sung, and shouted, and flung themselves down on the straw, just crazy and wild.

Well, the first I knowed, the king got agoing; and you could hear him over everybody; and next he went a-charging up on to the platform and the preacher he begged him to speak to the people, and he done it. He told them he was a pirate—been a pirate for thirty years, out in the Indian Ocean, and his crew was thinned out considerable, last spring, in a fight, and he was home now, to take out some fresh men, and thanks to goodness he'd been robbed last night, and put ashore off of a steamboat without a cent, and he was glad of it, it was the blessedest thing that ever happened to him, because he was a changed man now, and happy for the first time in his life; and poor as he was, he was going to start right off and work his way back to the Indian Ocean and put in the rest of his life trying to turn the pirates into the true path; for he could do it better than anybody else, being acquainted with all the pirate crews in that ocean; and though it would take him a long time to get there, without money, he would get there anyway, and every time he convinced a pirate he would say to him, "Don't you thank me, don't you give me no credit, it all belongs to them dear people in Pokeville camp-meeting, natural brothers and benefactors of the race—and that dear preacher there, the truest friend a pirate ever had!"

And then he busted into tears, and so did everybody. Then somebody sings out, "Take up a collection for him, take up a collection!" Well, a half a dozen made a jump to do it, but somebody sings out, "Let *him* pass the hat around!" Then everybody said it, the preacher too.

So the king went all through the crowd with his hat, swabbing his eyes, and blessing the people and praising them and thanking them for being so good to the poor pirates away off there; and every little while the prettiest kind of girls, with the tears running down their cheeks, would up and ask him would he let them kiss him, for to remember him by; and he always done it; and some of them he hugged and kissed as many as five or six times—and he was invited to stay a week; and everybody wanted him to live in their houses, and said they'd think it was an honor; but he said as this was the last day of the camp-meeting he couldn't do no good, and besides he was in a sweat to get to the Indian Ocean right off and go to work on the pirates.

When we got back to the raft and he come to count up, he found he had collected eighty-seven dollars and seventy-five cents. And then he had fetched away a three-gallon jug of whisky, too, that he found under a wagon when we was starting home through the woods. The king said, take it all around, it laid over any day he'd ever put in in the missionarying line. He said it warn't no use talking, heathens don't amount to shucks, alongside of pirates, to work a campmeeting with.

The duke was thinking *he'd* been doing pretty well, till the king

come to show up, but after that he didn't think so so much. He had
set up and printed off two little jobs for farmers, in that printing
office—horse bills—and took the money, four dollars. And he had
got in ten dollars worth of advertisements for the paper, which he
said he would put in for four dollars if they would pay in advance—
so they done it. The price of the paper was two dollars a year, but
he took in three subscriptions for half a dollar apiece on condition
of them paying him in advance; they were going to pay in cord-
wood and onions, as usual. but he said he had just bought the concern and knocked down the price as low as he could afford it, and
was going to run it for cash. He set up a little piece of poetry, which
he made, himself, out of his own head—three verses—kind of sweet
and saddish—the name of it was, "Yes, crush, cold world, this
breaking heart"—and he left that all set up and ready to print in
the paper and didn't charge nothing for it. Well, he took in nine
dollars and a half, and said he'd done a pretty square day's work for
it.

Then he showed us another little job he'd printed and hadn't
charged for, because it was for us. It had a picture of a runaway
nigger, with a bundle on a stick, over his shoulder, and "$200 re-
ward" under it. The reading was all about Jim, and just described
him to a dot. It said he run away from St. Jacques' plantation, forty
mile below New Orleans, last winter, and likely went north, and
whoever would catch him and send him back, he could have the
reward and expenses.

"Now," says the duke, "after to-night we can run in the daytime
if we want to. Whenever we see anybody coming, we can tie Jim
hand and foot with a rope, and lay him in the wigwam and show
this handbill and say we captured him up the river, and were too
poor to travel on a steamboat, so we got this little raft on credit
from our friends and are going down to get the reward. Handcuffs
and chains would look still better on Jim, but it wouldn't go well
with the story of us being so poor. Too much like jewelry. Ropes
are the correct thing—we must preserve the unities, as we say on
the boards."

We all said the duke was pretty smart, and there couldn't be no
trouble about running daytimes. We judged we could make miles
enough that night to get out of the reach of the pow-wow we reckoned the duke's work in the printing office was going to make in that
little town—then we could boom right along, if we wanted to.

We laid low and kept still, and never shoved out till nearly ten
o'clock; then we slid by, pretty wide away from the town, and didn't
hoist our lantern till we was clear out of sight of it.

When Jim called me to take the watch at four in the morning,
he says—

"Huck, does you reck'n we gwyne to run acrost any mo' kings on dis trip?"

"No," I says, "I reckon not."

"Well," says he, "dat's all right, den. I doan' mine one er two kings, but dat's enough. Dis one's powerful drunk, en de duke ain much better."

I found Jim had been trying to get him to talk French, so he could hear what it was like; but he said he had been in this country so long, and had so much trouble, he'd forgot it.

Chapter XXI

It was after sun-up, now, but we went right on, and didn't tie up. The king and the duke turned out, by-and-by, looking pretty rusty; but after they'd jumped overboard and took a swim, it chippered them up a good deal. After breakfast the king he took a seat on a corner of the raft, and pulled off his boots and rolled up his britches, and let his legs dangle in the water, so as to be comfortable, and lit his pipe, and went to getting his Romeo and Juliet by heart. When he had got it pretty good, him and the duke begun to practice it together. The duke had to learn him over and over again, how to say every speech; and he made him sigh, and put his hand on his heart, and after while he said he done it pretty well; "only," he says, "you mustn't bellow out *Romeo!* that way, like a bull— you must say it soft, and sick, and languishy, so—R-o-o-meo! that is the idea; for Juliet's a dear sweet mere child of a girl, you know, and she don't bray like a jackass."

Well, next they got out a couple of long swords that the duke made out of oak laths, and begun to practice the sword-fight—the duke called himself Richard III.; and the way they laid on, and pranced around the raft was grand to see. But by-and-by the king tripped and fell overboard, and after that they took a rest, and had a talk about all kinds of adventures they'd had in other times along the river.

After dinner, the duke says:

"Well, Capet,[5] we'll want to make this a first-class show, you know, so I guess we'll add a little more to it. We want a little something to answer encores with, anyway."

"What's onkores, Bilgewater?"

The duke told him, and then says:

"I'll answer by doing the Highland fling or the sailor's hornpipe; and you—well, let me see—oh, I've got it—you can do Hamlet's soliloquy."

"Hamlet's which?"

---

5. In convicting Louis XVI the National Convention used his family name, Louis Capet. The duke may also be garbling Juliet's family name, Capulet.

"Hamlet's soliloquy, you know; the most celebrated thing in Shakespeare. Ah, it's sublime, sublime! Always fetches the house. I haven't got it in the book—I've only got one volume—but I reckon I can piece it out from memory. I'll just walk up and down a minute, and see if I can call it back from recollection's vaults."

So he went to marching up and down, thinking, and frowning horrible every now and then; then he would hoist up his eyebrows; next he would squeeze his hand on his forehead and stagger back and kind of moan; next he would sigh, and next he'd let on to drop a tear. It was beautiful to see him. By-and-by he got it. He told us to give attention. Then he strikes a most noble attitude, with one leg shoved forwards, and his arms stretched away up, and his head tilted back, looking up at the sky; and then he begins to rip and rave and grit his teeth; and after that, all through his speech he howled, and spread around, and swelled up his chest, and just knocked the spots out of any acting ever *I* see before. This is the speech—I learned it, easy enough, while he was learning it to the king:[6]

To be, or not to be; that is the bare bodkin
That makes calamity of so long life;
For who would fardels bear, till Birnam Wood do come to Dun-
    sinane,
But that the fear of something after death
Murders the innocent sleep,
Great nature's second course,
And makes us rather sling the arrows of outrageous fortune
Than fly to others that we know not of.
There's the respect must give us pause:
Wake Duncan with thy knocking! I would thou couldst;
For who would bear the whips and scorns of time,
The oppressor's wrong, the proud man's contumely,
The law's delay, and the quietus which his pangs might take,
In the dead waste and middle of the night, when churchyards yawn
In customary suits of solemn black,
But that the undiscovered country from whose bourne no traveler
    returns,
Breathes forth contagion on the world,
And thus the native hue of resolution, like the poor cat i' the adage,
Is sicklied o'er with care,
And all the clouds that lowered o'er our housetops,
With this regard their currents turn awry,
And lose the name of action.
'Tis a consummation devoutly to be wished. But soft you, the fair

6. The duke's fractured Shakespeare, which is in the best impromptu frontier tradition, picks up and pieces together some of Shakespeare's most quotable lines.

Ophelia:
Ope not thy ponderous and marble jaws,
But get thee to a nunnery—go!

Well, the old man he liked that speech, and he mighty soon got
it so he could do it first rate. It seemed like he was just born for it;
and when he had his hand in and was excited, it was perfectly lovely
the way he would rip and tear and rair up behind when he was getting it off.

The first chance we got, the duke he had some show bills printed;
and after that, for two or three days as we floated along, the raft
was a most uncommon lively place, for there warn't nothing but
sword-fighting and rehearsing—as the duke called it—going on all
the time. One morning, when we was pretty well down the State
of Arkansaw, we come in sight of a little one-horse town in a big
bend; so we tied up about three-quarters of a mile above it, in the
mouth of a crick which was shut in like a tunnel by the cypress
trees, and all of us but Jim took the canoe and went down there to
see if there was any chance in that place for our show.

We struck it mighty lucky; there was going to be a circus there
that afternoon, and the country people was already beginning to
come in, in all kinds of old shackly wagons, and on horses. The
circus would leave before night, so our show would have a pretty
good chance. The duke he hired the court house, and we went
around and stuck up our bills. They read like this:[7]

Shaksperean Revival! ! !
Wonderful Attraction!
For One Night Only!
The world renowned tragedians,
David Garrick the younger, of Drury Lane Theatre, London,
and
Edmund Kean the elder, of the Royal Haymarket Theatre, White-
chapel, Pudding Lane, Piccadilly, London, and the
Royal Continental Theatres, in their sublime
Shaksperean Spectacle entitled
The Balcony Scene
in
Romeo and Juliet! ! !

Romeo . . . . Mr. Garrick.
Juliet . . . . Mr. Kean.

Assisted by the whole strength of the company!
New costumes, new scenery, new appointments!
Also:
The thrilling, masterly, and blood-curdling
Broad-sword conflict

7. The duke blithely confuses three great English Shakespearian actors, David Garrick (1717–1779), Edmund Kean (the Elder; 1787?–1833), and Charles John Kean (the Younger; 1811?–1868), all of whom were prominent tragedians at Drury Lane Theatre in London. He carries forward this error in the poster for the "Royal Nonesuch" in Chapter XXII.

In Richard III.! ! !

Richard III .... Mr. Garrick.
Richmond .... Mr. Kean.

also:
(by special request,)
Hamlet's Immortal Soliloquy! !
By the Illustrious Kean!
Done by him 300 consecutive nights in Paris!
For One Night Only,
On account of imperative European engagements!
Admission 25 cents; children and servants, 10 cents.

Then we went loafing around the town.[8] The stores and houses was most all old shackly dried-up frame concerns that hadn't ever been painted; they was set up three or four foot above ground on stilts, so as to be out of reach of the water when the river was over-flowed. The houses had little gardens around them, but they didn't seem to raise hardly anything in them but jimpson weeds, and sun-flowers, and ash-piles, and old curled-up boots and shoes, and pieces of bottles, and rags, and played-out tin-ware. The fences was made of different kinds of boards, nailed on at different times; and they leaned every which-way, and had gates that didn't generly have but one hinge—a leather one. Some of the fences had been white-washed, some time or another, but the duke said it was in Clumbus's time, like enough. There was generly hogs in the garden, and people driving them out.

All the stores was along one street. They had white-domestic awnings in front, and the country people hitched their horses to the awning-posts. There was empty dry-goods boxes under the awn-ings, and loafers roosting on them all day long, whittling them with their Barlow knives; and chawing tobacco, and gaping and yawning and stretching—a mighty ornery lot. They generly had on yellow straw hats most as wide as an umbrella, but didn't wear no coats nor waistcoats; they called one another Bill, and Buck, and Hank, and Joe, and Andy, and talked lazy and drawly, and used consider-able many cuss-words. There was as many as one loafer leaning up against every awning-post, and he most always had his hands in his britches pockets, except when he fetched them out to lend a chaw of tobacco or scratch. What a body was hearing amongst them, all the time was—

"Gimme a chaw 'v tobacker, Hank."

"Cain't—I hain't got but one chaw left. Ask Bill."

Maybe Bill he gives him a chaw; maybe he lies and says he ain't got none. Some of them kinds of loafers never has a cent in the world, nor a chaw of tobacco of their own. They get all their chaw-

8. The following is Twain's expression of contempt for the shiftless type of frontiersman and his unkempt town, showing another aspect of Hannibal, which Twain usually nostalgically de-scribed as idyllic.

ing by borrowing—they say to a fellow, "I wisht you'd len' me a chaw, Jack, I jist this minute give Ben Thompson the last chaw I had"—which is a lie, pretty much every time; it don't fool nobody but a stranger; but Jack ain't no stranger, so he says—

"*You* give him a chaw, did you? so did your sister's cat's grand-mother. You pay me back the chaws you've awready borry'd off'n me, Lafe Buckner, then I'll loan you one or two ton of it, and won't charge you no back intrust, nuther."

"Well, I *did* pay you back some of it wunst."

"Yes, you did—'bout six chaws. You borry'd store tobacker and paid back nigger-head."

Store tobacco is flat black plug, but these fellows mostly chaws the natural leaf twisted. When they borrow a chaw, they don't generly cut it off with a knife, but they set the plug in between their teeth, and gnaw with their teeth and tug at the plug with their hands till they get it in two—then sometimes the one that owns the tobacco looks mournful at it when it's handed back, and says, sar-castic—

"Here, gimme the *chaw*, and you take the *plug*."

All the streets and lanes was just mud, they warn't nothing else *but* mud—mud as black as tar, and nigh about a foot deep in some places; and two or three inches deep in *all* the places. The hogs loafed and grunted around, everywheres. You'd see a muddy sow and a litter of pigs come lazying along the street and whollop herself down in the way, where folks had to walk around her, and she'd stretch out, and shut her eyes, and wave her ears, whilst the pigs was milking her, and look as happy as if she was on salary. And pretty soon you'd hear a loafer sing out, "Hi! *so* boy! sick him, Tige!" and away the sow would go, squealing most horrible, with a dog or two swinging to each ear, and three or four dozen more a-coming; and then you would see all the loafers get up and watch the thing out of sight, and laugh at the fun and look grateful for the noise. Then they'd settle back again till there was a dog-fight. There couldn't anything wake them up all over, and make them happy all over, like a dog-fight—unless it might be putting turpentine on a stray dog and setting fire to him, or tying a tin pan to his tail and see him run himself to death.

On the river front some of the houses was sticking out over the bank, and they was bowed and bent, and about ready to tumble in. The people had moved out of them. The bank was caved away under one corner of some others, and that corner was hanging over. People lived in them yet, but it was dangersome, because sometimes a strip of land as wide as a house caves in at a time. Sometimes a belt of land a quarter of a mile deep will start in and cave along and cave along till it all caves into the river in one summer. Such a town as that has to be always moving back, and back, and back, because the river's always gnawing at it.

The nearer it got to noon that day, the thicker and thicker was the wagons and horses in the streets, and more coming all the time. Families fetched their dinners with them, from the country, and eat them in the wagons. There was considerable whiskey drinking going on, and I seen three fights. By-and-by somebody sings out—

"Here comes old Boggs![9]—in from the country for his little old monthly drunk—here he comes, boys!"

All the loafers looked glad—I reckoned they was used to having fun out of Boggs. One of them says—

"Wonder who he's a gwyne to chaw up this time. If he'd a chawed up all the men he's ben a gwyne to chaw up in the last twenty year, he'd have considerble ruputation, now."

Another one says, "I wisht old Boggs'd threaten me, 'cuz then I'd know I warn't gwyne to die for a thousan' year."

Boggs comes a-tearing along on his horse, whooping and yelling like an Injun, and singing out—

"Cler the track, thar. I'm on the waw-path, and the price uv coffins is a gwyne to raise."

He was drunk, and weaving about in his saddle; he was over fifty year old, and had a very red face. Everybody yelled at him, and laughed at him, and sassed him, and he sassed back, and said he'd attend to them and lay them out in their regular turns, but he couldn't wait now, because he'd come to town to kill old Colonel Sherburn, and his motto was, "meat first, and spoon vittles to top off on."

He see me, and rode up and says—

"Whar'd you come f'm, boy? You prepared to die?"

Then he rode on. I was scared; but a man says—

"He don't mean nothing; he's always a carryin' on like that, when he's drunk. He's the best-naturedest old fool in Arkansaw—never hurt nobody, drunk nor sober."

Boggs rode up before the biggest store in town and bent his head down so he could see under the curtain of the awning, and yells—

"Come out here, Sherburn! Come out and meet the man you've swindled. You're the houn' I'm after, and I'm a gwyne to have you, too!"

And so he went on, calling Sherburn everything he could lay his tongue to, and the whole street packed with people listening and laughing and going on. By-and-by a proud-looking man about fifty-five—and he was a heap the best dressed man in that town, too—steps out of the store, and the crowd drops back on each side to let him come. He says to Boggs, mighty ca'm and slow—he says:

9. The following episode is based on an actual case in Hannibal, tried by Twain's father, Judge Clemens. *Cf.* Dixon Wecter, *Sam Clemens of Hannibal*, pp. 106–109.

"I'm tired of this; but I'll endure it till one o'clock. Till one o'clock, mind—no longer. If you open your mouth against me only once, after that time, you can't travel so far but I will find you."

Then he turns and goes in. The crowd looked mighty sober; nobody stirred, and there warn't no more laughing. Boggs rode off blackguarding Sherburn as loud as he could yell, all down the street; and pretty soon back he comes and stops before the store, still keeping it up. Some men crowded around him and tried to get him to shut up, but he wouldn't; they told him it would be one o'clock in about fifteen minutes, and so he *must* go home—he must go right away. But it didn't do no good. He cussed away, with all his might, and throwed his hat down in the mud and rode over it, and pretty soon away he went a-raging down the street again, with his gray hair a-flying. Everybody that could get a chance at him tried their best to coax him off of his horse so they could lock him up and get him sober; but it warn't no use—up the street he would tear again, and give Sherburn another cussing. By-and-by somebody says—

"Go for his daughter!—quick, go for his daughter; sometimes he'll listen to her. If anybody can persuade him, she can."

So somebody started on a run. I walked down street a ways, and stopped. In about five or ten minutes, here comes Boggs again—but not on his horse. He was a-reeling across the street towards me, bareheaded, with a friend on both sides of him aholt of his arms and hurrying him along. He was quiet, and looked uneasy; and he warn't hanging back any, but was doing some of the hurrying himself. Somebody sings out—

"Boggs!"

I looked over there to see who said it, and it was that Colonel Sherburn. He was standing perfectly still, in the street, and had a pistol raised in his right hand—not aiming it, but holding it out with the barrel tilted up towards the sky. The same second I see a young girl coming on the run, and two men with her. Boggs and the men turned round, to see who called him, and when they see the pistol the men jumped to one side, and the pistol barrel come down slow and steady to a level—both barrels cocked. Boggs throws up both of his hands, and says, "O Lord, don't shoot!" Bang! goes the first shot, and he staggers back clawing at the air—bang! goes the second one, and he tumbles backwards onto the ground, heavy and solid, with his arms spread out. That young girl screamed out, and comes rushing, and down she throws herself on her father, crying, and saying, "Oh, he's killed him, he's killed him!" The crowd closed up around them, and shouldered and jammed one another, with their necks stretched, trying to see, and people on the inside trying to shove them back, and shouting, "Back, back! give him air, give him air!"

Colonel Sherburn he tossed his pistol onto the ground, and turned around on his heels and walked off.

They took Boggs to a little drug store, the crowd pressing around, just the same, and the whole town following, and I rushed and got a good place at the window, where I was close to him and could see in. They laid him on the floor, and put one large Bible under his head, and opened another one and spread it on his breast—but they tore open his shirt first, and I seen where one of the bullets went in. He made about a dozen long gasps, his breast lifting the Bible up when he drawed in his breath, and letting it down again when he breathed it out—and after that he laid still; he was dead. Then they pulled his daughter away from him, screaming and crying, and took her off. She was about sixteen, and very sweet and gentle-looking, but awful pale and scared.

Well, pretty soon the whole town was there, squirming and scrouging and pushing and shoving to get at the window and have a look, but people that had the places wouldn't give them up, and folks behind them was saying all the time, "Say, now, you've looked enough, you fellows; 'taint right and 'taint fair, for you to stay thar all the time, and never give nobody a chance; other folks has their rights as well as you."

There was considerable jawing back, so I slid out, thinking maybe there was going to be trouble. The streets was full, and everybody was excited. Everybody that seen the shooting was telling how it happened, and there was a big crowd packed around each one of these fellows, stretching their necks and listening. One long lanky man, with long hair and a big white fur stove-pipe hat on the back of his head, and a crooked-handled cane, marked out the places on the ground where Boggs stood, and where Sherburn stood, and the people following him around from one place to t'other and watching everything he done, and bobbing their heads to show they understood, and stooping a little and resting their hands on their thighs to watch him mark the places on the ground with his cane; and then he stood up straight and stiff where Sherburn had stood, frowning and having his hat-brim down over his eyes, and sung out, "Boggs!" and then fetched his cane down slow to a level, and says "Bang!" staggered backwards, says "Bang!" again, and fell down flat on his back. The people that had seen the thing said he done it perfect; said it was just exactly the way it all happened. Then as much as a dozen people got out their bottles and treated him.

Well, by-and-by somebody said Sherburn ought to be lynched. In about a minute everybody was saying it; so away they went, mad and yelling, and snatching down every clothes-line they come to, to do the hanging with.

Chapter XXII

They swarmed up the street towards Sherburn's house, a-whooping and yelling and raging like Injuns, and everything had to clear

the way or get run over and tromped to mush, and it was awful **to**
see. Children was heeling it ahead of the mob, screaming and trying
to get out of the way; and every window along the road was full of
women's heads, and there was nigger boys in every tree, and bucks
and wenches looking over every fence; and as soon as the mob
would get nearly to them they would break and skaddle back out
of reach. Lots of the women and girls was crying and taking on,
scared most to death.

They swarmed up in front of Sherburn's palings as thick as they
could jam together, and you couldn't hear yourself think for the
noise. It was a little twenty-foot yard. Some sung out "Tear down
the fence! tear down the fence!" Then there was a racket of ripping
and tearing and smashing, and down she goes, and the front wall
of the crowd begins to roll in like a wave.

Just then Sherburn steps out on to the roof of his little front
porch, with a double-barrel gun in his hand, and takes his stand,
perfectly ca'm and deliberate, not saying a word. The racket stopped,
and the wave sucked back.

Sherburn never said a word—just stood there, looking down. The
stillness was awful creepy and uncomfortable. Sherburn run his eye
slow along the crowd; and wherever it struck, the people tried a little
to outgaze him, but they couldn't; they dropped their eyes and
looked sneaky. Then pretty soon Sherburn sort of laughed; not the
pleasant kind, but the kind that makes you feel like when you are
eating bread that's got sand in it.

Then he says, slow and scornful:

"The idea of *you* lynching anybody! It's amusing. The idea of
you thinking you had pluck enough to lynch a *man!* Because you're
brave enough to tar and feather poor friendless cast-out women that
come along here, did that make you think you had grit enough to
lay your hands on a *man?* Why, a *man's* safe in the hands of ten
thousand of your kind—as long as it's day-time and you're not behind him.

"Do I know you? I know you clear through. I was born and raised
in the South, and I've lived in the North; so I know the average all
around. The average man's a coward. In the North he lets anybody
walk over him that wants to, and goes home and prays for a humble
spirit to bear it. In the South one man, all by himself, has stopped a
stage full of men, in the day-time, and robbed the lot. Your newspapers call you a brave people so much that you think you *are*
braver than any other people—whereas you're just *as* brave, and no
braver. Why don't your juries hang murderers? Because they're
afraid the man's friends will shoot them in the back, in the dark—
and it's just what they *would* do.

"So they always acquit; and then a *man* goes in the night, with a
hundred masked cowards at his back, and lynches the rascal. Your

mistake is, that you didn't bring a man with you; that's one mistake, and the other is that you didn't come in the dark, and fetch your masks. You brought *part* of a man—Buck Harkness, there—and if you hadn't had him to start you, you'd a taken it out in blowing.

"You didn't want to come. The average man don't like trouble and danger. *You* don't like trouble and danger. But if only *half* a man—like Buck Harkness, there—shouts 'Lynch him, lynch him!' you're afraid to back down—afraid you'll be found out to be what you are—*cowards*—and so you raise a yell, and hang yourselves onto that half-a-man's coat tail, and come raging up here, swearing what big things you're going to do. The pitifulest thing out is a mob; that's what an army is—a mob; they don't fight with courage that's born in them, but with courage that's borrowed from their mass, and from their officers. But a mob without any *man* at the head of it, is *beneath* pitifulness. Now the thing for *you* to do, is to droop your tails and go home and crawl in a hole. If any real lynching's going to be done, it will be done in the dark, Southern fashion; and when they come they'll bring their masks, and fetch a *man* along. Now *leave*—and take your half-a-man with you"—tossing his gun up across his left arm and cocking it, when he says this.

The crowd washed back sudden, and then broke all apart and went tearing off every which way, and Buck Harkness he heeled it after them, looking tolerable cheap. I could a staid, if I'd a wanted to, but I didn't want to.

I went to the circus, and loafed around the back side till the watchman went by, and then dived in under the tent. I had my twenty-dollar gold piece and some other money, but I reckoned I better save it, because there ain't no telling how soon you are going to need it, away from home and amongst strangers, that way. You can't be too careful. I ain't opposed to spending money on circuses, when there ain't no other way, but there ain't no use in *wasting* it on them.

It was a real bully circus. It was the splendidest sight that ever was, when they all come riding in, two and two, a gentleman and lady, side by side, the men just in their drawers and under-shirts, and no shoes nor stirrups, and resting their hands on their thighs, easy and comfortable—there must a' been twenty of them—and every lady with a lovely complexion, and perfectly beautiful, and looking just like a gang of real sure-enough queens, and dressed in clothes that cost millions of dollars, and just littered with diamonds. It was a powerful fine sight; I never see anything so lovely. And then one by one they got up and stood, and went a-weaving around the ring so gentle and wavy and graceful, the men looking ever so tall and airy and straight, with their heads bobbing and skimming along, away up there under the tent-roof, and every lady's rose-leafy dress flapping soft and silky around her hips, and she looking like the most loveliest parasol.

And then faster and faster they went, all of them dancing, first one foot stuck out in the air and then the other, the horses leaning more and more, and the ring-master going round and round the centre-pole, cracking his whip and shouting "hi!—hi!" and the clown cracking jokes behind him; and by-and-by all hands dropped the reins, and every lady put her knuckles on her hips and every gentleman folded his arms, and then how the horses did lean over and hump themselves! And so, one after the other they all skipped off into the ring, and made the sweetest bow I ever see, and then scampered out, and everybody clapped their hands and went just about wild.

Well, all through the circus they done the most astonishing things; and all the time that clown carried on so it most killed the people. The ring-master couldn't ever say a word to him but he was back at him quick as a wink with the funniest things a body ever said; and how he ever *could* think of so many of them, and so sudden and so pat, was what I couldn't noway understand. Why, I couldn't a thought of them in a year. And by-and-by a drunk man tried to get into the ring—said he wanted to ride; said he could ride as well as anybody that ever was. They argued and tried to keep him out, but he wouldn't listen, and the whole show come to a standstill. Then the people begun to holler at him and make fun of him, and that made him mad, and he begun to rip and tear; so that stirred up the people, and a lot of men began to pile down off of the benches and swarm towards the ring, saying, "Knock him down! throw him out!" and one or two women begun to scream. So, then, the ring-master he made a little speech, and said he hoped there wouldn't be no disturbance, and if the man would promise he wouldn't make no more trouble, he would let him ride, if he thought he could stay on the horse. So everybody laughed and said all right, and the man got on. The minute he was on, the horse begun to rip and tear and jump and cavort around, with two circus men hanging onto his bridle trying to hold him, and the drunk man hanging onto his neck, and his heels flying in the air every jump, and the whole crowd of people standing up shouting and laughing till the tears rolled down. And at last, sure enough, all the circus men could do, the horse broke loose, and away he went like the very nation, round and round the ring, with that sot laying down on him and hanging to his neck, with first one leg hanging most to the ground on one side, and the t'other one on t'other side, and the people just crazy. It warn't funny to me, though; I was all of a tremble to see his danger. But pretty soon he struggled up astraddle and grabbed the bridle, a-reeling this way and that; and the next minute he sprung up and dropped the bridle and stood! and the horse agoing like a house afire too. He just stood up there, a-sailing around as easy and comfortable as if he warn't ever drunk in his life —and then he begun to pull off his clothes and sling them. He shed them so thick they kind of clogged up the air, and altogether he shed seventeen suits. And then, there he was, slim and handsome, and dressed the gaudiest and prettiest you ever saw, and he lit into that horse with his whip and made him fairly hum—and finally skipped off, and made his bow and danced off to the dressing-room, and everybody just a-howling with pleasure and astonishment.

Then the ring-master he see how he had been fooled, and he *was* the sickest ring-master you ever see, I reckon. Why, it was one of his own men! He had got up that joke all out of his own head, and never let on to nobody. Well, I felt sheepish enough, to be took in so, but I wouldn't a been in that ring-master's place, not for a thousand dollars. I don't know; there may be bullier circuses than what that one was, but I never struck them yet. Anyways it was plenty good enough for *me*; and wherever I run across it, it can have all of *my* custom, every time.

Well, that night we had *our* show; but there warn't only about twelve people there; just enough to pay expenses. And they laughed all the time, and that made the duke mad; and everybody left, any-way, before the show was over, but one boy which was asleep. So the duke said these Arkansaw lunkheads couldn't come up to Shak-speare; what they wanted was low comedy—and may be something ruther worse than low comedy, he reckoned. He said he could size their style. So next morning he got some big sheets of wrapping-paper and some black paint, and drawed off some handbills and stuck them up all over the village. The bills said:

AT THE COURT HOUSE!
FOR 3 NIGHTS ONLY!
The World-Renowned Tragedians
DAVID GARRICK THE YOUNGER
AND
EDMUND KEAN THE ELDER!
*Of the London and Continental
Theatres,*
In their Thrilling Tragedy of
THE KING'S CAMELOPARD
OR
THE ROYAL NONESUCH! ! !
Admission 50 cents.

Then at the bottom was the biggest line of all—which said:

LADIES AND CHILDREN NOT ADMITTED.

"There," says he, "if that line don't fetch them, I dont know Arkansaw!"

Chapter XXIII

Well, all day him and the king was hard at it, rigging up a stage, and a curtain, and a row of candles for footlights; and that night the house was jam full of men in no time. When the place couldn't hold no more, the duke he quit tending door and went around the back way and come onto the stage and stood up before the curtain, and made a little speech, and praised up this tragedy, and said it was the most thrillingest one that ever was; and so he went on a-bragging about the tragedy and about Edmund Kean the Elder, which was to play the main principal part in it; and at last when he'd got everybody's expectations up high enough, he rolled up the curtain, and the next minute the king come a-prancing out on all fours, naked; and he was painted all over, ring-streaked-and-striped, all sorts of colors, as splendid as a rainbow. And—but never mind the rest of his outfit, it was just wild, but it was awful funny. The people most killed themselves laughing; and when the king got done capering, and capered off behind the scenes, they roared and clapped and stormed and haw-hawed till he come back and done it over again; and after that, they made him do it another time. Well, it would a made a cow laugh to see the shines that old idiot cut.

Then the duke he lets the curtain down, and bows to the people, and says the great tragedy will be performed only two nights more, on accounts of pressing London engagements, where the seats is all sold aready for it in Drury Lane; and then he makes them another bow, and says if he has succeeded in pleasing them and instructing them, he will be deeply obleeged if they will mention it to their friends and get them to come and see it.

Twenty people sings out:

"What, is it over? Is that *all?*"[1]

The duke says yes. Then there was a fine time. Everybody sings out "sold," and rose up mad, and was agoing for that stage and them tragedians. But a big fine-looking man jumps up on a bench, and shouts:

"Hold on! Just a word, gentlemen." They stopped to listen. "We are sold—mighty badly sold. But we don't want to be the laughing-stock of this whole town, I reckon, and never hear the last of this thing as long as we live. *No.* What we want, is to go out of here quiet, and talk this show up, and sell the *rest* of the town! Then we'll all be in the same boat. Ain't that sensible?" ("You bet it is! —the jedge is right!" everybody sings out.) "All right, then—not a word about any sell. Go along home, and advise everybody to come and see the tragedy."

1. Reportedly based on an obscene tale that the raconteur Jim Gillis called to Twain's attention in the California days. The fraudulent dramatic performance was also prevalent in humorous frontier literature.

Next day you couldn't hear nothing around that town but how splendid that show was. House was jammed again, that night, and we sold this crowd the same way. When me and the king and the duke got home to the raft, we all had a supper; and by-and-by. about midnight, they made Jim and me back her out and float her down the middle of the river and fetch her in and hide her about two mile below town.

The third night the house was crammed again—and they warn't new-comers, this time, but people that was at the show the other two nights. I stood by the duke at the door, and I see that every man that went in had his pockets bulging, or something muffled up under his coat—and I see it warn't no perfumery neither, not by a long sight. I smelt sickly eggs by the barrel, and rotten cabbages. and such things; and if I know the signs of a dead cat being around. and I bet I do, there was sixty-four of them went in. I shoved in there for a minute, but it was too various for me, I couldn't stand it. Well, when the place couldn't hold no more people, the duke he give a fellow a quarter and told him to tend door for him a minute, and then he started around for the stage door, I after him; but the minute we turned the corner and was in the dark, he says:

"Walk fast, now, till you get away from the houses, and then shin for the raft like the dickens was after you!"

I done it, and he done the same. We struck the raft at the same time, and in less than two seconds we was gliding down stream, all dark and still, and edging towards the middle of the river, nobody saying a word. I reckoned the poor king was in for a gaudy time of it with the audience; but nothing of the sort; pretty soon he crawls out from under the wigwam, and says:

"Well, how'd the old thing pan out this time, Duke?"

He hadn't been up town at all.

We never showed a light till we was about ten mile below that village. Then we lit up and had a supper, and the king and the duke fairly laughed their bones loose over the way they'd served them people. The duke says:

"Greenhorns, flatheads! *I* knew the first house would keep mum and let the rest of the town get roped in; and I knew they'd lay for us the third night, and consider it was *their* turn now. Well, it *is* their turn, and I'd give something to know how much they'd take for it. I *would* just like to know how they're putting in their opportunity. They can turn it into a picnic, if they want to—they brought plenty provisions."

Them rapscallions took in four hundred and sixty-five dollars in that three nights. I never see money hauled in by the wagon-load like that, before.

By-and-by, when they was asleep and snoring, Jim says:

"Don't it 'sprise you, de way dem kings carries on, Huck?"

"No," I says, "it don't."

"Why don't it, Huck?"

"Well, it don't, because it's in the breed. I reckon they're all alike."

"But, Huck, dese kings o' ourn is regular rapscallions; dat's jist what dey is; dey's reglar rapscallions."

"Well, that's what I'm a-saying; all kings is mostly rapscallions, as fur as I can make out."

"Is dat so?"

"You read about them once—you'll see. Look at Henry the Eight; this'n 's a Sunday-School Superintendent to *him*. And look at Charles Second, and Louis Fourteen, and Louis Fifteen, and James Second, and Edward Second, and Richard Third, and forty more; besides all them Saxon heptarchies that used to rip around so in old times and raise Cain. My, you ought to seen old Henry the Eight when he was in bloom.[2] He *was* a blossom. He used to marry a new wife every day, and chop off her head next morning. And he would do it just as indifferent as if he was ordering up eggs. 'Fetch up Nell Gwynn,' he says. They fetch her up. Next morning, 'Chop off her head!' And they chop it off. 'Fetch up Jane Shore,' he says; and up she comes. Next morning 'Chop off her head'—and they chop it off. 'Ring up Fair Rosamun.' Fair Rosamun answers the bell. Next morning, 'Chop off her head.' And he made every one of them tell him a tale every night; and he kept that up till he had hogged a thousand and one tales that way, and then he put them all in a book, and called it Domesday Book—which was a good name and stated the case. You don't know kings, Jim, but I know them; and this old rip of ourn is one of the cleanest I've struck in history. Well, Henry he takes a notion he wants to get up some trouble with this country. How does he go at it—give notice? —give the country a show? No. All of a sudden he heaves all the tea in Boston Harbor overboard, and whacks out a declaration of independence, and dares them to come on. That was *his* style—he never give anybody a chance. He had suspicions of his father, the Duke of Wellington. Well, what did he do?—ask him to show up? No—drownded him in a butt of mamsey, like a cat. Spose people left money laying around where he was—what did he do? He collared it. Spose he contracted to do a thing; and you paid him, and didn't set down there and see that he done it—what did he do? He always done the other thing. Spose he opened his mouth—what then? If he didn't shut it up powerful quick, he'd lose a lie, every time. That's the kind of a bug Henry was; and if we'd a had him along 'stead of our kings, he'd a fooled that town a heap worse than ourn done. I don't say that ourn is lambs, because they ain't,

2. Huck's following description of Henry VIII (1509–1547) is a grand confusion of history with fiction (he confuses the historical *Domesday Book*

when you come right down to the cold facts; but they ain't nothing to *that* old ram, anyway. All I say is, kings is kings, and you got to make allowances. Take them all around, they're a mighty ornery lot. It's the way they're raised."

"But dis one do *smell* so like de nation, Huck."

"Well, they all do, Jim. *We* can't help the way a king smells; history don't tell no way."

"Now de duke, he's a tolerble likely man, in some ways."

"Yes, a duke's different. But not very different. This one's a middling hard lot, for a duke. When he's drunk, there ain't no near-sighted man could tell him from a king."

"Well, anyways, I doan' hanker for no mo' un um, Huck. Dese is all I kin stan'."

"It's the way I feel, too, Jim. But we've got them on our hands, and we got to remember what they are, and make allowances. Sometimes I wish we could hear of a country that's out of kings."

What was the use to tell Jim these warn't real kings and dukes? It wouldn't a done no good; and besides, it was just as I said; you couldn't tell them from the real kind.

I went to sleep, and Jim didn't call me when it was my turn. He often done that. When I waked up, just at day-break, he was setting there with his head down betwixt his knees, moaning and mourning to himself. I didn't take notice, nor let on. I knowed what it was about. He was thinking about his wife and his children, away up yonder, and he was low and homesick; because he hadn't ever been away from home before in his life; and I do believe he cared just as much for his people as white folks does for their'n. It don't seem natural, but I reckon it's so. He was often moaning and mourning that way, nights, when he judged I was asleep, and saying, "Po' little 'Lizabeth! po' little Johnny! its mighty hard; I spec' I ain't ever gwyne to see you no mo', no mo'!" He was a mighty good nigger, Jim was.

But this time I somehow got to talking to Jim about his wife and young ones; and by-and-by he says:

"What makes me feel so bad dis time, 'uz bekase I hear sumpn over yonder on de bank like a whack, er a slam, while ago, en it mine me er de time I treat my little 'Lizabeth so ornery. She warn't on'y 'bout fo' year ole, en she tuck de sk'yarlet-fever, en had a powful rough spell; but she got well, en one day she was a-stannin' aroun', en I says to her, I says:

" 'Shet de do'.'

with the fictional Scheherazade's *Arabian Nights*) and of persons, incidents, and even centuries that could have no connection with Henry's life or times. He makes sixteenth-century Henry VIII the son of the nineteenth-century Duke of Wellington, whom he confuses with the fifteenth-century Duke of Clarence (who was supposedly drowned in a butt of malmsey); he also has Henry VIII creating the eighteenth-century American Declaration of Independence; finally, Fair Rosamond was mistress to twelfth-century Henry II, Jane Shore to fifteenth-century Edward IV, Nell Gwyn to seventeenth-century Charles II.

"She never done it; jis' stood dah, kiner smilin' up at me. It make me mad; en I says again, mighty loud, I says:

" 'Doan' you hear me?—shet de do'!'

"She jis' stood de same way, kiner smilin' up. I was a-bilin'! I says:

" 'I lay I *make* you mine!'

"En wid dat I fetch' her a slap side de head dat sont her a-sprawlin'. Den I went into de yuther room, en 'uz gone 'bout ten minutes; en when I come back, dah was dat do' a-stannin' open *yit*, en dat chile stannin' mos' right in it, a-lookin' down and mournin', en de tears runnin' down. My, but I *wuz* mad, I was agwyne for de chile, but jis' den—it was a do' dat open innerds—jis' den, 'long come de wind en slam it to, behine de chile, ker-*blam!* —en my lan', de chile never move'! My breff mos' hop outer me; en I feel so—so—I doan' know *how* I feel. I crope out, all a-tremblin', en crope aroun' en open de do' easy en slow, en poke my head in behine de chile, sof' en still, en all uv a sudden, I says *pow!* jis' as loud as I could yell. *She never budge!* Oh, Huck, I bust out a-cryin' en grab her up in my arms, en say, 'Oh, de po' little thing! de Lord God Amighty fogive po' ole Jim, kaze he never gwyne to fogive hisself as long's he live!' Oh, she was plumb deef en dumb, Huck, plumb deef en dumb—en I'd ben a'treat'n her so!"

Chapter XXIV

Next day, towards night, we laid up under a little willow towhead out in the middle, where there was a village on each side of the river, and the duke and the king begun to lay out a plan for working them towns. Jim he spoke to the duke, and said he hoped it wouldn't take but a few hours, because it got mighty heavy and tiresome to him when he had to lay all day in the wigwam tied with the rope. You see, when we left him all alone we had to tie him, because if anybody happened on him all by himself and not tied, it wouldn't look much like he was a runaway nigger, you know. So the duke said it *was* kind of hard to have to lay roped all day, and he'd cipher out some way to get around it.

He was uncommon bright, the duke was, and he soon struck it. He dressed Jim up in King Lear's outfit—it was a long curtain-calico gown, and a white horse-hair wig and whiskers; and then he took his theatre-paint and painted Jim's face and hands and ears and neck all over a dead dull solid blue, like a man that's been drownded nine days. Blamed if he warn't the horriblest looking outrage I ever see. Then the duke took and wrote out a sign on a shingle so—

Sick Arab—but harmless when not out of his head.

And he nailed that shingle to a lath, and stood the lath up four or five foot in front of the wigwam. Jim was satisfied. He said it was a sight better than laying tied a couple of years every day and trembling all over every time there was a sound. The duke told him to make himself free and easy, and if anybody ever come meddling around, he must hop out of the wigwam, and carry on a little, and fetch a howl or two like a wild beast, and he reckoned they would light out and leave him alone. Which was sound enough judgment; but you take the average man, and he wouldn't wait for him to howl. Why, he didn't only look like he was dead, he looked considerable more than that.

These rapscallions wanted to try the Nonesuch again, because there was so much money in it, but they judged it wouldn't be safe, because maybe the news might a worked along down by this time. They couldn't hit no project that suited, exactly; so at last the duke said he reckoned he'd lay off and work his brains an hour or two and see if he couldn't put up something on the Arkansaw village; and the king he allowed he would drop over to t'other village, without any plan, but just trust in Providence to lead him the profitable way —meaning the devil, I reckon. We had all bought store clothes where we stopped last; and now the king put his'n on, and he told me to put mine on. I done it, of course. The king's duds was all black, and he did look real swell and starchy. I never knowed how clothes could change a body before. Why, before, he looked like the orneriest old rip that ever was; but now, when he'd take off his new white beaver and make a bow and do a smile, he looked that grand and good and pious that you'd say he had walked right out of the ark, and maybe was old Leviticus himself. Jim cleaned up the canoe, and I got my paddle ready. There was a big steamboat laying at the shore away up under the point, about three mile above town—been there a couple of hours, taking on freight. Says the king:

"Seein' how I'm dressed, I reckon maybe I better arrive down from St. Louis or Cincinnati, or some other big place. Go for the steamboat, Huckleberry; we'll come down to the village on her."

I didn't have to be ordered twice, to go and take a steamboat ride. I fetched the shore a half a mile above the village, and then went scooting along the bluff bank in the easy water. Pretty soon we come to a nice innocent-looking young country jake setting on a log swabbing the sweat off of his face, for it was powerful warm weather; and he had a couple of big carpet-bags by him.

"Run her nose in shore," says the king. I done it. "Wher' you bound for, young man?"

"For the steamboat; going to Orleans."

"Git aboard," says the king. "Hold on a minute, my servant 'll he'p you with them bags. Jump out and he'p the gentleman, Adolphus"—meaning me, I see.

I done so, and then we all three started on again. The young chap was mighty thankful; said it was tough work toting his baggage such weather. He asked the king where he was going, and the king told him he'd come down the river and landed at the other village this morning, and now he was going up a few mile to see an old friend on a farm up there. The young fellow says:

"When I first see you, I says to myself, 'It's Mr. Wilks, sure, and he come mighty near getting here in time.' But then I says again, 'No, I reckon it ain't him, or else he wouldn't be paddling up the river.' You *ain't* him, are you?"

"No, my name's Blodgett—Elexander Blodgett—*Reverend* Elexander Blodgett, I spose I must say, as I'm one o' the Lord's poor servants. But still I'm jist as able to be sorry for Mr. Wilks for not arriving in time, all the same, if he's missed anything by it—which I hope he hasn't."

"Well, he don't miss any property by it, because he'll get that all right; but he's missed seeing his brother Peter die—which he mayn't mind, nobody can tell as to that—but his brother would a give anything in this world to see *him* before he died; never talked about nothing else all these three weeks; hadn't seen him since they was boys together—and hadn't ever seen his brother William at all— that's the deef and dumb one—William ain't more than thirty or thirty-five. Peter and George was the only ones that come out here; George was the married brother; him and his wife both died last year. Harvey and William's the only ones that's left now; and, as I was saying, they haven't got here in time."

"Did anybody send 'em word?"

"Oh, yes; a month or two ago, when Peter was first took; because Peter said then that he sorter felt like he warn't going to get well this time. You see, he was pretty old, and George's g'yirls was too young to be much company for him, except Mary Jane the red-headed one; and so he was kinder lonesome after George and his wife died, and didn't seem to care much to live. He most desperately wanted to see Harvey—and William too, for that matter—because he was one of them kind that can't bear to make a will. He left a letter behind for Harvey, and said he'd told in it where his money was hid, and how he wanted the rest of the property divided up so George's g'yirls would be all right—for George didn't leave nothing. And that letter was all they could get him to put a pen to."

"Why do you reckon Harvey don't come? Wher' does he live?"

"Oh, he lives in England—Sheffield—preaches there—hasn't ever been in this country. He hasn't had any too much time—and besides he mightn't a got the letter at all, you know."

"Too bad, too bad he couldn't a lived to see his brothers, poor soul. You going to Orleans, you say?"

"Yes, but that ain't only a part of it. I'm going in a ship, next Wednesday, for Ryo Janeero, where my uncle lives."

"It's a pretty long journey. But it'll be lovely; I wisht I was agoing. Is Mary Jane the oldest? How old is the others?"

"Mary Jane's nineteen, Susan's fifteen, and Joanna's about fourteen—that's the one that gives herself to good works and has a hare-lip."

"Poor things! to be left alone in the cold world so."

"Well, they could be worse off. Old Peter had friends, and they ain't going to let them come to no harm. There's Hobson, the Babtis' preacher; and Deacon Lot Hovey, and Ben Rucker, and Abner Shackleford, and Levi Bell, the lawyer; and Dr. Robinson, and their wives, and the widow Bartley, and—well, there's a lot of them; but these are the ones that Peter was thickest with, and used to write about sometimes, when he wrote home; so Harvey'll know where to look for friends when he gets[3] here."

Well, the old man he went on asking questions till he just fairly emptied that young fellow. Blamed if he didn't inquire about everybody and everything in that blessed town, and all about all the Wilkses; and about Peter's business—which was a tanner; and about George's—which was a carpenter; and about Harvey's—which was a dissentering minister; and so on, and so on. Then he says:

"What did you want to walk all the way up to the steamboat for?"

"Because she's a big Orleans boat, and I was afeard she mightn't stop there. When they're deep they won't stop for a hail. A Cincinnati boat will, but this is a St. Louis one."

"Was Peter Wilks well off?"

"Oh, yes, pretty well off. He had houses and land, and it's reckoned he left three or four thousand in cash hid up som'ers."

"When did you say he died?"

"I didn't say, but it was last night."

"Funeral to-morrow, likely?"

"Yes, 'bout the middle of the day."

"Well, it's all terrible sad; but we've all got to go, one time or another. So what we want to do is to be prepared; then we're all right."

"Yes, sir, it's the best way. Ma used to always say that."

When we struck the boat, she was about done loading, and pretty soon she got off. The king never said nothing about going aboard, so I lost my ride, after all. When the boat was gone, the king made me paddle up another mile to a lonesome place, and then he got ashore, and says:

"Now hustle back, right off, and fetch the duke up here, and the new carpet-bags. And if he's gone over to t'other side, go over there and git him. And tell him to git himself up regardless. Shove along,

---

3. Erroneously printed "get's" in 1885.

now."

I see what *he* was up to; but I never said nothing, of course. When I got back with the duke, we hid the canoe and then they set down on a log, and the king told him everything, just like the young fellow had said it—every last word of it. And all the time he was a doing it, he tried to talk like an Englishman; and he done it pretty well too, for a slouch. I can't imitate him, and so I ain't agoing to try to; but he really done it pretty good. Then he says:

"How are you on the deef and dumb, Bilgewater?"

The duke said, leave him alone for that; said he had played a deef and dumb person on the histrionic boards. So then they waited for a steamboat.

About the middle of the afternoon a couple of little boats come along, but they didn't come from high enough up the river; but at last there was a big one, and they hailed her. She sent out her yawl, and we went aboard, and she was from Cincinnati; and when they found we only wanted to go four or five mile, they was booming mad, and give us a cussing, and said they wouldn't land us. But the king was ca'm. He says:

"If gentlemen kin afford to pay a dollar a mile apiece, to be took on and put off in a yawl, a steamboat kin afford to carry 'em, can't it?"

So they softened down and said it was all right; and when we got to the village, they yawled us ashore. About two dozen men flocked down, when they see the yawl a coming; and when the king says—

"Kin any of you gentlemen tell me wher' Mr. Peter Wilks lives?" they give a glance at one another, and nodded their heads, as much as to say, "What d' I tell you?" Then one of them says, kind of soft and gentle:

"I'm sorry, sir, but the best we can do is to tell you where he *did* live yesterday evening."

Sudden as winking, the ornery old cretur went all to smash, and fell up against the man, and put his chin on his shoulder, and cried down his back, and says:

"Alas, alas, our poor brother—gone, and we never got to see him; oh, it's too, *too* hard!"

Then he turns around, blubbering, and makes a lot of idiotic signs to the duke on his hands,[4] and blamed if *he* didn't drop a carpet-bag and bust out a-crying. If they warn't the beatenest lot, them two frauds, that ever I struck.

Well, the men gethered around, and sympathized with them, and said all sorts of kind things to them, and carried their carpet-bags up the hill for them, and let them lean on them and cry, and told the king all about his brother's last moments, and the king

4. Twain uses this deaf-and-dumb jape again in *Tom Sawyer, Detective* (1896).

he told it all over again on his hands to the duke, and both of them took on about that dead tanner like they'd lost the twelve disciples. Well, if ever I struck anything like it, I'm a nigger. It was enough to make a body ashamed of the human race.[5]

Chapter XXV

The news was all over town in two minutes, and you could see the people tearing down on the run, from every which way, some of them putting on their coats as they come. Pretty soon we was in the middle of a crowd, and the noise of the tramping was like a soldier-march. The windows and dooryards was full; and every minute somebody would say, over a fence:

"Is it *them?*"

And somebody trotting along with the gang would answer back and say,

"You bet it is."

When we got to the house, the street in front of it was packed, and the three girls was standing in the door. Mary Jane *was* red-headed, but that don't make no difference, she was most awful beautiful, and her face and her eyes was all lit up like glory, she was so glad her uncles was come. The king he spread his arms, and Mary Jane she jumped for them, and the hare-lip jumped for the duke, and there they *had* it! Everybody most, leastways women, cried for joy to see them meet again at last and have such good times.

Then the king he hunched the duke, private—I see him do it—and then he looked around and see the coffin, over in the corner on two chairs; so then, him and the duke, with a hand across each other's shoulder, and t'other hand to their eyes, walked slow and solemn over there, everybody dropping back to give them room, and all the talk and noise stopping, people saying "Sh!" and all the men taking their hats off and drooping their heads, so you could a heard a pin fall. And when they got there, they bent over and looked in the coffin, and took one sight, and then they bust out a crying so you could a heard them to Orleans, most; and then they put their arms around each other's necks, and hung their chins over each other's shoulders; and then for three minutes, or maybe four, I never see two men leak the way they done. And mind you, everybody was doing the same; and the place was that damp I never see anything like it. Then one of them got on one side of the coffin, and t'other on t'other side, and they kneeled down and rested their foreheads on the coffin, and let on to pray all to theirselves. Well,

5. In the Wilks episode the schemes of the king and the duke, hitherto at the level of Halloween frauds, for the first time sink to the depths of absolute immorality in the proposed exploitation of the grief-stricken family. Huck realized it was "enough to make a body ashamed of the human race" but did not expose them because he thought they knew that Jim was a runaway; see his conversation with Mary Jane, Chapter XXVIII.

when it come to that, it worked the crowd like you never see anything like it, and so everybody broke down and went to sobbing
right out loud—the poor girls, too; and every woman, nearly, went
up to the girls, without saying a word, and kissed them, solemn,
on the forehead, and then put their hand on their head, and looked
up towards the sky, with the tears running down, and then busted
out and went off sobbing and swabbing, and give the next woman
a show. I never see anything so disgusting.

Well, by-and-by the king he gets up and comes forward a little,
and works himself up and slobbers out a speech, all full of tears
and flapdoodle about its being a sore trial for him and his poor
brother to lose the diseased, and to miss seeing diseased alive, after
the long journey of four thousand mile, but its a trial that's sweetened and sanctified to us by this dear sympathy and these holy
tears, and so he thanks them out of his heart and out of his brother's
heart, because out of their mouths they can't, words being too weak
and cold, and all that kind of rot and slush, till it was just sickening;
and then he blubbers out a pious goody-goody Amen, and turns
himself loose and goes to crying fit to bust.

And the minute the words was out of his mouth somebody over
in the crowd struck up the doxolojer,[6] and everybody joined in with
all their might, and it just warmed you up and made you feel as
good as church letting out. Music *is* a good thing; and after all that
soul-butter and hogwash, I never see it freshen up things so, and
sound so honest and bully.

Then the king begins to work his jaw again, and says how him
and his nieces would be glad if a few of the main principal friends
of the family would take supper here with them this evening, and
help set up with the ashes of the diseased; and says if his poor
brother laying yonder could speak, he knows who he would name,
for they was names that was very dear to him, and mentioned often
in his letters; and so he will name the same, to-wit, as follows, vizz:
—Rev. Mr. Hobson, and Deacon Lot Hovey, and Mr. Ben Rucker,
and Abner Shackleford, and Levi Bell, and Dr. Robinson, and their
wives, and the widow Bartley.

Rev. Hobson and Dr. Robinson was down to the end of the town,
a-hunting together; that is, I mean the doctor was shipping a sick
man to t'other world, and the preacher was pinting him right.
Lawyer Bell was away up to Louisville on some business. But the
rest was on hand, and so they all come and shook hands with the
king and thanked him and talked to him; and then they shook
hands with the duke, and didn't say nothing but just kept a-smiling
and bobbing their heads like a passel of sapheads whilst he made
all sorts of signs with his hands and said "Goo-goo—goo-goo-goo,"
all the time, like a baby that can't talk.

6. The Doxology.

So the king he blatted along, and managed to inquire about pretty much everybody and dog in town, by his name, and mentioned all sorts of little things that happened one time or another in the town, or to George's family, or to Peter; and he always let on that Peter wrote him the things, but that was a lie, he got every blessed one of them out of that young flathead that we canoed up to the steamboat.

Then Mary Jane she fetched the letter her father left behind, and the king he read it out loud and cried over it. It give the dwelling-house and three thousand dollars, gold, to the girls; and it give the tanyard (which was doing a good business), along with some other houses and land (worth about seven thousand), and three thousand dollars in gold to Harvey and William, and told where the six thousand cash was hid, down cellar. So these two frauds said they'd go and fetch it up, and have everything square and above-board; and told me to come with a candle. We shut the cellar door behind us, and when they found the bag they spilt it out on the floor, and it was a lovely sight, all them yallerboys. My, the way the king's eyes did shine! He slaps the duke on the shoulder, and says:

"Oh, *this* ain't bully, nor noth'n! Oh, no, I reckon not! Why, Biljy, it beats the Nonesuch, *don't* it!"

The duke allowed it did. They pawed the yaller-boys, and sifted them through their fingers and let them jingle down on the floor; and the king says:

"It ain't no use talkin'; bein' brothers to a rich dead man, and representatives of furrin heirs that's got left, is the line for you and me, Bilge. Thish-yer comes of trust'n to Providence. It's the best way, in the long run. I've tried 'em all, and ther' ain't no better way."

Most everybody would a been satisfied with the pile, and took it on trust; but no, they must count it. So they counts it, and it comes out four hundred and fifteen dollars short. Says the king:

"Dern him, I wonder what he done with that four hundred and fifteen dollars?"

They worried over that a while, and ransacked all around for it. Then the duke says:

"Well, he was a pretty sick man, and likely he made a mistake —I reckon that's the way of it. The best way's to let it go, and keep still about it. We can spare it."

"Oh, shucks, yes, we can *spare* it. I don't k'yer noth'n 'bout that —it's the *count* I'm thinkin' about. We want to be awful square and open and aboveboard, here, you know. We want to lug this h-yer money up stairs and count it before everybody—then ther' ain't noth'n suspicious. But when the dead man says ther's six thous'n dollars, you know, we don't want to—"

"Hold on," says the duke. "Less make up the deffisit"—and he begun to haul out yallerboys out of his pocket.

"It's a most amaz'n' good idea, duke—you *have* got a rattlin' clever head on you," says the king. "Blest if the old Nonesuch ain't a heppin' us out agin"—and *he* begun to haul out yallerjackets and stack them up.

It most busted them, but they made up the six thousand clean and clear.

"Say," says the duke, "I got another idea. Le's go up stairs and count this money, and then take and *give it to the girls.*"

"Good land, duke, lemme hug you! It's the most dazzling idea 'at ever a man struck. You have cert'nly got the most astonishin' head I ever see. Oh, this is the boss dodge, ther' ain't no mistake 'bout it. Let 'em fetch along their suspicions now, if they want to—this'll lay 'em out."

When we got up stairs, everybody gethered around the table, and the king he counted it and stacked it up, three hundred dollars in a pile—twenty elegant little piles. Everybody looked hungry at it, and licked their chops. Then they raked it into the bag again, and I see the king begin to swell himself up for another speech. He says:

"Friends all, my poor brother that lays yonder, has done generous by them that's left behind in the vale of sorrers. He has done generous by these-yer poor little lambs that he loved and sheltered, and that's left fatherless and motherless. Yes, and we that knowed him, knows that he would a done *more* generous by 'em if he hadn't been afeard o' woundin' his dear William and me. Now, *wouldn't* he? Ther' ain't no question 'bout it, in *my* mind. Well, then—what kind o' brothers would it be, that 'd stand in his way at sech a time? And what kind o' uncles would it be that 'd rob—yes, *rob* —sech poor sweet lambs as these 'at he loved so, at sech a time? If I know William—and I *think* I do—he—well, I'll jest ask him." He turns around and begins to make a lot of signs to the duke with his hands; and the duke he looks at him stupid and leather-headed a while, then all of a sudden he seems to catch his meaning, and jumps for the king, goo-gooing with all his might for joy, and hugs him about fifteen times before he lets up. Then the king says, "I knowed it; I reckon *that* 'll convince anybody the way *he* feels about it. Here, Mary Jane, Susan, Joanner, take the money—take it *all.* It's the gift of him that lays yonder, cold but joyful."

Mary Jane she went for him, Susan and the hare-lip went for the duke, and then such another hugging and kissing I never see yet. And everybody crowded up with the tears in their eyes, and most shook the hands off of them frauds, saying all the time:

"You *dear* good souls!—how *lovely!*—how *could* you!"

Well, then, pretty soon all hands got to talking about the diseased

again, and how good he was, and what a loss he was, and all that;
and before long a big iron-jawed man worked himself in there
from outside, and stood a listening and looking, and not saying
anything; and nobody saying anything to him either, because the
king was talking and they was all busy listening. The king was saying—in the middle of something he'd started in on—

"—they bein' partickler friends o' the diseased. That's why
they're invited here this evenin'; but to-morrow we want *all* to
come—everybody; for he respected everybody, he liked everybody,
and so it's fitten that his funeral orgies sh'd be public."

And so he went a-mooning on and on, liking to hear himself talk,
and every little while he fetched in his funeral orgies again, till
the duke he couldn't stand it no more; so he writes on a little scrap
of paper, *"obsequies,* you old fool," and folds it up and goes to
goo-gooing and reaching it over people's heads to him. The king
he reads it, and puts it in his pocket, and says:

"Poor William, afflicted as he is, his *heart's* aluz right. Asks me
to invite everybody to come to the funeral—wants me to make
'em all welcome. But he needn't a worried—it was jest what I was
at."

Then he weaves along again, perfectly ca'm, and goes to dropping in his funeral orgies again every now and then, just like he
done before. And when he done it the third time, he says:

"I say orgies, not because it's the common term, because it ain't
—obsequies bein' the common term—but because orgies is the
right term. Obsequies ain't used in England no more, now—it's
gone out. We say orgies now, in England. Orgies is better, because
it means the thing you're after, more exact. It's a word that's made
up out'n the Greek *orgo,* outside, open, abroad; and the Hebrew
jeesum, to plant, cover up; hence in*ter.* So, you see, funeral orgies
is an open er public funeral."

He was the *worst* I ever struck. Well, the iron-jawed man he
laughed right in his face. Everybody was shocked. Everybody says,
"Why *doctor!*" and Abner Shackleford says:

"Why, Robinson, hain't you heard the news? This is Harvey
Wilks."

The king he smiled eager, and shoved out his flapper, and says:
"*Is* it my poor brother's dear good friend and physician? I—"

"Keep your hands off of me!" says the doctor. "*You* talk like an
Englishman—*don't* you? It's the worse imitation I ever heard. *You*
Peter Wilks's brother. You're a fraud, that's what you are!"

Well, how they all took on! They crowded around the doctor,
and tried to quiet him down, and tried to explain to him, and tell
him how Harvey'd showed in forty ways that he *was* Harvey, and
knowed everybody by name, and the names of the very dogs, and
begged and *begged* him not to hurt Harvey's feelings and the poor

girls' feelings, and all that; but it warn't no use, he stormed right along, and said any man that pretended to be an Englishman and couldn't imitate the lingo no better than what he did, was a fraud and a liar. The poor girls was hanging to the king and crying; and all of a sudden the doctor ups and turns on *them*. He says:

"I was your father's friend, and I'm your friend; and I warn you *as* a friend, and an honest one, that wants to protect you and keep you out of harm and trouble, to turn your backs on that scoundrel, and have nothing to do with him, the ignorant tramp, with his idiotic Greek and Hebrew as he calls it. He is the thinnest kind of an impostor—has come here with a lot of empty names and facts which he has picked up somewheres, and you take them for *proofs*, and are helped to fool yourselves by these foolish friends here, who ought to know better. Mary Jane Wilks, you know me for your friend, and for your unselfish friend, too. Now listen to me; turn this pitiful rascal out—I *beg* you to do it. Will you?"

Mary Jane straightened herself up, and my, but she was handsome! She says:

"*Here* is my answer." She hove up the bag of money and put it in the king's hands, and says, "Take this six thousand dollars, and invest it[7] for me and my sisters any way you want to, and don't give us no receipt for it."

Then she put her arm around the king on one side, and Susan and the hare-lip done the same on the other. Everybody clapped their hands and stomped on the floor like a perfect storm, whilst the king held up his head and smiled proud. The doctor says:

"All right, I wash *my* hands of the matter. But I warn you all that a time's coming when you're going to feel sick whenever you think of this day"—and away he went.

"All right, doctor," says the king, kinder mocking him, "we'll try and get 'em to send for you"—which made them all laugh, and they said it was a prime good hit.

Chapter XXVI

Well, when they was all gone, the king he asks Mary Jane how they was off for spare rooms, and she said she had one spare room, which would do for Uncle William, and she'd give her own room to Uncle Harvey, which was a little bigger, and she would turn into the room with her sisters and sleep on a cot; and up garret was a little cubby, with a pallet in it. The king said the cubby would do for his valley—meaning me.

So Mary Jane took us up, and she showed them their rooms, which was plain but nice. She said she'd have her frocks and a lot of other traps took out of her room if they was in Uncle Harvey's

7. "It" omitted in 1885.

way, but he said they warn't. The frocks was hung along the wall, and before them was a curtain made out of calico that hung down to the floor. There was an old hair trunk in one corner, and a guitar box in another, and all sorts of little knickknacks and jimcracks around, like girls brisken up a room with. The king said it was all the more homely and more pleasanter for these fixings, and so don't disturb them. The duke's room was pretty small, but plenty good enough, and so was my cubby.

That night they had a big supper, and all them men and women was there, and I stood behind the king and the duke's chairs and waited on them, and the niggers waited on the rest. Mary Jane she set at the head of the table, with Susan along side of her, and said how bad the biscuits was, and how mean the preserves was, and how ornery and tough the fried chickens was—and all that kind of rot, the way women always do for to force out compliments; and the people all knowed everything was tip-top, and said so—said "How *do* you get biscuits to brown so nice?" and "Where, for the land's sake *did* you get these amaz'n pickles?" and all that kind of humbug talky-talk, just the way people always does at a supper, you know.

And when it was all done, me and the hare-lip had supper in the kitchen off of the leavings, whilst the others was helping the niggers clean up the things. The hare-lip she got to pumping me about England, and blest if I didn't think the ice was getting mighty thin, sometimes. She says:

"Did you ever see the king?"

"Who? William Fourth? Well, I bet I have—he goes to our church." I knowed he was dead years ago, but I never let on. So when I says he goes to our church, she says:

"What—regular?"

"Yes—regular. His pew's right over opposite ourn—on 'tother side the pulpit."

"I thought he lived in London?"

"Well, he does. Where *would* he live?"

"But I thought *you* lived in Sheffield?"

I see I was up a stump. I had to let on to get choked with a chicken bone, so as to get time to think how to get down again. Then I says:

"I mean he goes to our church regular when he's in Sheffield. That's only in the summer-time, when he comes there to take the sea baths."

"Why, how you talk—Sheffield ain't on the sea."

"Well, who said it was?"

"Why, you did."

"I *didn't*, nuther."

"You did!"

"I didn't."

"You did."

"I never said nothing of the kind."

"Well, what *did* you say, then?"

"Said he come to take the sea *baths*—that's what I said."

"Well, then! how's he going to take the sea baths if it ain't on the sea?"

"Looky here," I says; "did you ever see any Congress water?"[8]

"Yes."

"Well, did you have to go to Congress to get it?"

"Why, no."

"Well, neither does William Fourth have to go to the sea to get a sea bath."

"How does he get it, then?"

"Gets it the way people down here gets Congress water—in barrels. There in the palace at Sheffield they've got furnaces, and he wants his water hot. They can't bile that amount of water away off there at the sea. They haven't got no conveniences for it."

"Oh, I see, now. You might a said that in the first place and saved time."

When she said that, I see I was out of the woods again, and so I was comfortable and glad. Next, she says:

"Do you go to church, too?"

"Yes—regular."

"Where do you set?"

"Why, in our pew."

"*Whose* pew?"

"Why, *ourn*—your Uncle Harvey's."

"His'n? What does *he* want with a pew?"

"Wants it to set in. What did you *reckon* he wanted with it?"

"Why, I thought he'd be in the pulpit."

Rot him, I forgot he was a preacher. I see I was up a stump again, so I played another chicken bone and got another think. Then I says:

"Blame it, do you suppose there ain't but one preacher to a church?"

"Why, what do they want with more?"

"What!—to preach before a king? I never see such a girl as you. They don't have no less than seventeen."

"Seventeen! My land! Why, I wouldn't set out such a string as that, not if I *never* got to glory. It must take 'em a week."

"Shucks, they don't *all* of 'em preach the same day—only *one* of 'em."

"Well, then, what does the rest of 'em do?"

"Oh, nothing much. Loll around, pass the plate—and one thing

8. Mineral water from the Congress Spring at Saratoga, New York.

or another. But mainly they don't do nothing."

"Well, then, what are they *for?*"

"Why, they're for *style*. Don't you know nothing?"

"Well, I don't *want* to know no such foolishness as that. How is servants treated in England? Do they treat 'em better 'n we treat our niggers?"

"No! A servant ain't nobody there. They treat them worse than dogs."

"Don't they give 'em holidays, the way we do, Christmas and New Year's week, and Fourth of July?"

"Oh, just listen! A body could tell *you* hain't ever been to England, by that. Why, Hare-l—why, Joanna, they never see a holiday from year's end to year's end; never go to the circus, nor theatre, nor nigger shows, nor nowheres."

"Nor church?"

"Nor church."

"But *you* always went to church."

Well, I was gone up again. I forgot I was the old man's servant. But next minute I whirled in on a kind of an explanation how a valley was different from a common servant, and *had* to go to church whether he wanted to or not, and set with the family, on account of it's being the law. But I didn't do it pretty good, and when I got done I see she warn't satisfied. She says:

"Honest injun, now, hain't you been telling me a lot of lies?"

"Honest injun," says I.

"None of it at all?"

"None of it at all. Not a lie in it," says I.

"Lay your hand on this book and say it."

I see it warn't nothing but a dictionary, so I laid my hand on it and said it. So then she looked a little better satisfied, and says:

"Well, then, I'll believe some of it; but I hope to gracious if I'll believe the rest."

"What is it you won't believe, Joe?" says Mary Jane, stepping in with Susan behind her. "It ain't right nor kind for you to talk so to him, and him a stranger and so far from his people. How would you like to be treated so?"

"That's always your way, Maim—always sailing in to help somebody before they're hurt. I hain't done nothing to him. He's told some stretchers, I reckon; and I said I wouldn't swallow it all; and that's every bit and grain I *did* say. I reckon he can stand a little think like that, can't he?"

"I don't care whether 'twas little or whether 'twas big, he's here in our house and a stranger, and it wasn't good of you to say it. If you was in his place, it would make you feel ashamed; and so you ought'nt to say a thing to another person that will make *them* feel ashamed."

"Why, Maim, he said—"

"It don't make no difference what he *said*—that ain't the thing. The thing is for you to treat him *kind*, and not be saying things to make him remember he ain't in his own country and amongst his own folks."

I says to myself, *this* is a girl that I'm letting that old reptile rob her of her money!

Then Susan *she* waltzed in; and if you'll believe me, she did give Hare-lip hark from the tomb!

Says I to myself, And this is *another* one that I'm letting him rob her of her money!

Then Mary Jane she took another inning, and went in sweet and lovely again—which was her way—but when she got done there warn't hardly anything left o' poor Hare-lip. So she hollered.

"All right, then," says the other girls, "you just ask his pardon."

She done it, too. And she done it beautiful. She done it so beautiful it was good to hear; and I wished I could tell her a thousand lies, so she could do it again.

I says to myself, this is *another* one that I'm letting him rob her of her money. And when she got through, they all jest laid theirselves out to make me feel at home and know I was amongst friends. I felt so ornery and low down and mean, that I says to myself, My mind's made up; I'll hive that money for them or bust.

So then I lit out—for bed, I said, meaning some time or another. When I got by myself, I went to thinking the thing over. I says to myself, shall I go to that doctor, private, and blow on these frauds? No—that won't do. He might tell who told him; then the king and the duke would make it warm for me. Shall I go, private, and tell Mary Jane? No—I dasn't do it. Her face would give them a hint, sure; they've got the money, and they'd slide right out and get away with it. If she was to fetch in help, I'd get mixed up in the business, before it was done with, I judge. No, there ain't no good way but one. I got to steal that money, somehow; and I got to steal it some way that they won't suspicion that I done it. They've got a good thing, here; and they ain't agoing to leave till they've played this family and this town for all they're worth, so I'll find a chance time enough. I'll steal it, and hide it; and by-and-by, when I'm away down the river, I'll write a letter and tell Mary Jane where it's hid. But I better hive it to-night, if I can, because the doctor maybe hasn't let up as much as he lets on he has; he might scare them out of here, yet.

So, thinks I, I'll go and search them rooms. Up stairs the hall was dark, but I found the duke's room, and started to paw around it with my hands; but I recollected it wouldn't be much like the king to let anybody else take care of that money but his own self; so then I went to his room and begun to paw around there. But I see I couldn't do nothing without a candle, and I dasn't light one, of course. So I judged I'd got to do the other thing—lay for them, and eavesdrop. About that time, I hears their footsteps coming, and was going to skip under the bed; I reached for it, but it wasn't where I thought it would be; but I touched the curtain that hid Mary Jane's frocks, so I jumped in behind that and snuggled in amongst the gowns, and stood there perfectly still.

They come in and shut the door; and the first thing the duke done was to get down and look under the bed. Then I was glad I hadn't found the bed when I wanted it. And yet, you know, it's kind of natural to hide under the bed when you are up to anything private. They sets down, then, and the king says:

"Well, what is it? and cut it middlin' short, because it's better for us to be down there a whoopin'-up the mournin', than up here givin' 'em a chance to talk us over."

"Well, this is it, Capet. I ain't easy; I ain't comfortable. That doctor lays on my mind. I wanted to know your plans. I've got a notion, and I think it's a sound one."

"What is it, duke?"

"That we better glide out of this, before three in the morning, and clip it down the river with what we've got. Specially, seeing we got it so easy—*given* back to us, flung at our heads, as you may say, when of course we allowed to have to steal it back. I'm for knocking off and lighting out."

That made me feel pretty bad. About an hour or two ago, it would a been a little different, but now it made me feel bad and disappointed. The king rips out and says:

"What! And not sell out the rest o' the property? March off like a passel o' fools and leave eight or nine thous'n' dollars' worth o' property layin' around jest sufferin' to be scooped in?—and all good salable stuff, too."

The duke he grumbled; said the bag of gold was enough, and he didn't want to go no deeper—didn't want to rob a lot of orphans of *everything* they had.

"Why, how you talk!" says the king. "We shan't rob 'em of nothing at all but jest this money. The people that *buys* the property is the suff'rers; because as soon's it's found out 'at we didn't own it—which won't be long after we've slid—the sale won't be valid, and it'll all go back to the estate. These-yer orphans 'll git their house back agin, and that's enough for *them*; they're young and spry, and k'n easy earn a livin'. *They* ain't agoing to suffer. Why, jest think—there's thous'n's and thous'n's that ain't nigh so well off. Bless you, *they* ain't got noth'n to complain of."

Well, the king he talked him blind; so at last he give in, and said all right, but said he believed it was blame foolishness to stay, and that doctor hanging over them. But the king says:

"Cuss the doctor! What do we k'yer for *him*? Hain't we got all the fools in town on our side? and ain't that a big enough majority in any town?"

So they got ready to go down stairs again. The duke says:

"I don't think we put that money in a good place."

That cheered me up. I'd begun to think I warn't going to get a hint of no kind to help me. The king says:

"Why?"

"Because Mary Jane 'll be in mourning from this out; and first you know the nigger that does up the rooms will get an order to box these duds up and put 'em away; and do you reckon a nigger can run across money and not borrow some of it?"

"Your head's level, agin, duke," says the king; and he come a fumbling under the curtain two or three foot from where I was. I stuck tight to the wall, and kept mighty still, though quivery; and I wondered what them fellows would say to me if they catched me; and I tried to think what I'd better do if they did catch me. But the king he got the bag before I could think more than about a half a thought, and he never suspicioned I was around. They took and shoved the bag through a rip in the straw tick that was under the feather bed, and crammed it in a foot or two amongst the straw and said it was all right, now, because a nigger only makes up the feather bed, and don't turn over the straw tick only about twice a year, and so it warn't in no danger of getting stole, now.

But I knowed better. I had it out of there before they was half-way down stairs. I groped along up to my cubby, and hid it there till I could get a chance to do better. I judged I better hide it outside of the house somewheres, because if they missed it they would give the house a good ransacking. I knowed that very well. Then I turned in, with my clothes all on; but I couldn't a gone to sleep, if I'd a wanted to, I was in such a sweat to get through with the business. By-and-by I heard the king and the duke come up; so I rolled off of my pallet and laid with my chin at the top of my ladder and waited to see if anything was going to happen. But nothing did.

So I held on till all the late sounds had quit and the early ones hadn't begun, yet; and then I slipped down the ladder.

Chapter XXVII

I crept to their doors and listened; they was snoring, so I tip-toed along, and got down stairs all right. There warn't a sound anywheres. I peeped through a crack of the dining-room door, and see the men that was watching the corpse all sound asleep on their chairs. The door was open into the parlor, where the corpse was laying, and there was a candle in both rooms. I passed along, and the parlor door was open; but I see there warn't nobody in there but the remainders of Peter; so I shoved on by; but the front door was locked, and the key wasn't there. Just then I heard somebody coming down the stairs, back behind me. I run in the parlor, and took a swift look around, and the only place I see to hide the bag was in the coffin. The lid was shoved along about a foot, showing the dead man's face down in there, with a wet cloth over it, and his shroud on. I tucked the money-bag in under the lid, just down beyond where his hands was crossed, which made me creep, they was so cold, and then I run back across the room and in behind the door.

The person coming was Mary Jane. She went to the coffin, very soft, and kneeled down and looked in; then she put up her hand-kerchief and I see she begun to cry, though I couldn't hear her, and her back was to me. I slid out, and as I passed the dining-room I thought I'd make sure them watchers hadn't seen me; so I looked through the crack and everything was all right. They hadn't stirred.

I slipped up to bed, feeling ruther blue, on accounts of the thing playing out that way after I had took so much trouble and run so much resk about it. Says I, if it could stay where it is, all right; because when we get down the river a hundred mile or two, I could write back to Mary Jane, and she could dig him up again and get it; but that ain't the thing that's going to happen; the thing that's going to happen is, the money 'll be found when they come to screw on the lid. Then the king 'll get it again, and it 'll be a long day before he gives anybody another chance to smouch it from him. Of course I *wanted* to slide down and get it out of there, but I dasn't try it. Every minute it was getting earlier, now, and pretty soon some of them watchers would begin to stir, and I might get catched—catched with six thousand dollars in my hands that no-body hadn't hired me to take care of. I don't wish to be mixed up in no such business as that, I says to myself.

When I got down stairs in the morning, the parlor was shut up, and the watchers was gone. There warn't nobody around but the family and the widow Bartley and our tribe. I watched their faces to see if anything had been happening, but I couldn't tell.

Towards the middle of the day the undertaker come, with his man, and they set the coffin in the middle of the room on a couple of chairs, and then set all our chairs in rows, and borrowed more from the neighbors till the hall and the parlor and the dining-room was full. I see the coffin lid was the way it was before, but I dasn't go to look in under it, with folks around.

Then the people begun to flock in, and the beats and the girls took seats in the front row at the head of the coffin, and for a half an hour the people filed around slow, in single rank, and looked down at the dead man's face a minute, and some dropped in a tear, and it was all very still and solemn, only the girls and the beats holding handkerchiefs to their eyes and keeping their heads bent, and sobbing a little. There warn't no other sound but the scraping of the feet on the floor, and blowing noses—because people always blows them more at a funeral than they do at other places except church.

When the place was packed full, the undertaker he slid around in his black gloves with his softy soothering ways, putting on the last touches, and getting people and things all shipshape and comfortable, and making no more sound than a cat. He never spoke; he moved people around, he squeezed in late ones, he opened up passage-ways, and done it all with nods, and signs with his hands. Then he took his place over against the wall. He was the softest, glidingest, stealthiest man I ever see; and there warn't no more smile to him than there is to a ham.

They had borrowed a melodeum—a sick one; and when everything was ready, a young woman set down and worked it, and it was pretty skreeky and colicky, and everybody joined in and sung, and Peter was the only one that had a good thing, according to my notion. Then the Reverend Hobson opened up, slow and solemn, and begun to talk; and straight off the most outrageous row busted out in the cellar a body ever heard; it was only one dog, but he made a most powerful racket, and he kept it up, right along; the parson he had to stand there, over the coffin, and wait—you couldn't hear yourself think. It was right down awkward, and nobody didn't seem to know what to do. But pretty soon they see that long-legged undertaker make a sign to the preacher as much as to say, "Don't you worry—just depend on me." Then he stooped down and begun to glide along the wall, just his shoulders showing over the people's heads. So he glided along, and the pow-wow and racket getting more and more outrageous all the time; and at last, when he had gone around two sides of the room, he disappears down cellar. Then, in about two seconds we heard a whack, and the dog he finished up with a most amazing howl or two, and then everything was dead still, and the parson begun his solemn talk where he left off. In a minute or two here comes this undertaker's back and shoulders gliding along the wall again; and so he glided, and glided, around three sides of the room, and then rose up, and shaded his mouth with his hands, and stretched his neck out towards the preacher, over the people's heads, and says, in a kind of a coarse whisper, *"He had a rat!"* Then he drooped down and glided along the wall again to his place. You could see it was a great satisfaction to the people, because naturally they wanted to know. A little thing like that don't cost nothing, and it's just the little things that makes a man to be looked up to and liked. There warn't no more popular man in town than what that undertaker was.

Well, the funeral sermon was very good, but pison long and tiresome; and then the king he shoved in and got off some of his usual rubbage, and at last the job was through, and the undertaker begun to sneak up on the coffin with his screw-driver. I was in a sweat then, and watched him pretty keen. But he never meddled at all; just slid the lid along, as soft as mush, and screwed it down tight and fast. So there I was! I didn't know whether the money was in there, or not. So, says I, spose somebody has hogged that bag on the sly?—now how do *I* know whether to write to Mary Jane or not? 'Spose she dug him up and didn't find nothing— what would she think of me? Blame it, I says, I might get hunted up and jailed; I'd better lay low and keep dark, and not write at all; the thing's awful mixed, now; trying to better it, I've worsened it a hundred times, and I wish to goodness I'd just let it alone, dad fetch the whole business!

They buried him, and we come back home, and I went to watching faces again—I couldn't help it, and I couldn't rest easy. But nothing come of it; the faces didn't tell me nothing.

The king he visited around, in the evening, and sweetened every body up, and made himself ever so friendly; and he give out the idea that his congregation over in England would be in a sweat about him, so he must hurry and settle up the estate right away, and leave for home. He was very sorry he was so pushed, and so was everybody; they wished he could stay longer, but they said they could see it couldn't be done. And he said of course him and Wil-liam would take the girls home with them; and that pleased every-body too, because then the girls would be well fixed, and amongst their own relations; and it pleased the girls, too—tickled them so they clean forgot they ever had a trouble in the world; and told him to sell out as quick as he wanted to, they would be ready. Them poor things was that glad and happy it made my heart ache to see them getting fooled and lied to so, but I didn't see no safe way for me to chip in and change the general tune.

Well, blamed if the king didn't bill the house and the niggers and all the property for auction straight off—sale two days after the funeral; but anybody could buy private beforehand if they wanted to.

So the next day after the funeral, along about noontime, the girls' joy got the first jolt; a couple of nigger traders come along, and the king sold them the niggers reasonable, for three-day drafts as they called it, and away they went, the two sons up the river to Memphis, and their mother down the river to Orleans. I thought them poor girls and them niggers would break their hearts for grief; they cried around each other, and took on so it most made me down sick to see it. The girls said they hadn't ever dreamed of seeing the family separated or sold away from the town. I can't ever get it out of my memory, the sight of them poor miserable girls and niggers hanging around each other's necks and crying; and I reckon I couldn't a stood it all but would a had to bust out and tell on our gang if I hadn't knowed the sale warn't no account and the niggers would be back home in a week or two.

The thing made a big stir in the town, too, and a good many come out flatfooted and said it was scandalous to separate the mother and the children that way. It injured the frauds some; but the old fool he bulled right along, spite of all the duke could say or do, and I tell you the duke was powerful uneasy.

Next day was auction day. About broad-day in the morning, the king and the duke come up in the garret and woke me up, and I see by their look that there was trouble. The king says:

"Was you in my room night before last?"

"No, your majesty"—which was the way I always called him when nobody but our gang warn't around.

"Was you in there yisterday er last night?"

"No, your majesty."

"Honor bright, now—no lies."

"Honor bright, your majesty, I'm telling you the truth. I hain't been anear your room since Miss Mary Jane took you and the duke and showed it to you."

The duke says:

"Have you seen anybody else go in there?"

"No, your grace, not as I remember, I believe."

"Stop and think."

I studied a while, and see my chance, then I says:

"Well, I see the niggers go in there several times."

Both of them give a little jump; and looked like they hadn't ever expected it, and then like they *had*. Then the duke says:

"What, *all* of them?"

"No—leastways not all at once. That is, I don't think I ever see them all come *out* at once but just one time."

"Hello—when was that?"

"It was the day we had the funeral. In the morning. It warn't early, because I overslept. I was just starting down the ladder, and I see them."

"Well, go on, *go* on—what did they do? How'd they act?"

"They didn't do nothing. And they didn't act anyway, much, as fur as I see. They tip-toed away; so I seen, easy enough, that they'd shoved in there to do up your majesty's room, or something, sposing you was up; and found you *warn't* up, and so they was hoping to slide out of the way of trouble without waking you up, if they hadn't already waked you up."

"Great guns, *this* is a go!" says the king; and both of them looked pretty sick, and tolerable silly. They stood there a thinking and scratching their heads, a minute, and then the duke he bust into a kind of a little raspy chuckle, and says:

"It does beat all, how neat the niggers played their hand. They let on to be *sorry* they was going out of this region! and I believed they *was* sorry. And so did you, and so did everybody. Don't ever tell *me* any more that a nigger ain't got any histrionic talent. Why, the way they played that thing, it would fool *anybody*. In my opinion there's a fortune in 'em. If I had capital and a theatre, I wouldn't want a better lay out than that—and here we've gone and sold 'em for a song. Yes, and ain't privileged to sing the song, yet. Say, where *is* that song?—that draft."

"In the bank for to be collected. Where *would* it be?"

"Well, *that's* all right then, thank goodness."

Says I, kind of timid-like:

"Is something gone wrong?"

The king whirls on me and rips out:

"None o' your business! You keep your head shet, and mind y'r own affairs—if you got any. Long as you're in this town, don't you forget *that*, you hear?" Then he says to the duke, "We got to jest swaller it, and say noth'n: mum's the word for *us*."

As they was starting down the ladder, the duke he chuckles again, and says:

"Quick sales *and* small profits! It's a good business—yes."

The king snarls around on him and says,

"I was trying to do for the best, in sellin' 'm out so quick. If the profits has turned out to be none, lackin' considable, and none to carry, is it my fault any more'n it's yourn?"

"Well, *they'd* be in this house yet, and we *wouldn't* if I could a got my advice listened to."

The king sassed back, as much as was safe for him, and then swapped around and lit into *me* again. He give me down the banks for not coming and *telling* him I see the niggers come out of his room acting that way—said any fool would a *knowed* something was up. And then waltzed in and cussed *himself* a while; and said it all come of him not laying late and taking his natural rest that morning, and he'd be blamed if he'd ever do it again. So they went off a jawing; and I felt dreadful glad I'd worked it all off onto the niggers and yet hadn't done the niggers no harm by it.

Chapter XXVIII

By-and-by it was getting-up time; so I come down the ladder and started for down stairs, but as I come to the girls' room, the door was open, and I see Mary Jane setting by her old hair trunk, which was open and she'd been packing things in it—getting ready to go to England. But she had stopped now, with a folded gown in her lap, and had her face in her hands, crying. I felt awful bad to see it; of course anybody would. I went in there, and says:

"Miss Mary Jane, you can't abear to see people in trouble, and I can't—most always. Tell me about it."

So she done it. And it was the niggers—I just expected it. She said the beautiful trip to England was most about spoiled for her; she didn't know *how* she was ever going to be happy there, know-ing the mother and the children warn't ever going to see each other no more—and then busted out bitterer than ever, and flung up her hands, and says

"Oh, dear, dear, to think they ain't *ever* going to see each other any more!"

"But they *will*—and inside of two weeks—and I *know* it!" says I.

Laws it was out before I could think!—and before I could budge, she throws her arms around my neck, and told me to say it *again*, say it *again*, say it *again*!

I see I had spoke too sudden, and said too much, and was in a close place. I asked her to let me think a minute; and she set there, very impatient and excited, and handsome, but looking kind of happy and eased-up, like a person that's had a tooth pulled out. So I went to studying it out. I says to myself, I reckon a body that ups and tells the truth when he is in a tight place, is taking con-siderable many resks, though I ain't had no experience, and can't say for certain; but it looks so to me, anyway; and yet here's a case where I'm blest if it don't look to me like the truth is better, and actuly *safer*, than a lie. I must lay it by in my mind, and think it over some time or other, it's so kind of strange and unregular. I never see nothing like it. Well, I says to myself at last, I'm agoing to chance it; I'll up and tell the truth this time, though it does seem most like setting down on a kag of powder and touching it off just to see where you'll go to. Then I says:

"Miss Mary Jane, is there any place out of town a little ways, where you could go and stay three or four days?"

"Yes—Mr. Lothrop's. Why?"

"Never mind why, yet. If I'll tell you how I know the niggers will see each other again—inside of two weeks—here in this house—and *prove* how I know it—will you go to Mr. Lothrop's and stay four days?"

"Four days!" she says; "I'll stay a year!"

"All right," I says, "I don't want nothing more out of *you* than just your word—I druther have it than another man's kiss-the-Bible." She smiled, and reddened up very sweet, and I says, "If you don't mind it, I'll shut the door—and bolt it."

Then I come back and set down again, and says:

"Don't you holler. Just set still, and take it like a man. I got to tell the truth, and you want to brace up, Miss Mary, because it's a bad kind, and going to be hard to take, but there ain't no help for it. These uncles of yourn ain't no uncles at all—they're a couple[9] of frauds—regular dead-beats. There, now we're over the worst of it—you can stand the rest middling easy."

It jolted her up like everything, of course; but I was over the shoal water now, so I went right along, her eyes a blazing higher and higher all the time, and told her every blame thing, from where we first struck that young fool going up to the steamboat, clear through to where she flung herself onto the king's breast at the front door and he kissed her sixteen or seventeen times—and then up she jumps, with her face afire like sunset, and says:

"The brute! Come—don't waste a minute—not a *second*—we'll have them tarred and feathered, and flung in the river!"

Says I:

"Cert'nly. But do you mean, *before* you go to Mr. Lothrop's, or—"

"Oh," she says, "what am I *thinking* about!" she says, and set right down again. "Don't mind what I said—please don't—you *won't*, now, *will* you?" Laying her silky hand on mine in that kind of a way that I said I would die first. "I never thought, I was so stirred up," she says; "now go on, and I won't do so any more. You tell me what to do, and whatever you say, I'll do it."

"Well," I says, "it's a rough gang, them two frauds, and I'm fixed so I got to travel with them a while longer, whether I want to or not—I druther not tell you why—and if you was to blow on them this town would get me out of their claws, and I'd be all right, but there'd be another person that you don't know about who'd be in big trouble.[1] Well, we got to save *him*, hain't we? Of course. Well, then, we won't blow on them."

Saying them words put a good idea in my head. I see how maybe I could get me and Jim rid of the frauds; get them jailed here, and then leave. But I didn't want to run the raft in day-time, without anybody aboard to answer questions but me; so I didn't want the plan to begin working till pretty late to-night. I says:

"Miss Mary Jane, I'll tell you what we'll do—and you won't have to stay at Mr. Lothrop's so long, nuther. How fur is it?"

"A little short of four miles—right out in the country, back here."

"Well, that'll answer. Now you go along out there, and lay low till nine or half-past, to-night, and then get them to fetch you home again—tell them you've thought of something. If you get here before eleven, put a candle in this window, and if I don't turn up, wait *till* eleven, and *then* if I don't turn up it means I'm gone,

---

9. Erroneously printed "couples" in the first edition.

1. The Negro, Jim. *Cf.* the end of Chapter XXIV.

and out of the way, and safe. Then you come out and spread the news around, and get these beats jailed."

"Good," she says, "I'll do it."

"And if it just happens so that I don't get away, but get took up along with them, you must up and say I told you the whole thing beforehand, and you must stand by me all you can."

"Stand by you, indeed I will. They sha'n't touch a hair of your head!" she says, and I see her nostrils spread and her eyes snap when she said it, too.

"If I get away, I sha'n't be here," I says, "to prove these rapscallions ain't your uncles, and I couldn't do it if I *was* here. I could swear they was beats and bummers, that's all; though that's worth something. Well, there's others can do that better than what I can—and they're people that ain't going to be doubted as quick as I'd be. I'll tell you how to find them. Gimme a pencil and a piece of paper. There—'*Royal Nonesuch, Bricksville.*' Put it away, and don't lose it. When the court wants to find out something about these two, let them send up to Bricksville and say they've got the men that played the Royal Nonesuch, and ask for some witnesses—why, you'll have that entire town down here before you can hardly wink, Miss Mary. And they'll come a-biling, too."

I judged we had got everything fixed about right, now. So I says:

"Just let the auction go right along, and don't worry. Nobody don't have to pay for the things they buy till a whole day after the auction, on accounts of the short notice, and they ain't going out of this till they get that money—and the way we've fixed it the sale ain't going to count, and they ain't going to *get* no money. It's just like the way it was with the niggers—it warn't no sale, and the niggers will be back before long. Why, they can't collect the money for the *niggers*, yet—they're in the worst kind of a fix, Miss Mary."

"Well," she says, "I'll run down to breakfast now, and then I'll start straight for Mr. Lothrop's."

" 'Deed, *that* ain't the ticket, Miss Mary Jane," I says, "by no manner of means; go *before* breakfast."

"Why?"

"What did you reckon I wanted you to go at all for, Miss Mary?"

"Well, I never thought—and come to think, I don't know. What was it?"

"Why, it's because you ain't one of these leather-face people. I don't want no better book than[2] what your face is. A body can set down and read it off like coarse print. Do you reckon you can go and face your uncles, when they come to kiss you good-morning, and never—"

"There, there, don't! Yes, I'll go before breakfast—I'll be glad

2. Erroneously printed "that" in 1885.

to. And leave my sisters with them?"

"Yes—never mind about them. They've got to stand it yet a while. They might suspicion something if all of you was to go. I don't want you to see them, nor your sisters, nor nobody in this town—if a neighbor was to ask how is your uncles this morning, your face would tell something. No, you go right along, Miss Mary Jane, and I'll fix it with all of them. I'll tell Miss Susan to give your love to your uncles and say you've went away for a few hours for to get a little rest and change, or to see a friend, and you'll be back to-night or early in the morning."

"Gone to see a friend is all right, but I won't have my love given to them."

"Well, then, it sha'n't be." It was well enough to tell *her* so—no harm in it. It was only a little thing to do, and no trouble; and it's the little things that smoothes people's roads the most, down here below; it would make Mary Jane comfortable, and it wouldn't cost nothing. Then I says: "There's one more thing—that bag of money."

"Well, they've got that; and it makes me feel pretty silly to think *how* they got it."

"No, you're out, there. They hain't got it."

"Why, who's got it?"

"I wish I knowed, but I don't. I *had* it, because I stole it from them: and I stole it to give to you; and I know where I hid it, but I'm afraid it ain't there no more. I'm awful sorry, Miss Mary Jane, I'm just as sorry as I can be; but I done the best I could; I did, honest. I come nigh getting caught, and I had to shove it into the first place I come to, and run—and it warn't a good place."

"Oh, stop blaming yourself—it's too bad to do it, and I won't allow it—you couldn't help it; it wasn't you fault. Where did you hide it?"

I didn't want to set her to thinking about her troubles again; and I couldn't seem to get my mouth to tell her what would make her see that corpse laying in the coffin with that bag of money on his stomach. So for a minute I didn't say nothing—then I says:

"I'd ruther not *tell* you where I put it, Miss Mary Jane, if you don't mind letting me off; but I'll write it for you on a piece of paper, and you can read it along the road to Mr. Lothrop's, if you want to. Do you reckon that'll do?"

"Oh, yes."

So I wrote: "I put it in the coffin. It was in there when you was crying there, away in the night. I was behind the door, and I was mighty sorry for you, Miss Mary Jane."

It made my eyes water a little, to remember her crying there all by herself in the night, and them devils laying there right under her own roof, shaming her and robbing her; and when I folded it up and give it to her, I see the water come into her eyes, too; and she shook me by the hand, hard, and says:

"*Good*-bye—I'm going to do everything just as you've told me; and if I don't ever see you again, I sha'n't ever forget you, and I'll think of you a many and a many a time, and I'll *pray* for you, too!"—and she was gone.

Pray for me! I reckoned if she knowed me she'd take a job that was more nearer her size. But I bet she done it, just the same—she was just that kind. She had the grit to pray for Judus if she took the notion—there warn't no backdown to her, I judge. You may say what you want to, but in my opinion she had more sand in her than any girl I ever see; in my opinion she was just full of sand. It sounds like flattery, but it ain't no flattery. And when it comes to beauty—and goodness too—she lays over them all. I hain't ever seen her since that time that I see her go out of that door; no, I hain't ever seen her since, but I reckon I've thought of her a many and a many a million times, and of her saying she would pray for me; and if ever I'd a thought it would do any good for me to pray for *her*, blamed if I wouldn't a done it or bust.

Well, Mary Jane she lit out the back way, I reckon; because nobody see her go. When I struck Susan and the hare-lip, I says:

"What's the name of them people over on t'other side of the river that you all goes to see sometimes?"

They says:

"There's several; but it's the Proctors, mainly."

"That's the name," I says; "I most forgot it. Well, Miss Mary Jane she told me to tell you she's gone over there in a dreadful hurry—one of them's sick."

"Which one?"

"I don't know; leastways I kinder forget; but I think it's—"

"Sakes alive, I hope it ain't *Hanner*?"

"I'm sorry to say it," I says, "but Hanner's the very one."

"My goodness—and she so well only last week! Is she took bad?"

"It ain't no name for it. They set up with her all night, Miss Mary Jane said, and they don't think she'll last many hours."

"Only think of that, now! What's the matter with her!"

I couldn't think of anything reasonable, right off that way, so I says:

"Mumps."

"Mumps your granny! They don't set up with people that's got the mumps."

"They don't, don't they? You better bet they do with *these* mumps. These mumps is different. It's a new kind, Miss Mary Jane said."

"How's it a new kind?"

"Because it's mixed up with other things."

"What other things?"

"Well, measles, and whooping-cough, and erysiplas, and consumption, and yaller janders, and brain fever, and I don't know what all."

"My land! And they call it the *mumps?*"

"That's what Miss Mary Jane said."

"Well, what in the nation do they call it the *mumps* for?"

"Why, because it *is* the mumps. That's what it starts with."

"Well, ther' ain't no sense in it. A body might stump his toe, and take pison, and fall down the well, and break his neck, and bust his brains out, and somebody come along and ask what killed him, and some numskull up and say, 'Why, he stumped his *toe.*' Would ther' be any sense in that? No. And ther' ain't no sense in *this*, nuther. Is it ketching?"

"Is it *ketching?* Why, how you talk. Is a *harrow* catching?—in the dark? If you don't hitch onto one tooth, you're bound to on another, ain't you? And you can't get away with that tooth without fetching the whole harrow along, can you? Well, these kind of mumps is a kind of a harrow, as you may say—and it ain't no slouch of a harrow, nuther, you come to get it hitched on good."

"Well, it's awful, *I* think," says the hare-lip. "I'll go to Uncle Harvey and—"

"Oh, yes," I says, "I *would*. Of *course* I would. I wouldn't lose no time."

"Well, why wouldn't you?"

"Just look at it a minute, and maybe you can see. Hain't your uncles obleeged to get along home to England as fast as they can? And do you reckon they'd be mean enough to go off and leave you to go all that journey by yourselves? *You* know they'll wait for you. So fur, so good. Your uncle Harvey's a preacher, ain't he? Very well, then; is a *preacher* going to deceive a steamboat clerk? is he going to deceive a *ship clerk?*—so as to get them to let Miss Mary Jane go aboard? Now *you* know he ain't. What *will* he do, then? Why, he'll say, 'It's a great pity, but my church matters has got to get along the best way they can; for my niece has been exposed to the dreadful pluribus-unum mumps, and so it's my bounden duty to set down here and wait the three months it takes to show on her if she's got it.' But never mind, if you think it's best to tell your uncle Harvey—"

"Shucks, and stay fooling around here when we could all be having good times in England whilst we was waiting to find out whether Mary Jane's got it or not? Why, you talk like a muggins."

"Well, anyway, maybe you better tell some of the neighbors."

"Listen at that, now. You do beat all, for natural stupidness. Can't you *see* that *they'd* go and tell? Ther' ain't no way but just to not tell anybody at *all*."

"Well, maybe you're right—yes, I judge you *are* right."

"But I reckon we ought to tell Uncle Harvey she's gone out a while, anyway, so he wont be uneasy about her?"

"Yes, Miss Mary Jane she wanted you to do that. She says, 'Tell them to give Uncle Harvey and William my love and a kiss, and say I've run over the river to see Mr.—Mr.—what *is* the name of that rich family your uncle Peter used to think so much of?—I mean the one that—"

"Why, you must mean the Apthorps, ain't it?"

"Of course; bother them kind of names, a body can't ever seem to remember them, half the time, somehow. Yes, she said, say she has run over for to ask the Apthorps to be sure and come to the auction and buy this house, because she allowed her uncle Peter would ruther they had it than anybody else; and she's going to stick to them till they say they'll come, and then, if she ain't too tired, she's coming home; and if she is, she'll be home in the morning anyway. She said, don't say nothing about the Proctors, but only about the Apthorps—which'll be perfectly true, because she *is* going there to speak about their buying the house; I know it, because she told me so, herself."

"All right," they said, and cleared out to lay for their uncles, and give them the love and the kisses, and tell them the message.

Everything was all right now. The girls wouldn't say nothing because they wanted to go to England; and the king and the duke would ruther Mary Jane was off working for the auction than around in reach of Doctor Robinson. I felt very good; I judged I had done it pretty neat—I reckoned Tom Sawyer couldn't a done it no neater himself. Of course he would a throwed more style into it, but I can't do that very handy, not being brung up to it.

Well, they held the auction in the public square, along towards the end of the afternoon, and it strung along, and strung along, and the old man he was on hand and looking his level piousest,[3] up there longside of the auctioneer, and chipping in a little Scripture, now and then, or a little goody-goody saying, of some kind, and the duke he was around goo-gooing for sympathy all he knowed how, and just spreading himself genery.

But by-and-by the thing dragged through, and everything was sold. Everything but a little old trifling lot in the graveyard. So they'd got to work *that* off—I never see such a girafft as the king was for wanting to swallow *everything*. Well, whilst they was at it, a steamboat landed, and in about two minutes up comes a crowd a whooping and yelling and laughing and carrying on, and singing out:

"*Here's* your opposition line! here's your two sets o' heirs to old Peter Wilks—and you pays your money and you takes your choice!"

3. In the first and many subsequent editions, this was printed as "pisonest," but the manuscript shows the correct reading.

Chapter XXIX

They was fetching a very nice looking old gentleman along, and a nice looking younger one, with his right arm in a sling. And my souls, how the people yelled, and laughed, and kept it up. But I didn't see no joke about it, and I judged it would strain the duke and the king some to see any. I reckoned they'd turn pale. But no, nary a pale did *they* turn. The duke he never let on he suspicioned what was up, but just went a goo-gooing around, happy and satisfied, like a jug that's googling out buttermilk; and as for the king, he just gazed and gazed down sorrowful on them newcomers like it give him the stomach-ache in his very heart to think there could be such frauds and rascals in the world. Oh, he done it admirable. Lots of the principal people gethered around the king, to let him see they was on his side. That old gentleman that had just come looked all puzzled to death. Pretty soon he begun to speak, and I see, straight off, he pronounced *like* an Englishman, not the king's way, though the king's *was* pretty good, for an imitation. I can't give the old gent's words, nor I can't imitate him; but he turned around to the crowd, and says, about like this:

"This is a surprise to me which I wasn't looking for; and I'll acknowledge, candid and frank, I ain't very well fixed to meet it and answer it; for my brother and me has had misfortunes, he's broke his arm, and our baggage got put off at a town above here, last night in the night by a mistake. I am Peter Wilks's brother Harvey, and this is his brother William, which can't hear nor speak—and can't even make signs to amount to much, now 't he's only got one hand to work them with. We are who we say we are; and in a day or two, when I get the baggage, I can prove it. But, up till then, I won't say nothing more, but go to the hotel and wait."

So him and the new dummy started off; and the king he laughs, and blethers out:

"Broke his arm—*very* likely *ain't* it?—and very convenient, too, for a fraud that's got to make signs, and hain't learnt how. Lost their baggage! That's *mighty* good!—and mighty ingenious—under the *circumstances!*"

So he laughed again; and so did everybody else, except three or four, or maybe half a dozen. One of these was that doctor; another one was a sharp looking gentleman, with a carpet-bag of the old-fashioned kind made out of carpet-stuff, that had just come off of the steamboat and was talking to him in a low voice, and glancing towards the king now and then and nodding their heads—it was Levi Bell, the lawyer that was gone up to Louisville; and another one was a big rough husky that come along and listened to all the old gentleman said, and was listening to the king now. And when the king got done, this husky up and says:

"Say, looky here; if you are Harvey Wilks, when'd you come to this town?"

"The day before the funeral, friend," says the king.

"But what time o' day?"

"In the evenin'—'bout an hour er two before sundown."

"*How'd* you come?"

"I come down on the *Susan Powell*, from Cincinnati."

"Well, then, how'd you come to be up at the Pint in the *mornin'* —in a canoe?"

"I warn't up at the Pint in the mornin'."

"It's a lie."

Several of them jumped for him and begged him not to talk that way to an old man and a preacher.

"Preacher be hanged, he's a fraud and a liar. He was up at the Pint that mornin'. I live up there, don't I? Well, I was up there, and he was up there. I *see* him there. He come in a canoe, along with Tim Collins and a boy."

The doctor he up and says:

"Would you know the boy again if you was to see him, Hines?"

"I reckon I would, but I don't know. Why, yonder he is, now. I know him perfectly easy."

It was me he pointed at. The doctor says:

"Neighbors, I don't know whether the new couple is frauds or not; but if *these* two ain't frauds, I am an idiot, that's all. I think it's our duty to see that they don't get away from here till we've looked into this thing. Come along, Hines; come along, the rest of you. We'll take these fellows to the tavern and affront them with t'other couple, and I reckon we'll find out *something* before we get through."

It was nuts for the crowd, though maybe not for the king's friends; so we all started. It was about sundown. The doctor he led me along by the hand, and was plenty kind enough, but he never let *go* my hand.

We all got in a big room in the hotel, and lit up some candles, and fetched in the new couple. First, the doctor says:

"I don't wish to be too hard on these two men, but I think they're frauds, and they may have complices that we don't know nothing about. If they have, won't the complices get away with that bag of gold Peter Wilks left? It ain't unlikely. If these men ain't frauds, they won't object to sending for that money and letting us keep it till they prove they're all right—ain't that so?"

Everybody agreed to that. So I judged they had our gang in a pretty tight place, right at the outstart. But the king he only looked sorrowful, and says:

"Gentlemen, I wish the money was there, for I ain't got no

disposition to throw anything in the way of a fair, open, out-and-out investigation o' this misable business; but alas, the money ain't there; you k'n send and see, if you want to."

"Where is it, then?"

"Well, when my niece give it to me to keep for her, I took and hid it inside o' the straw tick o' my bed, not wishin' to bank it for the few days we'd be here, and considerin' the bed a safe place, we not bein' used to niggers, and suppos'n' 'em honest, like servants in England. The niggers stole it the very next mornin' after I had went down stairs; and when I sold 'em, I hadn't missed the money yit, so they got clean away with it. My servant here k'n tell you 'bout it gentlemen."

The doctor and several said "Shucks!" and I see nobody didn't altogether believe him. One man asked me if I see the niggers steal it. I said no, but I see them sneaking out of the room and hustling away, and I never thought nothing, only I reckoned they was afraid they had waked up my master and was trying to get away before he made trouble with them. That was all they asked me. Then the doctor whirls on me and says:

"Are *you* English too?"

I says yes; and him and some others laughed, and said, "Stuff!"

Well, then they sailed in on the general investigation, and there we had it, up and down, hour in, hour out, and nobody never said a word about supper, nor ever seemed to think about it—and so they kept it up, and kept it up; and it *was* the worst mixed-up thing you ever see. They made the king tell his yarn, and they made the old gentleman tell his'n; and anybody but a lot of prejudiced chuckleheads would a *seen* that the old gentleman was spinning truth and t'other one lies. And by-and-by they had me up to tell what I knowed. The king he give me a left-handed look out of the corner of his eye, and so I knowed enough to talk on the right side. I begun to tell about Sheffield, and how we lived there, and all about the English Wilkses, and so on; but I didn't get pretty fur till the doctor begun to laugh; and Levi Bell, the lawyer, says:

"Set down, my boy, I wouldn't strain mself, if I was you. I reckon you ain't used to lying, it don't seem to come handy; what you want is practice. You do it pretty awkward."

I didn't care nothing for the compliment, but I was glad to be let off, anyway.

The doctor he started to say something, and turns and says:

"If you'd been in town at first, Levi Bell—"

The king broke in and reached out his hand, and says:

"Why, is this my poor dead brother's old friend that he's wrote so often about?"

The lawyer and him shook hands, and the lawyer smiled and

looked pleased, and they talked right along a while, and then got
to one side and talked low; and at last the lawyer speaks up and
says:

"That'll fix it. I'll take the order and send it, along with your
brother's, and then they'll know it's all right."

So they got some paper and a pen, and the king he set down
and twisted his head to one side, and chawed his tongue, and
scrawled off something; and then they give the pen to the duke—
and then for the first time, the duke looked sick. But he took the
pen and wrote. So then the lawyer turns to the new old gentleman
and says:

"You and your brother please write a line or two and sign your
names."

The old gentleman wrote, but nobody couldn't read it. The lawyer looked powerful astonished, and says:

"Well, it beats *me*"—and snaked a lot of old letters out of his
pocket, and examined them, and then examined the old man's
writing, and then *them* again; and then says: "These old letters is
from Harvey Wilks; and here's *these* two's handwritings, and anybody can see *they* didn't write them" (the king and the duke
looked sold and foolish, I tell you, to see how the lawyer had took
them in), "and here's *this* old gentleman's handwriting, and anybody can tell, easy enough, *he* didn't write them—fact is, the
scratches he makes ain't properly *writing*, at all. Now here's some
letters from—"

The new old gentleman says:

"If you please, let me explain. Nobody can read my hand but
my brother there—so he copies for me. It's *his* hand you've got
there, not mine."

"*Well!*" says the lawyer, "this *is* a state of things. I've got some
of William's letters too; so if you'll get him to write a line or so
we can com—"

"He *can't* write with his left hand," says the old gentleman. "If
he could use his right hand, you would see that he wrote his own
letters and mine too. Look at both, please—they're by the same
hand."

The lawyer done it, and says:

"I believe it's so—and if it ain't so, there's a heap stronger resemblance than I'd noticed before, anyway. Well, well, well! I
thought we was right on the track of a slution, but it's gone to
grass, partly. But anyway, *one* thing is proved—*these* two ain't
either of 'em Wilkses"—and he wagged his head towards the king
and the duke.

Well, what do you think?—that muleheaded old fool wouldn't
give in *then*! Indeed he wouldn't. Said it warn't no fair test. Said
his brother William was the cussedest joker in the world, and

hadn't *tried* to write—*he* see William was going to play one of his jokes the minute he put the pen to paper. And so he warmed up and went warbling and warbling right along, till he was actuly beginning to believe what he was saying, *himself*—but pretty soon the new old gentleman broke in, and says:

"I've thought of something. Is there anybody here that helped to lay out my br—helped to lay out the late Peter Wilks for burying?"

"Yes," says somebody, "me and Ab Turner done it. We're both here."

Then the old man turns towards the king, and says:

"Peraps this gentleman can tell me what was tatooed on his breast?"

Blamed if the king didn't have to brace up mighty quick, or he'd a squshed down like a bluff bank that the river has cut under, it took him so sudden—and mind you, it was a thing that was calculated to make most *anybody* sqush to get fetched such a solid one as that without any notice—because how was *he* going to know what was tatooed on the man? He whitened a little; he couldn't help it; and it was mighty still in there, and everybody bending a little forwards and gazing at him. Says I to myself, *Now* he'll throw up the sponge—there ain't no more use. Well, did he? A body can't hardly believe it, but he didn't. I reckon he thought he'd keep the thing up till he tired them people out, so they'd thin out, and him and the duke could break loose and get away. Anyway, he set there, and pretty soon he begun to smile, and says:

"Mf! It's a *very* tough question, *ain't* it! *Yes,* sir, I k'n tell you what's tatooed on his breast. It's jest a small, thin, blue arrow—that's what it is; and if you don't look clost, you can't see it. *Now* what do you say—hey?"

Well, *I* never see anything like that old blister for clean out-and-out cheek.

The new old gentleman turns brisk towards Ab Turner and his pard, and his eye lights up like he judged he'd got the king *this* time, and says:

"There—you've heard what he said! Was there any such mark on Peter Wilks's breast?"

Both of them spoke up and says:

"We didn't see no such mark."

"Good!" says the old gentleman. "Now, what you *did* see on his breast was a small dim P, and a B (which is an initial he dropped when he was young), and a W, with dashes between them, so: P—B—W"—and he marked them that way on a piece of paper. "Come—ain't that what you saw?"

Both of them spoke up again, and says:

"No, we *didn't*. We never seen any marks at all."

Well, everybody *was* in a state of mind, now; and they sings out:

"The whole *bilin'* of 'm 's frauds! Le's duck 'em! le's drown 'em! le's ride 'em on a rail!" and everybody was whooping at once, and there was a rattling pow-wow. But the lawyer he jumps on the table and yells, and says:

"Gentlemen—gentle*men!* Hear me just a word—just a *single* word—if you PLEASE! There's one way yet—let's go and dig up the corpse and look."

That took them.

"Hooray!" they all shouted, and was starting right off; but the lawyer and the doctor sung out:

"Hold on, hold on! Collar all these four men and the boy, and fetch *them* along, too!"

"We'll do it!" they all shouted: "and if we don't find them marks we'll lynch the whole gang!"

I *was* scared, now, I tell you. But there warn't no getting away, you know. They gripped us all, and marched us right along, straight for the graveyard, which was a mile and a half down the river, and the whole town at our heels, for we made noise enough, and it was only nine in the evening.

As we went by our house I wished I hadn't sent Mary Jane out of town; because now if I could tip her the wink, she'd light out and save me, and blow on our dead-beats.

Well, we swarmed along down the river road, just carrying on like wild-cats; and to make it more scary, the sky was darking up, and the lightning beginning to wink and flitter, and the wind to shiver amonst the leaves. This was the most awful trouble and most dangersome I ever was in; and I was kinder stunned; everything was going so different from what I had allowed for; stead of being fixed so I could take my own time, if I wanted to, and see all the fun, and have Mary Jane at my back to save me and set me free when the close-fit come, here was nothing in the world betwixt me and sudden death but just them tatoo-marks. If they didn't find them—

I couldn't bear to think about it; and yet, somehow, I couldn't think about nothing else. It got darker and darker, and it was a beautiful time to give the crowd the slip; but that big husky had me by the wrist—Hines—and a body might as well try to give Goliar[4] the slip. He dragged me right along, he was so excited; and I had to run to keep up.

When they got there they swarmed into the graveyard and washed over it like an overflow. And when they got to the grave, they found they had about a hundred times as many shovels as they wanted, but nobody hadn't thought to fetch a lantern. But they sailed into digging, anyway, by the flicker of the lightning,

4. Goliath.

and sent a man to the nearest house a half a mile off, to borrow one.

So they dug and dug, like everything; and it got awful dark, and the rain started, and the wind swished and swushed along, and the lightning come brisker and brisker, and the thunder boomed; but them people never took no notice of it, they was so full of this business; and one minute you could see everything and every face in that big crowd, and the shovelfuls of dirt sailing up out of the grave, and the next second the dark wiped it all out, and you couldn't see nothing at all.

At last they got out the coffin, and begun to unscrew the lid, and then such another crowding, and shouldering, and shoving as there was, to scrouge in and get a sight, you never see; and in the dark, that way, it was awful. Hines he hurt my wrist dreadful, pulling and tugging so, and I reckon he clean forgot I was in the world, he was so excited and panting.

All of a sudden the lightning let go a perfect sluice of white glare, and somebody sings out:

"By the living jingo, here's the bag of gold on his breast!"

Hines let out a whoop, like everybody else, and dropped my wrist and give a big surge to bust his way in and get a look, and the way I lit out and shinned for the road in the dark, there ain't nobody can tell.

I had the road all to myself, and I fairly flew—leastways I had it all to myself except the solid dark, and the now-and-then glares, and the buzzing of the rain, and the thrashing of the wind, and the splitting of the thunder; and sure as you are born I did clip it along!

When I struck the town, I see there warn't nobody out in the storm, so I never hunted for no back streets, but humped it straight through the main one; and when I begun to get towards our house I aimed my eye and set it. No light there; the house all dark—which made me feel sorry and disappointed, I didn't know why. But at last, just as I was sailing by, *flash* comes the light in Mary Jane's window! and my heart swelled up sudden, like to bust; and the same second the house and all was behind me in the dark, and wasn't ever going to be before me no more in this world. She *was* the best girl I ever see, and had the most sand.

The minute I was far enough above the town to see I could make the tow-head, I begun to look sharp for a boat to borrow; and the first time the lightning showed me one that wasn't chained, I snatched it and shoved. It was a canoe, and warn't fastened with nothing but a rope. The tow-head was a rattling big distance off, away out there in the middle of the river, but I didn't lose no time; and when I struck the raft at last, I was so fagged I would a just laid down to blow and gasp if I could afforded it. But I didn't. As I sprung aboard I sung out:

"Out with you Jim, and set her loose! Glory be to goodness, we're shut of them!"

Jim lit out, and was a coming for me with both arms spread, he was so full of joy; but when I glimpsed him in the lightning, my heart shot up in my mouth, and I went overboard backwards; for I forgot he was old King Lear and a drownded A-rab all in one, and it most scared the livers and lights out of me. But Jim fished me out, and was going to hug me and bless me, and so on, he was so glad I was back and we was shut of the king and the duke, but I says:

"Not now—have it for breakfast, have it for breakfast! Cut loose and let her slide!"

So, in two seconds, away we went, a sliding down the river, and it *did* seem so good to be free again and all by ourselves on the big river and nobody to bother us. I had to skip around a bit, and jump up and crack my heels a few times, I couldn't help it; but about the third crack, I noticed a sound that I knowed mighty well—and held my breath and listened and waited—and sure enough, when the next flash busted out over the water, here they come!—and just a laying to their oars and making their skiff hum! It was the king and the duke.

So I wilted right down onto the planks, then, and give up; and it was all I could do to keep from crying.

Chapter XXX

When they got aboard, the king went for me, and shook me by the collar, and says:

"Tryin' to give us the slip, was ye, you pup! Tired of our company—hey?"

I says:

"No, your majesty, we warn't—*please* don't, your majesty!"

"Quick, then, and tell us what *was* your idea, or I'll shake the insides out o' you!"

"Honest, I'll tell you everything, just as it happened, your majesty. The man that had aholt of me was very good to me, and kept saying he had a boy about as big as me that died last year, and he was sorry to see a boy in such a dangerous fix; and when they was all took by surprise by finding the gold, and made a rush for the coffin, he lets go of me and whispers, 'Heel it, now, or they'll hang ye, sure!' and I lit out. It didn't seem no good for *me* to stay—I couldn't do nothing, and I didn't want to be hung if I could get away. So I never stopped running till I found the canoe; and when I got here I told Jim to hurry, or they'd catch me and hang me yet, and said I was afeard you and the duke wasn't alive, now, and I was awful sorry, and so was Jim, and was awful glad when we see you coming, you may ask Jim if I didn't."

Jim said it was so; and the king told him to shut up, and said, "Oh, yes, it's *mighty* likely!" and shook me up again, and said he reckoned he'd drownd me. But the duke says:

"Leggo the boy, you old idiot! Would *you* a done any different? Did you inquire around for *him*, when you got loose? *I* don't remember it."

So the king let go of me, and begun to cuss that town and everybody in it. But the duke says:

"You better a blame sight give *yourself* a good cussing, for you're the one that's entitled to it most. You hain't done a thing, from the start, that had any sense in it, except coming out so cool and cheeky with that imaginary blue-arrow mark. That *was* bright —it was right down bully; and it was the thing that saved us. For if it hadn't been for that, they'd a jailed us till them Englishmen's baggage come—and then—the penitentiary, you bet! But that trick took 'em to the graveyard, and the gold done us a still bigger kindness; for if the excited fools hadn't let go all holts and made that rush to get a look, we'd a slept in our cravats to-night— cravats warranted to *wear*, too—longer than *we'd* need 'em."

They was still a minute—thinking—then the king says, kind of absent-minded like:

"Mf! And we reckoned the *niggers* stole it!"

That made me squirm!

"Yes," says the duke, kinder slow, and deliberate, and sarcastic, "*We* did."

After about a half a minute, the king drawls out:

"Leastways—*I* did."

The duke says, the same way:

"On the contrary—*I* did."

The king kind of ruffles up, and says:

"Looky here, Bilgewater, what'r you referrin' to?"

The duke says, pretty brisk:

"When it comes to that, maybe you'll let me ask, what was *you* referring to?"

"Shucks!" says the king, very sarcastic; "but *I* don't know— maybe you was asleep, and didn't know what you was about."

The duke bristles right up, now, and says:

"Oh, let *up* on this cussed nonsense—do you take me for a blame' fool? Don't you reckon *I* know who hid that money in that coffin?"

"*Yes*, sir! I know you *do* know—because you done it yourself!"

"It's a lie!"—and the duke went for him. The king sings out:

"Take y'r hands off!—leggo my throat!—I take it all back!"

The duke says:

"Well, you just own up, first, that you *did* hide that money there, intending to give me the slip one of these days, and come back and dig it up, and have it all to yourself."

"Wait jest a minute, duke—answer me this one question, honest and fair; if you didn't put the money there, say it, and I'll b'lieve you, and take back everything I said."

"You old scoundrel, I didn't, and you know I didn't. There, now!"

"Well, then, I b'lieve you. But answer me only jest this one more—now *don't* git mad; didn't you have it in your *mind* to hook the money and hide it?"

The duke never said nothing for a little bit; then he says:

"Well—I don't care if I *did*, I didn't *do* it, anyway. But you not only had it in mind to do it, but you *done* it."

"I wisht I may never die if I done it, duke, and that's honest. I won't say I warn't *goin'* to do it, because I *was*; but you—I mean somebody—got in ahead o' me."

"It's a lie! You done it, and you got to *say* you done it, or—"

The king begun to gurgle, and then he gasps out:

" 'Nough!—*I own up!*"

I was very glad to hear him say that, it made me feel much more easier than what I was feeling before. So the duke took his hands off, and says:

"If you ever deny it again, I'll drown you. It's *well* for you to set there and blubber like a baby—it's fitten for you, after the way you've acted. I never see such an old ostrich for wanting to gobble everything—and I a trusting you all the time, like you was my own father. You ought to been ashamed of yourself to stand by and hear it saddled onto a lot of poor niggers and you never say a word for 'em. It makes me feel ridiculous to think I was soft enough to *believe* that rubbage. Cuss you, I can see, now, why you was so anxious to make up the deffesit—you wanted to get what money I'd got out of the Nonesuch and one thing or another, and scoop it *all!*"

The king says, timid, and still a snuffling:

"Why, duke, it was you that said make up the deffersit, it warn't me."

"Dry up! I don't want to hear no more *out* of you!" says the duke. "And *now* you see what you *got* by it. They've got all their own money back, and all of *ourn* but a shekel or two, *besides*. G'long to bed—and don't you deffersit *me* no more deffersits, long 's *you* live!"

So the king sneaked into the wigwam, and took to his bottle for comfort; and before long the duke tackled *his* bottle; and so in about a half an hour they was as thick as thieves again, and the tighter they got, the lovinger they got; and went off a snoring in each other's arms. They both got powerful mellow, but I noticed the king didn't get mellow enough to forget to remember to not deny about hiding the money-bag again. That made me feel easy and satisfied. Of course when they got to snoring, we had a long gabble, and I told Jim everything.

Chapter XXXI

We dasn't stop again at any town, for days and days; kept right along down the river. We was down south in the warm weather, now, and a mighty long ways from home. We begun to come to trees with Spanish moss on them, hanging down from the limbs like long gray beards. It was the first I ever see it growing, and it made the woods look solemn and dismal. So now the frauds reckoned they was out of danger, and they begun to work the villages again.

First they done a lecture on temperance; but they didn't make enough for them both to get drunk on. Then in another village they started a dancing school; but they didn't know no more how to dance than a kangaroo does; so the first prance they made, the general public jumped in and pranced them out of town. Another time they tried a go at yellocution; but they didn't yellocute long till the audience got up and give them a solid good cussing and made them skip out. They tackled missionarying, and mesmerizering, and doctoring, and telling fortunes, and a little of everything; but they couldn't seem to have no luck. So at last they got just about dead broke, and laid around the raft, as she floated along, thinking, and thinking, and never saying nothing, by the half a day at a time, and dreadful blue and desperate.

And at last they took a change, and begun to lay their heads together in the wigwam and talk low and confidential two or three hours at a time. Jim and me got uneasy. We didn't like the look of it. We judged they was studying up some kind of worse deviltry than ever. We turned it over and over, and at last we made up our minds they was going to break into somebody's house or store, or was going into the counterfeit-money business, or something. So then we was pretty scared, and made up an agreement that we wouldn't have nothing in the world to do with such actions, and if we ever got the least show we would give them the cold shake, and clear out and leave them behind. Well, early one morning we hid the raft in a good safe place about two mile below a little bit of a shabby village, named Pikesville, and the king he went ashore, and told us all to stay hid whilst he went up to town and smelt around to see if anybody had got any wind of the Royal Nonesuch there yet. ("House to rob, you *mean*," says I to myself; "and when you get through robbing it you'll come back here and wonder what's become of me and Jim and the raft—and you'll have to take it out in wondering.") And he said if he warn't back by midday, the duke and me would know it was all right, and we was to come along.

So we staid where we was. The duke he fretted and sweated around, and was in a mighty sour way. He scolded us for everything, and we couldn't seem to do nothing right; he found fault with every little thing. Something was a-brewing, sure. I was good and glad when midday come and no king; we could have a change, anyway—and maybe a chance for *the* change, on top of it. So me and the duke went up to the village, and hunted around there for the king, and by-and-by we found him in the back room of a little low doggery,[5] very tight, and a lot of loafers bullyragging him for sport, and he a cussing and threatening with all his might, and so tight he couldn't walk, and couldn't do nothing to them. The duke he began to abuse him for an old fool, and the king begun to sass back; and the minute they was fairly at it, I lit out, and shook the reefs out of my hind legs, and spun down the river road like a deer—for I see our chance; and I made up my mind that it would be a long day before they ever see me and Jim again. I got down there all out of breath but loaded up with joy, and sung out—

"Set her loose, Jim, we're all right, now!"

But there warn't no answer, and nobody come out of the wigwam. Jim was gone! I set up a shout—and then another—and then another one; and run this way and that in the woods, whooping and screeching; but it warn't no use—old Jim was gone. Then I set down and cried; I couldn't help it. But I couldn't set still long. Pretty soon I went out on the road, trying to think what I better do, and I run across a boy walking, and asked him if he'd seen a strange nigger, dressed so and so, and he says:

"Yes."

"Wherebouts?" says I.

"Down to Silas Phelps's place, two mile below here. He's a runaway nigger, and they've got him. Was you looking for him?"

"You bet I ain't! I run across him in the woods about an hour or two ago, and he said if I hollered he'd cut my livers out—and told me to lay down and stay where I was; and I done it. Been there ever since; afeard to come out."

"Well," he says, "you needn't be afeard no more, becuz they've got him. He run off f'm down South, som'ers."

"It's a good job they got him."

"Well, I *reckon!* There's two hunderd dollars reward on him. It's like picking up money out'n the road."

"Yes, it is—and *I* could a had it if I'd been big enough; I see him *first.* Who nailed him?"

5. Groggery, or low-type saloon.

"It was an old fellow—a stranger—and he sold out his chance in him for forty dollars, becuz he's got to go up the river and can't wait. Think o' that, now! You bet I'd wait, if it was seven year."

"That's me, every time," says I. "But maybe his chance ain't worth no more than that, if he'll sell it so cheap. Maybe there's something ain't straight about it."

"But it *is*, though—straight as a string. I see the handbill myself. It tells all about him, to a dot—paints him like a picture, and tells the plantation he's frum, below Newr*leans*. No-siree-*bob*, they ain't no trouble 'bout *that* speculation, you bet you. Say, gimme a chaw tobacker, won't ye?"

I didn't have none, so he left. I went to the raft, and set down in the wigwam to think. But I couldn't come to nothing. I thought till I wore my head sore, but I couldn't see no way out of the trouble. After all this long journey, and after all we'd done for them scoundrels, here was it all come to nothing, everything all busted up and ruined, because they could have the heart to serve Jim such a trick as that, and make him a slave again all his life, and amongst strangers, too, for forty dirty dollars.

Once I said to myself it would be a thousand times better for Jim to be a slave at home where his family was, as long as he'd *got* to be a slave, and so I'd better write a letter to Tom Sawyer and tell him to tell Miss Watson where he was. But I soon give up that notion, for two things: she'd be mad and disgusted at his rascality and ungratefulness for leaving her, and so she'd sell him straight down the river again; and if she didn't, everybody naturally despises an ungrateful nigger, and they'd make Jim feel it all the time, and so he'd feel ornery and disgraced. And then think of *me*! It would get all around, that Huck Finn helped a nigger to get his freedom; and if I was to ever see anybody from that town again, I'd be ready to get down and lick his boots for shame. That's just the way: a person does a low-down thing, and then he don't want to take no consequences of it. Thinks as long as he can hide it, it ain't no disgrace. That was my fix exactly. The more I studied about this, the more my conscience went to grinding me, and the more wicked and low-down and ornery I got to feeling. And at last, when it hit me all of a sudden that here was the plain hand of Providence slapping me in the face and letting me know my wickedness was being watched all the time from up there in heaven, whilst I was stealing a poor old woman's nigger that hadn't ever done me no harm, and now was showing me there's One that's always on the lookout, and ain't agoing to allow no such miserable doings to go only just so fur and no further, I most dropped in my tracks I was so scared. Well, I tried the best I could to kinder soften it up somehow for myself, by saying I was brung up wicked, and so I warn't so much to blame; but something inside of me kept saying,

"There was the Sunday school, you could a gone to it; and if you'd a done it they'd a learnt you, there, that people that acts as I'd been acting about that nigger goes to everlasting fire."

It made me shiver. And I about made up my mind to pray; and see if I couldn't try to quit being the kind of a boy I was, and be better. So I kneeled down. But the words wouldn't come. Why wouldn't they? It warn't no use to try and hide it from Him. Nor from *me*, neither. I knowed very well why they wouldn't come. It was because my heart warn't right; it was because I warn't square; it[6] was because I was playing double. I was letting *on* to give up sin, but away inside of me I was holding on to the biggest one of all. I was trying to make my mouth *say* I would do the right thing and the clean thing, and go and write to that nigger's owner and tell where he was; but deep down in me I knowed it was a lie—and He knowed it. You can't pray a lie—I found that out.

So I was full of trouble, full as I could be; and didn't know what to do. At last I had an idea; and I says, I'll go and write the letter—and *then* see if I can pray. Why, it was astonishing, the way I felt as light as a feather, right straight off, and my troubles all gone. So I got a piece of paper and a pencil, all glad and excited, and set down and wrote:

Miss Watson your runaway nigger Jim is down here two mile below Pikesville and Mr. Phelps has got him and he will give him up for the reward if you send.   Huck Finn.

I felt good and all washed clean of sin for the first time I had ever felt so in my life, and I knowed I could pray now. But I didn't do it straight off, but laid the paper down and set there thinking—thinking how good it was all this happened so, and how near I come to being lost and going to hell. And went on thinking. And got to thinking over our trip down the river; and I see Jim before me, all the time, in the day, and in the night-time, sometimes moonlight, sometimes storms, and we a floating along, talking, and singing, and laughing. But somehow I couldn't seem to strike no places to harden me against him, but only the other kind. I'd see him standing my watch on top of his'n, stead of calling me, so I could go on sleeping; and see him how glad he was when I come back out of the fog; and when I come to him again in the swamp, up there where the feud was; and such-like times; and would always call me honey, and pet me, and do everything he could think of for me, and how good he always was; and at last I struck the time I saved him by telling the men we had small-pox aboard, and he was so grateful, and said I was the best friend old Jim ever had in the world, and the *only* one he's got now; and then

6. Erroneously printed "is" in 1885.

I happened to look around, and see that paper.

It was a close place. I took it up, and held it in my hand. I was a trembling, because I'd got to decide, forever, betwixt two things, and I knowed it. I studied a minute, sort of holding my breath, and then says to myself:

"All right, then, I'll go to hell"—and tore it up.

It was awful thoughts, and awful words, but they was said. And I let them stay said; and never thought no more about reforming. I shoved the whole thing out of my head; and said I would take up wickedness again, which was in my line, being brung up to it, and the other warn't. And for a starter, I would go to work and steal Jim out of slavery again; and if I could think up anything worse, I would do that, too; because as long as I was in, and in for good, I might as well go the whole hog.

Then I set to thinking over how to get at it, and turned over considerable many ways in my mind; and at last fixed up a plan that suited me. So then I took the bearings of a woody island that was down the river a piece, and as soon as it was fairly dark I crept out with my raft and went for it, and hid it there, and then turned in. I slept the night through, and got up before it was light, and had my breakfast, and put on my store clothes, and tied up some others and one thing or another in a bundle, and took the canoe and cleared for shore. I landed below where I judged was Phelps's place, and hid my bundle in the woods, and then filled up the canoe with water, and loaded rocks into her and sunk her where I could find her again when I wanted her, about a quarter of a mile below a little steam sawmill that was on the bank.

Then I struck up the road, and when I passed the mill I see a sign on it, "Phelps's Sawmill," and when I come to the farm-houses, two or three hundred yards further along, I kept my eyes peeled, but didn't see nobody around, though it was good daylight, now. But I didn't mind, because I didn't want to see nobody just yet—I only wanted to get the lay of the land. According to my plan, I was going to turn up there from the village, not from below. So I just took a look, and shoved along, straight for town. Well, the very first man I see, when I got there, was the duke. He was sticking up a bill for the Royal Nonesuch—three-night performance—like that other time. *They* had the cheek, them frauds! I was right on him, before I could shirk. He looked astonished, and says:

"Hel-*lo*! Where'd *you* come from?" Then he says, kind of glad and eager, "Where's the raft?—got her in a good place?"

I says:

"Why, that's just what I was agoing to ask your grace."

Then he didn't look so joyful—and says:

"What was your idea for asking *me*?" he says.

"Well," I says, "when I see the king in that doggery yesterday, I says to myself, we can't get him home for hours, till he's soberer; so I went a loafing around town to put in the time, and wait. A man up and offered me ten cents to help him pull a skiff over the river and back to fetch a sheep, and so I went along; but when we was dragging him to the boat, and the man left me aholt of the rope and went behind him to shove him along, he was too strong for me, and jerked loose and run, and we after him. We didn't have no dog, and so we had to chase him all over the country till we tired him out. We never got him till dark, then we fetched him over, and I started down for the raft. When I got there and see it was gone, I says to myself, 'they've got into trouble and had to leave; and. they've took my nigger, which is the only nigger I've got in the world, and now I'm in a strange country, and ain't got no property no more, nor nothing, and no way to make my living;' so I set down and cried. I slept in the woods all night. But what *did* become of the raft then?—and Jim, poor Jim!"

"Blamed if *I* know—that is, what's become of the raft. That old fool had made a trade and got forty dollars, and when we found him in the doggery the loafers had matched half dollars with him and got every cent but what he'd spent for whisky; and when I got him home late last night and found the raft gone, we said, 'That little rascal has stole our raft and shook us, and run off down the river.' "

"I wouldn't shake my *nigger*, would I?—the only nigger I had in the world, and the only property."

"We never thought of that. Fact is, I reckon we'd come to consider him *our* nigger; yes, we did consider him so—goodness knows we had trouble enough for him. So when we see the raft was gone, and we flat broke, there warn't anything for it but to try the Royal Nonesuch another shake. And I've pegged along ever since, dry as a powderhorn. Where's that ten cents? Give it here."

I had considerable money, so I give him ten cents, but begged him to spend it for something to eat, and give me some, because it was all the money I had, and I hadn't had nothing to eat since yesterday. He never said nothing. The next minute he whirls on me and says:

"Do you reckon that nigger would blow on us? We'd skin him if he done that!"

"How can he blow? Hain't he run off?"

"No! That old fool sold him, and never divided with me, and the money's gone."

"*Sold* him?" I says, and begun to cry; "why, he was *my* nigger, and that was my money. Where is he?—I want my nigger."

"Well, you can't *get* your nigger, that's all—so dry up your blubbering. Looky here—do you think *you'd* venture to blow on us? Blamed if I think I'd trust you. Why, if you *was* to blow on us—·"

He stopped, but I never see the duke look so ugly out of his eyes before. I went on a-whimpering, and says:

"I don't want to blow on nobody; and I ain't got no time to blow, nohow. I got to turn out and find my nigger."

He looked kinder bothered, and stood there with his bills fluttering on his arm, thinking, and wrinkling up his forehead. At last he says:

"I'll tell you something. We got to be here three days. If you'll promise you won't blow, and won't let the nigger blow, I'll tell you where to find him."

So I promised, and he says:

"A farmer by the name of Silas Ph——" and then he stopped. You see he started to tell me the truth; but when he stopped, that way, and begun to study and think again, I reckoned he was changing his mind. And so he was. He wouldn't trust me; he wanted to make sure of having me out of the way the whole three days. So pretty soon he says: "The man that bought him is named Abram Foster—Abram G. Foster—and he lives forty mile back here in the country, on the road to Lafayette."

"All right," I says, "I can walk it in three days. And I'll start this very afternoon."

"No you won't, you'll start *now*; and don't you lose any time about it, neither, nor do any gabbling by the way. Just keep a tight tongue in your head and move right along, and then you won't get into trouble with *us*, d'ye hear?"

That was the order I wanted, and that was the one I played for. I wanted to be left free to work my plans.

"So clear out," he says; "and you can tell' Mr. Foster whatever you want to. Maybe you can get him to believe that Jim *is* your nigger—some idiots don't require documents—leastways I've heard there's such down South here. And when you tell him the handbill and the reward's bogus, maybe he'll believe you when you explain to him what the idea was for getting 'em out. Go 'long, now, and tell him anything you want to; but mind you don't work your jaw any *between* here and there."

So I left, and struck for the back country. I didn't look around, but I kinder felt like he was watching me. But I knowed I could tire him out at that. I went straight out in the country as much as a mile, before I stopped; then I doubled back through the woods towards Phelps's. I reckoned I better start in on my plan straight off, without fooling around, because I wanted to stop Jim's mouth till these fellows could get away. I didn't want no trouble with their kind. I'd seen all I wanted to of them, and wanted to get entirely shut of them.

Chapter XXXII

When I got there it was all still and Sunday-like, and hot and sunshiny—the hands was gone to the fields; and there was them kind of faint dronings of bugs and flies in the air that makes it seem so lonesome and like everybody's dead and gone; and if a breeze fans along and quivers the leaves, it makes you feel mournful, because you feel like it's spirits whispering—spirits that's been dead ever so many years—and you always think they're talking about *you*. As a general thing it makes a body wish *he* was dead, too, and done with it all.[7]

Phelps's was one of these little one-horse cotton plantations; and they all look alike.[8] A rail fence round a two-acre yard; a stile, made out of logs sawed off and up-ended, in steps, like barrels of a different length, to climb over the fence with, and for the women to stand on when they are going to jump onto a horse; some sickly grass-patches in the big yard, but mostly it was bare and smooth, like an old hat with the nap rubbed off; big double log house for the white folks—hewed logs, with the chinks stopped up with mud or mortar, and these mud-stripes been whitewashed some time or another; round-log kitchen, with a big broad, open but roofed passage joining it to the house; log smoke-house back of the kitchen; three little log nigger-cabins in a row t'other side the smokehouse; one little hut all by itself away down against the back fence, and some outbuildings down a piece the other side; ash-hopper, and big kettle to bile soap in, by the little hut; bench by the kitchen door, with bucket of water and a gourd; hound asleep there, in the sun; more hounds asleep, round about; about three shade-trees away off in a corner; some currant bushes and gooseberry bushes in one place by the fence; outside of the fence a garden and a water-melon patch; then the cotton fields begins; and after the fields, the woods.

I went around and clumb over the back stile by the ash-hopper, and started for the kitchen. When I got a little ways, I heard the dim hum of a spinning-wheel wailing along up and sinking along down again; and then I knowed for certain I wished I was dead—for that *is* the lonesomest sound in the whole world.

I went right along, not fixing up any particular plan, but just trusting to Providence to put the right words in my mouth when the time come; for I'd noticed that Providence always did put the right words in my mouth, if I left it alone.

When I got half-way, first one hound and then another got up

7. Almost the identical phrasing of this mood appears in the beginning paragraphs of *Tom Sawyer, Detective*, published eleven years later.
8. This plantation is much like the farm of Twain's uncle, John Quarles, near Hannibal. The Phelps place becomes the major locale and Aunt Sally and Uncle Silas important characters in *Tom Sawyer, Detective*, where Huck, again the narrator, and Tom become involved in a murder.

and went for me, and of course I stopped and faced them, and kept still. And such another pow-wow as they made! In a quarter of a minute I was a kind of a hub of a wheel, as you may say—spokes made out of dogs—circle of fifteen of them packed together around me, with their necks and noses stretched up towards me, a barking and howling; and more a coming; you could see them sailing over fences and around corners from everywheres.

A nigger woman come tearing out of the kitchen with a rolling-pin in her hand, singing out, "Begone! *you* Tige! you Spot! begone, sah!" and she fetched first one and then another of them a clip and sent him howling, and then the rest followed; and the next second, half of them come back, wagging their tails around me and making friends with me. There ain't no harm in a hound, nohow.

And behind the woman comes a little nigger girl and two little nigger boys, without anything on but tow-linen shirts, and they hung onto their mother's gown, and peeped out from behind her at me, bashful, the way they always do. And here comes the white woman running from the house, about forty-five or fifty year old, bare-headed, and her spinning-stick in her hand; and behind her comes her little white children, acting the same way the little niggers was doing. She was smiling all over so she could hardly stand—and says:

"It's *you*, at last!—*ain't* it?"

I out with a "Yes'm," before I thought.

She grabbed me and hugged me tight; and then gripped me by both hands and shook and shook; and the tears come in her eyes, and run down over; and she couldn't seem to hug and shake enough, and kept saying, "You don't look as much like your mother as I reckoned you would, but law sakes, I don't care for that, I'm *so* glad to see you! Dear, dear, it does seem like I could eat you up! Children, it's your cousin Tom!—tell him howdy."

But they ducked their heads, and put their fingers in their mouths, and hid behind her. So she run on:

"Lize, hurry up and get him a hot breakfast, right away—or did you get your breakfast on the boat?"

I said I had got it on the boat. So then she started for the house, leading me by the hand, and the children tagging after. When we got there, she set me down in a split-bottomed chair, and set herself down on a little low stool in front of me, holding both of my hands, and says:

"Now I can have a *good* look at you; and laws-a-me, I've been hungry for it a many and a many a time, all these long years, and it's come at last! We been expecting you a couple of days and more. What's kep' you?—boat get aground?"

"Yes'm—she—"

"Don't say yes'm—say Aunt Sally. Where'd she get aground?"

I didn't rightly know what to say, because I didn't know whether the boat would be coming up the river or down. But I go a good deal on instinct; and my instinct said she would be coming up— from down towards Orleans. That didn't[9] help me much, though; for I didn't know the names of bars down that way. I see I'd got to invent a bar, or forget the name of the one we got aground on—or— Now I struck an idea, and fetched it out:

"It warn't the grounding—that didn't keep us back but a little. We blowed out a cylinder-head."

"Good gracious! anybody hurt?"

"No'm. Killed a nigger."

"Well, it's lucky; because sometimes people do get hurt. Two years ago last Christmas, your uncle Silas was coming up from Newrleans on the old *Lally Rook*, and she blowed out a cylinder-head and crippled a man. And I think he died afterwards. He was a Babtist. Your uncle Silas knowed a family in Baton Rouge that knowed his people very well. Yes, I remember, now he *did* die. Mortification set in, and they had to amputate him. But it didn't save him. Yes, it was mortification—that was it. He turned blue all over, and died in the hope of a glorious resurrection. They say he was a sight to look at. Your uncle's been up to the town every day to fetch you. And he's gone again, not more'n an hour ago; he'll be back any minute, now. You must a met him on the road, didn't you?—oldish man, with a—"

"No, I didn't see nobody, Aunt Sally. The boat landed just at daylight, and I left my baggage on the wharf-boat and went looking around the town and out a piece in the country, to put in the time and not get here too soon; and so I come down the back way."

"Who'd you give the baggage to?"

"Nobody."

"Why, child, it'll be stole!"

"Not where *I* hid it I reckon it won't," I says.

"How'd you get your breakfast so early on the boat?"

It was kinder thin ice, but I says:

"The captain see me standing around, and told me I better have something to eat before I went ashore; so he took me in the texas to the officers' lunch, and give me all I wanted."

I was getting so uneasy I couldn't listen good. I had my mind on the children all the time; I wanted to get them out to one side, and pump them a little, and find out who I was. But I couldn't get no show, Mrs. Phelps kept it up and run on so. Pretty soon she made the cold chills streak all down my back, because she says:

"But here we're a running on this way, and you hain't told me a word about Sis, nor any of them. Now I'll rest my works a little, and you start up yourn; just tell me *everything*—tell me all about 'm all—every one of 'm; and how they are, and what they're doing,

9. Erroneously printed "did'nt" in 1885.

and what they told you to tell me; and every last thing you can think of."

Well, I see I was up a stump—and up it good. Providence had stood by me this fur, all right, but I was hard and tight aground, now. I see it warn't a bit of use to try to go ahead—I'd *got* to throw up my hand. So I says to myself, here's another place where I got to resk the truth. I opened my mouth to begin; but she grabbed me and hustled me in behind the bed, and says:

"Here he comes! stick your head down lower—there, that'll do; you can't be seen, now. Don't you let on you're here. I'll play a joke on him. Children, don't you say a word."

I see I was in a fix, now. But it warn't no use to worry; there warn't nothing to do but just hold still, and try and be ready to stand from under when the lightning struck.

I had just one little glimpse of the old gentleman when he come in, then the bed hid him. Mrs. Phelps she jumps for him and says:

"Has he come?"

"No," says her husband.

"Good-*ness* gracious!" she says, "what in the world *can* have become of him?"

"I can't imagine," says the old gentleman; "and I must say, it makes me dreadful uneasy."

"Uneasy!" she says, "I'm ready to go distracted! He *must* a come; and you've missed him along the road. I *know* it's so—something *tells* me so."

"Why Sally, I *couldn't* miss him along the road—*you* know that."

"But oh, dear, dear, what *will* Sis say! He must a come! You must a missed him. He—"

"Oh, don't distress me any more'n I'm already distressed. I don't know what in the world to make of it. I'm at my wit's end, and I don't mind acknowledging 't I'm right down scared. But there's no hope that he's come; for he *couldn't* come and me miss him. Sally, it's terrible—just terrible—something's happened to the boat, sure!"

"Why, Silas! Look yonder!—up the road!—ain't that somebody coming?"

He sprung to the window at the head of the bed, and that give Mrs. Phelps the chance she wanted. She stooped down quick, at the foot of the bed, and give me a pull, and out I come; and when he turned back from the window, there she stood, a-beaming and a-smiling like a house afire, and I standing pretty meek and sweaty alongside. The old gentleman stared, and says:

"Why, who's that?"

"Who do you reckon 't is?"

"I haint no idea. Who *is* it?"

"It's ~~Tom Sawyer~~!"

By jings, I most slumped through the floor. But there warn't no time to swap knives; the old man grabbed me by the hand and shook, and kept on shaking; and all the time, how the woman did dance around and laugh and cry; and then how they both did fire off questions about Sid, and Mary, and the rest of the tribe.

But if they was joyful, it warn't nothing to what I was; for it was like being born again, I was so glad to find out who I was. Well, they froze to me for two hours; and at last when my chin was so tired it couldn't hardly go, any more, I had told them more about my family—I mean the Sawyer family—than ever happened to any six Sawyer families. And I explained all about how we blowed out a cylinder-head at the mouth of White River and it took us three days to fix it. Which was all right, and worked first rate; because *they* didn't know but what it would take three days to fix it. If I'd a called it a bolt-head it would a done just as well.

Now I was feeling pretty comfortable all down one side, and pretty uncomfortable all up the other. Being Tom Sawyer was easy and comfortable; and it stayed easy and comfortable till by-and-by I hear a steamboat coughing along down the river—then I says to myself, spose Tom Sawyer come down on that boat?—and spose he steps in here, any minute, and sings out my name before I can throw him a wink to keep quiet? Well, I couldn't *have* it that way—it wouldn't do at all. I must go up the road and waylay him. So I told the folks I reckoned I would go up to the town and fetch down my baggage. The old gentleman was for going along with me, but I said no, I could drive the horse myself, and I druther he wouldn't take no trouble about me.

Chapter XXXIII

So I started for town, in the wagon, and when I was half-way I see a wagon coming, and sure enough it was Tom Sawyer, and I stopped and waited till he come along. I says "Hold on!" and it stopped alongside, and his mouth opened up like a trunk, and staid so; and he swallowed two or three times like a person that's got a dry throat, and then says:

"I hain't ever done you no harm. You know that. So then, what you want to come back and ha'nt *me* for?"

I says:

"I hain't come back—I hain't been *gone*."

When he heard my voice, it righted him up some, but he warn't quite satisfied yet. He says:

"Don't you play nothing on me, because I wouldn't on you. Honest injun, now, you ain't a ghost?"

"Honest injun, I ain't," I says.

"Well—I—I—well, that ought to settle it, of course; but I can't somehow seem to understand it, no way. Looky here, warn't you ever murdered *at all?*"

"No. I warn't ever murdered at all—I played it on them. You come in here and feel of me if you don't believe me."

So he done it; and it satisfied him; and he was that glad to see me again, he didn't know what to do. And he wanted to know all about it right off; because it was a grand adventure, and mysterious, and so it hit him where he lived. But I said, leave it alone till by-and-by; and told his driver to wait, and we drove off a little piece, and I told him the kind of a fix I was in, and what did he reckon we better do? He said, let him alone a minute, and don't disturb him. So he thought and thought, and pretty soon he says:

"It's all right, I've got it. Take my trunk in your wagon, and let on it's your'n; and you turn back and fool along slow, so as to get to the house about the time you ought to; and I'll go towards town a piece, and take a fresh start, and get there a quarter or a half an hour after you; and you needn't let on to know me, at first."

I says:

"All right; but wait a minute. There's one more thing—a thing that *nobody* don't know but me. And that is, there's a nigger here that I'm a-trying to steal out of slavery—and his name is *Jim*— old Miss Watson's Jim."

He says:

"What! Why Jim is—"

He stopped and went to studying. I says:

"*I* know what you'll say. You'll say it's dirty low-down business; but what if it is?—*I'm* low down; and I'm agoing to steal him, and I want you to keep mum and not let on. Will you?"

His eye lit up, and he says:

"I'll *help* you steal him!"

Well, I let go all holts then, like I was shot. It was the most astonishing speech I ever heard—and I'm bound to say Tom Sawyer fell, considerable, in my estimation. Only I couldn't believe it. Tom Sawyer a *nigger stealer!*[1]

"Oh, shucks," I says, "you're joking."

"I ain't joking, either."

"Well, then," I says, "joking or no joking, if you hear anything said about a runaway nigger, don't forget to remember that *you* don't know nothing about him, and *I* don't know nothing about him."

Then we took the trunk and put it in my wagon, and he drove off his way, and I drove mine. But of course I forgot all about

1. While Huck has reconciled *his* attitude toward freeing Jim, his recognition that Tom represents the "respectable" and law-abiding element of his community forces him to feel that Tom loses caste by entering into the plan for Jim's escape.

driving slow, on accounts of being glad and full of thinking; so I got home a heap too quick for that length of a trip. The old gentleman was at the door, and he says:

"Why, this is wonderful. Who ever would a thought it was in that mare to do it. I wish we'd a timed her. And she hain't sweated a hair—not a hair. It's wonderful. Why, I wouldn't take a hunderd dollars for that horse now; I wouldn't, honest; and yet I'd a sold her for fifteen before, and thought 'twas all she was worth."

That's all he said. He was the innocentest, best old soul I ever see. But it warn't surprising; because he warn't only just a farmer, he was a preacher, too, and had a little one-horse log church down back of the plantation, which he built it himself at his own expense, for a church and school-house, and never charged nothing for his preaching, and it was worth it, too. There was plenty other farmer-preachers like that, and done the same way, down South.

In about half an hour Tom's wagon drove up to the front stile, and Aunt Sally she see it through the window because it was only about fifty yards, and says:

"Why, there's somebody come! I wonder who 'tis? Why, I do believe it's a stranger. Jimmy" (that's one of the children), "run and tell Lize to put on another plate for dinner."

Everybody made a rush for the front door, because, of course, a stranger don't come *every* year, and so he lays over the yaller fever, for interest, when he does come. Tom was over the stile and starting for the house; the wagon was spinning up the road for the village, and we was all bunched in the front door. Tom had his store clothes on, and an audience—and that was always nuts for Tom Sawyer. In them circumstances it warn't no trouble to him to throw in an amount of style that was suitable. He warn't a boy to meeky along up that yard like a sheep; no, he come ca'm and important, like the ram. When he got afront of us, he lifts his hat ever so gracious and dainty, like it was the lid of a box that had butterflies asleep in it and he didn't want to disturb them, and says:

"Mr. Archibald Nichols, I presume?"

"No, my boy," says the old gentleman, "I'm sorry to say 't your driver has deceived you; Nichols's place is down a matter of three mile more. Come in, come in."

Tom he took a look back over his shoulder, and says, "Too late—he's out of sight."

"Yes, he's gone, my son, and you must come in and eat your dinner with us; and then we'll hitch up and take you down to Nichols's."

"Oh, I *can't* make you so much trouble; I couldn't think of it. I'll walk—I don't mind the distance."

"But we won't *let* you walk—it wouldn't be Southern hospitality to do it. Come right in."

"Oh, *do*," says Aunt Sally; "it ain't a bit of trouble to us, not a bit in the world. You *must* stay. It's a long, dusty three mile, and we *can't* let you walk. And besides, I've already told 'em to put on another plate, when I see you coming; so you mustn't disappoint us. Come right in, and make yourself at home."

So Tom he thanked them very hearty and handsome, and let himself be persuaded, and come in; and when he was in, he said he was a stranger from Hicksville, Ohio, and his name was William Thompson—and he made another bow.

Well, he run on, and on, and on, making up stuff about Hicksville and everybody in it he could invent, and I getting a little nervous, and wondering how this was going to help me out of my scrape; and at last, still talking along, he reached over and kissed Aunt Sally right on the mouth, and then settled back again in his chair, comfortable, and was going on talking; but she jumped up and wiped it off with the back of her hand, and says:

"You owdacious puppy!"

He looked kind of hurt, and says:

"I'm surprised at you, m'am."

"You're s'rp— Why, what do you reckon I am? I've a good notion to take and—say, what do you mean by kissing me?"

He looked kind of humble, and says:

"I didn't mean nothing, m'am. I didn't mean no harm. I—I—thought you'd like it."

"Why, you born fool!" She took up the spinning-stick, and it looked like it was all she could do to keep from giving him a crack with it. "What made you think I'd like it?"

"Well, I don't know. Only, they—they—told me you would."

"*They* told you I would. Whoever told you's *another* lunatic. I never heard the beat of it. Who's *they?*"

"Why—everybody. They all said so, m'am."

It was all she could do to hold in; and her eyes snapped, and her fingers worked like she wanted to scratch him; and she says:

"Who's 'everybody?' Out with their names—or ther'll be an idiot short."

He got up and looked distressed, and fumbled his hat, and says:

"I'm sorry, and I warn't expecting it. They told me to. They all told me to. They all said kiss her; and said she'll like it. They all said it—every one of them. But I'm sorry, m'am, and I won't do it no more—I won't, honest."

"You won't, won't you? Well, I sh'd *reckon* you won't!"

"No'm, I'm honest about it; I won't ever do it again. Till you ask me."

"Till I *ask* you! Well, I never see the beat of it in my born days! I lay you'll be the Methusalem-numskull of creation before ever I ask you—or the likes of you."

"Well," he says, "it does surprise me so. I can't make it out, somehow. They said you would, and I thought you would. But—" He stopped and looked around slow, like he wished he could run across a friendly eye, somewhere's; and fetched up on the old gentleman's, and says, "Didn't *you* think she'd like me to kiss her, sir?"

"Why, no, I—I—well, no, I b'lieve I didn't."

Then he looks on around, the same way, to me—and says:

"Tom, didn't *you* think Aunt Sally 'd open out her arms and say, 'Sid Sawyer—' "

"My land!" she says, breaking in and jumping for him, "you impudent young rascal, to fool a body so—" and was going to hug him, but he fended her off, and says:

"No, not till you've asked me, first."

So she didn't lose no time, but asked him; and hugged him and kissed him, over and over again, and then turned him over to the old man, and he took what was left. And after they got a little quiet again, she says:

"Why, dear me, I never see such a surprise. We warn't looking for *you*, at all, but only Tom. Sis never wrote to me about anybody coming but him."

"It's because it warn't *intended* for any of us to come but Tom," he says; "but I begged and begged, and at the last minute she let me come, too; so, coming down the river, me and Tom thought it would be a first-rate surprise for him to come here to the house first, and for me to by-and-by tag along and drop in and let on to be a stranger. But it was a mistake, Aunt Sally. This ain't no healthy place for a stranger to come."

"No—not impudent whelps, Sid. You ought to had your jaws boxed; I hain't been so put out since I don't know when. But I don't care, I don't mind the terms—I'd be willing to stand a thousand such jokes to have you here. Well, to think of that performance! I don't deny it, I was most putrified with astonishment when you give me that smack."

We had dinner out in that broad open passage betwixt the house and the kitchen; and there was things enough on that table for seven families—and all hot, too; none of your flabby tough meat that's laid in a cupboard in a damp cellar all night and tastes like a hunk of old cold cannibal in the morning. Uncle Silas he asked a pretty long blessing over it, but it was worth it; and it didn't cool it a bit, neither, the way I've seen them kind of interruptions do, lots of times.

There was a considerable good deal of talk, all the afternoon, and me and Tom was on the lookout all the time, but it warn't no use, they didn't happen to say nothing about any runaway nigger, and we was afraid to try to work up to it. But at supper, at night, one of the little boys says:

"Pa, mayn't Tom and Sid and me go to the show?"

"No," says the old man, "I reckon there ain't going to be any; and you couldn't go if there was; because the runaway nigger told Burton and me all about that scandalous show, and Burton said he would tell the people; so I reckon they've drove the owdacious loafers out of town before this time."

So there it was!—but I couldn't help it. Tom and me was to sleep in the same room and bed; so, being tired, we bid good-night and went up to bed, right after supper, and clumb out of the window and down the lightning-rod, and shoved for the town; for I didn't believe anybody was going to give the king and the duke a hint, and so, if I didn't hurry up and give them one they'd get into trouble sure.

On the road Tom he told me all about how it was reckoned I was murdered, and how pap disappeared, pretty soon, and didn't come back no more, and what a stir there was when Jim run away; and I told Tom all about our Royal Nonesuch rapscallions, and as much of the raft-voyage as I had time to; and as we struck into the town and up through the middle of it—it was as much as half-after eight, then—here comes a raging rush of people, with torches, and an awful whooping and yelling, and banging tin pans and blowing horns; and we jumped to one side to let them go by; and as they went by, I see they had the king and the duke astraddle of a rail—that is, I knowed it *was* the king and the duke, though they was all over tar and feathers, and didn't look like nothing in the world that was human—just looked like a couple of monstrous big soldier-plumes. Well, it made me sick to see it; and I was sorry for them poor pitiful rascals, it seemed like I couldn't ever feel any hardness against them any more in the world. It was a dreadful thing to see. Human beings *can* be awful cruel to one another.

We see we was too late—couldn't do no good. We asked some stragglers about it, and they said everybody went to the show looking very innocent; and laid low and kept dark till the poor old king was in the middle of his cavortings on the stage; then somebody give a signal, and the house rose up and went for them.

So we poked along back home, and I warn't feeling so brash as I was before, but kind of ornery, and humble, and to blame, somehow—though *I* hadn't done nothing. But that's always the way; it don't make no difference whether you do right or wrong, a person's conscience ain't got no sense, and just goes for him *anyway*. If I had a yaller dog that didn't know no more than a person's conscience does, I would pison him. It takes up more room than all the rest of a person's insides, and yet ain't no good, nohow. Tom Sawyer he says the same.

Chapter XXXIV

We stopped talking, and got to thinking. By-and-by Tom says:

"Looky here, Huck, what fools we are, to not think of it before! I bet I know where Jim is."

"No! Where?"

"In that hut down by the ash-hopper. Why, looky here. When we was at dinner, didn't you see a nigger man go in there with some vittles?"

"Yes."

"What did you think the vittles was for?"

"For a dog."

"So'd I. Well, it wasn't for a dog."

"Why?"

"Because part of it was watermelon."

"So it was—I noticed it. Well, it does beat all, that I never thought about a dog not eating watermelon. It shows how a body can see and don't see at the same time."

"Well, the nigger unlocked the padlock when he went in, and he locked it again when he come out. He fetched uncle a key, about the time we got up from table—same key, I bet. Watermelon shows man, lock shows prisoner; and it ain't likely there's two prisoners on such a little plantation, and where the people's all so kind and good. Jim's the prisoner. All right—I'm glad we found it out detective fashion; I wouldn't give shucks for any other way. Now you work your mind and study out a plan to steal Jim, and I will study out one, too; and we'll take the one we like the best."

What a head for just a boy to have! If I had Tom Sawyer's head, I wouldn't trade it off to be a duke, nor mate of a steamboat, nor clown in a circus, nor nothing I can think of. I went to thinking out a plan, but only just to be doing something; I knowed very well where the right plan was going to come from. Pretty soon, Tom says:

"Ready?"

"Yes," I says.

"All right—bring it out."

"My plan is this," I says. "We can easy find out if it's Jim in there. Then get up my canoe to-morrow night, and fetch my raft over from the island. Then the first dark night that comes, steal the key out of the old man's britches, after he goes to bed, and shove off down the river on the raft, with Jim, hiding daytimes and running nights, the way me and Jim used to do before. Wouldn't that plan work?"

"*Work?* Why cert'nly, it would work, like rats a fighting. But it's too blame' simple; there ain't nothing *to* it. What's the good of a plan that ain't no more trouble than that? It's as mild as goose-milk. Why, Huck, it wouldn't make no more talk than breaking into a soap factory."

I never said nothing, because I warn't expecting nothing different; but I knowed mighty well that whenever he got *his* plan ready it wouldn't have none of them objections to it.

And it didn't. He told me what it was, and I see in a minute it was worth fifteen of mine, for style, and would make Jim just as free a man as mine would, and maybe get us all killed besides. So I was satisfied, and said we would waltz in on it. I needn't tell what it was, here, because I knowed it wouldn't stay the way it was. I knowed he would be changing it around, every which way, as we went along, and heaving in new bullinesses wherever he got a chance. And that is what he done.

Well, one thing was dead sure; and that was, that Tom Sawyer was in earnest and was actuly going to help steal that nigger out of slavery. That was the thing that was too many for me. Here was a boy that was respectable, and well brung up; and had a character to lose; and folks at home that had characters; and he was bright and not leather-headed; and knowing and not ignorant; and not mean, but kind; and yet here he was, without any more pride, or rightness, or feeling, than to stoop to this business, and make himself a shame, and his family a shame, before everybody. I *couldn't* understand it, no way at all. It was outrageous, and I knowed I ought to just up and tell him so; and so be his true friend, and let him quit the thing right where he was, and save himself. And I *did* start to tell him; but he shut me up, and says:

"Don't you reckon I know what I'm about? Don't I generly know what I'm about?"

"Yes."

"Didn't I *say* I was going to help steal the nigger?"

"Yes."

"*Well* then."

That's all he said, and that's all I said. It warn't no use to say any more; because when he said he'd do a thing, he always done it. But *I* couldn't make out how he was willing to go into this thing; so I just let it go, and never bothered no more about it. If he was bound to have it so, *I* couldn't help it.

When we got home, the house was all dark and still; so we went on down to the hut by the ash-hopper, for to examine it. We went through the yard, so as to see what the hounds would do. They knowed us, and didn't make no more noise than country dogs is always doing when anything comes by in the night. When we got to the cabin, we took a look at the front and the two sides; and on the side I warn't acquainted with—which was the north side—we found a square window-hole, up tolerable high, with just one stout board nailed across it. I says:

"Here's the ticket. This hole's big enough for Jim to get through, if we wrench off the board."

Tom says:

"It's as simple as tit-tat-toe, three-in-a-row, and as easy as playing hooky. I should *hope* we can find a way that's a little more complicated than *that*, Huck Finn."

"Well then," I says, "how'll it do to saw him out, the way I done before I was murdered, that time?"

"That's more *like*," he says. "It's real mysterious, and troublesome, and good," he says; "but I bet we can find a way that's twice as long. There ain't no hurry; le's keep on looking around."

Betwixt the hut and the fence, on the back side, was a lean-to, that joined the hut at the eaves, and was made out of plank. It was as long as the hut, but narrow—only about six foot wide. The door to it was at the south end, and was padlocked. Tom he went to the soap kettle, and searched around and fetched back the iron thing they lift the lid with; so he took it and prized out one of the staples. The chain fell down, and we opened the door and went in, and shut it, and struck a match, and see the shed was only built against the cabin and hadn't no connection with it; and there warn't no floor to the shed, nor nothing in it but some old rusty played-out hoes, and spades, and picks, and a crippled plow. The match went out, and so did we, and shoved in the staple again, and the door was locked as good as ever. Tom was joyful. He says:

"Now we're all right. We'll *dig* him out. It'll take about a week!"

Then we started for the house, and I went in the back door—you only have to pull a buckskin latch-string, they don't fasten the doors—but that warn't romantical enough for Tom Sawyer: no way would do him but he must climb up the lightning-rod. But after he got up half-way about three times, and missed fire and fell every time, and the last time most busted his brains out, he thought he'd got to give it up; but after he was rested, he allowed he would give her one more turn for luck, and this time he made the trip.

In the morning we was up at break of day, and down to the nigger cabins to pet the dogs and make friends with the nigger that fed Jim—if it *was* Jim that was being fed. The niggers was just getting through breakfast and starting for the fields; and Jim's nigger was piling up a tin pan with bread and meat and things; and whilst the others was leaving, the key come from the house.

This nigger had a good-natured, chuckle-headed face, and his wool was all tied up in little bunches with thread. That was to keep witches off. He said the witches was pestering him awful, these nights, and making him see all kinds of strange things, and hear all kinds of strange words and noises, and he didn't believe he was ever witched so long, before, in his life. He got so worked up, and got to running[2] on so about his troubles, he forgot all about what he'd been agoing to do. So Tom says:

"What's the vittles for? Going to feed the dogs?"

The nigger kind of smiled around graduly over his face, like when you heave a brickbat in a mud puddle, and he says:

"Yes, Mars Sid, *a* dog. Cur'us dog, too. Does you want to go en look at 'im?"

"Yes."

I hunched Tom, and whispers:

"You going, right here in the day-break? *That* warn't the plan."

"No, it warn't—but it's the plan *now*."

So, drat him, we went along, but I didn't like it much. When we got in, we couldn't hardly see anything, it was so dark; but Jim was there, sure enough, and could see us; and he sings out:

"Why, *Huck!* En good *lan'!* ain' dat Misto Tom?"

I just knowed how it would be; I just expected it. *I* didn't know nothing to do; and if I had, I couldn't a done it; because that nigger busted in and says:

"Why, de gracious sakes! do he know you genlmen?"

We could see pretty well, now. Tom he looked at the nigger, steady and kind of wondering, and says:

"Does *who* know us?"

"Why, dish-yer runaway nigger."

"I don't reckon he does; but what put that into your head?"

"What *put* it dar? Didn' he jis' dis minute sing out like he knowed you?"

Tom says, in a puzzled-up kind of way:

"Well, that's mighty curious. *Who* sung out? *When* did he sing out. *What* did he sing out?" And turns to me, perfectly ca'm, and says, "Did *you* hear anybody sing out?"

Of course there warn't nothing to be said but the one thing; so I says:

"No; *I* ain't heard nobody say nothing."

Then he turns to Jim, and looks him over like he never see him before; and says:

"Did you sing out?"

"No, sah," says Jim; "*I* hain't said nothing, sah."

"Not a word?"

"No, sah, I hain't said a word."

"Did you ever see us before?"

"No, sah; not as *I* knows on."

2. Erroneously printed "runinng" in the first edition.

So Tom turns to the nigger, which was looking wild and distressed, and says, kind of severe:

"What do you reckon's the matter with you, anyway? What made you think somebody sung out?"

"Oh, it's de dad-blame' witches, sah, en I wisht I was dead, I do. Dey's awluz at it, sah, en dey do mos' kill me, dey sk'yers me so. Please to don't tell nobody 'bout it sah, er ole Mars Silas he'll scole me; 'kase he say dey *ain't* no witches. I jis' wish to goodness he was heah now—*den* what would he say! I jis' bet he couldn' fine no way to git aroun' it *dis* time. But it's awluz jis' so; people dat's *sot*, stays sot; dey won't look into nothn' en fine it out f'r deyselves, en when *you* fine it out en tell um 'bout it, dey doan' b'lieve you."

Tom give him a dime, and said we wouldn't tell nobody; and told him to buy some more thread to tie up his wool with; and then looks at Jim, and says:

"I wonder if Uncle Silas is going to hang this nigger. If I was to catch a nigger that was ungrateful enough to run away, *I* wouldn't give him up, I'd hang him." And whilst the nigger stepped to the door to look at the dime and bite it to see if it was good, he whispers to Jim, and says:

"Don't ever let on to know us. And if you hear any digging going on nights, it's us: we're going to set you free."

Jim only had time to grab us by the hand and squeeze it, then the nigger come back, and we said we'd come again some time if the nigger wanted us to; and he said he would, more particular if it was dark, because the witches went for him mostly in the dark, and it was good to have folks around then.

Chapter XXXV

It would be most an hour, yet, till breakfast, so we left, and struck down into the woods; because Tom said we got to have *some* light to see how to dig by, and a lantern makes too much, and might get us into trouble; what we must have was a lot of them rotten chunks that's called fox-fire[3] and just makes a soft kind of a glow when you lay them in a dark place. We fetched an armful and hid it in the weeds, and set down to rest, and Tom says, kind of dissatisfied:

"Blame it, this whole thing is just as easy and awkard as it can be. And so it makes it so rotten difficult to get up a difficult plan. There ain't no watchman to be drugged—now there *ought* to be a watchman. There ain't even a dog to give a sleeping-mixture to. And there's Jim chained by one leg, with a ten-foot chain, to the leg of his bed: why, all you got to do is to lift up the bedstead and

3. Phosphorescent glow from decaying wood.

slip off the chain. And Uncle Silas he trusts everybody; sends the key to the punkin-headed nigger, and don't send nobody to watch the nigger. Jim could a got out of that window hole before this, only there wouldn't be no use trying to travel with a ten-foot chain on his leg. Why, drat it, Huck, it's the stupidest arrangement I ever see. You got to invent *all* the difficulties. Well, we can't help it, we got to do the best we can with the materials we've got. Anyhow, there's one thing—there's more honor in getting him out through a lot of difficulties and dangers, where there warn't one of them furnished to you by the people who it was their duty to furnish them, and you had to contrive them all out of your own head. Now look at just that one thing of the lantern. When you come down to the cold facts, we simply got to *let on* that a lantern's resky. Why, we could work with a torchlight procession if we wanted to, *I* believe. Now, whilst I think of it, we got to hunt up something to make a saw out of, the first chance we get."

"What do we want of a saw?"

"What do we *want* of it? Hain't we got to saw the leg of Jim's bed off, so as to get the chain loose?"

"Why, you just said a body could lift up the bedstead and slip the chain off."

"Well, if that ain't just like you, Huck Finn. You *can* get up the infant-schooliest ways of going at a thing. Why, hain't you ever read any books at all?—Baron Trenck,[4] nor Casanova, nor Benvenuto Chelleeny, nor Henri IV., nor none of them heroes? Whoever heard of getting a prisoner loose in such an old-maidy way as that? No; the way all the best authorities does, is to saw the bedleg in two, and leave it just so, and swallow the sawdust, so it can't be found, and put some dirt and grease around the sawed place so the very keenest seneskal can't see no sign of it's being sawed, and thinks the bed-leg is perfectly sound. Then, the night you're ready, fetch the leg a kick, down she goes; slip off your chain, and there you are. Nothing to do but hitch your rope-ladder to the battlements, shin down it, break your leg in the moat—because a rope-ladder is nineteen foot too short, you know—and there's your horses and your trusty vassles, and they scoop you up and fling you across a saddle and away you go, to your native Langudoc, or Navarre, or wherever it is. It's gaudy, Huck. I wish there was a moat to this cabin. If we get time, the night of the escape, we'll dig one."

I says:

"What do we want of a moat, when we're going to snake him out from under the cabin?"

---

4. All four of these—Baron Friedrich von Trenck, officer of Frederick the Great's staff; Benvenuto Cellini, the brilliant and politically-minded sculptor; Giacomo Girolamo Casanova, the famous Italian lover and adventurer; and King Henry IV of France—made daring attempted or successful escapes. "Langudoc," below, is Tom's pronunciation of Languedoc.

But he never heard me. He had forgot me and everything else. He had his chin in his hand, thinking. Pretty soon, he sighs, and shakes his head; then sighs again, and says:

"No, it wouldn't do—there ain't necessity enough for it."

"For what?" I says.

"Why, to saw Jim's leg off," he says.

"Good land!" I says, "why, there ain't *no* necessity for it. And what would you want to saw his leg off for, anyway?"

"Well, some of the best authorities has done it. They couldn't get the chain off, so they just cut their hand off, and shoved. And a leg would be better still. But we got to let that go. There ain't necessity enough in this case; and besides, Jim's a nigger and wouldn't understand the reasons for it, and how it's the custom in Europe; so we'll let it go. But there's one thing—he can have a rope-ladder; we can tear up our sheets and make him a rope-ladder easy enough. And we can send it to him in a pie; it's mostly done that way. And I've et worse pies."

"Why, Tom Sawyer, how you talk," I says; "Jim ain't got no use for a rope-ladder."

"He *has* got use for it. How *you* talk, you better say; you don't know nothing about it. He's *got* to have a rope ladder; they all do."

"What in the nation can he *do* with it?"

"*Do* with it? He can hide it in his bed, can't he? That's what they all do; and *he's* got to, too. Huck, you don't ever seem to want to do anything that's regular; you want to be starting something fresh all the time. Spose he *don't* do nothing with it? ain't it there in his bed, for a clew, after he's gone? and don't you reckon they'll want clews? Of course they will. And you wouldn't leave them any? That would be a *pretty* howdy-do, *wouldn't* it! I never heard of such a thing."

"Well," I says, "if it's in the regulations, and he's got to have it, all right, let him have it; because I don't wish to go back on no regulations; but there's one thing, Tom Sawyer—if we go to tearing up our sheets to make Jim a rope-ladder, we're going to get into trouble with Aunt Sally, just as sure as you're born. Now, the way I look at it, a hickry-bark ladder don't cost nothing, and don't waste nothing, and is just as good to load up a pie with, and hide in a straw tick, as any rag ladder you can start; and as for Jim, he ain't had no experience, and so *he* don't care what kind of a—"

"Oh, shucks, Huck Finn, if I was as ignorant as you, I'd keep still—that's what *I'd* do. Who ever heard of a state prisoner escaping by a hickry-bark ladder? Why, it's perfectly ridiculous."

"Well, all right, Tom, fix it your own way; but if you'll take my advice, you'll let me borrow a sheet off of the clothes-line."

He said that would do. And that give him another idea, and he says:

"Borrow a shirt, too."

"What do we want of a shirt, Tom?"

"Want it for Jim to keep a journal on."

"Journal your granny—*Jim* can't write."

"Spose he *can't* write—he can make marks on the shirt, can't he, if we make him a pen out of an old pewter spoon or a piece of an old iron barrel-hoop?"

"Why, Tom, we can pull a feather out of a goose and make him a better one; and quicker, too."

"*Prisoners* don't have geese running around the donjon-keep to pull pens out of, you muggins. They *always* make their pens out of the hardest, toughest, troublesomest piece of old brass candlestick or something like that they can get their hands on; and it takes them weeks and weeks, and months and months to file it out, too, because they've got to do it by rubbing it on the wall. *They* wouldn't use a goose-quill if they had it. It ain't regular."

"Well, then, what'll we make him the ink out of?"

"Many makes it out of iron-rust and tears; but that's the common sort and women; the best authorities uses their own blood. Jim can do that; and when he wants to send any little common ordinary mysterious message to let the world know where he's captivated, he can write it on the bottom of a tin plate with a fork and throw it out of the window. The Iron Mask[5] always done that, and it's a blame' good way, too."

"Jim ain't got no tin plates. They feed him in a pan."

"That aint' anything; we can get him some."

"Can't nobody *read* his plates."

"That ain't got nothing to *do* with it, Huck Finn. All *he's* got to do is to write on the plate and throw it out. You don't *have* to be able to read it. Why, half the time you can't read anything a prisoner writes on a tin plate, or anywhere else."

"Well, then, what's the sense in wasting the plates?"

"Why, blame it all, it ain't the *prisoner's* plates."

"But it's *somebody's* plates, ain't it?"

"Well, spos'n it is? What does the *prisoner* care whose—"

He broke off there, because we heard the breakfast-horn blowing. So we cleared out for the house.

Along during that morning I borrowed a sheet and a white shirt off of the clothes-line; and I found an old sack and put them in it, and we went down and got the fox-fire, and put that in too. I called it borrowing, because that was what pap always called it; but Tom said it warn't borrowing, it was stealing. He said we was representing prisoners; and prisoners don't care how they get a thing so they get it, and nobody don't blame them for it, either. It ain't no

5. Another source of Tom's romantic maunderings: the subject of Alexandre Dumas' novel *Vicomte de Bragelonne,* the mysterious masked prisoner who died unknown in the Bastille in 1703.

crime in a prisoner to steal the thing he needs to get away with, Tom said; it's his right; and so, as long as we was representing a prisoner, we had a perfect right to steal anything on this place we had the least use for, to get ourselves out of prison with. He said if we warn't prisoners it would be a very different thing, and nobody but a mean ornery person would steal when he warn't a prisoner. So we allowed we would steal everything there was that come handy. And yet he made a mighty fuss, one day, after that, when I stole a watermelon out of the nigger patch and eat it; and he made me go and give the niggers a dime, without telling them what it was for. Tom said that what he meant was, we could steal anything we *needed*. Well, I says, I needed the watermelon. But he said I didn't need it to get out of prison with, there's where the difference was. He said if I'd a wanted it to hide a knife in, and smuggle it to Jim to kill the seneskal with, it would a been all right. So I let it go at that, though I couldn't see no advantage in my representing a prisoner, if I got to set down and chaw over a lot of gold-leaf distinctions like that, every time I see a chance to hog a watermelon.

Well, as I was saying, we waited that morning till everybody was settled down to business, and nobody in sight around the yard; then Tom he carried the sack into the lean-to whilst I stood off a piece to keep watch. By-and-by he come out, and we went and set down on the wood-pile, to talk. He says:

"Everything's all right, now, except tools; and that's easy fixed."

"Tools?" I says.

"Yes."

"Tools for what?"

"Why, to dig with. We ain't agoing to *gnaw* him out, are we?"

"Ain't them old crippled picks and things in there good enough to dig a nigger out with?" I says.

He turns on me looking pitying enough to make a body cry, and says:

"Huck Finn, did you *ever* hear of a prisoner having picks and shovels, and all the modern conveniences in his wardrobe to dig himself out with? Now I want to ask you—if you got any reasonableness in you at all—what kind of a show would *that* give him to be a hero? Why, they might as well lend him the key, and done with it. Picks and shovels—why they wouldn't furnish 'em to a king."

"Well, then," I says, "if we don't want the picks and shovels, what do we want?"

"A couple of case-knives."

"To dig the foundations out from under that cabin with?"

"Yes."

"Confound it, it's foolish, Tom."

"It don't make no difference how foolish it is, it's the *right* way —and it's the regular way. And there ain't no *other* way, that ever *I* heard of, and I've read all the books that gives any information about these things. They always dig out with a case-knife—and not through dirt, mind you; generly it's through solid rock. And it takes them weeks and weeks and weeks, and for ever and ever. Why, look at one of them prisoners in the bottom dungeon of the Castle Deef, in the harbor of Marseilles, that dug himself out that way; how long was *he* at it, you reckon?"[6]

"I don't know."

"Well, guess."

"I don't know. A month and a half?"

"*Thirty-seven year*—and he come out in China. *That's* the kind. I wish the bottom of *this* fortress was solid rock."

"*Jim* don't know nobody in China."

"What's *that* got to do with it? Neither did that other fellow. But you're always a-wandering off on a side issue. Why can't you stick to the main point?"

"All right—*I* don't care where he comes out, so he *comes* out; and Jim don't, either, I reckon. But there's one thing, anyway— Jim's too old to be dug out with a case-knife. He won't last."

"Yes he will *last*, too. You don't reckon it's going to take thirty- seven years to dig out through a *dirt* foundation, do you?"

"How long will it take, Tom?"

"Well, we can't resk being as long as we ought to, because it mayn't take very long for Uncle Silas to hear from down there by New Orleans. He'll hear Jim ain't from there. Then his next move will be to advertise Jim, or something like that. So we can't resk being as long digging him out as we ought to. By rights I reckon we ought to be a couple of years; but we can't. Things being so uncertain, what I recommend is this: that we really dig right in, as quick as we can; and after that, we can *let on*, to ourselves, that we was at it thirty-seven years. Then we can snatch him out and rush him away the first time there's an alarm. Yes, I reckon that'll be the best way."

"Now, there's *sense* in that," I says. "Letting on don't cost noth- ing; letting on ain't no trouble; and if it's any object, I don't mind letting on we was at it a hundred and fifty year. It wouldn't strain me none, after I got my hand in. So I'll mosey along now, and smouch a couple of case-knives."

"Smouch three," he says; "we want one to make a saw out of."

"Tom, if it ain't unregular and irreligious to sejest it," I says, "there's an old rusty saw-blade around yonder sticking under the weatherboarding behind the smoke-house."

6. The Dumas influence on Tom again—this time, the hero of *The Count of Monte Cristo* at the Chateau d'If.

He looked kind of weary and discouraged-like, and says:

"It ain't no use to try to learn you nothing, Huck. Run along and smouch the knives—three of them." So I done it.

Chapter XXXVI

As soon as we reckoned everybody was asleep, that night, we went down the lightning-rod, and shut ourselves up in the lean-to, and got out our pile of fox-fire, and went to work. We cleared everything out of the way, about four or five foot along the middle of the bottom log. Tom said he was right behind Jim's bed now, and we'd dig in under it, and when we got through there couldn't nobody in the cabin ever know was any hole there, because Jim's counterpin hung down most to the ground, and you'd have to raise it up and look under to see the hole. So we dug and dug, with the case-knives, till most midnight; and then we was dog-tired, and our hands was blistered, and yet you couldn't see we'd done anything, hardly. At last I says:

"This ain't no thirty-seven year job, this is a thirty-eight year job, Tom Sawyer."

He never said nothing. But he sighed, and pretty soon he stopped digging, and then for a good little while I knowed he was thinking. Then he says:

"It ain't no use, Huck, it ain't agoing to work. If we was prisoners it would, because then we'd have as many years as we wanted, and no hurry; and we wouldn't get but a few minutes to dig, every day, while they was changing watches, and so our hands wouldn't get blistered, and we could keep it up right along, year in and year out, and do it right, and the way it ought to be done. But *we* can't fool along, we got to rush; we ain't got no time to spare. If we was to put in another night this way, we'd have to knock off for a week to let our hands get well—couldn't touch a case-knife with them sooner."

"Well, then, what we going to do, Tom?"

"I'll tell you. It ain't right, and it ain't moral, and I wouldn't like it to get out—but there ain't only just the one way; we got to dig him out with the picks, and *let on* its's case-knives."

"*Now* you're *talking!*" I says; "your head gets leveler and leveler all the time, Tom Sawyer," I says. "Picks is the thing, moral or no moral; and as for me, I don't care shucks for the morality of it, nohow. When I start in to steal a nigger, or a watermelon, or a Sunday-school book, I ain't no ways particular how it's done so it's done. What I want is my nigger; or what I want is my watermelon; or what I want is my Sunday-school book; and if a pick's the handiest thing, that's the thing I'm agoing to dig that nigger or that watermelon or that Sunday-school book out with; and I don't give a dead rat what the authorities thinks about it nuther."

"Well," he says, "there's excuse for picks and letting-on in a case like this; if it warn't so, I wouldn't approve of it, nor I wouldn't stand by and see the rules broke—because right is right, and wrong is wrong, and a body ain't got no business doing wrong when he ain't ignorant and knows better. It might answer for *you* to dig Jim out with a pick, *without* any letting-on, because you don't know no better; but it wouldn't for me, because I do know better. Gimme a case-knife."

He had his own by him, but I handed him mine. He flung it down, and says:

"Gimme a *case-knife*."

I didn't know just what to do—but then I thought. I scratched around amongst the old tools, and got a pick-ax and give it to him, and he took it and went to work, and never said a word.

He was always just that particular. Full of principle.

So then I got a shovel, and then we picked and shoveled, turn about, and made the fur fly. We stuck to it about a half an hour, which was as long as we could stand up; but we had a good deal of a hole to show for it. When I got up stairs, I looked out at the window and see Tom doing his level best with the lightning-rod, but he couldn't come it, his hands was so sore. At last he says:

"It ain't no use, it can't be done. What you reckon I better do? Can't you think up no way?"

"Yes," I says, "but I reckon it ain't regular. Come up the stairs, and let on it's a lightning-rod."

So he done it.

Next day Tom stole a pewter spoon and a brass candlestick in the house, for to make some pens for Jim out of, and six tallow candles; and I hung around the nigger cabins, and laid for a chance, and stole three tin plates. Tom said it wasn't enough; but I said nobody wouldn't ever see the plates that Jim throwed out, because they'd fall in the dog-fennel and jimpson weeds under the window-hole—then we could tote them back and he could use them over again. So Tom was satisfied. Then he says:

"Now, the thing to study out is, how to get the things to Jim."

"Take them in through the hole," I says, "when we get it done."

He only just looked scornful, and said something about nobody ever heard of such an idiotic idea, and then he went to studying. By-and-by he said he had ciphered out two or three ways, but there warn't no need to decide on any of them yet. Said we'd got to post Jim first.

That night we went down the lightning-rod a little after ten, and took one of the candles along, and listened under the window-hole, and heard Jim snoring; so we pitched it in, and it didn't wake him. Then we whirled in with the pick and shovel, and in about two hours and a half the job was done. We crept in under Jim's bed and into the cabin, and pawed around and found the candle and lit it, and stood over Jim a while, and found him looking hearty and healthy, and then we woke him up gentle and gradual. He was so glad to see us he most cried; and called us honey, and all the pet names he could think of; and was for having us hunt up a cold chisel to cut the chain off of his leg with, right away, and clearing out without losing any time. But Tom he showed him how unregular it would be, and set down and told him all about our plans, and how we could alter them in a minute any time there was an alarm; and not to be the least afraid, because we would see he got away, *sure*. So Jim he said it was all right, and we set there and talked over old times a while, and then Tom asked a lot of questions, and when Jim told him Uncle Silas come in every day or two to pray with him, and Aunt Sally come in to see if he was comfortable and had plenty to eat, and both of them was kind as they could be, Tom says:

"*Now* I know how to fix it. We'll send you some things by them."

I said, "Don't do nothing of the kind; it's one of the most jackass ideas I ever struck;" but he never paid no attention to me; went right on. It was his way when he'd got his plans set.

So he told Jim how we'd have to smuggle in the rope-ladder pie, and other large things, by Nat, the nigger that fed him, and he must be on the lookout, and not be surprised, and not let Nat see him open them; and we would put small things in uncle's coat pockets and he must steal them out; and we would tie things to aunt's apron strings or put them in her apron pocket, if we got a chance; and told him what they would be and what they was for. And told him how to keep a journal on the shirt with his blood, and all that. He told him everything. Jim he couldn't see no sense in the most of it, but he allowed we was white folks and knowed better than him; so he was satisfied, and said he would do it all just as Tom said.

Jim had plenty corn-cob pipes and tobacco; so we had a right down good sociable time; then we crawled out through the hole, and so home to bed, with hands that looked like they'd been chawed. Tom was in high spirits. He said it was the best fun he ever had in his life, and the most intellectural; and said if he only could see his way to it we would keep it up all the rest of our lives and leave Jim to our children to get out; for he believed Jim would come to like it better and better the more he got used to it. He said that in that way it could be strung out to as much as eighty year, and would be the best time on record. And he said it would make us all celebrated that had a hand in it.

In the morning we went out to the wood-pile and chopped up the brass candlestick into handy sizes, and Tom put them and the pewter spoon in his pocket. Then we went to the nigger cabins, and while I got Nat's notice off, Tom shoved a piece of candlestick into the middle of a corn-pone that was in Jim's pan, and we went along with Nat to see how it would work, and it just worked noble; when Jim bit into it it most mashed all his teeth out; and there warn't ever anything could a worked better. Tom said so himself. Jim he never let on but what it was only just a piece of rock or something like that that's always getting into bread, you know; but after that he never bit into nothing but what he jabbed his fork into it in three or four places, first.

And whilst we was a standing there in the dimmish light, here comes a couple of the hounds bulging in, from under Jim's bed; and they kept on piling in till there was eleven of them, and there warn't hardly room in there to get your breath. By jings, we forgot to fasten that lean-to door. The nigger Nat he only just hollered "witches!" once, and keeled over onto the floor amongst the dogs, and begun to groan like he was dying. Tom jerked the door open and flung out a slab of Jim's meat, and the dogs went for it, and in two seconds he was out himself and back again and shut the door, and I knowed he'd fixed the other door too. Then he went to work on the nigger, coaxing him and petting him, and asking him if he'd been imagining he saw something again. He raised up, and blinked his eyes around, and says:

"Mars Sid, you'll say I's a fool, but if I didn't b'lieve I see most a million dogs, er devils, er some'n, I wisht I may die right heah in dese tracks. I did, mos' sholy. Mars Sid, I *felt* um—I *felt* um, sah; dey was all over me. Dad fetch it, I jis' wisht I could git my han's on one er dem witches jis' wunst—on'y jis' wunst—it's all I'd ast. But mos'ly I wisht dey'd lemme 'lone, I does."

Tom says:

"Well, I tell you what *I* think. What makes them come here just at this runaway nigger's breakfast-time? It's because they're hungry; that's the reason. You make them a witch pie; that's the thing for *you* to do."

"But my lan', Mars Sid, how's *I* gwyne to make 'm a witch pie? I doan' know how to make it. I hain't ever hearn er sich a thing b'fo.'"

"Well, then, I'll have to make it myself."

"Will you do it, honey?—will you? I'll wusshup de groun' und' yo' foot, I will!"

"All right, I'll do it, seeing it's you, and you've been good to us and showed us the runaway nigger. But you got to be mighty careful. When we come around, you turn your back; and then whatever we've put in the pan, don't you let on you see it at all. And don't you look, when Jim unloads the pan—something might happen, I don't know what. And above all, don't you *handle* the witch-things."

"*Hannel* 'm Mars Sid? What *is* you a talkin' 'bout? I wouldn' lay de weight er my finger on um, not f'r ten hund'd thous'n' billion dollars, I wouldn't."

Chapter XXXVII

That was all fixed. So then we went away and went to the rubbage-pile in the back yard where they keep the old boots, and rags, and pieces of bottles, and wore-out tin things, and all such truck, and scratched around and found an old tin washpan and stopped up the holes as well as we could, to bake the pie in, and took it down cellar and stole it full of flour, and started for breakfast and found a couple of shingle-nails that Tom said would be handy for a prisoner to scrabble his name and sorrows on the dungeon walls with, and dropped one of them in Aunt Sally's apron pocket which was hanging on a chair, and t'other we stuck in the band of Uncle Silas's hat, which was on the bureau, because we heard the children say their pa and ma was going to the runaway nigger's house this morning, and then went to breakfast, and Tom dropped the pewter spoon in Uncle Silas's coat pocket, and Aunt Sally wasn't come yet, so we had to wait a little while.

And when she come she was hot, and red, and cross, and couldn't hardly wait for the blessing; and then she went to sluicing out coffee with one hand and cracking the handiest child's head with her thimble with the other, and says:

"I've hunted high, and I've hunted low, and it does beat all, what *has* become of your other shirt."

My heart fell down amongst my lungs and livers and things, and a hard piece of corn-crust started down my throat after it and got met on the road with a cough and was shot across the table and took one of the children in the eye and curled him up like a fishing-worm, and let a cry out of him the size of a war-whoop, and Tom he turned kinder blue around the gills, and it all amounted to a considerable state of things for about a quarter of a minute or as much as that, and I would a sold out for half price if there was a bidder. But after that we was all right again—it was the sudden surprise of it that knocked us so kind of cold. Uncle Silas he says:

"It's most uncommon curious, I can't understand it. I know perfectly well I took it *off*, because——"

"Because you hain't got but one *on*. Just *listen* at the man! I know you took it off, and know it by a better way than your wool-gethering memory, too, because it was on the clo'es-line yester-day—I see it there myself. But it's gone—that's the long and the short of it, and you'll just have to change to a red flann'l one till

I can get time to make a new one. And it'll be the third I've made in two years; it just keeps a body on the jump to keep you in shirts; and whatever you do manage to *do* with 'm all, is more'n I can make out. A body'd think you *would* learn to take some sort of care of 'em, at your time of life."

"I know it, Sally, and I do try all I can. But it oughtn't to be altogether my fault, because you know I don't see them nor have nothing to do with them except when they're on me; and I don't believe I've ever lost one of them *off* of me."

"Well, it ain't *your* fault if you haven't, Silas—you'd a done it if you could, I reckon. And the shirt ain't all that's gone, nuther. Ther's a spoon gone; and *that* ain't all. There was ten, and now ther's only nine. The calf got the shirt I reckon, but the calf never took the spoon, *that's* certain."

"Why, what else is gone, Sally?"

"Ther's six *candles* gone—that's what. The rats could a got the candles, and I reckon they did; I wonder they don't walk off with the whole place, the way you're always going to stop their holes and don't do it; and if they warn't fools they'd sleep in your hair, Silas—*you'd* never find it out; but you can't lay the *spoon* on the rats, and that I *know*."

"Well, Sally, I'm in fault, and I acknowledge it; I've been remiss; but I won't let to-morrow go by without stopping up them holes."

"Oh, I wouldn't hurry, next year'll do. Matilda Angelina Araminta *Phelps!*"

Whack comes the thimble, and the child snatches her claws out of the sugar-bowl without fooling around any. Just then, the nigger woman steps onto the passage, and says:

"Missus, dey's a sheet gone."

"A *sheet* gone! Well, for the land's sake!"

"I'll stop up them holes *to-day*," says Uncle Silas, looking sorrowful.

"Oh, *do* shet up!—spose the rats took the *sheet?* *Where's* it gone, Lize?"

"Clah to goodness I hain't no notion, Miss Sally. She wuz on de clo's-line yistiddy, but she done gone; she ain' dah no mo', now."

"I reckon the world *is* coming to an end. I *never* see the beat of it, in all my born days. A shirt, and a sheet, and a spoon, and six can—"

"Missus," comes a young yaller wench, "dey's a brass cannel-stick miss'n."

"Cler out from here, you hussy, er I'll take a skillet to ye!"

Well, she was just a biling. I begun to lay for a chance; I reckoned I would sneak out and go for the woods till the weather moderated. She kept a raging right along, running her insurrection all by herself, and everybody else mighty meek and quiet; and at last Uncle Silas, looking kind of foolish, fishes up that spoon out of his pocket. She stopped, with her mouth open and her hands up; and as for me, I wished I was in Jeruslem or somewheres. But not long; because she says:

"It's *just* as I expected. So you had it in your pocket all the time; and like as not you've got the other things there, too. How'd it get there?"

"I reely don't know, Sally," he says, kind of apologizing, "or you know I would tell. I was a-studying over my text in Acts Seventeen, before breakfast, and I reckon I put it in there, not noticing, meaning to put my Testament in, and it must be so, because my Testament ain't in, but I'll go and see, and if the Testament is where I had it, I'll know I didn't put it in, and that will show that I laid the Testament down and took up the spoon, and——"

"Oh, for the land's sake! Give a body a rest! Go 'long now, the whole kit and biling of ye; and don't come nigh me again till I've got back my peace of mind."

I'd a heard her, if she'd a said it to herself, let alone speaking it out; and I'd a got up and obeyed her, if I'd a been dead. As we was passing through the setting-room, the old man he took up his hat, and the shingle-nail fell out on the floor, and he just merely picked it up and laid it on the mantel-shelf, and never said nothing, and went out. Tom see him do it, and remembered about the spoon, and says:

"Well, it ain't no use to send things by *him* no more, he ain't reliable." Then he says: "But he done us a good turn with the spoon, anyway, without knowing it, and so we'll go and do him one without *him* knowing it—stop up his rat-holes."

There was a noble good lot of them, down cellar, and it took us a whole hour, but we done the job tight and good, and ship-shape. Then we heard steps on the stairs, and blowed out our light, and hid; and here comes the old man, with a candle in one hand and a bundle of stuff in t'other, looking as absent-minded as year before last. He went a mooning around, first to one rat-hole and then another, till he'd been to them all. Then he stood about five minutes, picking tallow-drip off of his candle and thinking. Then he turns off slow and dreamy towards the stairs, saying:

"Well, for the life of me I can't remember when I done it. I could show her now that I warn't to blame on account of the rats. But never mind—let it go. I reckon it wouldn't do no good."

And so he went on a mumbling up stairs, and then we left. He was a mighty nice old man. And always is.

Tom was a good deal bothered about what to do for a spoon, but he said we'd got to have it; so he took a think. When he had ciphered it out, he told me how we was to do; then we went and waited around the spoon-basket till we see Aunt Sally coming, and then Tom went to counting the spoons and laying them out to one side, and I slid one of them up my sleeve, and Tom says:

"Why, Aunt Sally, there ain't but nine spoons, *yet*."

She says:

"Go 'long to your play, and don't bother me. I know better, I counted 'm myself."

"Well, I've counted them twice, Aunty, and I can't make but nine."

She looked out of all patience, but of course she come to count —anybody would.

"I declare to gracious ther' *ain't* but nine!" she says. "Why, what in the world—plague *take* the things, I'll count 'm again."

So I slipped back the one I had, and when she got done counting, she says:

"Hang the troublesome rubbage, ther's *ten*, now!" and she looked huffy and bothered both. But Tom says:

"Why, Aunty, I don't think there's ten."

"You numskull, didn't you see me *count* 'm?"

"I know, but—"

"Well, I'll count 'm *again*."

So I smouched one, and they come out nine same as the other time. Well, she *was* in a tearing way—just a trembling all over, she was so mad. But she counted and counted, till she got that addled she'd start to count-in the *basket* for a spoon, sometimes; and so, three times they come out right, and three times they come out wrong. Then she grabbed up the basket and slammed it across the house and knocked the cat galley-west; and she said cle'r out and let her have some peace, and if we come bothering around her again betwixt that and dinner, she'd skin us. So we had the odd spoon; and dropped it in her apron pocket whilst she was a giving us our sailing-orders, and Jim got it all right, along with her shingle-nail, before noon. We was very well satisfied with this business, and Tom allowed it was worth twice the trouble it took, because he said *now* she couldn't ever count them spoons twice alike again to save her life; and wouldn't believe she'd counted them right, if she *did*; and said that after she'd about counted her head off, for the next three days, he judged she'd give it up and offer to kill anybody that wanted her to ever count them any more.

So we put the sheet back on the line, that night, and stole one out of her closet; and kept on putting it back and stealing it again, for a couple of days, till she didn't know how many sheets she had, any more, and said she didn't *care*, and warn't agoing to bullyrag the rest of her soul out about it, and wouldn't count them again not to save her life, she druther die first.

So we was all right now, as to the shirt and the sheet and the spoon and the candles, by the help of the calf and the rats and the mixed-up counting; and as to the candlestick, it warn't no consequence, it would blow over by-and-by.

But that pie was a job; we had no end of trouble with that pie. We fixed it up away down in the woods, and cooked it there; and we got it done at last, and very satisfactory, too; but not all in one day; and we had to use up three washpans full of flour, before we got through, and we got burnt pretty much all over, in places, and eyes put out with the smoke; because, you see, we didn't want nothing but a crust, and we couldn't prop it up right, and she would always cave in. But of course we thought of the right way at last; which was to cook the ladder, too, in the pie. So then we laid in with Jim, the second night, and tore up the sheet all in little strings, and twisted them together, and long before daylight we had a lovely rope, that you could a hung a person with. We let on it took nine months to make it.

And in the forenoon we took it down to the woods, but it wouldn't go in the pie. Being made of a whole sheet, that way, there was rope enough for forty pies, if we'd a wanted them, and plenty left over for soup, or sausage, or anything you choose. We could a had a whole dinner.

But we didn't need it. All we needed was just enough for the pie, and so we throwed the rest away. We didn't cook none of the pies in the washpan, afraid the solder would melt; but Uncle Silas he had a noble brass warming-pan which he thought considerable of, because it belonged to one of his ancestors with a long wooden handle that come over from England with William the Conqueror in the *Mayflower* or one of them early ships and was hid away up garret with a lot of other old pots and things that was valuable, not on acount of being any account because they warn't, but on account of them being relicts, you know, and we snaked her out, private, and took her down there, but she failed on the first pies, because we didn't know how, but she come up smiling on the last one. We took and lined her with dough, and set her in the coals, and loaded her up with rag-rope, and put on a dough roof, and shut down the lid, and put hot embers on top, and stood off five foot, with the long handle, cool and comfortable, and in fifteen minutes she turned out a pie that was a satisfaction to look at. But the person that et it would want to fetch a couple of kags of toothpicks along, for if that rope-ladder wouldn't cramp him down to business, I don't know nothing what I'm talking about, and lay him in enough stomach-ache to last him till next time, too.

Nat didn't look, when we put the witch-pie in Jim's pan; and

we put the three tin plates in the bottom of the pan under the
vittles; and so Jim got everything all right, and as soon as he was
by himself he busted into the pie and hid the rope-ladder inside
of his straw tick, and scratched some marks on a tin plate and
throwed it out of the window-hole.

Chapter XXXVIII

Making them pens was a distressid-tough job, and so was the
saw; and Jim allowed the inscription was going to be the toughest
of all. That's the one which the prisoner has to scrabble on the
wall. But we had to have it; Tom said we'd *got* to; there warn't no
case of a state prisoner not scrabbling his inscription to leave behind, and his coat of arms.

"Look at Lady Jane Grey," he says; "look at Gilford Dudley;
look at old Northumberland! Why, Huck, spose it *is* considerable
trouble?—what you going to do?—how you going to get around it?
Jim's *got* to do his inscription and coat of arms. They all do."

Jim says:

"Why, Mars Tom, I hain't got no coat o' arms; I hain't got
nuffn but dish-yer ole shirt, en you knows I got to keep de journal
on dat."

"Oh, you don't understand, Jim; a coat of arms is very different."

"Well," I says, "Jim's right, anyway, when he says he hain't got
no coat of arms, because he hain't."

"I reckon *I* knowed that," Tom says, "but you bet he'll have
one before he goes out of this—because he's going out *right*, and
there ain't going to be no flaws in his record."

So whilst me and Jim filed away at the pens on a brickbat apiece,
Jim a making his'n out of the brass and I making mine out of the
spoon, Tom set to work to think out the coat of arms. By-and-by
he said he'd struck so many good ones he didn't hardly know which
to take, but there was one which he reckoned he'd decide on. He
says:

"On the scutcheon we'll have a bend *or* in the dexter base, a
saltire *murrey* in the fess, with a dog, couchant, for common
charge, and under his foot a chain embattled, for slavery, with a
chevron *vert* in a chief engrailed, and three invected lines on a
field *azure*, with the nombril points rampant on a dancette in-
dented; crest, a runaway nigger, *sable*, with his bundle over his
shoulder on a bar sinister: and a couple of gules for supporters,
which is you and me; motto, *Maggiore fretta, minore atto*. Got it
out of a book—means, the more haste, the less speed."

"Geewhillikins," I says, "but what does the rest of it mean?"

"We ain't got no time to bother over that," he says, "we got
to dig in like all git-out."

"Well, anyway," I says, "what's *some* of it? What's a fess?"

"A fess—a fess is—*you* don't need to know what a fess is. I'll show him how to make it when he gets to it."

"Shucks, Tom," I says, "I think you might tell a person. What's a bar sinister?"

"Oh, *I* don't know. But he's got to have it. All the nobility does."

That was just his way. If it didn't suit him to explain a thing to you, he wouldn't do it. You might pump at him a week, it wouldn't make no difference.

He'd got all that coat of arms business fixed, so now he started in to finish up the rest of that part of the work, which was to plan out a mournful inscription—said Jim got to have one, like they all done. He made up a lot, and wrote them out on a paper, and read them off, so:

1. *Here a captive heart busted.*

2. *Here a poor prisoner, forsook by the world and friends, fretted out his sorrowful life.*

3. *Here a lonely heart broke, and a worn spirit went to its rest, after thirty-seven years of solitary captivity.*

4. *Here, homeless and friendless, after thirty-seven years of bitter captivity, perished a noble stranger, natural son of Louis XIV.*

Tom's voice trembled, whilst he was reading them, and he most broke down. When he got done, he couldn't no way make up his mind which one for Jim to scrabble onto the wall, they was all so good; but at last he allowed he would let him scrabble them all on. Jim said it would take him a year to scrabble such a lot of truck onto the logs with a nail, and he didn't know how to make letters, besides; but Tom said he would block them out for him, and then he wouldn't have nothing to do but just follow the lines. Then pretty soon he says:

"Come to think, the logs ain't agoing to do; they don't have log walls in a dungeon: we got to dig the inscriptions into a rock. We'll fetch a rock."

Jim said the rock was worse than the logs; he said it would take him such a pison long time to dig them into a rock, he wouldn't ever get out. But Tom said he would let me help him do it. Then he took a look to see how me and Jim was getting along with the pens. It was most pesky tedious hard work and slow, and didn't give my hands no show to get well of the sores, and we didn't seem to make no headway, hardly. So Tom says:

"I know how to fix it. We got to have a rock for the coat of arms and mournful inscriptions, and we can kill two birds with that same rock. There's a gaudy big grindstone down at the mill, and we'll smouch it, and carve the things on it, and file out the pens and the saw on it, too."

It warn't no slouch of an idea; and it warn't no slouch of a grindstone nuther; but we allowed we'd tackle it. It warn't quite midnight, yet, so we cleared out for the mill, leaving Jim at work. We smouched the grindstone, and set out to roll her home, but it was a most nation tough job. Sometimes, do what we could, we couldn't keep her from falling over, and she come mighty near mashing us, every time. Tom said she was going to get one of us, sure, before we got through. We got her half way; and then we was plumbed played out, and most drownded with sweat. We see it warn't no use, we got to go and fetch Jim. So he raised up his bed and slid the chain off of the bed-leg, and wrapt it round and round his neck, and we crawled out through our hole and down there, and Jim and me laid into that grindstone and walked her along like nothing;[7] and Tom superintended. He could out-superintend any boy I ever see. He knowed how to do everything.

Our hole was pretty big, but it warn't big enough to get the grindstone through; but Jim he took the pick and soon made it big enough. Then Tom marked out them things on it with the nail, and set Jim to work on them, with the nail for a chisel and an iron bolt from the rubbage in the lean-to for a hammer, and told him to work till the rest of his candle quit on him, and then he could go to bed, and hide the grindstone under his straw tick and sleep on it. Then we helped him fix his chain back on the bed-leg, and was ready for bed ourselves. But Tom thought of something, and says:

"You got any spiders in here, Jim?"

"No, sah, thanks to goodness I hain't, Mars Tom."

"All right, we'll get you some."

"But bless you, honey, I doan' *want* none. I's afeard un um. I jis' 's soon have rattlesnakes aroun'."

Tom thought a minute or two, and says:

"It's a good idea. And I reckon it's been done. It *must* a been done; it stands to reason. Yes, it's a prime good idea. Where could you keep it?"

"Keep what, Mars Tom?"

"Why, a rattlesnake."

"De goodness gracious alive, Mars Tom! Why, if dey was a rattlesnake to come in heah, I'd take en bust right out thoo dat log wall, I would, wid my head."

"Why, Jim, you wouldn't be afraid of it, after a little. You could

7. In these concluding chapters, the persistent horseplay may seem a cruelty toward Jim; yet here, as before, he participates in familiar antics with boys whom he trusts, although actually he could easily have escaped. The author, in this relaxed mood, employs the extravagance of comic statement and situation traditional with the frontier tall tale, but at the highest level of human understanding.

tame it."

"*Tame* it!"

"Yes—easy enough. Every animal is grateful for kindness and petting, and they wouldn't *think* of hurting a person that pets them. Any book will tell you that. You try—that's all I ask; just try for two or three days. Why, you can get him so, in a little while, that he'll love you; and sleep with you; and won't stay away from you a minute; and will let you wrap him round your neck and put his head in your mouth."

"*Please*, Mars Tom—*doan'* talk so! I can't *stan'* it! He'd *let* me shove his head in my mouf—fer a favor, hain't it? I lay he'd wait a pow'ful long time 'fo' I *ast* him. En mo' en dat, I doan' *want* him to sleep wid me."

"Jim, don't act so foolish. A prisoner's *got* to have some kind of a dumb pet, and if a rattlesnake hain't ever been tried, why, there's more glory to be gained in your being the first to ever try it than any other way you could ever think of to save your life."

"Why, Mars Tom, I doan' *want* no sich glory. Snake take 'n bite Jim's chin off, den *whah* is de glory? No, sah, I doan' want no sich doin's."

"Blame it, can't you *try*? I only *want* you to try—you needn't keep it up if it don't work."

"But de trouble all *done*, ef de snake bite me while I's a tryin' him. Mars Tom, I's willin' to tackle mos' anything 'at ain't on-reasonable, but ef you en Huck fetches a rattlesnake in heah for me to tame, I's gwyne to *leave*, dat's *shore*."

"Well, then, let it go, let it go, if you're so bullheaded about it. We can get you some garter-snakes and you can tie some buttons on their tails, and let on they're rattlesnakes, and I reckon that'll have to do."

"I k'n stan' *dem*, Mars Tom, but blame' 'f I couldn' get along widout um, I tell you dat. I never knowed b'fo', 't was so much bother and trouble to be a prisoner."

"Well, it *always* is, when it's done right. You got any rats around here?"

"No, sah, I hain't seed none."

"Well, we'll get you some rats."

"Why, Mars Tom, I doan' *want* no rats. Dey's de dad-blamedest creturs to sturb a body, en rustle roun' over 'im, en bite his feet, when he's tryin' to sleep, I ever see. No, sah, gimme g'yarter-snakes, 'f I's got to have 'm, but doan' gimme no rats, I ain' got no use f'r um, skasely."

"But Jim, you *got* to have 'em—they all do. So don't make no more fuss about it. Prisoners ain't ever without rats. There ain't no instance of it. And they train them, and pet them, and learn them tricks, and they get to be as sociables as flies. But you got to play music to them. You got anything to play music on?"

"I ain't got nuffn but a coase comb en a piece o' paper, en a juice-harp; but I reck'n dey wouldn' take no stock in a juice-harp."

"Yes they would. *They* don't care what kind of music 'tis. A jews-harp's plenty good enough for a rat. All animals likes music— in a prison they dote on it. Specially, painful music; and you can't get no other kind out of a jews-harp. It always interests them; they come out to see what's the matter with you. Yes, you're all right; you're fixed very well. You want to set on your bed, nights, before you go to sleep, and early in the mornings, and play your jews-harp; play The Last Link is Broken—that's the thing that'll scoop a rat, quicker'n anything else: and when you've played about two minutes, you'll see all the rats, and the snakes, and spiders, and things begin to feel worried about you, and come. And they'll just fairly swarm over you, and have a noble good time."

"Yes, *dey* will, I reck'n, Mars Tom, but what kine er time is *Jim* havin'? Blest if I kin see de pint. But I'll do it ef I got to. I reck'n I better keep de animals satisfied, en not have no trouble in de house."

Tom waited to think over, and see if there wasn't nothing else; and pretty soon he says:

"Oh—there's one thing I forgot. Could you raise a flower here, do you reckon?"

"I doan' know but maybe I could, Mars Tom; but it's tolable dark in heah, en I ain' got no use f'r no flower, nohow, en she'd be a pow'ful sight o' trouble."

"Well, you try it, anyway. Some other prisoners has done it."

"One er dem big cat-tail-lookin' mullen-stalks would grow in heah, Mars Tom, I reck'n, but she wouldn' be wuth half de trouble she'd coss."

"Don't you believe it. We'll fetch you a little one, and you plant it in the corner, over there, and raise it. And don't call it mullen, call it Pitchiola—that's its right name, when it's in a prison.[8] And you want to water it with your tears."

"Why, I got plenty spring water, Mars Tom."

"You don't *want* spring water; you want to water it with your tears. It's the way they always do."

"Why, Mars Tom, I lay I kin raise one er dem mullen-stalks twyste wid spring water whiles another man's a *start'n* one wid tears."

"That ain't the idea. You *got* to do it with tears."

"She'll die on my han's, Mars Tom, she sholy will; kase I doan' skasely ever cry."

So Tom was stumped. But he studied it over, and then said Jim would have to worry along the best he could with an onion. He

8. In J. X. Boniface's *Picciola* (1836) a plant sustains a noble prisoner.

promised he would go to the nigger cabins and drop one, private, in Jim's coffee-pot, in the morning. Jim said he would "jis' 's soon have tobacker in his coffee;" and found so much fault with it, and with the work and bother of raising the mullen, and jews-harping the rats, and petting and flattering up the snakes and spiders and things, on top of all the other work he had to do on pens, and inscriptions, and journals, and things, which made it more trouble and worry and responsibility to be a prisoner than anything he ever undertook, that Tom most lost all patience with him; and said he was just loadened down with more gaudier chances than a prisoner ever had in the world to make a name for himself, and yet he didn't know enough to appreciate them, and they was just about wasted on him. So Jim he was sorry, and said he wouldn't behave so no more, and then me and Tom shoved for bed.

Chapter XXXIX

In the morning we went up to the village and bought a wire rat trap and fetched it down, and unstopped the best rat hole, and in about an hour we had fifteen of the bulliest kind of ones; and then we took it and put it in a safe place under Aunt Sally's bed. But while we was gone for spiders, little Thomas Franklin Benjamin Jefferson Elexander Phelps found it there, and opened the door of it to see if the rats would come out, and they did; and Aunt Sally she come in, and when we got back she was a standing on top of the bed raising Cain, and the rats was doing what they could to keep off the dull times for her. So she took and dusted us both with the hickry, and we was as much as two hours catching another fifteen or sixteen, drat that meddlesome cub, and they warn't the likeliest, nuther, because the first haul was the pick of the flock. I never see a likelier lot of rats than what that first haul was.

We got a splendid stock of sorted spiders, and bugs, and frogs, and caterpillars, and one thing or another; and we like-to got a hornet's nest, but we didn't. The family was at home. We didn't give it right up, but staid with them as long as we could; because we allowed we'd tire them out or they'd got to tire us out, and they done it. Then we got allycumpain and rubbed on the places, and was pretty near all right again, but couldn't set down convenient. And so we went for the snakes, and grabbed a couple of dozen garters and house-snakes, and put them in a bag, and put it in our room, and by that time it was supper time, and a rattling good honest day's work; and hungry?—oh, no, I reckon not! And there warn't a blessed snake up there, when we went back—we didn't half tie the sack, and they worked out, somehow, and left. But it didn't matter much, because they was still on the premises somewheres. So we judged we could get some of them again. No, there warn't no real scarcity of snakes about the house for a considerable spell. You'd see them dripping from the rafters and places, every now and then; and they generly landed in your plate, or down the back of your neck, and most of the time where you didn't want them. Well, they was handsome, and striped, and there warn't no harm in a million of them; but that never made no difference to Aunt Sally, she despised snakes, be the breed what they might, and she couldn't stand them no way you could fix it; and every time one of them flopped down on her, it didn't make no difference what she was doing, she would just lay that work down and light out. I never see such a woman. And you could hear her whoop to Jericho. You couldn't get her to take aholt of one of them with the tongs. And if she turned over and found one in bed, she would scramble out and lift a howl that you would think the house was afire. She disturbed the old man so, that he said he could most wish there hadn't ever been no snakes created. Why, after every last snake had been gone clear out of the house for as much as a week, Aunt Sally warn't over it yet; she warn't near over it; when she was setting thinking about something, you could touch her on the back of her neck with a feather and she would jump right out of her stockings. It was very curious. But Tom said all women was just so. He said they was made that way; for some reason or other.

We got a licking every time one of our snakes come in her way; and she allowed these lickings warn't nothing to what she would do if we ever loaded up the place again with them. I didn't mind the lickings, because they didn't amount to nothing; but I minded the trouble we had, to lay in another lot. But we got them laid in, and all the other things; and you never see a cabin as blithesome as Jim's was when they'd all swarm out for music and go for him. Jim didn't like the spiders, and the spiders didn't like Jim; and so they'd lay for him and make it mighty warm for him. And he said that between the rats, and the snakes, and the grindstone, there warn't no room in bed for him, skasely; and when there was, a body couldn't sleep, it was so lively, and it was always lively, he said, because *they* never all slept at one time, but took turn about, so when the snakes was asleep the rats was on deck, and when the rats turned in the snakes come on watch, so he always had one gang under him, in his way, and t'other gang having a circus over him, and if he got up to hunt a new place, the spiders would take a chance at him as he crossed over. He said if he ever got out, this time, he wouldn't ever be a prisoner again, not for a salary.

Well, by the end of three weeks, everything was in pretty good shape. The shirt was sent in early, in a pie, and every time a rat bit Jim he would get up and write a little in his journal whilst the ink was fresh; the pens was made, the inscriptions and so on was all carved on the grindstone; the bed-leg was sawed in two, and we had et up the sawdust, and it give us a most amazing stomach-ache. We reckoned we was all going to die, but didn't. It was the most undigestible sawdust I ever see; and Tom said the same. But as I was saying, we'd got all the work done, now, at last; and we was all pretty much fagged out, too, but mainly Jim. The old man had wrote a couple of times to the plantation below Orleans tc come and get their runaway nigger, but hadn't got no answer, be-cause there warn't no such plantation; so he allowed he would ad-vertise Jim in the St. Louis and New Orleans papers; and when he mentioned the St. Louis ones, it give me the cold shivers, and I see we hadn't no time to lose. So Tom said, now for the nonnamous letters.

"What's them?" I says.

"Warnings to the people that something is up. Sometimes it's done one way, sometimes another. But there's always somebody spying around, that gives notice to the governor of the castle. When Louis XVI was going to light out of the Tooleries, a servant girl done it. It's a very good way, and so is the nonnamous letters. We'll use them both. And it's usual for the prisoner's mother to change clothes with him, and she stays in, and he slides out in her clothes. We'll do that too."

"But looky here, Tom, what do we want to *warn* anybody for, that something's up? Let them find it out for themselves—it's their lookout."

"Yes, I know; but you can't depend on them. It's the way they've acted from the very start—left us to do *everything*. They're so con-fiding and mullet-headed they don't take notice of nothing at all. So if we don't *give* them notice, there won't be nobody nor noth-ing to interfere with us, and so after all our hard work and trouble this escape 'll go off perfectly flat: won't amount to nothing—won't be nothing *to* it."

"Well, as for me, Tom, that's the way I'd like."

"Shucks," he says, and looked disgusted. So I says:

"But I ain't going to make no complaint. Anyway that suits you suits me. What you going to do about the servant-girl?"

"You'll be her. You slide in, in the middle of the night, and hook that yaller girl's frock."

"Why, Tom, that'll make trouble next morning; because of course she prob'bly hain't got any but that one."

"I know; but you don't want it but fifteen minutes, to carry the nonnamous letter and shove it under the front door."

"All right, then, I'll do it; but I could carry it just as handy in my own togs."

"You wouldn't look like a servant-girl *then*, would you?"

"No, but there won't be nobody to see what I look like, *any-*

way."

"That ain't got nothing to do with it. The thing for us to do, is just to do our *duty*, and not worry about whether anybody *sees* us do it or not. Hain't you got no principle at all?"

"All right, I ain't saying nothing; I'm the servant-girl. Who's Jim's mother?"

"I'm his mother. I'll hook a gown from Aunt Sally."

"Well, then, you'll have to stay in the cabin when me and Jim leaves."

"Not much. I'll stuff Jim's clothes full of straw and lay it on his bed to represent his mother in disguise, and Jim 'll take Aunt Sally's[9] gown off of me and wear it, and we'll all evade together. When a prisoner of style escapes, it's called an evasion. It's always called so when a king escapes, f'rinstance. And the same with a king's son; it don't make no difference whether he's a natural one or an unnatural one."

So Tom he wrote the nonamous letter, and I smouched the yaller wench's frock, that night, and put it on, and shoved it under the front door, the way Tom told me to. It said:

Beware. Trouble is brewing. Keep a sharp lookout.
UNKNOWN FRIEND.

Next night we stuck a picture which Tom drawed in blood, of a skull and crossbones, on the front door; and next night another one of a coffin, on the back door. I never see a family in such a sweat. They couldn't a been worse scared if the place had a been full of ghosts laying for them behind everything and under the beds and shivering through the air. If a door banged, Aunt Sally she jumped, and said "ouch!" if anything fell, she jumped and said "ouch!" if you happened to touch her, when she warn't noticing, she done the same; she couldn't face noway and be satisfied, because she allowed there was something behind her every time—so she was always a whirling around, sudden, and saying "ouch," and before she'd get two-thirds around, she'd whirl back again, and say it again; and she was afraid to go to bed, but she dasn't set up. So the thing was working very well, Tom said; he said he never see a thing work more satisfactory. He said it showed it was done right.

So he said, now for the grand bulge! So the very next morning at the streak of dawn we got another letter ready, and was wondering what we better do with it, because we heard them say at supper they was going to have a nigger on watch at both doors all night. Tom he went down the lightning-rod to spy around; and the nigger at the back door was asleep, and he stuck it in the back of his neck and come back. This letter said:

9. The original edition and standard editions based on it erroneously read "the nigger woman's gown."

Don't betray me, I wish to be your friend. There is a desprate gang of cutthroats from over in the Ingean Territory[1] going to steal your runaway nigger to-night, and they have been trying to scare you so as you will stay in the house and not bother them. I am one of the gang, but have got relligion and wish to quit it and lead a honest life again, and will betray the helish design. They will sneak down from northards, along the fence, at midnight exact, with a false key, and go in the nigger's cabin to get him. I am to be off a piece and blow a tin horn if I see any danger; but stead of that, I will BA *like a sheep soon as they get in and not blow at all; then whilst they are getting his chains loose, you slip there and lock them in, and can kill them at your leasure. Don't do anything but just the way I am telling you, if you do they will suspicion something and raise whoopjamboreehoo. I do not wish any reward but to know I have done the right thing.*

UNKNOWN FRIEND.

Chapter XL

We was feeling pretty good, after breakfast, and took my canoe and went over the river a fishing, with a lunch, and had a good time, and took a look at the raft and found her all right, and got home late to supper, and found them in such a sweat and worry they didn't know which end they was standing on, and made us go right off to bed the minute we was done supper, and wouldn't tell us what the trouble was, and never let on a word about the new letter, but didn't need to, because we knowed as much about it as anybody did, and as soon as we was half up stairs and her back was turned, we slid for the cellar cubboard and loaded up a good lunch and took it up to our room and went to bed, and got up about half-past eleven, and Tom put on Aunt Sally's dress that he stole and was going to start with the lunch, but says:

"Where's the butter?"

"I laid out a hunk of it," I says, "on a piece of a corn-pone."

"Well, you *left* it laid out, then—it ain't here."

"We can get along without it," I says.

"We can get along *with* it, too," he says; "just you slide down cellar and fetch it. And then mosey right down the lightning-rod and come along. I'll go and stuff the straw into Jim's clothes to represent his mother in disguise, and be ready to *ba* like a sheep and shove soon as you get there."

So out he went, and down cellar went I. The hunk of butter, big as a person's fist, was where I had left it, so I took up the slab of corn-pone with it on, and blowed out my light, and started up

1. Oklahoma, the Indian federal land grant which became also a refuge for gunmen and lawbreakers.

stairs, very stealthy, and got up to the main floor all right, but here comes Aunt Sally with a candle, and I clapped the truck in my hat, and clapped my hat on my head, and the next second she see me; and she says:

"You been down cellar?"

"Yes'm."

"What you been doing down there?"

"Noth'n."

"*Noth'n!*"

"No'm."

"Well, then, what possessed you to go down there, this time of night?"

"I don't know'm."

"You don't *know?* Don't answer me that way, Tom, I want to know what you been *doing* down there?"

"I hain't been doing a single thing, Aunt Sally, I hope to gracious if I have."

I reckoned she'd let me go, now, and as a generl thing she would; but I spose there was so many strange things going on she was just in a sweat about every little thing that warn't yard-stick straight; so she says, very decided:

"You just march into that setting-room and stay there till I come. You been up to something you no business to, and I lay I'll find out what it is before *I'm* done with you."

So she went away as I opened the door and walked into the setting-room. My, but there was a crowd there! Fifteen farmers, and every one of them had a gun. I was most powerful sick, and slunk to a chair and set down. They was setting around, some of them talking a little, in a low voice, and all of them fidgety and uneasy, but trying to look like they warn't; but I knowed they was, because they was always taking off their hats, and putting them on, and scratching their heads, and changing their seats, and fumbling with their buttons. I warn't easy myself, but I didn't take my hat off, all the same.

I did wish Aunt Sally would come, and get done with me, and lick me, if she wanted to, and let me get away and tell Tom how we'd overdone this thing, and what a thundering hornet's nest we'd got ourselves into, so we could stop fooling around, straight off, and clear out with Jim before these rips got out of patience and come for us.

At last she come, and begun to ask me questions, but I *couldn't* answer them straight, I didn't know which end of me was up; because these men was in such a fidget now, that some was wanting to start right *now* and lay for them desperadoes, and saying it warn't but a few minutes to midnight; and others was trying to get them to hold on and wait for the sheep-signal; and here was aunty

pegging away at the questions, and me a shaking all over and ready
to sink down in my tracks I was that scared; and the place getting
hotter and hotter, and the butter beginning to melt and run down
my neck and behind my ears: and pretty soon, when one of them
says, "*I'm* for going and getting in the cabin *first*, and right *now*,
and catching them when they come," I most dropped; and a streak
of butter come a trickling down my forehead, and Aunt Sally she
see it, and turns white as a sheet, and says:

"For the land's sake what *is* the matter with the child!—he's got
the brain fever as shore as you're born, and they're oozing out!"

And everybody runs to see, and she snatches off my hat, and
out comes the bread, and what was left of the butter, and she
grabbed me, and hugged me, and says:

"Oh, what a turn you did give me! and how glad and grateful I
am it ain't no worse; for luck's against us, and it never rains but it
pours, and when I see that truck I thought we'd lost you, for I
knowed by the color and all, it was just like your brains would be
if— Dear, dear, whyd'nt you *tell* me that was what you'd been
down there for, *I* wouldn't a cared. Now cler out to bed, and don't
lemme see no more of you till morning!"

I was up stairs in a second, and down the lightning-rod in another one, and shinning through the dark for the lean-to. I
couldn't hardly get my words out, I was so anxious; but I told Tom
as quick as I could, we must jump for it, now, and not a minute
to lose—the house full of men, yonder, with guns!

His eyes just blazed; and he says:

"No!—is that so? *Ain't* it bully! Why, Huck, if it was to do over
again, I bet I could fetch two hundred! If we could put it off
till—"

"Hurry! *hurry!*" I says. "Where's Jim?"

"Right at your elbow; if you reach out your arm you can touch
him. He's dressed, and everything's ready. Now we'll slide out and
give the sheep-signal."

But then we heard the tramp of men, coming to the door, and
heard them begin to fumble with the padlock; and heard a man
say:

"I *told* you we'd be too soon; they haven't come—the door is
locked. Here, I'll lock some of you into the cabin and you lay for
'em in the dark and kill 'em when they come; and the rest scatter
around a piece, and listen if you can hear 'em coming."

So in they come, but couldn't see us in the dark, and most trod
on us whilst we was hustling to get under the bed. But we got
under all right, and out through the hole, swift but soft—Jim first,
me next, and Tom last, which was according to Tom's orders. Now
we was in the lean-to, and heard trampings close by outside. So
we crept to the door, and Tom stopped us there and put his eye

to the crack, but couldn't make out nothing, it was so dark; and whispered and said he would listen for the steps to get further, and when he nudged us Jim must glide out first, and him last. So he set his ear to the crack and listened, and listened, and listened, and the steps a scraping around, out there, all the time; and at last he nudged us, and we slid out, and stooped down, not breathing, and not makin the least noise, and slipped stealthy towards the fence, in Injun file, and got to it, all right, and me and Jim over it; but Tom's britches catched fast on a splinter on the top rail, and then he hear the steps coming, so he had to pull loose, which snapped the splinter and made a noise; and as he dropped in our tracks and started, somebody sings out:

"Who's that? Answer, or I'll shoot!"

But we didn't answer; we just unfurled our heels and shoved. Then there was a rush, and a *bang, bang, bang!* and the bullets fairly whizzed around us! We heard them sing out:

"Here they are! They've broke for the river! after 'em, boys! And turn loose the dogs!"

So here they come, full tilt. We could hear them, because they wore boots, and yelled, but we didn't wear no boots, and didn't yell. We was in the path to the mill; and when they got pretty close onto us, we dodged into the bush and let them go by, and then dropped in behind them. They'd had all the dogs shut up, so they wouldn't scare off the robbers; but by this time somebody had let them loose, and here they come, making pow-wow enough for a million; but they was our dogs; so we stopped in our tracks till they catched up; and when they see it warn't nobody but us, and no excitement to offer them, they only just said howdy, and tore right ahead towards the shouting and clattering; and then we up steam again and whizzed along after them till we was nearly to the mill, and then struck up through the bush to where my canoe was tied, and hopped in and pulled for dear life towards the middle of the river, but didn't make no more noise than we was obleeged to. Then we struck out, easy and comfortable, for the island where my raft was; and we could hear them yelling and barking at each other all up and down the bank, till we was so far away the sounds got dim and died out. And when we stepped onto the raft, I says:

"*Now*, old Jim, you're a free man *again*, and I bet you won't ever be a slave no more."

"En a mighty good job it wuz, too, Huck. It 'uz planned beautiful, en it 'uz *done* beautiful; en dey ain't *nobody* kin git up a plan dat's mo' mixed-up en splendid den what dat one wuz."

We was all as glad as we could be, but Tom was the gladdest of all, because he had a bullet in the calf of his leg.

When me and Jim heard that, we didn't feel so brash as what

we did before. It was hurting him considerble, and bleeding; so we laid him in the wigwam and tore up one of the duke's shirts for to bandage him, but he says:

"Gimme the rags, I can do it myself. Don't stop, now; don't fool around here, and the evasion booming along so handsome; man the sweeps, and set her loose! Boys, we done it elegant!—'deed we did. I wish *we'd* a had the handling of Louis XVI, there wouldn't a been no 'Son of Saint Louis, ascend to heaven!' wrote down in *his* biography: no, sir, we'd a whooped him over the *border*— that's what we'd a done with *him*—and done it just as slick as nothing at all, too. Man the sweeps—man the sweeps!"

But me and Jim was consulting—and thinking. And after we'd thought a minute, I says:

"Say it, Jim."

So he says:

"Well, den, dis is de way it look to me, Huck. Ef it wuz *him* dat 'uz bein' sot free, en one er de boys wuz to git shot, would he say, 'Go on en save me, nemmine 'bout a doctor f'r to save dis one? Is dat like Mars Tom Sawyer? Would he say dat? You *bet* he wouldn't! *Well*, den, is *Jim* gwyne to say it? No, sah—I doan' budge a step out'n dis place, 'dout a *doctor*; not if it's forty year!"

I knowed he was white inside, and I reckoned he'd say what he did say—so it was all right, now, and I told Tom I was agoing for a doctor. He raised considerble row about it, but me and Jim stuck to it and wouldn't budge; so he was for crawling out and setting the raft loose himself; but we wouldn't let him. Then he give us a piece of his mind—but it didn't do no good.

So when he see me getting the canoe ready, he says:

"Well, then, if you're bound to go, I'll tell you the way to do, when you get to the village. Shut the door, and blindfold the doctor tight and fast, and make him swear to be silent as the grave, and put a purse full of gold in his hand, and then take and lead him all around the back alleys and everywheres, in the dark, and then fetch him here in the canoe, in a roundabout way amongst the islands, and search him and take his chalk away from him, and don't give it back to him till you get him back to the village, or else he will chalk this raft so he can find it again. It's the way they all do."

So I said I would, and left, and Jim was to hide in the woods when he see the doctor coming, till he was gone again.

Chapter XLI

The doctor was an old man; a very nice, kind-looking old man, when I got him up. I told him me and my brother was over on Spanish Island hunting, yesterday afternoon, and camped on a piece of a raft we found, and about midnight he must a kicked his gun in his dreams, for it went off and shot him in the leg, and we wanted him to go over there and fix it and not say nothing about it, nor let anybody know, because we wanted to come home this evening, and surprise the folks.

"Who is your folks?" he says.

"The Phelpses, down yonder."

"Oh," he says. And after a minute, he says: "How'd you say he got shot?"

"He had a dream," I says, "and it shot him."

"Singular dream," he says.

So he lit up his lantern, and got his saddle-bags, and we started. But when he see the canoe, he didn't like the look of her—said she was big enough for one, but didn't look pretty safe for two. I says:

"Oh, you needn't be afeard, sir, she carried the three of us, easy enough."

"What three?"

"Why, me and Sid, and—and—and *the guns*; that's what I mean."

"Oh," he says.

But he put his foot on the gunnel, and rocked her; and shook his head, and said he reckoned he'd look around for a bigger one. But they was all locked and chained; so he took my canoe, and said for me to wait till he come back, or I could hunt around further, or maybe I better go down home and get them ready for the surprise, if I wanted to. But I said I didn't; so I told him just how to find the raft, and then he started.

I struck an idea, pretty soon. I says to myself, spos'n he can't fix that leg just in three shakes of a sheep's tail, as the saying is? spos'n it takes him three or four days? What are we going to do?—lay around there till he lets the cat out of the bag? No, sir, I know what *I'll* do. I'll wait, and when he comes back, if he says he's got to go any more, I'll get down there, too, if I swim; and we'll take and tie him, and keep him, and shove out down the river; and when Tom's done with him, we'll give him what it's worth, or all we got, and then let him get shore.

So then I crept into a lumber pile to get some sleep; and next time I waked up the sun was away up over my head! I shot out and went for the doctor's house, but they told me he'd gone away in the night, some time or other, and warn't back yet. Well, thinks I, that looks powerful bad for *Tom*, and I'll dig out for the island, right off. So away I shoved, and turned the corner, and nearly rammed my head into Uncle Silas's stomach! He says:

"Why, *Tom!* Where you been, all this time, you rascal?"

"I hain't been nowheres," I says, "only just hunting for the runaway nigger—me and Sid."

"Why, where ever did you go?" he says. "Your aunt's been mighty uneasy."

"She needn't," I says, "because we was all right. We followed the men and the dogs, but they out-run us, and we lost them; but we thought we heard them on the water, so we got a canoe and took out after them, and crossed over but couldn't find nothing of them; so we cruised along up-shore till we got kind of tired and beat out; and tied up the canoe and went to sleep, and never waked up till about an hour ago, then we paddled over here to hear the news, and Sid's at the post-office to see what he can hear, and I'm a branching out to get something to eat for us, and then we're going home."

So then we went to the post-office to get "Sid"; but just as I suspicioned, he warn't there; so the old man he got a letter out of the office, and we waited a while longer but Sid didn't come; so the old man said come along, let Sid foot it home, or canoe-it, when he got done fooling around—but we would ride. I couldn't get him to let me stay and wait for Sid; and he said there warn't no use in it, and I must come along, and let Aunt Sally see we was all right.

When we got home, Aunt Sally was that glad to see me she laughed and cried both, and hugged me, and give me one of them lickings of hern that don't amount to shucks, and said she'd serve Sid the same when he come.

And the place was plumb full of farmers and farmers' wives, to dinner; and such another clack a body never heard. Old Mrs. Hotchkiss was the worst; her tongue was agoing all the time. She says:

"Well, Sister Phelps, I've ransacked that-air cabin over an' I b'lieve the nigger was crazy. I says so to Sister Damrell—didn't I, Sister Damrell?—s'I, he's crazy, s'I—them's the very words I said. You all hearn me: he's crazy, s'I; everything shows it, s'I. Look at that-air grindstone, s'I; want to tell *me*'t any cretur 'ts in his right mind 's agoin' to scrabble all them crazy things onto a grindstone, s'I? Here sich 'n' sich a person busted his heart; 'n' here so 'n' so pegged along for thirty-seven year, 'n' all that—natcherl son o' Louis somebody, 'n' sich everlast'n rubbage. He's plumb crazy, s'I; it's what I says in the fust place, it's what I says in the middle, 'n' it's what I says last 'n' all the time—the nigger's crazy—crazy's Nebokoodneezer, s'I."

"An' look at that-air ladder made out'n rags, Sister Hotchkiss," says old Mrs. Damrell, "what in the name o' goodness *could* he ever want of—"

"The very words I was a-sayin' no longer ago th'n this minute to Sister Utterback, 'n' she'll tell you so herself. Sh-she, look at that-air rag ladder, sh-she; 'n' s'I, yes, *look* at it, s'I—what *could* he a wanted of it, s'I. Sh-she, Sister Hotchkiss, sh-she—"

"But how in the nation'd they ever *git* that grindstone *in* there, *any*way? 'n' who dug that-air *hole*? 'n' who—"

"My very *words*, Brer Penrod! I was a-sayin'—pass that-air sasser o' m'lasses, won't ye?—I was a-sayin' to Sister Dunlap, jist this minute, how *did* they git that grindstone in there, s'I. Without *help*, mind you—'thout *help! Thar's* wher' 'tis. Don't tell *me*, s'I; there *wuz* help, s'I; 'n' ther' wuz a *plenty* help, too, s'I; ther's ben a *dozen* a-helpin' that nigger, 'n' I lay I'd skin every last nigger on this place, but *I'd* find out who done it, s'I; 'n' moreover, s'I—"

"A *dozen* says you!—*forty* couldn't a done everything that's been done. Look at them case-knife saws and things, how tedious they've been made; look at that bed-leg sawed off with 'em, a week's work for six men; look at that nigger made out'n straw on the bed; and look at—"

"You may *well* say it, Brer Hightower! It's jist as I was a-sayin' to Brer Phelps, his own self. S'e, what do *you* think of it, Sister Hotchkiss, s'e? think o' what, Brer Phelps, s'I? think o' that bed-leg sawed off that a way, s'e? *think* of it, s'I? I lay it never sawed *itself* off, s'I—somebody *sawed* it, s'I; that's my opinion, take it or leave it, it mayn't be no 'count, s'I, but sich as 't is, it's my opinion, s'I, 'n' if anybody k'n start a better one, s'I, let him *do* it, s'I, that's all. I says to Sister Dunlap, s'I—"

"Why, dog my cats, they must a ben a house-full o' niggers in there every night for four weeks, to a done all that work, Sister Phelps. Look at that shirt—every last inch of it kivered over with secret African writ'n done with blood! Must a ben a raft uv 'm at it right along, all the time, amost. Why, I'd give two dollars to have it read to me; 'n' as for the niggers that wrote it, I 'low I'd take 'n' lash 'm t'll—"

"People to *help* him, Brother Marples! Well, I reckon you'd *think* so, if you'd a been in this house for a while back. Why, they've stole everything they could lay their hands on—and we a watching, all the time, mind you. They stole that shirt right off o' the line! and as for that sheet they made the rag ladder out of ther' ain't no telling how many times they *didn't* steal that; and flour, and candles, and candlesticks, and spoons, and the old warming-pan, and most a thousand things that I disremember, now, and my new calico dress; and me, and Silas, and my Sid and Tom on the constant watch day *and* night, as I was a telling you, and not a one of us could catch hide nor hair, nor sight nor sound of them; and here at the last minute, lo and behold you, they slides right in under our noses, and fools us, and not only fools *us* but the

Injun Territory robbers too, and actuly gets *away* with that nigger,
safe and sound, and that with sixteen men and twenty-two dogs
right on their very heels at that very time! I tell you, it just bangs
anything I ever *heard* of. Why, *sperits* couldn't a done better, and
been no smarter. And I reckon they must a *been* sperits—because,
you know our dogs, and ther' ain't no better; well, them dogs never
even got on the *track* of 'm, once! You explain *that* to me, if you
can!—*any* of you!"

"Well, it does beat—"

"Laws alive, I never—"

"So help me, I wouldn't a be—"

"*House*-thieves as well as—"

"Goodnessgracioussakes, I'd a ben afeard to *live* in sich a—"

" 'Fraid to *live!*—why, I was that scared I dasn't[2] hardly go to
bed, or get up, or lay down, or *set* down, Sister Ridgeway. Why,
they'd steal the very—why, goodness sakes, you can guess what
kind of a fluster *I* was in by the time midnight come, last night. I
hope to gracious if I warn't afraid they'd steal some o' the family!
I was just to that pass, I didn't have no reasoning faculties no more.
It looks foolish enough, *now*, in the day-time; but I says to myself,
there's my two poor boys asleep, 'way up stairs in that lonesome
room, and I declare to goodness I was that uneasy 't I crep' up
there and locked 'em in! I *did*. And anybody would. Because, you
know, when you get scared, that way, and it keeps running on, and
getting worse and worse, all the time, and your wits gets to addling,
and you get to doing all sorts o' wild things, and by-and-by you
think to yourself, spos'n *I* was a boy, and was away up there, and
the door ain't locked, and you—" She stopped, looking kind of
wondering, and then she turned her head around slow, and when
her eye lit on me—I got up and took a walk.

Says I to myself, I can explain better how we come to not be in
that room this morning, if I go out to one side and study over it
a little. So I done it. But I dasn't go fur, or she'd a sent for me.
And when it was late in the day, the people all went, and then I
come in and told her the noise and shooting waked up me and
"Sid," and the door was locked, and we wanted to see the fun, so
we went down the lightning-rod, and both of us got hurt a little, and
we didn't never want to try *that* no more. And then I went on and
told her all what I told Uncle Silas before; and then she said
she'd forgive us, and maybe it was all right enough anyway, and
about what a body night expect of boys, for all boys was a pretty
harum-scarum lot, as fur as she could see; and so, as long as no harm
hadn't come of it, she judged she better put in her time being
grateful we was alive and well and she had us still, stead of fretting

2. Erroneously printed "das'nt" in 1885.

over what was past and done. So then she kissed me, and patted me on the head, and dropped into a kind of a brown study; and pretty soon jumps up, and says:

"Why, lawsamercy, it's most night, and Sid not come yet! What *has* become of that boy?"

I see my chance; so I skips up and says:

"I'll run right up to town and get him," I says.

"No you won't," she says. "You'll stay right wher' you are; *one's* enough to be lost at a time. If he ain't here to supper, your uncle 'll go."

Well, he warn't there to supper; so right after supper uncle went.

He come back about ten, a little bit uneasy; hadn't run across Tom's track. Aunt Sally was a good *deal* uneasy; but Uncle Silas he said there warn't no occasion to be—boys will be boys, he said, and you'll see this one turn up in the morning, all sound and right. So she had to be satisfied. But she said she'd set up for him a while, anyway, and keep a light burning, so he could see it.

And then when I went up to bed she come up with me and fetched her candle, and tucked me in, and mothered me so good I felt mean, and like I couldn't look her in the face; and she set down on the bed and talked with me a long time, and said what a splendid boy Sid was, and didn't seem to want to ever stop talking about him; and kept asking me every now and then, if I reckoned he could a got lost, or hurt, or maybe drownded, and might be laying at this minute, somewheres, suffering or dead, and she not by him to help him, and so the tears would drip down, silent, and I would tell her that Sid was all right, and would be home in the morning, sure; and she would squeeze my hand, or maybe kiss me, and tell me to say it again, and keep on saying it, because it done her good, and she was in so much trouble. And when she was going away, she looked down in my eyes, so steady and gentle, and says:

"The door ain't going to be locked, Tom; and there's the window and the rod; but you'll be good, *won't* you? And you won't go? For *my* sake."

Laws knows I *wanted* to go, bad enough, to see about Tom, and was all intending to go; but after that, I wouldn't a went, not for kingdoms.

But she was on my mind, and Tom was on my mind; so I slept very restless. And twice I went down the rod, away in the night, and slipped around front, and see her setting there by her candle in the window with her eyes towards the road and the tears in them; and I wished I could do something for her, but I couldn't, only to swear that I wouldn't never do nothing to grieve her any more.

And the third time, I waked up at dawn, and slid down, and she was there yet, and her candle was most out, and her old gray head was resting on her hand, and she was asleep.

Chapter XLII

The old man was up town again, before breakfast, but couldn't get no track of Tom; and both of them set at the table, thinking, and not saying nothing, and looking mournful, and their coffee getting cold, and not eating anything. And by-and-by the old man says:

"Did I give you the letter?"

"What letter?"

"The one I got yesterday out of the post-office."

"No, you didn't give me no letter."

"Well, I must a forgot it."

So he rummaged his pockets, and then went off somewheres where he had laid it down, and fetched it, and give it to her. She says:

"Why, it's from St. Petersburg—it's from Sis."

I allowed another walk would do me good; but I couldn't stir. But before she could break it open, she dropped it and run—for she see something. And so did I. It was Tom Sawyer on a mattress; and that old doctor; and Jim, in *her* calico dress, with his hands tied behind him; and a lot of people. I hid the letter behind the first thing that come handy, and rushed. She flung herself at Tom, crying, and says:

"Oh, he's dead, he's dead, I know he's dead!"

And Tom he turned his head a little, and muttered something or other, which showed he warn't in his right mind; then she flung up her hands, and says:

"He's alive, thank God! And that's enough!" and she snatched a kiss of him, and flew for the house to get the bed ready, and scattering orders right and left at the niggers and everybody else, as fast as her tongue could go, every jump of the way.

I followed the men to see what they was going to do with Jim; and the old doctor and Uncle Silas followed after Tom into the house. The men was very huffy, and some of them wanted to hang Jim, for an example to all the other niggers around there, so they wouldn't be trying to run away, like Jim done, and making such a raft of trouble, and keeping a whole family scared most to death for days and nights. But the others said, don't do it, it wouldn't answer at all, he ain't our nigger, and his owner would turn up and make us pay for him, sure. So that cooled them down a little, because the people that's always the most anxious for to hang a nigger that hain't done just right, is always the very ones that ain't the most anxious to pay for him when they've got their satisfaction out of him.

They cussed Jim considerble, though, and give him a cuff or two, side the head, once in a while, but Jim never said nothing, and he never let on to know me, and they took him to the same cabin, and put his own clothes on him, and chained him again, and not to no bed-leg, this time, but to a big staple drove into the bottom log, and chained his hands, too, and both legs, and said he warn't to have nothing but bread and water to eat, after this, till his owner come or he was sold at auction, because he didn't come in a certain length of time, and filled up our hole, and said a couple of farmers with guns must stand watch around about the cabin every night, and a bull-dog tied to the door in the day-time; and about this time they was through with the job and was tapering off with a kind of generl good-bye cussing, and then the old doctor comes and takes a look, and says:

"Don't be no rougher on him than you're obleeged to, because he ain't a bad nigger. When I got to where I found the boy, I see I couldn't cut the bullet out without some help, and he warn't in no condition for me to leave, to go and get help; and he got a little worse and a little worse, and after a long time he went out of his head, and wouldn't let me come anigh him, any more, and said if I chalked his raft he'd kill me, and no end of wild foolishness like that, and I see I couldn't do anything at all with him; so I says, I got to have *help*, somehow; and the minute I says it, out crawls this nigger from somewheres, and says he'll help, and he done it, too, and done it very well. Of course I judged he must be a runaway nigger, and there I *was!* and there I had to stick, right straight along all the rest of the day, and all night. It was a fix, I tell you! I had a couple of patients with the chills, and of course I'd of liked to run up to town and see them, but I dasn't, because the nigger might get away, and then I'd be to blame; and yet never a skiff come close enough for me to hail. So there I had to stick, plumb till daylight this morning; and I never see a nigger that was a better nuss or faithfuller, and yet he was resking his freedom to do it, and was all tired out, too, and I see plain enough he'd been worked main hard, lately. I liked the nigger for that; I tell you, gentlemen, a nigger like that is worth a thousand dollars—and kind treatment, too. I had everything I needed, and the boy was doing as well there as he would a done at home— better, maybe, because it was so quiet; but there I *was*, with both of 'm on my hands; and there I had to stick, till about dawn this morning; then some men in a skiff come by, and as good luck would have it, the nigger was setting by the pallet with his head propped on his knees, sound asleep; so I motioned them in, quiet, and they slipped up on him and grabbed him and tied him before

he knowed what he was about, and we never had no trouble. And
the boy being in a kind of a flighty sleep, too, we muffled the oars
and hitched the raft on, and towed her over very nice and quiet,
and the nigger never made the least row nor said a word, from the
start. He ain't no bad nigger, gentlemen; that's what I think about
him."

Somebody says:

"Well, it sounds very good, doctor, I'm obleeged to say."

Then the others softened up a little, too, and I was mighty
thankful to that old doctor for doing Jim that good turn; and I
was glad it was according to my judgment of him, too; because
I thought he had a good heart in him and was a good man, the
first time I see him. Then they all agreed that Jim had acted very
well, and was deserving to have some notice took of it, and reward.
So every one of them promised, right out and hearty, that they
wouldn't cuss him no more.

Then they come out and locked him up. I hoped they was going
to say he could have one or two of the chains took off, because
they was rotten heavy, or could have meat and greens with his
bread and water, but they didn't think of it, and I reckoned it
warn't best for me to mix in, but I judged I'd get the doctor's yarn
to Aunt Sally, somehow or other, as soon as I'd got through the
breakers that was laying just ahead of me. Explanations, I mean,
of how I forgot to mention about Sid being shot, when I was
telling how him and me put in that dratted night paddling around
hunting the runaway nigger.

But I had plenty time. Aunt Sally she stuck to the sick-room
all day and all night; and every time I see Uncle Silas mooning
around, I dodged him.

Next morning I heard Tom was a good deal better, and they
said Aunt Sally was gone to get a nap. So I slips to the sick-room,
and if I found him awake I reckoned we could put up a yarn for
the family that would wash. But he was sleeping, and sleeping
very peaceful, too; and pale, not fire-faced the way he was when
he come. So I set down and laid for him to wake. In about a half
an hour, Aunt Sally comes gliding in, and there I was, up a stump
again! She motioned me to be still, and set down by me, and
begun to whisper, and said we could all be joyful now, because
all the symptoms was first rate, and he'd been sleeping like that
for ever so long, and looking better and peacefuller all the time,
and ten to one he'd wake up in his right mind.

So we set there watching, and by-and-by he stirs a bit, and
opened his eyes very natural, and takes a look, and says:

"Hello, why I'm at *home!* How's that? Where's the raft?"

"It's all right," I says.

"And *Jim?*"

"The same," I says, but couldn't say it pretty brash. But he never noticed, but says:

"Good! Splendid! *Now* we're all right and safe! Did you tell Aunty?"

I was going to say yes; but she chipped in and says:

"About what, Sid?"

"Why, about the way the whole thing was done."

"What whole thing?"

"Why, *the* whole thing. There ain't but one; how we set the runaway nigger free—me and Tom."

"Good land! Set the run— What *is* the child talking about! Dear, dear, out of his head again!"

"*No*, I ain't out of my HEAD; I know all what I'm talking about. We *did* set him free—me and Tom. We laid out to do it, and we *done* it. And we done it elegant, too." He'd got a start, and she never checked him up, just set and stared and stared, and let him clip along, and I see it warn't no use for *me* to put in. "Why, Aunty, it cost us a power of work—weeks of it—hours and hours, every night, whilst you was all asleep. And we had to steal candles, and the sheet, and the shirt, and your dress, and spoons, and tin plates, and case-knives, and the warming-pan, and the grindstone, and flour, and just no end of things, and you can't think what work it was to make the saws, and pens, and inscriptions, and one thing or another, and you can't think *half* the fun it was. And we had to make up the pictures of coffins and things, and nonnamous letters from the robbers, and get up and down the lightning-rod, and dig the hole into the cabin, and make the rope-ladder and send it in cooked up in a pie, and send in spoons and things to work with, in your apron pocket"—

"Mercy sakes!"

—"and load up the cabin with rats and snakes and so on, for company for Jim; and then you kept Tom here so long with the butter in his hat that you come near spiling the whole business, because the men come before we was out of the cabin, and we had to rush, and they heard us and let drive at us, and I got my share, and we dodged out of the path and let them go by, and when the dogs come they warn't interested in us, but went for the most noise, and we got our canoe, and made for the raft, and was all safe, and Jim was a free man, and we done it all by ourselves, and *wasn't* it bully, Aunty!"

"Well, I never heard the likes of it in all my born days! So it was *you*, you little rapscallions, that's been making all this trouble, and turn everybody's wits clean inside out and scared us all most to death. I've as good a notion as ever I had in my life, to take it out o' you this very minute. To think, here I've been, night after night, a—*you* just get well once, you young scamp, and I lay

I'll tan the Old Harry out o' both o' ye!"

But Tom, he *was* so proud and joyful, he just *couldn't* hold in, and his tongue just *went* it—she a-chipping in, and spitting fire all along, and both of them going it at once, like a cat-convention; and she says:

"*Well*, you get all the enjoyment you can out of it *now*, for mind I tell you if I catch you meddling with him again—"

"Meddling with *who?*" Tom says, dropping his smile and looking surprised.

"With *who?* Why, the runaway nigger, of course. Who'd you reckon?"

Tom looks at me very grave, and says:

"Tom, didn't you just tell me he was all right? Hasn't he got away?"

"*Him?*" says Aunt Sally; "the runaway nigger? 'Deed he hasn't. They've got him back, safe and sound, and he's in that cabin again, on bread and water, and loaded down with chains, till he's claimed or sold!"

Tom rose square up in bed, with his eye hot, and his nostrils opening and shutting like gills, and sings out to me:

"They hain't no *right* to shut him up! *Shove!*—and don't you lose a minute. Turn him loose! he ain't no slave; he's as free as any cretur that walks this earth!"

"What *does* the child mean?"

"I mean every word I *say*, Aunt Sally, and if somebody don't go, *I'll* go. I've knowed him all his life, and so has Tom, there. Old Miss Watson died two months ago, and she was ashamed she ever was going to sell him down the river, and *said* so; and she set him free in her will."

"Then what on earth did *you* want to set him free for, seeing he was already free?"

"Well, that *is* a question, I must say; and *just* like women! Why, I wanted the *adventure* of it; and I'd a waded neck-deep in blood to—goodness alive, AUNT POLLY!"[3]

If she warn't standing right there, just inside the door, looking as sweet and contented as an angel half-full of pie, I wish I may never!

Aunt Sally jumped for her, and most hugged the head off of her, and cried over her, and I found a good enough place for me under the bed, for it was getting pretty sultry for *us*, seemed to me. And I peeped out, and in a little while Tom's Aunt Polly shook herself loose and stood there looking across at Tom over her spectacles—kind of grinding him into the earth, you know. And then she says:

"Yes, you *better* turn y'r head away—I would if I was you,

---

3. Aunt Polly, introduced in the first paragraph of the novel, is Tom's rela- tive and guardian, a major figure in *The Adventures of Tom Sawyer* (1876).

Tom."

"Oh, deary me!" says Aunt Sally; "*is* he changed so? Why, that ain't *Tom* it's Sid; Tom's—Tom's—why, where is Tom? He was here a minute ago."

"You mean where's Huck *Finn*—that's what you mean! I reckon I hain't raised such a scamp as my Tom all these years, not to know him when I *see* him. That *would* be a pretty howdy-do. Come out from under that bed, Huck Finn."

So I done it. But not feeling brash.

Aunt Sally she was one of the mixed-upest looking persons I ever see; except one, and that was Uncle Silas, when he come in, and they told it all to him. It kind of made him drunk, as you may say, and he didn't know nothing at all the rest of the day, and preached a prayer-meeting sermon that night that give him a rattling ruputation, because the oldest man in the world couldn't a understood it. So Tom's Aunt Polly, she told all about who I was, and what; and I had to up and tell how I was in such a tight place that when Mrs. Phelps took me for Tom Sawyer—she chipped in and says, "Oh, go on and call me Aunt Sally, I'm used to it, now, and 'tain't no need to change"—that when Aunt Sally took me for Tom Sawyer, I had to stand it—there warn't no other way, and I knowed he wouldn't mind, because it would be nuts for him, being a mystery, and he'd make an adventure out of it and be perfectly satisfied. And so it turned out, and he let on to be Sid, and made things as soft as he could for me.

And his Aunt Polly she said Tom was right about old Miss Watson setting Jim free in her will; and so, sure enough, Tom Sawyer had gone and took all that trouble and bother to set a free nigger free! and I couldn't ever understand, before, until that minute and that talk, how he *could* help a body set a nigger free, with his bringing-up.

Well, Aunt Polly she said that when Aunt Sally wrote to her that Tom and *Sid* had come, all right and safe, she says to herself:

"Look at that, now! I might have expected it, letting him go off that way without anybody to watch him. So now I got to go and trapse all the way down the river, eleven hundred mile, and find out what that creetur's up to, *this* time; as long as I couldn't seem to get any answer out of you about it."

"Why, I never heard nothing from you," says Aunt Sally.

"Well, I wonder! Why, I wrote to you twice, to ask you what you could mean by Sid being here."

"Well, I never got 'em, Sis."

Aunt Polly, she turns around slow and severe, and says:

"You, Tom!"

"Well—*what?*" he says, kind of pettish.

"Don't you what *me*, you impudent thing—hand out them

letters."

"What letters?"

"*Them* letters. I be bound, if I have to take aholt of you I'll—"

"They're in the trunk. There, now. And they're just the same as they was when I got them out of the office. I hain't looked into them, I hain't touched them. But I knowed they'd make trouble, and I thought if you warn't in no hurry, I'd—"

"Well, you *do* need skinning, there ain't no mistake about it. And I wrote another one to tell you I was coming; and I spose he—"

"No, it come yesterday; I hain't read it yet, but *it's* all right, I've got that one."

I wanted to offer to bet two dollars she hadn't, but I reckoned maybe it was just as safe to not to. So I never said nothing.

Chapter the Last

The first time I catched Tom, private, I asked him what was his idea, time of the evasion?—what it was he'd planned to do if the evasion worked all right and he managed to set a nigger free that was already free before? And he said, what he had planned in his head, from the start, if we got Jim out all safe, was for us to run him down the river, on the raft, and have adventures plumb to the mouth of the river, and then tell him about his being free, and take him back up home on a steamboat, in style, and pay him for his lost time, and write word ahead and get out all the niggers around, and have them waltz him into town with a torch-light procession and a brass band, and then he would be a hero, and so would we. But I reckened it was about as well the way it was.

We had Jim out of the chains in no time, and when Aunt Polly and Uncle Silas and Aunt Sally found out how good he helped the doctor nurse Tom, they made a heap of fuss over him, and fixed him up prime, and give him all he wanted to eat, and a good time, and nothing to do. And we had him up to the sick-room; and had a high talk; and Tom give Jim forty dollars for being prisoner for us so patient, and doing it up so good, and Jim was pleased most to death, and busted out, and says:

"*Dah*, now, Huck, what I tell you?—what I tell you up dah on Jackson islan'? I *tole* you I got a hairy breas', en what's de sign un it; en I *tole* you I ben rich wunst, en gwineter to be rich *agin*; en it's come true; en heah she *is*! *Dah*, now! doan' talk to *me*— signs is *signs*, mine I tell you; en I knowed jis' 's well 'at I 'uz gwineter be rich agin as I's a stannin' heah dis minute!"

And then Tom he talked along, and talked along, and says, le's all three slide out of here, one of these nights, and get an outfit, and go for howling adventures amongst the Injuns, over in the Territory, for a couple of weeks or two; and I says, all right, that suits me, but I aint got no money for to buy the outfit, and I reckon I couldn't get none from home, because it's likely pap's been back before now, and got it all away from Judge Thatcher and drunk it up.

"No he hain't," Tom says; "it's all there, yet—six thousand dollars and more; and your pap hain't ever been back since. Hadn't when I come away, anyhow."

Jim says, kind of solemn:

"He ain't a comin' back no mo', Huck."

I says:

"Why, Jim?"

"Nemmine why, Huck—but he ain't comin' back no mo'."

But I kept at him; so at last he says:

"Doan' you 'member de house dat was float'n down de river, en dey wuz a man in dah, kivered up, en I went in en unkivered him and didn' let you come in? Well, den, you k'n git yo' money when you wants it; kase dat wuz him."

Tom's most well, now, and got his bullet around his neck on a watch-guard for a watch, and is always seeing what time it is, and so there ain't nothing more to write about, and I am rotten glad of it, because if I'd a knowed what a trouble it was to make a book I wouldn't a tackled it and ain't[4] agoing to no more. But I reckon I got to light out for the Territory ahead of the rest, because Aunt Sally she's going to adopt me and sivilize me and I can't stand it. I been there before.

THE END. YOURS TRULY, HUCK FINN.

1876, 1879–80, 1883   1884, 1885

4. Erroneously printed "aint't" in 1885.

Backgrounds and Sources

SAMUEL LANGHORNE CLEMENS

From Life on the Mississippi

[*The Raft Passage*]¹

By way of illustrating keelboat talk and manners, and that now departed and hardly remembered raft life, I will throw in, in this place, a chapter from a book which I have been working at, by fits and starts, during the past five or six years, and may possibly finish in the course of five or six more. The book is a story which details some passages in the life of an ignorant village boy, Huck Finn, son of the town drunkard of my time out West, there. He has run away from his persecuting father, and from a persecuting good widow who wishes to make a nice, truth-telling, respectable boy of him; and with him a slave of the widow's has also escaped. They have found a fragment of a lumber-raft (it is high water and dead summer-time), and are floating down the river by night, and hiding in the willows by day—bound for Cairo,² whence the negro will seek freedom in the heart of the free states. But, in a fog, they pass Cairo without knowing it. By and by they begin to suspect the truth, and Huck Finn is persuaded to end the dismal suspense by swimming down to a huge raft which they have seen in the distance ahead of them, creeping aboard under cover of the darkness, and gathering the needed information by eavesdropping:

But you know a young person can't wait very well when he is impatient to find a thing out. We talked it over, and by and by Jim said it was such a black night, now, that it wouldn't be no risk to swim down to the big raft and crawl aboard and listen—they would talk about Cairo, because they would be calculating to go ashore there for a spree, maybe; or anyway they would send boats ashore to buy whisky or fresh meat or something. Jim had a wonderful level head, for a nigger: he could most always start a good plan when you wanted one.

I stood up and shook my rags off and jumped into the river, and struck out for the raft's light. By and by, when I got down nearly to her, I eased up and went slow and cautious. But everything was all right—nobody at

1. The so-called "Raft Passage" was part of the 1876 draft of *Huckleberry Finn*, where it appeared in present Chapter XVI, following the second paragraph. In 1883 Mark Twain inserted it in *Life on the Mississippi*, in Chapter III, following paragraph 6. It never reappeared in authorized editions of *Huck Finn*, although two modern editions of *Huck Finn* included it. It represents the boisterous Halloween fun and the bully and braggart, stock situations and characters of the frontier humor and epic, familiar to Twain's youth. The episode of Dick Allbright and the reappearance of his corpse-haunted barrel on the river at once represents the persistent hoax of Mississippi folk humor and the superstitions which Mark Twain associated with Huck and Jim.

2. In the southern tip of Illinois, where the Mississippi is joined by the Ohio. (Pronounced "Kay-ro.")

the sweeps. So I swum down along the raft till I was most abreast the camp-fire in the middle, then I crawled aboard and inched along and got in among some bundles of shingles on the weather side of the fire. There was thirteen men there—they was the watch on deck of course. And a mighty rough-looking lot, too. They had a jug, and tin cups, and they kept the jug moving. One man was singing—roaring, you may say; and it wasn't a nice song—for a parlor, anyway. He roared through his nose, and strung out the last word of every line very long. When he was done they all fetched a kind of Injun war-whoop, and then another was sung. It begun:

> "There was a woman in our towdn,
>   In our towdn did dwed'l [dwell],
> She loved her husband dear-i-lee,
>   But another man twyste as wed'l.

> "Singing too, riloo, riloo, riloo,
>   Ri-too, riloo, rilay - - - e,
> She loved her husband dear-i-lee,
>   But another man twyste as wed'l."

And so on—fourteen verses. It was kind of poor, and when he was going to start on the next verse one of them said it was the tune the old cow died on; and another one said: "Oh, give us a rest!" And another one told him to take a walk. They made fun of him till he got mad and jumped up and begun to cuss the crowd, and said he could lam any thief in the lot.

They was all about to make a break for him, but the biggest man there jumped up and says:

"Set whar you are, gentlemen. Leave him to me; he's my meat."

Then he jumped up in the air three times, and cracked his heels together every time. He flung off a buckskin coat that was all hung with fringes, and says, "You lay thar tell the chawin-up's done"; and flung his hat down, which was all over ribbons, and says, "You lay thar tell his sufferin's is over."

Then he jumped up in the air and cracked his heels together again, and shouted out:

"Whoo-oop! I'm the old original iron-jawed, brass-mounted, copper-bellied corpse-maker from the wilds of Arkansaw! Look at me! I'm the man they call Sudden Death and General Desolation! Sired by a hurricane, dam'd by an earthquake, half-brother to the cholera, nearly related to the smallpox on the mother's side! Look at me! I take nineteen alligators and a bar'l of whisky for breakfast when I'm in robust health, and a bushel of rattlesnakes and a dead body when I'm ailing. I split the everlasting rocks with my glance, and I squench the thunder when I speak! Whoo-oop! Stand back and give me room according to my strength! Blood's my natural drink, and the wails of the dying is music to my ear. Cast your eye on me, gentlemen! and lay low and hold your breath, for I'm 'bout to turn myself loose!"[3]

All the time he was getting this off, he was shaking his head and looking fierce, and kind of swelling around in a little circle, tucking up his wrist-bands, and now and then straightening up and beating his breast with his fist, saying, "Look at me, gentlemen!" When he got through, he jumped up and cracked his heels together three times, and let off a roaring "Whoo-

3. This speech, the characters, and epi-sode are in the tall-tale tradition of such backwoods heroes as Davy Crock-ett and Mike Fink, and illustrate the frontier brag, which echoed with whoops, boasting, and verbal thunder, and which reached its prime in the humor of the Old Southwest, 1830–1865.

oop! I'm the bloodiest son of a wildcat that lives!"

Then the man that had started the row tilted his old slouch hat down over his right eye; then he bent stooping forward, with his back sagged and his south end sticking out far, and his fists a-shoving out and drawing in in front of him, and so went around in a little circle about three times, swelling himself up and breathing hard. Then he straightened, and jumped up and cracked his heels together three times before he lit again (that made them cheer), and he began to shout like this:

"Whoo-oop! bow your neck and spread, for the kingdom of sorrow's a-coming! Hold me down to the earth, for I feel my powers a-working! whoo-oop! I'm a child of sin, *don't* let me get a start! Smoked glass, here, for all! Don't attempt to look at me with the naked eye, gentlemen! When I'm playful I use the meridians of longitude and parallels of latitude for a seine, and drag the Atlantic Ocean for whales! I scratch my head with the lightning and purr myself to sleep with the thunder! When I'm cold, I bile the Gulf of Mexico and bathe in it; when I'm hot I fan myself with an equinoctial storm; when I'm thirsty I reach up and suck a cloud dry like a sponge; when I range the earth hungry, famine follows in my tracks! Whoo-oop! Bow your neck and spread! I put my hand on the sun's face and make it night in the earth; I bite a piece out of the moon and hurry the seasons; I shake myself and crumble the mountains! Contemplate me through leather—*don't* use the naked eye! I'm the man with a petrified heart and biler-iron bowels! The massacre of isolated communities is the pastime of my idle moments, the destruction of nationalities the serious business of my life! The boundless vastness of the great American desert is my inclosed property, and I bury my dead on my own premises!" He jumped up and cracked his heels together three times before he lit (they cheered him again), and as he come down he shouted out: "Whoo-oop! bow your neck and spread, for the Pet Child of Calamity's a-coming!"

Then the other one went to swelling around and blowing again—the first one—the one they called Bob; next, the Child of Calamity chipped in again, bigger than ever; then they both got at it at the same time, swelling round and round each other and punching their fists most into each other's faces, and whooping and jawing like Injuns; then Bob called the Child names, and the Child called him names back again; next, Bob called him a heap rougher names, and the Child come back at him with the very worst kind of language; next, Bob knocked the Child's hat off, and the Child picked it up and kicked Bob's ribbony hat about six foot; Bob went and got it and said never mind, this warn't going to be the last of this thing, because he was a man that never forgot and never forgive, and so the Child better look out, for there was a time a-coming, just as sure as he was a living man, that he would have to answer to him with the best blood in his body. The Child said no man was willinger than he for that time to come, and he would give Bob fair warning, *now*, never to cross his path again, for he could never rest till he had waded in his blood, for such was his nature, though he was sparing him now on account of his family, if he had one.

Both of them was edging away in different directions, growling and shaking their heads and going on about what they was going to do; but a little black-whiskered chap skipped up and says:

"Come back here, you couple of chicken-livered cowards, and I'll thrash the two of ye!"

And he done it, too. He snatched them, he jerked them this way and that, he booted them around, he knocked them sprawling faster than they could get up. Why, it warn't two minutes till they begged like dogs—and

how the other lot did yell and laugh and clap their hands all the way
through, and shout, "Sail in, Corpse-Maker!" "Hi! at him again, Child of
Calamity!" "Bully for you, little Davy!" Well, it was a perfect pow-wow
for a while. Bob and the Child had red noses and black eyes when they got
through. Little Davy made them own up that they was sneaks and cowards
and not fit to eat with a dog or drink with a nigger; then Bob and the
Child shook hands with each other, very solemn, and said they had always
respected each other and was willing to let bygones be bygones. So then
they washed their faces in the river; and just then there was a loud order
to stand by for a crossing, and some of them went forward to man the
sweeps there, and the rest went aft to handle the after sweeps.

I laid still and waited for fifteen minutes, and had a smoke out of a
pipe that one of them left in reach; then the crossing was finished, and
they stumped back and had a drink around and went to talking and singing again. Next they got out an old fiddle, and one played, and another
patted juba, and the rest turned themselves loose on a regular old-fashioned
keelboat breakdown.⁴ They couldn't keep that up very long without getting
winded, so by and by they settled around the jug again.

They sung "Jolly, Jolly Raftsman's the Life for Me," with a rousing
chorus, and then they got to talking about differences betwixt hogs, and
their different kind of habits; and next about women and their different
ways; and next about the best ways to put out houses that was afire; and
next about what ought to be done with the Injuns; and next about what a
king had to do, and how much he got; and next about how to make cats
fight; and next about what to do when a man has fits; and next about
differences betwixt clear-water rivers and muddy-water ones. The man
they called Ed said the muddy Mississippi water was wholesomer to drink than
the clear water of the Ohio; he said if you let a pint of this yaller Mississippi
water settle, you would have about a half to three-quarters of an inch of
mud in the bottom, according to the stage of the river, and then it warn't
no better than Ohio water—what you wanted to do was to keep it stirred
up—and when the river was low, keep mud on hand to put in and thicken
the water up the way it ought to be.

The Child of Calamity said that was so; he said there was nutritiousness
in the mud, and a man that drunk Mississippi water could grow corn in
his stomach if he wanted to. He says:

"You look at the graveyards; that tells the tale. Trees won't grow worth
shucks in a Cincinnati graveyard, but in a Sent Louis graveyard they grow
upwards of eight hundred foot high. It's all on account of the water the
people drunk before they laid up. A Cincinnati corpse don't richen a soil
any."

And they talked about how Ohio water didn't like to mix with Mississippi
water. Ed said if you take the Mississippi on a rise when the Ohio is low,
you'll find a wide band of clear water all the way down the east side of
the Mississippi for a hundred mile or more, and the minute you get out a
quarter of a mile from shore and pass the line, it is all thick and yaller the
rest of the way across. Then they talked about how to keep tobacco from
getting moldy, and from that they went into ghosts and told about a lot
that other folks had seen; but Ed says:

"Why don't you tell something that you've seen yourselves? Now let me
have a say. Five years ago I was on a raft as big as this, and right along
here it was a bright moonshiny night, and I was on watch and boss of the
stabboard oar forrard, and one of my pards was a man named Dick Allbright,

4. Two dances of Negro origin: juba, a
lively tapdance accompanied by clap- ping; breakdown, a shuffling dance in
very rapid rhythm.

and he come along to where I was sitting, forrard—gaping and stretching, he was—and stooped down on the edge of the raft and washed his face in the river, and come and set down by me and got out his pipe, and had just got it filled, when he looks up and says:

" 'Why looky-here,' he says, 'ain't that Buck Miller's place, over yander in the bend?'

" 'Yes,' says I, 'it is—why?' He laid his pipe down and leaned his head on his hand, and says:

" 'I thought we'd be furder down.' I says:

" 'I thought it, too, when I went off watch'—we was standing six hours on and six off—'but the boys told me,' I says, 'that the raft didn't seem to hardly move, for the last hour,' says I, 'though she's a-slipping along all right now,' says I. He give a kind of a groan, and says:

" 'I've seed a raft act so before, along here,' he says. ' 'pears to me the current has most quit above the head of this bend durin' the last two years,' he says.

"Well, he raised up two or three times, and looked away off and around on the water. That started me at it, too. A body is always doing what he sees somebody else doing, though there mayn't be no sense in it. Pretty soon I see a black something floating on the water away off to stabboard and quartering behind us. I see he was looking at it, too. I says:

" 'What's that?' He says, sort of pettish:

" ' 'Tain't nothing but an old empty bar'l.'

" 'An empty bar'l!' says I, 'why,' says I, 'a spy-glass is a fool to *your* eyes. How can you tell it's an empty bar'l?' He says:

" 'I don't know; I reckon it ain't a bar'l, but I thought it might be,' says he.

" 'Yes,' I says, 'so it might be, and it might be anything else too; a body can't tell nothing about it, such a distance as that,' I says.

"We hadn't nothing else to do, so we kept on watching it. By and by I says:

" 'Why, looky-here, Dick Allbright, that thing's a-gaining on us, I believe.'

"He never said nothing. The thing gained and gained, and I judged it must be a dog that was about tired out. Well, we swung down into the crossing, and the thing floated across the bright streak of the moonshine, and by George, it *was* a bar'l. Says I:

" 'Dick Allbright, what made you think that thing was a bar'l, when it was half a mile off?' says I. Says he:

" 'I don't know.' Says I:

" 'You tell me, Dick Allbright.' Says he:

" 'Well, I knowed it was a bar'l; I've seen it before; lots has seen it; they says it's a ha'nted bar'l.'

"I called the rest of the watch, and they come and stood there, and I told them what Dick said. It floated right along abreast, now, and didn't gain any more. It was about twenty foot off. Some was for having it aboard, but the rest didn't want to. Dick Allbright said rafts that had fooled with it had got bad luck by it. The captain of the watch said he didn't believe in it. He said he reckoned the bar'l gained on us because it was in a little better current than what we was. He said it would leave by and by.

"So then we went to talking about other things, and we had a song, and then a breakdown; and after that the captain of the watch called for another song; but it was clouding up now, and the bar'l stuck right thar in the same place, and the song didn't seem to have much warm-up to it, somehow, and so they didn't finish it, and there warn't any cheers, but it sort of dropped flat, and nobody said anything for a minute. Then everybody tried to talk at once, and one chap got off a joke, but it warn't no use, they didn't laugh, and even the chap that made the joke didn't laugh at it, which ain't usual. We all just settled down glum, and watched the bar'l, and was oneasy and oncomfortable. Well, sir, it shut down black and still, and then the wind began to moan around, and next the lightning began to play and the thunder to grumble. And pretty soon there was a regular storm, and in the middle of it a man that was running aft stumbled and fell and sprained his ankle so that he had to lay up. This made the boys shake their heads. And every time the lightning come, there was that bar'l, with the blue lights winking around it. We was always on the lookout for it. But by and by, toward dawn, she was gone. When the day come we couldn't see her anywhere, and we warn't sorry, either.

"But next night about half-past nine, when there was songs and high jinks going on, here she comes again, and took her old roost on the stabboard side. There warn't no more high jinks. Everybody got solemn; nobody talked; you couldn't get anybody to do anything but set around moody and look at the bar'l. It begun to cloud up again. When the watch changed, the off watch stayed up, 'stead of turning in. The storm ripped and roared around all night, and in the middle of it another man tripped and sprained his ankle, and had to knock off. The bar'l left toward day, and nobody see it go.

"Everybody was sober and down in the mouth all day. I don't mean the kind of sober that comes of leaving liquor alone—not that. They was quiet, but they all drunk more than usual—not together, but each man sidled off and took it private, by himself.

"After dark the off watch didn't turn in; nobody sung, nobody talked; the boys didn't scatter around, neither; they sort of huddled together, forrard; and for two hours they set there, perfectly still, looking steady in the one direction, and heaving a sigh once in a while. And then, here comes the bar'l again. She took up her old place. She stayed there all night; nobody turned in. The storm come on again, after midnight. It got awful dark; the rain poured down; hail, too; the thunder boomed and roared and bellowed; the wind blowed a hurricane; and the lightning spread over everything in big sheets of glare, and showed the whole raft as plain as day; and the river lashed up white as milk as far as you could see for miles, and there was that bar'l jiggering along, same as ever. The captain ordered the watch to man the after sweeps for a crossing, and nobody would go—no more sprained ankles for them, they said. They wouldn't even *walk* aft. Well, then, just then the sky split wide open, with a crash, and the lightning killed two men of the after watch, and crippled two more. Crippled them how, say you? Why, *sprained their ankles!*

"The bar'l left in the dark betwixt lightnings, toward dawn. Well, not a body eat a bite at breakfast that morning. After that the men loafed around, in twos and threes, and talked low together. But none of them herded with Dick Allbright. They all give him the cold shake. If he come around where any of the men was, they split up and sidled away. They wouldn't man the sweeps with him. The captain had all the skiffs hauled up on the raft, alongside of his wigwam, and wouldn't let the dead men be took ashore to be planted; he didn't believe a man that got ashore would come back; and he was right.

"After night come, you could see pretty plain that there was going to be trouble if that bar'l come again; there was such a muttering going on. A good many wanted to kill Dick Allbright, because he'd seen the bar'l on other trips, and that had an ugly look. Some wanted to put him ashore.

Some said: 'Let's all go ashore in a pile, if the bar'l comes again.'

"This kind of whispers was still going on, the men being bunched together forrard watching for the bar'l, when lo and behold you! here she comes again. Down she comes, slow and steady, and settles into her old tracks. You could 'a' heard a pin drop. Then up comes the captain, and says:

" 'Boys, don't be a pack of children and fools; I don't want this bar'l to be dogging us all the way to Orleans, and *you* don't: Well, then, how's the best way to stop it? Burn it up—that's the way. I'm going to fetch it aboard,' he says. And before anybody could say a word, in he went.

"He swum to it, and as he come pushing it to the raft, the men spread to one side. But the old man got it aboard and busted in the head, and there was a baby in it! Yes, sir; a stark-naked baby. It was Dick Allbright's baby; he owned up and said so.

" 'Yes,' he says, a-leaning over it, 'yes, it is my own lamented darling, my poor lost Charles William Allbright deceased,' says he—for he could curl his tongue around the bulliest words in the language when he was a mind to, and lay them before you without a jint started anywheres. Yes, he said, he used to live up at the head of this bend, and one night he choked his child, which was crying, not intending to kill it—which was prob'ly a lie—and then he was scared, and buried it in a bar'l, before his wife got home, and off he went, and struck the northern trail and went to rafting; and this was the third year that the bar'l had chased him. He said the bad luck always begun light, and lasted till four men was killed, and then the bar'l didn't come any more after that. He said if the men would stand it one more night—and was a-going on like that—but the men had got enough. They started to get out a boat to take him ashore and lynch him, but he grabbed the little child all of a sudden and jumped overboard with it, hugged up to his breast and shedding tears, and we never see him again in this life, poor old suffering soul, nor Charles William neither."

"*Who* was shedding tears?" says Bob; "was it Allbright or the baby?"

"Why, Allbright, of course; didn't I tell you the baby was dead? Been dead three years—how could it cry?"

"Well, never mind how it could cry—how could it *keep* all that time?" says Davy. "You answer me that."

"I don't know how it done it," says Ed. "It done it, though—that's all I know about it."

"Say—what did they do with the bar'l?" says the Child of Calamity.

"Why, they hove it overboard, and it sunk like a chunk of lead."

"Edward, did the child look like it was choked?" says one.

"Did it have its hair parted?" says another.

"What was the brand on that bar'l, Eddy?" says a fellow they called Bill.

"Have you got the papers for them statistics, Edmund?" says Jimmy.

"Say, Edwin, was you one of the men that was killed by the lightning?" says Davy.

"Him? Oh, no! he was both of 'em," says Bob. Then they all haw-hawed.

"Say, Edward, don't you reckon you'd better take a pill? You look bad—don't you feel pale?" says the Child of Calamity.

"Oh, come, now, Eddy," says Jimmy, "show up; you must 'a' kept part of that bar'l to prove the thing by. Show us the bung-hole—*do*—and we'll all believe you."

"Say, boys," says Bill, "less divide it up. Thar's thirteen of us. I can swaller a thirteenth of the yarn, if you can worry down the rest."

Ed got up mad and said they could all go to some place which he ripped out pretty savage, and then walked off aft, cussing to himself, and they yelling and jeering at him, and roaring and laughing so you could hear them a mile.

"Boys, we'll split a watermelon on that," says the Child of Calamity; and he came rummaging around in the dark amongst the shingle bundles where I was, and put his hand on me. I was warm and soft and naked; so he says "Ouch!" and jumped back.

"Fetch a lantern or a chunk of fire here, boys—there's a snake here as big as a cow!"

So they run there with a lantern, and crowded up and looked in on me.

"Come out of that, you beggar!" says one.

"Who are you?" says another.

"What are you after here? Speak up prompt, or overboard you go."

"Snake him out, boys. Snatch him out by the heels."

I began to beg, and crept out amongst them trembling. They looked me over, wondering, and the Child of Calamity says:

"A cussed thief! Lend a hand and less heave him overboard!"

"No," says Big Bob, "less get out the paint-pot and paint him a sky-blue all over from head to heel, and *then* heave him over."

"Good! that's it. Go for the paint, Jimmy."

When the paint come, and Bob took the brush and was just going to begin, the others laughing and rubbing their hands, I begun to cry, and that sort of worked on Davy, and he says:

"'Vast there. He's nothing but a cub. I'll paint the man that teches him!"

So I looked around on them, and some of them grumbled and growled, and Bob put down the paint, and the others didn't take it up.

"Come here to the fire, and less see what you're up to here," says Davy. "Now set down there and give an account of yourself. How long have you been aboard here?"

"Not over a quarter of a minute, sir," says I.

"How did you get dry so quick?"

"I don't know, sir. I'm always that way, mostly."

"Oh, you are, are you? What's your name?"

I warn't going to tell my name. I didn't know what to say, so I just says:

"Charles William Allbright, sir."

Then they roared—the whole crowd; and I was mighty glad I said that, because, maybe, laughing would get them in a better humor.

When they got done laughing, Davy says:

"It won't hardly do, Charles William. You couldn't have growed this much in five year, and you was a baby when you come out of the bar'l, you know, and dead at that. Come, now, tell a straight story, and nobody'll hurt you, if you ain't up to anything wrong. What *is* your name?"

"Aleck Hopkins, sir. Aleck James Hopkins."

"Well, Aleck, where did you come from, here?"

"From a trading-scow. She lays up the bend yonder. I was born on her. Pap has traded up and down here all his life; and he told me to swim off here, because when you went by he said he would like to get some of you to speak to a Mr. Jonas Turner, in Cairo, and tell him—"

"Oh, come!"

"Yes, sir, it's as true as the world. Pap he says—"

"Oh, your grandmother!"

They all laughed, and I tried again to talk, but they broke in on me and stopped me.

"Now, looky-here," says Davy; "you're scared, and so you talk wild. Honest, now, do you live in a scow, or is it a lie?"

"Yes, sir, in a trading-scow. She lays up at the head of the bend. But I warn't born in her. It's our first trip."

"Now you're talking! What did you come aboard here for? To steal?"

"No sir, I didn't. It was only to get a ride on the raft. All boys does that."

"Well, I know that. But what did you hide for?"

"Sometimes they drive the boys off."

"So they do. They might steal. Looky-here; if we let you off this time, will you keep out of these kind of scrapes hereafter?"

" 'Deed I will, boss. You try me."

"All right, then. You ain't but little ways from shore. Overboard with you, and don't you make a fool of yourself another time this way. Blast it, boy, some raftsmen would rawhide you till you were black and blue!"

I didn't wait to kiss good-by, but went overboard and broke for shore. When Jim come along by and by, the big raft was away out of sight around the point. I swum out and got aboard, and was mighty glad to see home again.

JOHNSON JONES HOOPER

From Some Adventures of Captain Simon Suggs

Chapter the Tenth. The Captain Attends a Camp-Meeting[1]

* * * Captain Suggs drew on his famous old green-blanket overcoat, and ordered his horse, and within five minutes was on his way to a camp-meeting, then in full blast on Sandy creek, twenty miles distant, where he hoped to find amusement, at least. When he arrived there, he found the hollow square of the encampment filled with people, listening to the mid-day sermon and its dozen accompanying "exhortations." * * * Men and women rolled about on the ground, or lay sobbing or shouting in promiscuous heaps. More than all, the negroes sang and screamed and prayed. Several, under the influence of what is technically called "the jerks," were plunging and pitching about with convulsive energy. * * *

"Keep the thing warm!" roared a sensual seeming man, of stout

1. *Some Adventures of Captain Simon Suggs*, by Johnson Jones Hooper, Philadelphia, 1845, recaptured the picaresque literary tradition made classic by Cervantes. Hooper's book derives from the actualities of the American frontier and Mississippi River life, which produced a roguish literature of oral anecdote. In the "flush times" of frontier Alabama, Sugg's wholehearted devotion to rascality is fundamentally comic. Mark Twain knew this book in his youth, and he had a long acquaintance with the Mississippi customs and folklore that it represents. There must be more than coincidence in the resemblance between his "King" and "Duke" in *Huckleberry Finn* and the Captain Suggs of the Camp-meeting episode, below. It is also inescapable that, by the time of his revisiting the river in 1882, before completing *Huck*, Twain had come to share Hooper's evident disgust at the human riffraff of the Bricksvilles down the river, so unlike his earlier dream of St. Petersburg.

mould and florid countenance, who was exhorting among a bevy of young women, upon whom he was lavishing caresses. "Keep the thing warm, breethring!—come to the Lord, honey!" he added, as he vigorously hugged one of the damsels he sought to save.

"Oh, I've got him!" said another in exulting tones, as he led up a gawky youth among the mourners— "I've got him—he tried to git off, but—ha! Lord!"—shaking his head as much as to say, it took a smart fellow to escape him—"ha! Lord!"—and he wiped the perspiration from his face with one hand, and with the other, patted his neophyte on the shoulder—"he couldn't do it! No!" * * *

In another part of the square a dozen old women were singing. They were in a state of absolute extasy, as their shrill pipes gave forth,

"I rode on the sky,
Quite ondestified² I,
And the moon it was under my feet!"

* * *

Amid all this confusion and excitement Suggs stood unmoved. * * *

"Well, now," said he, as he observed the full-faced brother who was "officiating," among the women, "that ere feller takes *my* eye! —thar he's been this half-hour, a-figurin amongst them galls, and's never said the fust word to nobody else. Wonder what's the reason these here preachers never hugs up the old, ugly women? Never seed one do it in my life—the sperrit never moves 'em that way! It's nater tho'; and the women, *they* never flocks round one o' the old dried-up breethring—bet two to one old splinter-legs thar,"— nodding at one of the ministers—"won't git a chance to say turkey to a good-lookin gall to-day! Well! who blames 'em? Nater will be nater, all the world over; and I judge ef I was a preacher, I should save the purtiest souls fust, myself!"

While the Captain was in the middle of this conversation with himself, he caught the attention of the preacher in the pulpit, who inferring from an indescribable something about his appearance that he was a person of some consequence, immediately determined to add him at once to the church if it could be done; and to that end began a vigorous, direct personal attack.

"Breethring," he exclaimed, "I see yonder a man that's a sinner; I *know* he's a sinner! Thar he stands," pointing at Simon, "a missubble old crittur, with his head a-blossomin for the grave! A few more short years, and d-o-w-n he'll go to perdition, lessen the Lord have mer-cy on him! Come up here, you old hoary-headed sinner,

2. An example of the picturesque word coinage of the American frontier; here a combination of "unsanctified" with "predestined."

a-n-d git down upon your knees, a-n-d put up your cry for the Lord to snatch you from the bottomless pit! You're ripe for the devil— you're b-o-u-n-d for hell, and the Lord only knows what'll become on you!"

"D——n it," thought Suggs, "*ef* I only had you down in the krick swamp for a minit or so, *I'd* show you who's *old! I'd* alter your tune *mighty* sudden, you sassy, 'saitful[3] old rascal!'" But he judiciously held his tongue and gave no utterance to the thought.

The attention of many having been directed to the Captain by the preacher's remarks, he was soon surrounded by numerous well-meaning, and doubtless very pious persons, each one of whom seemed bent on the application of his own particular recipe for the salvation of souls. For a long time the Captain stood silent, or answered the incessant stream of exhortation only with a sneer; but at length, his countenance began to give token of inward emotion. First his eye-lids twitched—then his upper lip quivered—next a transparent drop formed on one of his eyelashes and a similar one on the tip of his nose—and, at last, a sudden bursting of air from nose and mouth, told that Captain Suggs was overpowered by his emotions. At the moment of the explosion, he made a feint as if to rush from the crowd, but he was in experienced hands, who well knew that the battle was more than half won.

"Hold to him!" said one—"it's a-working in him as strong as a Dick horse!"

"Pour it into him," said another, "it'll all come right directly!"

"That's the way I love to see 'em do," observed a third; "when you begin to draw water from their eyes, taint gwine to be long afore you'll have 'em on their knees!"

And so they clung to the Captain manfully, and half dragged, half led him to the mourner's bench; by which he threw himself down, altogether unmanned, and bathed in tears. Great was the rejoicing of the brethren, as they sang, shouted, and prayed around him—for by this time it had come to be generally known that the "convicted" old man was Captain Simon Suggs, the very "chief of sinners" in all that region.

The Captain remained grovelling in the dust during the usual time, and gave vent to even more than the requisite number of sobs, and groans, and heart-piercing cries. At length, when the proper time had arrived, he bounced up, and with a face radiant with joy commenced a series of vaultings and tumblings, which "laid in the shade" all previous performances of the sort at that camp-meeting. The brethren were in extasies at this demonstrative evidence of completion of the work; and whenever Suggs shouted "Gloree!" at the top of his lungs, every one of them shouted it

3. Deceitful.

back, until the woods rang with echoes. * * *

"Friends," he said, "it don't take long to curry a short horse, accordin' to the old sayin', and I'll give you the perticklers of the way I was brought to a knowledge"—here the Captain wiped his eyes, brushed the tip of his nose and snuffled a little—"in less'n no time."

"Praise the Lord!" ejaculated a bystander.

"You see I come here full o' romancin' and devilment, and jist to make game of all the purceedins. Well, sure enough, I done so for some time, and was a-thinkin how I should play some trick * * * to turn it all into redecule, when they began to come round me and talk. Long at fust I didn't mind it, but arter a little that brother"—pointing to the reverend gentleman who * * * Simon was convinced was the "big dog of the tanyard"—"that brother spoke a word that struck me kleen to the heart, and run all over me, like fire in dry grass——"

"I-I-I can bring 'em!" cried the preacher alluded to, in a tone of exultation—"Lord thou knows ef thy servant can't stir 'em up, nobody else needn't try—but the glory aint mine! I'm a poor worrum of the dust," he added, with ill-managed affectation.

"And so from that I felt somethin' a-pullin' me inside——"

"Grace! grace! nothin' but grace!" exclaimed one; meaning that "grace" had been operating in the Captain's gastric region.[4]

"And then," continued Suggs, "I wanted to git off, but they hilt me, and bimeby I felt so missuble, I had to go yonder"—pointing to the mourners' seat—"and when I lay down thar it got wuss and wuss, and 'peared like somethin' was a-mashin' down on my back—"

"That was his load o' sin," said one of the brethren—"never mind, it'll tumble off presently, see ef it don't!" and he shook his head professionally and knowingly.

"And it kept a-gittin heavier and heavier, ontwell it looked like it might be a four year old steer, or a big pine log, or somethin' of that sort—" * * *

"And arter awhile," Suggs went on, "'peared like I fell into a trance, like, and I seed—"

"Now we'll git the good on it" cried one of the sanctified.

"And I seed the biggest, longest, rip-roarenest, blackest, scaliest—" Captain Suggs paused, wiped his brow, and ejaculated "Ah, L-o-r-d!" so as to give full time for curiosity to become impatience to know what he saw.

"*Sarpent!* warn't it?" asked one of the preachers.

"No, not a sarpent," replied Suggs, blowing his nose.

4. The object of the camp-meeting "revival" was conversion—the recognition of grace, the divine love of God extended to fallen man.

"Do tell us *what* it war, soul alive!—whar *is* John?" said Mrs. Dobbs.

"Allegator!" said the Captain.

"Alligator!" repeated every woman present, and screamed for very life. * * *

"Well," said the Captain in continuation, "the allegator kept a-comin' and a-comin' to'ards me, with his great long jaws a-gapin' open like a ten-foot pair o' tailors' shears—"

"Oh! oh! oh! Lord! gracious above!" cried the woman.

"SATAN!" was the laconic ejaculation of the oldest preacher present, who thus informed the congregation that it was the devil which had attacked Suggs in the shape of an alligator.

"And then I concluded the jig was up, 'thout I could block his game some way; for I seed his idee was to snap off my head—"

The women screamed again.

"So I fixed myself jist like I was purfectly willin' for him to take my head, and rather he'd do it as not"—here the women shuddered perceptibly—"and so I hilt my head straight out"—the Captain illustrated by elongating his neck—"and when he come up and was a gwine to *shet down* on it, I jist pitched in a big rock which choked him to death, and that minit I felt the weight slide off, and I had the best feelins—sorter like you'll have from *good* sperrits— any body ever had!"

"Didn't I *tell* you so? Didn't I *tell* you so?" asked the brother who had predicted the off-tumbling of the load of sin. "Ha, Lord! fool *who?* I've been *all* along thar!—yes, *all along thar!* and I know every inch of the way jist as good as I do the road home!" and then he turned round and round, and looked at all, to receive a silent tribute to his superior penetration.

Captain Suggs was now the "lion of the day." Nobody could pray so well, or exhort so movingly, as "brother Suggs." Nor did his natural modesty prevent the performance of appropriate exercises. With the reverend Bela Bugg (him to whom, under providence, he ascribed his conversion) he was a most especial favourite. They walked, sang, and prayed together for hours. * * *

The next morning, when the preacher of the day first entered the pulpit, he announced that "brother Simon Suggs," mourning over his past iniquities, and desirous of going to work in the cause as speedily as possible, would take up a collection to found a church in his own neighborhood, at which he hoped to make himself useful as soon as he could prepare himself for the ministry, which the preacher didn't doubt, would be in a very few weeks, as brother Suggs was "a man of mighty good *judgment,* and of a *great discorse.*" The funds were to be collected by "brother Suggs," and held in trust by brother Bela Bugg, who was the financial officer of the circuit, until some arrangement could be made to build a suitable house.

"Yes, breethring," said the Captain, rising to his feet; "I want to start a little 'sociation close to me, and I want you all to help. I'm mighty poor myself, as poor as any of you—don't leave breethring"—observing that several of the well-to-do were about to go off—"don't leave; ef you aint able to afford any thing, jist give us your blessin' and it'll be all the same!"

This insinuation did the business, and the sensitive individuals re-seated themselves.

"It's mighty little of this world's goods I've got," resumed Suggs, pulling off his hat and holding it before him; "but I'll bury *that* in the cause any how," and he deposited his last five-dollar bill in the hat.

There was a murmur of approbation at the Captain's liberality throughout the assembly.

Suggs now commenced collecting, and very prudently attacked first the gentlemen who had shown a disposition to escape. These, to exculpate themselves from any thing like poverty, contributed handsomely.

"Look here, breethring," said the Captain, displaying the bank-notes thus received, "brother Snooks has drapt a five wi' me, and brother Snodgrass a ten! In course 'taint expected that you *that aint as well off as them*, will give *as much*; let every one give *accordin'* to ther means."

This was another chain-shot that raked as it went! "Who so low" as not to be able to contribute as much as Snooks and Snodgrass?

"Here's all the *small* money I've got about me," said a burly old fellow, ostentatiously handing to Suggs, over the heads of a half dozen, a ten dollar bill.

"That's what I call maganimus!" exclaimed the Captain; "that's the way *every* rich man ought to do!"

These examples were followed, more or less closely, by almost all present, for Simon had excited the pride of purse of the congregation, and a very handsome sum was collected in a very short time.

The reverend Mr. Bugg, as soon as he observed that our hero had obtained all that was to be had at that time, went to him and inquired what amount had been collected. The Captain replied that it was still uncounted, but that it couldn't be much under a hundred.

"Well, brother Suggs, you'd better count it and turn it over to me now. I'm goin' to leave presently."

"No!" said Suggs—"can't do it!"

"Why?—what's the matter?" inquired Bugg.

"It's got to be *prayed over*, fust!" said Simon, a heavenly smile illuminating his whole face.

"Well," replied Bugg, "less go one side and do it!"

"No!" said Simon, solemnly.

Mr. Bugg gave a look of inquiry,

"You see that krick swamp?" asked Suggs—"I'm gwine down in *thar*, and I'm gwine to lay this money down *so*"—showing how he would place it on the ground—"and I'm gwine to git on these here knees"—slapping the right one—"and I'm *n-e-v-e-r* gwine to quit the grit ontwell I feel it's got the blessin'! And nobody aint got to be thar but me!"

Mr. Bugg greatly admired the Captain's fervent piety, and bidding him God-speed, turned off.

Captain Suggs "struck for" the swamp sure enough, where his horse was already hitched. "Ef them fellers ain't done to a cracklin,'" he muttered to himself as he mounted, "*I*'ll never bet on two pair agin! They're peart at the snap game, theyselves; but they're badly lewed[5] this hitch! Well, Live and let live is a good old motter, and it's my sentiments adzactly!" And giving the spur to his horse, off he cantered.

1845

DAN DE QUILLE

From The Big Bonanza

Chapter LXXII. The Comical Story of Pike.[1] Tom sings—The joke successful—Pike vanishes—A pretty big story—Doubtful dreams— Self-deceived—Our journey's end

As soon as we were left to ourselves we built a roaring fire, in spite of all Pike's remonstrances. "It's jist as good a thing as the Injuns want," said he. "It's jist showin' 'em whar we are. We'll lose our skelps afore mornin'."

When we began to think of supper, we found that we had played a little joke on ourselves, in our hurry to get the other fellows away in order to make sure of Pike. We had nothing in the shape of provision except a few pounds of rice, which happened to be on Tom's

5. Brought low or outwitted.
1. From *History of the Big Bonanza, An Authentic Account of the Discovery, History, and Working of the * * * Comstock Lode of Nevada * * ** by Dan De Quille, Hartford, 1877. The signature is the pen name of William Wright (1829–98), who, like Artemus Ward and Mark Twain, followed the Argonauts to the Comstock and to California as newspaper man and humorist.

Associates in 1862 on the *Territorial Enterprise*, Virginia City, Nevada, they remained lifelong friends. De Quille's racy stories, and their authentic folklore, influenced Twain's writing. For example, the present western hoax recalls Huck's pathetic attempt to delude Jim into thinking that he dreamed that Huck had fallen from the raft and drowned.

horse. We put some of this into a gold-pan and boiled it, but it was rather poor eating without either butter or salt. As we were sitting about the pan scooping up this rice with knives and wooden paddles, Pike said: "I allers knowed I didn't like rice as well as I thought I did, and now I'm sure of it." But we had plenty of tobacco and what we lacked in "grub" we made up in smoke. As soon as it grew dark Pike became very restless.

"What was that?" he would say. "Did you hear the rocks rattle up on the hillside?" and he would peer out into the darkness.

Tom now began to sing as loud as he could roar:

"My name it is Joe Bowers, I've got a brother Ike,
I come from old Missouri, yes, all the way from Pike."

"Stop singin' so loud, Tom," cried Pike in alarm. "Don't!" But Tom roared the louder:

"I'll tell you why I left thar, and how I came to roam,
And leave my poor old mammy, so far away from home."

"Tom! Tom! Good Lord, don't!" begged Pike.

"I used to love a gal thar, they called her Sally Black,
I axed her for to marry me, she said it was a whack,
But says she to me: 'Joe Bowers, before we hitch for life,
You'd orter have a little home, to keep your little wife.' "

"If you've got a little home, Tom," said Pike, "I wish to God you was now in it!"

"Says I, 'My dearest Sally, O Sally, for your sake,
I'll go to Californy and try to raise a stake.' "

"That thar's a fool song," said Pike, "and nobody but a fool would sing it!"

"But one day I got a letter from my dear brother Ike,
It came from old Missouri, sent all the way from Pike."

"Whar I wish to the Lord I was now!" groaned Pike.

"It brought the goldarndest news that ever you did hear.
My heart is almost bustin', so pray excuse this tear.
It said my Sal was fickle, that her love for me had fled,
That she'd married with a butcher, whose har was orful red."

"Thar'll be butchers here 'fore long," groaned Pike.

"It told me more than that, oh! it's enough to make one swear
It said Sally had a baby, and the baby had red hair."

"Now, cuss yer pictur!" said Pike. "Yer done, air yer? I'll bet thar'll be red har enough here before mornin'. Your singin' has played thunder with us, sure as thar's wool on a nigger, but you'll not have a bit on the—"

"Top of his head, where the wool had orter be,"[2] roared Tom.

Pike was now at his wits' end and went off a rod or two from the fire and sat down by a dark clump of bushes, sullen and thoroughly disgusted. Tom called out to him: "Say, Pike, are you loadin' that revolver o' your'n?" but Pike had the sulks and would not condescend to answer. It was soon time to turn in for the night, and each man took his blankets and sought the smoothest place to be found. Pike and one of our party known as "Hank" spread their blankets together at some distance from the fire, which was now quite low, while the rest of us found places for our beds among some willows.

Pike lay awake a long time listening for Indians and would rise to his knees at the slightest sound, pulling the blankets off Hank, who was trying to make him lie still, so that he could get to sleep. There was a high hill on the east side of the canyon, covered on the side next to us with shelly slate rock, and whenever a fox, coyote, or even a rat ran over this it caused a great clatter, the scales of slate ringing like pieces of pottery. This was a place fruitful of alarms and caused Pike to be upon his knees about every five minutes, but about midnight he could keep his eyes open no longer. Hank made the signal agreed upon, by holding up his hat, when two of the boys crept cautiously out of the camp with six-shooters in their hands. By following up a little ravine they were able to gain the summit of the slaty hill without making the slightest noise, as there was no loose rock except on the slope. Presently they started down the slope through the loose rock, leaping and making as much noise as though old Winnemucca and half the Piute tribe were coming down the mountain. At the same time they began yelling and firing their revolvers. At the first racket made on the hill Pike was on his feet and came running toward us, who were returning the fire of the supposed Indians, and yelling as we fired, making altogether enough noise for half a dozen small battles. When Pike reached us, two or three of our men fell, crying out that they were killed, and at the same time Hank fell and caught him about the legs, crying: "I'm wounded. Carry me off and hide me in the bushes!"

"Let go of me, Hank, there's five hundred of 'em comin'!"

"I'll never let go of you," said Hank. "Carry me off!"

Pike then lifted Hank, who was groaning at a terrible rate, and carrying him about two rods, pitched him, neck and heels, into a clump of thorny bushes. This done, Pike rushed down the canyon at the speed of an antelope. Tom rolled on the ground and laughed until he almost smothered himself. "I'm even with Pike on the

2. In a folksong then familiar, the "old Negro, Uncle Ned, had no wool on the top of his head."

prickly-pear business!" cried he as soon as he was able to speak. "He shall never hear the last of this Injun fight!" For my part, now that the fun was all over, I began to feel quite miserable over the whole affair. I feared that in his great fright Pike might dash his brains out against a tree or break his neck among the rocks. I firmly resolved never to take part in another affair of the kind, calling to mind several sham fights and other deviltry in California that had been attended by fatal results to the victims.

In the morning we were ready for a start at sunrise. The first thing I saw was Pike's hat, lying near the place where he had spread his blankets the night before. The sight gave me quite a shock, as it seemed to be the hat of a dead man. I soon found that the others were beginning to feel much as I did about the matter, for as Pike's blankets were being rolled up to be packed on Tom's horse, one of the boys said: "I hope nothing has happened to Pike." Another said: "Oh, he's all right!" but at the same time it was easy to see that the speaker feared that he was not "all right."

As we passed down the canyon, I could not help thinking that we should presently find Pike lying wounded or already dead in some rocky pit or pile of boulders near the trail, and most of our party looked quite solemn. The man who carried Pike's hat looked as though he were in a funeral procession, carrying a portion of the corpse. At length we were through the canyon, and having reached the level plain without finding Pike's remains, we all felt quite jolly again and immediately set to work and planned another surprise for him when we should find him. Instead of fording the river, as we had done in going out, we went some two miles farther down and crossed at a ferry. We inquired of the colored man in charge if anyone had crossed during the night. He assured us that no one had crossed, as he found the boat tied up on the west bank as he had left it the evening before.

We now knew that Pike must have crossed at the ford and again began to feel uneasy, fearing that, reaching the river in a state of exhaustion, he had plunged in and had been swept under by the current. One of two things was certain: he was either safe across or was drowned, as the Mississippi itself would not have stayed his flight. On turning into the main street of Chinatown we came suddenly upon a group of men with Minié muskets in their hands and in their midst stood Pike, with a handkerchief tied about his head. He had a musket in his hand and was the center of attraction. We could see that he was telling those about him of the dreadful affair of the previous night. All those surrounding him were listening so intently that we approached without being observed. Pike was just saying: "Yes, Hank may be alive. I carried him about two miles on my back, with the red cusses yellin' at my heels, then laid him down and kivered him up with brush. But all the rest—" Here Pike turned and saw our party. His jaw dropped, and his eyes almost started from their sockets.

"Well, what of the rest?" said one of his auditors.

"Why, my God! They are all here!" said Pike. "There they all stand!"

The crowd now turned to us and began to ask: "Who was killed?" "Were there many Indians?" and many other like questions. Not a word of this, however, could we be made to understand. We had seen no Indians; we had never dreamed of any danger from Indians. The whole crowd at once turned to Pike for an explanation. Some of the men hinted that unless he gave a pretty satisfactory explanation of his strange stories he would get into trouble. Pike was thunderstruck and gazed at us with a look of utter helplessness. At last he stammered: "Tom, wasn't you killed?"

"If I was killed I wouldn't be here, would I?"

"I thought I saw you fall," and Pike's face wore the most puzzled look imaginable. His fingers sought the yellowish tuft of hair on his chin and, gazing at one and another of us, he sighed: "I don't understand it at all."

"We none of us understand it," said one of the crowd sneeringly.

"All here—all here!" said Pike, his countenance wearing the look of an insane person.

"Pike," said I, "you must have dreamt all this about Indians." Pike's face brightened for a moment, but soon resumed its old look of despair. "No, no," said he, "no dream. I saw them all killed."

"But, Pike, look at us; we are all here—all alive and well!"

Pike looked vacantly about him at the boys, and said: "Yes, I know, but I don't understand it at all."

"Well," said I, "all there is about it is that you were dreaming and suddenly rose up shouting: 'Injuns! Injuns!' and before we could stop you, you ran away down the canyon."

"Yes," said Pike, "it must have been a dream. You are all here— it must have been a dream. But it don't seem that way at all."

"Don't seem what way?"

"Why, the way you tell it."

"Well, how does it seem? Let us hear you tell it. Let us have your dream."

"Give us the dream!" "Let's have yer dream!" cried the crowd.

"Well, you see I was a-layin' thar in my blankets— But I'll be doggoned ef I believe I did dream it!" cried Pike. "I can almost hear the guns crack now!"

"Of course you dreamt it. Ain't we all here?"

"Yes, I know. But how did I act—what did I do?"

"Why, I've just told you all you did. You know that after you went to bed you was bouncing up on your knees every five minutes, and at last you bounced up and took to your heels."

"Yes, I know I was a little oneasy like. I kept a-hearin' somethin' rattle up on that hill, so I kinder kept on my guard like."

"Well, let us have the dream," all again cried.

"Well," began Pike, "at first I was a-dreamin' along kinder nice and easy like, when all at once I heard the rocks clatter—I mean I thought I heard 'em clatter. Then bang, bang! pop, pop! went the guns, and oh, sich yells—sich yells! I thought my hair riz straight on end, and I seed more'n five hundred Injuns, all a-hoppin' down the hill like turkeys. All this time I thought that you fellers was a-blazin' away at about two hundred of 'em that was all round you and about five hundred on the hill. Then I thought I grabbed up a pick and went right inter the thick of the cusses and fit and fit till I'd wore out the pick, and then fit a long time with the handle. By this time I thought you fellers was all killed and I thought I'd git up and dust. But jist then I thought that Hank got holt round my legs and said he was wounded, and wouldn't let go of me 'thout I'd carry him off. I thought I tuck him on my back and carried him 'bout four miles, and hid him in some brush. Then I thought I run on and waded across the river—"

"No, no! You didn't dream that! You did actually wade across the river."

"Well, then, what part of it did I dream? Can anybody tell me that?" and poor Pike looked more puzzled than ever.

"You must have waded the river, you know, or you would not be here."

"Well, yes; I s'pose I did, but that don't seem a bit plainer, nor hardly half as plain as the shootin' and yellin' part. That was the doggonest plainest dream I ever did hev!"

"Yet, as we are all here, alive and well, it must have been a dream?"

"Oh, yes, it was a dream, sartain and sure, but what gits me was its bein' so astonishin' plain—jist the same as bein' wide awake!"

Pike continued to tell his dream for some years, constantly adding new matter, till at last it was a wonderful yarn. He enlarged greatly on the part he took in the fight, and after wearing out the pick on the skulls of the Indians, wound up by thrusting the handle down the throat of a brave, as his last act before beating a retreat. Tom more than once told him the truth about the whole affair, bringing in half a dozen of the "boys" to corroborate what he said, but not a word of it would Pike believe.

"Do you think," he would say, "that I was fool enough to believe that sich things actually happened? No, it was all a dream from fust to last, and the biggest and plainest dream I ever had!"

* * *

ARTEMUS WARD

Artemus Ward and the Prince of Wales[1]

I was drawin' near to the Prince, when a red-faced man in Millingtery close grabd holt of me and axed me whare I was goin' all so bold?

"To see Albert Edard, the Prince of Wales," sez I; "who are you?"

He sed he was the Kurnal of the Seventy Fust Regiment, Her Magisty's troops. I told him I hoped the Seventy Onesters was in good helth, and was passin' by when he ceased hold of me agin, and sed in a tone of indigent cirprise:

"What? Impossible! It kannot be! Blarst my hize, sir, did I understan' you to say that you was actooally goin' into the presents of his Royal Iniss?"

"That's what's the matter with me," I replied.

"But blarst my hize, sir, its onprecedented. It's orful sir. Nothin' like it hain't happened sins the Gun Powder Plot of Guy Forks. Owdashus man, who air yu?"

"Sir," sez I, drawin' myself up & puttin' on a defiant air, "I'm a Amerycan sitterzen. My name is Ward. I'm a husband, & the father of twins, which I'm happy to state thay look like me. By perfession I'm a exhibiter of wax works & sich."

"Good God!" yelled the Kurnal; "the idee of a exhibiter of wax figgers goin' into the presents of Royalty! The British Lion may well roar with raje at the thawt!"

Sez I, "Speakin' of the British Lion, Kurnal, I'd like to make a bargin with you fur that beast fur a few weeks to add to my Show." I didn't meen nothin' by this. I was only gettin' orf a goak, but you orter hev seen the Old Kurnal jump up and howl. He actooally foamed at the mowth.

"This can't be real," he showtid. "No, no. It's a horrid dream. Sir, you air not a human bein'—you hav no existents—yu're a Myth!"

"Wall," sez I, "old hoss, yule find me a ruther oncomfortable

1. Charles Farrar Browne (1834–67), professionally known as Artemus Ward, was, like Mark Twain, a roving printer, newspaper man, and humorist when the two met in the early 'sixties at the silver-boom town of Virginia City, Nevada. Their friendship outlasted Ward's life and influenced Mark's writings. Both derided cultists, "Shakers," and Mormons; both comically burlesqued the extravagance of romance and the pretensions of royalty and social rank—compare Ward's sketch here with Huck Finn's discourse on kings. Clemens included this with other sketches by Artemus Ward in his popular compilation, *Mark Twain's Library of Humor*, New York, 1888.

Myth ef you punch my inards in that way agin." I began to git a
little riled, fur when he called me a Myth he puncht me putty hard.
The Kurnal now commenst showtin fur the Seventy Onesters. I at
fust thawt I'd stay & becum a Marter to British Outraje, as sich a
course mite git my name up & be a good advertisement fur my Show,
but it occurred to me that ef enny of the Seventy Onesters shood
happen to insert a baronet into my stummick it mite be onplesunt;
& I was on the pint of runnin' orf when the Prince hisself kum up
& axed me what the matter was. Sez I, "Albert Edard, is that you?"
& he smilt & sed it was. Sez I, "Albert Edard, hears my keerd. I cum
to pay my respecks to the futer King of Ingland. The Kurnal of the
Seventy Onesters hear is ruther smawl pertaters, but of course you
ain't to blame fur that. He puts on as many airs as tho he was the
Bully Boy with the glass eye."

"Never mind," sez Albert Edard, "I'm glad to see you, Mister
Ward, at all events," & he tuk my hand so plesunt like, & larfed so
sweet that I fell in love with him to onct. He handid me a segar, &
we sot down on the Pizarro & commenst smokin' rite cheerful.

"Wall," sez I, "Albert Edard, how's the old folks?"

"Her Majesty & the Prince are well," he sed.

"Duz the old man take his Lager beer reglar?" I inquired.

The Prince larfed, & intermatid that the old man didn't let many
kegs of that bevridge spile in the sellar in the coarse of a year. We
sot & tawked there sum time abowt matters & things, & bimeby I
axed him how he like bein' Prince, as fur as he'd got.

"To speak plain, Mister Ward," he sed, "I don't much like it.
I'm sick of all this bowin' & scrapin' & crawlin' & hurrain over a boy
like me. I would rather go through the country quietly & enjoy
myself in my own way, with the other boys, & not be made a Show
of to be gaped at by everybody. When the *peple* cheer me I feel
pleesed, fur I know they meen it; but if these one-horse offishuls
cood know how I see threw all their moves & understan' exactly
what they air after, & knowd how I larft at 'em in private, thayd stop
kissin' my hands & fawnin' over me as thay now do. But you know,
Mister Ward, I can't help bein' a Prince, & I must do all I kin to fit
myself for the persishun I must sumtime ockepy."

"That's troo," sez I; "sickness & the docters will carry the Queen
orf one of these dase, sure's yer born."

The time hevin' arove fur me to take my departer, I rose up &
sed: "Albert Edard, I must go, but previs to doin' so, I will obsarve
that you soot me. Yure a good feller, Albert Edard, & tho I'm agin
Princes as a gineral thing, I must say I like the cut of your Gib.
When you git to be King, try & be as good a man as your muther has
bin! Be just & be Jenerus, espeshully to showmen, who have allers
bin aboosed sins the dase of Noah, who was the fust man to go into

the Menagery bizniss, & ef the daily papers of his time air to be beleeved, Noah's colleckshun of livin' wild beests beet ennything ever seen sins, tho I make bold to dowt ef his snaiks was ahead of mine. Albert Edard, adoo!" I tuk his hand, which he shook warmly, & givin' him a perpetooal free pars to my show, & also parses to take hum for the Queen & Old Albert, I put on my hat and walkt away.

"Mrs. Ward," I solilerquized as I walkt along—"Mrs. Ward, ef you could see your husband now, just as he prowdly emerjis from the presunts of the futer King of Ingland, you'd be sorry you called him a Beest jest becaws he cum home tired 1 nite & wantid to go to bed without takin' off his boots. You'd be sorry for tryin' to deprive yure husband of the priceless Boon of liberty, Betsy Jane!"

Jest then I met a long perseshun of men with gownds onto 'em. The leader was on horseback, & ridin' up to me, he sed:

"Air you Orange?"

Sez I, "Which?"

"Air you a Orangeman?" he repeated, sternly.

"I used to peddle lemins," sed I, "but never delt in oranges. They are apt to spile on yure hands. What particler Loonatic Asylum hev you & yure friends escaped frum, if I may be so bold?" Just then a suddent thawt struck me, & I sed, "Oh, yure the fellers who air worryin' the Prince so, & givin' the Juke of Noocastle cold sweats at nite, by yure infernal catawalins, air you? Well, take the advice of a Amerykin sitterzen, take orf them gownds & don't try to get up a religious fite, which is 40 times wuss nor a prize fite, over Albert Edard, who wants to receive you all on a ekal footin' not keerin' a tinker's cuss what meetin'-house you sleep in Sundays. Go home & mind yure bisness, & not make noosenses of yourselves." With which observashuns I left 'em.

I shall leave British sile 4thwith.

THE POET LARIAT AND THE SWEET SINGER OF MICHIGAN[1]

BLOODGOOD H. CUTTER: On the Death of His Beloved Wife, March 24, 1881

The tyrant, Death did my home invade,
In his cold embrace my wife he laid;

1. Huck's quotation of Emmeline Grangerford's "Ode To Stephen Dowling Bots, Dec'd" reflects Twain's amusement with the lugubrious, sentimental and semi-literate verse produced by Bloodgood Haviland Cutter (1817?–1906) and Julia A. Moore (1847–1920). Cutter, the "poet lariat" of the

So sudden and fatal was the blow,
She had to yield and from me go.

When the doctor said her end was near,
It did affect me so severe;
It seemed to paralyze my brains,
And the circulation of my veins.

When I went up into her room,
I quickly did perceive her doom;
So fatal, then, did seem her case,
The mark of death was in her face.

Oh! 'twas the sad agony of my life,
To see the death gasping of my wife;
Then calmly yielding up her breath,
There in the cold embrace of death.

So quietly she seemed to rest,
With her cold hands across her breast;
Free from all pain and sorrow too,
Her face still looked lovely to my view.

As if her spirit was at rest
In the pure regions of the blest;
That, I sincerely do believe,
Though for my loss I sadly grieve.

In sadness now I mourn! I mourn,
For her who never will return;
Wife of my youth, my heart's delight,
Forever banished from my sight.

After I bade my last adieu,
The grave soon hid her from my view;
Tears from my eyes like fountains run,
When I did lose this faithful one.

If the Lord who gave took her away,
I must submit and to Him pray;

Quaker City excursion in *Innocents Abroad* (1869), was moved to verse during the voyage to the Holy Land in 1867 by every aspect of the trip, including seasickness, the health authorities at Naples, and his fellow passengers. Of one he wrote: "One droll person there was on board / The passengers called him 'Mark Twain;' / He'd talk and write all sort of stuff, / In his queer way, would it explain." Twain took delight in encouraging the publication of Cutter's effusions in *The Long Island Farmer's Poems, Lines Written on the "Quaker City" Excursion to Palestine,* *and other Poems* (New York, 1886), the source of Cutter's poem below. Julia Moore, the "Sweet Singer of Michigan," was poetically inspired by the death of little children, the perils of choking on roast beef, and the Ashtabula bridge disaster. One of her awestricken admirers, Twain said that she had "the touch that makes an intentionally humorous episode pathetic and an intentionally pathetic one funny." "Little Andrew" is taken from *The Sentimental Song Book* (Cleveland, 1877).

To enable me this trial to bear,
And trust to His Almighty care.

For forty years He did her spare,
And in my trials she did share;
When sick, to me she was so kind,
To ease my pain, to cheer my mind.

Bind up my wounds, to bathe my head,
Sit up by night by my sick bed;
Try many ways to me relieve—
Till that was done, would sit and grieve.

Now she is taken from the earth,
More keenly I do feel her worth!
On none like her I can depend,
I've lost! I've lost my dearest friend.

Perhaps my loss is now her gain:
She's free from sickness, care and pain;
But the debt of nature all must pay,
At a sooner or a later day.

Her spirit seems whispering in my ear,
"Weep not for me, my husband dear;
O! do your duty there below,
Until the Lord call you also."

(Little Neck, L. I., April, 1881)

JULIA A. MOORE: Little Andrew

Andrew was a little infant,
And his life was two years old;
He was his parents' eldest boy,
And he was drowned, I was told.
His parents never more can see him
In this world of grief and pain,
And Oh! they will not forget him
While on earth they do remain.

On one bright and pleasant morning
His uncle thought it would be nice
To take his dear little nephew
Down to play upon a raft,
Where he was to work upon it,
And this little child would company be—
The raft the water rushed around it,
Yet he the danger did not see.

This little child knew no danger—
Its little soul was free from sin—
He was looking in the water,
When, alas, this child fell in.
Beneath the raft the water took him,
For the current was so strong,
And before they could rescue him
He was drowned and was gone.

Oh! how sad were his kind parents
When they saw their drowned child,
As they brought him from the water,
It almost made their hearts grow wild.
Oh! how mournful was the parting
From that little infant son.
Friends, I pray you, all take warning,
Be careful of your little ones.

SAMUEL LANGHORNE CLEMENS

From Life on the Mississippi

[*The House Beautiful*][1]

* * *

Every town and village along that vast stretch of double river-frontage had a best dwelling, finest dwelling, mansion—the home of its wealthiest and most conspicuous citizen. It is easy to describe it: large grassy yard, with paling fence painted white—in fair repair; brick walk from gate to door; big, square, two-story "frame" house, painted white and porticoed like a Grecian temple—with this difference, that the imposing fluted columns and Corinthian capitals were a pathetic sham, being made of white pine, and painted; iron knocker; brass door-knob—discolored, for lack of polishing. Within, an uncarpeted hall, of planed boards; opening out of it, a parlor, fifteen feet by fifteen—in some instances five or ten feet larger; ingrain carpet; mahogany center-table; lamp on it, with green-paper shade—standing on a gridiron, so to speak, made of high-colored

1. From Mark Twain, *Life on the Mississippi*, Boston, 1883. This sketch may be regarded a background for an appreciation of the author's later sketches of dwellings, particularly that of the Grangerford plantation in Chapter XVII of *Huckleberry Finn*. Walter Blair says in this connection, "A comparison between this description written by the wry and critical humorist and that of the admiring Huck [at the Grangerford house] throws brilliant light on the comic values of Huck's angle of narrative" (*Mark Twain and Huck Finn*, p. 289).

yarns, by the young ladies of the house, and called a lamp-mat; several books, piled and disposed, with cast-iron exactness, according to an inherited and unchangeable plan; among them, Tupper, much penciled; also, *Friendship's Offering*, and *Affection's Wreath*, with their sappy inanities illustrated in die-away mezzotints; also, Ossian; *Alonzo and Melissa*; maybe *Ivanhoe*; also "Album," full of original "poetry" of the Thou-hast-wounded-the-spirit-that-loved-thee breed; two or three goody-goody works—*Shepherd of Salisbury Plain*, etc.; current number of the chaste and innocuous *Godey's Lady's Book*, with painted fashion-plate of wax-figure women with mouths all alike—lips and eyelids the same size—each five-foot woman with a two-inch wedge sticking from under her dress and letting on to be half of her foot. Polished air-tight stove (new and deadly invention), with pipe passing through a board which closes up the discarded good old fireplace. On each end of the wooden mantel, over the fireplace, a large basket of peaches and other fruits, natural size, all done in plaster, rudely, or in wax, and painted to resemble the originals—which they don't. Over middle of mantel, engraving— "Washington Crossing the Delaware"; on the wall by the door, copy of it done in thunder-and-lightning crewels by one of the young ladies—work of art which would have made Washington hesitate about crossing, if he could have foreseen what advantage was going to be taken of it. Piano—kettle in disguise—with music, bound and unbound, piled on it, and on a stand near by: "Battle of Prague"; "Bird Waltz"; "Arkansas Traveler"; "Rosin the Bow"; "Marseillaise Hymn"; "On a Lone Barren Isle" (St. Helena); "The Last Link Is Broken"; "She Wore a Wreath of Roses the Night When Last We Met"; "Go, Forget Me, Why Should Sorrow o'er That Brow a Shadow Fling"; "Hours That Were to Memory Dearer"; "Long, Long Ago"; "Days of Absence"; "A Life on the Ocean Wave, a Home on the Rolling Deep"; "Bird at Sea"; and spread open on the rack where the plaintive singer has left it, "*Ro*-holl on, silver *moo*-hoon, guide the *trav*-el-err on his *way*," etc. Tilted pensively against the piano, a guitar—guitar capable of playing the Spanish fandango by itself, if you give it a start. Frantic work of art on the wall—pious motto, done on the premises, sometimes in colored yarns, sometimes in faded grasses: progenitor of the "God Bless Our Home" of modern commerce. Framed in black moldings on the wall, other works of art, conceived and committed on the premises, by the young ladies; being grim black-and-white crayons; landscapes, mostly: lake, solitary sailboat, petrified clouds, pregeological trees on shore, anthracite precipice; name of criminal conspicuous in the corner. Lithograph, "Napoleon Crossing the Alps." Lithograph, "The Grave at St. Helena." Steel plates, Trumbull's "Battle of Bunker Hill," and the "Sally from Gibraltar." Copper plates, "Moses Smiting the Rock," and "Return of the Prodigal Son." In big gilt frame, slander of the family in oil: papa holding a book ("Constitution of the United States"); guitar leaning against mamma, blue ribbons fluttering from its neck; the young ladies, as children, in slippers and scalloped pantalettes, one embracing toy horse, the other beguiling kitten with ball of yarn, and both simpering up at mamma, who simpers back. These persons all fresh, raw, and red—apparently skinned. Opposite, in gilt frame, grandpa and grandma, at thirty and twenty-two, stiff, old-fashioned, high-collared, puff-sleeved, glaring pallidly out from a background of solid Egyptian night. Under a glass French clock dome, large bouquet of stiff flowers done in corpsy-white wax. Pyramidal what-not in the corner, the shelves occupied chiefly with bric-à-brac of the period, disposed with an eye to best effect: shell, with the Lord's Prayer carved on it; another shell—of the long-oval sort, narrow, straight orifice, three inches long, running from end to end—portrait of Washington carved on it; not well done; the shell had Washington's mouth, originally—artist should have built to that. These two are memorials of the long-ago bridal trip to New Orleans and the French Market. Other bric-à-brac: Californian "specimens"—quartz, with gold wart adhering; old Guinea-gold locket, with circlet of ancestral hair in it; Indian arrow-heads, of flint; pair of bead moccasins, from uncle who crossed the Plains; three "alum" baskets of various colors— being skeleton-frame of wire, clothed on with cubes of crystallized alum in the rock-candy style—works of art which were achieved by the young ladies; their doubles and duplicates to be found upon all what-nots in the land; convention of desiccated bugs and butterflies pinned to a card; painted toy dog, seated upon bellows attachment—drops its under-jaw and squeaks when pressed upon; sugar-candy rabbit—limbs and features merged together, not strongly defined; pewter presidential-campaign medal; miniature cardboard wood-sawyer, to be attached to the stovepipe and operated by the heat; small Napoleon, done in wax; spread-open daguerreotypes of dim children, parents, cousins, aunts, and friends, in all attitudes but customary ones; no templed portico at back, and manufactured landscape stretching away in the distance—that came in later, with the photograph; all these vague figures lavishly chained and ringed— metal indicated and secured from doubt by stripes and splashes of vivid gold bronze; all of them too much combed, too much fixed up; and all of them uncomfortable in inflexible Sunday clothes of a pattern which the spectator cannot realize could ever have been in fashion; husband and wife generally grouped together—husband sitting, wife standing, with hand on his shoulder—and both preserving, all these fading years, some traceable effect of the daguerreo-

typist's brisk "Now smile, if you please!" Bracketed over what-not—
place of special sacredness—an outrage in water-color, done by the
young niece that came on a visit long ago, and died. Pity, too; for
she might have repented of this in time. Horsehair chairs, horse-
hair sofa which keeps sliding from under you. Window-shades, of oil
stuff, with milkmaids and ruined castles stenciled on them in fierce
colors. Lambrequins dependent from gaudy boxings of beaten tin,
gilded. Bedrooms with rag carpets; bedsteads of the "corded" sort,
with a sag in the middle, the cords needing tightening; snuffy
feather-bed—not aired often enough; cane-seat chairs, splint-
bottomed rocker; looking-glass on wall, school-slate size, veneered
frame; inherited bureau; wash-bowl and pitcher, possibly—but not
certainly; brass candlestick, tallow candle, snuffers. Nothing else in
the room. Not a bathroom in the house; and no visitor likely to
come along who has ever seen one.

That was the residence of the principal citizen, all the way from
the suburbs of New Orleans to the edge of St. Louis. * * *

DIXON WECTER

[The Formative Experience: Sam Clemens of Hannibal]†

[*The Prototype of Nigger Jim*]

The most memorable servant of the Quarleses was middle-aged
Uncle Dan'l, sensible, honest, patient, the children's comrade in
adventure, their adviser and ally in time of trouble. "It was on the
farm that I got my strong liking for his race," wrote Mark, "and
my appreciation of certain of its fine qualities." Mark made a trial
sketch of him, under that name, in *The Gilded Age*. Later he became
the acknowledged original of Huck Finn's friend "Nigger Jim,"
whose unshakable loyalty, generous heart, and unconscious dignity
—even when Huck makes game of his credulity—raise him to the
rank of Mark Twain's noblest creation. He probably intended Joan
of Arc for that niche; in his hands she turns to plaster saint. But
Nigger Jim is as vital and earth-bound as one of the lofty hickories
that towered over the old farmstead.

† The selection from Dixon Wecter, *Sam Clemens of Hannibal*, copyright 1952, is reprinted by permission of and arrangement with Houghton Mifflin Company, the authorized publishers. Pp. 106–9; 147–51; 187–89. Compare these sketches with the article by Henry Nash Smith, "Mark Twain's Images of Hannibal." By contrast, Dixon Wecter, in his book on young Sam Clemens, reproduces from the Mark Twain papers, from the author's *Autobiography*, and from other primary sources, the actual records of the town of Twain's boyhood, which his literary memory recalled in various ways, both idealized and disagreeable.

[Murder at Bricksville]

On January 24, 1845, Hannibal witnessed its first premeditated murder, which left among its relics twenty-eight depositions set down by the hand of John M. Clemens, J.P., and the recollection which his son recaptured in one of *Huckleberry Finn*'s most vivid episodes—the shooting of old Boggs by Colonel Sherburn.‡ The village shoemaker named Boggs may have furnished this name, but the real victim was "Uncle Sam" Smarr, "as honest a man as any in the state" a neighbor testified to Judge Clemens, but "when drinking he was a little turbulent," yet "I did not consider him a dangerous man at all." Curiously enough, one of the "damned rascals" against whom Uncle Sam liked to rail when in his cups was "big Ira Stout," of unhappy association with John M. Clemens' business affairs. Another target was a prosperous merchant named William Owsley, whom old Smarr when drinking liked to describe to all within earshot as "a damned pickpocket . . . a damned son of a bitch . . . if he ever does cross my path I will kill him." He believed that Owsley "had stole" two thousand dollars from a friend at Palmyra named Thompson, and had also swindled old Smarr's drinking crony Tom Davis, "and for that he intended to have Owsley whipped." Two or three weeks before the shooting, "Smarr and Davis had been in town, spreeing around and cutting up smart . . . and shooting off pistols." Probably on this same evening, stated another witness named Caldwell, "when on my way home, when opposite to Judge Clemens' office, I heard Mr. Smarr five times call out at different points in the street 'O yes! O yes, here is Bill Owsley, has got a big stack of goods here, and stole two thousand dollars from Thompson in Palmyra.' . . . I returned and went to Mr. Selms' store—Mr. Davis and Mr. Smarr were in there —Davis then went out and I heard the report of a pistol—Mr. Davis and Jimmy Finn then both came in, Jim remarked, 'that would have made a hole in a man's belly. . . .'" (Jimmy Finn, original of Huck's pappy who slept with the hogs in the tanyard, held the distinction of being the village drunkard.) Other witnesses called Smarr sober, "as kind and good a neighbor as any man amongst us," and doubted that he ever carried a pistol, but agreed that he had walked or ridden up in front of Owsley's store shouting drunken abuse, while Owsley within, hearing these words in the presence of his customers, "had a kind of twitching and turned white around the mouth—and said it was insufferable."

The general forecast that "Smarr would catch hell" was fulfilled at noon a few days later, when Smarr came back to town to sell

‡ The episode occurs in *Huckleberry Finn*, Chapters XXI and XXII. For identification of Bricksville with Han- nibal see Chapter XXI, note 8, but the name of the town is not mentioned until Chapter XXVIII [Editors].

some beef. At the corner of Hill and Main—a few steps from the Clemens doorway—Owsley came up behind Smarr and a friend named Brown, and as the latter told Judge Clemens, the merchant cried out,

" 'You Sam Smarr'—Mr. Smarr turned around, seeing Mr. Owsley in the act of drawing a pistol from his pocket, said Mr. Owsley don't fire, or something to that effect. Mr. Owsley was within about four paces of Mr. Smarr when he drew the pistol and fired twice in succession, after the second fire, Mr. Smarr fell, when Mr. Owsley turned on his heel and walked off. After Mr. Smarr fell he raised his head and called, 'Brown come take me up I am shot and will soon be a dead man.' Dr. Grant then came up and invited us to take him to his store. We did so. The while he was begging us to lay him on his back. He then begged me not to leave him saying he must soon die. In about a half an hour from the time he was shot he expired."

Another witness added the detail that Smarr fell backward when shot, while "the gentleman that I saw shoot" kept his arm extended as he fired a second time. Thus, almost without a hairsbreadth of variation, the description in *Huckleberry Finn* of how the Colonel dispatched old Boggs.

In the depositions taken by Judge Clemens no mention is made of the heavy Bible laid by some pious fool upon the dying man's chest, though this "torture of its leaden weight" haunted young Sam's dreams and figured long afterward in his inspired retelling of the story. But Dr. Orville Grant, over whose drugstore at Hill and Main the Clemenses soon took up their abode, attested that the dying man was carried into this shop—where he and a fellow physician opened the victim's clothing and made hasty examination of the wounds, but "he then shewed signs of fainting and we . . . then stood by to see him die."

Owsley, a proud Kentuckian who smoked "fragrant cigars—regalias" and was regarded as something of a swell, may have repelled the threat of mob violence with the same cold contempt displayed by the fictitious Colonel Sherburn. Of this the court record makes no mention, but clearly the first deliberate murder on Hannibal's streets caused uproar and feverish excitement. Long afterward, in writing about the cowardice of lynch mobs, Mark reflected that in such a group "of a certainty there are never ten men in it who would not prefer to be somewhere else—and would be, if they had but the courage to go. When I was a boy I saw a brave gentleman deride and insult a mob and drive it away." Whatever threats Owsley may have faced down in the heat of the hour, he was not brought to trial until more than a year later. A man of wealth and influence, he had friends who were ready from the start to swear that his provocation had been great. At Palmyra on March 14, 1846, a jury returned a verdict of acquittal. Mark Twain's notes tell the sequel: "His party brought him huzzaing in from Palmyra at midnight. But there was a cloud upon him—a social chill—and he presently moved away."

The paltriness of a justice's fees is shown well enough by a note on the docket of papers which John M. Clemens prepared in this case—revealing that his fee for writing these 13,500 words was $13.50, and for administering oaths to twenty-nine witnesses, $1.81. Clerical drudgery, in fact, seems to have become the essence of his life. To his daughter Pamela, now helping to support the family by giving piano and guitar lessons in Florida and Paris, in adjoining Monroe County, he wrote a letter on May 5, 1845: "I have removed my office of Justice to Messrs McCune & Holliday's counting room where I have taken Mr. Dawes' place as clerk—I did not succeed in making such arrangements as would enable me to go into business advantageously on my acct—and thought it best therefore not to attempt it at present." The tradition that John M. Clemens "obtained employment for a time in a commission-house on the levee" doubtless belongs to this stage in his ill fortunes.

But under all the batterings of poverty Judge Clemens clung to his pride, his intellectual fastidiousness, and his sense of civic duty. Every letter that survives from his pen is redolent of an old-fashioned dignity. With the loose grammar and slovenly speech of river towns and backwoods—"the fruit of careless habit, not ignorance," as his famous son described it in *Life on the Mississippi* —the Judge made no truce or concession. In August 1845 he began to attend a course of "twenty oral lectures on Grammar . . . by Professor Hull," and made a careful précis of "Rules for Parsing by Transposition" for the benefit of Orion, the prentice printer in St. Louis.

[Tom Blankenship and His Family]

* * * In *Life on the Mississippi* Mark observes that if, in one of his penitential moods he had dared to carry a basket of victuals to the poor, "I knew we had none so poor but they would smash the basket over my head for my pains."

One such family, whose invincible cheerfulness seemed no less a communal scandal than its indolence, is thus sketched in Mark's reminiscent notes: "*Blankenships*. The parents paupers and drunkards; the girls charged with prostitution—not proven. Tom, a kindly young heathen. Bence, a fisherman. These children were never sent to school or church. Played out and disappeared." They lived in a ramshackle old barn of a house on Hill Street—a distance quickly covered by Sam when summoned with stealthy catcalls from Tom. The site is now cherished by the Chamber of Commerce as that of "Huck Finn's home,"† although the house no longer stands, following several generations of habitation by Negro families whose petty thefts, cutting scrapes, and the didos of a one-time denizen called Cocaine Nell Smith lent it a repute still more dubious than it enjoyed in the Blankenships' day.

Head of the family was Woodson Blankenship, a ne'er-do-well from South Carolina, who fitfully worked at the old sawmill but drank whenever possessed of cash to jingle in his jeans. In 1845 he appears on the roll of tax delinquents as owing twenty-nine cents. His eldest boy Benson, called Bence, did odd jobs but preferred to angle for catfish and tease the playmates of Sam Clemens by knotting their clothes when they went swimming, or clodding them when they came ashore. But he had a kind streak too—probably furnishing the original for Tom and Huck's friend Muff Potter,‡ who loafed and drank, but shared his catch if they were hungry, and mended their kites. In the summer of 1847 Bence befriended secretly a runaway Negro whom he found hiding among the swampy thickets of Sny Island, a part of Illinois's Pike County that hugged the opposite bank of the river from Hannibal. Ignoring the reward posted for the black man, Bence carried food to him week after week and kept mum about his hiding place—thus inspiring that rare tribute to loyalty in *Huckleberry Finn*, in which the homeless river rat rejects all temptations of gain and even elects to "go to Hell" rather than betray his friend Nigger Jim. But one day woodchoppers flushed the fugitive and chased him into a morass called Bird Slough, where he disappeared. Some days later, Sam Clemens, John Briggs, and the Bowen boys were fishing and roaming about the island as they often did—for the sake of its berries, and a fine grove of Illinois pecans such as the woods behind Hannibal did not bear—and made a discovery thus reported in the Hannibal *Journal* of August 19: "While some of our citizens were fishing a few days since on the Sny Island, they discovered in what is called Bird Slough the body of a negro man. On examination of the body, they found it to answer the description of a negro recently advertised in handbills as a runaway from Neriam Todd, of Howard County. He had on a brown jeans frock coat, home-made linen pants, and a new pair of lined and bound shoes. The body when discovered was much mutilated." One account says that the gruesome thing, released from a snag by their poling about in the drift, rose headfirst like an apparition before their eyes. Endless seem the variations upon terror in the boyhood of Sam Clemens.

† Tom Blankenship was the real-life prototype for the fictional Huck Finn, although the family as a whole is reflected in various characters and episodes [Ed.].

‡ Muff Potter will be recalled as a character in *The Adventures of Tom Sawyer* [Editors].

Among the Blankenships, whose society was a forbidden pleasure and therefore sought as often as possible, Sam's special joy was the younger brother Tom. Like Huck Finn, whose image Mark Twain repeatedly identified with him, Tom was ill-fed, an outrageous wreck of rags, dirty, ignorant, cheerful, carefree, and altogether enviable, being "the only really independent person—boy or man—in the community."† Tom went barefoot all the time, both from freedom and necessity, whereas boys from "quality" families were forbidden by parents to "come out barefoot" until warm weather—meanwhile often mocked as "Miss Nancys" by the more emancipated. The woods and the waters around Hannibal were his education. Living by his wits, suspicious of every attempt to civilize him, "to comb him all to hell," he had none of the unimportant virtues and all the essential ones. The school of hard knocks had given him a tenacious grasp on reality, despite his faith in dreams, omens, and superstitions. But it had not toughened him into cynicism or crime, and "he had as good a heart as ever any boy had." The testimony of another witness is interesting, a lad named Ayres, grandson of a pioneer Hannibal settler named Richmond. Younger than Sam Clemens, he knew him slightly and was his fellow member in the Cadets of Temperance, but Tom he knew well and admiringly:

"My grandmother told us that Tom Blankenship was a bad boy and we were forbidden to play with him, but when we went on a rabbit chase he joined us. . . . Black John (a half-grown negro belonging to my grandmother) and Tom Blankenship were naturally leading spirits and they led us younger 'weaker' ones through all our sports. Both were 'talented,' bold, kind, and just, and we all liked them both and were easily led by them. We also played down around the old Robards mill and the school house in the city park."

Long years after, in 1902, Mark heard that his old crony Tom had become justice of the peace and a respected citizen "in a remote village in Montana."

Objects of equal juvenile interest with the Blankenship boys, but naturally less comradeship, were those ultimate dregs of Hannibal society, the village drunkards. Besides old Blankenship himself, the list began with "General" Gaines—an ancient and disreputable relic of the Indian wars, who when full of rotgut used to fancy himself one of the half-man, half-alligator breed, and roar, "Whoop! bow your neck and spread!" like one of the raftmen whose mixture of cockalorum with cowardice Mark hit off in the third chapter of *Life on the Mississippi*. From him the title of town drunkard, "an exceedingly well-defined and unofficial office of those days," descended to Jimmy Finn, who furnished the name and most of the

† The quoted words are Mark Twain's [Editors].

attributes for Huck's pappy. "He was a monument of rags and dirt; he was the profanest man in town; he had bleary eyes, and a nose like a mildewed cauliflower; he slept with the hogs in an abandoned tanyard." Judge Clemens once tried without success to reform him; the Judge's son merely enjoyed him. To Will Bowen in later years Sam recalled how "we stole his dinner while he slept in the vat and fed it to the hogs in order to keep them still till we could mount them and have a ride." It was probably with Jimmy Finn in mind that a town ordinance passed in the spring of 1845 made it a misdemeanor to be "found drunk or intoxicated in any streat, alley, avinue, market place, or public square . . . or found a sleep in any such place not his own." But Finn was not long destined to plague the good citizens of Hannibal. On November 6 of that year, among the county records we find the sum of $8.25 allowed "for making a coffin, furnishing a shroud and burying James Finn a pauper." Mark insisted that he died a natural death in a tan vat, from delirium tremens combined with spontaneous combustion— "I mean it was a natural death for Jimmy Finn to die."

[*The Burning Shame*]

Mark recalls how in his school days a couple of young Englishmen sojourning in Hannibal "one day . . . got themselves up in cheap royal finery and did the Richard III sword-fight with maniac energy and prodigious powwow, in the presence of the village boys" —another favorite in the repertory of Huck's renegades. A cryptic note among further Hannibal memories, "Uncle Tom Cabin '53" may refer to some wandering troupe's offering a year after the appearance of Mrs. Stowe's novel—though its theme could hardly have been popular in slave-owning Hannibal.

In 1845 Hannibal's city fathers penalized anyone daring to "exhibit any indecent or lewd book, picture, statute [*sic*] or other things, or who shall exhibit or perform any immoral or lewd play or other representation." Probably, as one Mark Twain expert has suggested, "The Royal Nonesuch"† or "The Burning Shame," as originally called—from which all details are suppressed in *Huckleberry Finn* save that the king came prancing out on all fours as the "cameleopard," naked save for rings and stripes of many-colored paint, and capered to the base instincts of the Arkansas loafers— had to do with a mythical phallic beast known to the old southwest frontier as the "Gyascutus." Although the king and duke "fetched" their loafers by handbills barring ladies and children, the beast was sometimes exhibited a shade more decently. In Palmyra, the *Whig* on October 9, 1845, announced that the Gyascutus is "loose" and

† See Huckleberry Finn, Chapters XXII and XXIII, and see note 1, Chapter XXIII. The original story and the dramatic performance that resulted was part of the more racy oral tradition of the western frontier [Editors].

the public should be warned. It related that a couple of Yankees roving through the South, finding themselves short of cash and "determined to take advantage of the passion for shows which possessed our people," decided that one should "personate a rare beast, for which they invented the name of 'Gyascutus,' while the other was to be keeper or showman." At the next village they advertised their find, "captured . . . in the wilds of the Arostook . . . more ferocious and terrible than the gnu, the hyena, or ant-eater of the African desert! Admittance 25 cents, children and servants half price." A great crowd gathered, all agog. Beneath the curtain stretched across a corner of the hall could be seen "four horrible feet, which to less excited fancies would have born a wonderful resemblance to the feet and hands of a live Yankee, with strips of coonskin sewed round his wrists and ankles." While this monster flapped about and growled, the keeper Jonathan—his pockets heavy with silver—started a lecture on the beast's ferocity, all the while prodding him behind the curtain with a stick. Then came a savage roar, and the warning cry, "Ladies and gentlemen— *save yourselves—the Gyascutus is loose!*" In the pell-mell flight, Jonathan and the Gyascutus retired through the back door. From the old frontier of Missouri, the legendary beast later traveled to the Far West, as newspaper witticisms show. Out there in January 1865 Mark saw some miners on Jackass Hill enact a ribald skit, and jotted cautiously in his notebook in phonetic shorthand, "The 'Tragedians' and the Burning Shame. No Women admitted."

A similar "sell" in Hannibal is reported by Orion Clemens' *Journal* on March 18, 1852, captioned "The ———— Troupe." Sam Clemens' playful touch may be suspected in this account, rather than the heavy hand of Orion. It relates how a few days earlier the town had suddenly blossomed with posters announcing that wonders were imminent at Benton Hall.

"All the little boys·in town gazed on the groups of astonishing pictures which appeared on the above mentioned bills, and were thereby wrought up to an intense pitch of excitement. It was to be a real theatre, and the 'troupe' (which nobody had ever heard of before,) was so 'celebrated.' Well, the momentous evening came. Those who enjoyed the felicity of paying a quarter, to see the show, found a large man on the first story, who received the money, and a small man at the top of the second pair of steps, who received the tickets . . . the very persons who were afterwards transformed into heroes and soldiers by the power of paint. In the hall we found forty or fifty of our citizens, sitting in front of a striped curtain, behind which was all the mysterious paraphernalia of the theatre.

When the curtain was pulled to one side, the first appearance on the stage was the large man. . . . He was evidently a novice, and acted his part about as you have seen boys, in a thespian society.

He was intended to be a lover of the distinguished danseuse, who played the part of a miss in short dresses, though her apparent age would have justified her in wearing them longer, and we have seen spectacles on younger people. Then the small man, who came in first as a corporal in the army, and then pretended to be drunk, for the amusement of the audience, made up the third character in this burlesque of a farce, the dullness of which was not relieved even by the disgusting blackguardisms with which it was profusely interlarded."

Beyond much doubt, the antics of the king and the duke in *Huckleberry Finn* owe something to the experiences of that night in Benton Hall.

A Sampler:
Autobiography, Biography, and Correspondence

The following passages, selected from the writings concerning Mark Twain and the large body of primary material relating to him, are intended to illustrate what these sources contributed to the identification of characters, to the authority of Twain's transcript of life and the interest of his contemporaries and later observers, and to the picture of Mark Twain as a writer and as an individual. In particular we have here the identification of the real-life Huck in Tom Blankenship; Twain's own description of the farm of his uncle, John Quarles, the memory of which, as here recorded, was the source of his early idealization of the St. Petersburg of *Tom Sawyer*, and the early scenes of *Huckleberry Finn*; and biographical comments culled from two of the author's closest friends, Albert Bigelow Paine and William Dean Howells.

From Mark Twain's Autobiography†

In *Huckleberry Finn* I have drawn Tom Blankenship exactly as he was. He was ignorant, unwashed, insufficiently fed; but he had as good a heart as ever any boy had. His liberties were totally unrestricted. He was the only really independent person—boy or man—in the community, and by consequence he was tranquilly and continuously happy, and was envied by all the rest of us. We liked him; we enjoyed his society. And as his society was forbidden us by our parents, the prohibition trebled and quadrupled its value, and therefore we sought and got more of his society than of any other boy's. I heard, four years ago, that he was justice

† From *Mark Twain's Autobiography*. Copyright 1924 by Clara Gabrilowitsch. Reprinted by permission of Harper and Brothers. The bracketed references following each excerpt are to the volume and pages in this edition.

of the peace in a remote village in Montana, and was a good citizen and greatly respected.

[II, 174–75]

My uncle, John A. Quarles, was a farmer, and his place was in the country four miles from Florida. He had eight children and fifteen or twenty negroes, and was also fortunate in other ways, particularly in his character. I have not come across a better man than he was. I was his guest for two or three months every year, from the fourth year after we removed to Hannibal till I was eleven or twelve years old. I have never consciously used him or his wife in a book, but his farm has come very handy to me in literature once or twice. In *Huck Finn* and in *Tom Sawyer, Detective* I moved it down to Arkansas. It was all of six hundred miles, but it was no trouble; it was not a very large farm—five hundred acres, perhaps—but I could have done it if it had been twice as large. And as for the morality of it, I cared nothing for that; I would move a state if the exigencies of literature required it.

It was a heavenly place for a boy, that farm of my uncle John's. The house was a double log one, with a spacious floor (roofed in) connecting it with the kitchen. In the summer the table was set in the middle of that shady and breezy floor, and the sumptuous meals—well, it makes me cry to think of them. Fried chicken, roast pig; wild and tame turkeys, ducks, and geese; venison just killed; squirrels, rabbits, pheasants, partridges, prairie-chickens; biscuits, hot batter cakes, hot buckwheat cakes, hot "wheat bread," hot rolls, hot corn pone; fresh corn boiled on the ear, succotash, butterbeans, stringbeans, tomatoes, peas, Irish potatoes, sweet potatoes; buttermilk, sweet milk, "clabber"; watermelons, muskmelons, cantaloupes—all fresh from the garden; apple pie, peach pie, pumpkin pie, apple dumplings, peach cobbler—I can't remember the rest. The way that the things were cooked was perhaps the main splendor—particularly a certain few of the dishes. For instance, the corn bread, the hot biscuits and wheat bread, and the fried chicken. These things have never been properly cooked in the North—in fact, no one there is able to learn the art, so far as my experience goes. The North thinks it knows how to make corn bread, but this is mere superstition. Perhaps no bread in the world is quite so good as Southern corn bread, and perhaps no bread in the world is quite so bad as the Northern imitation of it. The North seldom tries to fry chicken, and this is well; the art cannot be learned north of the line of Mason and Dixon, nor anywhere in Europe. This is not hearsay; it is experience that is speaking. In Europe it is imagined that the custom of serving various kinds of bread blazing hot is "American," but that is too broad a spread; it is custom in the

South, but is much less than that in the North. In the North and in Europe hot bread is considered unhealthy. This is probably another fussy superstition, like the European superstition that ice-water is unhealthy. Europe does not need ice-water and does not drink it; and yet, notwithstanding this, its word for it is better than ours, because it describes it, whereas ours doesn't. Europe calls it "iced" water. Our word describes water made from melted ice— a drink which has a characterless taste and which we have but little acquaintance with.

It seems a pity that the world should throw away so many good things merely because they are unwholesome. I doubt if God has given us any refreshment which, taken in moderation, is unwholesome, except microbes. Yet there are people who strictly deprive themselves of each and every eatable, drinkable, and smokable which has in any way acquired a shady reputation. They pay this price for health. And health is all they get for it. How strange it is! It is like paying out your whole fortune for a cow that has gone dry.

The farmhouse stood in the middle of a very large yard, and the yard was fenced on three sides with rails and on the rear side with high palings; against these stood the smoke-house; beyond the palings was the orchard; beyond the orchard were the negro quarters and the tobacco fields. The front yard was entered over a stile made of sawed-off logs of graduated heights; I do not remember any gate. In a corner of the front yard were a dozen lofty hickory trees and a dozen black walnuts, and in the nutting season riches were to be gathered there.

Down a piece, abreast the house, stood a little log cabin against the rail fence; and there the woody hill fell sharply away, past the barns, the corn-crib, the stables, and the tobacco-curing house, to a limpid brook which sang along over its gravelly bed and curved and frisked in and out and here and there and yonder in the deep shade of overhanging foliage and vines—a divine place for wading, and it had swimming pools, too, which were forbidden to us and therefore much frequented by us. For we were little Christian children and had early been taught the value of forbidden fruit.

[I, 96–99]

ALBERT BIGELOW PAINE

From Mark Twain: A Biography†

* * * he loved the river in its every mood and aspect and detail, and not only the river, but a steamboat; and still more, perhaps, the freedom of the pilot's life and its prestige. Wherever he has written of the river—and in one way or another he was always writing of it—we feel the claim of the old captivity and that it still holds him. In the *Huckleberry Finn* book, during those nights and days with Huck and Nigger Jim on the raft—whether in stormlit blackness, still noontide, or the lifting mists of morning—we can fairly "smell" the river, as Huck himself would say, and we know that it is because the writer loved it with his heart of hearts and literally drank in its environment and atmosphere during those halcyon pilot days.

[I, 122–23]

A quotation from the childish biography of Susy, about Mrs. Clemens' expurgation of certain materials in Huckleberry Finn.

* * * Papa read *Huckleberry Finn* to us in manuscript, just before it came out, and then he would leave parts of it with mama to expergate, while he went off to the study to work, and sometimes Clara and I would be sitting with mama while she was looking the manuscript over, and I remember so well, with what pangs of regret we used to see her turn down the leaves of the pages, which meant that some delightfully terrible part must be scratched out. And I remember one part pertickularly which was perfectly fascinating it was so terrible, that Clara and I used to delight in and oh, with what despair we saw mama turn down the leaf on which it was written, we thought the book would almost be ruined without it. But we gradually came to think as mama did.

[II, 774–75]

The story of *Huck Finn* will probably stand as the best of Mark Twain's purely fictional writings. A sequel to *Tom Sawyer*, it is greater than its predecessor; greater artistically, though perhaps with less immediate interest for the juvenile reader * * * The tale of Huck and Nigger Jim drifting down the mighty river on a raft, cross-secting the various primitive aspects of human existence,

† From *Mark Twain: A Biography*, edited by Albert Bigelow Paine. Copy-   right 1912 by Harper and Brothers. Reprinted by permission.

constitutes one of the most impressive examples of picaresque fiction in any language. It has been ranked greater than *Gil Blas,* greater even than *Don Quixote;* certainly it is more convincing, more human, than either of these tales.

[II, 793–94]

Take the story as a whole, it is a succession of startling and unique pictures. * * * these are of no time or literary fashion and will never lose their flavor nor change their freshness so long as humanity itself does not change. * * * It is the way things happen in reality; and the quiet, unexcited frame of mind in which Huck is prompted to set them down would seem to be the last word in literary art.

[II, 795–96]

It was Huck Finn's morality that caused the book to be excluded from the Concord Library, and from other libraries here and there at a later day. The orthodox mental attitude of certain directors of juvenile literature could not condone Huck's looseness in the matter of statement and property rights. * * *

[II, 797]

Able critics have declared that the psychology of Huck Finn is the book's large feature: Huck's moral point of view—the struggle between his heart and his conscience concerning the sin of Jim's concealment, and his final decision of self-sacrifice. Time may show that as an epic of the river, the picture of a vanished day, it will rank even greater. The problems of conscience we have always with us, but periods once passed are gone forever.

[II, 797]

Huck is what he is because, being made so, he cannot well be otherwise. He is a boy throughout—such a boy as Mark Twain had known and in some degree had been. One may pettily pick a flaw here and there in the tale's construction if so minded, but the moral character of Huck himself is not open to criticism. And indeed any criticism of this the greatest of Mark Twain's tales of modern life would be as the mere scratching of the granite of an imperishable structure. *Huck Finn* is a monument that no puny pecking will destroy. It is built of indestructible blocks of human nature; and if the blocks do not always fit, and the ornaments do not always agree, we need not fear. Time will blur the incongruities and moss over the mistakes. The edifice will grow more beautiful with the years.

[II, 798]

A letter from Clemens to a librarian in Brooklyn about the banning of Tom Sawyer *and* Huckleberry Finn *from the children's room of the library.*

* * * I wrote *Tom Sawyer* & *Huck Finn* for adults exclusively, & it always distresses me when I find that boys & girls have been allowed access to them. The mind that becomes soiled in youth can never again be washed clean. I know this by my own experience, & to this day I cherish an unappeasable bitterness against the unfaithful guardians of my young life, who not only permitted but compelled me to read an unexpurgated Bible through before I was 15 years old. * * * More honestly do I wish that I could say a softening word or two in defense of Huck's character since you wish it, but really, in my opinion, it is no better than those of Solomon, David, & the rest of the sacred brotherhood. * * *

[II, 1280–81]

WILLIAM DEAN HOWELLS
From My Mark Twain†

* * * Even now I think he should rather be called a romancer, though such a book as *Huckleberry Finn* takes itself out of the order of romance and places itself with the great things in picaresque fiction. Still, it is more poetic than picaresque, and of a deeper psychology. The probable and credible soul that the author divines in the son of the town-drunkard is one which we might each own brother, and the art which portrays this nature at first hand in the person and language of the hero, without pose or affectation, is fine art. In the boy's history the author's fancy works realistically to an end as high as it has reached elsewhere, if not higher; and I who like *The Connecticut Yankee in King Arthur's Court* so much have half a mind to give my whole heart to *Huckleberry Finn.*

Both *Huckleberry Finn* and *Tom Sawyer* wander in episodes loosely related to the main story, but they are of a closer and more logical advance from the beginning to the end than the fiction which preceded them, and which I had almost forgotten to name before them.

† From *My Mark Twain* by William Dean Howells. Reprinted by permission of Harper and Brothers.

Mark Twain's Correspondence: Letters to William Dean Howells†

August 9, 1876

* * * The double-barreled novel [perhaps *The Prince and The Pauper*] lies torpid. I found I could not go on with it. The chapters I had written were still too new and familiar to me. I may take it up next winter, but cannot tell yet; I waited and waited to see if my interest in it would not revive, but gave it up a month ago and began another boys' book—more to be at work than anything else. I have written 400 pages on it—therefore it is very nearly half done. It is Huck Finn's Autobiography. I like it only tolerably well, as far as I have got, and may possibly pigeonhole or burn the MS when it is done. * * *

July 20, 1883

* * * I have finished one small book, and am away along in a big one that I half-finished two or three years ago. I expect to complete it in a month or six weeks or two months more. And *I* shall *like* it, whether anybody else does or not.

It is a kind of companion to Tom Sawyer. There's a raft episode from it in second or third chapter of *Life on the Mississippi*. * * *

† Excerpts from letters Aug. 9, 1876, and Jul. 20, 1883, from Mark Twain to W. D. Howells from *Mark Twain's* *Letters,* edited by Albert Bigelow Paine. Reprinted by permission of Harper & Brothers.

Essays in Criticism

BRANDER MATTHEWS

[*Huckleberry Finn:* A Review]†

The boy of to-day is fortunate indeed, and, of a truth, he is to
be congratulated. While the boy of yesterday had to stay his stomach
with the unconscious humour of *Sandford and Merton,* the boy of
to-day may get his fill of fun and of romance and of adventure in
Treasure Island and in *Tom Brown* and in *Tom Sawyer,* and now
in a sequel to *Tom Sawyer,* wherein Tom himself appears in the
very nick of time, like a young god from the machine. Sequels of
stories which have been widely popular are not a little risky. *Huckleberry Finn* is a sharp exception to this general rule. Although it is
a sequel, it is quite as worthy of wide popularity as *Tom Sawyer.*
An American critic once neatly declared that the late G. P. R.
James hit the bull's-eye of success with his first shot, and that for
ever thereafter he went on firing through the same hole. Now this
is just what Mark Twain has not done. *Huckleberry Finn* is not an
attempt to do *Tom Sawyer* over again. It is a story quite as unlike
its predecessor as it is like. Although Huck Finn appeared first in
the earlier book, and although Tom Sawyer reappears in the later,
the scenes and the characters are otherwise wholly different. Above
all, the atmosphere of the story is different. *Tom Sawyer* was a tale
of boyish adventure in a village in Missouri, on the Mississippi river,
and it was told by the author. *Huckleberry Finn* is autobiographic;
it is a tale of boyish adventure along the Mississippi river told as
it appeared to Huck Finn. There is not in *Huckleberry Finn* any
one scene quite as funny as those in which Tom Sawyer gets his
friends to whitewash the fence for him, and then uses the spoils
thereby acquired to attain the highest situation of the Sunday
school the next morning. Nor is there any distinction quite as
thrilling as that awful moment in the cave when the boy and the
girl are lost in the darkness, and when Tom Sawyer suddenly sees a
human hand bearing a light, and then finds that the hand is the
hand of Indian Joe, his one mortal enemy; we have always thought
that the vision of the hand in the cave in *Tom Sawyer* is one of
the very finest things in the literature of adventure since Robinson
Crusoe first saw a single footprint in the sand of the seashore. But
though *Huckleberry Finn* may not quite reach these two highest
points of *Tom Sawyer,* we incline to the opinion that the general

† Published in the *Saturday Review*
(London), January 31, 1885, p. 153.
The earliest review recorded, this dealt
with the English release of the novel,
which antedated the American issue.
Brander Matthews, an American, then
thirty-three and author of two plays
and several books on the theater, was
contributing to both British and American periodicals, and later became a
professor at Columbia University.

level of the later story is perhaps higher than that of the earlier. For one thing, the skill with which the character of Huck Finn is maintained is marvellous. We see everything through his eyes— and they are his eyes and not a pair of Mark Twain's spectacles. And the comments on what he sees are his comments—the comments of an ignorant, superstitious, sharp, healthy boy, brought up as Huck Finn had been brought up; they are not speeches put into his mouth by the author. One of the most artistic things in the book— and that Mark Twain is a literary artist of a very high order all who have considered his later writings critically cannot but confess— one of the most artistic things in *Huckleberry Finn* is the sober self-restraint with which Mr. Clemens lets Huck Finn set down, without any comment at all, scenes which would have afforded the ordinary writer matter for endless moral and political and socio-logical disquisition. We refer particularly to the account of the Grangerford-Shepherdson feud, and of the shooting of Boggs by Colonel Sherburn. Here are two incidents of the rough old life of the South-Western States, and of the Mississippi Valley forty or fifty years ago, of the old life which is now rapidly passing away under the influence of advancing civilization and increasing com-mercial prosperity, but which has not wholly disappeared even yet, although a slow revolution in public sentiment is taking place. The Grangerford-Shepherdson feud is a vendetta as deadly as any Cor-sican could wish, yet the parties to it were honest, brave, sincere, good Christian people, probably people of deep religious sentiment. Not the less we see them taking their guns to church, and, when occasion serves, joining in what is little better than a general mas-sacre. The killing of Boggs by Colonel Sherburn is told with equal sobriety and truth; and the later scene in which Colonel Sherburn cows and lashes the mob which has set out to lynch him is one of the most vigorous bits of writing Mark Twain has done.

In *Tom Sawyer* we saw Huckleberry Finn from the outside; in the present volume we see him from the inside. He is almost as much a delight to any one who has been a boy as was Tom Sawyer. But only he or she who has been a boy can truly enjoy this record of his adventures, and of his sentiments and of his sayings. Old maids of either sex will wholly fail to understand him or to like him, or to see his significance and his value. Like Tom Sawyer, Huck Finn is a genuine boy; he is neither a girl in boy's clothes like many of the modern heroes of juvenile fiction, nor is he a "little man," a full-grown man cut down; he is a boy, just a boy, only a boy. And his ways and modes of thought are boyish. As Mr. F. Anstey understands the English boy, and especially the English boy of the middle classes, so Mark Twain understands the American boy, and especially the American boy of the Mississippi Valley of forty or fifty years ago. The contrast between Tom Sawyer, who is the child of respectable parents, decently brought up, and Huckleberry Finn, who is the child of the town drunkard, not brought up at all, is made distinct by a hundred artistic touches, not the least natural of which is Huck's constant reference to Tom as his ideal of what a boy should be. When Huck escapes from the cabin where his drunken and worthless father had confined him, carefully manufacturing a mass of very circumstantial evidence to prove his own murder by robbers, he cannot help saying, "I did wish Tom Sawyer was there, I knowed he would take an interest in this kind of business, and throw in the fancy touches. Nobody could spread himself like Tom Sawyer in such a thing as that." Both boys have their full share of boyish imagination; and Tom Sawyer, being given to books, lets his imagination run on robbers and pirates and genies, with a perfect understanding with himself that, if you want to get fun out of this life, you must never hesitate to make believe very hard; and, with Tom's youth and health, he never finds it hard to make believe and to be a pirate at will, or to summon an attendant spirit, or to rescue a prisoner from the deepest dungeon 'neath the castle moat. But in Huck this imagination has turned to superstition; he is a walking repository of the juvenile folklore of the Mississippi Valley —a folklore partly traditional among the white settlers, but largely influenced by intimate association with the negroes. When Huck was in his room at night all by himself waiting for the signal Tom Sawyer was to give him at midnight, he felt so lonesome he wished he was dead:—

"The stars was shining and the leaves rustled in the woods ever so mournful; and I heard an owl, away off, who-whooing about somebody that was dead, and a whippowill and a dog crying about somebody that was going to die; and the wind was trying to whisper something to me, and I couldn't make out what it was, and so it made the cold shivers run over me. Then away out in the woods I heard that kind of a sound that a ghost makes when it wants to tell about something that's on its mind and can't make itself understood, and so can't rest easy in its grave, and has to go about that way every night grieving. I got so downhearted and scared I did wish I had some company. Pretty soon a spider went crawling up my shoulders, and I flipped it off and it lit in the candle; and before I could budge it was all shrivelled up. I didn't need anybody to tell me that that was an awful bad sign and would fetch me some bad luck, so I was scared and most shook the clothes off me. I got up and turned around in my tracks three times and crossed my breast every time; and then I tied up a little lock of my hair with a thread to keep witches away. But I hadn't no confidence. You do that when you've lost a horse-shoe that you've found, instead of nailing it up over the door, but I hadn't ever heard anybody say it was any way to keep off bad luck when you'd killed a spider."

And, again, later in the story, not at night this time, but in broad daylight, Huck walks along a road:—

"When I got there it was all still and Sunday-like, and hot and sunshiny—the hands was gone to the fields; and there was them kind of faint dronings of bugs and flies in the air that makes it seem so lonesome and like everybody's dead and gone; and if a breeze fans along and quivers the leaves, it makes you feel mournful, because you feel like it's spirits whispering—spirits that's been dead ever so many years—and you always think they're talking about *you*. As a general thing it makes a body wish *he* was dead, too, and done with it all."

Now, none of these sentiments are appropriate to Tom Sawyer, who had none of the feeling for nature which Huck Finn had caught during his numberless days and nights in the open air. Nor could Tom Sawyer either have seen or set down this instantaneous photograph of a summer storm:—

"It would get so dark that it looked all blue-black outside, and lovely; and the rain would thrash along by so thick that the trees off a little ways looked dim and spider-webby; and here would come a blast of wind that would bend the trees down and turn up the pale underside of the leaves; and then a perfect ripper of a gust would follow along and set the branches to tossing their arms as if they was just wild; and next, when it was just about the bluest and blackest—fst! it was as bright as glory, and you'd have a little glimpse of tree-tops a-plunging about, away off yonder in the storm, hundreds of yards further than you could see before; dark as sin again in a second, and now you'd hear the thunder let go with an awful crash, and then go rumbling, grumbling, tumbling down the sky towards the under side of the world, like rolling empty barrels down stairs, where it's long stairs and they bounce a good deal, you know."

The romantic side of Tom Sawyer is shown in most delightfully humorous fashion in the account of his difficult devices to aid in the easy escape of Jim, a runaway negro. Jim is an admirably drawn character. There have been not a few fine and firm portraits of negroes in recent American fiction, of which Mr. Cable's Bras-Coupé in the *Grandissimes* is perhaps the most vigorous, and Mr. Harris's Mingo and Uncle Remus and Blue Dave are the most gentle. Jim is worthy to rank with these; and the essential simplicity and kindliness and generosity of the Southern negro have never been better shown than here by Mark Twain. Nor are Tom Sawyer and Huck Finn and Jim the only fresh and original figures in Mr.

Clemens's new book; on the contrary, there is scarcely a character of the many introduced who does not impress the reader at once as true to life—and therefore as new, for life is so varied that a portrait from life is sure to be as good as new. That Mr. Clemens draws from life, and yet lifts his work from the domain of the photograph to the region of art, is evident to any one who will give his work the honest attention which it deserves. Mr. John T. Raymond, the American comedian, who performs the character of Colonel Sellers to perfection, is wont to say that there is scarcely a town in the West and South-West where some man did not claim to be the original of the character. And as Mark Twain made Colonel Sellers, so has he made the chief players in the present drama of boyish adventure; they are taken from life, no doubt, but they are so aptly chosen and so broadly drawn that they are quite as typical as they are actual. They have one great charm, all of them—they are not written about and about; they are not described and dissected and analysed; they appear and play their parts and disappear; and yet they leave a sharp impression of indubitable vitality and individuality. No one, we venture to say, who reads this book will readily forget the Duke and the King, a pair of as pleasant "confidence operators" as one may meet in a day's journey, who leave the story in the most appropriate fashion, being clothed in tar and feathers and ridden on a rail. Of the more broadly humorous passages—and they abound—we have not left ourselves space to speak; they are to the full as funny as in any of Mark Twain's other books; and, perhaps, in no other book has the humourist shown so much artistic restraint, for there is in *Huckleberry Finn* no mere "comic copy," no straining after effect; one might almost say that there is no waste word in it * * *

ANDREW LANG

The Art of Mark Twain†

The duty of self-examination is frequently urged upon us by moralists. No doubt we should self-examine our minds as well as our conduct now and then, especially when we have passed the age in which we are constantly examined by other people. When I attempt to conduct this delicate inquiry I am puzzled and alarmed at finding that I am losing Culture. I am backsliding, I have not final perseverance, unless indeed it is Culture that is backsliding and

† First published in *Illustrated News of the World* (London), XCVIII (February 14, 1891), 222. This Scottish historian, poet, and man of letters had by 1885 translated Homer and Theocritus and collected and rewritten several volumes of folk tales.

getting on to the wrong lines. For I ought to be cultured; it is my own fault if I have not got Culture.

I have been educated till I nearly dropped; I have lived with the earliest Apostles of Culture, in the days when Chippendale was first a name to conjure with, and Japanese art came in like a raging lion, and Ronsard was the favorite poet, and Mr. William Morris was a poet too, and blue and green were the only wear, and the name of paradise was Camelot. To be sure, I cannot say that I took all this quite seriously, but "we too have played" at it, and know all about it. Generally speaking, I have kept up with Culture. I can talk (if desired) about Sainte-Beuve, and Mérimée, and Félicien Rops; I could rhyme "Ballades" when they were "in," and knew what a *pantoom* was. I am acquainted with the scholia on the Venetus A. I have a pretty taste in Greek gems. I have got beyond the stage of thinking Mr. Cobden Sanderson a greater binder than Bauzonnet. With practice I believe I could do an epigram of Meleager's into a bad imitation of a sonnet by Joachim du Bellay, or a sonnet of Bellay's into a bad imitation of a Greek epigram. I could pass an examination in the works of M. Paul Bourget. And yet I have not Culture. My works are but a tinkling brass, because I have not Culture. For Culture has got into new regions where I cannot enter, and, what is perhaps worse, I find myself delighting in a great many things which are under the ban of Culture.

This is a dreadful position, which makes a man feel like one of those Liberal politicians who are always "sitting on the fence," and who follow their party, if follow it they do, with the reluctant acquiescence of the prophet's donkey. Not that I do follow it. I cannot rave with pleasure over Tolstoi, especially as he admits that "The Kreutzer Sonata" is not "only his fun" but a kind of Manifesto. I have tried Hartmann, and I prefer Plato. I don't like poems by young ladies in which the verses neither scan nor rhyme, and the constructions are all linguistically impossible. I am shaky about Blake, though I am stalwart about Mr. Rudyard Kipling.

This is not the worst of it. Culture has hardly a new idol but I long to hurl things at it. Culture can scarcely burn anything, but I am impelled to sacrifice to that same. I am coming to suspect that the majority of Culture's modern disciples are a mere crowd of very slimly educated people, who have no natural taste or impulse; who do not really know the best things in literature; who have a feverish desire to admire the newest thing, to follow the latest artistic fashion; who prate about "style" without the faintest acquaintance with the ancient examples of style, in Greek, French, or English; who talk about the classics and criticise the classical critics and poets, without being able to read a line of them in the original. Nothing of the natural man is left in these people; their intellectual equipment is made up of ignorant vanity, and eager desire of novelty, and a yearning to be in the fashion.

Take, for example—and we have been a long time in coming to him—Mark Twain. If you praise him among the persons of Culture, they cannot believe that you are serious. They call him a Barbarian. They won't hear of him, they hurry from the subject; they pass by on the other side of the way. Now I do not mean to assert that Mark Twain is "an impeccable artist," but he is just as far from being a mere coarse buffoon. Like other people, he has his limitations. Even Mr. Gladstone, for instance, does not shine as a Biblical critic, nor Mark Twain as a critic of Italian art nor as a guide to the Holy Land. I have abstained from reading his work on an American at the Court of King Arthur, because here Mark Twain is not, and cannot be, at the proper point of view. He has not the knowledge which would enable him to be a sound critic of the ideal of the Middle Ages. An Arthurian Knight in New York or in Washington would find as much to blame, and justly, as a Yankee at Camelot. Let it be admitted that Mark Twain often and often sins against good taste, that some of his waggeries are mechanical, that his books are full of passages which were only good enough for the corner of a newspaper. Even so, the man who does not "let a laugh out of him"—like the Gruagach Gaire—at the story of the Old Ram, or of the Mexican Plug, or of the editing of the country newspaper, or of the Blue Jay, or at the lecture on the German language, can hardly have a laugh in him to let out. Chesterfield very gravely warns his son that it is wrong and vulgar to laugh; but the world has agreed to differ from Chesterfield. To "Homo Ridens" Mark Twain is a benefactor beyond most modern writers, and the Cultured, who do not laugh, are merely to be pitied.

* * * I have no hesitation in saying that Mark Twain is one among the greatest contemporary makers of fiction. For some reason, which may perhaps be guessed, he has only twice chosen to exercise this art seriously, in *Tom Sawyer* and in *Huckleberry Finn*. The reason, probably, is that old life on the Mississippi is the only form of life in which Mark Twain finds himself so well versed that he can deal with it in seriousness. Again, perhaps his natural and cultivated tendency to extravagance and caricature is only to be checked by working on the profound and candid seriousness of boyhood. These are unlucky limitations, if they really exist, for they have confined him, as a novelist, to a pair of brief works, masterpieces which a fallacious appearance has confounded with boys' books and facetiae. Of the two, by an unheard-of stroke of luck, the second, the sequel, is by far the better. I can never forget nor be ungrateful for the exquisite pleasure with which I read *Huckleberry Finn* for the first time, years ago. I read it again last night, deserting *Kenilworth* for

Huck. I never laid it down till I had finished it. I perused several passages more than once, and rose from it with a higher opinion of its merits than ever.

What is it that we want in a novel? We want a vivid and original picture of life; we want character naturally displayed in action, and if we get the excitement of adventure into the bargain, and that adventure possible and plausible, I so far differ from the newest school of criticism as to think that we have additional cause for gratitude. If, moreover, there is an unstrained sense of humour in the narrator, we have a masterpiece, and *Huckleberry Finn* is nothing less. Once more. If the critics are right who think that art should so far imitate nature as to leave things at loose ends, as it were, not pursuing events to their conclusions, even here *Huckleberry Finn* should satisfy them. It is the story of the flight down the Mississippi of a white boy and a runaway slave. The stream takes them through the fringes of life on the riverside; they pass feuds and murders of men, and towns full of homicidal loafers, and are intermingled with the affairs of families, and meet friends whom they would wish to be friends always. But the current carries them on: they leave the murders unavenged, the lovers in full flight; the friends they lose for ever; we do not know, any more than in reality we would know, "what became of them all." They do not return, as in novels, and narrate their later adventures.

As to the truth of the life described, the life in little innocent towns, the religion, the Southern lawlessness, the feuds, the lynchings, only persons who have known this changed world can say if it be truly painted, but it looks like the very truth, like an historical document. Already *Huckleberry Finn* is an historical novel, and more valuable, perhaps, to the historian than *Uncle Tom's Cabin*, for it is written without partisanship, and without "a purpose." The drawing of character seems to be admirable, unsurpassed in its kind. By putting the tale in the mouth of the chief actor, Huck, Mark Twain was enabled to give it a seriousness not common in his work, and to abstain from comment. Nothing can be more true and more humorous than the narrative of this outcast boy, with a heart naturally good, with a conscience torn between the teachings of his world about slavery and the promptings of his nature. In one point Mark Twain is Homeric, probably without knowing it. In the Odyssey, Odysseus frequently tells a false tale about himself, to account for his appearance and position when disguised on his own island. He shows extraordinary fertility and appropriateness of invention, wherein he is equalled by the feigned tales of Huckleberry Finn.

The casual characters met on the way are masterly: the woman who detects Huck in a girl's dress; the fighting families of Shepherdson and Grangerford; the homicidal Colonel Sherburn, who cruelly shoots old Boggs, and superbly quells the mob of would-be lynchers; the various old aunts and uncles; the negro Jim; the two wandering impostors; the hateful father of Huck himself. Then Huck's compliment to Miss Mary Jane, whom he thought of afterwards "a many and a many million times," how excellent it is! "In my opinion she had more sand in her than any girl I ever see; in my opinion she was just full of sand. It sounds like flattery, but it ain't no flattery. And when it comes to beauty—and goodness, too—she lays over them all."

No novel has better touches of natural description: the starlit nights on the great river, the storms, the whole landscape, the sketches of little rotting towns, of the woods, of the cotton-fields, are simple, natural, and visible to the mind's eye. The story, to be sure, ends by lapsing into burlesque, when Tom Sawyer insists on freeing the slave whom he knows to be free already, in a manner accordant with "the best authorities." But even the burlesque is redeemed by Tom's real unconscious heroism. There are defects of taste, or passages that to us seem deficient in taste, but the book remains a nearly flawless gem of romance and of humour. The world appreciates it, no doubt, but "cultural critics" are probably unaware of its singular value. A two-shilling novel by Mark Twain, with an ugly picture on the cover, "has no show," as Huck might say, and the great American novel has escaped the eyes of those who watch to see this new planet swim into their ken. And will Mark Twain never write such another? One is enough for him to live by, and for our gratitude, but not enough for our desire.

VAN WYCK BROOKS

From The Ordeal of Mark Twain†

There was a reason for Mark Twain's pessimism, a reason for that chagrin, that fear of solitude, that tortured conscience, those fantastic self-accusations, that indubitable self-contempt. It is an established fact, if I am not mistaken, that these morbid feelings of sin, which have no evident cause, are the result of having trans-

† From the book *The Ordeal of Mark Twain*, by Van Wyck Brooks. Copyright, 1920, by E. P. Dutton & Co. Inc. Renewal, 1948, by Van Wyck Brooks. Reprinted by permission of the publishers. The editors have selected, *cursim* from the volume, passages intended to represent the so-called "Brooks thesis." This supported certain controversial ideas of the period: namely, that the American experience, especially that of the frontier, and the genteel tradition as reportedly represented in the attitudes of Mark's mother, his wife, and his editorial friend, Howells, would handicap the creative freedom of the artist. (Bracketed page numbers follow each selection.)

gressed some inalienable life-demand peculiar to one's nature. It is as old as Milton that there are talents which are "death to hide," and I suggest that Mark Twain's "talent" was just so hidden. That bitterness of his was the effect of a certain miscarriage in his creative life, a balked personality, an arrested development of which he himself was almost wholly unaware, but which for him destroyed the meaning of life. The spirit of the artist in him, like the genie at last released from the bottle, overspread in a gloomy vapor the mind it had never quite been able to possess. [p. 14]

He was, as Arnold Bennett says, a "divine amateur"; his appeal is, on the whole, what Henry James called it, an appeal to rudimentary minds. But is not that simply another way of saying, in the latter case, that his was a mind that had not developed, and in the former, that his was a splendid genius which had never found itself? [p. 17]

The life of a Mississippi pilot had, in some special way, satisfied the instinct of the artist in him; in quite his way, the instinct of the artist in him had never been satisfied again. We do not have to look beyond this in order to interpret, if not the fact, at least the obsession. He felt that, in some way, he had been as a pilot on the right track; and he felt that he had lost this track. * * * Is it possible that he had, in fact, found himself in his career as a pilot and lost himself with that career? It is a bold hypothesis, and yet I think a glance at Mark Twain's childhood will bear it out. * * *
What a social setting it was, that little world into which Mark Twain was born! It was drab, it was tragic. In *Huckleberry Finn* and *Tom Sawyer* we see it in the color of rose; and besides, we see there only a later phase of it, after Mark Twain's family had settled in Hannibal, on the Mississippi. He was five at the time; his eyes had opened on such a scene as we find in the early pages of *The Gilded Age*. That weary, discouraged father, struggling against conditions amid which, as he says, a man can do nothing but rot away, that kind, worn, wan, desperately optimistic, fanatically energetic mother, those ragged, wretched little children, sprawling on the floor, "sopping corn-bread in some gravy left in the bottom of a frying-pan"—it is the epic not only of Mark Twain's infancy but of a whole phase of American civilization. [pp. 28–29]

If Jane Clemens had been a woman of wide experience and independent mind, in proportion to the strength of her character, Mark Twain's career might have been wholly different. Had she been catholic in her sympathies, in her understanding of life, then, no matter how more than maternal her attachment to her son was, she might have placed before him and encouraged him to pursue interests and activities amid which he could eventually have recovered his balance, reduced the filial bond to its normal measure and stood on his own feet. But that is to wish for a type of woman our old pioneer society could never have produced. We are told that the Aunt Polly of *Tom Sawyer* is a speaking portrait of Jane Clemens, and Aunt Polly, as we know, was the symbol of all the taboos. The stronger her will was, the more comprehensive were her repressions, the more certainly she became the inflexible guardian of tradition in a social regime where tradition was inalterably opposed to every sort of personal deviation from the accepted type. [p. 34]

Already, I think we divine what was bound to happen in the soul of Mark Twain. The story of Huckleberry Finn turns, as we remember, upon a conflict: "The author," says Mr. Paine, "makes Huck's struggle a psychological one between conscience and the law, on one side, and sympathy on the other." In the famous episode of Nigger Jim, "sympathy," the cause of individual freedom, wins. "We found," says the boy who tells the story [of "The Mysterious Stranger"], "that we were not manly enough nor brave enough to do a generous action when there was a chance that it could get us into trouble." Conscience and the law, we see, had long prevailed in the spirit of Mark Twain, but what is the conscience of a boy who checks a humane impulse but "boy terror," as Mr. Paine calls it, an instinctive fear of custom, of tribal authority? The conflict in *Huckleberry Finn* is simply the conflict of Mark Twain's own childhood. He solved it successfully, he fulfilled his desire, in the book, as an author can. In actual life he did not solve it at all; he surrendered. [pp. 35–36]

As we can see now, it was affection rather than material self-interest that was leading Mark Twain onward and upward. It had always been affection! He had never at bottom wanted to "make good" for any other reason than to please his mother, and in order to get on he had had to adopt his mother's values of life; he had had to repress the deepest instinct in him and accept the guidance of those who knew the ropes of success. As the ward of his mother, he had never consciously broken with the traditions of Western society. Now, a candidate for gentility on terms wholly foreign to his nature, he found the filial bond of old renewed with tenfold intensity in a fresh relationship. He had to "make good" in his wife's eyes, and that was a far more complicated obligation. As we shall see, Mark Twain rebelled against her will, just as he had rebelled against his mother's, yet could not seriously or finally question anything she thought or did. "He adored her as little less than a saint," we are told: which is only another way of saying that, automatically, her gods had become his. [p. 106]

It was, this marriage, as we perceive, a case of the blind leading the blind. Mark Twain had thrown himself into the hands of his wife; she, in turn, was merely the echo of her environment. "She was very sensitive about me," he wrote in his Autobiography. "It distressed her to see me do heedless things which could bring me under criticism." That was partly, of course, because she wished him to succeed for his own sake, but it was also because she was not sure of herself. We can see, between the lines of Mr. Paine's record, not only what a shy little provincial body she was, how easily thrown out of her element, how ill-at-ease in their journeyings about the world, but how far from unambitious she was also. It was for her own sake, therefore, that she trimmed him and tried to turn Caliban into a gentleman. [p. 116]

Profane art, the mature expression of life, in short, was outside Mrs. Clemens's circle of ideas; she could not breathe in that atmosphere with any comfort; her instinctive notion of literature was of something that is read at the fireside, out loud, under the lamp, a family institution, vaguely associated with the Bible and a father tempering the wind of King James's English to the sensitive ears and blushing cheek of the youngest daughter. Her taste, in a word, was quite infantile. "Mrs. Clemens says my version of the blindfold novelette, A Murder and a Marriage, is 'good.' Pretty strong language for her," writes Mark Twain in 1876; and we know that when he was at work on Huckleberry Finn and The Prince and the Pauper, she so greatly preferred the latter that Mark Twain really felt it was rather discreditable of him to pay any attention to Huckleberry Finn at all. [pp. 120–21]

It was The Prince and the Pauper, a book that anybody might have written but whose romantic medievalism was equally respectable in its tendency and infantile in its appeal, that Mrs. Clemens felt so proud of: "Nobody," adds Mr. Paine, "appears to have been especially concerned about Huck, except, possibly the publisher." Plainly it was very little encouragement that Mark Twain's natural genius received from these relentless critics to whom he stood in such subjection, to whom he offered such devotion; for Mr. Howells, too, if we are to accept Mr. Paine's record, seconded him as often as not in these innocuous, infantile ventures, abetting him in the production of "blindfold novelettes" and plays of an abysmal foolishness. As for Mark Twain's unique masterpiece, *Huckleberry Finn*, "I like it only tolerably well, as far as I have got," he writes, "and may possibly pigeonhole or burn the MS when it is done"; to which Mr. Paine adds: "It did not fascinate him as did the story of the wandering prince. He persevered only as the story moved him. * * * Apparently, he had not yet acquired confidence or pride enough in poor Huck to exhibit him, even to friends." [p. 121]

Through the character of Huck, that disreputable, illiterate little boy, as Mrs. Clemens no doubt thought him, he was licensed to let himself go. We have seen how indifferent his sponsors were to the writing and the fate of this book. * * * The more indifferent they were, the freer was Mark Twain! Anything that little vagabond said might be safely trusted to pass the censor, just because he was a little vagabond, just because, as an irresponsible boy, he could not, in the eyes of the mighty ones of this world, know anything in any case about life, morals and civilization. That Mark Twain was almost, if not quite, conscious of his opportunity, we can see from his introductory note to the book: "Persons attempting to find a motive in this narrative will be prosecuted; persons attempting to find a moral in it will be banished; persons attempting to find a plot in it will be shot." He feels so secure of himself that he can actually challenge the censor to accuse him of having a motive! Huck's illiteracy, Huck's disreputableness and general outrageousness are so many shields behind which Mark Twain can let all the cats out of the bag with impunity. He must, I say, have had a certain sense of his unusual security when he wrote some of the more cynically satirical passages of the book, when he permitted Colonel Sherburn to taunt the mob, when he drew that picture of the audience who had been taken in by the Duke proceeding to sell the rest of their townspeople, when he had the King put up the notice, "Ladies and Children not Admited," and add: "There, if that line don't fetch them, I don't know Arkansaw!" The withering contempt for humankind expressed in these episodes was of the sort that Mark Twain expressed more and more openly, as time went on, in his own person; but he was not indulging in that costly kind of cynicism in the days when he wrote *Huckleberry Finn*. He must, therefore, have appreciated the license that little vagabond, like the puppet on the lap of a ventriloquist, afforded him. This, however, was only a trivial detail in his general sense of happy expansion, of ecstatic liberation. "Other places do seem so cramped up and smothery, but a raft don't," says Huck, on the river; "you feel mighty free and easy and comfortable on a raft." Mark Twain himself was free at last!—that raft and river to him were something more than mere material facts. His whole unconscious life, the pent-up river on his own soul, had burst its bonds and rushed forth, a joyous torrent! Do we need any other explanation of the abandon, the beauty, the eternal freshness of *Huckleberry Finn?* Perhaps we can say that a lifetime of moral slavery and repression was not too much to pay for it. Certainly, if it flies like a gay, bright, shining arrow through the tepid atmosphere of American literature, it is because of the straining of the bow, the tautness of the string, that gave it its momentum.

Yes, if we did not know, if we did not feel, that Mark Twain was intended for a vastly greater destiny, for the role of a demiurge, in fact, we might have been glad of all those pretty restrictions and misprisions he had undergone, restrictions that had prepared the way for this joyous release. No smoking on Sundays! No "swearing" allowed! Neckties having to be bothered over! That everlasting diet of Ps and Qs, petty Ps and pettier Qs, to which Mark Twain had had to submit, the domestic diet of Mrs. Clemens, the literary diet of Mr. Howells, those second parents who had taken the place of his first—we have to thank it, after all, for the vengeful solace we find in the promiscuous and general revolt of Huckleberry Finn.

[pp. 194–96]

BERNARD DeVOTO

[Mark Twain: The Artist As American]†

* * *

As an accessory of literature, American journalism attained its highest reach in the February or Midwinter number of the *Century Magazine* for 1885. That issue carried "Royalty on the Mississippi" the last of three selections from *The Adventures of Huckleberry Finn*. It had also the ninth and tenth chapters of *The Rise of Silas Lapham* and began the serialization of *The Bostonians*. No comparable enterprise has ever been undertaken by a magazine.

To Mark, Howells's novel seemed "dazzling—masterly—incomparable." But as for Henry James's, he "would rather be damned to John Bunyan's heaven than read that." Both judgments were in-

† The selection from Bernard DeVoto, *Mark Twain's America*, copyright 1932, is reprinted by permission of and arrangement with Houghton Mifflin Company, the authorized publishers. Pp. 308; 310–20. By emphasizing the creative inspiration which Twain derived from his frontier origins and his knowledge of common American life, DeVoto opposed the hypothesis of Van Wyck Brooks (see *The Ordeal of Mark Twain*, 1920, quoted above) and the official biography by Twain's secretary, Albert Bigelow Paine (1912); the latter portrayed the author and man in the image of Hartford gentility, whereas Brooks suggested that Twain as an artist was betrayed by genteel censorship and the traumatic effect of his frontier boyhood.

evitable to him, but they neglect to understand a coincidence that joined the two novels with his in the climax of the national literature which followed the Civil War. The coincidence provides a yardstick for comparative measurements.

The two studies of amenities in the Back Bay are a chapter in the amiable difference between Howells and James which seems to have been, through the course of several novels on intersecting themes, an almost deliberate debate. Neither went beyond this chapter. *The Rise of Silas Lapham* is the most effective of Howells's stenotypes. After *The Bostonians* James began to submerge in the psychological perplexity through which only members of a school can follow him with complete belief; it was his last confrontation of an objective world. In the two books, two realisms, each in its way formidable, deal with American theorems—in so far as there remained, on the water side of Beacon Street, something recognizable as American.

* * *

Both novels are exquisitely conceived and written. Both employ a more mature technique than our fiction had experienced before them. Both, to the full extent of their powers, embody the truth about their themes sensitively studied and imaginatively projected. But both are wonderfully innocent of the world, their time and their nation. They are insulated from America. They are the genteel tradition attaining its complete expression in fiction but also irrevocably revealing its anæmia. Their impotence could be no more dramatically exhibited than by Gilder's accompanying them with selections from the novel in which nineteenth-century America exists with a vitality, a finality, and a greatness it has had nowhere else.

The kernel of *Huckleberry Finn* is in a speech of Huck's toward the end of *Tom Sawyer*. At the foot of the dead-limb tree t'other side of Still-House branch, he doubts the value of finding buried treasure. "Pap would come back to thish yer town some day and get his claws on it if I didn't hurry up, and I tell you he'd clean it out pretty quick." *Old Times on the Mississippi*, contains a passage as integral with Huck's journey as anything in his book, and *Life on the Mississippi*, written over the period when Huck was gestated, has many incidents on their way to fruition.[1] The Darnell-Watson feud is the Grangerford-Shepherdson trouble in chrysalis, a desultory tale told by a passenger as the *Gold Dust* passes through the chute of Island Number 8. On the upstream voyage as yet anonymous

1. Critics who enjoy dealing with the unconscious mind as the womb of art are offered such passages for amusement. I reluctantly confess, however, my fear that they will not indicate a father fixation, Mark's incestuous love of his sister, a forgotten reading of Nathaniel Wanley, or zoöphily.

strollers forecast David Garrick the younger and Edmund Keen the elder. John A. Murrell's inheritors hint at revenge in the state-rooms of a wrecked steamboat and other creatures of midnight presage the turmoil of search and escape through underbrush. Nor are these volumes the only ones in which pupal stages of incidents in *Huckleberry Finn* may be observed: most of the books that precede have passages of premonition. Why not? It was a book he was foreordained to write: it brought harmoniously to a focus everything that had a basic reality in his mind.

The opening is just *Tom Sawyer* and pretty poor *Tom Sawyer* at that. Huck's report of his emotions while ghosts are talking to him in the wind is a promise of what is to come, but Tom Sawyer's gang commenting on *Don Quixote* lacks the fineness of its predecessor. Discussions of ransom and Tom's exposition of Aladdin's lamp are feeble; such finish as they have comes from Huck's tolerant but obstinate common sense, here making its first experiments. But no flavor of the real Odyssey appears until Miss Watson forbids him to avert by magic the bad luck made inevitable by spilled salt, thus precipitating his trouble, and he immediately finds in the snow the impression of a boot heel in which nails make a cross to keep off the devil. . . . It is expedient to list here the book's obvious faults. After a first half in which, following the appearance of old man Finn, no touch is unsure, Mark's intuition begins to falter occasionally. When the Duke has Louis XVII learn a Shakespearian speech compounded out of Sol Smith and George Ealer, high and poetic reality lapses into farce. (Predictably. The humorist's necessity to write burlesque had frequently ruined fine things in the earlier books.) The King's conversion is weakened by his use of pirates instead of the neighborhood church which his predecessor Simon Suggs had more persuasively employed. (Predictably. The necessity to carry a joke into cosmic reaches had betrayed him often enough before.) Huck's discourse on the domestic manners of royalty is a blemish. (Extravaganza had diluted satire in many earlier contexts.) Huck's confusion when he tries to lie to the hare-lipped girl is perfunctory. (Improvisation had substituted for structure sufficiently often in Mark's previous fiction.) The concluding episodes of the attempted fraud on the Wilks family are weak in their technical devices—the manipulation required to postpone the detection of imposture, for instance, is annoying. Thereafter the narrative runs downhill through a steadily growing incredibility. The use of ghosts, the deceptions practiced on Aunt Sally and Uncle Silas, the whole episode built around the delivery of Jim from prison—all these are far below the accomplishment of what has gone before. Mark was once more betrayed. He intended a further chapter in his tireless attack on romanticism, especially Southern romanticism, and nothing in his mind or training enabled him to understand that this extemporized burlesque was a defacement of his purer work. His boundless gusto expended itself equally on the true and the false. . . . Predictably. It has been observed that he was incapable of sustained and disciplined imagination. One could expect it no more reasonably here than in *The Innocents Abroad.*

So, though I regard comparisons as worthless in æsthetics, the obligation of a critic of Mark Twain rests on me to point out these selfsame faults in the only American novel which even enthusiasm can offer to dispute the preëminence of *The Adventures of Huckleberry Finn.* Much more identity than has ever been noticed in print exists in the careers of Mark Twain and Herman Melville, whose minds were as antipathetic as religion and reality or the subjective and the objective world can be. Similarly, Jonathan Edwards's successor, when he came to write his masterpiece, plentifully anticipated the errors of Mark Twain and went beyond them. *Moby Dick* has, as fiction, no structure whatever. Its lines of force mercilessly intercept one another. Its improvisations are commoner and falser than those in Huck Finn. It does not suffer from burlesque (exuberant vitality had no place in Melville's nature) but its verbal humor is sometimes more vicariously humiliating than such passages as Huck's discussion of kings—a miracle, no doubt, withheld Mark Twain from the mere jokes habitual to him. And, though Melville could write great prose, his book frequently escapes into a passionately swooning rhetoric that is unconscious burlesque. He was no surer than Mark, he was in fact less sure, of the true object of his book, and much less sure of the technical instruments necessary to achieve it. That much of weakness the two novels have in common. It is convenient to point out, this much having been said, that they are otherwise antipathies. *Moby Dick* opposes metaphysics to the objective reality of *Huckleberry Finn.* It is a study in demonology, bound to the world of experience by no more durable threads than a few passages in the lives of mates, harpooners and sailors who are otherwise mostly symbol or mist. They were the book's disregarded possibility of great realism. Melville preferred to sigh through eternity after the infinite. It is a search which has an eternal value for some minds. Other minds, if they look to fiction for values of time instead of eternity and of the finite instead of the infinite, are likely to relinquish the *Pequod's* voyage toward fulfillment of man's destiny and prefer a lumber raft's voyage down inland waters after no more ambitious purpose than to see what the world is like.

The title announces the structure: a picaresque novel concerned with the adventures of Huckleberry Finn. The form is the one most native to Mark Twain and so best adapted to his use. No more than

Huck and the river's motion gives continuity to a series of episodes which are in essence only developed anecdotes. They originate in the tradition of newspaper humor, but the once uncomplicated form becomes here the instrument of great fiction. The lineage goes back to a native art; the novel derives from the folk and embodies their mode of thought more purely and more completely than any other ever written. Toward the beginning of this preface it was asserted that the life of the southwestern frontier was umbilical to the mind of Mark Twain. The blood and tissue of *Huckleberry Finn* have been formed in no other way. That life here finds issue more memorably than it has anywhere else, and since the frontier is a phase through which most of the nation has passed, the book comes nearer than any other to identity with the national life. The gigantic amorphousness of our past makes impossible, or merely idle, any attempt to fix in the form of idea the meaning of nationality. But more truly with *Huckleberry Finn* than with any other book, inquiry may satisfy itself: here is America.

The book has the fecundity, the multiplicity, of genius. It is the story of a wandering—so provocative a symbol that it moved Rudyard Kipling to discover another sagacious boy beneath a cannon and conduct him down an endless road, an enterprise that enormously fell short of its model. It is a passage through the structure of the nation. It is an exploration of the human race, whose adjective needs no explicit recording. It is an adventure of pageantry, horror, loveliness, and the tropisms of the mind. It is a faring-forth with inexhaustible delight through the variety of America. It is the restlessness of the young democracy borne southward on the river—the energy, the lawlessness, the groping ardor of the flux perfectly comprehended in a fragment of lumber raft drifting on the June flood. In a worn phrase—it is God's plenty.

The arrival of Huck's father lifts the narrative from the occupations of boyhood to as mature intelligence as fiction has anywhere. The new interest begins on a major chord, for old man Finn is the perfect portrait of the squatter. Behind him are the observations of hundreds of anonymous or forgotten realists who essayed to present the clay eaters or piney-woods people, as well as a lifelong interest of Mark Twain's. It is amazing how few pages of type he occupies; the effect is as of a prolonged, minute analysis. There is no analysis; a clear light is focused on him and the dispassionate, final knowledge of his creator permits him to reveal himself. We learn of him only that he had heard about Huck's money "away down the river," but a complete biography shines through his speech. This rises to the drunken monologue about a government that can't take a-hold of a prowling, thieving, white-shirted free nigger. The old man subsides to an attack of snakes, is heard rowing his skiff in darkness, and then is just a frowsy corpse, shot in the back, which drifts downstream with the flood.

Something exquisite and delicate went into that creation—as into the casuals of the riverside. Mrs. Judith Loftus is employed to start Huck and Jim upon their voyage. She is just a device, but she outtops a hundred-odd patient attempts of fiction to sketch the pioneer wife. In her shrewdness, curiosity, initiative and brusque humanity one reads an entire history. Mere allusions—the ferryboat owner, the oarsmen who flee from smallpox, even raftsmen heard joking in the dark—have an incomparable authenticity. There is also the crowd. The loafers of Bricksville whittle under the store fronts. They set a dog upon a sow that has "wholloped" herself right down in the way and "laugh and look grateful for the noise." Presently a bubble rises through this human mire: the drunken Boggs, the best-naturedest old fool in Arkansaw, comes riding into Bricksville, on the warpath. Colonel Sherburn finds it necessary to shoot him; and then, in one of the most blinding flashlights in all fiction, a "long, lanky man, with long hair and a big white fur stovepipe hat on the back of his head" rehearses the murder. "The people that had seen the thing said he done it perfect." So Buck Harkness leads a mob to Sherburn's house for a lynching but the Colonel breaks up the mob with a speech in which contempt effervesces like red nitric.

But in such passages as this, the clearly seen individuals merge into something greater, a social whole, a civilization, seen just as clearly. Pokeville, where the King is converted at the camp meeting, Bricksville, and the town below the P'int where a tanner has died are one with Dawson's Landing and Napoleon—but more concentrated and thereby more final. It seems unnecessary to linger in consideration of this society. At the time of its appearance in 1885 a number of other novelists, perhaps fecundated by *The Gilded Age*, were considering similar themes. The name of any one of them—Charles Egbert Craddock or Mary E. Wilkins or Edward Eggleston will do—is enough to distinguish honest talent from genius. The impulse weakened under the æstheticism of the Nineties, and it was not till after the World War that the countryside again received consideration in these terms. To set Bricksville against Gopher Prairie or Winesburg is to perceive at once the finality of Mark Twain. The long lanky man in a white stovepipe hat who rehearses the death of Boggs has recorded this society with an unemotional certainty beside which either Mr. Lewis's anger or Mr. Anderson's misery seems a transitory hysterics.

The completeness of the society must be insisted upon. One should scrutinize the family of the dead tanner and their friends and neighbors, and orient them by reference to the family of Colonel

Grangerford. The Wilkses belong to the industrious respectability of the towns. Their speech and thinking, the objects of their desire, the circumstances of their relationships are the totality of their kind. The funeral of Peter Wilks is, as fiction, many themes blended together; it is, among them, a supreme exhibition of the mid-continental culture of its time—almost an archæological display. When the undertaker tiptoes among the mourners to silence a howling dog and returns to whisper "He had a rat," something final has been said about this life. But Colonel Grangerford is a gentle-man. Incidentally to the feud, which is the principal occupation of this episode, Southern gentility is examined. James's Basil Ransom was an embraced tradition; Colonel Grangerford is a reality. His daughter's elopement, a device for the precipitation of the plot, is out of fiction; the feud itself, with all the lovingly studied details of the scene, are from life. Gentility decorates the parlor with Em-maline Grangerford's verse and sketches. Its neurons show in the management of more than a hundred niggers quite as positively as in the parlor, or in the ceremonies of family intercourse and the simple code of honor, so indistinguishable from that of the Iroquois, which results in mass murder.

The portraiture which begins among the dregs with old man Finn ends with the Grangerfords. Between these strata has come every level of the South. What is the integrity of an artist? It would seem to consist in an intelligence which holds itself to the statement of a perceived truth, refusing to color it with an emotion of the artist's consequent to the truth. . . . These scenes are warm with an originality and a gusto that exist nowhere else in American fic-tion, and yet they are most notable for Mark Twain's detachment. There is no coloration, no resentment, no comment of any kind. The thing itself is rendered. If repudiation is complete, it exists im-plicitly in the thing.[2]

The differentiation of the speech these people use is so subtly done that Mark had to defend himself against an accusation of carelessness. He did not want readers to "suppose that all these characters were trying to talk alike and not succeeding." Superla-tives are accurate once more: no equal sensitiveness to American speech has ever been brought to fiction. But a triumph in dialect is after all one of the smaller triumphs of novel-writing, and the important thing to be observed about Huckleberry's speech is its achievement in making the vernacular a perfect instrument for all the necessities of fiction. Like Melville, Mark Twain could write

2. Criticism has spent some pain on Mark Twain's deletion from *Life on the Mississippi* of a passage which, he was persuaded, might affect sales in the South. Apparently those who were out-raged by this pandering to prejudice did not bother to read the suppressed passage. It is considerably less offensive to Southern sensibilities than several passages which remain in *Life on the Mississippi* and beside a good half of *Huckleberry Finn* it is innocuous.

empty rhetoric enough when the mood was on him, and the set pieces of description in the travel books are as trying as the Mc-Guffey selections which may have influenced them, while a willingness to let tears flow menaces a good many effects elsewhere. Yet his writing is never mediocre and is mostly, even in the least pretentious efforts, a formidable strength. Beginning with *Life on the Mississippi* it becomes, as Mr. Ford has remarked, one of the great styles of English literature. No analysis need be made here: its basis is simplicity, adaptability, an intimate liaison with the senses, and fidelity to the idioms of speech. Against the assertions of criticism, it should be remembered that such a style is not developed inattentively, nor are infants born with one by God's providence. Mark's lifelong pleasure in the peculiarities of language, which has distressed commentators, was the interest of any artist in his tools. . . . The successful use of an American vernacular as the sole prose medium of a masterpiece is a triumph in technique. Such attempts have been common in two and a half centuries of English fiction, but no other attempt on the highest level has succeeded. In this respect, too, *Huckleberry Finn* is unique. Patently, American literature has nothing to compare with it. Huck's language is a sensitive, subtle, and versatile instrument—capable of every effect it is called upon to manage. Whether it be the purely descriptive necessity of recording the river's mystery, or the notation of psychological states so minute and transitory as the effect on a boy of ghosts crying in the wind, or the fixation of individuality in dialogue, or the charged finality that may be typified by the King's "Hain't we got all the fools in town on our side? And ain't that a big enough majority in any town?"—the prose fulfills its obligation with the casual competence of genius. The fiction of Mark Twain had brought many innovations to the national literature—themes, lives, and interests of the greatest originality. This superb adaptation of vernacular to the purposes of art is another innovation, one which has only in the last few years begun to have a dim and crude but still perceptible fruition.

A tradition almost as old as prose narrative joins to the novel another tributary of world literature when a purely American wandering brings two further creatures of twilight to the raft. The Duke of Bilgewater and the Lost Dauphin were born of Mark's inexhaustible delight in worthlessness, but are many-sided. Pretension of nobility is one of his commonest themes, here wrought into pure comedy. The Duke is akin to characters in the other books; the King embodies a legend widespread and unimaginably glorious on the frontier. The ambiguity surrounding the death of Louis XVII gave to history riots, dynasties and social comedies that still absorb much reverence in Florence and Paris. It gave mythology a superb legend, which at once accommodated itself to American belief. Up the river from New Orleans, one of the most pious repositories of allegiance, stories of the dethroned Bourbon gratified believers during three generations. The legend must have entertained Mark's boyhood but the circumstances of his Dauphin suggest that he more enjoyed the appearance of Eleazar Williams, who became an international celebrity in 1853. The whole course of his life probably gave him no more satisfying exhibition of the race's folly than the discovery of a Bourbon king in the person of this Mohawk half-breed turned Christian and missionary, who had systematically defrauded his church and his people. The story is one of the occasional ecstasies with which history rewards the patient mind.

The two rogues are formed from the nation's scum. They are products of chance and opportunity, drifters down rivers and across the countryside in the service of themselves. The Duke has sold medicines, among them a preparation to remove tartar from the teeth; he has acted tragedy and can sling a lecture sometimes; he can teach singing-geography school or take a turn to mesmerism or phrenology when there's a chance. The King can tell fortunes and can cure cancer or paralysis by the laying on of hands; but preaching, missionarying, and the temperance revival are his best lines. American universals meet here; once more, this is a whole history, and into these drifters is poured an enormous store of the nation's experience. They have begotten hordes of successors since 1885 but none that joins their immortality. They belong with Colonel Sellers: they are the pure stuff of comedy. Their destiny is guile: to collect the tax which freedom and wit levy on respectability. Their voyage is down a river deep in the American continent; they are born of a purely American scene. Yet the river becomes one of the world's roads and these disreputables join, of right, a select fellowship. They are Diana's foresters: the brotherhood that receives them, approving their passage, is immortal in the assenting dreams of literature. Such freed spirits as Panurge, Falstaff, Gil Blas and the Abbé Coignard are of that fellowship; no Americans except the Duke and the Dauphin have joined it. None seems likely to.

Yet the fabric on which all this richness is embroidered is the journey of Huck and Jim down the Mississippi on the June rise. There, finally, the book's glamour resides. To discuss that glamour would be futile. In a sense, Huck speaks to the national shrewdness, facing adequately what he meets, succeeding by means of native intelligence whose roots are ours—and ours only. In a sense, he exists for a delight or wonder inseparable from the American race. This passage down the flooded river, through pageantry and spectacle, amidst an infinite variety of life, something of surprise or gratification surely to be met with each new incident—it is the heritage of a nation not unjustly symbolized by the river's flow. Huck sleeping under the stars or wakefully drifting through an immensity dotted only by far lights or scurrying to a cave while the forest bends under a cloudburst satisfies blind gropings of the mind. The margin widens to obscurity. Beyond awareness, a need for freedom, an insatiable hunger for its use, finds in him a kind of satisfaction. At the margin, too, the endless flow speaks for something quite as immediate. It is movement, not quiet. By day or darkness the current is unceasing; its rhythm, at the obscure margin, speaks affirmatively. For life is movement—a down-river voyage amidst strangeness.

Go warily in the obscurity. One does not care to leave Huck in the twilight at such a threshold, among the dim shapes about which no one can speak with authority. Unquestionably something of him is resident there—with something of Tom, the disreputables, Colonel Sellers and some others. But first he is a shrewd boy who takes a raft down the Mississippi, through a world incomparably alive. With him goes a fullness made and shaped wholly of America. It is only because the world he passes through is real and only because it is American that his journey escapes into universals and is immortal. His book is American life formed into great fiction.

Somewhere in the person of Mark Twain, who wrote it, must have been an artist—as American.

* * *

DeLANCEY FERGUSON

Huck Finn Aborning†

No American critical theory has taken deeper root than Mr. Van Wyck Brooks's thesis that Mark Twain was a thwarted satirist whose bitterness toward the damned human race was the fruit of a lifelong prostitution of his talents. Despite the counter-attacks of Bernard DeVoto and others, it flourishes everywhere from the London *Times Literary Supplement* to the last semester paper turned in by an English major at the University of Middletown. Past question, it is picturesque and dramatic, but—as Braxfield said of the clever chiel who would be none the worse for a hanging—it would be better if it were supported by a few facts.

A new interpretation of a great writer cannot have too many facts to stand on. The books published by the man himself or his literary executors are not enough; one must study him in his un-

† Published in *Colophon*, III, N. S. (Spring, 1938), 171–80. Among the earliest critical articles substantiated by the evidence of the Mark Twain manuscripts. Reprinted by permission of DeLancey Ferguson.

guarded moments, in the letters withheld from his biography and in the first drafts of his books. Had Mr. Brooks thus studied Mark Twain, he would have found out many things. But he could not have written his book.

If a writer either consciously or unconsciously withholds anything of himself in his public utterances, traces of the buried talents are bound to show in the early drafts that are not yet groomed and sleeked for print. If nothing appears there which is not in the finished book, then the author is not censored, either by himself, his wife, or his literary advisors.

Everyone, including Mr. Brooks, agrees that *Huckleberry Finn* is Mark Twain's masterpiece. Written at the height of his creative power, it includes all he had to say, for good and ill, of the Mississippi world of his boyhood. Mr. DeVoto, while rejecting the Brooks thesis, admits it is impossible to pass final judgment on Mark Twain as an artist until we know, among other things, what was deleted from the early drafts of Huck, and why. For here, if Mark Twain had any more to say about the damned human race than he admitted to print, is where he would have said it.

It speaks little for the enterprise of the critics that a large part of the original manuscript of *Huck Finn* has for the past fifty years lain in the Buffalo Public Library without attracting the least notice. Its author gave it to James Fraser Gluck of Buffalo in 1886; soon afterward Mr. Gluck gave it to the library, along with a lot of other literary documents. It has been there ever since, most of the time on public exhibition.

True, the manuscript represents a little less than three-fifths of the book. Beginning in the middle of Chapter XII, it extends to the end of Chapter XIV, resumes at Chapter XXII, and is complete from there on. (The manuscript chapters are not numbered, and the few signs of division seldom coincide with those in the book.) Nevertheless, incomplete as it is, it is fully representative. Some strong scenes are missing, among them the Shepherdson-Grangerford feud, the camp meeting, and the shooting of Boggs, but it includes the attempt to lynch Col. Sherburn, "The Royal Nonesuch," the whole Wilks episode, and Huck's struggle with his conscience over surrendering Jim. The presence of the weak Tom Sawyer chapters at the end is offset by the absence of those at the beginning.

Furthermore, it is genuinely the *original* manuscript, not a specially revised fair copy. Though it bears no printer's marks, it must be the text from which the book was set up, for it includes the original title page, with the author's instructions to the printer, and similar instructions are written here and there in the margins. Without counting the innumerable differences in punctuation, the manuscript contains more than nine hundred textual changes, ranging from single words to whole paragraphs added or deleted, and shows, moreover, several distinct layers of correction, done at different times. Some changes were made at first writing, or almost immediately afterward; others indicate the direction taken in rejected passages not now in the manuscript; still others must have been made in proof. Besides these, a number of penciled marginalia show a critical reading intermediate between first composition and proofs.

But whatever their date, nature, or extent, all the revisions are the same sort. They are not the excision of scathing passages which Mrs. Clemens or Howells would disapprove of, neither are they the dilution of grim realism to make it meat for babes. They are the work of a skilled craftsman removing the unessential, adding vividness to dialog and description, and straightening out incongruities. Not more than two or three of the lot are the sort Olivia Clemens is reputed to have insisted on, and these two or three are so trifling that Mark may well have made them himself, without his wife's orders.

The only clear evidence of change of plan in a main section of the story will scarcely hearten the believers in censorship. When Huck and Tom arrived at Silas Phelps's plantation their creator originally intended them to find there a boy and a girl about their own age, named Phil and Mat. Fragmentary deleted passages, on renumbered pages, show that Mark Twain had developed this idea as far as where Tom passes himself off as Sid. Huck had confided Tom's impending arrival to Phil and Mat. But about that time Mark plainly realized that Tom and Huck, unaided, were going to furnish quite as many complications as the story would hold. He destroyed the older children, leaving only the brood of youngsters who were too small to share in the excitement. But he neglected to revise downward the ages of Silas and Sally (at first called Ruth) Phelps, who therefore appear in the book as somewhat elderly for the parents of so young a family.

So far, then, as the surviving manuscript shows, the general plan was little altered. Most of the changes are of detail. Thus when Huck and Jim visit the wrecked steamboat, Huck talks down Jim's fears by pointing out the untold riches, in five-cent cigars and other things, of steamboat captains. This whole long speech was added overleaf in the manuscript, to replace the unimaginative sentence, "Steamboat captains is always rich, and have everything they want, you know." Some of the best phrases were inserted in proof. The King's "soul-butter and hogwash" was only "humbug and hogwash" in the manuscript. Later on, when the King has "to brace up mighty quick, or he'd 'a squshed down like a bluff bank that the river has cut under," the simile was an afterthought. In the manuscript he merely "kerflummoxed." Again, the mob tears down Sherburn's fence, and begins "to roll in like a wave." When the Colonel appears with his shotgun, the book says, "The racket stopped, and the wave sucked back." For the last phrase, the manuscript has only "the crowd fell back." In the next paragraph, the book says, "Then pretty soon Sherburn sort of laughed; not the pleasant kind, but the kind that makes you feel like when you are eating bread that's got sand in it." This replaces, "not the kind of laugh you hear at the circus, but the kind that's fitten for a funeral—the kind that makes you feel crawly."

Many substitutions are dramatic. The first thoughts may be picturesque, but are out of character. Huck's summing up of Mary Jane Wilks was first, "She *was* the best girl that ever was! and you could depend on her like the everlasting sun and the stars, every time." The speech might have fitted the mouth of the Playboy of the Western World, but not Huck's. It was changed in proof to, "She *was* the best girl I ever see, and had the most sand." A sentimental reference to "the big friendly river stretching out so homelike before us" was deleted entirely. Huck, telling Jim of the ways and works of kings, at first said that Henry VIII made each wife tell him a tale every night, "and he kept that up till he had hogged a thousand and one tales that way, and then he got out a copyright and published them all in a book, and called it Domesday Book—which was a good name and stated the case. Of course most any publisher would do that, but you wouldn't think a king would. If you didn't know kings." . . . But copyright is outside Huck's range of knowledge. Mark Twain, author and publisher, had taken his place. The passage was struck out of the proofs.

Remarks, again, might be right in character, but wrong in tone. Some of the more serious persons tended at first to orate in the style of Drury Lane melodrama. Col. Sherburn's speeches are full of passages like the one here italicised: "Because you're brave enough to tar and feather poor friendless cast-out women that come along here *lowering themselves to your level to earn a bite of bitter bread to eat,* did it fool you into thinking you had courage enough to lay your hands on a MAN?" And when Dr. Robinson denounces the King and Duke as imposters, his oration originally wound up thus:

"He is the thinnest of thin imposters—has come here with a lot of empty names and facts which he picked up somewhere; and you weakly take them for proofs, and are assisted in deceiving yourselves by these thoughtless unreasoning friends here, who ought to know better. Mary Jane Wilks, you know me for your friend, and your honest and unselfish friend. Now listen to me: cast this paltry villain out—I beg you, I beseech you to do it. Will you?"

As any reader of Victorian novels knows, this was a natural literary idiom in the 1870's. But even if Dr. Robinson had really talked that way, it was not the natural idiom for Huck to report him in.

Another sort of revision marks the King's two speeches, "all full of tears and flapdoodle," over Peter Wilks's coffin. Their permanent form, like the immortal phrase which introduces them, was an afterthought. They were first written in direct discourse, thus:

"Friends, good friends of the deceased, and ourn too, I trust—it's indeed a sore trial to lose him, and a sore trial to miss seeing him alive, after the wearisome long journey of four thousand mile; but it's a trial ·that's sweetened and sanctified to us by this dear sympathy and these holy tears; and so, out of our hearts we thank you, for out of our mouths we cannot, words being too weak and cold. May you find such friends and such sympathy yourselves, when your own time of trial comes, and may this affliction be softened to you as ourn is today, by the soothing ba'm of earthly love and the healing of heavenly grace. Amen."

In this speech and its companion, every phrase in the draft is carried over into the final text, but the indirect reporting, by implying compression from much greater length, immeasurably heightens the effect. It also gives Stephen Leacock, who says that Mark Twain never could convey the idea of prolixity except by getting prolix, something to ponder.

For still other effects, entire situations are expanded or reduced. Apparently almost the whole plan of the Wilks auction and its consequences came to Mark Twain as he wrote. After reporting the sale of the slaves, he at first went on with merely, "Next day was auction. They sold off the girls' house, and the tanyard and the rest of the property, but the prices wasn't the very highest." He immediately struck this out, and developed the narrative much as it stands in the book. Mark's invention, like most people's, did not always run smooth. Some passages, such as the chapter recording Huck's efforts to warn Mary Jane of impending trouble with the King and the Duke, have as many as twenty or twenty-five textual changes on a single page of print; at other times, whole pages of the book stand unchanged from the manuscript. There is no relation between the level of the work and the number of changes: Tom's arrival at the Phelps's is almost as much revised as Huck's interview with Mary Jane, and more than the attempted lynching of Sherburn.

Earlier in the Wilks episode, at the opening of Chapter XXVI, Mark originally began:

"Well, when they was all gone the king asked Mary Jane how they was off for spare rooms, and she said they had two; so he said they could put his valley in the same bed with him—meaning me. He said in England it warn't usual for a valley to sleep with his master, but in Rome he always done the way the Romans done, and besides he warn't proud, and reckoned he could stand Adolphus very well. Maybe he could; but I couldn't a stood him, only I was long ago used to sleeping with the other kind of hogs. So Mary Jane showed us all up, and they was plain rooms but nice."

Here again deletion was immediate. Huck's nocturnal prowls, and his hiding the Wilks gold, would have been impossible had he slept in the same room with the King. This, like the auction passage, shows Mark composing as he went along, with only the vaguest general plan in mind.

In the earlier adventure on the wrecked steamboat some changes are in the manuscript; others were not made until the proofs. At first writing, when Huck and Jim board the wreck, "rip comes a flash of lightning out of the sky, and shows us a skiff tied to the skylight pretty close beyond the door, for all that side was under water." This was struck out at once; it destroyed both the surprise of discovering the ruffians on the boat and the suspense when the raft went adrift. But later in the chapter the manuscript elaborates the plans of Bill and Jake for silencing their treacherous companion, Jim Turner. They are going to gag him, to keep him quiet till the wreck breaks up and drowns him. Bill objects,

" 'But s'pose she don't break up and wash off?'
" 'Well, we can wait the two hours, can't we? Then, if the thing don't work, it'll still be long enough befo' daylight, and we'll come back and do the next best thing—tie a rock to him and dump him into the river.'
" 'All right, then: come along and less gag him.' "

And later, when the ruffians come out just as Huck and Jim are getting away in the skiff, a wail from Turner calls them back to replace the gag he has worked loose. In the book, all references to the gagging disappear, apparently because it merely complicated the action without intensifying it.

In this same episode appears the first of the marginalia indicating critical revision between first writing and sending to press. When Huck cuts the skiff loose, his creator has penciled in the margin, "Provide him with a knife." This reminder is no doubt what allowed Huck to find, among the junk in the wrecked house floating down river in Chapter IX, "a bran-new Barlow knife worth two bits in any store."

Several such notes appear on the pages telling of the flight after the Wilks fiasco. When the crooks are plotting to sell Jim, the Duke, says Huck, "found fault with every little thing, and he even cussed Jim for being a fool and keeping his blue paint and King Lear clothes on, and made him take them off and wash himself off; and yet it warn't no fault of Jim's, for nobody hadn't ever told him he might do it." This passage is scored through, and a note says, "This is lugged—shove it back yonder to where they escape lynching and regain raft." But Mark failed to shove it, and so never told how or when Jim shed his "sick Arab" make-up. But the next note was acted on. When Huck, trying to find what the scoundrels have done with Jim, arrives at the Phelps's, a penciled note says, "Has good clothes on." Consequently, in the previous chapter, when Huck leaves the raft, the book has him putting on his store clothes, instead of "some old rough clothes" that he wore in the manuscript. There also, when he is going ashore in the canoe, one note says, "The skiff being new and worth advertising;" another, "Go back and [*sink* deleted] burn the skiff when they escape lynching;" a third, on the next leaf, "Go back and put on old clothes after escape from lynching." All these were finally ignored. So were a couple during Tom's elaborate schemes to free Jim. Where Tom instructs Huck about famous escapes, his author added in the margin, "Edmond Dantes," but let the book text stand as "them prisoners in the bottom dungeon of the Castle Deef." In the next chapter, when the boys are working in Jim's shack, a note says, "They always take along a lunch." But no change was made, and so far as the book reveals they carried on their night work without extra nourishment.

Most interesting of all is the note on the leaf which describes the King's make-up in "The Royal Nonesuch." It is the single word, scored through, "scandalous." Here, if anywhere, we might expect censorship. No one acquainted with fraternity initiations and other gatherings where Greek phallic comedy survives, has ever been in doubt as to the sort of show the King provided for the male population of Bricksville, Arkansas. Mark's canceled comment shows that he knew it was dangerous ground; the text shows exactly how much censorship he—or possibly Olivia—exercised. One phrase is deleted: the King originally "said he judged he could caper to their base instincts; 'lowed he could size their style." The title of the "play" is changed: throughout the manuscript it is "The Burning Shame" instead of "The Royal Nonesuch." The description of the King's makeup is modified in two places. In the manuscript he is "stark naked;" in the book merely "naked." The next sentence was first, "And—but I won't describe the rest of his outfit, because it was just outrageous, although it was awful funny." In the book Huck says, "And—but never mind the rest of his outfit; it was just wild, but it was awful funny." Out of the vast laboring mountain of charges that Mark Twain was a blighted Hemingway emerges this tiny and ineffectual mouse. If this was the utmost he suffered in revising what by implication is probably the bawdiest passage he ever conceived for publication, he was one of the freest authors who ever lived, instead of one of the most repressed.

The complete list of other changes which were, or may have been, made for decorum's sake bears out the impression from "The Royal Nonesuch." "Drunk," used twice in one paragraph, becomes "tight" and "mellow." Kings "hang," instead of "wallow," round the harem. "Rotten eggs" is changed to "sickly eggs," but since "rotten cabbages" stands in the same line, the change may be mere avoidance of repetition. The smells "too various" for Huck in the book were "too rancid" in the manuscript, and "the signs of a dead cat being around" replace "the smell of a dead cat." In several other places Mark's second thought modified his unhappy fondness for seeking humor in death, decay, and viscera. Jim, made up as the sick Arab, "didn't only look like he was dead, he looked considerably more than that." It may be doubted if realism would have gained much had the phrase been let stand as "he looked like he was mortified." It would be a questionable improvement to describe unappetizing meat as "a hunk of your old cold grandfather" instead of the "hunk of old cold cannibal," which again was second thought. And is it any better to say your conscience "takes up more room than a person's bowels" instead of "all the rest of a person's insides"?

A very few alterations considered the feelings of the churchly. Huck first said that the King rigged out in his store clothes looked as if "he had walked right out of the Bible;" this was changed to "the ark," but he still might be "old Leviticus himself." "Judas Iscarott" is softened to "Judus"; the King looks up towards the sky instead of the Throne. Two of Tom's jibes are altered, "mild as Sunday School" becoming "mild as goose-milk," and "Sunday-schooliest ways" becoming "infant-schooliest." On the other hand, when Huck trusts "to Providence to put the right words in [his] mouth when the time come," Mark changed "Providence" to "luck" in the manuscript, but restored the original reading in the proofs. And once he inadvertently wrote "damn," but immediately changed it to "dern."

In the Wilks episode, the manuscript allows the King and Duke to be a trifle more goatish towards Mary Jane and her sisters than the book does. The description of their welcome by the girls originally included this:

"Soon as he could, the duke shook the hair-lip, and sampled Susan, which was better looking. After the king had kissed Mary Jane fourteen or fifteen times, he give the duke a show, and tapered off on the others."

When Huck is getting Mary Jane away as the show-down approaches, he asks, "Do you reckon you can face your uncles, and take your regular three or four good-morning smacks?" The earlier passage was deleted, and this one softened. The motive is obviously artistic, not prudish. Mary Jane is a heroine, Huck's ideal of spirited young womanhood. The canceled passages are esthetically out of key with his feelings towards her.

Out of all the hundreds of changes, just one deletion is sincerely to be regretted as a masterly sample of Mark Twain's invective. When the scoundrels quarrel after the Wilks fisasco, the Duke's denunciation of the King originally ended as here italicised: "You wanted to get what money I'd got out of the 'Burning Shame' and one thing or another, and scoop it *all, you unsatisfiable, tunnel-bellied old sewer!*" Mark may well have canceled it himself, without his wife's help, but it is the sole instance in the entire manuscript which gives her critics a chance to score, and they had better make the most of it.

In short, the Mark Twain who emerges from this study is a man of letters practising his art, a humorist who knows what he is doing and making the most of his materials. Of the thwarted Swift invented by Mr. Brooks and his followers there is not a trace. Mark Twain didn't write humor because his wife forced him to prostitute his genius; he wrote it because he was Mark Twain.

V. S. PRITCHETT

[*Huckleberry Finn* and the Cruelty of American Humor]†

After reading Hemingway and Faulkner and speculating upon the breach of American with English literature, the mind goes back to the two decisive, indigenous Americans who opened the new vein—Mark Twain and Edgar Allan Poe. Everything really American, really non-English, comes out of that pair of spiritual derelicts, those two scarecrow figures with their half-lynched minds. We have never had the obverse of Puritanism in England, for the political power of Puritanism lasted only a decade. If an Englishman hated Puritanism, he could fall back on the rest of the elaborate English tradition; if an American hated that philosophy (which had become

† Published in *New Statesman and Nation* (London), XXII, No. 545 (August 2, 1941), 113, in the column, "Books in General." A prominent British reviewer finds that the novel rose above the supposedly ingrained defects of culture in America, to become "its first truly indigenous masterpiece." Reprinted by permission of the *New Statesman.*

almost totalitarian in the United States), he found himself alone in a wilderness, with nothing but bottomless cynicism and bitterness for his consolation. There has never been in English literature a cynicism to compare with the American; at any rate we have never had the American kind, with its broken chopper edge and its ugly wound. We have also never had its by-product: the humorous practical philosophers, the Josh Billings, Artemus Wards, Will Rogers, the Pudd'nhead Wilsons with their close-fisted proverbs.

"Training is everything. The peach was once a bitter almond: cauliflower is nothing but cabbage with a college education."

Or:

"Consider well the proportions of things. It is better to be a young June bug than an old bird of Paradise."

Pudd'nhead Wilson was, of course, Twain's invention.

I say we have never had this kind of rumination, but there is one exception to prove the rule and to prove it very well, for he also is an uprooted and, so to speak, colonial writer. The Anglo-Indian Kipling with his "A woman is always a woman, but a good cigar is a smoke," is our first writer in the American school, with a cynicism, a brand of humour and a jungle book of beliefs which, I think, would be characteristic of our literature if we become seriously totalitarian in the future. For English totalitarianism would create the boredom and bitterness of the spiritual wilderness, as surely as Puritanism did in America.

When Mark Twain turned upon the religion of his childhood because it was intolerable, he was unaware that it would destroy him by turning him into a money-grubber of the most disastrously Puritan kind. Fortunately the resources of the imagination are endless even when a fanatical philosophy wrecks human life, genius and happiness. Out of the mess which Twain made of his life, amid the awful pile of tripe which he wrote, there does rise one book which has the serenity of a thing of genius. *Huckleberry Finn* takes the breath away. Knowing Mark Twain's life, knowing the hell of vulgarity from which the book has ascended, one dreads as one turns from page to page the seemingly inevitable flop. How can a low comedian, so tortured and so angry, refrain from blackguarding God, Man and Nature for the narrow boredom of his early life, and ruining the perfect comedy and horror of this story? But imaginative writers appear to get at least one lucky break in their careers; for a moment the conflicts are assimilated, the engine ceases to work against itself. *Huckleberry Finn* does not flop. America gets its first truly indigenous masterpiece. The small boyhood of Huck Finn is the small boyhood of a new culture.

The curious thing about *Huckleberry Finn* is that, although it is one of the funniest books in all literature and really astonishing in the variety of its farce and character, we are even more moved than we are amused by it. Why are we moved? Do we feel the sentiment of sympathy only? Are we sighing with some envy and self-pity? "Alas, Huck Finn is just what I would have been in my boyhood if I had had half a chance?" Are we sorry for the vagrant, or are we moved by his rebellion? These minor feelings may play their part; but they are only sighs on the surface of the main stream of our emotion. Mark Twain has brought to his subject far more than this personal longing; he has become the channel of the generic emotion which floods all really American literature—the emotion of nostalgia. In that absurd, brilliant, hit-or-miss book, *Studies in Classical American Literature*, which is so often dead right, D. H. Lawrence called this feeling the longing of the rebel for a master. It may be simply the longing for a spiritual home, but it is as strong in Mark Twain as it is implicit in Hemingway. One finds this feeling in Anglo-Irish literature which is also colonial and, in a less lasting way, in the work of Kipling. The peculiar power of American nostalgia is that it is not only harking back to something lost in the past, but suggests also the tragedy of a lost future. As Huck Finn and old Jim drift down the Mississippi from one horrifying little town to the next and hear the voices of men quietly swearing at one another across the water; as they pass the time of day with the scroungers, rogues, murderers, the lonely women, the frothing revivalists, the maundering boatmen and fantastic drunks of the river towns, we see the human wastage that is left in the wake of a great effort of the human will, the hopes frustrated, the idealism which has been whittled down to eccentricity and craft. These people are the price paid for building a new country. It is not, once you have faced it—which Dickens did not do in *Martin Chuzzlewit*, obsessed as he was with the negative pathos of the immigrant—it is not a disheartening spectacle; for the value of a native humour like Twain's is that it expresses a profound reality in human nature: the ability of man to adjust himself to circumstance and to live somehow.

Movement is one of the great consolers of human woe; movement, a sense of continual migration, is the history of America. This factor gives Twain's wonderful descriptions of the journey down the Mississippi their haunting overtone. His natural sensibility which is shown nowhere else in his writings and which is indeed vulgarly repressed in them is awakened:

". . . then we set down on the sandy bottom where the water was about knee-deep and watched the daylight come. Not a sound anywhere—perfectly still—just like the whole world was asleep, only sometimes the bullfrogs a-clattering maybe. The first thing to see, looking away over the water, was a kind of dull line—that was the woods on t'other side—you couldn't make nothing else out; then a pale place in the sky; then more paleness, spreading around; then the river softened up, away off, and wasn't black any more but grey; you could see little dark spots drifting along, ever so far away—trading scows and such things; and long black streaks —rafts; sometimes you could hear a sweep screaking; or jumbled-up voices, it was so still, and sounds come so far; and by-and-by you could see a streak on the water which you know by the look of the streak that there's a snag in the swift current which breaks on it and that makes that streak look that way; and you see the mist curl up off the water, and the east reddens up, and the river, and you make out a log cabin in the edge of the woods, away on the bank t'other side of the river, being a woodyard likely, and piled by them cheats so you can throw a dog through it anywheres. . . ."

The subject of *Huckleberry Finn* is the comical but also brutal effect of an anarchic rebellion against civilisation and especially its traditions:

"I reckon I got to light out for the Territory ahead of the rest, because Aunt Sally she's going to adopt me and sivilize me and I can't stand it. I been there before."

Huck isn't interested in "Moses and the Bulrushers" because Huck "don't take no stock of dead people." He garbles European history when he is discussing Kings with Jim, the negro. Whether Huck is the kind of boy who will grow up to build a new civilisation is doubtful; Tom Sawyer obviously would do so because he is imaginative. Huck never imagines anything except fears. Huck is "lowdown plain ornery," in trouble because of the way he was brought up with "Pap." He is a natural anarchist and bum. He can live without civilisation, depending on simple affections and workaday loyalties. He is the first of those typical American portraits of the underdog, which have culminated in the "poor white" literature and Charlie Chaplin—an underdog who gets along on horse sense, so to speak. Romanticism, ideas, ideals, are repugnant to Huck.

Mark Twain obliges you to accept the boy as the humorous norm. Without him the violence of the book would be stark reporting of low life. For if this is a great comic book it is also a book of terror and brutality. Think of the scenes: Pap with d.t.'s chasing Huck round the cabin with a knife; Huck sitting up all night with a gun preparing to shoot the old man; Huck's early familiarity with corpses; the pig killing scene; the sight of the frame house (evidently some sort of brothel) floating down the Mississippi with a murdered man in it; the fantastic events at the Southerner's house where two families are shooting each other down in a vendetta; the drunken

Boggs who comes into town to pick a quarrel and is eventually coolly shot dead before the eyes of his screaming young daughter by the man he has insulted. The "Duke" and "the King," those cynical rascals whose adventures liven up the second half of the story, are sharpers, twisters and crooks of the lowest kind. Yet a child is relating all this with a child's detachment and with a touch of morbidity. Marvellous as it all is as picaresque episode and as a description of the mess of frontier life, it is strong meat. Sometimes we wonder how Twain's public stomached such illusionless reporting. The sardonic humour and the important fact that in this one book Mark Twain never forced a point nor overwrote—in the Dickens way, for example—are of course the transfiguring and beguiling forces. The corpse and coffin humour is a dry wine which raises his animal spirits. Old Jim not only looked like a dead man after "the King" had painted him blue, but like one "who had been dead a considerable time." Judiciousness is carried to the comic limit.

Is *Huckleberry Finn* one of the great works of picaresque literature? It is, granting the limits of a boy's mind in the hero and the author, a comic masterpiece; but this limitation is important. It is not a book which grows spiritually, if we compare it to *Quixote*, *Dead Souls* or even *Pickwick*; and it is lacking in that civilised quality which you are bound to lose when you throw over civilisation —the quality of pity. One is left with the cruelty of American humour, a cruelty which is softened by the shrewd moralisings of the humorous philosophers—the Josh Billings, the Artemus Wards, the Will Rogers. And once Mark Twain passed this exquisite moment of his maturity, he went to bits in that morass of sentimentality, cynicism, melodrama and vulgarity which have damned him for the adult reader. I advise those who haven't read *Huckleberry Finn* since their school days to read it again.

Critics' Debate:
Symbolism *vs.* Structure

The publication of essays by Lionel Trilling (1948) and T. S. Eliot (1950) praising *Huckleberry Finn* as a masterpiece on grounds of symbolic excellence touched off a lively controversy about the structure of the novel. Certain critics took exception to the Trilling and Eliot articles, alleging that serious flaws exist in the structure of the novel's sociological patterns and sensibility. The Trilling and Eliot articles are included here, with three essays by critics who have participated in the debate.

LIONEL TRILLING

The Greatness of *Huckleberry Finn*†

In 1876 Mark Twain published *The Adventures of Tom Sawyer* and in the same year he began what he called "another boys' book." He set little store by the new venture and said that he had undertaken it "more to be at work than anything else." His heart was not in it—"I like it only tolerably well as far as I have got," he said, "and may possibly pigeonhole or burn the MS when it is done." He pigeonholed it long before it was done and for as much as four years. In 1880 he took it out and carried it forward a little, only to abandon it again. He had a theory of unconscious composition and believed that a book must write itself; the book which he referred to as "Huck Finn's Autobiography" refused to do the job of its own creation and he would not coerce it.

But then in the summer of 1882 Mark Twain was possessed by a charge of literary energy which, as he wrote to a friend, was more intense than any he had experienced for many years. He worked all day and every day, and periodically he so fatigued himself that he had to recruit his strength by a day or two of smoking and reading in bed. It is impossible not to suppose that this great creative

† From Lionel Trilling's Introduction to *The Adventures of Huckleberry Finn*, Rinehart Editions. Copyright 1948 by Lionel Trilling. Reprinted by permission of the publishers, Holt, Rinehart and Winston, Inc. Collected in *The Liberal Imagination*, by Lionel Trilling, New York, 1950.

drive was connected with—was perhaps the direct result of—the
visit to the Mississippi he had made earlier in the year, the trip
which forms the matter of the second part of *Life on the Mississippi*.
His boyhood and youth on the river he so profoundly loved had
been at once the happiest and most significant part of Mark Twain's
life; his return to it in middle age stirred vital memories which
revived and refreshed the idea of *Huckleberry Finn*. Now at last the
book was not only ready but eager to write itself. But it was not
to receive much conscious help from its author. He was always full
of second-rate literary schemes and now, in the early weeks of the
summer, with *Huckleberry Finn* waiting to complete itself, he
turned his hot energy upon several of these sorry projects, the completion of which gave him as much sense of satisfying productivity
as did his eventual absorption in *Huckleberry Finn*.

When at last *Huckleberry Finn* was completed and published
and widely loved, Mark Twain became somewhat aware of what he
had accomplished with this book that had been begun as journey-
work and depreciated, postponed, threatened with destruction. It is
his masterpiece, and perhaps he learned to know that. But he could
scarcely have estimated it for what it is, one of the world's great
books and one of the central documents of American culture.

2

Wherein does its greatness lie? Primarily in its power of telling
the truth. An awareness of this quality as it exists in *Tom Sawyer*
once led Mark Twain to say of the earlier work that "it is *not* a
boys' book at all. It will be read only by adults. It is written only
for adults." But this was only a manner of speaking, Mark Twain's
way of asserting, with a discernible touch of irritation, the degree of
truth he had achieved. It does not represent his usual view either
of boys' books or of boys. No one, as he well knew, sets a higher
value on truth than a boy. Truth is the whole of a boy's conscious
demand upon the world of adults. He is likely to believe that the
adult world is in a conspiracy to lie to him, and it is this belief, by
no means unfounded, that arouses Tom and Huck and all boys to
their moral sensitivity, their everlasting concern with justice, which
they call fairness. At the same time it often makes them skillful and
profound liars in their own defense, yet they do not tell the ultimate
lie of adults: they do not lie to themselves. That is why Mark
Twain felt that it was impossible to carry Tom Sawyer beyond boyhood—in maturity "he would lie just like all the other one-horse
men of literature and the reader would conceive a hearty contempt
for him."

Certainly one element in the greatness of *Huckleberry Finn*—as
also in the lesser greatness of *Tom Sawyer*—is that it succeeds first
as a boys' book. One can read it at ten and then annually ever after,

and each year find that it is as fresh as the year before, that it has changed only in becoming somewhat larger. To read it young is like planting a tree young—each year adds a new growth-ring of meaning, and the book is as little likely as the tree to become dull. So, we may imagine, an Athenian boy grew up together with the *Odyssey*. There are few other books which we can know so young and love so long.

The truth of *Huckleberry Finn* is of a different kind from that of *Tom Sawyer*. It is a more intense truth, fiercer and more complex. *Tom Sawyer* has the truth of honesty—what it says about things and feelings is never false and always both adequate and beautiful. *Huckleberry Finn* has this kind of truth, too, but it has also the truth of moral passion; it deals directly with the virtue and depravity of man's heart.

Perhaps the best clue to the greatness of *Huckleberry Finn* has been given to us by a writer who is as different from Mark Twain as it is possible for one Missourian to be from another. T. S. Eliot's poem, "The Dry Salvages," the third of his *Four Quartets*, begins with a meditation on the Mississippi, which Mr. Eliot knew in his St. Louis boyhood. These are the opening lines:

> I do not know much about gods; but I think that the river
> Is a strong brown god . . .

And the meditation goes on to speak of the god as

> almost forgotten
> By the dwellers in cities—ever, however, implacable,
> Keeping his seasons and rages, destroyer, reminder of
> What men choose to forget. Unhonoured, unpropitiated
> By worshippers of the machine, but waiting, watching and waiting.[1]

Huckleberry Finn is a great book because it is about a god—about, that is, a power which seems to have a mind and will of its own, and which, to men of moral imagination, appears to embody a great moral idea.

Huck himself is the servant of the river-god, and he comes very close to being aware of the divine nature of the being he serves. The world he inhabits is perfectly equipped to accommodate a deity, for it is full of presences and meanings which it conveys by natural signs and also by preternatural omens and taboos: to look at the moon over the left shoulder, to shake the tablecloth after sundown, to handle a snakeskin, are ways of offending the obscure and prevalent spirits. Huck is at odds, on moral and aesthetic grounds, with the only form of Christianity he knows, and his very intense moral life may be said to derive from his love of the river. He lives

1. Copyright, 1943, by T. S. Eliot, reprinted by permission of Harcourt, Brace and Company.

in a perpetual adoration of the Mississippi's power and charm. Huck, of course, always expresses himself better than he can know, but nothing draws upon his gift of speech like his response to his deity. After every sally into the social life of the shore, he returns to the river with relief and thanksgiving; and at each return, regular and explicit as a chorus in a Greek tragedy, there is a hymn of praise to the god's beauty, mystery, and strength, and to his noble grandeur in contrast with the pettiness of men.

Generally the god is benign, a being of long sunny days and spacious nights. But, like any god, he is also dangerous and deceptive. He generates fogs which bewilder, and he contrives echoes and false distances which confuse. His sandbars can ground and his hidden snags can mortally wound a great steamboat. He can cut away the solid earth from under a man's feet and take his house with it. The sense of the danger of the river is what saves the book from any touch of the sentimentality and moral ineptitude of most works of the imagination which contrast the life of nature with the life of society.

The river itself is only divine; it is not ethical and good. But its nature seems to foster the goodness of those who love it and try to fit themselves to its ways. And we must observe that we cannot make —that Mark Twain does not make—an absolute opposition between the river and human society. To Huck much of the charm of the river life is human: it is the raft and the wigwam and Jim. He has not run away from Miss Watson and the Widow Douglas and his brutal father to a completely individualistic liberty, for in Jim he finds his true father, very much as Stephen Dedalus in James Joyce's *Ulysses* finds his true father in Leopold Bloom.[2] The boy and the Negro slave form a family, a primitive community—and it is a community of saints.

Huck's intense and even complex moral quality may possibly not appear on a first reading, for one may be caught and convinced by his own estimate of himself, by his brags about his lazy hedonism, his avowed preference for being alone, his dislike of civilization. The fact is, of course, that he is involved in civilization up to his ears. His escape from society is but his way of reaching what society ideally dreams of for itself. Responsibility is the very essence of his character, and it is perhaps to the point that the original of Huck, a boyhood companion of Mark Twain's named Tom Blankenship, did, like Huck, "light out for the Territory," only to become a justice of the peace in Montana, "a good citizen and greatly re-

2. In Joyce's *Finnegans Wake* both Mark Twain and Huckleberry Finn appear frequently. The theme of rivers is, of course, dominant in the book; and Huck's name suits Joyce's purpose, as so many names do, for Finn is one of the many names of his hero. Mark Twain's love of and gift for the spoken language makes another reason for Joyce's interest in him.

spected."

Huck does indeed have all the capacities for simple happiness he says he has, but circumstances and his own moral nature make him the least carefree of boys—he is always "in a sweat" over the predicament of someone else. He has a great sense of the sadness of human life, and although he likes to be alone, the words "lonely" and "loneliness" are frequent with him. The note of his special sensibility is struck early in the story: "Well, when Tom and me got to the edge of the hilltop we looked away down into the village and could see three or four lights twinkling where there were sick folks, maybe; and the stars over us was sparkling ever so fine; and down by the village was the river, a whole mile broad, and awful still and grand." The identification of those three or four lonely lights as the lamps of sick-watches defines Huck's character.

His sympathy is quick and immediate. When the circus audience laughs at the supposedly drunken man who tries to ride the horse, Huck is only miserable: "It wasn't funny to me . . . ; I was all of a tremble to see his danger." When he imprisons the intending murderers on the wrecked steamboat, his first thought is of how to get someone to rescue them, for he considers "how dreadful it was, even for murderers, to be in such a fix. I says to myself, there ain't no telling but I might come to be a murderer myself yet, and then how would I like it?" But his sympathy is never sentimental. When at last he knows that the murderers are beyond help, he has no inclination to false pathos. "I felt a little bit heavy-hearted about the gang, but not much, for I reckoned that if they could stand it I could." His will is genuinely good and therefore he has no need to torture himself with guilty second thoughts.

Not the least remarkable thing about Huck's feeling for people is that his tenderness goes along with the assumption that his fellow men are likely to be dangerous and wicked. He travels incognito, never telling the truth about himself and never twice telling the same lie, for he trusts no one and the lie comforts him even when it is not necessary. He instinctively knows that the best way to keep a party of men away from Jim on the raft is to beg them to come aboard to help his family stricken with smallpox. And if he had not already had the knowledge of human weakness and stupidity and cowardice, he would soon have acquired it, for all his encounters forcibly teach it to him—the insensate feud of the Grangerfords and Shepherdsons, the invasion of the raft by the Duke and the King, the murder of Boggs, the lynching party, and the speech of Colonel Sherburn. Yet his profound and bitter knowledge of human depravity never prevents him from being a friend to man.

No personal pride interferes with his well-doing. He knows what status is and on the whole he respects it—he is really a very *re-*

spectable person and inclines to like "quality folks"—but he himself is unaffected by it. He himself has never had status, he has always been the lowest of the low, and the considerable fortune he had acquired in *The Adventures of Tom Sawyer* is never real to him. When the Duke suggests that Huck and Jim render him the personal service that accords with his rank, Huck's only comment is, "Well, that was easy so we done it." He is injured in every possible way by the Duke and the King, used and exploited and manipulated, yet when he hears that they are in danger from a mob, his natural impulse is to warn them. And when he fails of his purpose and the two men are tarred and feathered and ridden on a rail, his only thought is, "Well, it made me sick to see it; and I was sorry for them poor pitiful rascals, it seemed like I couldn't ever feel any hardness against them any more in the world."

And if Huck and Jim on the raft do indeed make a community of saints, it is because they do not have an ounce of pride between them. Yet this is not perfectly true, for the one disagreement they ever have is over a matter of pride. It is on the occasion when Jim and Huck have been separated by the fog. Jim has mourned Huck as dead, and then, exhausted, has fallen asleep. When he awakes and finds that Huck has returned, he is overjoyed; but Huck convinces him that he has only dreamed the incident, that there has been no fog, no separation, no chase, no reunion, and then allows him to make an elaborate "interpretation" of the dream he now believes he has had. Then the joke is sprung, and in the growing light of the dawn Huck points to the debris of leaves on the raft and the broken oar.

"Jim looked at the trash, and then looked at me, and back at the trash again. He had got the dream fixed so strong in his head that he couldn't seem to shake it loose and get the facts back into its place again right away. But when he did get the thing straightened around he looked at me steady without ever smiling, and says:

" 'What do dey stan' for? I'se gwyne to tell you. When I got all wore out wid work, en wid de callin' for you, en went to sleep, my heart wuz mos' broke bekase you wuz los', en I didn' k'yer no mo' what became er me en de raf'. En when I wake up en fine you back agin, all safe en soun', de tears come, en I could a got down on my knees en kiss yo' foot, I's so thankful. En all you wuz thinkin' 'bout wuz how you could make a fool uv ole Jim wid a lie. Dat truck dah is *trash*; en trash is what people is dat puts dirt on de head er dey fren's en makes 'em ashamed.'

"Then he got up slow and walked to the wigwam, and went in there without saying anything but that."

The pride of human affection has been touched, one of the few prides that has any true dignity. And at its utterance, Huck's one last dim vestige of pride of status, his sense of his position as a white man, wholly vanishes: "It was fifteen minutes before I could work myself up to go and humble myself to a nigger; but I done it, and I warn't sorry for it afterward, neither."

This incident is the beginning of the moral testing and development which a character so morally sensitive as Huck's must inevitably undergo. And it becomes an heroic character when, on the urging of affection, Huck discards the moral code he has always taken for granted and resolves to help Jim in his escape from slavery. The intensity of his struggle over the act suggests how deeply he is involved in the society which he rejects. The satiric brilliance of the episode lies, of course, in Huck's solving his problem not by doing "right" but by doing "wrong." He has only to consult his conscience, the conscience of a Southern boy in the middle of the last century, to know that he ought to return Jim to slavery. And as soon as he makes the decision according to conscience and decides to inform on Jim, he has all the warmly gratifying emotions of conscious virtue. "Why, it was astonishing, the way I felt as light as a feather right straight off, and my troubles all gone . . . I felt good and all washed clean of sin for the first time I had ever felt so in my life, and I knowed I could pray now." And when at last he finds that he cannot endure his decision but must change it and help Jim in his escape, it is not because he has acquired any new ideas about slavery—he believes that he detests Abolitionists; he himself answers when he is asked if the explosion of a steamboat boiler had hurt anyone, "No'm, killed a nigger," and of course he finds nothing wrong in the responsive comment, "Well, it's lucky because sometimes people do get hurt." Ideas and ideals can be of no help to him in his moral crisis. He no more condemns slavery than Tristram and Lancelot condemn marriage; he is as consciously *wicked* as any illicit lover of romance and he consents to be damned for a personal devotion, never questioning the justice of the punishment he has incurred.

Huckleberry Finn was once barred from certain libraries and schools for its alleged subversion of morality. The authorities had in mind the book's endemic lying, the petty thefts, the denigrations of respectability and religion, the bad language and the bad grammar. We smile at that excessive care, yet in point of fact *Huckleberry Finn* is indeed a subversive book—no one who reads thoughtfully the dialectic of Huck's great moral crisis will ever again be wholly able to accept without some question and some irony the assumptions of the respectable morality by which he lives, nor will ever again be certain that what he considers the clear dictates of moral reason are not merely the engrained customary beliefs of his time and place.

3

We are not likely to miss in *Huckleberry Finn* the subtle, implicit moral meaning of the great river. But we are likely to understand these moral implications as having to do only with personal and individual conduct. And since the sum of individual pettiness is on the whole pretty constant, we are likely to think of the book as applicable to mankind in general and at all times and in all places, and we praise it by calling it "universal." And so it is; but like many books to which that large adjective applies, it is also local and particular. It has a particular moral reference to the United States in the period after the Civil War. It was then when, in Mr. Eliot's phrase, the river was forgotten, and precisely by the "dwellers in cities," by the "worshippers of the machine."

The Civil War and the development of the railroads ended the great days when the river was the central artery of the nation. No contrast could be more moving than that between the hot, turbulent energy of the river life of the first part of *Life on the Mississippi* and the melancholy reminiscence of the second part. And the war that brought the end of the rich Mississippi days also marked a change in the quality of life in America which, to many men, consisted of a deterioration of American moral values. It is of course a human habit to look back on the past and to find it a better and more innocent time than the present. Yet in this instance there seems to be an objective basis for the judgment. We cannot disregard the testimony of men so diverse as Henry Adams, Walt Whitman, William Dean Howells, and Mark Twain himself, to mention but a few of the many who were in agreement on this point. All spoke of something that had gone out of American life after the war, some simplicity, some innocence, some peace. None of them was under any illusion about the amount of ordinary human wickedness that existed in the old days, and Mark Twain certainly was not. The difference was in the public attitude, in the things that were now accepted and made respectable in the national ideal. It was, they all felt, connected with new emotions about money. As Mark Twain said, where formerly "the people had desired money," now they "fall down and worship it." The new gospel was, "Get money. Get it quickly. Get it in abundance. Get it in prodigious abundance. Get it dishonestly if you can, honestly if you must."[3]

With the end of the Civil War capitalism had established itself. The relaxing influence of the frontier was coming to an end. Americans increasingly became "dwellers in cities" and "worshippers of the machine." Mark Twain himself became a notable part of this new dispensation. No one worshipped the machine more than he did, or thought he did—he ruined himself by his devotion to the

3. *Mark Twain in Eruption*, edited by Bernard De Voto, p. 77.

Paige typesetting machine by which he hoped to make a fortune even greater than he had made by his writing, and he sang the praises of the machine age in *A Connecticut Yankee in King Arthur's Court*. He associated intimately with the dominant figures of American business enterprise. Yet at the same time he hated the new way of life and kept bitter memoranda of his scorn, commenting on the low morality or the bad taste or the smugness and dullness of the men who were shaping the national ideal and directing the destiny of the nation.

Mark Twain said of *Tom Sawyer* that it "is simply a hymn, put into prose form to give it a worldly air." He might have said the same, and with even more reason, of *Huckleberry Finn*, which is a hymn to an older America forever gone, an America which had its great national faults, which was full of violence and even of cruelty, but which still maintained its sense of reality, for it was not yet enthralled by money, the father of ultimate illusion and lies. Against the money-god stands the river-god, whose comments are silent—sunlight, space, uncrowded time, stillness and danger. It was quickly forgotten once its practical usefulness had passed, but, as Mr. Eliot's poem says, "The river is within us. . . ."

4

In form and style *Huckleberry Finn* is an almost perfect work. Only one mistake has ever been charged against it, that it concludes with Tom Sawyer's elaborate, too elaborate, game of Jim's escape. Certainly this episode is too long—in the original draft it was much longer—and certainly it is a falling-off, as almost anything would have to be, from the incidents of the river. Yet it has a certain formal aptness—like, say, that of the Turkish initiation which brings Molière's *Le Bourgeois Gentilhomme* to its close. It is a rather mechanical development of an idea, and yet some device is needed to permit Huck to return to his anonymity, to give up the role of hero, to fall into the background which he prefers, for he is modest in all things and could not well endure the attention and glamour which attend a hero at a book's end. For this purpose nothing could serve better than the mind of Tom Sawyer with its literary furnishings, its conscious romantic desire for experience and the hero's part, and its ingenious schematization of life to achieve that aim.

The form of the book is based on the simplest of all novel-forms, the so-called picaresque novel, or novel of the road, which strings its incidents on the line of the hero's travels. But, as Pascal says, "rivers are roads that move," and the movement of the road in its own mysterious life transmutes the primitive simplicity of the form: the road itself is the greatest character in this novel of the road, and the hero's departures from the river and his returns to it compose a subtle and significant pattern. The linear simplicity of the picaresque novel is further modified by the story's having a clear dramatic organization: it has a beginning, a middle and an end, and a mounting suspense of interest.

As for the style of the book, it is not less than definitive in American literature. The prose of *Huckleberry Finn* established for written prose the virtues of American colloquial speech. This has nothing to do with pronunciation or grammar. It has something to do with ease and freedom in the use of language. Most of all it has to do with the structure of the sentence, which is simple, direct, and fluent, maintaining the rhythm of the word-groups of speech and the intonations of the speaking voice.

In the matter of language, American literature had a special problem. The young nation was inclined to think that the mark of the truly literary product was a grandiosity and elegance not to be found in the common speech. It therefore encouraged a greater breach between its vernacular and its literary language than, say, English literature of the same period ever allowed. This accounts for the hollow ring one now and then hears even in the work of our best writers in the first half of the last century. English writers of equal stature would never have made the lapses into rhetorical excess that are common in Cooper and Poe and that are to be found even in Melville and Hawthorne.

Yet at the same time that the language of ambitious literature was high and thus always in danger of falseness, the American reader was keenly interested in the actualities of daily speech. No literature, indeed, was ever so taken up with matters of speech as ours was. "Dialect," which attracted even our serious writers, was the accepted common ground of our popular humorous writing. Nothing in social life seemed so remarkable as the different forms which speech could take—the brogue of the immigrant Irish or the mispronunciation of the German, the "affectation" of the English, the reputed precision of the Bostonian, the legendary twang of the Yankee farmer, and the drawl of the Pike County man. Mark Twain, of course, was in the tradition of humor that exploited this interest, and no one could play with it nearly so well. Although today the carefully spelled-out dialects of nineteenth-century American humor are likely to seem dull enough, the subtle variations of speech of *Huckleberry Finn*, of which Mark Twain was justly proud, are still part of the liveliness and flavor of the book.

Out of his knowledge of the actual speech of America Mark Twain forged a classic prose. The adjective may seem a strange one, yet it is apt. Forget the misspellings and the faults of grammar, and the prose will be seen to move with the greatest simplicity, directness, lucidity, and grace. These qualities are by no means accidental. Mark Twain, who read widely, was passionately interested in the problems of style; the mark of the strictest literary sensibility is everywhere to be found in the prose of *Huckleberry Finn*.

It is this prose that Ernest Hemingway had chiefly in mind when he said that "all modern American literature comes from one book by Mark Twain called *Huckleberry Finn*." Hemingway's own prose stems from it directly and consciously; so does the prose of the two modern writers who most influenced Hemingway's early style, Gertrude Stein and Sherwood Anderson (although neither of them could maintain the robust purity of their model); so, too, does the best of William Faulkner's prose, which, like Mark Twain's own, reinforces the colloquial tradition with the literary tradition. Indeed, it may be said that almost every contemporary writer who deals conscientiously with the problems and possibility of prose must feel, directly or indirectly, the influence of Mark Twain. He is the master of the style that escapes the fixity of the printed page, that sounds in our ears with the immediacy of the heard voice, the very voice of unpretentious truth.

T. S. ELIOT

[An Introduction to *Huckleberry Finn*]†

The Adventures of Huckleberry Finn is the only one of Mark Twain's various books which can be called a masterpiece. I do not suggest that it is his only book of permanent interest; but it is the only one in which his genius is completely realized, and the only one which creates its own category. There are pages in *Tom Sawyer* and in *Life on the Mississippi* which are, within their limits, as good as anything with which one can compare them in *Huckleberry Finn*; and in other books there are drolleries just as good of their kind. But when we find one book by a prolific author which is very much superior to all the rest, we look for the peculiar accident or concourse of accidents which made that book possible. In the writing of *Huckleberry Finn* Mark Twain had two elements which, when treated with his sensibility and his experience, formed a great book: these two are the Boy and the River.

Huckleberry Finn is, no doubt, a book which boys enjoy. I cannot speak from memory: I suspect that a fear on the part of my parents lest I should acquire a premature taste for tobacco, and perhaps other habits of the hero of the story, kept the book out of my way. But *Huckleberry Finn* does not fall into the category of juvenile

† From T. S. Eliot's Introduction to *The Adventures of Huckleberry Finn*. The Cresset Press, London, 1950, Pp. vii–xvi. Published in the U. S. by Chanticleer Press, New York, 1950. Reprinted by permission of T. S. Eliot

fiction. The opinion of my parents that it was a book unsuitable for boys left me, for most of my life, under the impression that it was a book suitable only for boys. Therefore it was only a few years ago that I read for the first time, and in that order, *Tom Sawyer* and *Huckleberry Finn.*

Tom Sawyer did not prepare me for what I was to find its sequel to be. *Tom Sawyer* seems to me to be a boys' book, and a very good one. The River and *the* Boy make their appearance in it; the narrative is good; and there is also a very good picture of society in a small mid-Western river town (for St. Petersburg is more Western than Southern) a hundred years ago. But the point of view of the narrator is that of an adult observing a boy. And Tom is the ordinary boy, though of quicker wits, and livelier imagination, than most. Tom is, I suppose, very much the boy that Mark Twain had been: he is remembered and described as he seemed to his elders, rather than created. Huck Finn, on the other hand, is the boy that Mark Twain still was, at the time of writing his adventures. We look at Tom as the smiling adult does: Huck we do not look at— we see the world through his eyes. The two boys are not merely different types; they were brought into existence by different processes. Hence in the second book their roles are altered. In the first book Huck is merely the humble friend—almost a variant of the traditional valet of comedy; and we see him as he is seen by the conventional respectable society to which Tom belongs, and of which, we feel sure, Tom will one day become an eminently respectable and conventional member. In the second book their nominal relationship remains the same; but here it is Tom who has the secondary role. The author was probably not conscious of this, when he wrote the first two chapters: *Huckleberry Finn* is not the kind of story in which the author knows, from the beginning, what is going to happen. Tom then disappears from our view; and when he returns, he has only two functions. The first is to provide a foil for Huck. Huck's persisting admiration for Tom only exhibits more clearly to our eyes the unique qualities of the former and the commonplaceness of the latter. Tom has the imagination of a lively boy who has read a good deal of romantic fiction: he might, of course, become a writer—he might become Mark Twain. Or rather, he might become the more commonplace aspect of Mark Twain. Huck has not imagination, in the sense in which Tom has it: he has, instead, vision. He sees the real world; and he does not judge it—he allows it to judge itself.

Tom Sawyer is an orphan. But he has his aunt; he has, as we learn later, other relatives; and he has the environment into which he fits. He is wholly a social being. When there is a secret band to be formed, it is Tom who organizes it and prescribes the rules.

Huck Finn is alone: there is no more solitary character in fiction. The fact that he has a father only emphasizes his loneliness; and he views his father with a terrifying detachment. So we come to see Huck himself in the end as one of the permanent symbolic figures of fiction; not unworthy to take a place with Ulysses, Faust, Don Quixote, Don Juan, Hamlet and other great discoveries that man has made about himself.

It would seem that Mark Twain was a man who—perhaps like most of us—never became in all respects mature. We might even say that the adult side of him was boyish, and that only the boy in him, that was Huck Finn, was adult. As Tom Sawyer grown up, he wanted success and applause (Tom himself always needs an audience). He wanted prosperity, a happy domestic life of a conventional kind, universal approval, and fame. All of these things he obtained. As Huck Finn he was indifferent to all these things; and being composite of the two, Mark Twain both strove for them, and resented their violation of his integrity. Hence he became the humorist and even clown: with his gifts, a certain way to success, for everyone could enjoy his writings without the slightest feeling of discomfort, self-consciousness or self-criticism. And hence, on the other hand, his pessimism and misanthropy. To be a misanthrope is to be in some way divided; or it is a sign of an uneasy conscience. The pessimism which Mark Twain discharged into *The Man That Corrupted Hadleyburg* and *What is Man?* springs less from observation of society, than from his hatred of himself for allowing society to tempt and corrupt him and give him what he wanted. There is no wisdom in it. But all this personal problem has been diligently examined by Mr. Van Wyck Brooks; and it is not Mark Twain, but *Huckleberry Finn*, that is the subject of this introduction.

You cannot say that Huck himself is either a humorist or a misanthrope. He is the impassive observer: he does not interfere, and, as I have said, he does not judge. Many of the episodes that occur on the voyage down the river, after he is joined by the Duke and the King (whose fancies about themselves are akin to the kind of fancy that Tom Sawyer enjoys) are in themselves farcical; and if it were not for the presence of Huck as the reporter of them, they would be no more than farce. But, seen through the eyes of Huck, there is a deep human pathos in these scoundrels. On the other hand, the story of the feud between the Grangerfords and the Shepherdsons is a masterpiece in itself: yet Mark Twain could not have written it so, with that economy and restraint, with just the right details and no more, and leaving to the reader to make his own moral reflections, unless he had been writing in the person of Huck. And the *style* of the book, which is the style of Huck, is what makes it a far more convincing indictment of slavery than the sensationalist propaganda of *Uncle Tom's Cabin*. Huck is passive and impassive, apparently always the victim of events; and yet, in his acceptance of his world and of what it does to him and others, he is more powerful than his world, because he is more *aware* than any other person in it.

Repeated readings of the book only confirm and deepen one's admiration of the consistency and perfect adaptation of the writing. This is a style which at the period, whether in America or in England, was an innovation, a new discovery in the English language. Other authors had achieved natural speech in relation to particular characters—Scott with characters talking Lowland Scots, Dickens with cockneys: but no one else had kept it up through the whole of a book. Thackeray's Yellowplush, impressive as he is, is an obvious artifice in comparison. In *Huckleberry Finn* there is no exaggeration of grammar or spelling or speech, there is no sentence or phrase to destroy the illusion that these are Huck's own words. It is not only in the way in which he tells his story, but in the details he remembers, that Huck is true to himself. There is, for instance, the description of the Grangerford interior as Huck sees it on his arrival; there is the list of the objects which Huck and Jim salvaged from the derelict house:

"We got an old tin lantern, and a butcher-knife without any handle, and a bran-new Barlow knife worth two bits in any store, and a lot of tallow candles, and a tin candlestick, and a gourd, and a tin cup, and a ratty old bedquilt off the bed, and a reticule with needles and pins and beeswax and buttons and thread and all such truck in it, and a hatchet and some nails, and a fish-line as thick as my little finger, with some monstrous hooks on it, and a roll of buckskin, and a leather dog-collar, and a horseshoe, and some vials of medicine that didn't have no label on them; and just as we was leaving I found a tolerable good curry-comb, and Jim he found a ratty old fiddle-bow, and a wooden leg. The straps was broke off of it, but barring that, it was a good enough leg, though it was too long for me and not long enough for Jim, and we couldn't find the other one, though we hunted all round.

"And so, take it all round, we made a good haul."

This is the sort of list that a boy reader should pore over with delight; but the paragraph performs other functions of which the boy reader would be unaware. It provides the right counterpoise to the horror of the wrecked house and the corpse; it has a grim precision which tells the reader all he needs to know about the way of life of the human derelicts who had used the house; and (especially the wooden leg, and the fruitless search for its mate) reminds us at the right moment of the kinship of mind and the sympathy between the boy outcast from society and the negro fugitive from the injustice of society.

Huck in fact would be incomplete without Jim, who is almost as notable a creation as Huck himself. Huck is the passive observer of men and events, Jim the submissive sufferer from them; and they are equal in dignity. There is no passage in which their relationship is brought out more clearly than the conclusion of the chapter in which, after the two have become separated in the fog, Huck in the canoe and Jim on the raft, Huck, in his impulse of boyish mischief, persuades Jim for a time that the latter had dreamt the whole episode.

". . . my heart wuz mos' broke bekase you wuz los', en I didn' k'yer no mo' what become er me en de raf'. En when I wake up en fine you back agin', all safe en soun', de tears come en I could a got down on my knees en kiss' yo' foot, I's so thankful. En all you wuz thinkin' 'bout wuz how you could make a fool uv ole Jim wid a lie. Dat truck dah is *trash*; en trash is what people is dat puts dirt on de head er dey fren's en makes 'em ashamed.' . . .

"It was fifteen minutes before I could work myself up to go and humble myself to a nigger—but I done it, and I warn't ever sorry for it afterwards, neither."

This passage has been quoted before; and if I quote it again, it is because I wish to elicit from it one meaning that is, I think, usually overlooked. What is obvious in it is the pathos and dignity of Jim, and this is moving enough; but what I find still more disturbing, and still more unusual in literature, is the pathos and dignity of the boy, when reminded so humbly and humiliatingly, that his position in the world is not that of other boys, entitled from time to time to a practical joke; but that he must bear, and bear alone, the responsibility of a man.

It is Huck who gives the book style. The River gives the book its form. But for the River, the book might be only a sequence of adventures with a happy ending. A river, a very big and powerful river, is the only natural force that can wholly determine the course of human peregrination. At sea, the wanderer may sail or be carried by winds and currents in one direction or another; a change of wind or tide may determine fortune. In the prairie, the direction of movement is more or less at the choice of the caravan; among mountains there will often be an alternative, a guess at the most likely pass. But the river with its strong, swift current is the dictator to the raft or to the steamboat. It is a treacherous and capricious dictator. At one season, it may move sluggishly in a channel so narrow that, encountering it for the first time at that point, one can hardly believe that it has travelled already for hundreds of miles, and has yet many hundreds of miles to go; at another season, it may obliterate the low Illinois shore to a horizon of water, while in its bed it runs with a speed such that no man or beast can survive in it. At such times, it carries down human bodies, cattle and houses. At least twice, at St. Louis, the western and the eastern shores have been separated by the fall of bridges, until the designer of the great Eads Bridge devised a structure which could resist the floods. In my own childhood, it was not unusual for the spring freshet to interrupt railway travel; and then the traveller to the East had to take steamboat from the levee up to Alton, at a higher level on the Illinois shore, before he could begin his rail journey. The river is never wholly chartable; it changes its pace, it shifts its channel, unaccountably; it may suddenly efface a sandbar, and throw up another bar where before was navigable water.

It is the River that controls the voyage of Huck and Jim; that will not let them land at Cairo, where Jim could have reached freedom; it is the River that separates them and deposits Huck for a time in the Grangerford household; the River that re-unites them, and then compels upon them the unwelcome company of the King and the Duke. Recurrently we are reminded of its presence and its power.

"When I woke up, I didn't know where I was for a minute. I set up and looked around, a little scared. Then I remembered. The river looked miles and miles across. The moon was so bright I could a counted the drift-logs that went a-slipping along, black and still, hundreds of yards out from shore. Everything was dead quiet, and it looked late, and *smelt* late. You know what I mean— I don't know the words to put it in.

"It was kind of solemn, drifting down the big still river, laying on our backs looking up at the stars, and we didn't ever feel like talking loud, and it warn't often that we laughed, only a little kind of a low chuckle. We had mighty good weather as a general thing, and nothing ever happened to us at all, that night, nor the next, nor the next.

"Every night we passed towns, some of them away up on black hillsides, nothing but just a shiny bed of lights, not a house could you see. The fifth night we passed St. Louis, and it was like the whole world lit up. In St. Petersburg they used to say there was twenty or thirty thousand people in St. Louis, but I never believed it till I see that wonderful spread of lights at two o'clock that still night. There warn't a sound there; everybody was asleep."

We come to understand the River by seeing it through the eyes of the Boy; but the Boy is also the spirit of the River. *Huckleberry Finn*, like other great works of imagination, can give to every reader whatever he is capable of taking from it. On the most superficial level of observation, Huck is convincing as a boy. On the same level, the picture of social life on the shores of the Mississippi a hundred years ago is, I feel sure, accurate. On any level, Mark Twain makes you see the River, as it is and was and always will be, more clearly than the author of any other description of a river known to me. But you do not merely see the River, you do not merely become acquainted with it through the senses: you experience the River. Mark Twain, in his later years of success and fame, referred to his early life as a steamboat pilot as the happiest he had known. With all allowance for the illusions of age, we can agree that those years were the years in which he was most fully alive. Certainly, but for his having practised that calling, earned his living by that profession, he would never have gained the understanding which his genius for expression communicates in this book. In the pilot's daily struggle with the River, in the satisfaction of activity, in the constant attention to the River's unpredictable vagaries, his consciousness was fully occupied, and he absorbed knowledge of which, as an artist, he later made use. There are, perhaps, only two ways in which a writer can acquire the understanding of environment which he can later turn to account: by having spent his childhood in that environment—that is, living in it at a period of life in which one experiences much more than one is aware of; and by having had to struggle for a livelihood in that environment—a livelihood bearing no direct relation to any intention of writing about it, of *using* it as literary material. Most of Joseph Conrad's understanding came to him in the latter way. Mark Twain knew the Mississippi in both ways: he had spent his childhood on its banks, and he had earned his living matching his wits against its currents.

Thus the River makes the book a great book. As with Conrad, we are continually reminded of the power and terror of Nature, and the isolation and feebleness of Man. Conrad remains always the European observer of the tropics, the white man's eye contemplating the Congo and its black gods. But Mark Twain is a native, and the River God is his God. It is as a native that he accepts the River God, and it is the subjection of Man that gives to Man his dignity. For without some kind of God, Man is not even very interesting.

Readers sometimes deplore the fact that the story descends to the level of *Tom Sawyer* from the moment that Tom himself re-appears. Such readers protest that the escapades invented by Tom, in the attempted "rescue" of Jim, are only a tedious development of themes with which we were already too familiar—even while admitting that the escapades themselves are very amusing, and some of the incidental observations memorable.[1] But it is right that the mood of the end of the book should bring us back to that of the beginning. Or, if this was not the right ending for the book, what ending would have been right?

In *Huckleberry Finn* Mark Twain wrote a much greater book

1. *e.g.*, "*Jim* don't know anybody in China."

than he could have known he was writing. Perhaps all great works of art mean much more than the author could have been aware of meaning: certainly, *Huckleberry Finn* is the one book of Mark Twain's which, as a whole, has this unconsciousness. So what seems to be the rightness, of reverting at the end of the book to the mood of *Tom Sawyer*, was perhaps unconscious art. For Huckleberry Finn, neither a tragic nor a happy ending would be suitable. No worldly success or social satisfaction, no domestic consummation would be worthy of him; a tragic end also would reduce him to the level of those whom we pity. Huck Finn must come from nowhere and be bound for nowhere. His is not the independence of the typical or symbolic American Pioneer, but the independence of the vaga-bond. His existence questions the values of America as much as the values of Europe; he is as much an affront to the "pioneer spirit" as he is to "business enterprise"; he is in a state of nature as de-tached as the state of the saint. In a busy world, he represents the loafer; in an acquisitive and competitive world, he insists on living from hand to mouth. He could not be exhibited in any amorous encounters or engagements, in any of the juvenile affections which are appropriate to Tom Sawyer. He belongs neither to the Sunday School nor to the Reformatory. He has no beginning and no end. Hence, he can only disappear; and his disappearance can only be accomplished by bringing forward another performer to obscure the disappearance in a cloud of whimsicalities.

Like Huckleberry Finn, the River itself has no beginning or end. In its beginning, it is not yet the River; in its end, it is no longer the River. What we call its headwaters is only a selection from among the innumerable sources which flow together to compose it. At what point in its course does the Mississippi become what the Mississippi *means?* It is both one and many; it is the Mississippi of this book only after its union with the Big Muddy—the Missouri; it derives some of its character from the Ohio, the Tennessee and other confluents. And at the end it merely disappears among its deltas: it is no longer there, but it is still where it was, hundreds of miles to the North. The River cannot tolerate any design, to a story which is its story, that might interfere with its dominance. Things must merely happen, here and there, to the people who live along its shores or who commit themselves to its current. And it is as impossible for Huck as for the River to have a beginning or end —a *career.* So the book has the right, the only possible concluding sentence. I do not think that any book ever written ends more certainly with the right words:

"But I reckon I got to light out for the Territory ahead of the rest, because Aunt Sally she's going to adopt me and civilize me, and I can't stand it. I been there before."

LEO MARX

Mr. Eliot, Mr. Trilling, and *Huckleberry Finn*†

In the losing battle that the plot fights with the characters, it often takes a cowardly revenge. Nearly all novels are feeble at the end. This is because the plot requires to be wound up. Why is this necessary? Why is there not a convention which allows a novelist to stop as soon as he feels muddled or bored? Alas, he has to round things off, and usually the characters go dead while he is at work, and our final impression of them is through deadness.—E. M. Forster

The *Adventures of Huckleberry Finn* has not always occupied its present high place in the canon of American literature. When it was first published in 1885, the book disturbed and offended many reviewers, particularly spokesmen for the genteel tradition.[1] In fact, a fairly accurate inventory of the narrow standards of such critics might be made simply by listing epithets they applied to Clemens' novel. They called it vulgar, rough, inelegant, irreverent, coarse, semi-obscene, trashy and vicious.[2] So much for them. Today (we like to think) we know the true worth of the book. Everyone now agrees that *Huckleberry Finn* is a masterpiece: it is probably the one book in our literature about which highbrows and lowbrows can agree. Our most serious critics praise it. Nevertheless, a close look at what two of the best among them have recently written will likewise reveal, I believe, serious weaknesses in current criticism. Today the problem of evaluating the book is as much obscured by unqualified praise as it once was by parochial hostility.

I have in mind essays by Lionel Trilling and T. S. Eliot.[3] Both praise the book, but in praising it both feel obligated to say something in justification of what so many readers have felt to be its great flaw: the disappointing "ending," the episode which begins when Huck arrives at the Phelps place and Tom Sawyer reappears.

† Reprinted from *The American Scholar*, Vol. 22, No. 4 (Autumn, 1953), pp. 423–40. Copyright © 1953 by the United Chapters of Phi Beta Kappa. By permission of the publishers.
1. I use the term "genteel tradition" as George Santayana characterized it in his famous address "The Genteel Tradition in American Philosophy," first delivered in 1911 and published the following year in his *Winds of Doctrine*. Santayana described the genteel tradition as an "old mentality" inherited from Europe. It consists of the various dilutions of Christian theology and morality, as in transcendentalism—a fastidious and stale philosophy of life no longer relevant to the thought and activities of the United States. "America," he said, "is a young country with an old mentality." (Later references to Santayana also refer to this essay.)
2. For an account of the first reviews, see A. L. Vogelback, "The Publication and Reception of *Huckleberry Finn* in America," *American Literature*, XI (November, 1939), 260–272.
3. Mr. Eliot's essay is the introduction to the edition of *Huckleberry Finn* published by Chanticleer Press, New York, 1950. Mr. Trilling's is the introduction to an edition of the novel published by Rinehart, New York, 1948, and later reprinted in his *The Liberal Imagination*, Viking, New York, 1950.

There are good reasons why Mr. Trilling and Mr. Eliot should feel the need to face this issue. From the point of view of scope alone, more is involved than the mere "ending"; the episode comprises almost one-fifth of the text. The problem, in any case, is unavoidable. I have discussed *Huckleberry Finn* in courses with hundreds of college students, and I have found only a handful who did not confess their dissatisfaction with the extravagant mock rescue of Nigger Jim and the denouement itself. The same question always comes up: "What went wrong with Twain's novel?" Even Bernard De Voto, whose wholehearted commitment to Clemens' genius is well known, has said of the ending that "in the whole reach of the English novel there is no more abrupt or more chilling descent."[4] Mr. Trilling and Mr. Eliot do not agree. They both attempt, and on similar grounds, to explain and defend the conclusion.

Of the two, Mr. Trilling makes the more moderate claim for Clemens' novel. He does admit that there is a "falling off" at the end; nevertheless he supports the episode as having "a certain formal aptness." Mr. Eliot's approval is without serious qualification. He allows no objections, asserts that "it is right that the mood of the end of the book should bring us back to the beginning." I mean later to discuss their views in some detail, but here it is only necessary to note that both critics see the problem as one of form. And so it is. Like many questions of form in literature, however, this one is not finally separable from a question of "content," of value, or, if you will, of moral insight. To bring *Huckleberry Finn* to a satisfactory close, Clemens had to do more than find a neat device for ending a story. His problem, though it may never have occurred to him, was to invent an action capable of placing in focus the meaning of the journey down the Mississippi.

I believe that the ending of *Huckleberry Finn* makes so many readers uneasy because they rightly sense that it jeopardizes the significance of the entire novel. To take seriously what happens at the Phelps farm is to take lightly the entire downstream journey. What is the meaning of the journey? With this question all discussion of *Huckleberry Finn* must begin. It is true that the voyage down the river has many aspects of a boy's idyl. We owe much of its hold upon our imagination to the enchanting image of the raft's unhurried drift with the current. The leisure, the absence of constraint, the beauty of the river—all these things delight us. "It's lovely to live on a raft." And the multitudinous life of the great valley we see through Huck's eyes has a fascination of its own. Then, of course, there is humor—laughter so spontaneous, so free of bitterness present almost everywhere in American humor that readers often forget how grim a spectacle of human existence Huck con-

4. *Mark Twain at Work* (Cambridge, 1942), p. 92.

templates. Humor in this novel flows from a bright joy of life as remote from our world as living on a raft.

Yet along with the idyllic and the epical and the funny in *Huckleberry Finn*, there is a coil of meaning which does for the disparate elements of the novel what a spring does for a watch. The meaning is not in the least obscure. It is made explicit again and again. The very words with which Clemens launches Huck and Jim upon their voyage indicate that theirs is not a boy's lark but a quest for freedom. From the electrifying moment when Huck comes back to Jackson's Island and rouses Jim with the news that a search party is on the way, we are meant to believe that Huck is enlisted in the cause of freedom. "Git up and hump yourself, Jim!" he cries. "There ain't a minute to lose. They're after us!" What particularly counts here is the *us*. No one is after Huck; no one but Jim knows he is alive. In that small word Clemens compresses the exhilarating power of Huck's instinctive humanity. His unpremeditated identification with Jim's flight from slavery is an unforgettable moment in American experience, and it may be said at once that any culmination of the journey which detracts from the urgency and dignity with which it begins will necessarily be unsatisfactory. Huck realizes this himself, and says so when, much later, he comes back to the raft after discovering that the Duke and the King have sold Jim:

"After all this long journey . . . here it was all come to nothing, everything all busted up and ruined, because they could have the heart to serve Jim such a trick as that, and make him a slave again all his life, and amongst strangers, too, for forty dirty dollars."

Huck knows that the journey will have been a failure unless it takes Jim to freedom. It is true that we do discover, in the end, that Jim is free, but we also find out that the journey was not the means by which he finally reached freedom.

The most obvious thing wrong with the end, then, is the flimsy contrivance by which Clemens frees Jim. In the end we not only discover that Jim has been a free man for two months, but that his freedom has been granted by old Miss Watson. If this were only a mechanical device for terminating the action, it might not call for much comment. But it is more than that: it is a significant clue to the import of the last ten chapters. Remember who Miss Watson is. She is the Widow's sister whom Huck introduces in the first pages of the novel. It is she who keeps "pecking" at Huck, who tries to teach him to spell and to pray and to keep his feet off the furniture. She is an ardent proselytizer for piety and good manners, and her greed provides the occasion for the journey in the first place. She is Jim's owner, and he decides to flee only when he realizes that she is about to break her word (she cannot resist a slave trader's offer of eight hundred dollars) and sell him down the river away from his family.

Miss Watson, in short, is the Enemy. If we except a predilection for physical violence, she exhibits all the outstanding traits of the valley society. She pronounces the polite lies of civilization that suffocate Huck's spirit. The freedom which Jim seeks, and which Huck and Jim temporarily enjoy aboard the raft, is accordingly freedom *from* everything for which Miss Watson stands. Indeed, the very intensity of the novel derives from the discordance between the aspirations of the fugitives and the respectable code for which she is a spokesman. Therefore, her regeneration, of which the death-bed freeing of Jim is the unconvincing sign, hints a resolution of the novel's essential conflict. Perhaps because this device most transparently reveals that shift in point of view which he could not avoid, and which is less easily discerned elsewhere in the concluding chapters, Clemens plays it down. He makes little attempt to account for Miss Watson's change of heart, a change particularly surprising in view of Jim's brazen escape. Had Clemens given this episode dramatic emphasis appropriate to its function, Miss Watson's bestowal of freedom upon Jim would have proclaimed what the rest of the ending actually accomplishes—a vindication of persons and attitudes Huck and Jim had symbolically repudiated when they set forth downstream.

It may be said, and with some justice, that a reading of the ending as a virtual reversal of meanings implicit in the rest of the novel misses the point—that I have taken the final episode too seriously. I agree that Clemens certainly did not intend us to read it so solemnly. The ending, one might contend, is simply a burlesque upon Tom's taste for literary romance. Surely the tone of the episode is familiar to readers of Mark Twain. The preposterous monkey business attendant upon Jim's "rescue," the careless improvisation, the nonchalant disregard for common-sense plausibility—all these things should not surprise readers of Twain or any low comedy in the tradition of "Western humor." However, the trouble is, first, that the ending hardly comes off as burlesque: it is *too* fanciful, *too* extravagant; and it is tedious. For example, to provide a "gaudy" atmosphere for the escape, Huck and Tom catch a couple of dozen snakes. Then the snakes escape.

"No, there warn't no real scarcity of snakes about the house for a considerable spell. You'd see them dripping from the rafters and places every now and then; and they generly landed in your plate, or down the back of your neck. . . ."

Even if this were *good* burlesque, which it is not, what is it doing here? It is out of keeping; the slapstick tone jars with the underlying seriousness of the voyage.

Huckleberry Finn is a masterpiece because it brings Western humor to perfection and yet transcends the narrow limits of its conventions. But the ending does not. During the final extravaganza we are forced to put aside many of the mature emotions evoked earlier by the vivid rendering of Jim's fear of capture, the tenderness of Huck's and Jim's regard for each other, and Huck's excruciating moments of wavering between honesty and respectability. None of these emotions are called forth by the anticlimactic final sequence. I do not mean to suggest that the inclusion of low comedy per se is a flaw in *Huckleberry Finn*. One does not object to the shenanigans of the rogues; there is ample precedent for the place of extravagant humor even in works of high seriousness. But here the case differs from most which come to mind: the major characters themselves are forced to play low comedy roles. Moreover, the most serious motive in the novel, Jim's yearning for freedom, is made the object of nonsense. The conclusion, in short, is farce, but the rest of the novel is not.

That Clemens reverts in the end to the conventional manner of Western low comedy is most evident in what happens to the principals. Huck and Jim become comic characters; that is a much more serious ground for dissatisfaction than the unexplained regeneration of Miss Watson. Remember that Huck has grown in stature throughout the journey. By the time he arrives at the Phelps place, he is not the boy who had been playing robbers with Tom's gang in St. Petersburg the summer before. All he has seen and felt since he parted from Tom has deepened his knowledge of human nature and of himself. Clemens makes a point of Huck's development in two scenes which occur just before he meets Tom again. The first describes Huck's final capitulation to his own sense of right and wrong: "All right, then, I'll *go* to Hell." This is the climactic moment in the ripening of his self-knowledge. Shortly afterward, when he comes upon a mob riding the Duke and the King out of town on a rail, we are given his most memorable insight into the nature of man. Although these rogues had subjected Huck to every indignity, what he sees provokes this celebrated comment:

"Well, it made me sick to see it; and I was sorry for them poor pitiful rascals, it seemed like I couldn't ever feel any hardness against them any more in the world. It was a dreadful thing to see. Human beings can be awful cruel to one another."

The sign of Huck's maturity here is neither the compassion nor the skepticism, for both had been marks of his personality from the first. Rather, the special quality of these reflections is the extraordinary combination of the two, a mature blending of his instinctive suspicion of human motives with his capacity for pity.

But at this point Tom reappears. Soon Huck has fallen almost completely under his sway once more, and we are asked to believe that the boy who felt pity for the rogues is now capable of making Jim's capture the occasion for a game. He becomes Tom's helpless accomplice, submissive and gullible. No wonder that Clemens has Huck remark, when Huck first realizes Aunt Sally has mistaken him for Tom, that "it was like being born again." Exactly. In the end, Huck regresses to the subordinate role in which he had first appeared in *The Adventures of Tom Sawyer*. Most of those traits which made him so appealing a hero now disappear. He had never, for example, found pain or misfortune amusing. At the circus, when a clown disguised as a drunk took a precarious ride on a prancing horse, the crowd loved the excitement and danger; "it warn't funny to me, though," said Huck. But now, in the end, he submits in awe to Tom's notion of what is amusing. To satisfy Tom's hunger for adventure he makes himself a party to sport which aggravates Jim's misery.

It should be added at once that Jim doesn't mind too much. The fact is that he has undergone a similar transformation. On the raft he was an individual, man enough to denounce Huck when Huck made him the victim of a practical joke. In the closing episode, however, we lose sight of Jim in the maze of farcical invention. He ceases to be a man. He allows Huck and "Mars Tom" to fill his hut with rats and snakes, "and every time a rat bit Jim he would get up and write a line in his journal whilst the ink was fresh." This creature who bleeds ink and feels no pain is something less than human. He has been made over in the image of a flat stereotype: the submissive stage-Negro. These antics divest Jim, as well as Huck, of much of his dignity and individuality.[5]

What I have been saying is that the flimsy devices of plot, the discordant farcical tone, and the disintegration of the major characters all betray the failure of the ending. These are not aspects merely of form in a technical sense, but of meaning. For that matter, I would maintain that this book has little or no formal unity independent of the joint purpose of Huck and Jim. What components of the novel, we may ask, provide the continuity which links one adventure with another? The most important is the unifying consciousness of Huck, the narrator, and the fact that we follow the same principals through the entire string of adventures. Events, moreover, occur in a temporal sequence. Then there is the river; after each adventure Huck and Jim return to the raft and the river. Both Mr. Trilling and Mr. Eliot speak eloquently of the river as a

5. For these observations on the transformation of Jim in the closing episodes, I am indebted to the excellent unpublished essay by Mr. Chadwick Hansen on the subject of Clemens and Western humor.

source of unity, and they refer to the river as a god. Mr. Trilling says that Huck is "the servant of the river-god." Mr. Eliot puts it this way: "The River gives the book its form. But for the River, the book might be only a sequence of adventures with a happy ending." This seems to me an extravagant view of the function of the neutral agency of the river. Clemens had a knowledgeable respect for the Mississippi and, without sanctifying it, was able to provide excellent reasons for Huck's and Jim's intense relation with it. It is a source of food and beauty and terror and serenity of mind. But above all, it provides motion; it is the means by which Huck and Jim move away from a menacing civilization. They return to the river to continue their journey. The river cannot, does not, supply purpose. That purpose is a facet of their consciousness, and without the motive of escape from society, *Huckleberry Finn* would indeed "be only a sequence of adventures." Mr. Eliot's remark indicates how lightly he takes the quest for freedom. His somewhat fanciful exaggeration of the river's role is of a piece with his neglect of the theme at the novel's center.

That theme is heightened by the juxtaposition of sharp images of contrasting social orders: the microcosmic community Huck and Jim establish aboard the raft and the actual society which exists along the Mississippi's banks. The two are separated by the river, the road to freedom upon which Huck and Jim must travel. Huck tells us what the river means to them when, after the Wilks episode, he and Jim once again shove their raft into the current: "It *did* seem so good to be free again and all by ourselves on the big river, and nobody to bother us." The river is indifferent. But its sphere is relatively uncontaminated by the civilization they flee, and so the river allows Huck and Jim some measure of freedom at once, the moment they set foot on Jackson's Island or the raft. Only on the island and the raft do they have a chance to practice that idea of brotherhood to which they are devoted. "Other places do seem so cramped and smothery," Huck explains, "but a raft don't. You feel mighty free and easy and comfortable on a raft." The main thing is freedom.

On the raft the escaped slave and the white boy try to practice their code: "What you want, above all things, on a raft, is for everybody to be satisfied, and feel right and kind towards the others." This human credo constitutes the paramount affirmation of *The Adventures of Huckleberry Finn,* and it obliquely aims a devastating criticism at the existing social order. It is a creed which Huck and Jim bring to the river. It neither emanates from nature nor is it addressed to nature. Therefore I do not see that it means much to talk about the river as a god in this novel. The river's connection with this high aspiration for man is that it provides a means of escape, a place where the code can be tested. The truly profound meanings of the novel are generated by the impingement of the actual world of slavery, feuds, lynching, murder, and a spurious Christian morality upon the ideal of the raft. The result is a tension which somehow demands release in the novel's ending.

But Clemens was unable to effect this release and at the same time control the central theme. The unhappy truth about the ending of *Huckleberry Finn* is that the author, having revealed the tawdry nature of the culture of the great valley, yielded to its essential complacency. The general tenor of the closing scenes, to which the token regeneration of Miss Watson is merely one superficial clue, amounts to just that. In fact, this entire reading of *Huckleberry Finn* merely confirms the brilliant insight of George Santayana, who many years ago spoke of American humorists, of whom he considered Mark Twain an outstanding representative, as having only "half escaped" the genteel tradition. Santayana meant that men like Clemens were able to "point to what contradicts it in the facts; but not in order to abandon the genteel tradition, for they have nothing solid to put in its place." This seems to me the real key to the failure of *Huckleberry Finn*. Clemens had presented the contrast between the two social orders but could not, or would not, accept the tragic fact that the one he had rejected was an image of solid reality and the other an ecstatic dream. Instead he gives us the cozy reunion with Aunt Polly in a scene fairly bursting with approbation of the entire family, the Phelpses included.

Like Miss Watson, the Phelpses are almost perfect specimens of the dominant culture. They are kind to their friends and relatives; they have no taste for violence; they are people capable of devoting themselves to their spectacular dinners while they keep Jim locked in the little hut down by the ash hopper, with its lone window boarded up. (Of course Aunt Sally visits Jim to see if he is "comfortable," and Uncle Silas comes in "to pray with him.") These people, with their comfortable Sunday-dinner conviviality and the runaway slave padlocked nearby, are reminiscent of those solid German citizens we have heard about in our time who tried to maintain a similarly *gemütlich* way of life within virtual earshot of Buchenwald. I do not mean to imply that Clemens was unaware of the shabby morality of such people. After the abortive escape of Jim, when Tom asks about him, Aunt Sally replies: "Him? . . . the runaway nigger? . . . They've got him back, safe and sound, and he's in the cabin again, on bread and water, and loaded down with chains, till he's claimed or sold!" Clemens understood people like the Phelpses, but nevertheless he was forced to rely upon them to provide his happy ending. The satisfactory outcome of Jim's quest for freedom must be attributed to the benevolence of the very people whose inhumanity first made it necessary.

But to return to the contention of Mr. Trilling and Mr. Eliot that the ending is more or less satisfactory after all. As I have said, Mr. Trilling approves of the "formal aptness" of the conclusion. He says that "some device is needed to permit Huck to return to his anonymity, to give up the role of hero," and that therefore "nothing could serve better than the mind of Tom Sawyer with its literary furnishings, its conscious romantic desire for experience and the hero's part, and its ingenious schematization of life. . . ." Though more detailed, this is essentially akin to Mr. Eliot's blunt assertion that "it is right that the mood at the end of the book should bring us back to that of the beginning." I submit that it is wrong for the end of the book to bring us back to that mood. The mood of the beginning of *Huckleberry Finn* is the mood of Huck's attempt to accommodate himself to the ways of St. Petersburg. It is the mood of the end of *The Adventures of Tom Sawyer*, when the boys had been acclaimed heroes, and when Huck was accepted as a candidate for respectability. That is the state in which we find him at the beginning of *Huckleberry Finn*. But Huck cannot stand the new way of life, and his mood gradually shifts to the mood of rebellion which dominates the novel until he meets Tom again. At first, in the second chapter, we see him still eager to be accepted by the nice boys of the town. Tom leads the gang in re-enacting adventures he has culled from books, but gradually Huck's pragmatic turn of mind gets him in trouble. He has little tolerance for Tom's brand of make-believe. He irritates Tom. Tom calls him a "numb-skull," and finally Huck throws up the whole business:

"So then I judged that all that stuff was only just one of Tom Sawyer's lies. I reckoned he believed in the A-rabs and the elephants, but as for me I think different. It had all the marks of a Sunday school."

With this statement, which ends the third chapter, Huck parts company with Tom. The fact is that Huck has rejected Tom's romanticizing of experience; moreover, he has rejected it as part of the larger pattern of society's make-believe, typified by Sunday school. But if he cannot accept Tom's harmless fantasies about the A-rabs, how are we to believe that a year later Huck is capable of awe-struck submission to the far more extravagant fantasies with which Tom invests the mock rescue of Jim?

After Huck's escape from his "pap," the drift of the action, like that of the Mississippi's current, is *away* from St. Petersburg. Huck leaves Tom and the A-rabs behind, along with the Widow, Miss Watson, and all the pseudo-religious ritual in which nice boys must partake. The return, in the end, to the mood of the beginning therefore means defeat—Huck's defeat; to return to that mood *joyously* is to portray defeat in the guise of victory.

Mr. Eliot and Mr. Trilling deny this. The overriding consideration for them is form—form which seems largely to mean symmetry of structure. It is fitting, Mr. Eliot maintains, that the book should come full circle and bring Huck once more under Tom's sway. Why? Because it begins that way. But it seems to me that such structural unity is *imposed* upon the novel, and therefore is meretricious. It is a jerry-built structure, achieved only by sacrifice of characters and theme. Here the controlling principle of form apparently is unity, but unfortunately a unity much too superficially conceived. Structure, after all, is only one element—indeed, one of the more mechanical elements—of unity. A unified work must surely manifest coherence of meaning and clear development of theme, yet the ending of *Huckleberry Finn* blurs both. The eagerness of Mr. Eliot and Mr. Trilling to justify the ending is symptomatic of that absolutist impulse of our critics to find reasons, once a work has been admitted to the highest canon of literary reputability, for admiring every bit of it.

What is perhaps most striking about these judgments of Mr. Eliot's and Mr. Trilling's is that they are so patently out of harmony with the basic standards of both critics. For one thing, both men hold far more complex ideas of the nature of literary unity than their comments upon *Huckleberry Finn* would suggest. For another, both critics are essentially moralists, yet here we find them turning away from a moral issue in order to praise a dubious structural unity. Their efforts to explain away the flaw in Clemens' novel suffer from a certain narrowness surprising to anyone who knows their work. These facts suggest that we may be in the presence of a tendency in contemporary criticism which the critics themselves do not fully recognize.

Is there an explanation? How does it happen that two of our most respected critics should seem to treat so lightly the glaring lapse of moral imagination in *Huckleberry Finn?* Perhaps—and I stress the conjectural nature of what I am saying—perhaps the kind of moral issue raised by *Huckleberry Finn* is not the kind of moral issue to which today's criticism readily addresses itself. Today our critics, no less than our novelists and poets, are most sensitively attuned to moral problems which arise in the sphere of individual behavior. They are deeply aware of sin, of individual infractions of our culture's Christian ethic. But my impression is that they are, possibly because of the strength of the reaction against the mechanical sociological criticism of the thirties, less sensitive to questions of what might be called social or political morality.

By social or political morality I refer to the values implicit in a social system, values which may be quite distinct from the personal morality of any given individual within the society. Now *The Adventures of Huckleberry Finn*, like all novels, deals with the behavior of individuals. But one mark of Clemens' greatness is his deft presentation of the disparity between what people do when they behave as individuals and what they do when forced into roles imposed upon them by society. Take, for example, Aunt Sally and Uncle Silas Phelps, who consider themselves Christians, who are by impulse generous and humane, but who happen also to be staunch upholders of certain degrading and inhuman social institutions. When they are confronted with an escaped slave, the imperatives of social morality outweigh all pious professions.

The conflict between what people think they stand for and what social pressure forces them to do is central to the novel. It is present to the mind of Huck and, indeed, accounts for his most serious inner conflicts. He knows how he feels about Jim, but he also knows what he is expected to do about Jim. This division within his mind corresponds to the division of the novel's moral terrain into the areas represented by the raft on the one hand and society on the other. His victory over his "yaller dog" conscience therefore assumes heroic size: it is a victory over the prevailing morality. But the last fifth of the novel has the effect of diminishing the importance and uniqueness of Huck's victory. We are asked to assume that somehow freedom can be achieved in spite of the crippling power of what I have called the social morality. Consequently the less importance we attach to that force as it operates in the novel, the more acceptable the ending becomes.

Moreover, the idea of freedom, which Mr. Eliot and Mr. Trilling seem to slight, takes on its full significance only when we acknowledge the power which society exerts over the minds of men in the world of *Huckleberry Finn*. For freedom in this book specifically means freedom from society and its imperatives. This is not the traditional Christian conception of freedom. Huck and Jim seek freedom not from a burden of individual guilt and sin, but from social constraint. That is to say, evil in *Huckleberry Finn* is the product of civilization, and if this is indicative of Clemens' rather too simple view of human nature, nevertheless the fact is that Huck, when he can divest himself of the taint of social conditioning (as in the incantatory account of sunrise on the river), is entirely free of anxiety and guilt. The only guilt he actually knows arises from infractions of a social code. (The guilt he feels after playing the prank on Jim stems from his betrayal of the law of the raft.) Huck's and Jim's creed is secular. Its object is harmony among men, and so Huck is not much concerned with his own salvation. He repeatedly renounces prayer in favor of pragmatic solutions to his problems. In other words, the central insights of the novel belong to the tradition of the Enlightenment. The meaning of the quest itself is hardly reconcilable with that conception of human nature embodied in the myth of original sin. In view of the current fashion of reaffirming man's innate depravity, it is perhaps not surprising to find the virtues of *Huckleberry Finn* attributed not to its meaning but to its form.

But "if this was not the right ending for the book," Mr. Eliot asks, "what ending would have been right?" Although this question places the critic in an awkward position (he is not always equipped to rewrite what he criticizes), there are some things which may justifiably be said about the "right" ending of *Huckleberry Finn*. It may be legitimate, even if presumptuous, to indicate certain conditions which a hypothetical ending would have to satisfy if it were to be congruent with the rest of the novel. If the conclusion is not to be something merely tacked on to close the action, then its broad outline must be immanent in the body of the work.

It is surely reasonable to ask that the conclusion provide a plausible outcome to the quest. Yet freedom, in the ecstatic sense that Huck and Jim knew it aboard the raft, was hardly to be had in the Mississippi Valley in the 1840's, or, for that matter, in any other known human society. A satisfactory ending would inevitably cause the reader some frustration. That Clemens felt such disappointment to be inevitable is borne out by an examination of the novel's clear, if unconscious, symbolic pattern. Consider, for instance, the inferences to be drawn from the book's geography. The river, to whose current Huck and Jim entrust themselves, actually carries them to the heart of slave territory. Once the raft passes Cairo, the quest is virtually doomed. Until the steamboat smashes the raft, we are kept in a state of anxiety about Jim's escape. (It may be significant that at this point Clemens found himself unable to continue work on the manuscript, and put it aside for several years.) Beyond Cairo, Clemens allows the intensity of that anxiety to diminish, and it is probably no accident that the fainter it becomes, the more he falls back upon the devices of low comedy. Huck and Jim make no serious effort to turn north, and there are times (during the Wilks episode) when Clemens allows Huck to forget all about Jim. It is as if the author, anticipating the dilemma he had finally to face, instinctively dissipated the power of his major theme.

Consider, too, the circumscribed nature of the raft as a means of moving toward freedom. The raft lacks power and maneuverability. It can only move easily with the current—southward into slave country. Nor can it evade the mechanized power of the steamboat. These impotencies of the raft correspond to the innocent helplessness of its occupants. Unresisted, the rogues invade and take over the raft. Though it is the symbolic locus of the novel's central affirmations, the raft provides an uncertain and indeed precarious mode of traveling toward freedom. This seems another confirmation of Santayana's perception. To say that Clemens only half escaped the genteel tradition is not to say that he failed to note any of the creed's inadequacies, but rather that he had "nothing solid" to put in its place. The raft patently was not capable of carrying the burden of hope Clemens placed upon it.[6] (Whether this is to be attributed to the nature of his vision or to the actual state of American society in the nineteenth century is another interesting question.) In any case, the geography of the novel, the raft's powerlessness, the goodness and vulnerability of Huck and Jim, all prefigure a conclusion quite different in tone from that which Clemens gave us. These facts constitute what Hart Crane might have called the novel's "logic of metaphor," and this logic—probably inadvertent—actually takes us to the underlying meaning of *The Adventures of Huckleberry Finn*. Through the symbols we reach a truth which the ending obscures: the quest cannot succeed.

Fortunately, Clemens broke through to this truth in the novel's last sentences:

"But I reckon I got to light out for the territory ahead of the rest, because Aunt Sally she's going to adopt me and civilize me, and I can't stand it. I been there before."

Mr. Eliot properly praises this as "the only possible concluding sentence." But one sentence can hardly be advanced, as Mr. Eliot advances this one, to support the rightness of ten chapters. Moreover, if this sentence is right, then the rest of the conclusion is wrong, for its meaning clashes with that of the final burlesque. Huck's decision to go west ahead of the inescapable advance of civilization is a confession of defeat. It means that the raft is to be abandoned. On the other hand, the jubilation of the family reunion and the proclaiming of Jim's freedom create a quite different mood. The tone, except for these last words, is one of unclouded success. I believe this is the source of the almost universal dissatisfaction with the conclusion. One can hardly forget that a bloody civil war did not resolve the issue.

Should Clemens have made Huck a tragic hero? Both Mr. Eliot and Mr. Trilling argue that that would have been a mistake, and they are very probably correct. But between the ending as we have it and tragedy in the fullest sense, there was vast room for invention.

6. Gladys Bellamy (*Mark Twain as a Literary Artist*, Norman, Oklahoma, 1950, p. 221) has noted the insubstantial, dream-like quality of the image of the raft. Clemens thus discusses travel by raft in *A Tramp Abroad:* "the motion of the raft is . . . gentle, and gliding, and smooth, and noiseless; it calms down all feverish activities, it soothes to sleep all nervous . . . impatience; under its restful influence all the troubles and vexations and sorrows that harass the mind vanish away, and existence becomes a dream . . . a deep and tranquil ecstasy."

Clemens might have contrived an action which left Jim's fate as much in doubt as Huck's. Such an ending would have allowed us to assume that the principals were defeated but alive, and the quest unsuccessful but not abandoned. This, after all, would have been consonant with the symbols, the characters, and the theme as Clemens had created them—and with history.

Clemens did not acknowledge the truth his novel contained. He had taken hold of a situation in which a partial defeat was inevitable, but he was unable to—or unaware of the need to—give imaginative substance to that fact. If an illusion of success was indispensable, where was it to come from? Obviously Huck and Jim could not succeed by their own efforts. At this point Clemens, having only half escaped the genteel tradition, one of whose preeminent characteristics was an optimism undaunted by disheartening truth, returned to it. Why he did so is another story, having to do with his parents and his boyhood, with his own personality and his wife's, and especially with the character of his audience. But whatever the explanation, the faint-hearted ending of *The Adventures of Huckleberry Finn* remains an important datum in the record of American thought and imagination. It has been noted before, both by critics and non-professional readers. It should not be forgotten now.

To minimize the seriousness of what must be accounted a major flaw in so great a work is, in a sense, to repeat Clemens' failure of nerve. This is a disservice to criticism. Today we particularly need a criticism alert to lapses of moral vision. A measured appraisal of the failures and successes of our writers, past and present, can show us a great deal about literature and about ourselves. That is the critic's function. But he cannot perform that function if he substitutes considerations of technique for considerations of truth. Not only will such methods lead to errors of literary judgment, but beyond that, they may well encourage comparable evasions in other areas. It seems not unlikely, for instance, that the current preoccupation with matters of form is bound up with a tendency, by no means confined to literary quarters, to shy away from painful answers to complex questions of political morality. The conclusion to *The Adventures of Huckleberry Finn* shielded both Clemens and his audience from such an answer. But we ought not to be as tender-minded. For Huck Finn's besetting problem, the disparity between his best impulses and the behavior the community attempted to impose upon him, is as surely ours as it was Twain's.

RICHARD P. ADAMS

The Unity and Coherence of *Huckleberry Finn*†

Huckleberry Finn received very little critical attention of any kind before 1948. Students up to then were more interested in the life of Samuel Clemens than in the esthetic qualities of his work. It was generally felt that he was not an artist, and that any esthetic consideration of his writing would be a waste of time.

In 1948, however, Lionel Trilling published his brilliant introduction to the Rinehart edition.[1] His defense of the ending of the book, which had always been deplored, led to a controversy. T. S. Eliot, in another brilliant introduction, published in 1950, agreed with Trilling.[2] In 1953 Leo Marx dissented, attacking Trilling, Eliot, and the book.[3] Others, such as E. M. Branch, Gladys Bellamy, J. M. Cox, Lewis Leary, and Frank Baldanza, have approached the story from various esthetic points of view and offered various critical opinions.[4] Several theories and suggestions emerge concerning theme and structure, style and technique, and the esthetic value of the work. But no discussion has yet presented a formula that fully or systematically accounts for the greatness of *Huckleberry Finn* as a work of literary art.

Tom Sawyer has been more fortunate. In 1939 Walter Blair made an analysis of it which shows clearly and fairly completely the principles of construction and of unity that Clemens used in his better fiction. There are, Blair says, four "lines of action" in *Tom Sawyer*, all concerned with the boy's development toward manhood and moral maturity.

"Each one of these is initiated by a characteristic and typically boyish action. The love story begins with Tom's childishly fickle desertion of his fiancée, Amy Lawrence; the Potter narrative with the superstitious trip to the graveyard; the Jackson's Island episode with the adolescent revolt of the boy against Aunt Polly, and Tom's

† Reprinted from *Tulane Studies in English*, VI (1956), 87–103, by permission of Richard P. Adams.

1. Reprinted in *The Liberal Imagination* (New York, 1950), pp. 104–117.
2. *The Adventures of Huckleberry Finn* (London, 1950), pp. vii–xvi.
3. Leo Marx, "Mr. Eliot, Mr. Trilling, and *Huckleberry Finn*," *Am. Schol.*, XXII (Autumn, 1953), 423–440.
4. Edgar M. Branch, *The Literary Apprenticeship of Mark Twain* (Urbana, 1950), pp. 199–216; Gladys C. Bellamy, *Mark Twain as a Literary Artist* (Norman, 1950), pp. 340–347; James M. Cox, "Remarks on the Sad Initiation of Huckleberry Finn," *SR*, LXII (Summer, 1954), 389–405; Lewis Leary, "Tom and Huck: Innocence on Trial," *VQR*, XXX (Summer, 1954), 417–430; and Frank Baldanza, "The Structure of *Huckleberry Finn*," *AL*, XXVII (Nov. 1955), 347–355. All of these, except the last, more or less strongly disagree with Trilling and Eliot about the ending.

youthful ambition to be a pirate; the Injun Joe story with the juvenile search for buried treasure. Three of these narrative strands, however, are climaxed by a characteristic and mature sort of action, a sort of action, moreover, directly opposed to the initial action. Tom chivalrously takes Becky's punishment and faithfully helps her in the cave; he defies boyish superstition and courageously testifies for Muff Potter; he forgets a childish antipathy and shows mature concern for his aunt's uneasiness about him. The Injun Joe story, though it is the least useful of the four so far as showing Tom's maturing is concerned, by showing Huck conquering fear to rescue the widow, has a value as a repetition—with variations—of the motif of the book.[5]

The interweaving of these four lines of developing action, Blair feels, gives "reason for believing that the theme, the main action, and the character portrayal in the novel are one—the developing of Tom's character in a series of crucial situations."[6] That is to say, quite correctly I think, that *Tom Sawyer*, for all its apparent casualness of construction, has a high degree of organic unity. Blair does not say that it has a coherent plot, nor would I, but the clear implication is that it does not need one. Its unity and coherence are thematic and symbolic—imaginative in the Coleridgean sense. Its elements are not related by the logic of cause and effect. Instead, they are fused in an organization of imagery that transcends any concept of plot or story line as a series of casually related events.

Huck Finn has a somewhat different structure, but the principle is the same or very similar. It has a symbolic pattern or organization of imagery, not a plot in the traditional sense. Critics who ignore Clemens's warning and come to it looking for a plot are likely to go astray, fall foul of Trilling and Eliot, and bog down in a fruitless effort to prove that the ending, or the whole book, is a failure. When a critic gets that far out on a limb it is not necessary to shoot him.

The most obvious element of structure in *Huck Finn*, and the one most often noticed, is the picaresque journey down the river, full of inconsequently interspersed and apparently aimless adventures. But it is dangerous to say that much and stop, for the inconsequence does not preclude a plan, and the aimlessness is only apparent. Trilling, in discussing the special qualities of the river as a road, points out some profitable directions for further inquiry. The important thing, he says, is that the river is a moving road,

". . . and the movement of the road in its own mysterious life transmutes the primitive simplicity of the form: the road itself is

5. Walter Blair, "On the Structure of *Tom Sawyer,*" *MP*, XXXVII (Aug. 1939), 84–85.
6. *Ibid.*, p. 86. Leary, pp. 419–423, in his discussion of *Tom Sawyer*, confirms Blair's theory, but he does not apply it to *Huck Finn*.

the greatest character in this novel of the road, and the hero's departures from the river and his returns to it compose a subtle and significant pattern. The linear simplicity of the picaresque novel is further modified by the story's having a clear dramatic organization: it has a beginning, a middle, and an end, and a mounting suspense of interest."[7]

Trilling perhaps oversimplifies the linear quality of the picaresque novel as Clemens knew it, but he does not over-estimate the complexity of *Huck Finn*, and his observations on the "living" quality of the river and on the alternation of Huck's river and shore experiences are valuable clues.

Another clue, of perhaps even greater value, is furnished by James M. Cox's discussion of Huck's "initiation." According to Cox, the "fake murder" that Huck stages in order to get away from his father "is probably the most vital and crucial incident of the entire novel,"[8] and Cox's observations on this event come close to defining the basic structure of the novel. The basic structure, which expresses the theme of the boy's growth and which carries the weight of the incidents and the imagery throughout, is a pattern of symbolic death and rebirth. As Cox points out, the central action on the river begins with Huck's pretended death. It ends with his mistaken recognition as Tom by Aunt Sally Phelps, when he feels that "it was like being born again, I was so glad to find out who I was." This pattern is kept in the focus of the reader's attention, as Cox also observes, by repeated deaths and escapes occurring between, before, and after the main events.

The pattern of death and rebirth is reinforced by the pattern Trilling observes in Huck's departures from and returns to the river; only we need to reverse Trilling's terms, for it is Huck's departures from and returns to shore which are cognate and parallel to the pattern of death and rebirth. The same pattern provides the framework for the "clear dramatic organization" which Trilling notices, and it roughly determines the kind of beginning, middle, and end that the story has. Putting Cox and Trilling together, and over-simplifying for the sake of initial clarity, we can state a more nearly complete definition of the structure of *Huckleberry Finn*. The beginning is Huck's life on shore in and around the village of St. Petersburg with the Widow Douglas and Pap. The middle, initiated by Huck's fake death, is his withdrawal from the life of society and civilization to the river; this withdrawal is repeated after each of his adventures on land. The end is his equivocal rebirth, his qualified return, under a false identity and with many reservations, to civilized life at the Phelps plantation.

The pattern of death and rebirth is also intimately concerned in

7. Trilling, p. 115.   8. Cox, p. 395.

the "mounting suspense of interest" which Trilling notes. The theme of the book, as we have hinted, is the same as that of *Tom Sawyer:* the growth of a boy to manhood, and his final acceptance of adult moral responsibilities. In this connection the pattern of death and rebirth is more than a technical device. In the tradition of romantic literature, to which *Huck Finn* belongs, it is a form with a meaning. The growth of a boy to manhood is perhaps the most popular of all themes for romantic fiction, and the structure which best expresses it is that of the death-and-rebirth pattern. The reason for this association is based in romantic philosophy, according to which the individual human personality is conceived as an organism which cannot undergo a fundamental change of any kind without being totally reconstituted. Its old self "dies" and its new self, an unpredictably different organism, is "born." Huck's initiation, his transformation from boy to man, is such a change. It is a radical reconstitution of his moral attitude toward the society in which he lives. He grows, therefore, during the time of crucial change, by "dying" out of society, withdrawing into nature on the river, and then returning or being "reborn" into society with a new and different attitude toward it.

It should not have to be said that this return is by no means an uncritical acceptance of conventional social values. The process of Huck's moral growth is, in fact, most emphatically indicated by his decision, made on three separate but closely related occasions, to free Jim from slavery, which is an act of rebellion against society. In a superficial sense the three decisions are the same, but each means more than the one before, because Huck knows more about the society he is deciding to oppose and because he sees more fully and clearly the implications of the decision and its probable consequences.

The context, which becomes increasingly solid and massive as Huck's knowledge increases, is a complex interrelationship of social, cultural, political, and economic forces. We might skeletonize it by making three simple statements, which we can then elaborate. First, slavery is evil. Second, the pseudo-aristocratic society of the antebellum South which fosters and depends on slavery is also evil. Third, the sentimental culture veneer with which that society conceals its evil from itself, if not from others, is evil as well. These propositions apply with increasing cogency to Huck's three decisions, as he learns more about the character and workings, the concrete personal meanings and moral values, of Southern slave-holding aristocracy. The relations among these three intertwined thematic strands in *Huck Finn* are so complex and pervasive that a thorough explication of them would be longer than the book. I shall not try to exhaust them here, but rather to indicate their general character and, by exploring a few of them in some detail, to show how they work.

Huck's first decision to help Jim escape is made casually enough in the process of his own flight from civilization and from the domination of his father. When he comes across his fellow runaway on Jackson's Island, he is so glad to have his lonesomeness relieved by any sort of company that he hardly thinks of difficulties. "People would call me a low-down Abolitionist and despise me for keeping mum," he admits to Jim, "—but that don't make no difference. I ain't a-going to tell, and I ain't a-going back there, anyways." But even this first and easiest decision is preceded by a fairly substantial development of motives and of symbolic motifs. Huck has been introduced to respectable society at the Widow's, where gentility is manifested painfully to him in regular hours, formal meals, and stiff clothing. When Miss Watson tells him about the bad place, he says he wishes he were there. "She got mad then, but I didn't mean no harm. All I wanted was to go somewheres. . . ." Later the same night, in harmony with the fake murder which is to come, he says, "I felt so lonesome I most wished I was dead." Then, in the planning and organization of Tom Sawyer's gang, we see Huck's indirect exposure to the culture of popular books and the sentimental proprieties of "high-toned" robbery and exploitation. Tom and the gang, of course, are completely unrealistic about the crimes they propose to commit, and blissfully unaware that crime, as gilded by the popular romances, is morally wrong. Farther on, Huck is regaled with Pap's reverse snobbishness on the subject of education and with his poor-white's groundless assertion of superiority over the much better educated "free nigger."

These lights and others like them are placed so as to reveal what Clemens considered to be the characteristic weaknesses, follies, and injustices of prewar Southern society. The essentially false and hypocritical gentility of the would-be aristocracy, the febrile and morally confusing sentimentalism of its favorite literature, and the crime of slavery which was the real basis of its economic and social system are continually brought home to Huck and the reader, in all kinds of dramatic, representative, and symbolic ways. The incidents are not haphazardly chosen or arranged. Each has its revealing gleam to contribute to Huck's unconsciously dawning awareness of the true values of the civilization to which he is being asked to belong. The result is that he runs away and, without any great misgivings at first, agrees to help Jim do the same.

The second decision is made necessary by a qualm of conscience. The fugitives are approaching Cairo, or think they are, and they both believe that Jim is almost free. Says Huck, "It hadn't ever come home to me before, what this thing was that I was doing. But now it did; and it stayed with me, and scorched me more and more." The point of difficulty is that freeing Jim involves robbing his owner, Miss Watson, of the eight hundred dollars he is worth on the market; and Jim makes the difficulty greater by threatening to have his children stolen, if necessary, by an Abolitionist. Huck is immediately and properly horrified. "It most froze me to hear such talk. . . . Here was this nigger, which I had as good as helped to run away, coming right out flat-footed and saying he would steal his children—children that belonged to a man I didn't even know; a man that hadn't ever done me no harm." The juxtaposition of "his" and "belonged" in this sentence, so carefully calculated to drive home the shocking injustice of property rights in human flesh, should not obscure the fact that there is a real moral issue. The great wrong of slavery does not make the lesser wrong of robbery right; a point which most pre-Civil War anti-slavery propagandists preferred to overlook. The issue is resolved by the fact that Huck finds himself unable to turn Jim in, for reasons which he does not fully understand but which the reader can surmise. To put it most simply, his human feelings are stronger than the commercial morality with which they are in conflict—as of course they should be. Unable to do entirely right, he chooses the lesser evil and goes on helping Jim.

When he repudiates his own conscience in this way, Huck takes a long step farther in his repudiation of Southern society, which has formed his conscience. He says to himself, in his usual innocent way, "what's the use you learning to do right when it's troublesome to do right and ain't no trouble to do wrong, and the wages is just the same? . . . So I reckoned I wouldn't bother no more about it, but after this always do whichever come handiest at the time." The innocence is of Huck, not Clemens, and it represents a remarkably keen penetration into the difficult question of personal or individual morality in relation to social conventions. Huck realizes in practice, though never in conscious theory, that the question is not one of a simple conflict between the individual and the mass, or the social institution, but that the two interpenetrate, and that the individual conscience is usually an ally of the social pressure for conformity.

Thoreau, in "Civil Disobedience," feels himself on solid ground when his conscience tells him to oppose the extension of slavery and the government that sanctions and promotes it. "If," he says, "the injustice . . . is of such a nature that it requires you to be the agent of injustice to another, then, I say, break the law." That seems comparatively easy; all that is needed is the courage to stand up against the government, which Southerners have always had in abundance. But, when the ante-bellum conscience is formed in

Missouri instead of Massachusetts, the battle becomes intensely complicated. Its lines are drawn mostly inside the personality, which is then divided against itself. As Trilling remarks, it is the paradox in Huck's own thinking, by the terms of which he does right by doing what he thoroughly believes, in his conscious mind, to be wrong, that makes his character heroic and Clemens's satire brilliant.[9] His battle is desperate, his victory sublime. If it is fine to follow as Thoreau does the dictates of conscience over law, it is finer and much more difficult to follow those of the right over conscience and law combined.

It is fair to say, as it is for the first decision, that everything leading up to this second one contributes to Huck's preparation for making it as he does. We can examine the process most efficiently, perhaps, by focussing on one incident, and tracing its relations to see how they bear on the larger meanings of the action. Let us take, for example, the adventure of Huck and Jim with the murderers on the wrecked steamboat *Walter Scott*.

This event has a number of bearings, mostly ironic, on the related themes of aristocracy and sentimental literature. One of the antipathies which Clemens cherished most warmly and flourished most often was his detestation of Sir Walter Scott and all or almost all his works. In *Life on the Mississippi* Scott is blamed for having checked the "wave of progress" in the South with his propaganda for medieval feudalism, which, according to Clemens, "sets the world in love with dreams and phantoms; with decayed and swinish forms of religion; with decayed and degraded systems of government; with the sillinesses and emptinesses, sham grandeurs, sham gauds, and sham chivalries of a brainless and worthless long-vanished society." The reality behind these shams was, Clemens felt, a sordid and quite common crime. He remarked in a notebook entry, probably made in 1888, that the establishment of a monarchy "is the same sort of crime that surprise and seizure of a weak community's property by a robber gang, and the conversion of the community itself into slaves, is. . . . A monarchy is perpetuated piracy. In its escutcheon should always be the skull and crossbones."[10]

In these terms, the presence of three murderous robbers on a wrecked steamboat named *Walter Scott* is neatly satirical. It echoes, on a note of considerably greater seriousness, the earlier activities of Tom's gang, one of which is a seizure of doughnuts and jam from "a Sunday-school picnic, and only a primer class at that," which Tom insists is a rich caravan—as if that would make the act less shamefully cruel. The American function of Scott and others like him, Clemens implies, is to excuse and gloss over the exploitation

9. Trilling, pp. 111–112.
10. *Mark Twain's Notebook*, ed. A. B.

Paine (New York and London, 1935), p. 197.

of slaves and poor whites, and to glamorize the exploiters as Southern chivalry. The actual behavior of the slave-owning class, according to Clemens's double-edged suggestion, is on the one hand as evil as that of a gang of thieves and murderers, and on the other as silly as that of Tom's infatuated band.

Part of the loot of the *Walter Scott*, which the robbers unknowingly bequeath to Huck and Jim, is a number of appropriate books "about kings and dukes and earls and such, and how gaudy they dressed, and how much style they put on, and called each other your majesty, and your grace, and your lordship, and so on, 'stead of mister. . . ." Huck's reading to Jim from these books leads to a good deal of talk about Solomon and his wisdom, which Jim rather shrewdly questions, and about Louis XVI and "the dolphin," which prepares for the later advent of the bogus king and duke. The whole incident, in all its ramifications, contributes to the satirical exploration in Huck's experience of the various meanings, pretended and real, false and true, of the aristocratic idea in the South.

This incident is balanced as well as followed by the much more important one of Huck's separation from Jim in the fog and his practical joke in making Jim think that it was a dream. In this event Huck is made to realize that Jim is a proud and sensitive human being, not livestock or chattel goods, and that the joke has been a cruel and humiliating betrayal of a friend's feelings. Corrupted by his life in a slave society and by the propaganda with which that society tries to justify the crime of slavery, Huck has never before considered that a slave might have feelings as worthy of respect as anyone else's. The speech in which Jim shows him his error, full of simple dignity and a pathos that beautifully consists with its righteous indignation, opens Huck's eyes in a way that is likely to stay in his memory. His reaction is worthy. "It was fifteen minutes," he says, "before I could work myself up to go and humble myself to a nigger; but I done it, and I warn't ever sorry for it afterward, neither. I didn't do him no more mean tricks, and I wouldn't done that one if I'd 'a' knowed it would make him feel that way." This realization, occurring shortly before the second decision to help Jim escape, makes any other decision practically impossible. With his indirect, unconscious realization of the falseness of aristocracy to balance his new awareness of the humanity of the slave, Huck would find it the meanest trick of all to betray Jim and send him back into the status of a piece of property to be exploited by the robber gang which is the reality behind the sham front of Southern aristocracy.

The third and final decision is led up to by a more personal and extensive experience of upper-class Southerners than before. Shortly after the second crisis, Huck and Jim realize that they have passed

Cairo in the fog, but before they can do anything to get back, the raft is wrecked by a steamboat and they are separated again. Huck finds himself ashore, beginning a new phase of the story and of his education. His shore adventures alternate, from this point on, with repeated escapes to the river, until he comes to the Phelps plantation. These adventures bring him more dramatically than before into contact, and more often into conflict, with aristocrats of various kinds. The increase of experience, knowledge, and understanding which he gains in this phase leads convincingly to his ultimate decision to repudiate aristocratic society by freeing its victim Jim.

The first aristocrats he meets in person, leaving aside the Widow, Miss Watson, and Judge Thatcher, are the Grangerfords, by whom he is strongly impressed and who are genuinely impressive in many ways. They have the typical aristocratic virtues: they are dignified, hospitable, proud, handsome, cultured (after a fashion), courteous, devout, and kind to strangers and dependents. But the more Huck learns of them, the more uneasy he becomes about their character and behavior. Clemens, through Huck's observations and comments, gradually undercuts the value of their culture. The description of the house, which is parallel to the account of "The House Beautiful" in *Life on the Mississippi*, is a skillful piece of irony. Huck admires the place immensely, while Clemens mercilessly exposes the queer mixture of arrogant show and pathetic provincialism that it presents to even a moderately sophisticated eye. The description leads up to and is ludicrously topped off by Huck's account of Emmeline Grangerford's esthetic misdeeds in crayon and verse, of the graveyard school run wild and gone to seed. The cultural pretensions of the aristocracy are, by this report, sufficiently harmless in themselves but crude, anachronistic, and highly absurd from any civilized modern point of view.

The feud which is going on between the Grangerfords and the Shepherdsons is a much more serious matter, and it does not depend on the same kind of irony for its effect. It is as deeply horrifying to Huck as it could possibly be to Clemens. The brutal killing of the two boys makes Huck so sick that he cannot even tell about it in detail without getting sick again; and his admiration for the better qualities of the aristocrats is more than canceled by this result of their violence.

The incident is a direct expression of feeling on the part of its author. In *Life on the Mississippi* Clemens goes somewhat out of his way to comment on a published opinion that the South had "the highest type of civilization this continent has seen. . . ." He demonstrates the hollowness of the brag in a footnote with "Illustrations of it thoughtlessly omitted by the advertiser," consisting of newspaper accounts of four fights in which five Southern gentlemen

were killed and one injured, with the usual incidental damage to
bystanders, reference also being made to four other murders and
one nonfatal stabbing in previous engagements involving some
of the same gentlemen. The people concerned were of the highest
class that Southern civilization had produced, including a general
and his son, a bank president, a college professor, and "two 'highly
connected' young Virginians" who fought a duel with butcher
knives. It is from this kind of violence that Huck escapes to the
river again, wishing that he "hadn't ever come ashore that night to
see such things. I ain't ever going to get shut of them—lots of
times I dream about them." Clemens had often dreamed about
some violent episodes he witnessed as a boy.

Huck's reaction leads to one of his most lyric descriptions of
the freedom, comfort, and beauty of the river, and the loveliness
of life on a raft. But evil comes into this world also, in the shape
of the two confidence men who palm themselves off as "the rightful
Duke of Bridgewater" and "the late Dauphin. . . . Looy the
Seventeen, son of Looy the Sixteen and Marry Antonette," and
who take over in the true aristocratic robber-gang fashion. The
cream of the jest is that the duke's claim is accepted by the other
rogue so that he may in turn make his higher claim. The cream
of the cream is that the duke then has to admit the king's superior
status and rights in order that both may exploit the plebeian members of the little commonwealth. But the richest layer of all is
Huck's good-naturedly cynical accommodation to the whole arrangement. He sees immediately what frauds these are, but he is
pleased when the duke knuckles under; "for what you want, above
all things, on a raft, is for everybody to be satisfied, and feel right
and kind towards the others."

Clemens's feeling about the kind of imposition practiced—or at
least attempted—here is given in another notebook entry: "There
are shams and shams; there are frauds and frauds, but the trans-
parentest of all is the sceptered one. We see monarchs meet and
go through solemn ceremonies, farces, with straight countenances;
but it is not possible to imagine them meeting in private and not
laughing in each other's faces."[11] The fraud practiced by the
bogus king and duke is no different from the frauds put over by
real kings and dukes, except that the latter are bigger. As Huck
explains to Jim, after the confidence men have worked over their
first town together, they are lucky not to have Henry VIII on their
hands, for he was a really accomplished crook; "If we'd 'a' had him
along 'stead of our kings he'd 'a' fooled that town a heap worse
than ourn done. I don't say that ourn is lambs, because they ain't,

11. *Ibid.*, p. 196. Clemens neglected this view when he later met some royal
persons himself.

when you come right down to the cold facts; but they ain't nothing to *that* old ram, anyway." This observation reinforces the point already made, implicitly, that the Grangerfords and Shepherdsons, by their more serious imitation of aristocratic ways, are only presenting a more pernicious version of something which at best is a sham and a fraud.

Perhaps the most emphatic impression of the ugly side of Southern chivalry is given by the incident in which Huck witnesses the cold-blooded murder of old Boggs by Colonel Sherburn. Boggs is a noisy but harmless fool, Sherburn a fine example of aristocratic pride—brave and intelligent in his own way, but narrow, selfish, inconsiderate, harsh, and brutal. It is, again, a sickening scene, and it is based on a murder that Clemens witnessed as a boy. But it may be that the importance of the incident for the satirical aspect of the book lies mainly in the character of the townspeople, who are by and large a degraded lot. "There couldn't anything wake them up all over," says Huck, "and make them happy all over, like a dog-fight—unless it might be putting turpentine on a stray dog and setting fire to him, or tying a tin pan to his tail and see him run himself to death." They try half-heartedly to get Boggs to stop his offensive yelling and go home, but they also perversely enjoy the shooting and the old man's death, the view of the body in the drug store window, and the re-enactment of the murder by one of the onlookers. When they go to Sherburn's house with the announced intention of lynching him, he lectures them contemptuously and drives them off with a shotgun, which he does not have to fire.

His contempt seems justified, on the face of things. These are the same people who, after hooting the Shakespearean efforts of the king and duke, prove ripe for the Royal Nonesuch hoax. The duke, in his estimate of them, agrees with Sherburn. He prints at the foot of his handbill "LADIES AND CHILDREN NOT ADMITTED," remarking, "There . . . if that line don't fetch them, I don't know Arkansaw!" It does. But the deeper point is not explicitly stated here, or anywhere else in *Huck Finn*, nor is it fully understood, we may suppose, by either Sherburn or the duke. They see well enough that the people are ignorant, cowardly, and gullible; they do not see that the reason for that fact is the apparently opposite fact that an aristocracy is in power. Clemens, however, was aware of it and well convinced that poverty, both of the flesh and of the spirit, is the mirror image of aristocratic splendor and that universal cruelty is inevitably characteristic of any society divided into rigid classes with hereditary inequalities of function, privilege, and status.

This principle is explained more clearly in *A Connecticut Yankee*. The Yankee is shocked at the way poor peasants in Arthurian England rush out, heedless of right or justice, and help each other hang their neighbors in their lord's behalf, apparently unable "to see anything horrible about it." His comment is almost a direct reference to the satire in *Huck Finn*.

"It reminded me of a time thirteen centuries away, when the 'poor whites' of our South who were always despised and frequently insulted by the slave-lords around them, and who owed their base condition simply to the presence of slavery in their midst, were yet pusillanimously ready to side with the slave-lords in all political moves for the upholding and perpetuating of slavery, and did also finally shoulder their muskets and pour out their lives in an effort to prevent the destruction of that very institution which degraded them. And there was only one redeeming feature connected with that pitiful piece of history; and that was, that secretly the 'poor white' did detest the slave-lord, and did feel his own shame."

The Yankee also remarks that "It is enough to make a body ashamed of his race to think of the sort of froth that has always occupied its thrones without shadow of right or reason," and what Clemens obviously means is that any respectable race would blow such froth to the moon before letting it settle into power.

Huck, whose background is about as purely poor-white as it could be, is given almost exactly the same words— "It was enough to make a body ashamed of the human race"—to describe his feelings about the next incident. The king and duke are having a fine run of initial success in playing their confidence game on the Wilks girls and most of their neighbors. It is a game that Huck perfectly understands, and he becomes so much ashamed of himself for being involved in it, though unwillingly, that he takes the risky measure of telling the truth in order to break it up. The most painful aspect of the affair applies directly to the theme of slavery, being the inhumanity of the fake aristocrats in the sale of the Wilks family slaves, "the two sons up the river to Memphis, and their mother down the river to Orleans." Huck says again that "it most made me down sick to see it. . . . I can't ever get it out of my memory, the sight of them poor miserable girls and niggers hanging around each other's necks and crying. . . ." The reader is likely to recall, as Clemens must have done, that this is not something only fakers do; it is precisely what Miss Watson does in planning to sell Jim "down to Orleans"; the general truth is that, as the Connecticut Yankee remarks in another place, "a privileged class, an aristocracy, is but a band of slaveholders under another name." The function of the king and duke is to show this basic identity, and underscore its meaning. Are these two scoundrels the most absurd, unmitigated, bare-faced buffoons of wickedness imaginable? So, Clemens wishes us to feel and understand, are all aristocrats. Kings, dukes, pirates,

robbers, confidence men, and slaveholders are the same, and all
sorry. Anyone who respects them is a fool, anyone who fears them
is a coward, and anyone who supports them or submits to them is
a slave himself.

Huck is none of these things, though he is almost infinitely good-
natured and accommodating. He goes along with the king and
duke as well and as long as he can, and he feels sorry for them when
the mob escorts them out of town, in tar and feathers, on a rail.
But he spoils their game with the Wilkses, and he leaves them
when the king sells Jim into bondage again. For him, their function
has been to complete his education in the social realities of slavoc-
racy and to put the finishing touches on his preparation for the final
decision he has to make. They have done the job effectively; he is
ready now to see Jim through to freedom in spite of anything. Unconsciously, but with deep conviction, he understands the society
to which by accident of birth he belongs, and refuses to submit
to it.

On this last occasion, Huck sees his problem as being more
difficult than it has ever seemed to him before, because it presents
itself to him in terms of the religious sanction which the institution of slavery enjoyed in the prewar South. His conscience, unable
to win the battle alone, now tells him, in accordance with the
Sunday-school teaching he feels he should have had, "that people
that acts as I'd been acting about the nigger goes to everlasting
fire." Again, Huck is expressing one of his author's ideas. Clemens
remarks of his mother in the *Autobiography* that,

"kind-hearted and compassionate as she was, I think she was not
conscious that slavery was a bald, grotesque, and unwarrantable
usurpation. She had never heard it assailed in any pulpit, but had
heard it defended and sanctified in a thousand; her ears were familiar
with Bible texts that approved it, but if there were any that dis-
approved it they had not been quoted by her pastors; as far as her
experience went, the wise and the good and the holy were unanimous
in the conviction that slavery was right, righteous, sacred, the peculiar pet of the Deity, and a condition which the slave himself
ought to be daily and nightly thankful for."[12]

Huck has easily won out over public opinion, less easily over public
opinion reinforced by his own conscience. The addition of the
Deity to the list of powers with which he has to contend raises his
battle to its ultimate pitch of intensity.

His first maneuver is to pray for the improvement of his character,
but he realizes at once that the plea is hypocritical. To make it
good, he writes a letter to Miss Watson to tell her where Jim is,

12. *Mark Twain's Autobiography*, ed. A. B. Paine (New York and London. 1924),
I, 123.

but he gets to thinking about Jim's goodness and loyalty and kindness, and all the times they have helped each other, and again he makes up his mind.

"I was a-trembling, because I'd got to decide, forever, betwixt two things, and I knowed it. I studied a minute, a sort of holding my breath, and then says to myself:

" 'All right, then, I'll go to hell'—and tore it up.

"It was awful thoughts and awful words, but they was said. And I let them stay said; and never thought no more about reforming."

With this decision, the middle or river section comes to its conclusion, and the ending of the book begins.

Clemens obviously had difficulty handling the ending. The reason seems to be that once Huck's final decision is made there is no longer any important part for Jim to play. His function in relation to the theme has been to test, or to furnish occasions when events would test, Huck's growing moral strength and mature independence. When that has been done, to the last possible extreme, Jim needs simply to be got out of the book as quickly and as unobtrusively as possible. Instead, Clemens plays up Tom Sawyer's long, elaborate, and almost meaningless escape plot. The final solution to the problem, the disclosure that Miss Watson has died and freed Jim in her will, is all that is needed, and the less said about it the better. And yet the escape plot is not altogether irrelevant. It furthers and completes the satire on sentimental literature, from which Tom draws his inspirations. It caps the ridicule of aristocratic pretensions by identifying Jim, the imprisoned slave, with the noble persons on whose renowned adventures his liberation is modeled. It is an immense expression of contempt for adult society, so easily and so thoroughly hoodwinked by a pair of audacious children; and the more absurd Tom's antics become, the more the satire is built up. It is as much an attack on conventional respectability as Huck's discomforts at the Widow Douglas's, or his observations on the culture of the Grangerfords, or his rebellion against slavery itself.

Huck's attitude at the end is a mixture, full of ironies and reservations of many kinds. Having made the great decision to repudiate society, physically, morally, and spiritually, he can hardly return to it without equivocation. In a sense, his acceptance of the name and status of Tom Sawyer on the Phelps plantation is a return, but it is made on completely false premises. Also Huck is glad in a way to submit to Tom's leadership and direction. The burden of lonely responsibility has weighed long and heavily. But he is not fooled for a minute into thinking that there is any validity in Tom's adherence to bookish or aristocratic authority. "When I start in to steal a nigger," he says, "I ain't no ways particular how it's done so it's done. What I want is my nigger . . . and I don't give a dead rat what the authorities thinks about it nuther." He has arrived at maturity and self-sufficiency, and he is poised at the end in a delicate balance, ready at any moment "to light out for the territory" in order to escape Aunt Sally's threatened continuation of the civilizing process begun by the Widow Douglas.

This aspect of the conclusion is exactly right. It would have been wrong—impossible in fact—for Clemens to bring the story to a stop, as he might have tried to do by having Huck accept the moral values of society and return to it uncritically in a "happy ending." The whole process of his development runs counter to any such result. The impression that Clemens has to leave, and does leave, in the reader's mind and feelings is that Huck will continue to develop. He will escape again, as many times as he needs to, from society and any of its restrictions which would hamper or prevent his growth. He will die and be reborn whenever his character needs to break the mold that society would place upon it. Accordingly, the structure of the story is left open; the conclusion is deliberately inconclusive.

Frank Baldanza, who has made the most direct attack so far on the problem of structure in *Huck Finn*, believes that the basic principle can be defined as rhythmic repetition, with variation and development, of many thematic motifs, which have the effect of stitching the book together internally. He further suggests that each recurrence "was impulsive on Twain's part, and that any pattern we find in the repetitions is either unconsciously or accidentally ordained."[13] My analysis would seem to bear out the observation that rhythmic, varied, and developmental repetition is important. It is not basic to the structure, but it certainly does support it and supply it with a texture of rich and complex harmony. However, this effect is not and cannot possibly be accidental; it fits too well with the larger thematic repetition of Huck's decision. And I suspect very strongly too that Clemens must have been aware of it, in some way, as being appropriate to the pattern of the work he meant to make. A close examination will show that the motifs most often repeated are those most intimately concerned with the aristocracy-slavery-sentimentalism relationship. Moreover the variations add up to a steady intensification of Huck's and the reader's awareness of the injustice, the hypocrisy, and the general moral ugliness and weakness of Southern society before the war. This intensification provides the milieu and the measure of Huck's development through the death-and-rebirth pattern from irresponsible boyhood to moral maturity.

The total result of these thematic, structural, and symbolic work-

13. Baldanza, p. 353.

ings is a novel which has a remarkably high degree of consistency, coherence, and unity. Its theme is the growth of an individual personality. Its crisis is the moral decision, repeated three times, to repudiate the conventions of society and do the individually, humanly right thing. Its rising interest is given by the sharply increasing complexity of the individual awareness of the implications of such an action. Its structure is defined by the extinction of the old childish organization of mind and feelings, the symbolic death of the individual as he was, his withdrawal from society into nature, and his reconstitution, or symbolic rebirth, on a higher and more mature level of organization, as a better, more capable person. The theme and structure are concretely embodied and related in the texture, which reinforces both with a rhythmically repeated and varied pattern of appropriate motifs and images. The functional, organic interrelations of all these factors must have something to do with the effect of unity which readers generally feel in *Huckleberry Finn*, but which we are now only beginning to understand and be able to explain.

THOMAS ARTHUR GULLASON

The "Fatal" Ending of *Huckleberry Finn*†

Some recent critics have made attempts to discredit *Huckleberry Finn* by pointing to its final episode—where Tom Sawyer reappears and masterminds Jim's escape from prison. They have called this episode "irrelevant,"[1] a "flimsy" contrivance,[2] "a serious anti-climax."[3] Only T. S. Eliot and Lionel Trilling have tried to defend the pattern of the novel. Both present weak arguments. Eliot feels the end of the book rounds off the story and brings the reader back to the level of the childish, boyish beginning,[4] while Trilling sees the close of the novel as a device which permits Huck to fall back into the anonymity he prefers.[5]

I suggest that Mark Twain had a very definite plan in the final episode which depends on repetitions and variations of themes presented earlier in the novel.[6] His primary objective in the "fatal"

† From *American Literature*, XXIX (March 1957), 86–91.
1. Philip Young, *Hemingway* (New York, 1952), pp. 200–201.
2. Leo Marx, "Mr. Eliot, Mr. Trilling and *Huckleberry Finn*," *American Scholar*, XXII, 426, 430 (Autumn, 1953).
3. William Van O'Connor, "Why *Huckleberry Finn* Is Not The Great American Novel," *College English*, XVII, 6 (Oct., 1955).
4. Marx, *op. cit.*, pp. 424, 433–434.

5. *Huckleberry Finn*, ed. Lionel Trilling (New York, 1952), pp. xv–xvi. All later references to the novel are to this edition.
6. Frank Baldanza, "The Structure of *Huckleberry Finn*," *American Literature*, XXVII, 347–355 (Nov., 1955). Mr. Baldanza refers to "repetition plus variation" in the novel, but he does not attempt to show how this necessary rhythm makes the ending relevant.

last chapters is to ridicule, in the manner of *Don Quixote*, the romantic tradition as exemplified by Tom Sawyer, who lacks character, who is full of purposeless fun; and to win final sympathy for the realistic tradition and its hero, Huck, who has achieved a sense of responsibility and a meaningful vision of life. In *Life on the Mississippi* (1883), Twain had already suggested his deep concern with the unwholesome effects of romanticism:

"A curious exemplification of the power of a single book for good or harm is shown in the effects wrought by *Don Quixote* and those wrought by *Ivanhoe*. The first swept the world's admiration for the medieval chivalry silliness out of existence; and the other restored it. As far as our South is concerned, the good work done by Cervantes is pretty nearly a dead letter, so effectually has Scott's pernicious work undermined it."[7]

With *Huckleberry Finn*, Twain tries to "kill" romanticism. He suggests this obliquely by recording the fate of two ships prior to the last episode of the novel: the *Lally Rook* (a reference to Thomas Moore's romantic poem, *Lalla Rookh*) blows up (p. 222), and the *Walter Scott* becomes a "wreck" (p. 73).

There are other objectives in the last chapters. Besides ridiculing Tom's romantic vision, Twain neatly finishes off with other dominant themes dealt with in previous episodes: man's inhumanity to man, and Huck's faith in Jim's humanity.

To understand the romantic-realistic dilemma clearly, one needs to pick up an important thread in Chapter II, where Tom Sawyer convinces his gang that they are bold highwaymen—he wants to be in romantic "style"—and not common burglars. In Chapter III, Tom, who is influenced by the romantic novels he has read, sees turnips as "julery," hogs as ingots, and a picnic as enemy warriors. While this is all harmless fun, the realistic Huck argues with his own conscience: "So then I judged that all that stuff was only just one of Tom Sawyer's lies. I reckoned he believed in the A-rabs and the elephants, but as for me I think different. It had all the marks of a Sunday-school" (p. 14).

This theme, made so much of in the first chapters, is reintroduced in Chapter XXXIII, just prior to the final episode. Here Huck learns that Tom will actively support him in a liberal cause—leading Jim to freedom. Huck does not know that Jim has already been made free by Miss Watson; only Tom knows, and he withholds this information so that he can have another romantic adventure. The unsuspecting Huck reveals surprise at his conservative friend's promise: "It was the most astonishing speech I ever heard—and I'm bound to say Tom Sawyer fell considerable in my estimation. Only I couldn't believe it. Tom Sawyer a nigger-stealer!"

7. *Life on the Mississippi* (New York, 1917), pp. 377–378.

(p. 226).

In Chapter XXXIV, this theme is developed further. Reassured that Tom will become a "nigger-stealer," Huck innocently sets up what could be termed the irony of anticipation; for Tom and the "folks at home" will lose character—and Huck will gain more of it—in the last chapters. Huck says:

"Well, one thing was dead sure, and that was that Tom Sawyer was in earnest, and was actuly going to help steal that nigger out of slavery. That was the thing that was too many for me. Here was a boy that was respectable and well brung up; and had a character to lose; and folks at home that had characters; and he was bright and not leather-headed; and knowing and not ignorant; and not mean, but kind. . . ." (p. 234)

Only because of a complete faith in Tom's "serious" promise Huck remains the lieutenant that he was in the first chapters of the story and helps his leader in tireless, extravagant preparations (reminiscent of Scott's improbabilities) for Jim's escape from prison. Among other things, they prepare a rope ladder, a journal, and a coat of arms. Still, one becomes aware of an important change in Huck's attitude toward Tom.

For with Chapter XXXIV, Huck is no longer the lieutenant who blindly submits to his leader's romantic schemes—which are not harmless ones now because Jim's life is at stake. For every exaggerated plan Tom proposes in the final episode (each one proves he is sinning against Jim), Huck comes up with a practical one in such a way that the reader realizes that he is challenging Tom's previously unquestioned authority. This is evident when Tom plans Jim's escape. First, Tom says: "I wish there was a moat to this cabin. If we get time, the night of the escape, we'll dig one." Huck replies: "What do we want of a moat when we're going to snake him out from under the cabin?" They continue on in this way as Huck reports the conversation:

" 'No, it wouldn't do—there ain't necessity enough for it.'
" 'For what?' I says.
" 'Why, to saw Jim's leg off,' he says.
" 'Good land!' I says; 'why, there ain't no necessity for it. And what would you want to saw his leg off for, anyway?'
". . . 'But there's one thing—he can have a rope ladder. . . .'
". . . 'Why, Tom Sawyer, how you talk,' I says; 'Jim ain't got no use for a rope ladder." (pp. 240–241)

In this scene, Huck clearly demonstrates the childishness and impracticability of Tom's romantic view, and, as a sharp contrast, the practicality of his realistic view. And though he momentarily says that Tom's head is getting "leveler," Huck openly criticizes the "authorities" (the romantic books of the past) which Tom has depended upon since Chapter II as his code of conduct:

"When I start in to steal a nigger or a watermelon, or a Sunday-school book, I ain't no ways particular how it's done so it's done. What I want is my nigger; or what I want is my watermelon; or what I want is my Sunday-school book; and if a pick's the handiest thing, that's the thing I'm a-going to dig that nigger or that watermelon or that Sunday-school book out with; and I don't give a dead rat what the authorities think about it nuther." (p. 247)

This romantic-realistic quarrel is part of Mark Twain's conscious plot against the real antagonist of the novel, Tom Sawyer. He returns at the end because, like Huck, he is a major character who needs to be set in a final position. The story has come a long way. It is not the child's tale that it was in the beginning where Tom played the leader of the gang. Tom remains the child of the first chapters and, try as he may, he cannot pass himself off as the hero in the last episode because he toys inhumanly with Jim. His life has been a continuous lie, and it is this final harmful lie in a serious adult situation—after all, Tom himself is wounded when Jim does escape—that epitomizes his romantic nonsense.

Huck, on the other hand, by involving himself in the Shepherdson-Grangerford feud, by serving the whims of the treacherous Duke and Dauphin, by watching Colonel Sherburn kill a man, has developed before the last episode a soberer insight into man's inhumanity to man, into life as it is. He is no longer the prankster, who in an early chapter planted a dead rattlesnake next to Jim merely to amuse himself (p. 52). In the last episode he is the educated, morally responsible person. Therefore, he *is* concerned when he learns that Tom plotted Jim's escape to freedom only for the "adventure" of it (p. 289). Certainly Jim's plight was not a game to the serious-minded Huck, and though he does not openly condemn Tom for his romantic foolishness, he becomes the "innocent" ironist (where the author intrudes and speaks through his hero—a favorite device of Twain's) who intimates that Tom had a bad "bringing-up": . . . "so, sure enough, Tom Sawyer had gone and took all that trouble and bother to set a free nigger free! and I couldn't ever understand before, until that minute and that talk, how he *could* help a body set a nigger free with his bringing-up" (p. 290).

Even Tom's society carries on a theme—man's inhumanity to man—to its logical conclusion. The last working out of this theme occurred when the Duke and Dauphin tried to dupe the Wilks family out of their money. In Chapter XLII, Huck listens to Tom's adult world agree that Jim was "white" for having nursed the wounded Tom instead of escaping to freedom. Then one of these admirers suddenly speaks of Jim as something less than a human being: "I liked that nigger for that; I tell you, gentlemen, a nigger like that is worth a thousand dollars—and kind treatment, too" (p. 285). Huck quickly sees the irony of the situation. He observes that these same adults, who treated Jim like a hero, "come out and locked him up" (p. 286). These hypocrites, Tom included, are more than partially responsible for Huck's final decision to "light out for the territory," to leave an inhuman civilization (p. 293).

The last episode has still another purpose. It resolves Huck's greatest problem—the question of a slave's humanity. Before this, Huck had not been fully convinced that he was justified in being an Abolitionist and that society was wrong in its attitude. In Chapter XVI, Huck reveals his uncertainty: "Give a nigger an inch and he'll take an ell" (p. 88). In Chapter XXXI, he decides to free Jim, yet he knows that he is wicked—a sinner against Tom's society; he says: "All right, then, I'll *go* to hell . . ." (p. 214). In the last episode he no longer feels evil because he is overwhelmed by Jim's nobility. He listens eagerly as Jim explains why he stayed behind to nurse Tom when he could have escaped to freedom:

" 'Well, den, dis is de way it look to me, Huck. Ef it wuz *him* [Tom] dat 'uz bein' sot free, en one er de boys wuz to git shot, would he say, "Go on en save me, nemmine 'bout a doctor f'r to save dis one"? Is dat like Mars Tom Sawyer? Would he say dat? You *bet* he wouldn't! Well, den, is Jim gwyne to say it?' " (pp. 275–276)

All that Huck can say to Jim's reasoning is: "I knowed he was white inside. . . ."

This entire episode, based on Tom's lie, cannot be considered fatal because Huck settles conflicts presented earlier in the novel. Important themes, which are repeated and varied, furnish the key. It is only in the last chapters that Huck completely rejects both Tom's romantic irresponsibility (which he first suspected in Chapter II) and society's cruel nature. It is only here that he understands Jim's true worth, after battling his conscience through many chapters. Finally, it is the honest and humble way in which he faces and then resolves each of the above-mentioned conflicts that shows Huck's developing strength of character—and this makes him the hero of the novel.

[Gullason's article is the final essay of "Critics' Debate: Symbolism vs. Structure"]

JOSEPH WOOD KRUTCH

[Huckleberry Finn: "A Bad Novel"]†

This spring a great many people must have been reading *Huckle-berry Finn* at the same moments I was. How many of them, I wonder, were reminded again how conclusively it proves that a great work of fiction does not need to be what is called a "good novel" or, indeed, a merely "good" anything else.

In his recent *A Writer's Notebook* Somerset Maugham commented briefly on the fact that all of the novelists whom he would be willing to call great without reservation—especially Balzac, Dickens, Tolstoy and Dostoevsky—wrote their language rather badly, at least in the limited sense that they did not very often achieve either the polish or the adroitness which constitutes the excellence of many lesser writers. He might have gone on to point out that many of the very greatest novels exhibit also glaring imperfections which go far beyond a mere lack of verbal felicity. Not a few of them, perhaps even most of them, are what a disciple of Flaubert or of Henry James would call "bad novels," no matter how interesting or impressive they may be.

In the case of *Huckleberry Finn* the "badness" is not a matter of carelessly inelegant sentences. In this respect the book is actually extremely "well written" because Mark Twain seems to have polished his style until he achieved precisely that effect of colloquial semi-literacy at which he was aiming. But everybody knows that it is also and unintentionally "a bad novel" in certain fundamental respects. Much of it is so improbable as to become at times wholly unconvincing on one level of understanding. It is also episodic, clumsily plotted, and sometimes as crudely melodramatic as a dime novel. One could reasonably argue that, as a whole, it is a botched job just as, in another way, the whole last quarter of *Life on the Mississippi* is botched. But both books are also uniquely delightful and never to be forgotten by anyone who has ever read either.

When Huck explains a mysterious absence by inventing a wonderfully complicated case of the mumps involving symptoms hitherto unknown to medical history, or when he describes the collection of lachrymose crayons and assorted elegiac verses left behind by a departed maiden, the pages are howlingly comic on several different levels from that of pure farce to high intellectual

† From "Speaking of Books," published in *The New York Times Book Review,* May 23, 1954, p. 2. By permission of the author and *The New York Times Book Review.*

comedy. Obviously Mark had been visited by that same wise counselor who advised Cervantes three hundred years before how he should write so that the simple would be entertained while the wise were finding something which the simple had missed. But the best episodes will not make a "bad novel" into a great book. Some largeness of plan is also necessary.

That largeness of plan *Huckleberry Finn* does have. The whole conception of the journey down the river remains in the mind like the large conception of an epic, and it justifies an interpretation of the book in epic terms which might have surprised the author. The river journey is as unforgettable as the March of the Ten Thousand or as the wanderings of Ulysses. By comparison with that fact the badness of the plotting or the "unconvincing" aspects of the episodes is as irrelevant as the "unconvincing" aspects of the story of the Cyclops.

Once a certain degree of imaginative intensity has been reached we lose all concern with what is ordinarily called "realism." The question whether or not something is "probable" or "convincing" becomes mere fiddle-faddle. One no longer needs to be convinced; one simply knows. Huck floated down the river as indubitably as Hamlet saw a ghost or the Greeks hid in a wooden horse.

Even the intellectual, even the sociological, points are made so much the better because Mark Twain scorns the careful "realism" of the problem novelist. Huck's incredulity in face of the fact that Nigger Jim is as grief-stricken by a personal loss as a white man would have been, his remark that "it doesn't seem natural that he should be," is worth, artistically at least, not only all of *Uncle Tom's Cabin* but also the complete corpus of recent novels about "prejudice." Such a passage is like certain ones in *The Merchant of Venice*. "If a jew is cut does he not bleed?"

Not all the "bad novels" which are also great books are such because they are really not novels at all but epics. There are other good things which "bad novels" may sometimes be—romances, poems, even autobiographies. Perhaps nothing except great energy of some sort is absolutely indispensable. Balzac once declared that "the important point was not to avoid mistakes but to have a quality that sweeps everything in front of it." In the case of *Huckleberry Finn* this quality is essentially epic. And there are ways in which an epic is better than even a "good" novel.

Critics' Debate:
How Great?

In 1955 a debate was staged in the pages of the journal *College English* between Professor Lauriat Lane, Jr., who contended that *Huckleberry Finn* was a great *world* novel, and Professor William Van O'Connor, who denied that it was even the great *American* novel. In subsequent issues of the journal other critics entered the debate with commentaries, letters to the editor, and full-length essays of their own. The articles that opened the debate and two of the rebuttals are included in this section.

LAURIAT LANE, JR.

Why *Huckleberry Finn* Is a Great World Novel†

Of all forms of literature, the novel is in many ways the hardest to describe with any precision. Its relative newness as a form and its varied and complex nature combine to make this so. Whenever we try to view such a full and living book as *The Adventures of Huckleberry Finn*, some of it always escapes our gaze. In fact, apart from its mere physical presence, paper, ink, glue, covers, and so forth, it is often easiest to assume that the novel does not exist at all, but only the experience of reading it. Each time we read *Huckleberry Finn* we read a certain book, and each time we read it we read a different book. No one of these books is the real *Huckleberry Finn*; in a sense, they all are.

At the heart of *Huckleberry Finn* lies a story about real human figures with genuine moral and ethical problems and decisions, figures placed in a society which we recognize as having everywhere in it the flavor of authenticity—the whole combination treated, for the most part, as directly and realistically as possible. I would like to move beyond this primary description or definition of *Huckleberry Finn*, however, and suggest that the novel may contain other elements equally important to a full appreciation. I would like to

† From *College English*, XVII (October 1955), 1–5. By permission of the author and *College English*.

extend the novel in three directions, in space, in time, and in degree: in space, by considering some of the ways in which the book extends beyond its position as one of the masterworks of American fiction and becomes, if the term be allowed, a world novel; in time, by considering how much *Huckleberry Finn* resembles a literary form much older than the novel, the epic poem; and in degree, by considering just how much *Huckleberry Finn* transcends its position as a realistic novel and takes on the forms and qualities of allegory.

I

A world novel may be defined as that kind of novel whose importance in its own literature is so great, and whose impact on its readers is so profound and far-reaching, that it has achieved worldwide distinction. In the total picture of world literature, such a novel stands out as a work always to be reckoned with. The world novel, however, achieves its position not only through its importance but also because of its essential nature. And in discussing *Huckleberry Finn* as a world novel I shall deal not so much with this importance, as measured by permanent popularity and influence, as with the special qualities *Huckleberry Finn* has in common with certain other world novels.

The first real novel and the first world novel is, by almost universal consent, Cervantes' *The Adventures of Don Quixote*. The most important thing which *Don Quixote* has bequeathed to the novels after it (apart of course from the all-important fact of there being such a thing as a novel at all) is the theme which is central to *Don Quixote* and to almost every great novel since, the theme of appearance versus reality. This theme is also central to *Huckleberry Finn*.

Even on the simplest plot level the world of *Huckleberry Finn* is one of deception. The very existence of Huck at all is a continual deception—he is supposed to be dead. This falseness in his relations with the world at large merely reflects the difference between his standards and those of the outside world. Huck's truth and the truth of the world are diametrically opposed. Throughout the novel his truth is always cutting through the surfaces of the world's appearance and learning the contrary reality beneath. At the climax Huck tells himself, "You can't pray a lie—I found that out." That is to say, the lie of appearance is always far different from the truth of reality, and to the truly heroic and individual conscience no amount of self-delusion can ever bridge the gap lying between.

In the final section of the book, the theme of appearance versus reality reaches almost philosophical proportions. Both because of the way in which Jim's escape is carried out and because of the underlying fact of there being no need for him to escape at all, the situation is one of total dramatic and moral irony. At the end, however, Twain relaxes the tone, straightens out the plot complications, and lets the moral issue fade away. He avoids, in fact, the logical conclusion to the kind of disorder he has introduced into his world-in-fiction, a world in which the distinction between appearance and reality has, from the reader's point of view, been lost forever. For if we cannot tell appearance from reality, if the two do become totally confused and impossible to distinguish, the only answer can be the one Twain eventually came to in his most pessimistic work, *The Mysterious Stranger;* that all is illusion, and nothing really exists. In *Huckleberry Finn,* Twain does not yet reach this point of despair. By centering his action within the essentially balanced mind of the boy, Huck, he keeps his hold on reality and manages to convey this hold to the reader. But the main issue of the novel, between the way things seem and the way they are, is nevertheless one that trembles in the balance almost up to the final page.

Huckleberry Finn also gains its place as a world novel by its treatment of one of the most important events of life, the passage from youth into maturity. The novel is a novel of education. Its school is the school of life rather than of books, but Huck's education is all the more complete for that reason. Huck, like so many other great heroes of fiction—Candide, Tom Jones, Stephen Dedalus, to mention only a few—goes forth into life that he may learn. One of the central patterns of the novel is the progress of his learning.

Yet another theme which *Huckleberry Finn* shares with most of the world's great novels is that of man's obsession with the symbols of material wealth. The book opens with an account of the six thousand dollars Huck got from the robbers' hoard and ends on the same note. Throughout the intervening pages gold is shown to be not only the mainspring of most human action, but usually the only remedy mankind can offer to atone for the many hurts they are forever inflicting on one another. And as Mr. Lionel Trilling has remarked, in a certain sense all fiction is ultimately about money.

The world novel may also convey a total vision of the nation or people from which it takes its origin. It not only addresses the world in a language which is uniquely the language of that nation or people, but it brings before the view of the world at large many character types which are especially national. In *Huckleberry Finn* we recognize in Jim, in the Duke and the Dauphin, in Aunt Sally, and in Huck himself, typically American figures whom Twain has presented for inspection by the world's eye. *Huckleberry Finn* gains much of its justification as a world novel from the fact that it is an intensely American novel as well.

II

In his essay on "The Poetic Principle" Poe remarks that "no very long poem will ever be popular again." In part, no doubt, Poe bases this remark on his own special definition of poetry. But he is also recognizing that during the eighteenth and nineteenth centuries the epic poem was gradually dying out as a literary form. Or, to be more precise, it was gradually merging with another form, the novel. Much of the poetic form of the epic came from the requirements of oral rendition; with the invention of printing, these requirements vanished. More and more writers gradually turned to prose fiction as the appropriate form to accomplish what had once been accomplished in the epic poem. Some novelists, such as Fielding or Scott, drew quite consciously on epic tradition; other novelists and novels, by a more indirect drawing on tradition, took over some of the qualities originally associated with epic poetry.

One quality of the epic poem is simply scope. Some novels confine themselves to treating exhaustively and analytically a limited segment of life. But others seem to be constantly trying to gather all life into their pages and to say, within a single story, all the important things that need to be said. Such novels derive much of their strength from the epic tradition, and *Huckleberry Finn* is such a novel. It has geographical scope. It ranges down the length of the great river and cuts through the center of a whole nation. As it does so, it gains further scope by embracing all levels of society, from the lowest to the highest. And it has the added scope of its own varying qualities, ranging from high comedy to low farce, from the poetic tranquility of life on the raft to the mob violence and human depravity always waiting on the shore.

Epic poetry gives literary form to the national destiny of the people for whom it is written. *Huckleberry Finn* gives literary form to many aspects of the national destiny of the American people. The theme of travel and adventure is characteristically American, and in Twain's day it was still a reality of everyday life. The country was still very much on the move, and during the novel Huck is moving with it. Huck's movements also embody a desire to escape from the constrictions of civilized society. Such a desire is of course not uniquely American, but during the nineteenth century Americans took it and made it their own. The American of that time could always say, as did Huck at the very end of the story, "I reckon I got to light out for the territory ahead of the rest, because Aunt Sally she's going to adopt me and sivilize me, and I can't stand it. I been there before." Another specially American theme is that of the Negro, and Huck is faced with this problem throughout the story. Starting with the typically American prejudices and easy generalizations about Jim, he is gradually shocked into an increasingly complex awareness of Jim as a human being. And although Huck's relations with Jim do not so much embody a national attitude as suggest how the nation may purge itself of one, the theme of the Negro is still one which achieves epic stature in *Huckleberry Finn*.

The epic hero is usually an embodiment of some virtue or virtues valued highly by the society from which he has sprung. Huck has many such virtues. He holds a vast store of practical knowledge which makes itself felt everywhere in the story. He knows the river and how to deal with it; and he knows mankind and how to deal with it. And he has the supreme American virtue of never being at a loss for words. In fact Huck, though he still keeps some of the innocence and naïveté of youth, has much in common with one of the greatest of epic heroes, Odysseus, the practical man. Jim also has some of the qualities of an epic hero. He has strength and courage, and he possesses the supreme virtue of epic poetry, loyalty. It is part of Twain's irony that in Huck and Jim we have, in one sense, the two halves of an epic hero. In Huck, the skill and canniness; in Jim, the strength and simple loyalty.

In the society along the shore we see traces of other epic values, values which have survived from a more primitive world. The Grangerford-Shepherdson feud strikes the modern reader as a senseless mess, but as Huck says, "There ain't a coward amongst them Shepherdsons—not a one. And there ain't no cowards amongst the Grangerfords either." Huck sees the essential folly behind this courage, but the reader, one degree further removed from the harsh reality, is allowed the luxury of a double vision. Similarly, Colonel Sherburn, destroying a lynching mob merely by the courage of his presence, illustrates another epic theme, the bravery of one against many.

One final quality which *Huckleberry Finn* derives from its epic ancestry is its poetry. The novel is full of poetry. Not just the passages of lyric description, which mark a pause between the main actions and give a heightened and more literary tone just as they often did in the traditional epic, but also the many similes and turns of speech Huck uses, which, if they are not quite Homeric, are certainly unforgettable. And much of the exaggerated language of the frontier world, one not far removed in kind from that of the primitive migrations, is also a natural part of the epic style.

III

Allegory may be defined simply as the representation of one thing in the form of another. A second definition, more germane to literature, is that allegory is a process by which the spiritual is embodied in the physical. To go one step further, the main purpose of allegory is somehow to embody a spiritual action in a physical action. By making a suitable physical object stand for some metaphysical one, or at least for one which cannot be contained in the terms of normal, everyday life, the writer carries out one of the main purposes of all art, which is to bring to its audience, through the representation of real objects, an awareness and knowledge which transcend the limitations of such reality. Allegory, that is, deals primarily with matters of the spirit.

This assumption helps to explain why the great allegories deal either with a physical journey or a physical conflict or both. For a spiritual change, when embodied allegorically, will take the form of a meaningful physical journey through symbolic space. And a spiritual conflict, when embodied allegorically, will take the form of a real physical conflict between significant forces, each of them representing some metaphysical quality.

Although all novels are in a certain sense descended from *Don Quixote*, it is also true that in another sense all novels, and especially English ones, are descended from Bunyan's *Pilgrim's Progress*. The main difference between the allegorical novel as we know it today and Bunyan's narrative of the human soul is that whereas in *Pilgrim's Progress* we have an allegory that tends to turn into a novel, in most modern instances we have a novel that tends to turn into an allegory. As the author, whether he be Melville or Mann or Twain, develops and elaborates his original materials, he may become aware of certain meaningful connections which are tending to establish themselves between the physical objects and the physical narrative he is describing and the related spiritual values and conflicts. Drawing on a tradition which has existed for a long time in literature and which is a natural part of the artistic process in any form, the author finds himself writing allegory. And this is what happened to Mark Twain. Writing as he was a great novel, his masterpiece in fact, he organized and related certain physical materials to certain metaphysical conditions so that their relationship became meaningful in a special way—became, in short, allegory.

Huckleberry Finn is the story of a journey, a real journey. If we are to find any meaning in Huck's journey beyond the literal level, we must seek it first in the medium through which Huck journeys, in the great river down which he drifts during much of the story. And Huck's movements take on at least the external form of a basic symbolic pattern, one seen in such poems as Shelley's *Alastor*, Arnold's *The Future*, and Rimbaud's *Bateau Ivre*, a pattern stated most directly in *Prometheus Unbound*, "My soul is an enchanted boat." Implicit in this pattern is the suggestion that the river journey can have a distinctly metaphysical quality, that it can be, in fact, a journey of the soul as well as of the body. This suggestion is not at all arbitrary. Of all forms of physical progression, that of drifting downstream in a boat, or on a raft, is the most passive one possible. The mind under such conditions is lulled, as Huck's mind is, into the illusion that it has lost all contact with reality and is drifting bodilessly through a world of sleep and of dreams. Thus the nakedness of Huck and Jim when they are alone on the raft becomes a symbol of how they have shucked off the excrescences of the real world, their clothes, and have come as close as possible to the world of the spirit.

All journeys, even allegorical ones, must have a goal. What is the goal of Huck's journey? We find the answer in what happens while Huck and Jim float down the river. The pattern is, very simply, one of an ever-increasing engagement of the world of the raft, of the spirit, with the world of the shore, of reality. As the book progresses, more and more Huck tells about events that take place on the banks, and less and less he tells about those that take place out on the river. No matter how hard Huck and Jim try to escape, the real world is always drawing them back into it. Finally, in the Duke and the Dauphin, themselves fleeing for the moment from the harsh reality of the river's shores, the real world invades the world of the raft, and the latter loses forever the dream-like and idyllic quality it has often had for the two voyagers. The climax of Huck's lyric praise of the river comes significantly just before this mood is shattered forever by the arrival of the Duke and the Dauphin.

Parallel to this pattern of the ever-increasing engagement of the world of the shore with that of the raft is a pattern which begins with Huck's pretended death, a death which is actual to all the world but Huck and Jim. The symbolic fact of his death accomplished, Huck must find an identity with which he can face the real world. His assumption of various such identities forms a significant pattern. The various masks he assumes, starting with that of a girl, as far removed from the reality as possible, gradually draw back nearer the truth. Huck's final disguise, as Tom Sawyer, is only slightly removed from his real self. When he is about to reveal this real self and is instead taken for Tom, Huck almost recognizes the meaning of his journey. For he says to himself, "But if they was joyful, it warn't nothing to what I was; for it was like being born again, I was so glad to find out who I was."

This, then, is the allegory of *Huckleberry Finn*. Dying symbolically almost at the opening of the novel, Huck journeys through the world of the spirit, ever working out a pattern of increasing involvement with the world of reality and with his own self, both cast aside at the beginning of the journey. Only when he is finally forced to assume this real self in the eyes of the world, through the sudden arrival of *Aunt Polly*, is he allowed to learn the all-important truth Jim has kept from him throughout the novel, that his Pap "ain't comin back no mo." We cannot say that Huck has undergone a total initiation and is now fully prepared to take on adulthood, but neither can we doubt that he has undergone a knowledgeful and maturing experience. And at the end of the story he is about to undertake another journey, this time to the west, in search of further experience and further knowledge.

WILLIAM VAN O'CONNOR

Why *Huckleberry Finn* Is Not the Great American Novel†

From the late nineteenth century to World War I, and even after, there was much discussion of the great American novel. Eventually the idea died, apparently of its own inanity. But in recent years the idea, though not the phrase, has returned to life, for we are informed, from a variety of critical positions, that *The Adventures of Huckleberry Finn* is the truly American novel.

A novel wants to be circumscribed to live in its own terms, to fulfill itself imaginatively. On the other hand, it speaks to a people and to their beliefs about themselves. Huck is said to live for us somewhat as Roland lives for France or Arthur for England. If Huck is firmly enshrined in myth it would be futile to try to dislodge him. But his place in an American myth would not of itself be assurance that *Huckleberry Finn* is a great novel.

The following observations maintain that the book owes much of its eminence to our mythologizing of the West and, further, that the claims made for it as a source book for all later "American" fiction is not a valid claim. In making such observations it is helpful to refer to the introductions of *Huckleberry Finn* written by T. S. Eliot and Lionel Trilling. It is also necessary, on occasion, to disagree with them. Mr. Eliot reads it—Twain's only masterpiece he says—as the story of the Boy and the River, the former being the unconscious or all but unconscious critic of civilization, its pursuits, wickedness, and vagaries, and the latter the symbol of time that is timeless and of human affairs carried downstream, often capriciously. Lionel Trilling also writes of the unblinking honesty of the boy Huck, and of the river as a god. He finds it a central American document and one of the world's great books.

Both Eliot and Trilling suggest that there is only one flaw, and this not a very serious one, to be charged against the structure of the book: the overly elaborate scheme for Jim's escape engineered by Tom Sawyer in the closing section of the story. Trilling does say the episode is far too long but, like Eliot, he justifies it as a way

† From *College English*, XVII (October 1955), 6–10. By permission of the author and *College English*.

of returning the reader to civilization, and of freeing Huck, allowing him to disappear. The Tom Sawyer episode is certainly a method for bringing off the dénouement, but involved with it is a serious anti-climax. Miss Watson's will had already freed Jim, and all the high-jinks and genuine danger have been merely to satisfy Tom's desire to keep things hopping. Tom is the Practical Joker of American literature and Twain has a streak of it himself, which interferes with his true sense of comedy.

I

The critical acumen of Eliot and Trilling notwithstanding, there are a number of flaws in *Huckleberry Finn*, some of them attributable to Twain's refusal to respect the "work of art" and others attributable to his imperfect sense of tone. The downstream movement of the story (theme as well as action) runs counter to Jim's effort to escape. Life on the raft may indeed be read as implied criticism of civilization—but it doesn't get Jim any closer to freedom. One may also ask (it has been asked before) why it never occurred to Jim, or to Huck, to strike out for the Illinois shore and freedom. It is possible that Twain felt Tom's highjinks were necessary not merely to prepare for the disappearance of Huck but to shift attention away from his conflicting themes.

For the downward movement of the novel, of course, the picaresque form serves its subject very well, allowing for innumerable and rapid adventures, afloat and ashore, and for the sort of ponderings that are peculiar to Huck. The picaresque form is also a clue to the kind of unity the book does have, a melodramatic mixture of reality and unreality and of comedy and horror. It is frequently theatrical in a good sense of the word. But the unity depends on Huck's mind, and too often there are bits of action, dialogue, and observation which are not appropriate to him. There are two sorts of theatricality in the novel, melodrama and claptrap.

Huck's relationship with his father is melodrama. So is the shooting of Boggs, or the tar and feathering of the Duke and King. A proof of their being melodrama is the ease with which one moves from a scene of violence to a humorous dialogue. For example, the encounter of Huck and Jim with the thieves and murderers aboard the *Walter Scott* is followed by the minstrel show, end-men sort of humor of "Was Solomon Wise?" Verisimilitude offers no problem when reality merges with unreality or horror dissolves innocently into comedy, but sometimes Twain's sense of proper distance, the degree and nature of the stylization he is employing, fails him and the action becomes gruesomely real. An instance of this is Huck's telling of the murders in "Why Harney Rode Away for His Hat." The starkness is too unrelieved. The scene does not respect the premises nor the general tone of the novel, and, even though it might work in another novel, it does not work here.

A good deal is made, quite justly, of Huck's affection for Jim, and the example commonly given is Huck's apology to Jim after having tormented him with a lie about there having been no storm. "It was fifteen minutes," Huck says, "before I could work myself up to go and humble myself to a nigger, but I done it, and I warn't sorry for it afterwards neither." But Twain sometimes loses sight of Huck's moral sensitivity. An instance is in Chapters XVII and XVIII.

Near the close of Chapter XVI the raft is run over by an upstream steamboat. In the darkness, after he and Jim have dived into the water, Huck cannot see Jim and his calls go unanswered. Huck then strikes out for shore. The following chapter, "The Grangerfords Take Me In," is a humorous introduction to the Grangerford family. Huck stays with the Grangerfords for many days, perhaps weeks, getting involved in their affairs, notably as courier between the lovers Miss Sophia Grangerford and Harney Shepherdson. No thought about Jim enters Huck's head! It doesn't occur to him to search for the old Negro. Jack, Huck's "nigger servant," finally invites him to see a "stack o' water-moccasins" in a swamp, a trick for leading him to the spot where Jim is hiding. "I poked into the place a ways and come to a little open patch as big as a bedroom all hung round with vines, and found a man lying there asleep—and, by jingo, it was my old Jim!" There is not much indication that Huck is greatly relieved or moved at finding Jim alive: "I waked him up, and I reckoned it was going to be a grand surprise to him to see me again. . . . He nearly cried he was so glad. . . ." Huck says nothing about being glad himself. Perhaps we are to read this passage ironically, as an instance of a boy's self-centeredness and believe that true affection lies beneath it. This might be so, but it doesn't explain away Huck's absence of grief over Jim's "death," or his failure to search for him if alive, or his general indifference to Jim's fate.

Technically, too, the device for getting rid of Jim so that Huck can move into the Grangerford-Shepherdson world is awkward and unconvincing. Jim tells Huck he had heard him call for him when they were swimming toward shore but hadn't answered for fear of being detected. Presumably one reply would have quieted Huck and made detection much less likely. And if Huck had been allowed to help Jim hide, or even to maintain some awareness of him, he would be the Huck known to us in "Fooling Old Jim."

Huck's parody (Chapter XVII) of the activities of Emmeline Grangerford, poetess, is extremely amusing, but the "voice" is more nearly Twain's than Huck's. Many other things are put into the mouth of the twelve or thirteen year old Huck that, sometimes only weakly humorous themselves, are Twain himself speaking. This, for example, from a boy with almost no schooling:

"Look at Henry the Eight; this 'n' a Sunday-school Superintendent to *him*. And look at Charles Second, and Louis Fourteen, and Louis Fifteen, and James Second, and Edward Second, and Richard Third, and forty more; besides all them Saxon heptarchies that used to rip around so in oldtimes and raise Cain. . . ."

There are other witticisms about kings, a theme appropriate enough to *Huckleberry Finn*, but Twain might have found some other way of introducing them. In "An Arkansas Difficulty," where Twain is giving a sense of life in a small river-town, he makes Huck relate an observation on "chawing tobacker" that one would expect to find as "filler" in a nineteenth-century newspaper or magazine. Most incongruous of all, perhaps, is Huck's account of the Duke's rendition of Hamlet's soliloquy.

A more self-conscious artist would not have allowed such discrepancies to mar the tone of his novel. The truth is that Twain, however gifted a raconteur, however much genius he had as an improviser, was not, even in *Huckleberry Finn*, a great novelist.

A glance at Twain's biography reveals attitudes that, if they were related about another "major" writer, would appear highly damaging. In *My Mark Twain* William Dean Howells reported: "He once said to me, I suppose after he had been reading some of my unsparing praise of [Jane Austen]: 'You seem to think that woman could write,' and he forbore withering me with his scorn. . . ." Howells also wrote: "I fancy his pleasure in poetry was not great, and I do not believe he cared much for the conventionally accepted masterpieces of literature." And of Henry James, whose *The Bostonians* was serialized in the same magazine with *Huckleberry Finn*, Twain said, "I would rather be damned to John Bunyan's heaven than read that."

II

Huckleberry Finn is involved with the mystique of America. The chief symbols are the Boy and the River. Huck is the break not merely with Europe but with civilization, the westward push. Self-sufficient and yet dependable, he is the proper kind of individualist. He is also youth, a rugged Peter Pan who lives eternally. Huck belongs also with Cooper's Leatherstocking and Faulkner's Ike McCaslin, symbolic figures who reject the evils of civilization. (A weakness in all of them is that they do not acknowledge the virtues of civilization or try to live, as one must, inside it.) Huck is, finally, a sentimental figure, not in himself of course, since he is a boy, but in the minds of those who unduly admire his departure for the territory.

The River, as Eliot says, is time and timelessness, "a strong brown god" with his own thoughts about the machine, the hurry and fuss of cities, the illusions and struggles that make us lie, steal, or cheat. But the River is also the Mississippi as it borders the state of Missouri, the very heart of America. If Twain helped create a mythic river, the mythic river also helped Twain find his place as a legendary writer. Having such a place, he is sometimes, by sheer association, given more: he is made into the "Lincoln of American literature."

My Mark Twain concludes with Howells' account of seeing Twain in his coffin, the face "patient with the patience I had often seen in it; something of a puzzle, a great silent dignity, an assent to what must be from the depths of a nature whose tragical seriousness broke in the laughter which the universe took for the whole of him." Howells then adds: "Longfellow, Lowell, Holmes—I knew them all and all the rest of our sages, poets, seers, critics, humorists; they were like one another and like other literary men; but Clemens was sole, incomparable, the Lincoln of our literature." Stuart Pratt Sherman in the *Cambridge History of American Literature* also compares Twain with Lincoln: "In the retrospect he looms for us with Whitman and Lincoln, recognizably his countrymen, out of the shadows of the Civil War, an unmistakable native son of an eager, westward moving people—unconventional, self-reliant, mirthful, profane, realistic, cynical, boisterous, popular, tender-hearted, touched with chivalry, and permeated to the marrow of his bones with the sentiment of a democratic society and with loyalty to American institutions."

The association of Lincoln and Twain may seem appropriate at first glance—but only at first glance. Presumably Howells meant that both men discovered their need for comedy in the pathos and tragedy of the human condition, that both men were sons of a frontier society. To a degree, then, the comparison holds. But to allow for a detailed comparison, Lincoln should have to have written novels, or Twain to have been a politician, statesman, or writer of speeches. Insofar as Lincoln the writer and Twain the writer can be compared, Lincoln is the greater. Lincoln's wit, also in a vernacular idiom, is frequently more subtle than Twain's and may be expected to be more lasting. Lincoln's ability in writing an analytical prose, flexible and closely reasoned, and his ability in writing a serious and, when the occasion required, solemn rhetoric were also greater than Twain's. The seriousness and solemnity in Twain's are of innocence betrayed, as in the concluding paragraph of *The Mysterious Stranger*. Lincoln's seriousness is that of a man dealing with the world, in its own terms when forced to, but also above it, urging it to create its destiny in ways that make for the fullest sense of achievement and dignity. If Lincoln had written novels, he would, without doubt, have been a greater novelist than Twain. His virtues include Twain's and surpass them.

III

It was in *The Green Hills of Africa* that Hemingway made his now famous assertion that "All modern American literature comes from one book by Mark Twain called *Huckleberry Finn.*" The genealogy, as commonly worked out, is as follows:

Huckle-	⎰ Crane ⎱	Hem-	Modern
berry → ⎨ Stein ⎬ →	ing- →	American
Finn	⎩ Anderson ⎭	way	fiction

Obviously there are other strands of American fiction. Writers like Willa Cather, Scott Fitzgerald, and Faulkner do not derive from Twain. Nor from Hemingway. Again, an English reader could undoubtedly point out much in the prose of Melville or Hawthorne or Poe that is "peculiarly American." In other words, several semiliterate Missouri idioms are not exclusively "pure American language." Perhaps one can say that these idioms bear the same relationship to general American English that the tall tale bears to American fiction as a whole. At any rate, the strand of language that Hemingway is concerned with is—though vigorous, vital, and concrete—unsuited to speculation or subtle distinctions.

It is interesting to compare Hemingway's prose[1] with Lincoln's in "The Gettysburg Address." In the latter, one finds not merely the simplicity and repetition of the Hemingway prose but an ennobling rhetoric; Lincoln's prose both meets the Hemingway esthetic and transcends it.

Probably it is a time and a place, with a language appropriate to them, that appeals to the followers of Twain. In a series of letters addressed to Van Wyck Brooks, Sherwood Anderson made many references to Twain, to the midwest, and to *the* book. In Brooks's introduction to the letters one reads:

"I can remember how struck I was by his [Anderson's] fresh healthy mind and his true Whitmanian feeling for comradeship, his beautiful humility, his lovely generosity, and the 'proud conscious innocence' of his nature. This was his own phrase for Mark Twain's mind at the time he was writing *Huckleberry Finn*; and it goes for Sherwood also. He was the most natural of men, as innocent as any animal or flowering tree."

This passage, in language reminiscent of Anderson's own, of Hemingway's too, but a little thin and nostalgic to have been Twain's, is obviously intended as wholly a compliment. If one wonders why

1. Perhaps the best summary of the style Hemingway admires and employs is Gertrude Stein's "How Writing is Written." There are also good discussions of it in Frederick Hoffman's *The Modern Novel in America* and in Philip Young's *Ernest Hemingway*.

an American quality, innocence, and superior writing go together, there is Anderson's reasoning on the matter: "He [Twain] belonged out here in the Middle West and was only incidentally a writer." Presumably craftsmanship, wide experience, or even thought in any complexity inhibit a truly American writer. Innocence, that strange word in American life, helps to account for Twain's place, and the place of *Huckleberry Finn*, in the hierarchy of American literature.

Innocence, to pursue the subject a little further, also helps account for the two writers who most clearly come in the wake of Twain—Anderson and Hemingway. The protagonists in Anderson's stories, as Trilling points out, are ensnared or caught: in poverty (*Marching Men*), in marriage (*Many Marriages*), by inhibitions (*Dark Laughter*). Anderson's message is that we must be "free," economically, emotionally, intellectually, but in his stories to be free is to escape. Anderson did not accept the conditions of human existence and responsibility. The child, or the boy, is his chief protagonist, and the reader watches him confront and be offended by the adult world. In "I Want to Know Why," the point of which Hemingway borrowed and improved upon, Anderson has the young protagonist use one of Huck's phrases, "It gave me the fantods." In the context of Anderson's story the phrase sounds dated and ineffectual, but it may be a clue to what Anderson was attempting, to live in the nineteenth century, or, better, in the boy's world which Huck symbolized for him.

Nick Adams, the protagonist in *In Our Time* (1925), suffers, as Philip Young points out, a trauma, or to use the more literary term, a wound, the result of the anguish and evil he has experienced. He is the first of the Hemingway heroes. As Nick Adams this hero breaks with a pious and righteous mother. As Jake Barnes in *The Sun Also Rises* he is an expatriate in more senses than one. As Lt. Henry in *A Farewell to Arms* he makes a separate peace. As Harry Morgan in *To Have and Have Not* he is an outlaw. As Robert Jordan in *For Whom the Bell Tolls* he is a soldier adventurer. As Colonel Cantwell in *Across the River and into the Trees* he conducts a private war against stupid generals. As the old man in *The Old Man and the Sea* he fights his battle alone, except for a small boy admirer. The Hemingway hero, in addition to other characteristics, refuses the compromises all civilized people make. It is not fair to say he is Huck Finn grown up—but he is in part Huck Finn. Except for an occasional tribute to humanity as one, the Hemingway hero looks at civilization and says what Huck said: "I been there before."

Beyond the Huck aspect in Hemingway is the irony that not even in the territory is there peace. In the simplest of his phrases there is a suggestion of terror. His protagonists would like to find innocence, and in a way they search for it, but they never expect to find it. And perhaps this suggests a reasonable way of viewing *Huckleberry Finn*. It appeals to our desire for a condition of innocence. The difficulty we have in conceiving what Huck might be as an adult is an indication of the limited usefulness of Huck as a symbol. If we refuse to over-value him as a symbol, we may be less inclined to over-value the novel, or to over-value the language in which it is written.

GILBERT M. RUBENSTEIN

The Moral Structure of *Huckleberry Finn*†

The greatness of *Huckleberry Finn* has always seemed so self-evident that we are distinctly surprised to find it obscured or actually denied by two articles in a recent number (October 1955) of *College English*. But perhaps it is a good thing to have our most cherished convictions examined, if only that we may more firmly realize the ground on which we stand. Beginning with an analysis of each of the aforementioned articles, the present paper will attempt to show how a more constructive evaluation may be achieved by concentrating attention upon the undeniable moral structure of the book. It is my contention that *Huckleberry Finn* should be approached simply, directly, *realistically*—precisely as Mark Twain wrote it.

I

The first article, by Mr. Lauriat Lane, Jr., does indeed pay a passing tribute to the moral realism of the book, but then "extends" it into fantastic patterns of allegory and symbolism. For example, the river journey becomes something out of Rimbaud. Huck is described as "drifting" and "passive"; the "nakedness" of the two friends becomes a symbol of their shucking off "the excrescences of the real world" and their coming "as close as possible to the world of the spirit." Now the actual facts are plain. The very last word one should use to describe Huck is "passive." He is no drifter but a plucky, lovable boy who, after painful self-examination, achieves an iron determination to help his friend Jim reach free territory. Their journey together *has* a destination, and it is not, as Lane suggests, an "escape" from "the real world"; it is rather an escape from slavery into freedom, *within* a real world which amply contains both conditions of mankind. They are bound for Cairo, Illinois, there to find passage for Jim up the Ohio River into a free land. And if they occasionally relax and enjoy the trip by swimming, loafing, or fishing,

† From *College English*, XVIII (November 1956), 72–76. By permission of the author and *College English*.

what harm is done? Their major goal is never forgotten—as witness
Jim's eager expectation of reaching Cairo and his bitter, fearful
disappointment at having overshot it during the fog. The river is
not an end but a means to an end. It has no "basic symbolic pattern" beyond the general connotation of freedom. Nor are Huck
and Jim noticeably more naked on the raft than they are ashore,
except when swimming, possibly! Mr. Lane has evidently been influenced by Eliot's "strong brown god" interpretation of the river
(repeated with variations by Trilling in his famous and otherwise
excellent essay on the novel). But the symbolic interpretation is
quite misleading and unnecessary, to say the least. Huck Finn,
though no churchgoer, is *not* a pagan; and the moral structure of
the book is deeply moving, in the best Judaeo-Christian tradition.

The article winds up with some ultra-profound observations about
Huck's "symbolic death" and assumption of various identities, "as
far removed from . . . reality as possible." Once again a simpler,
more realistic interpretation would be preferable. There are sound
reasons in the plot for Huck to pretend to be dead (he must escape
the ever-present threat of his father) and to assume the disguises he
takes (he must shield Jim and himself and obtain information to
facilitate their mutual escape). His lies and evasions, as Trilling
correctly recognizes, are the boy's only weapons against physically
stronger adult foes. Huck's courage and dedication are truly inspiring. It is a pity, then, that Mr. Lane chose to defend the book
by "extending" it into a symbolic pattern that it simply does not
possess. At other points in the article, however, he makes some more
meaningful attempts at extension—though these are never adequately explored. For instance, Lane speaks of the book as being related to *Don Quixote* in its theme of "appearance versus reality";
but he fails to relate the character of Huck and Jim to the realistic
Sancho Panza or Tom Sawyer to the romantic knight. Lane makes
still another comparison in a very brief paragraph linking the book
to other novels of education (*Candide, Tom Jones,* and *Ulysses*), in
which the hero "goes forth into life that he may learn." But *what*
Huck learns Lane never makes clear.

II

If Mr. Lane's analysis of the novel goes astray because of un-
rewarding "extensions" of reality into allegory and symbolism, the
second article, by William Van O'Connor, commits the graver fault
of misreading the realities of the book entirely. In a harsh attack on
Huckleberry Finn, O'Connor finds it not to be a work of art because of serious "flaws," primarily an "imperfect sense of tone."
First he criticizes Jim for using the raft to escape downstream and
asks why Jim didn't simply "strike out for the Illinois shore and
freedom." But these objections are answered very clearly in Ch. 8

(p. 44, Rinehart ed.), where Jim tells of his original plans for escape: he was afraid to flee on foot for fear of being tracked by dogs, and it would have been unwise to steal a skiff to cross over the river because the skiff would have been missed and traced to a likely position on the Illinois shore. He intended to slip ashore some twenty-five miles downstream, by taking hold of a passing raft, but was prevented—luckily for him, as Huck later discovers (in Ch. 11), for Jim would surely have been captured by eager people on the Illinois shore who were on the lookout for a runaway Negro "murderer" of Huck Finn. The only possible goal then was Cairo, far downstream.

The second example of "imperfect tone" involves what O'Connor calls Tom's "highjinks" at the end of the book which are "anticlimactic" because Miss Watson's will has already freed Jim. Properly understood, however, the ending is but the final example of one of the main themes—the contrast between realism and romance (to be explained further below); it is in perfect keeping with Tom's imaginative nature (see Chs. 2 and 3) and ends the book on a stimulating note of dramatic irony. O'Connor finds additional evidence of what he calls "melodrama" in Huck's relationship with his father, in the shooting of Boggs, and in the tarring and feathering of the Duke and Dauphin; but he does not explain *why* any of these examples is melodramatic. Thousands of upright boys have had the misfortune of a bullying, worthless father. The Boggs episode gives Twain a splendid chance to expose mass cowardice in addition to the cowardice of Boggs himself; perhaps Boggs did not deserve his end, but nobody can say he didn't ask for it. As to the tarring and feathering of the Duke and Dauphin, it seems perfectly clear that sooner or later their confidence game would backfire, and their particular kind of punishment was usual then on the frontier— not only usual but eminently just. They have assumed different aliases and costumes throughout the book: let them get out of *that* costume!

It would be wearisome to refute the few additional examples that O'Connor gives of "imperfect tone," but one major charge must still be answered. This is the very specious claim that Twain once lost sight of Huck's moral sensitivity towards Jim after they were separated by the steamboat which smashed their raft and Huck was taken in by the Grangerfords. Huck is condemned for not thinking of Jim during his involvement "for many days, perhaps weeks" with the affairs of the other people; and O'Connor does not find Huck sufficiently demonstrative when the servant Jack leads him to the overjoyed Jim. But he has neglected to say that when they were separated Huck "sung out for Jim about a dozen times" (p. 94); Huck may well have concluded that Jim had been drowned. Anyhow, the moment he sets foot on shore he is stopped in his tracks by the Grangerfords' dogs, and events thereafter move so rapidly toward a climax that Huck, a virtual prisoner, has no opportunity to look for Jim even if he should think Jim to be alive. In the Grangerford-Shepherdson feud, incidentally, Huck shows plenty of his usual "moral sensitivity" to the tragic death of little Buck. O'Connor tries to give the impression that Twain has forgotten the Huck-Jim relationship too long, but in fact less than two chapters elapse before the two are reunited; and into those chapters Twain has packed a world of meaning relevant to his major theme (as I shall show below). Finally Huck is *not* cold to Jim when they meet. He is shocked, as well he might be! "I poked into the place a ways and . . . found a man laying there asleep—and, by jings, it was my old Jim!" After Jim's brief account of their separation he asks the natural question: "Why didn't you tell my Jack to fetch me here sooner, Jim?" Considering all these circumstances and also considering what we already know about Huck's attachment to Jim (remember the famous apology which Huck makes only a chapter before he is separated from Jim), is it fair to say, as O'Connor does, that Huck is "indifferent" to Jim's fate? O'Connor also finds fault with Jim, incidentally, for not replying to Huck's calls when they were separated in the river. "Presumably one reply would have quieted Huck and made detection much less likely." Would it have been heard against the "booming current" and the noisy steamboat that "started her engines ten seconds after she stopped them"? (p. 94). Additional calls would certainly have brought upon Jim the dogs which trapped Huck. Jim did not *know* that there were dogs there; but he was shrewd enough to expect dogs everywhere on shore and to fear them (see p. 111).

All these critical distortions—and more—about Mark Twain's masterpiece he has managed to cram into less than three pages of text, but these are "pie" to the irrelevancies that fill the remaining half of O'Connor's article in which he speaks about the author's life, about Abraham Lincoln, and other persons. There is, particularly, a long discussion of the uncivilized, passive hero in Hemingway's novels—like the "uncivilized" and "passive" Huck, presumably; in this digression O'Connor sneers at the "innocence" and "irresponsibility" of Hemingway's characters and those of Sherwood Anderson. He equates irresponsibility with a refusal to "make the [unspecified] compromises all civilized people make."

III

What then is *Huckleberry Finn* about? Nothing that the ordinary reader—not given to supersubtle speculations and distortions, but possessed only of common sense and a responsive heart—would fail to understand and appreciate. The clarity and directness of insight, the humorous but sharp exposure of human failings on the one hand and the warm faith in human goodness and equality on the other—these are the substance of the novel; these are the qualities that have endeared the book to common humanity all over the world and have indeed made it a "great world novel."

The major theme is stated succinctly at the end of Ch. 33 (p. 232), when Huck feels compassion even for the feathered frauds: "Human beings *can* be awful cruel to one another." This theme is central to every aspect of the plot and characterization. Human cruelty applies primarily, of course, to the life of the saintly but hunted Jim, whose history personifies all of the evils of slavery. Twain makes a sharp distinction between two types of cruelty—the deliberate callousness of the hard-hearted, and the unintentional or thoughtless indifference of the normally kind-hearted Examples of the first type are Pap's cruelty toward Huck, or the Duke and Dauphin's cruelty toward Jim (the Dauphin actually sells Jim for forty dollars—forty pieces of silver) and toward the three Wilks girls they attempt to defraud. As examples of less deliberate cruelty there is Miss Watson's initial throughtless desire to sell faithful Jim, the event which starts the entire plot; there is the senseless, ancient feud which ends the lives of so many good Grangerfords and Shepherdsons, including the pathetic thirteen-year-old Buck; there is the unthinking, automatic chaining of Jim by kindly Uncle Silas and Aunt Sally (he can preach lofty sermons, and she can weep for "Sid"). Most notably there is Huck's one fault, his earlier attitude of "superiority" to Jim, a feeling quite understandable in any Southern white boy of that day but one which—to his everlasting credit—he forces himself to reject. It should be added that his prejudice never does Jim any harm except for the one practical joke, which backfires on Huck and teaches him a permanent lesson.

This idea of the two types of cruelty relates Twain's world view to those other novelists of the realistic tradition that he resembles most closely—Fielding and Dickens. All three authors look at people in much the same way, dividing them into three classes. On the one hand, we have a few saintly characters, those who are almost always naturally good—like Huck, Jim, Widow Douglas, Aunt Polly, and the three sweet Wilks girls; examples in Fielding and Dickens include Parson Adams, Joseph Andrews, Fanny, Pickwick, Joe Gargery, and Biddy. On the other hand, there are also the two more faulty types mentioned above: numerous well-meaning but sometimes thoughtless ones, who in the English novelists include Squire Western, Tom Jones, David Copperfield, Pip, or Provis; and a few cold-blooded ones—for example, Lady Booby, Parson Trulliber, Bill Sykes, Estella, and Jaggers.

The saintly persons, of course, require no major alteration of character; and the cold-blooded ones are usually beyond redemption, as the new judge, for example, can testify with his efforts to "reform" Pap. It is the large middle group, particularly, in all three novelists which can be redeemed out of their false pride or selfishness—these are usually the besetting sins. But their redemption, if it comes at all, comes only as a result of deep searching by the individual into his own heart; it does not come by merely paying lip service to the dogmas or rituals of organized religion. A good example of this fact may be found in Ch. 18 of *Huckleberry Finn,* in which Huck describes the Grangerfords and Shepherdsons going to church, carrying their guns along. "It was pretty ornery preaching— all about brotherly love, and suchlike tiresomeness; but everybody said it was a good sermon, and they all talked it over going home, and had such a powerful lot to say about good works and free grace and preforeordestination, and I don't know what all, that it did seem to me to be one of the roughest Sundays I had run across yet." The next day the feud is resumed, and Buck is shot down. Only the lovers get away from their murderous families. The false pride inherent in the whole unexamined, traditional code of "quality" is here clearly exposed, and so is the solution to the evils that false pride brings. The solution, simply, is human love, the generally unapplied lesson of the sermon—love between Sophia and Harney, between Huck and Jim, between black and white, between human beings everywhere.

Another important theme in the book, which runs parallel to the main idea already discussed and which frequently fuses with it, is the conflict between romance and realism. This opposition comes out clearly in the contrast between Huck and Tom. Tom is an imaginative boy, who must invest the most prosaic facts of life with a glamorous aura (a Sunday-school picnic becomes a "whole parcel of Spanish merchants and rich A-rabs") and who never does anything in a simple way when there is a more complicated method available which will appeal to his romantic fancy; Huck is just the reverse—to him a spade is always a spade. Of course Twain prefers Huck's mature, forthright directness to Tom's day-dreaming, which results in unintentional cruelty to Jim. This distinction between the two boys explains the nature of the overlong conclusion of the novel, but the distinction is applied to other persons and situations throughout the book, in perhaps more meaningful ways. The whole idea of monarchy, in the persons of the Duke and Dauphin and in the very funny and pertinent colloquy between Huck and Jim about King Solomon's wisdom, is satirized as a cruel romantic delusion; the colloquy is all the funnier because, for once, Huck himself has been trapped by the romantic lore he has picked up from Tom, as Jim realistically explodes Huck's "logic." Also the cruelty inherent in the concept of chivalry and aristocracy, as embodied by the Granger-fords and Shepherdsons, is exposed as being the inevitable result of the senseless romantic tradition of duelling and feuding. Most important of all, the notion of race superiority, the whole code of white supremacy, is revealed as romantic nonsense. We see this idea not only in the story of Huck and Jim but also in the foul anti-Negro rantings of Pap Finn, earlier in the book (Ch. 6), a superb example of Know-Nothingism. The spirit of democracy, according to Mark Twain, is not to be found in the romantic myths of class or racial superiority. Human beings are superior to one another only in the goodness of their hearts and in their love for other people.

This is not the place to enlarge upon the many other fine qualities of Twain's masterpiece—his wonderfully accurate ear for colloquial speech, the naturalness with which the story begins and ends, the photographic eye for realistic physical detail, the inclusion of national types, and so on. But meanwhile it can surely be said that the moral structure of the book alone teaches timeless lessons to all humanity.

R. W. STALLMAN

[Reality and Parody in *Huckleberry Finn*]†

In *College English* for Oct. 1955, William Van O'Connor, echoing De Voto and Wecter, questions the plausibility of Jim's not striking out directly for the Illinois shore and freedom. De Voto contended that Jim "could have reached free soil simply by paddling to the Illinois shore," but this notion is upset by the text itself as quoted in Walter Blair's "Why Huck and Jim Went Downstream" (Nov. 1956). Mr. Blair answers the question at the literal level. His detailed note (as you put it)‡ lays the ghost raised by De Voto, Wecter, O'Connor, and Spiller.

Your own editorial note raises a question about the post-Cairo journey, namely Huck's failure to carry out the plan of buying a canoe and going north up the Ohio (Ch. 16). When Huck finds a canoe (in Ch. 19), instead of going north up the Ohio he paddles up a creek in search of berries and meets the Duke and the Dauphin. Twain sacrifices the Jim-escape business, so you complain, for the Duke-Dauphin business; but what a godsend that he did it that way, for without the Duke and Dauphin, *Huckleberry Finn* isn't worth our attempts to save it. The seemingly chance occasion of

† From *College English*, XVIII (May 1957), 425–26. By permission of the   author and *College English*.
‡ I.e., the editor of *College English*.

the appearance of the Duke and Dauphin has in fact been prepared for in Ch. 14 with the discussion of "kings and dukes and earls and such," and again by Jim's expressed scorn for Frenchmen who don't talk like other men. Twain's example is the Dauphin, a "Frenchman" who doesn't speak French but talks like other men!

The Duke and Dauphin humbugs represent in parody form one side of Huck's double consciousness, namely the Huck who fabricates his past and his identity; his other selfhood, his true self or conscience, is represented by Jim and finds sanctuary in darkness, nakedness, and the river. When Huck is misidentified as Tom Sawyer (Ch. 32), he feels "like being born again, I was so glad to find out who I was." But this is a false rebirth, and a mockery of his quest to find himself. The quest began with his drowning himself in order to find himself; true rebirth occurs not on land but only by water. Everything in the novel goes by pairs. Doubleness is the dominant leit-motif, notably in the two Hucks: "Now I was feeling pretty comfortable *all down one side*, and pretty uncomfortable *all up the other*" (Ch. 32). "That was my fix exactly." It "was because I was playing double. . . . You can't pray a lie—I found that out" (Ch. 31).

Doubleness patterns the book thus: (a) the real thing is presented, as in the death of Boggs, and then (b) the parody of it, as in the mock imitation of his tragic death (Ch. 21). The structure of *Huckleberry Finn*, as I see it, consists of a recurrent counterpointing of the real or true thing or event with the juxtaposed parody of it. Nothing is not parodied. Everything exists thus in doubleness, by contraries. Twain pairs, for example, the real circus (Ch. 22) with the King's Royal Nonesuch, a peepshow parody of the real thing: "the king come a-prancing out on all fours, naked; and he was painted all over, ring-streaked-and-striped, all sorts of colors, as splendid as a rainbow" (Ch. 23). Here's the naked truth, a parody of it.

With doubleness of selfhood goes masked selfhood in clothes, false fronts and false words, false identities, maudlin sentiments and lies. While disguise occurs not only on land but also on the river, the river on the contrary is the sole sanctuary for nakedness, literally and spiritually. Even the raft, when it touches land, is masked. Twain manages the death-and-rebirth motif on the same principle as for the mask motif; namely that while the river is not exempt from death, it is the sole sanctuary for rebirth. On land occur only false rebirths, false reformations (e.g., Pap's fraudulent reformation in Ch. 5). In *American Scholar* for Autumn 1953 Leo Marx contends: "The river cannot, does not, supply purpose." It supplies, by my reading, the central purpose of representing conscience, spiritual integrity, the baptismal source for rebirth and self-recognition of true identity— Who am I?

That the river represents conscience is indicated by the fact that the river gnaws at the land. At Parkville the stores and houses are "set up three or four feet above ground on stilts, *so as to be out of reach of the water* when the river was overflowed." Their gardens grow nothing but "jimpson-weeds, and sunflowers, and ashpiles"; and the houses are as dead as their gardens. These Houses of Death stick out over the bank—"bowed and bent, and about ready to tumble in. People lived in them yet, but it was dangersome, because sometimes a strip of land as wide as a house caves in at a time. Sometimes a belt of land a quarter of a mile deep will start in and cave along and cave along till it all caves into the river in one summer. Such a town as that has to be always moving back, and back, and back, because the river's always gnawing at it" (Ch. 21). In *Sewanee Review* for Summer 1954, in which same issue appeared an essay on *Huckleberry Finn* by James M. Cox, I transposed this situation into the concluding stanza of my poem "Come Back to the Raft":

> They can't out-trick
> The river. Nor
> Pray the lies
> They pray on shore.
> Which is all bluff.
> When rivers rise
> There's not a lick
> Of bluff can stand.
> The river pries.
> Gnaws at the land.
> That shack, no wonder
> It tilts at skies.
> On edge it juts.
> The river cuts
> Bluffs asunder.

That the river cuts bluffs asunder is manifested literally in the passage quoted above from Ch. 21, and allegorically in the fact that the King, when asked what Wilks had tattooed on his breast, feels "squashed down like a bluff bank that the river has cut under" (Ch. 29). That bluff of land is personified by the King. In the river's always gnawing at the land and the town's always drawing back from it Twain provides the analogy for Huck's own plight. Huckleberry, having paddled up a creek in search of berries, confronts instead his other self—personified in the pair of frauds.

To return now to the initial question about the journeying southward by Huck and Jim, their journeying southward in order to go northward strikes me as justifiable both at the literal and the

thematic level. Their journeying southward masks their true intention. Everything in the novel goes masked, even Moses in the bull-
rushes; and that's what saved him. (In Ch. 18 Jim, like Moses, is
saved by the disguise of marsh-bushes.) Doubleness and the corol-
lary motif of mask dominate the patterns of the book. "Was Jim a
runaway nigger?" ask the Frauds (in Ch. 20); to which question
Huck fakes the reply: "Goodness sakes! would a runaway nigger
run *south?*"

> [Stallman's article is the final essay of "Critics' Debate:
> How Great?"]

W. R. MOSES

The Pattern of Evil in *Adventures*
of Huckleberry Finn†

Adventures of Huckleberry Finn (whatever its superficial re-
semblances to the picaresque type) possesses various modes of unity.
There is the geographical and psychological continuum of the river.
There is the matter of Huck's changing and deepening relationships
with Jim. There is the hovering question of whether Jim will ever
become free. (This is something like the hovering question, in the
latter portion of *Typee*, of whether anyone will ever actually get
eaten by cannibals—not in the forefront of the action, usually, but
always present.) There is Huck's running problem of coming to
bearable terms with the civilization of his times as he encounters it
along the shore. I believe there is at least one other. I want to suggest an element of developing tension that in itself furnishes a vital
unity, and to me accounts in considerable part for the forcefulness
and appeal of Clemens' many-faceted novel.

Let us—odd as the concept seems at first glance—try *Adventures
of Huckleberry Finn* in terms of Dante's *Inferno*. They are long
centuries and long miles, to be sure, that separate the Florentine's
vision from the American's. Yet a fascinating parallel between them
may be traced, and the distance, I should think, only bears witness
to the universality of both. I offer no fact, and I disclaim speculation, about what Clemens himself had read, or about what use he
meant to make of his reading if he had it. (This essay is of the
type that deals with works of literature as entities separate from
their authors; regards works of literature as documents which may
have more significance, or less or different significance, than their
authors consciously intended.)

It may be well to keep in mind that the categorizing of sin or evil

† From *The Georgia Review*, XIII (Summer, 1959), 161–66. Reprinted by permission of *The Georgia Review*.

is not an activity peculiar to Dante alone, or to Christianity alone. A few examples should establish that point sufficiently: there is always Aristotle, who observed that there are three kinds of moral state to be avoided—vice, incontinence, and brutishness; and Cicero, who found either violence or fraud to be the medium of all injurious conduct. Dante took the step of arranging sin in specific order of seriousness; his vision of Hell is a descent, more dreadful and offensive circle by circle, through the areas of (1) Incontinence, (2) Violence, and (3) Fraud. The first includes the lustful, the gluttonous, hoarders and spendthrifts, and the wrathful. The second, those violent against their neighbors, against themselves (i.e. suicides), against God, and against Nature or Art (e.g. sodomites and usurers.) The third includes those guilty of simple fraud—panders and seducers, flatterers, simoniacs, sorcerers, barrators, hypocrites, thieves, counsellors of fraud, sowers of discord, and falsifiers; and those guilty of complex fraud—traitors to their kindred, to their country, to guests, or to their lords.

Probably certain adjustments or adaptations are necessary to give the *Inferno* the greatest possible availability to twentieth century readers. We confront the ancient, still vexed problem of quotidian, non-literary belief versus literary construct, and this is no place to debate it again. I suggest, summarily, that for nearly everyone a skeleton of belief exists to support the dazzling vision, though in many readers the effort to accept some details of Dantean beliefs may bring about resistance that can destroy the effectiveness of the vision. One potential objection to the whole thing is that, to people who have not a theological conception of sin, the citation of Dante's arrangement is not necessarily significant. Here it should be recalled that the judgment reflected in Dante's sequence seems generally parallel to that implied both in our legal codes and in our popular morality. Most people, I believe, regard a "cold-blooded" murderer (one of the violent) as worse than a drunkard or glutton (one of the incontinent), and a traitor to his country (who would be a perpetrator of complex fraud) as worse than either. A further objection is that, to the secular conscience and perhaps to the typical twentieth century religious conscience as well, the sins classified as simple fraud are likely to seem venial affairs. Some of them seem very remote, and others we tend to think of in watered-down versions—many a man believes he sees a hypocrite every time he looks into his shaving mirror, but devalues himself very little on that account. I fancy that most readers today (most readers in their capacity as believers, that is) must regard the simple fraud section of the *Inferno* as a sacrifice to time, from which the vitality and significance have been drained by the passing centuries. We still have the vision, resting on acceptance of the main outline of the progression of sin or evil: incontinence; below that violence; below that *complex* fraud, i.e., the worst varieties of treachery.

Huck's adventures are a progression from contact with and endangerment by incontinence, through violence, through fraud. The moral, emotional, and psychological strains he must endure, and perhaps the physical danger as well, increase accordingly. That the three aspects are not quite mutually exclusive—specifically, that violence is not entirely confined to the middle section, but hovers and threatens throughout—does not invalidate the proposition. The tension mounts as the evil worsens, until, apparently, Clemens could think of no way out except that prolonged knocking-at-the-gate scene which is the episode of the Phelps plantation.

Pap, of course, is the personification of incontinence. As opportunity presents, he is a spendthrift, and he would like to get hold of Huck's fortune in order to be a spendthrift on a grand scale. He is indiscriminately drunken, again as opportunity permits. He is sullenly or frantically wrathful against the world in general, especially the "civilized" portion of it: angry because Huck is attending school and may "get religion" and possess such "frills" as good clothes, comfortable surroundings, and money; so hostile toward Huck's "civilized" friends that he gives as reason for abducting Huck the desire to show who "was Huck Finn's boss"; so enraged by the law that permits a Negro to be free under any circumstances that he delivers a long anti-Negro, anti-government tirade and on the same occasion curses "everything and everybody he could think of." One time, out of his head with drink, he seriously threatens Huck's life—but I believe we must take account of the fact that he is unable to recognize Huck at the time, and believes himself to be pursuing the Angel of Death.

Bad as all this is, there are certain palliating features. Though Huck had been terrified of his father in earlier childhood (so much so that he felt "comfortable" on hearing a report that Pap was drowned, and "uncomfortable" when he decided the report must be untrue), when he actually faces Pap in the bedroom at the Widow's he finds that he is no longer seriously afraid of him. In spite of occasional beatings, he is able to make a kind of game of defying Pap's order that he quit attending school. After the kidnapping, Huck enjoys the life with Pap in the cabin on the Illinois shore, "all but the cowhide part." Finally, let it be repeated that though Pap's drunken efforts with his clasp knife imperil the material Huck, they are not directed at Huck as a personality. Though that fact does not matter physically, morally it does matter.

Though *Adventures* . . . contains several episodes that include violence, especially the violence against neighbors which is one of the subdivisions of Dante's central category, the principal episode is that of the Shepherdson-Grangerford feud. The essence of that feud, as Clemens presents it, is an exchange of witless murders that can no longer even be rationalized in plausible terms, at least not by the one youthful Grangerford who is permitted to try to explain the situation to Huck. It all began with a lawsuit, following which the loser shot the winner ("which he would naturally do, of course"), but Buck cannot say whether Shepherdson or Grangerford did the original shooting, or what the lawsuit was about. Anyhow, there have been "right smart chance of funerals," Buck's father and his two older brothers have all been wounded at one time or another, each clan has had a member killed during the current year, and Buck himself, in Huck's presence, tries to bushwhack a Shepherdson who presents himself for the purpose. The episode ends in something approaching a massacre of the Grangerford clan, a massacre that, save for the mere accident that none of the attacking Shepherdsons raised his eyes to see Huck sitting in his tree, presumably would have included Huck as well.

To Huck the feud is violence on a larger scale than he has had to witness before, perpetrated for almost incomprehensible motives. Though the cross-clan elopement provided a motive of sorts for the final flare-up, it is apparently a motive less comprehensible to Huck than Pap's drunkenness, or than the lust for money and fear of detection felt by the potential murderers on the wrecked *Walter Scott*. Huck does not suffer physically in the feud. Yet there seems no doubt that, had a Shepherdson seen him in the heat of the action, Huck would have been killed, not as the Angel of Death, but as a person—anonymous, but recognized to be human—who had committed the crime of being friendly with Grangerfords. He does suffer the emotional shock of seeing others, including his friend Buck, wantonly killed. We are invited to consider that shock a trauma from which Huck can never fully recover: "I wish I hadn't ever come ashore that night to see such things. I ain't ever going to get shut of them—lots of times I dream about them."

Huck has no such persistent nightmares, or at least never mentions any, about his troubles with Pap. The strain increases with the degree of evil encountered.

No sooner is Huck free of the feud than he is set upon by fraud personified by the King and the Duke, fraud which will have the effect, among others, of stirring up more violence around his innocent head. So far as we learn their antecedents, the King and the Duke have been petty grafters for a long time, living by whatever combinations of lying, hypocrisy, and theft serve best to victimize their audiences. After joining Huck and Jim on the raft they continue for some time to be petty grafters, victimizing in different ways both their raftmates and certain communities ashore. When opportunity presents, they try to become large-scale grafters. It is always a matter of obtaining some desired thing under false pretenses: service and subservience from Huck and Jim under pretense of inherited merit; money from various landsmen under pretense of furnishing entertainment, or using the take in order to convert pirates, or whatever comes handy. Their big killing would have been stealing the orphaned Wilks girls' fortune by the device of impersonating hitherto unseen relatives.

Though Huck and circumstances thwart them, their vicious attempt to defraud the girls causes Huck to suffer both deep moral disgust and severe emotional pain. ("I can't ever get it out of my memory, the sight of them poor miserable girls and niggers hanging around each other's necks and crying. . . .") Furthermore, the undiscriminating mob which finally turns on the King and Duke puts Huck in the gravest physical peril of his life to date, or he thinks it does: "This was the most awful trouble and the most dangersome I ever was in. . . ." The fraud perpetrated by the two rascals is, of course, responsible for the mob violence and the danger. It almost gets Huck killed, not as the Angel of Death, not as the associate of an honorable though hostile clan, but as a person supposed to be a partner in villainy.

Finally, the King and the Duke commit the nearly supreme treachery of selling Jim; so far as intention goes, they "make him a slave again all his life, and amongst strangers, too, for forty dirty dollars." Though their sin is not quite on a level with those of Brutus and Cassius, Judas and Lucifer (who are the beings who exist at the nadir of Dante's Hell), it is surely complex fraud, involving as it does the treatment of a human being (Huck, at least, knows that he is a human being) as though he were non-human, and treachery toward a person who in his relationship with them partook of the character both of host and of dependent.

This greatest treachery brings Huck to no serious physical danger, but it does reduce him to the lowest spiritual point he is to reach. Though loyalty to his friend overcomes all objections, and Huck determines to steal Jim out of slavery, the price he pays is a sense of alienation both from society and from God. "It would get all around that Huck helped a nigger to get his freedom; and if I was ever to see anybody from that town again I'd be ready to get down and lick his boots for shame." But the sacrifice must be made: " 'All right, then, I'll *go* to hell.' "

But really, by now, Huck's tour of Hell is virtually completed. Unless he encounters the arch-fiend in person, he can go no deeper. Since Clemens was apparently unwilling either to kill his character, to leave him in the infernal regions, or to conduct him through Purgatory and Paradise, there was nothing left to do except laugh

and shatter the vision with some such device as the Phelps planta-
tion sequence. (Since at the end of the book Sally is threatening
Huck with adoption and civilization, I suppose one may say that
Huck is headed for Purgatory if it pleases his fancy to do so.)

Since its subject—one of its subjects—is a boy in conflict with
and flight from increasingly deadly forms of sin and evil, probably
it is neither incongruous nor contradictory, but something like
necessary, that *Adventures . . .* is a humorous book. Throughout
the course of Huck's troubles, effect after effect is softened or
blunted or turned aside by one kind or another of humorous treatment; probably the book would be very nearly unbearable reading
if this were not true. Huck becomes deeply involved in the evil,
fights against it and suffers under it as a hero should and must. Yet
he is a *boy*; that he should finally elude evil or be arbitrarily
rescued from it—see the abominable vision but live to tell the tale—
is appropriate. The evil he sees, though wearing guises appropriate
to its historical time and place, fits a pattern once given concrete-
ness by one of the strongest and bitterest of the world's literary im-
aginations. Where even Dante escaped alive, it would *not* be appropriate for the American waif to bear the ultimate burden of the
tragic hero.

WALTER BLAIR

Tom and Huck†

A year after finishing *Tom Sawyer*, while reading chapter proofs
for that book, Mark Twain started, as a sequel, *Adventures of
Huckleberry Finn*, subtitled "Tom Sawyer's Comrade." Because of
juxtapositions in time and subject matter the two books were closely
related. One result was that, just as other writings had rehearsed
parts of *Tom Sawyer*, that book rehearsed parts of the later novel.

On Jackson's Island, in chapter xiii of the book bearing his name,
Tom talks about the superiority of a pirate's life over a hermit's:

" 'You see,' said Tom, 'people don't go much on hermits, now-
a-days . . . but a pirate's always respected. And a hermit's got to
sleep on the hardest place he can find, and put sack-cloth and ashes
on his head, and stand out in the rain, and—'

" 'What does he put sack-cloth and ashes on his head for?' inquired Huck.

" '*I* dono. But they've *got* to do it. Hermits always do. You'd
have to do that if you was a hermit.'

† Chapter 5 (pp. 71–76) of *Mark Twain and Huck Finn* by Walter Blair. University of California Press, 1960. By permission of the publisher.

" 'Dern'd if I would,' said Huck.

" 'Well what would you do?'

" 'I dono. But I wouldn't do that.'

" 'Why Huck, you'd *have* to. How'd you get around it?'

" 'Why I just wouldn't stand it. I'd run away.'

" 'Run away! Well you *would* be a nice old slouch of a hermit. You'd be a disgrace.' "

Tom's skimpy knowledge and his pedantic acceptance of books as authorities as contrasted with Huck's ignorance, his respect for Tom's learning, and his common sense are ingredients of this passage. The same incongruities occur in chapters xxv, xxxiii, and xxxv, when Tom and Huck discuss robber gangs, and in chapter xxvi, when they consider Robin Hood.

At the start of *Huck*, the same pair have an almost identical talk about robbers, and in chapter iii Tom discourses on genies—"as tall as a tree and as big around as a church":

" 'Well,' I says, 's'pose we got some genies to help *us*—can't we lick the other crowd then?'

" 'How you going to get them?'

" 'I don't know. How do *they* get them?'

" 'Why, they rub an old tin lamp or an iron ring, and then the genies come tearing in . . . and everything they're told to do they up and do it. . . .'

" 'Who makes them tear around so?'

" 'Why, whoever rubs the lamp or the ring. They belong to whoever rubs the lamp or the ring, and they've got to do whatever he says. . . .'

" 'Well,' says I, 'I think they are a pack of flat-heads. . . . And what's more—if I was one of them I would see a man in Jericho before I would drop my business and come to him for the rubbing of an old tin lamp. . . .'

" 'Shucks, it ain't no use to talk to you. . . . You don't seem to know anything, somehow—perfect sap-head.' "

The humor is essentially the same. At the end of the new novel, Tom again lectures—this time on prisoners' escapes—through a series of chapters.

A prediction made by Huck in chapter xxv of the earlier novel about what would happen if he found a treasure is fulfilled in the sequel; indeed, it may have suggested an inciting force: "Pap would come back to thish-yer town some day and get his claws on it if I didn't hurry up [and get rid of it]." Pap does return and in an attempt to get hold of the treasure seizes his son. To avoid Pap's abuse and being "sivilized" by Widow Douglas, Huck escapes to Jackson's Island.

There, just as he and Tom and Joe Harper do in chapter xiv of

Tom Sawyer, Huck watches the ferryboat hunt for his drowned body:

"Well, I was dozing off again, when I thinks I hears a deep sound of 'boom!' away up the river. I rouses up and rests on my elbow and listens; pretty soon I hears it again. I hopped up, and went and looked out at a hole in the leaves, and I see a bunch of smoke laying on the water a long ways up—about abreast the ferry. And there was the ferry-boat full of people, floating along down. I knowed what was the matter now. 'Boom!' I see the white smoke squirt out of the ferry-boat's side. You see, they was firing cannon over the water, trying to make my carcass come to the top."

In chapter xxviii of *Tom Sawyer*, Huck plans to sleep in the Rogers' hayloft with the consent of the slave, Uncle Jake:

"I tote water for Uncle Jake whenever he wants me to, and any time I ask him he gives me a little something to eat if he can spare it. That's a mighty good nigger, Tom. He likes me, becuz I don't ever act as if I was above him. Sometimes I've set right down and eat *with* him. But you needn't tell that. A body's got to do things when he's awful hungry he wouldn't want to do as a steady thing."

This is a crude pencil sketch of the escaping slave Jim, who joins Huck on the island and later goes down the river with him. And the vein of satire dealing with moral anomalies in a slaveholding society here briefly exposed was to be brilliantly exploited.

During the journey downstream, Huck does some reading and for a time he is to uneducated but commonsensible Jim what Tom is to Huck in *Tom Sawyer*—an argumentative instructor. The two investigate such topics as King Solomon, the French language, and the ways of royalty and nobility.

These and other repetitions relate the two novels. Nevertheless, there would be tremendous differences between these books, close in time though they were.

Comparison of even brief excerpts indicates one great difference—in the styles. The descriptions of daybreak preceding this chapter are an instance. In *Tom*, two squirrels (one in apologetic quotation marks) "skurry along . . . to inspect and to chatter at the boys"; in *Huck*, "a couple of squirrels set on a limb and jabbered at me very friendly." In *Tom*, "All Nature [with a capital N] was awake and stirring, now"; in *Huck*, "I could see the sun out at one or two holes." In *Tom*, "long lances of sunlight pierced down through the dense foliage far and near"; in *Huck*, "it was big trees all about, and gloomy in there," and "there was freckled places on the ground where the light sifted down through the leaves." If the earlier passage misses the contrived "prettiness" and artiness of a Victorian description, it barely does so; but the later passage appears to have no more concern with prettiness or artiness than Huck does. If the earlier passage gets its effect, it does so despite the handicap of its all but trite style. If the latter passage gets its effect, it does so largely because it is in a style which handles the detail naturally and in phrases striking enough to be memorable.

The shift to Huck as narrator would liberate Mark Twain from many limitations which an overweening desire to haul off and be literary in the third person had imposed. Huck's character, of course, would have a great deal to do with this. A boy so sensitive and so shrewd was bound to record scenes and actions with insight; but since he was unabashedly uncouth, he was bound to do this naturally and unpretentiously. Since he was almost completely humorless, he was bound to be incongruously naïve and somber on many laugh-provoking occasions. The author's experience would help him climb into Huck's skin. He too was sensitive and perceptive, and he too had been informed of his lack of manners and culture. And for purposes of both written and oral humor he had often impersonated a similar character, using language homely to him which had given him a freedom that the literary language of the day could not afford.

And the ideas in the new book would be more vital to Twain—and to his readers—than those in the earlier novel. *Tom* is a light book suitable for children and for adults satisfied with a funny story; *Huck* is a funny book suitable for children, too; but grownups who read it find depths in its humor and in its meanings which as childish readers they completely missed.

In *Tom Sawyer*, Mark Twain pictures with amusement and sympathy youngsters who were currently labeled Bad Boys, and he concludes by showing such youngsters triumphant. In a sense, therefore, the book was rebellious. But its attack was a playful one. The boys can resist civilization blamelessly and comically—blamelessly because they are not responsible, comically because their innocent insurrections contrast incongruously with the tensions of responsible grownups. Tom and his companions—even Huck—do not question the standards, nor does Mark. In 1875, when he finished this novel, he could make his happy ending a boy's attainment of respectability.

But in the new book, while Tom's character would be greatly simplified, Huck's would be made far more complex, and this outcast would be the narrator and the protagonist. Pap Finn, not on the scene in *Tom Sawyer*, would figure prominently because Huck was to live with him and escape from him. Jim would be pictured at full length because Huck would spend days and nights with him out on Jackson's Island, on the raft drifting downstream or ashore away from everybody else. On his journey, this waif would meet and come to know many other characters who could not have invaded Tom's childhood world except as melodramatic figures. Most of them would be adults. The civilization which they represent would differ greatly from that of godly St. Petersburg. Twain's attitude toward this civilization, moreover, would be very different. Many of its standards he would not accept but would question and reject. Huck would struggle with his own problems not in a childish but in an adult fashion. And whereas the ending of *Tom* shows the boy initiated into society, the new book would show the much more mature Huck fleeing from society.

These changes would come about because of the life the author led, the books he read, his ponderings, and the conclusions he reached about humanity during the seven-year period of the book's composition.

DANIEL G. HOFFMAN

Black Magic—and White—in *Huckleberry Finn*†

One

The most universal book to have come out of the United States of America begins with this preamble:

NOTICE

Persons attempting to find a motive in this narrative will be prosecuted; persons attempting to find a moral in it will be banished; persons attempting to find a plot in it will be shot.

What a way to begin: "No Trespassing!" This, of course, is only the first of the innumerable jokes, pranks, disguises, tricks, deceptions, ruses, and verbal extravagances that make *Adventures of Huckleberry Finn* a book that has won the world's heart. At the start Mark Twain establishes its tone of frontier humor. His preamble is nailed to a stake, and it posts the limits of his claim, and of ours, on the golden lode of his own remembered boyhood on the Mississippi.

But why such caution behind his bumptious fooling?

What a way to begin a book. Think, for instance, of the "Author's Prologue" to *Gargantua*, exactly three and a half centuries earlier. Rabelais began by comparing his book to the Sileni of old, "little boxes . . . painted on the outside with wanton toyish

† Chapter 15 (pp. 317–42) of *Form and Fable in American Fiction* by Daniel G. Hoffman. © 1961 by Daniel G. Hoffman and reprinted by permission of Oxford University Press, Inc.

figures . . . and other such counterfeited pictures, at pleasure, to excite people unto laughter." But within those caskets lay "many rich and fine drugs . . . balm, ambergreese, amonomon . . . and other things of great price." And he goes on to speak of Socrates, for whose outer appearance "you would not have given the peel of an onion . . . always laughing, tippling, and merry, carousing to everyone, with continual gibes and jeers, the better by those means to conceal his divine knowledge."

Divine knowledge, of course, is not a commodity much in demand in the world, and those who find it burdening their souls are often hard-pressed to put a good face on the matter. The faces of Silenus, god of mirth, are as good a disguise as any.

Even Rabelais, in his mock-monkery fashion, drives a stake against the scholiasts, just as Mark Twain would do. If you believe, he says, that "Homer, whilst he was couching his Iliads and Odysseys, had any thought upon those allegories" which the critics have "squeezed out of him," you may as well take the gospel sacraments to be written by Ovid. Now Mark Twain could be just as bookish, as well as just as truly comic, as Rabelais, but in posting his "Notice" he intuitively chose the vernacular way of warning off the critics who would squeeze the juice of allegorical lemons from a work which he had freshened with the juices of life. To divine knowledge he makes no claims. Yet what can explain his cautious parrying of critical exegesis but that he well knew the motive, the moral, and the plot of his own book—he had recognized the divine knowledge that came to him when he finally plumbed the images of his deepest recollection—and this he did not want abstracted from the only form in which it could retain the fullness of its truth: *Adventures of Huckleberry Finn*.

Despite his "Notice," scholars, annotators, and critics have poached all over Mark's place. Indeed, in the past generation there has been an unparalleled exploration of motive, moral, and plot in *Huckleberry Finn*. As regards the plot, many readers have taken Mark Twain literally, or at least assumed that the book has no more intrinsic a plot than the picaresque pattern of a journey imposes. Certainly their contention was strengthened by Bernard DeVoto's publication in *Mark Twain at Work* of the author's plan for a concluding episode—mercifully never carried out—which involved Huck, Jim and Tom's encountering an escaped circus elephant in the Louisiana bayous. The ending that he actually did give the book—Tom Sawyer's burlesque liberation of the already-freed slave—has been much criticized as disastrously out of key with the fundamental themes of the rest of the story. Yet T. S. Eliot and Lionel Trilling have found this ending satisfactory; other recent critics have contended the contrary against them as well as against Mark Twain.

As for the first two clauses in the author's "Notice," both motive and moral have been scrutinized with Geiger-counter sensitivity by critics of a dozen different persuasions. Where some find the theme of the book to be the search for freedom, another proposes the "theme of appearance versus reality." J. M. Cox suggests initiation and rebirth as its besetting theme, while Philip Young discovers that "an excessive exposure to violence and death" have produced "an ideal symbol" for dying, namely, a "supremely effortless flight into a dark and silent unknown." Yet again "death and rebirth" and "Huck's journey in search of a father" are urged by K. S. Lynn as themes, while R. W. Frantz terms Huck "a creature of fear." As for motive, the ingenious Leslie Fiedler reads the book as a wish-fulfillment of homosexual miscegenation. On the other hand Mr. Trilling has made a definitive case for "Huck's intense and even complex moral quality."[1]

Mark Twain should have known better; in Academe, as in Missouri, a notice without a sheriff proves utterly unavailing. This chapter is itself yet another act of trespass. An assortment of critical readings such as those just enumerated suggests that if the disguises Mark Twain painted upon his Sileni have been baffling in their variety, there is yet indeed a divine knowledge concealed within them. Although each of these essays is helpful in noting valuable themes and structures of the book, a most important pattern has not been sufficiently explored. This is the pattern of relationships in *Huckleberry Finn* between the human and the divine.

Mr. Eliot and Mr. Trilling agree in their readings that the River is a god, presiding over the action, its divinity everywhere implied though nowhere stated outright. But there is a more explicit supernaturalism in this book. Or, more properly, there is an exemplification and a testing of three attitudes toward the imaginative fulfillment of life, and these are largely indicated in supernatural terms. Each typifies the moral nature of those who profess it. Two of these imaginary supernatural worlds prove morally inadequate; the third —which pays homage to the river god—gives dignity to human life.

These attitudes, so compellingly dramatized by Mark Twain, are the conventional piety of the villagers; the irrelevant escape of the

1. T. S. Eliot, "Introduction" to *Adventures of Huckleberry Finn* (London, 1950); Lionel Trilling, "*Huckleberry Finn*," *The Liberal Imagination* (New York, 1951), pp. 104–17; William Van O'Connor, "Why *Huckleberry Finn* Is Not the Great American Novel," *College English*, XVII (Oct. 1955), 6–10; Leo Marx, "Mr. Eliot, Mr. Trilling, and *Huckleberry Finn*," *American Scholar*, XXII (Autumn 1953), 423–40; Lauriat Lane, Jr., "Why *Huckleberry Finn* Is a Great World Novel." *College English*, XVII (Oct., 1955), 1–5; James M. Cox, "Remarks on the Sad Initiation of Huckleberry Finn," *Sewanee Review*, LXII (Summer 1954), 389–405; Philip Young, *Ernest Hemingway* (New York, 1952), chap. 6; Kenneth S. Lynn, "Huck and Jim," *Yale Review*, XLVII (Spring 1958), 421–31; Ray W. Frantz, "The Role of Folklore in *Huckleberry Finn*," *American Literature*, XXVIII (Nov. 1956), 314–27; Leslie Fiedler, "Come Back to the Raft, Huck, Honey!" *An End to Innocence* (Boston, 1955), pp. 142–57.

romantic imagination (as played by Tom Sawyer and an assorted adult cast of rapscallions and Southern gentlemen), and the world of supernatural omens which Jim, the runaway slave, best understands. Huck Finn is the sorcerer's apprentice. The superstitious imagination recognizes evil as a dynamic force; it acknowledges death. It is truer to the moral demands of life than is either the smug piety of Christian conformity or the avoidance of choice by escaping to fantasy and romance.

Bernard DeVoto has made it impossible for us to miss Mark Twain's indebtedness to Negro superstitions. Yet their significance in *Huckleberry Finn* has not adequately been shown. Jim's and Huck's beliefs in witches, ghosts, and omens are not merely authentic touches of local color; they are of signal importance in the thematic development of the book and in the growth toward maturity of its principal characters. When understood as a commentary upon and criticism of the two conventional traditions of white society in reconciling the moral sense with the realities of life on the Mississippi, this folklore of the supernatural becomes a structural element essential to the work of art.

In working out the conflicts between the three otherworlds and their human representatives in *Huckleberry Finn* I hope to do full justice to the character of Jim. Insufficient notice has been taken of the ways in which Jim, as well as Huck, grows to maturity and assumes a man's full obligations. Some of the most important evidence of his development is given us in his role as seer and shaman, interpreter of the dark secrets of nature which the white folks in the church deny, secrets which Tom Sawyer and all the other romanticists along the Mississippi cannot discover.

These three commitments of the imagination allow Mark Twain to explore the possibilities of establishing sympathetic relations between man and nature and between man and man. The local conditions of Huck Finn's world are those of the sleepy village of "St. Petersburg"—or, to be more accurate biographically, of Hannibal, Missouri, the riverfront town where young Sam Clemens grew up, played with the outcast boy Tom Blankenship (the original of Huck), and listened to the Negroes speak of ghosts and omens. His best two books of boyhood create this river hamlet for us; several of the themes of *Huckleberry Finn* have their beginnings in *The Adventures of Tom Sawyer*. We should consider both books in order to explore the three otherworlds of Hannibal.

* * *

Four

The third imaginary realm is the world of superstition, a world we enter as soon as we meet Huckleberry Finn. As DeVoto observes, "On page 64 of *Tom Sawyer*, Huckleberry Finn wanders into immortality swinging a dead cat." Huck and his cat symbolize freedom to Tom, who meets them on a Monday morning between his bondage at church the day before and his approaching incarceration in the district school. That dead cat also represents the lure of an unknown and forbidden world of spirits, omens, and dark powers, a world which attracts Tom not only by its Gothicism and horror but because, unlike his romantic escapades, this imaginary realm succeeds in transcending reality by rendering life itself in mythic terms. The boys exchange cures for warts; yet try as he will, Tom can never really enter Huck's world. When he tries to recover by incantation all the marbles he ever lost Tom's charm is bound to fail, for the first allegiance of his imagination—as we have seen—lies elsewhere. Besides, he is after all a village boy, nephew of the respectable Aunt Polly, brother of the model prig Sid Sawyer; Tom shares their status, and to him Huck is a "romantic outcast." Therefore Tom will never share Huck's secret wisdom—or his freedom.

The association of these superstitions in Mark Twain's mind with freedom from restraint is reiterated in the first chapter of *Huckleberry Finn*. This time it is Huck who sweats through the lessons, about Moses and "the Bulrushers." At last the widow "let it out that Moses had been dead a considerable long time; so then I didn't care no more about him, because I don't take no stock in dead people." Huck is then lectured on going to Heaven by Miss Watson; this is so depressing that by nighttime "I felt so lonesome I most wished I was dead."

"The stars were shining, and the leaves rustled in the woods ever so mournful; and I heard an owl, away off, who-whooing about somebody that was dead, and a whippoorwill and a dog crying about somebody that was going to die; and the wind was trying to whisper something to me, and I couldn't make out what it was, and so it made the cold shivers run over me. Then away out in the woods I heard that kind of a sound that a ghost makes when it wants to tell about something that's on its mind and can't make itself understood, and so can't rest easy in its grave, and has to go about that way every night grieving. I got so downhearted and scared I did wish I had some company. Pretty soon a spider went crawling up my shoulder, and I flipped it off and it lit in the candle; and before I could budge it was all shriveled up. I didn't need anybody to tell me that that was an awful bad sign and would fetch me some bad luck, so I was scared and most shook the clothes off of me. I got up and turned around in my tracks three times and crossed my breast every time; and then I tied up a little lock of my hair to keep witches away. But I hadn't no confidence."

Freedom from the restraints of civilization, yes; but such freedom has its dangers too. For Huck, the omens are an acknowledgment of the fact of death. "I didn't take no stock in dead people" applies to the dead lessons in Bible or school, not to these immanent realities. These portents are an admission of evil as a positive force in the natural world. His exorcisms attempt to control the operation of malevolent powers. But while he knows far more about such things than Tom does, Huck is still a mere disciple. The magus is Nigger Jim.

But when we first meet him, Jim is a slave. His superstitions, like the hagiolatry of the ignorant peasants in *The Innocents Abroad*, are the manacles upon his soul. Mark Twain dramatizes his bondage by the quality of his beliefs. Far from controlling nature, Jim in slavery is helpless before the dark powers, a gullible prey to every chance or accident which befalls him. This is made humorously manifest in chapter 2, when Tom and Huck find Jim snoozing on the widow's kitchen steps. Tom hangs his hat on a branch and leaves a five-cent piece on the table. "Afterward Jim said the witches bewitched him and put him in a trance, and rode him all over the state, and then set him down under the trees again, and hung his hat on a limb to show who done it." Other slaves come from miles around to hear Jim's expanding account of this marvel. It gives him status! But he is more than ever enslaved to his fears; and a week later Miss Watson decides to sell him down the river to a more arduous bondage. That is a fear he cannot transform into personal distinction through the artistic control of a tall tale. Jim runs away to Jackson's Island.

On the island he lives in terror of capture. Huck, having escaped from Pap, is there before him. Still the fearful, haunt-ridden manchild, Jim takes Huck for a ghost and drops to his knees, imploring, "Doan' hurt me—don't! I hain't ever done no harm to a ghos'. I alwuz liked dead people, en done all I could for 'em. You go en git in de river ag'in, wah you b'longs." But once he learns in earnest that Huck is alive, Jim realizes that he himself is free. The mighty river rises and the two move camp to a womb-like cavern. Animals take refuge in the trees, and "they got so tame, on account of being hungry, that you could paddle right up and put your hand on them if you wanted to; but not the snakes and turtles." This is an uneasy Eden, menaced by the implacable flooding river.

Now that he is free in this ambiguous paradise the nature of Jim's superstitious belief undergoes a change. We hear no more of ghosts and witches. Instead, Jim instructs Huck in the lore of weather, in the omens of luck, in the talismans of death. "Jim knowed all kinds of signs." Seeing young birds skip along means rain; catching one brings death. You must tell the bees when their owner dies or they will weaken and perish. Death is never far from the superstitious imagination. Jim goes on—don't shake the table-cloth after sundown, or count the things you cook for dinner, or look at the moon over your left shoulder—these bring bad luck. "It looked to me like all the signs was about bad luck, and so I asked him if there warn't any good-luck signs. He says: 'Mighty few—an' *dey* ain't no use to a body. What you want to know when good luck's a-comin' for? Want to keep it off?' " Luck is the folk concept of what the Greeks called Fate, the Anglo-Saxons, Wyrd. There is a stoical wisdom in Jim's resignation before it which makes a manly contrast to the psalm-singing optimism of Miss Watson and the revivalists, and to Tom's romantic evasions of reality.

Soon after they see the young birds flying, sure enough, it rains: a huge, frightening storm that reasserts the dominance of nature over man. The river rises, and as was foretold in so many of their omens, the House of Death floats by. When Jim's omens come true he is no more a gullible supplicant to witches. He is a magus now, a magician in sympathetic converse with the spirits that govern—often by malice or caprice—the world of things and men.

As soon as Jim begins to feel his freedom, his attitude toward Huck develops. One of the grand ironies of this book is that while it seems to show Huck protecting Jim, Jim is also taking care of Huck all along. Jim's folk wisdom saved Huck from the storm; Jim builds the wigwam on the raft. "I'd see him standing my watch on top of his'n, 'stead of calling me, so I could go on sleeping." Just after the storm, when the House of Death floats by, it is Jim who goes aboard first, sees the corpse, and won't let Huck behold it. Huck boyishly salvages an old straw hat, a Barlow knife, "a ratty old bedquilt. . . . And so, take it all around, we made a good haul." These squalid remnants, we discover much later, constitute Huck's patrimony from Pap, the father whose savagery he fled. So terrible was the self-destructive anarchic energy of Pap that Huck had to simulate self-destruction to escape him. But now it is Jim who comprehends the degradation of Pap's death and protects Huck from that cruel knowledge. Jim is now free to take the place that Pap was never worthy to hold as Huck's spiritual father. When Jim and Huck shove off from the House of Death their odyssey begins. Jim can now act as Huck's father, and Huck's first act is to protect him, as a son might do.

Because of this filial relationship, Huck cannot play tricks on Jim as he could on Tom or Ben Rogers. This he discovers when he kills a rattler and coils it in Jim's bed. Jim had warned him, "it was the worst bad luck in the world to touch a snake-skin." The dead snake's mate coils round it and bites poor Jim. But Jim has a folk cure—eating the snake's head roasted, tying the rattles around his wrist, and drinking whiskey. Just as his omens come true, his cures cure. Again we see Jim as medicine man, free to control—within mortal limits—his universe.

Another aspect of Jim's shamanistic role is his power to interpret oracles and dreams. Here, too, when in slavery this attribute parodies itself because Jim then held pretensions without power. He had a hairball from the fourth stomach of an ox with which he "used to do magic." Huck consults him after seeing Pap's footprints in the snow, to learn what Pap would do. Accepting Huck's counterfeit quarter, Jim reels off a counterfeit prophecy, concluding, "You wants to keep 'way fum de water as much as you kin." But when Huck returns to his room, "there sat Pap—his own self!" and the only escape from Pap is to flee by water. Jim's next oracular occasion comes when he and Huck find each other after being separated by the fog. Huck, as a joke, convinces Jim that they had been to-gether on the raft all the time; Jim must have dreamed their sep-aration. So Jim "said he must start in and 'terpret it, for it was sent for a warning." Towheads and currents stand for men who will aid or hinder them; their cries were warnings of trouble ahead, but all would work out well in the end. Then Huck points to the leaves, the rubbish, the smashed oar. Jim ponders:

"What do they stan' for? I's gwyne tell you. When I got all wore out wid work, en wid de callin' for you, en went to sleep, my heart wuz mos' broke bekase you wuz los', en I didn' k'yer no mo' what become er me en de raf'. En when I wake up en find you back ag'in, all safe en soun', de tears come, en I could 'a' got down on my knees en kiss yo' foot, I's so thankful. En all you wuz thinkin' 'bout wuz how you could make a fool uv ole Jim wid a lie. Dat truck dah is *trash*; en trash is what people is dat puts dirt on de head er dey fren's en makes 'em ashamed."

This speech, so moving in its avowal of dignity, combines Jim's attempt at magical interpretation (which is in fact accurate) with the realism that underlies it, and with his staunch adherence to the code of simple decencies by which good men must live. It is indeed the first major turning-point of the romance. It reinforces the lesson of the snakeskin: Huck now realizes that he is bound to Jim by ties too strong for mischievous trifling, ties so strong that he must break the strongest mores of the society he was raised in to acknowledge them. "It was fifteen minutes before I could work myself up to go and humble myself to a nigger; but I done it, and I warn't ever sorry for it afterward, neither."

Now that Huck has learned how he and Jim are inseparable, circumstances at once thrust them apart. In the next chapter their raft is run over by a paddlewheeler; when Huck gets ashore and sings out for Jim he finds himself alone. This, he thinks, is what comes of handling that snakeskin. He is taken in by the Granger-fords and does not find Jim again until after the shooting. Then the Duke and Dauphin come aboard. From this point on Jim and Huck are never again alone together, and Jim does not act as magus again. His powers have their mysterious source in the river, par-taking of its inscrutable might. For if the river is a god, Jim is its priest. The river god is indifferent to humanity; he runs on, uncon-taminated by the evils along his shores, asserting now and then in storms and floods which sweep the House of Death downstream his dominance and power over "the damned human race." Only when Jim is alone with Huck on the river island or drifting on the current is he so free from the corruption of civilization that he can partake of the river god's dark power. Jim responds on a primitive level to that power, through which he can interpret the signs that are older than Christianity.

But now he is on the sidelines while Huck observes the Duke and King play out their grasping roles. After their failure to filch Mary Jane Wilkes' patrimony, the King sells Jim to Tom Sawyer's Uncle Silas. Huck sets out to find him. Suddenly aware of his guilt in having aided a runaway slave, Huck wrestles again with his con-science. In a memorable climax to his discovery of his own natural goodness, Huck dares to defy the codes of Miss Watson's church and of Tom Sawyer's village by stealing Jim out of slavery again: "All right, then, I'll go to hell."

There are witches again on Uncle Silas's farm, for this is slave territory. Silas's slave, Nat, wears wool in his hair to ward them away, thinks he is bewitched when Tom tells him he is, knows this is true when a pack of hounds leap into Jim's cell through the escape hole the boys had Jim dig beneath the bed. But Jim knows better. Although manacled while Nat has the run of the place, Jim is spiritually free. Now that he has experienced the freedom of life on the raft, life in accord with the rhythms of nature, mere chains will not reduce him to subjection again. As Tom knows, he is legally free anyway. But Jim does not know this; his fortitude during his imprisonment is one of the signs of his moral stature.

Jim's stature is made manifest at the end of the book when, having suffered such needless discomfitures at Tom's hands, he voluntarily gives himself up in the swamp to help the doctor nurse back to health the boy who had plagued him. Then, brought back to the farm as he knew he would be—in chains, suffering the abuse of an angry mob, in momentary danger of lynching—Jim refuses to recognize Huck in the crowd lest he involve this other, truer friend in his own misfortunes. Jim's loyalty is so great that he is willing to sacrifice his freedom for his young friends' sakes. His selflessness is truly noble, a far cry from the chuckle-headedness of the slave who was ridden all over the country by witches when Tom Sawyer lifted his hat.

Five

During the decade when critical opinion at last recognized the inherent dignity of Jim, *Adventures of Huckleberry Finn,* in response to strong pressure from the N.A.A.C.P., was removed from the high school curriculum in our largest city.[5] The most eloquent statement of the objections of a Negro reader to Mark Twain's characterization of Jim is that of the novelist Ralph Ellison:

"Writing at a time when the blackfaced minstrel was still popular, and shortly after a war which left even the abolitionists weary of those problems associated with the Negro, Twain fitted Jim into the outlines of the minstrel tradition, and it is from behind this stereotype mask that we see Jim's dignity and human capacity— and Twain's complexity—emerge. Yet it is his source in this same tradition which creates that ambivalence between his identification as an adult and parent and his 'boyish' naïveté, and which by contrast makes Huck, with his street-sparrow sophistication, seem more adult. . . . Jim's friendship for Huck comes across as that of a boy for another boy rather than as the friendship of an adult for a junior; thus there is implicit in it not only a violation of the manners sanctioned by society for relations between Negroes and whites, there is a violation of our conception of adult maleness."[6]

Speaking of the blackfaced minstrel, the "smart-man-playing-dumb," Mr. Ellison remarks that his role grows "out of the white American's manichean fascination with the symbolism of blackness and whiteness." This color symbolism is openly appropriated in *Huckleberry Finn;* it is used in full awareness of its ironies. We remember Pap's first appearance in the book—his face "was white . . . a white to make a body's flesh crawl—a treetoad white, a fish-belly white"; he it is who out of pride of color would secede from the government because it permits "a free nigger from Ohio—a mulatter, most as white as a white man," to vote. This early in the book the falsity of the manichean color symbolism is dramatized.

But there is no gainsaying Mr. Ellison that when Jim analyzes the stock market, or asks "Was Sollerman Wise?" or kowtows to the bogus royalty or endures his torturous liberation for Tom's amusement he is indeed akin to the Mr. Bones of minstrel fame. I hope to have shown, however, that this is what he begins as, what he emerges from. Jim plays his comic role in slavery, when he bears

5. New York *Times,* Sept. 12, 1957, pp. 1–2.
6. 'The Negro Writer in America: An Exchange,' *Partisan Review* XXV (Spring 1958), 215–16.

the status society or Tom imposes upon him; not when he lives in his intrinsic human dignity, alone on the raft with Huck.

If Jim emerges from the degradation of slavery to become as much a man as Mark Twain could make him be, we must remember that Jim's growth marks a progress in Twain's spiritual maturity too. "In my school days I had no aversion to slavery. I was not aware that there was anything wrong with it. No one arraigned it in my hearing . . . the local pulpit taught us that God approved it, that it was a holy thing."[7] In 1855 Sam Clemens wrote home to his mother that a nigger had a better chance than a white man of getting ahead in New York. Mark Twain began with all the stereotypes of racial character in his mind, the stereotypes that he as well as Jim outgrows.

It is clear that supernatural folklore plays an important part in Twain's handling of Jim. Since this lore is used to differentiate Jim from the white characters, there remains the question of Mark Twain's accuracy in assigning folk belief to the black man.[8] In the preface to *Tom Sawyer*, Mark Twain makes explicit his assumption about the provenience of folk beliefs: "The odd superstitions touched upon were all prevalent among children and slaves in the West at the period of its story—that is to say, thirty or forty years ago" (1835–45). In both books the only whites who are superstitious are either young boys or riffraff like Pap—the two categories of white folks who might have picked up the lore of slave quarter. The only "white" superstition in *Huckleberry Finn*, attributed to the villagers in general, is belief in the power of bread and quicksilver to discover a drowned corpse.[9] More typical of the attitude of white characters toward superstition is the derision of the raftsmen when their companion tells the ghost story of the murderer pursued by the corpse of his slain child floating in a barrel beside the raft.[10] Twain's usual assumption is that white persons of any status higher than trash like Pap have little knowledge of, and no belief in, superstition.[11]

Mark Twain's memory played him wrong. Every one of the beliefs in witch-lore and in omens he used in *Huckleberry Finn* proves

7. *Mark Twain's Autobiography*, ed. Albert Bigelow Paine (New York, 1924), p. 101.

8. 'Regarding the feelings, emotions, and the spiritual life of the Negro the average white man knows little,' writes Newbell Niles Puckett in his magisterial *Folk Beliefs of the Southern Negro* (Chapel Hill, 1926), vii. 'Should some weird, archaic, Negro doctrine be brought to his attention he almost invariably considers it a "relic of African heathenism," though in four cases out of five it is a European dogma from which only centuries of patient education

could wean even his own ancestors.'

9. The identical belief is reported by Harry Middleton Hyatt in *Folklore from Adams County Illinois* (New York, 1935), a region on the opposite shore of river above Hannibal; item no.10283.

10. I followed Bernard De Voto (*The Portable Mark Twain*) in considering this episode, usually printed as chapter 3 of *Life on the Mississippi,* an integral part of the book for which it was originally written.

11. Pap wears a cross of nails in the heel of his boot as a charm against the devil.

to be of European rather than African origin and to have been held widely among the whites as well as among the Negroes of the region. The witch who is warded off by tying one's hair with threads and who rides her victims by night is an old familiar European folk figure:

> This is that very Mab
> That plaits the manes of horses in the night

whom Mercutio described in *Romeo and Juliet* (I, iv, 88–9). Jim's fear of snakeskins, his belief that one must tell the bees of their keeper's death, his conviction that counting the things you cook for supper, or shaking the tablecloth after sundown, or speaking of the dead, or seeing the moon over your left shoulder all bring bad luck, and that a hairy chest means he's "gwine be rich"—all these were known among the white folk of the Mississippi valley.[12] Only his divination with a hairball from the stomach of an ox is a Negro belief of voodoo origin.

Why, then, does Mark Twain make such a point of having only Negroes, children, and riffraff as the bearers of folk superstitions in the re-created world of his childhood? *Huckleberry Finn* was written while Twain lived among the insurance magnates, the manufacturing millionaires, and the wealthy literati of the Nook Farm colony in Hartford, Connecticut. It had been many years since he had lived in a superstitious frontier community, and in his own not-too-reliable memory this folklore became associated with the slaves he had known in his boyhood. The original of Jim, he writes in his *Autobiography*, was " 'Uncle Dan'l,' a middle-aged slave" on the farm of Mrs. Clemens' brother John Quarles. "I can see the white and black children grouped around the hearth" of the slave's kitchen, "and I can hear Uncle Dan'l telling the immortal tales which Uncle Remus Harris was to gather into his book and charm the world with."[13] On such nights Dan'l's favorite encore was no animal fable but—as Twain wrote it down years later, in 1881, for Joel Chandler Harris's benefit—"De Woman wid de Gold'n Arm,"[14] a ghost story widely collected by folklorists since. In those days, "every old woman" was an herb doctor; in Hannibal and Florida the young Sam Clemens knew also old Aunt Hannah, so old she had talked with Moses, who tied threads in her hair against witches. A subtle emotional complex binds together *superstition: slaves: boyhood freedom* in Mark Twain's mind. These three aspects of his experience had occurred most vividly together,

---

12. I have traced in detail the European origins and white provenience of these beliefs in 'Jim's Magic: Black or White?' *American Literature*, XXXII (March 1960), 47–54.

13. *Autobiography*, pp. 100, 112.

14. *Mark Twain to Uncle Remus*, ed. Thomas H. English (Atlanta, 1953), pp. 11–13. Mark Twain gives another version of the tale in 'How to Tell a Story.'

and he seems, in his greatest book, not to have thought of any one of them without invoking both of the others. There is, then, no invidious intention behind his characterizing Jim by the superstitions common to both races.

I hope in the foregoing pages to have cleared Mark Twain of the imputation that "the humor of those scenes of superstition . . . illustrate the ridiculous inadequacy and picturesque inventiveness of the fearful human responses to the powers of evil," for such an interpretation—it is that of Francis Brownell[15]—would put all of Jim's folk beliefs in the service of the degrading minstrel characterization to which Mr. Ellison objects. The minstrel stereotype, as we have seen, was the only possible starting-point for a white author attempting to deal with Negro character a century ago. How else could young Sam Clemens have known a Negro in the Missouri of the 1840's except as the little white boy on familiar terms with his uncle's household retainer? The measure of Mark Twain's human understanding—Mr. Ellison calls it his complexity—is evident when we compare Jim to the famous Negro character in the writings of Mark Twain's friend, Joel Chandler Harris, remembering that Sam Clemens was in real life to "Uncle" Dan'l as the little boy in Harris's books is to Uncle Remus. The Georgia author's Negro fablist never ceases to be the minstrel in blackface. The poetic irony in the Uncle Remus books is one of which Harris was probably unaware: the Negro's human dignity survives the minstrel mask not in Uncle Remus's character but in the satirical stories he tells the white boy. That many of these were thinly veiled avowals of the Negro's pride and dignity and refusal to submit his spirit to the unjust yoke of custom would not seem to have occurred to Joel Chandler Harris, whose conscious literary strategy was to palliate Northern antagonism of the South by idealizing antebellum plantation life.[16] But Mark Twain tries to make Jim stride out of his scapegoat minstrel's role to stand before us in the dignity of his own manhood. It is true that Mark Twain's triumph here is incomplete: despite the skillful gradation of folk belief and other indications of Jim's emergent stature, what does come through for many readers is, as Mr. Ellison remarks, Jim's boy-to-boy relationship with Huck, "a violation of our conception of adult maleness." We remember that Mark Twain himself admired Uncle Remus extravagantly, and much as he means for us to admire Jim—much as he admires Jim himself—the portrait, though drawn in deepest sympathy, is yet seen from the outside. The closest that Mark

15. 'The Role of Jim in *Huckleberry Finn*,' *Boston Univ. Studies in English*, I (1955), 81.
16. This is a point I have discussed in some detail in a review of *Joel Chandler Harris—Folklorist* by Stella Brewer Brookes, in *Midwest Folklore*, I (Summer 1951), 133–8. See also John Stafford, 'Patterns of Meaning in *Nights with Uncle Remus*,' *American Literature*, XVIII (May 1946), 89–108.

Twain gets to Jim's soul, and the furthest from the stereotyped minstrel mask, is the ethical coherence with which the author's manipulation of folk superstitions allows him to endow the slave. In both his emergence toward manhood through the exercise of his freedom and in his supernatural power as interpreter of the oracles of nature, Jim comes to be the hero of his own magic. The test and proof of natural goodness, which raises Jim and Huck above religious hypocrisy and selfish romanticism, is its transforming power upon him. The fear-ridden slave becomes in the end a source of moral energy. The shifting of Jim's shape is reversed at the end, as he sinks back from his heroism to become the bewildered freed darky of reconstruction days, grateful to the young white boss for that guilt-payment of forty dollars. (It did bring true his only good luck omen: a hairy breast and arms meant that he's "gwineter be rich . . . signs is signs!") For Jim has status now, a status imposed by society, not, as was his moral eminence, determined by his inner nature. And it is status of which Huck is now afraid; for at the end he is preparing to flee again, this time to "light out for the territory ahead of the rest. . . . Aunt Sally she's going to adopt and sivilize me, and I can't stand it. I been there before." For Huck, *"there"* means the stasis of being a part of society. His voyage, like Jim's, was a quest for freedom too; after their idyll and their ordeals, both find only the equivocal freedom of status at the end of their odyssey. The pattern of action in this double quest depended upon their freedom of movement—of both spatial movement and social mobility. Freedom to die in each identity, freedom to be reborn anew in another—this pattern of action is the theme of the next chapter.

The Long Journey: Escape and Return

HENRY NASH SMITH

[Two Faces of Hannibal]†

* * *

Mark Twain mentions Hannibal occasionally in articles written for newspapers in Nevada and California during the 1860's, and he revisited the town briefly in 1867. But the memories of his boyhood first really surge up into consciousness in his reply to a letter from his old friend Will Bowen in 1870:

"Your letter has stirred me to the bottom. The fountains of my great deep are broken up & I have rained reminiscences for four & twenty hours. The old life has swept before me like a panorama; the old days have trooped by in their old glory again; the old faces have looked out of the mists of the past; . . . & the songs I loved ages & ages ago have come wailing down the centuries!"[2]

Then for several pages he pours out a catalogue of remembered characters and incidents. Perhaps a score of items that were to be used in *Tom Sawyer* or *Huckleberry Finn* appear here—the Hannibal tan-yard, the Sunday School, the swimming-hole in the still-house branch, the game of Robin Hood in the forest.

Significantly enough, this letter recording the discovery of the Matter of Hannibal was written four days after Mark Twain's marriage to Livy. He was indeed stirred to the depths, and buried

† From "Mark Twain's Images of Hannibal: From St. Petersburg to Eseldorf," published in *Texas Studies in English*, Vol. 37, (1958), pp. 3–23. By permission of the author and *Texas Studies in Literature and Language*. With respect to the *Adventures of Huckleberry Finn*, the following selection reproduces the central portion of this article. In its entirety the article deals with the significance of Mark Twain's changing attitudes toward Hannibal. Missouri, the scene of his boyhood and (as St. Petersburg) that of Tom Sawyer and Huck Finn. Hannibal had two "faces" from the beginning: one was the idyllic face of *The Adventures of Tom Sawyer;* the other was that represented by desperadoes and drunks such as Injun Joe and Huck's Pap. Henry Nash Smith is curator of the Mark Twain papers at Berkeley, California.
2. *Mark Twain's Letters to Will Bowen*, ed. Theodore Hornberger, Austin, 1941, p. 18.

memories of the past rose to the surface of his mind. Although Mark Twain speaks of the "glory" of the olden days, the list of things he remembers includes, along with schoolboy pranks and good times, some very painful items, such as the time when "we accidentally burned up that poor fellow in the calaboose. . . ." The death of this tramp when the Hannibal jail caught fire and no one could find the key to let him out became a recurrent nightmare for young Sam Clemens, who considered himself responsible for the man's death because he had given him matches with which to light his pipe. The Matter of Hannibal embraced the glory of boyhood but it also embraced the terror and the guilt.

Later in the same year (1870) Mark Twain composed a "Boy's Manuscript" that is recognizable as the germ from which *The Adventures of Tom Sawyer* developed, even though it is so empty of promise the author abandoned it after writing less than eight thousand words.[3] The story of how Tom Sawyer got the fence whitewashed came back into Mark Twain's mind while he was in England in 1872, and he wrote it down,[4] but probably did not write more of the book at that time. He began to work steadily on it during the summer of 1874, and his full recovery of the Matter of Hannibal should be dated from this period. The writing of *Tom Sawyer* brought other memories to his mind. The opening pages of the first instalment of "Old Times on the Mississippi" (written in November, 1874, and published in the *Atlantic Monthly* for January, 1875) present a vivid image of "our village on the west bank of the Mississippi River":

"Once a day a cheap, gaudy packet arrived upward from St. Louis, and another downward from Keokuk. Before these events had transpired, the day was glorious with expectancy; after they had transpired, the day was a dead and empty thing. Not only the boys, but the whole village, felt this. After all these years I can picture that old time to myself now, just as it was then: the white town drowsing in the sunshine of a summer's morning; the streets empty, or pretty nearly so; one or two clerks sitting in front of the Water Street stores, with their splint-bottomed chairs tilted back against the wall, chins on breasts, hats slouched over their faces, asleep— with shingle-shavings enough around to show what broke them down; a sow and a litter of pigs loafing along the sidewalk, doing a good business in water-melon rinds and seeds; . . . a pile of "skids" on the slope of the stone-paved wharf, and the fragrant town drunkard asleep in the shadow of them; . . . the great Mississippi, the majestic, the magnificent Mississippi, rolling its mile-wide tide along, shining in the sun; the dense forest away on the other side; the "point" above the town, and the "point" below,

3. Published in Bernard DeVoto, *Mark Twain at Work*, Cambridge, Mass.,   1942, pp. 25–44.
4. DeVoto, *Mark Twain at Work*, p. 4.

bounding the river-glimpse and turning it into a sort of sea, and withal a very still and brilliant and lonely one."[5]

The relatively static quality of this description suggests a distinction worth keeping in mind, between images that do not involve significant action and the various acts and events included along with visual images in the Matter of Hannibal. Here the emphasis is on what is seen rather than on what happens. The town, without conscious symbolism no doubt but still significantly, is "white," and the river is "shining" and "brilliant." The town is isolated; the steamer arrives in its glory from an unimaginably remote great world, and is the only link between this great world and the village. Otherwise everything is quiet—the community as a whole and various individuals are said to be drowsing or sleeping. The white town has its shadows: the town drunkard, mentioned three times in less than a page, shows that Huck's Pap was integral to the image of Hannibal from the very first, as was the sow with her litter, who would reappear in Bricksville in *Huckleberry Finn* and in the Camelot of King Arthur's Britain. It was these sordid touches that led Howells in commenting on this first instalment to speak of the "low-lived little town." On the other hand, the majestic natural setting of forest and river is benign; it is described with an emotion that anticipates the tranquil delight of Huck and Jim alone on their raft.

Looking back on *Tom Sawyer* ten years after it was published, Mark Twain said it was "simply a hymn, put into prose form to give it a worldly air."[6] Much of this lyric quality results from the projection of emotion into the landscape, so that it reflects Tom's moods. The white-washing scene, for example, begins as follows:

"Saturday morning was come, and all the summer world was bright and fresh, and brimming with life. . . . The locust trees were in bloom and the fragrance of the blossoms filled the air. Cardiff Hill, beyond the village and above it, was green with vegetation, and it lay just far enough away to seem a Delectable Land, dreamy, reposeful, and inviting."[7]

The mood of innocence and peace was not a characteristic of fiction alone; it could invest Hannibal, in memory, just as surely as it could invest St. Petersburg in fiction. In 1887 Mark Twain wrote that thinking and dreaming of "that old day" in Hannibal made him feel "like some banished Adam who is revisiting his half-forgotten Paradise and wondering how the arid outside world could ever have seemed green and fair to him."[8] This statement reveals much about

5. *Atlantic*, XXXV, 69–70, January, 1875.
6. *Mark Twain's Letters*, ed. Albert B. Paine, 2 vols., New York, 1917, II, 477.
7. *The Adventures of Tom Sawyer*, in *The Writings of Mark Twain*, Definitive Edition, 37 vols., New York, 1922–25 (hereafter DE), VIII, 12.
8. Samuel L. Clemens to Mrs. Boardman, Hartford, 25 March 1887, Berg Collection, New York Public Library

the "white" Hannibal that was called St. Petersburg, for Eden had been domesticated in America a long time. Mark Twain's village realizes the dream of the good life in the New World that had been cherished by Utopian thinkers in Europe for centuries before the Republic was established. In the earlier chapters of *Tom Sawyer* we seem to be witnessing the fictional embodiment of Crèvecoeur's memorable incantation: "Here are no aristocratical families, no courts, no kings, no bishops, no ecclesiastical dominion, . . . no great manufacturers employing thousands, no great refinements of luxury. The rich and the poor are not so far removed from each other as they are in Europe. . . . We have no princes, for whom we toil, starve, and bleed: we are the most perfect society now existing in the world."[9]

The St. Petersburg image gains much of its power from the fact that it incorporates this long tradition of faith and assertion about the possibilities of life in America. It is the appropriate habitat of the American Adam whom Mr. R. W. B. Lewis has described recently with such persuasive examples.[10] To be sure, the episodes in *Tom Sawyer* involving Injun Joe and Muff Potter are provided with appropriately sinister settings—the ill-kept graveyard, the haunted house, the tavern, the old tannery, the cave—but these Gothic materials are not really a part of the environment in which Tom lives his daily life. They have no moral significance; they are stage properties. Tom's St. Petersburg is a village of absolute innocence, an innocence that is not in the least impaired by the venerable notion that a half-breed—that is, an outsider—is capable of robbery and murder. In this respect, as in others, the St. Petersburg of the novel must be recognized as a deliberate creation, not an effort to reproduce the actual town of Hannibal. The "Villagers" MS, written more than twenty years after *Tom Sawyer*, shows that Mark Twain's recollections of Hannibal were considerably more complex than is his description of St. Petersburg. He made a careful selection of the materials provided by his memory when he created the child's world of the novel.

Even so, St. Petersburg does not conform in every respect to the specifications of Crèvecoeur's optimistic blueprint. Like Hannibal, it bears the dark shadow of slavery, although this may not have seemed so dark in pre-War Hannibal as it does now, and in St. Petersburg it is hardly noticeable. Yet quite apart from slavery, neither St. Petersburg nor Hannibal could claim to exemplify complete social equality. "In the small town of Hannibal, Missouri,

(TS in MTP); copyright 1958 by the Mark Twain Company. I am grateful to the New York Public Library for access to the MS and to the Trustees of the Mark Twain Estate for permission to publish this passage.

9. *Letters from an American Farmer*, ed. Ludwig Lewisohn, New York, 1904, 49–50.
10. In *The American Adam: Innocence, Tragedy and Tradition in the Nineteenth Century*, Chicago, 1955.

when I was a boy," Mark Twain wrote in the late 1890's, "everybody was poor, but didn't know it; and everybody was comfortable, and did know it." Nevertheless, ". . . there were grades of society —people of good family, people of unclassified family, people of no family. Everybody knew everybody, and was affable to everybody, and nobody put on any visible airs; yet the class lines were quite clearly drawn and the familiar social life of each class was restricted to that class. It was a little democracy which was full of liberty, equality, and Fourth of July, and sincerely so, too; yet you perceived that the aristocratic taint was there."[11] The relations among social classes in St. Petersburg resemble those which Mark Twain recalled in Hannibal. It is true that no one seems to have social status markedly higher than Tom's. The Widow Douglas, whose mansion on the summit of Cardiff Hill is "the only palace in the town," is not separated by social barriers from the bulk of the community. She is hospitable and "lavish in the matter of festivities."[12] On the day of Becky Thatcher's picnic and excursion to the cave, Tom takes it for granted that anyone of the party who wishes may "stop at the Widow Douglas's" that evening to eat ice cream, without invitation; ". . . she'll be awful glad to have us," he declares, and Becky agrees with him.[13] But although there is no clear line between middle and upper class, the line between middle and lower is well defined. Huck is not invited to the picnic and it does not occur to him to join the evening party at the Widow's. For Huck is "the juvenile pariah of the village," "cordially hated and dreaded by all the mothers of the town, because he was idle and lawless and vulgar and bad . . ." "Tom," we learn, "was like the rest of the respectable boys, in that he envied Huckleberry his gaudy outcast condition, and was under strict orders not to play with him."[14]

The difference in social status between the middle-class Tom and the clearly lower-class Huck becomes important in *Adventures of Huckleberry Finn* because after writing the first novel more or less from Tom's point of view, in the sequel, which he began at once, Mark Twain commits himself to the viewpoint and therefore the perspective of Huck. This technical decision involves a drastic change in the image of Hannibal. *Huckleberry Finn* focuses attention on aspects of St. Petersburg that are barely mentioned in the earlier novel. The town drunkard who was seen sleeping near the steamboat landing in "Old Times on the Mississippi" now appears as the Pap from whom Huck has to run away literally to save his life. In his flight Huck encounters another fugitive, Jim, who has

11. *Mark Twain's Autobiography*, ed. Albert B. Paine, 2 vols., New York, 1924, I, 119–120.
12. DE, VIII, 43. See footnote 7. Here and throughout, "DE" refers to the Definitive Edition.
13. DE, VIII, 230.
14. DE, VIII, 54.

been threatened with being sold down the river. The blissful security in which Tom can play at being a bad boy is seen to be only accidental: not every boy in St. Petersburg is so fortunate. Slavery, which was blandly taken for granted in *Tom Sawyer*, is now made real in the figure of Jim sitting on the raft at daybreak "with his head down betwixt his knees, moaning and mourning to himself" for his wife and children.[15] Both Pap's bestiality and Jim's escape pose moral problems for Huck that transcend the carefully limited child's universe of the earlier story.

The first release of creative energy in 1876 carried Mark Twain only to Chapter XVI of his new book.[16] Yet even in this fragment certain characteristics of the novel are established beyond the possibility of change. The image of Hannibal has lost its magical power to generate the sense of security that defines Tom's world. The dream of innocence has not entirely vanished, but it is now associated not with the town but with the natural setting, and even here it is qualified by the physical and moral squalor that Pap brings to the cabin on the Illinois shore, and by the danger of pursuit that compels Huck and Jim to flee from Jackson's Island. Happiness, peace, freedom are to be found, if at all, only on the River, on the raft.

In the magnificent middle section of *Huckleberry Finn* (Chapters XIX–XXXIII), written between 1880 and the late summer of 1883, the contrast between the peace and freedom of the raft and the predominantly unattractive life of the towns along the shore becomes a recurrent theme. These squalid towns are very different from the idyllic St. Petersburg of *Tom Sawyer*, but they belong just as clearly to the Matter of Hannibal. Mark Twain gives them many details of setting and incident remembered from his boyhood. Most conspicuous among these autobiographical materials, because it is so prominent in the novel, is the shooting of old Boggs by Colonel Sherburn in the main street of Bricksville (Chapter XXI). The incident is based on the shooting of one Uncle Sam Smarr by William Owsley in Hannibal on January 24, 1845, when Sam Clemens was nine years old. It is not certain that the child actually saw the murder, but he probably did witness Owsley's confrontation of a mob.[17] It had all come back into his mind when he was writing to Will Bowen in 1870. The loafers in front of the stores of Bricksville are familiar from the description of Hannibal in "Old Times on the Mississippi." But let us recall some of the details of this celebrated chapter:

"The stores and houses was most all old, shackly, dried-up frame concerns that hadn't ever been painted; they was set up three or

15. DE, XIII, 215.
16. Walter Blair, "When Was *Huckleberry Finn* Written?" *American Litera-* *ture,* XXX, 1–25 (March, 1958).
17. Dixon Wecter, *Sam Clemens of Hannibal,* Boston, 1952, p. 108.

four foot above ground on stilts, so as to be out of reach of the water when the river was overflowed. The houses had little gardens around them, but they didn't seem to raise hardly anything in them but jimpson-weeds, and sunflowers, and ash-piles, and old curled-up boots and shoes, and pieces of bottles, and rags, and played-out tinware. . . ."

The loafers "roost" on empty drygoods boxes under the awnings, whittling "and chawing tobacco, and gaping and yawning and stretching—a mighty ornery lot." "All the streets and lanes was just mud . . . The hogs loafed and grunted around everywheres. You'd see a muddy sow and a litter of pigs come lazying along the street and whollop herself right down in the way, where folks had to walk around her, and she'd stretch out and shut her eyes and wave her ears whilst the pigs was milking her, and look as happy as if she was on salary."[18]

The difference in atmosphere between Bricksville and St. Peters burg is emphasized by the fact that St. Petersburg is white, while this town is dingy and weatherbeaten. Possibly St. Petersburg's whiteness is due to actual paint on houses in a historical Hannibal and Bricksville's shabbiness is borrowed from some actual unpainted town in Arkansas.[19] But one suspects that St. Petersburg has been whitened and Bricksville darkened in color mainly by projected emotion. Mark Twain meant to affirm St. Petersburg; he means to reject Bricksville. He describes at length the murder of Boggs, the idiotic behavior of the townspeople, and their futile effort to muster enough courage to lynch Colonel Sherburn; and he becomes so deeply involved in Sherburn's denunciation of the mob that he casts aside the mask of Huck Finn to speak in unmistakable accents of his own disgust.

The recognition that the image of Hannibal has altered so much between the composition of *Tom Sawyer* and that of *Huckleberry Finn* inevitably raises the question of causes. Can we account for the change? Probably not; but several possible reasons for it suggest themselves. One was certainly Mark Twain's fortunate decision to have Huck tell the story of the later novel. Huck's vernacular was a language in which it was difficult to endorse the smug, comfortable attitudes of the little southern towns. Another factor making

18. DE, XIII, 192–194.
19. Group A of the notes of *Huckleberry Finn* reproduced by Bernard De Voto in *Mark Twain at Work* contains the phrase, "The Burning Shame at Napoleon, Ark." (p. 64). Napoleon was an actual town near the confluence of the Arkansas and the Mississippi. Since "The Burning Shame" was the original name of the obscene skit staged by the Duke and the King in Bricksville under the title of "The Royal Nonesuch," it seems likely that Mark Twain had in mind some relation between Bricksville and Napoleon. In *Life on the Mississippi* he tells an elaborate story of how he learned of ten thousand dollars hidden behind a stone in the wall of a livery stable in Napoleon and intended to stop there to search for it in the course of his trip down the River in 1882. But he discovered that the town had been washed away in a flood years before (DE, XII, 285).

for change in the image of Hannibal was Mark Twain's own greater sophistication. When he wrote *Tom Sawyer*, Hannibal existed for him primarily in the memory of his experiences as a boy growing up in the town. He had no perspective on it except a man's nostalgia for his own childhood. He had paid only a couple of brief visits to Hannibal since he had left it in 1853 as a youth of eighteen.[20] But when he returned to the river in 1882 he was a wealthy and famous writer. He had worked as a newspaperman in Virginia City and San Francisco and New York and Washington, he had lived in Hartford ten years, he had visited every part of the East and the Middle West on lecture tours, and he had made four trips to Europe. Through his marriage and his success as a writer he had gained an unmistakably higher social position. This change in perspective is not noticeable in what he says about the Hannibal of 1882, which was a thriving railroad center with fifteen thousand inhabitants, having little apparent relation to the town of his boyhood. The chapters about Hannibal are almost entirely given over to reminiscences. But elsewhere, except when he can note signs of commercial prosperity and growth, he views the society along the banks of the River with marked condescension. His sardonic attitude is projected back into the past in the celebrated description of "The House Beautiful," which summarizes his recollections of the typical "best dwelling, finest dwelling, mansion" of the wealthiest citizen in every town and village along the River thirty or forty years before.[21]

The House Beautiful reappears with only slight revisions as the Grangerford house in *Huckleberry Finn*, and the description of Bricksville in the novel also expresses the attitude toward the South as a whole that is set forth at length in the later chapters of *Life on the Mississippi*. Here Mark Twain draws an emphatic contrast between North and South as representing, respectively, Progress and feudal backwardness. This cult of Progress was to have a profound influence on the image of Hannibal.

Like many Southerners, Mark Twain both loved and hated his native region. He had strong emotional ties with it but condemned it with his reason—especially when he was under the sway of the attitudes current in New England, where he had lived for ten years. From the perspective of Hartford, Connecticut, not only was the South's history stained by its defense of slavery; with the emancipation of the slaves the issue had become broader: the South

---

20. In *Life on the Mississippi*, describing his visit to Hannibal in 1882, he wrote (DE, XII, 428): "I had had a glimpse of it fifteen years ago, and another glimpse six years earlier, but both were so brief that they hardly counted. The only notion of the town that remained in my mind was the memory of it as I had known it when I first quitted it twenty-nine years ago. That picture of it was still as clear and vivid to me as a photograph."

21. DE, XII, 317–322.

seemed perversely determined to identify itself with the past. It was anti-progressive. The chapters in *Life on the Mississippi* describing the South in 1882 were written from this point of view. On the other hand, when Mark Twain made his way upriver past Quincy and Burlington and Rock Island and other busy towns of the Northwest, he grew enthusiastic over the spirit of enterprise, the growth of population, the building of railroads, in a word the visible Progress which distinguished the bustling North from the backward-looking decadent South:

"From St. Louis northward there are all the enlivening signs of the presence of active, energetic, intelligent, prosperous, practical nineteenth-century populations. The people don't dream; they work. The happy result is manifest all around in the substantial outside aspect of things, and the suggestions of wholesome life and comfort that everywhere appear."

.   .   .   .

"In the beginning Quincy had the aspect and ways of a model New England town: and these she has yet; broad, clean streets, trim, neat dwellings and lawns, fine mansions, stately blocks of commercial buildings. And there are ample fair-grounds, a well-kept park, and many attractive drives; library, reading-rooms, a couple of colleges, some handsome and costly churches, and a grand court-house, with grounds which occupy a square. The population of the city is thirty thousand. There are some large factories here, and manufacturing, of many sorts, is done on a great scale."[22]

We stand here close to the throbbing heart of Philistinism. One feels that a truly great writer of real-estate advertising was lost in the author of this ode to Quincy, Illinois. To be sure, Mark Twain is straining to produce the requisite number of pages for a proper subscription book. Nevertheless, to part of his mind, the part that (in T. S. Eliot's phrase) had been violated by ideas, Quincy with its grand courthouse was undoubtedly more pleasing than Baton Rouge with its pseudo-Gothic capitol. He preferred the nineteenth-century smell of the railway to the suffocating perfume of the magnolia.

Yet Mark Twain also had strong feelings that ran exactly counter to this cult of Progress. Remembering old times on the river, he regretted that lights maintained by the federal government had "knocked the romance out of piloting," and that the lumber rafts he saw in 1882 were not "floating leisurely along, in the old-fashioned way, manned with joyous and reckless crews of fiddling, song-singing, whisky-drinking, breakdown-dancing rapscallions," but instead were being "shoved swiftly along by a powerful stern-wheeler, modern fashion," whose crew were "quiet, orderly men,

22. DE, XII, 461–462.

of a sedate business aspect, with not a suggestion of romance about them anywhere."[23]

In Mark Twain's previous work this conflict of attitudes had not found full expression. *Tom Sawyer* had embodied a relatively simple image of Hannibal as Eden, and even *Huckleberry Finn*, for all its attention to the sordid details of life in the river towns, would give the author no occasion for proclaiming the doctrine of Progress. This greatest of Mark Twain's books bears hardly a trace of general ideas not rendered concretely. But his passionate interest in the question of Progress versus Reaction, the Future versus the Past, was certain eventually to find expression in fiction. The occasion came when George W. Cable gave him a copy of Malory's *Morte d'Arthur* and he conceived the notion of writing a burlesque of it. The result was *A Connecticut Yankee in King Arthur's Court*, published in 1889, four years after the publication of *Huckleberry Finn*.

In *A Connecticut Yankee* Progress is seen primarily as technological development, but a high level of technology necessarily implies republicanism, separation of church and state, abolition of slavery, and a number of other social and political tendencies which Mark Twain considered "modern." This alignment of values made necessary yet a further reinterpretation of the image of Hannibal. For as we have seen, Hannibal—in its guise of St. Petersburg at least—had been conceived of as "a little democracy" in which a general equality of condition and freedom from oppression more than compensated for the absence of the traits of a high civilization. But if Hannibal was perceived as being Southern, that is as backward and unprogressive, such claims could no longer be made for it. In the course of the 1880's the image of Hannibal ceased to be for Mark Twain the repository of the values of democracy. Instead, he adopted the view that democracy is one of the fruits of Progress, that it comes at the end of the historical process begun by industrialization.

* * *

The final catastrophe which destroys Arthur's kingdom through civil war is explicitly represented as an outgrowth of financial conflict. Sir Lancelot buys up the "wildcat" stock of the London, Canterbury & Dover railway while it is still under construction. The other knights of the Round Table are selling the stock short, and when he has his corner he skins them alive. Sir Agravaine and Sir Mordred, nephews of the king, take revenge on Lancelot by calling the king's attention to the adulterous affair of long standing between Lancelot and Guinevere. The outcome is civil war, as in Malory and Tennyson.

Mark Twain believed that something comparable to this had hap-

23. DE, XII, 232, 476.

pened to the United States during his lifetime. He had spent his boyhood in a village hardly touched by machines. But at the age of fifty he found himself living in a society that had moved far along the road toward industrialization and was accelerating every year the pace of its economic transformation. Progress had undoubtedly taken place, on a scale and at a rate without precedent in history. All the premises of the Enlightenment had been validated and all its promises fulfilled, as far as any tangible measure of fulfillment could be applied. And yet the outcome somehow failed to live up to the millennial expectations that the doctrines of Progress had fostered. What was the matter? Where had history gone astray?

To these questions Mark Twain would never find satisfactory answers, but he wrestled with them the rest of his life. The conclusion he most often came to was that the love of money had debauched America and frustrated the promise of the Great Civilization. In the Hannibal of his youth, he wrote in 1897 in the "Villagers" MS, "To get rich was no one's ambition—it was not in any young person's thoughts. . . . It was an intensely sentimental age, but it took no sordid form. The Californian rush for wealth in '49 introduced the change & begot the lust for money which is the rule of life today, & the hardness & cynicism which is the spirit of today." * * *

Mark Twain came nearer registering in fiction the death of nineteenth-century culture than did such contemporaries as Howells, whose remarkable gifts as a novelist could not in the end overcome his intellectual confusion, or James, who created the technique of the modern novel but paid the price for his single-minded devotion to art by failing to recognize the countenance of the twentieth century until the outbreak of the First World War. From the 1890's onward Mark Twain was struggling with his perception that democracy had been corrupted by money and that war was the normal behavior of modern as well as of ancient nations. When he tried to ignore these insights his work had no vitality, yet he could not devise a form to embody them. *The Mysterious Stranger*, his nearest approach to such a feat, was left unfinished at his death. He had bet too much on the doctrine of Progress and the belief in an orderly benign universe to be able to emulate the younger writers who in his old age were finding literary capital in the master image of the Waste Land and were beginning to produce a whole literature of alienation.

Nevertheless the image of Hannibal had served him better than he or anyone else knew in his day. As we have slowly become aware, the development of twentieth-century American literature, its dominant themes and above all its language, began on the day in 1876 when Mark Twain conceived the idea of treating the Matter of Hannibal from the viewpoint of the outcast, Huckleberry Finn.

KENNETH S. LYNN

You Can't Go Again†

In *Huckleberry Finn,* * * * Twain proposed to develop for the first time on a major scale the conflict adumbrated in the story. The novel was to be told in the first person, and the action was to be essentially psychological: in his own words, the boy would tell of being caught in the crossfire between his environment-trained conscience and his "Voices," as Twain's Joan would say, and of his agonizing struggle to decide whether or not to become a liberator.

* * *

The liberation theme is announced in the title of the novel's very first chapter: "I Discover Moses and the Bulrushers." For although Huck soon loses all interest in the Moses story, "because I don't take no stock in dead people," the humorous introduction of the Biblical saga at the very start of the book effectively ushers in the majestic theme of slavery and freedom, and inextricably associates Huck—a native of the river valley which its most famous citizen, Abraham Lincoln, called the "Egypt of the West"—with the little Jewish child who, abandoned in a great, continental river, grew up to lead an enslaved people to freedom. In the early chapters the liberation theme is developed *a verso* in terms of the idea of confinement, for these describe Huck's life at the Widow's which Twain had been tempted to include in *Tom Sawyer* and then had decided not to on the grounds that they were not a part of Tom's story. Once again the tribe is attempting to administer the ephebic rites to a free-spirited boy, with comic results. When Huck is sworn into Tom Sawyer's gang and introduced to Miss Watson's and the Widow Douglas's piety, he is in both cases being shown how a respectable St. Petersburg boy is expected to behave, and in both initiations he resists the mysteries. Sancho Panza to Tom's Quixote, Huck sees only turnips and Sunday school picnickers where Tom imagines "julery" and "rich A-rabs." For his down-to-earth honesty, Tom calls him a "numskull," a judgment which is echoed by Miss Watson when she discovers that he has called on God for fishhooks

† Chapter IX, Sections iii, vii, and viii, of *Mark Twain and Southwestern Humor* by Kenneth S. Lynn, by permission of Little, Brown & Co. Copyright © 1959, by Kenneth S. Lynn.

as a result of her having told him that he would receive whatever he prayed for. But revealing as these incidents are, the most telling indication of Huck's spiritual difference from the rest of the community, as well as a premonition of the stirring drama of liberation that lies ahead, is his refusal to help Tom Sawyer tie up Nigger Jim "for fun."

Restless in his confinement to respectability, Huck echoes the narrator of *Roughing It* in his confession that "All I wanted was to go somewheres; all I wanted was a change." Yet in these early chapters, his rebellion does not seem much more serious, finally, than Tom's had been. His occasional forays into the freedom of his cast-off rags and his hogsheads are short-lived; by the time that winter comes we find him admitting that whereas he still prefers his old ways, "I was getting so I liked the new ones, too, a little bit." When his outcast Pap reappears and takes him off to the woods, Huck at first thinks he has regained his lost freedom, only to find that freedom means being locked up in a lonely cabin for days on end— means being a captive audience for his Pap's tirades about "free niggers"; and that for all the delights of shoelessness and pipe-smoking, he has in fact exchanged the discomforts and restrictions of respectability for a disreputable prison.

In writing the episode of Huck and Pap in their cabin home, Twain in all likelihood was drawing on the memory of his relationship with his own father. Although Twain's mother was warm-hearted, the family atmosphere in the Clemens household was dominated by the personality of his father, John Marshall Clemens. Thanks to this strange, austere, loveless man, the Clemenses were reserved and formal with one another to an almost unbelievable degree; at night, they shook hands before going to bed—a warmer gesture would have been unthinkable. Indeed, in later years Twain could remember only one time when a kiss was ever exchanged between members of the Clemens family. The story that Mrs. Clemens was disappointed in love and married her husband out of spite has never been satisfactorily verified, but there is no doubt as to the nature of the relationship between the father and his son Sam. As Twain recalled, "My father and I were always on the most distant terms when I was a boy—a sort of armed neutrality, so to speak." In such an atmosphere, Twain must have suffered almost daily from rejection, but the instance that seemed to him to epito-mize all his experiences of parental neglect was the time when his family, moving from Florida, Missouri, to a new home in Hannibal, drove off without him. Writing an article in later years for the *North American Review*, Twain could still remember the "grisly deep silence" that fell upon the locked house after his family had gone, and the nameless terrors that gripped him as the afternoon waned into evening. The story is engrossing, but as Dixon Wecter has pointed out, untrue, for Twain was here describing as a personal experience something that in fact happened to his brother, Orion. So acute, apparently, was Twain's sense of rejection that in looking back on his early life he was convinced that it was surely he who had suffered the agony of being locked up and forgotten.

Huck's lonesome vigil in the locked-up cabin is the equivalent of the experience that Twain believed had happened to him. And Huck's outlaw Pap is a nightmare version of Twain's hardhearted father: "He was most fifty, and he looked it. His hair was long and tangled and greasy, and hung down, and you could see his eyes shining through like he was behind vines. . . . There warn't no color in his face, where his face showed; it was white to make a body's flesh crawl—a tree-toad white, a fish-belly white." Between this terrible father and his son armed neutrality is but the prelude to open war. The day after Pap tries to kill Huck with a claspknife, Huck manages to escape from the cabin by committing symbolic suicide and murder. So that his Pap will not pursue him, Huck simulates his own death by killing a wild pig and distributing its blood around the cabin; but this act has a double meaning, which emerges only when we recall Pap Finn's notorious habit of lying drunk amongst the hogs in the tanyard, as well as the drunkard's slobberingly self-pitying identification of himself with his sleeping companions: "There's the hand that was the hand of a hog." Huck's slaughter of the pig not only symbolizes his desire to end his own miserable life, but to slay his father and the sordid animality of his ways.

Bursting clear of the locked-up cabin, Huck is simply running away from his past, rather than toward any definable future. On the one hand, he is not prepared to go back and be "cramped up and sivilized" at the Widow's, while on the other—as his symbolic murder of his Pap makes clear—he has also rejected the life of a social outcast. He has neither embraced St. Petersburg nor turned his back on it. Slipping into the river, an officially dead Huck is "reborn." Yet he has no ideas about a new life and a new identity for himself. Irresolute and uncertain, Huck instinctively turns toward a familiar goal: Jackson's Island, Tom Sawyer's halfway-house of rebellion where all irrevocable decisions are magically held in abeyance.

The means by which Huck will find out who he now is is illustrated by a parable in Chapter XVI. The parable is a part of an episode which did not appear in the novel when it was finally completed, because Twain had already thrown it—the verb is his—into *Life on the Mississippi*. Unsure as to when, if ever, he would finish *Huckleberry Finn*, and wishing to flesh out his history of the river with a dramatization of "keelboat talk and manners" as they had existed in the 1840s, Twain improved a good book at the cost of looting his masterpiece of an episode of extraordinary richness, of great beauty and humor, which takes us to the heart of the novel.

The episode begins immediately after Huck and Jim's terrifying experience of getting lost in the fog. Drifting down an unfamiliar and "monstrous big river," the boy and the Negro decide that Huck should find out where they are by swimming over to a huge raft they have seen in the distance and gathering the information by eavesdropping. Under cover of darkness, Huck reaches the raft, climbs on board without being noticed, and settles down to listen to the talk of the raftsmen—to their colossal boasting, their roaring songs, and above all, to the fantastic tall tale about a man named Dick Allbright and the mysterious barrel that followed him on the river wherever he went rafting, bringing terror and death to his companions. Nothing, the teller of the tale assures his audience, could keep the barrel off Dick Allbright's trail, or mitigate its inexorable fatality, until finally a raft captain swam out to the barrel and hauled it aboard. Inside its wooden walls, the captain and his men found a stark naked baby—

". . . Dick Allbright's baby; he owned up and said so. 'Yes,' he says, a-leaning over it, 'yes, it is my own lamented darling, my poor lost Charles William Allbright deceased,' says he—for he could curl his tongue around the bulliest words in the language when he was a mind to. . . . Yes, he said he used to live up at the head of this bend, and one night he choked his child, which was crying, not intending to kill it—which was prob'ly a lie—and then he was scared, and buried it in a bar'l, before his wife got home, and off he went, and struck the northern trail and went to rafting; and this was the third year that the bar'l had chased him."

Crouched in the darkness, naked and afraid, Huck seems utterly apart from these coarse, rough men. Nevertheless, the fantasy of violence and terror which the raftsman has spun for the scoffing delight of his fellows vitally involves the runaway boy, an involvement which Huck himself acknowledges. For when he is suddenly seized from his hiding-place and surrounded by strange men demanding to know his name, he jokingly replies, "Charles William Allbright, sir." Always in Twain the best jokes reveal the profoundest connections, and with the release of laughter triggered by this superbly timed response we are made aware that we have been eavesdropping on a parable about Huck Finn's life. The entire incident magnificently exemplifies how Mark Twain could exploit for the purposes of high art the tradition of Southwestern humor—and shows, too, what very different effects he achieved. The ignorant river waif who has replaced the Self-controlled Gentleman as auditor is deeply and personally involved in the story he hears, rather than amusedly aloof from it. Charles William Allbright afloat in his barrel mirrors the situation of Huck on the raft: having died, both boys have come alive again in the flowing waters of the great Mississippi. Charles William Allbright in his barrel also calls up once again the infant Moses hidden in the ark of bulrushes in the Nile, and in so doing associates the drama of liberating an enslaved people with the ideas of freedom and renewal of life that the river connotes. At the very heart of the parable there is an even more breathtaking illumination. Charles William Allbright, having lost his father, has taken to the river to go in search of him. In telling us that, the parable tells us things about Huck Finn that Huck himself cannot possibly communicate. Drifting down the river toward a goal he can neither define nor scarcely imagine, Huck is in fact looking for another father to replace the one he has lost. And this quest is also a quest for himself, because once Huck has found his new father he will know at last who he himself really is. Upon that recognition, in turn, rests the resolution of the struggle between Huck's conscience and the impulse of his generous heart as to what to do about Jim. The novel's grand theme, then, the Mosaic drama of liberation, depends ultimately upon the outcome of Huck's search for a father.

The parenthood problem is officially introduced in the fifth chapter of the novel, when Judge Thatcher and the Widow Douglas go to court to get permission to take Huck away from his Pap. Who should be his parents, the respectable aristocrats who are no blood relation to him, or his violent, drunken father? Nothing less than a human life is at stake; the decision would seem to call for the wisdom of Solomon. Echoing Huck's judgment of Moses, Nigger Jim "doan' take no stock" in the wisdom of Solomon, yet in Chapter XIV—entitled "Was Solomon Wise?"—our laughter at Jim's stupidity carries with it the realization that the parenthood problem, like the liberation theme, has been given a deeper moral seriousness through a Biblical association. Jim regards it as utter foolishness that Solomon should have attempted to settle the parenthood dispute by offering to cut the child in two and give half to each mother —"De 'spute warn't 'bout half a chile, de 'spute was 'bout a whole chile; en de man dat think he kin settle a 'spute 'bout a whole chile wid a half a chile doan' know enough to come in out'n de rain." Twain himself was very fond of this chapter and delighted in reading it aloud in public lectures. But if it can be successfully taken out of context, the scene is also a vital element in the moral pattern of the novel. For Huck, like Solomon, is listening for the voice of truth and the accents of love as a means of identifying the true parent he seeks. Neither side in the legal contest so identifies itself, and therefore Huck retreats from both respectability and hoggishness to the way station of Jackson's Island. In doing so he is certainly not acting self-consciously: he is simply drifting with the tide—quite literally—and not even wondering what will happen to him next. All that this ignorant and inexperienced child is able to tell us directly about himself is that it is awful to be so "dreadful lonesome." Encountering the outcast colored man in hiding on the island, Huck is at first merely amused and exasperated by the black man's stupidity, but part of the drama of their relationship is Huck's gathering awareness that Jim is "most always right" about things that really matter, about how certain movements of the birds mean a storm is coming, about the dangers of messing with snakes, and the meaning of dreams. But while Jim's relationship to Huck is fatherly in the sense that he constantly is correcting and admonishing the boy, forever telling him some new truth about the world, he is identified even more unmistakably as Huck's father by the love that he gives him. As Huck is searching for a father, so Jim is attempting to rejoin his family, and he lavishes on the love-starved boy all of his parental affection. Jim's ludicrous horror at Solomon's apparent willingness to split a child in two is seen in retrospect to be a humorous statement of his loving care for the integrity of his white child.

As it gradually dawns on Huck—and the gradualness of his realization is very delicately controlled by Twain—that Jim loves him, the psychological battle within Huck's mind intensifies accordingly. * * * In Chapter XVI of *Huckleberry Finn*, an environment-trained conscience punishes Huck for his subversive association with the runaway slave with an even greater ferocity:

"Jim said it made him all over trembly and feverish to be so close to freedom. Well, I can tell you it made me all over trembly and feverish, too, to hear him, because I begun to get it through my head that he *was* most free—and who was to blame for it? Why, *me*. I couldn't get that out of my conscience, no how nor no way. It got to troubling me so I couldn't rest; I couldn't stay still in one place. It hadn't ever come home to me before, what this thing was that I was doing. But now it did; and it stayed with me, and scorched me more and more. I tried to make out to myself that *I* warn't to blame, because *I* didn't run Jim off from his rightful owner; but it warn't no use, conscience up and says, ever/ time, 'But you knowed he was running for his freedom, and you could a paddled ashore and told somebody.' That was so—I couldn't get around that noway. That was where it pinched. Conscience says to me, 'What had poor Miss Watson done to you that you could see her nigger go off right under your eyes and never say one single word? What did that poor woman do to you that you could treat her so mean? Why, she tried to learn you your book, she tried to learn you your manners, she tried to be good to you every way she knowed how. *That's* what she done.'

I got to feeling so mean and so miserable I most wished I was dead."

With these words, the first of the novel's really notable representations of moral doubt, Huck at last comes to understand the dilemma confronting him. The battle in his mind is at this point fully joined.

And at this point, Twain could go no further. Having brought a rich and various novel to a moment of psychological crisis; having managed all the complexities of the action with superb facility; Twain abandoned *Huckleberry Finn* at the end of Chapter XVI and threatened to burn the manuscript. The author did not, probably could not, analyze why he was unable to go on. To Twain—accustomed as he was to writing by fits and starts—the failure of his inspiration may not even have bothered him as much as his bitter letter to Will Bowen might suggest. At least, not at first. For Twain was also accustomed to having his "tank" fill up again in a reasonable period of time. In this case, seven long years would pass before he would find himself able to finish the novel. Renewed efforts to get the book moving again during this Biblical period of barrenness resulted in a few additional chapters, but nothing more. Clearly, Twain in August of 1876 had run into unprecedented difficulties which his usual remedy for a recalcitrant manuscript of pigeonholing it for a time could not overcome.

The question—the fascinating question—is: What was the nature of those difficulties? What was the problem that arose in Chapter XVI and that so stubbornly resisted solution? Some of Twain's most knowledgeable critics, including Bernard DeVoto and Henry Nash Smith, have pointed to the fact that in Chapter XVI Huck and Jim discover they have drifted past Cairo in the fog, and that therefore Jim's plan of taking a steamboat up the Ohio toward a free state could no longer be used by Twain as an excuse for moving Huck and Jim downstream on the Mississippi. Now, Twain obviously wanted to have the two runaways continue their voyage southward, if only because it was the Mississippi Valley, not the Ohio, that he knew so well from his piloting days; yet to have a slave seek for freedom by heading deeper and deeper into the heart of the slave country was quite incredible. Baffled as to how to resolve this problem—so Professor Smith has argued—Twain abandoned the novel at the end of Chapter XVI; picked it up in the winter of 1879–1880 long enough to add Chapters XVII and XVIII; but was unable really to get rolling again until he struck upon the idea of introducing the King and the Duke. For once the King and the

Duke come aboard the raft in Chapter XIX, they master it, and the desire of Nigger Jim to head for a free state perforce gives way to the plan of the two confidence men to proceed downstream in search of sucker money. Thus did Twain logically account for the continued southward progress of Huck and Jim. Once he had done this, he was able to go on with the book.

The flaw in this argument is that the introduction of the King and the Duke emphatically did not enable Twain to proceed very far or very fast. Thanks to the ingenious detective work of Walter Blair, we know that Chapter XIX—in which the two con men first appear—was probably written in the summer of 1880, as in all likelihood was Chapter XX. But having written these chapters, Twain's inspiration once again failed him, for on the basis of the evidence he has assembled Professor Blair suspects that Chapter XXI was not written until the spring of 1883, almost three years later. Therefore, the invention of the King and the Duke can hardly be said to have released Twain's pent-up imagination, and in view of that fact it does not seem very likely that whatever was stymieing him had much to do with the question of how to account for Huck and Jim's continuing to move south. (When one recalls the unexplained illogicalities and improbabilities with which his books are replete, it seems even less likely that a little detail like the direction of a slave's escape route would have delayed as resourceful a writer as Mark Twain for very long.) Yet what other explanation is there? The text of Chapter XVI itself supplies the clue to an alternative theory.

The chapter, to repeat, shows Huck for the first time fully acknowledging his moral dilemma. Perhaps in some way the boy's dilemma was the author's as well; perhaps Mark Twain no more than Huck Finn could decide what Huck should do about Nigger Jim. To a de-Southernized Twain, it was of course unthinkable that the boy should return the Negro to slavery. On the other hand, once Huck committed the "sin" of helping Jim to freedom he would place himself forever beyond the pale of heavenly St. Petersburg; he would be carrying his irresolute rebellion against the Happy Valley to the point of no return; he would be electing to become an outcast and a renegade, like his vile Pap. As *The Adventures of Tom Sawyer* unforgettably shows, the vision of an unfallen American Eden meant an enormous amount to Twain. And that vision was validated and defined by the thought of innocent boys playing there, in a dreaming and eternal summertime. That Huck should be cast out of St. Petersburg was thus equally unthinkable to Twain. Tom Sawyer's rebellion against this magic place had been simply child's play, ending in reconciliation and acceptance. But Huck Finn's rebellion had turned into a far more drastic business. It was as if Joan of Arc had been called on to save France by flouting Heaven's decrees.

Unlike the hero of "Carnival,"† Huck did not bear a vindictive grudge against respectable society; for antebellum Missouri, unlike post-Civil War Connecticut, was seen by Twain at long distance in both space and time, a perspective which reduced all motives for hatred, all social coercions, to delightful jokes. Without a single exception, the respectable inhabitants of the Happy Valley whom Huck encounters in the first sixteen chapters of the novel—the Widow Douglas, Judge Thatcher, Tom Sawyer, Miss Watson, Judith Loftus, the night watchman, even Mr. Parker, the slave-hunter—are fundamentally decent people. What, indeed, had they done to Huck that he should treat them so mean? Twain in 1876 could present Huck's dilemma—brilliantly present it, because it sprang directly out of a deep conflict in his own feelings—but he was completely unable to resolve it.

* * *

vii

Chapter XXI of the novel, Professor Blair suspects, was written in the spring of 1883—exactly a year after Twain's visit to the river.‡ It was the first sign that the long drought in his "tank" was over. Then the following summer, at Elmira, inspiration came like a flood. Soon Twain was writing to Howells that "I haven't piled up MS so in years as I have done since we came here to the farm three weeks and a half ago. Why, it's like old times, to step right into the study, damp from the breakfast table, and sail right in and sail right on, the whole day long, without thought of running short of stuff or words. I wrote 4000 words today and I touch 3000 and upwards pretty often, and don't fall below 2600 any working day." To Orion and his family Twain averred that "I am piling up manuscript in a really astonishing way. I believe I shall complete, in two months, a book which I have been fooling over for 7 years. This summer it is no more trouble to me to write than it is to lie." Shortly thereafter, the book was done.

Twain's altered view of the Valley society is immediately established in two sets of interrelated and successive chapters, XXI–XXII and XXIII–XXIV, the first four chapters written subsequent to the 1882 trip.

In Chapter XXII, Huck goes to a circus, sees a drunken man weaving around the ring on horseback, and is terribly distressed—although the crowd roars with delight. But it is not Huck's charming naïveté in not recognizing that the drunkard is a clown that Twain condemns, it is the callousness of the crowd. For this circus scene

† Twain's comic self-portrait, entitled "Facts Concerning the Recent Carnival of Crime in Connecticut," 1876 [Editors].
‡ In the spring of 1882, preparatory to finishing the descriptive *Life on the Mississippi*. It is conjectured that this renewal of boyhood scenes influenced his return to *Huck*, abandoned at Chapter XX in 1880 [Editors].

depends upon the preceding Chapter XXI, which really does involve a drunk, the drunken Boggs, who weaves down the street on
horseback, shouting insults at Colonel Sherburn. When Sherburn
mortally wounds Boggs, a crowd gathers excitedly around the drunkard to watch him die. Everyone is tremendously pleased—except
Huck, and the dying man's daughter. By this juxtaposition of episodes, each of which contrasts the boy's sympathetic concern with
the gleeful howling of the crowd, Twain lays bare the moral callousness of a society that views life romantically—that regards suffering
as a circus.

The Arkansas town in which these two chapters take place is
another version of Hannibal, but the place has nothing in common
with the lovely, white-painted town that had sustained Twain's
imagination for twenty-nine years. In contrast to the heavenly St.
Petersburg he had summoned up in *Tom Sawyer*, Bricksville, Arkansas, is a squalid hole:

> "The houses had little gardens around them, but they didn't
> seem to raise hardly anything in them but jimpson-weeds, and
> sun-flowers, and ash piles, and old curled-up boots and shoes, and
> pieces of bottles, and rags, and played-out tinware. . . . There was
> generly hogs in the garden, and people driving them out. . . . All
> the streets and lanes was just mud; they warn't nothing else *but*
> mud—mud as black as tar and nigh about a foot deep in some
> places, and two or three inches deep in *all* places. The hogs loafed
> and grunted around everywhere."

Images of whiteness have been replaced by images of blackness
and filth; gardens no longer bloom in this fallen Eden; and everywhere there are hogs, heretofore associated not with organized
society but with violent and unscrupulous outlaws. Twain once
observed that the Negroes he knew as a boy feared being sold
"down the river" as the equivalent of being sent to Hell, and Nigger
Jim has run away precisely because of this fear. In Bricksville, the
Negro's nightmare becomes the novel's reality. The 1883 version of
Hannibal is a veritable Hell, populated by a company of the
damned. Huck and Jim's voyage southward from St. Petersburg has
in fact become—like the course of the stars that were hove out of
the nest—a downward fall.

As if he were worried that the contrast between the two drunks
was too subtle a condemnation, Twain chose—for the first and only
time in the novel—to violate Huck's point of view in Chapter
XXII and speak to the reader through another mask, in order that
he might ram home his moral judgment of the society in explicit
and unmistakable terms. The mask he chose to assume for this
brief moment was a familiar one in Southwestern humor: the mask
of a Southern aristocrat. Not, to be sure, the cool and collected

Gentleman of the Whig myth, for Colonel Sherburn is self-admittedly a killer. Nor is Sherburn concerned to instruct the mob in the virtues of the temperate life. His furiously contemptuous opinion of the townspeople carries with it no hope that they will ever improve:

"Do I know you? I know you clear through. I was born and raised in the South, and I've lived in the North; so I know the average all around. The average man's a coward. In the North he lets anybody walk over him that wants to. . . . In the South one man, all by himself, has robbed a stage full of men in the daytime, and robbed the lot. . . . Why don't your juries hang murderers? Because they're afraid the man's friends will shoot them in the back in the dark—and it's just what they *would* do. So they always acquit; and then a *man* goes in the night with a hundred masked cowards at his back, and lynches the rascal. Your mistake is, that you didn't bring a man with you; that's one mistake, and the other is that you didn't come in the dark and fetch your masks."

The speech, as Professor Blair was the first to point out, is very like the passage that Twain cut from *Life on the Mississippi* about the withering-away of independent thought and action in Southern life. Sherburn's condemnation has been broadened out somewhat to make a more inclusive judgment of Americans everywhere, but it centers none the less on the degradation of human character in the monolithic South.

The point of ironic connection between Chapters XXIII and XXIV occurs in their conclusions. The last paragraph of Chapter XXIII is perhaps the most poignant moment in the entire novel, for it is here that Jim relates to Huck how his daughter, after recovering from scarlet fever, became a mysteriously disobedient child. Even when Jim had slapped her and sent her sprawling, she refused to obey his orders, but just as he was going for her again, he realized what was wrong: "De Lord God Almighty fogive po' ole Jim, kaze he never gwyne to fogive hisself as long's he live! Oh, she was plumb deef en dumb, Huck, plumb deef en dumb—en I'd ben a-treat'n her so!" On the last page of Chapter XXIV, the King and the Duke arrive at the little Tennessee town where they expect to rob the Wilks girls of their inheritance by playing the parts, respectively, of a parson and a deaf mute. When viewed beside Jim's sorrow and compassion for his deaf-and-dumb daughter, the spectacle of the two frauds talking on their hands is sickening— "It was enough," says Huck, "to make a body ashamed of the human race."

The striking difference between Huck's account of the confidence game that the King and the Duke work on the Tennessee town and the King's swindle of the Pokeville camp meeting is that the gullible townspeople now seem as subhuman as the crooks who defraud them. As Henry Nash Smith has pointed out, when the townspeople move rapidly up the street to have a look at the newly-arrived "parson" and "deaf mute," Huck likens them to soldiers marching along, thereby calling attention to their regimented minds and lives. A moment later, he refers to them as a "gang" which is "trotting along," as if they reminded him of a herd of squealing pigs. The people of what was once the Happy Valley are now not only associated with, but have actually become, the dirty animals which are the novel's leading symbol of degradation and sordidness. Huck Finn—and Mark Twain—have come a long way from St. Petersburg.

Sickened by society, Huck finds refuge in the fatherly bosom of Nigger Jim, even as Little Eva had turned to Uncle Tom. To what extent Twain had *Uncle Tom's Cabin* in mind when he conceived of the relationship between Huck and Jim can never be known, for with neighborly good manners he did not make public comments about Mrs. Stowe's famous book. We know that George Washington Cable burst into tears when he read the novel as a child; we know that the character of Uncle Tom had such a profound effect on Joel Chandler Harris that he seriously considered the novel to be a defense of slavery—on the grounds that any system which could produce such a holy man must necessarily be good; we know, indeed, the reaction of a vast number of individual Americans to *Uncle Tom's Cabin*; but not Mark Twain's. Yet Uncle Tom and little Eva, talking rapturously about reunion in Heaven, clearly have something to do with Huck's decision to go to Hell rather than send Jim back to slavery: in both instances, the black man and the white child are morally united against the organized world. Little Eva and Uncle Tom are brought together by their unquestioning acceptance of the Will of God; Huck and Jim are also united by their common beliefs—in the comparative harmlessness of stealing an occasional chicken or watermelon; in the delights of going naked in the starlight, and of smoking a pipe after breakfast; in the undoubted existence of ghosts, and the significance of "signs." In both novels, the child-Negro relationship exists on a level of emotional ecstasy, the extraordinary intensity of which derived from an unappeased longing of the author's.

For just as the religious ecstasy of Uncle Tom and Little Eva illuminates the spiritual biography of the doubt-ridden daughter of Lyman Beecher, so the raft life of Huck and Jim tells us much about the emotional hunger of John Marshall Clemens's son. Seeking for release from the emotional austerity of the Clemens household, the young Mark Twain had turned almost inevitably to the warm, black underworld of the slaves. Many, many years later, Twain could still recall

"the look of Uncle Dan'l's kitchen as it was on the privileged nights, when I was a child, and I can see the white and black children grouped on the hearth, with the firelight playing on their faces and the shadows flickering upon the walls, clear back toward the cavernous gloom of the rear, and I can hear Uncle Dan'l telling the immortal tales which Uncle Remus Harris was to gather into his book and charm the world with, by and by; and I can feel again the creepy joy which quivered through me when the time for the ghost story was reached—and the sense of regret, too, which came over me, for it was always the last story of the evening and there was nothing between it and the unwelcome bed."

Uncle Dan'l, Twain said, was the prototype of Nigger Jim, but as the above passage implies, Twain's memory of him was mixed up in his mind with his response to yet another literary image of the Negro, Uncle Remus. With characteristic modesty, Joel Chandler Harris felt that the only talent he had as a writer lay in his ability to transcribe accurately the Negro tales he had been listening to—on street corners, at railroad stations, along country roads—ever since the days when, as an impoverished and illegitimate child, he had found solace in the companionship of slaves. But Mark Twain assured Harris that "in reality the stories are only alligator pears—one eats them merely for the sake of the dressing." To Twain, the most meaningful part of the Uncle Remus stories was the part that Harris had contributed—the "frame," which dramatized the relationship between Uncle Remus and the little boy who comes to listen to his stories. The comment says as much about Twain as it does about Harris. Seeking for a quality of experience they could not find in their white lives, both men sent their boy-heroes in search of the companionship and understanding of the black man. He was a mythical figure, this Negro of Twain's and Harris's, a figure out of a dream, passionate, loyal, immensely dignified—a Black Christ, in sum, but with a very human sense of humor that Mrs. Stowe's great prototype notably lacked. In Uncle Remus's cabin, or spinning down the big river at night with Nigger Jim, there were beauty, and mystery, and laughter.

"It needs no scientific investigation," Harris wrote in the preface of his first book, "to show why [the Negro] selects as his hero the weakest and most harmless of all animals, and brings him out victorious in contest with the bear, the wolf, and the fox." Nor is any scientific investigation necessary to understand why Twain's and Harris's boys were drawn so irresistibly toward the black storyteller. In a world of wolves and foxes—and hogs—he was a bulwark and a refuge. The cave in *Tom Sawyer*, that vast, subterranean realm of darkness, was a place of ambivalent meaning: a place of magical excitement, full of mysterious chambers with exotic names, a dream-world where one could find the love of a young girl and buried treasure; yet death was down there, too, in the lurking presence of an "underground man" whose skin was not white; all in all, it was safer for Tom Sawyer to return to the white-painted Heaven above. But by the summer of 1883, the "cavernous gloom" of Uncle Dan'l's cabin had come to figure in Mark Twain's mind as a lonely boy's only haven. When the moment comes for Huck to choose whether to live by the precepts of his society-trained conscience or in spite of them, a Valley of Bricksvilles can offer no comparable image of love and warmth to his vision of the black man: "I see Jim there before me all the time: in the day and in the night-time, sometimes moonlight, sometimes storm, and we a-floating along, talking and singing and laughing." Unlike Tom Sawyer, Huck does not flee the "underground man"; he joins him.

viii

When Moses led the Israelites to freedom he also moved toward his prophesied appointment with death; *Huckleberry Finn* likewise moves simultaneously toward triumph and tragedy. For the liberation of Jim inexorably enforces the tragic separation of the boy and the Negro. Throughout the long, final sequence at the Phelps farm,[11] the information is withheld from the reader that a repentant Miss Watson has freed Jim on her deathbed. Yet it is perfectly clear from the moment that Tom Sawyer arrives that something is terribly wrong. Although Huck works night and day to liberate Jim from the locked-up cabin, the two of them are never really "in touch" again. They have become strangers to one another. Evidently, Mark Twain was only capable of imagining Huck and Jim's relationship as existing in the condition of slavery and under the aspect of flight—as an "underground" affair—although he tried very hard to imagine it otherwise. Hating to bring the story of the two runaways to a close, striving vainly to recreate the intense emotion that had lifted the middle section of the novel into the most memorable idyll in American literature, Twain prolonged and prolonged the final sequence into by far the longest—and the least

11. The Phelps farm is another version of John A. Quarles's farm at Florida, Missouri, but it is a "one-horse" affair by comparison with the Grangerford establishment. Nothing more clearly illustrates the effect of the 1882 trip on the images of Mark Twain's memory than the difference in size and attractiveness between the "before" and "after" portraits of the Quarles farm. As Twain observed to Howells in 1887, "When a man goes back to look at the house of his childhood it has always *shrunk;* there is no instance of such a house being as big as the picture that memory and imagination call for. Shrunk how? Why, to its correct dimensions: the house hasn't altered; this is the first time it has been in focus." Although Twain did not visit the Quarleses in 1882, the general effect of the trip was to deflate all his childhood memories.

successful—in the book.

Even the humor is not up to par. In certain moments, as Huck (masquerading as Tom Sawyer) and Tom (masquerading as his half-brother Sid) go cavorting through Aunt Sally's house, it is possible to believe that we are back once again in the high-spirited, comic world of *The Adventures of Tom Sawyer*. But Aunt Sally is Aunt Polly with a difference—the difference created by Twain's 1882 trip:

> " 'Good gracious! anybody hurt?'
> " 'No'm. Killed a nigger.'
> " 'Well, it's lucky; because people sometimes do get hurt.'

Huck and Tom are no longer playing in Heaven; a shadow has fallen across their boyish good fun, stilling the reader's laughter.

If the Phelps farm sequence fails as humor, perhaps it succeeds as anguish. For Huck is pathetically reluctant to see his beautiful dream of the raft and the river come to an end. In "Chapter the Last" he responds excitedly to Tom Sawyer's gorgeous schemes for running Jim "down the river on the raft, . . . plumb to the mouth," and for having "howling adventures amongst the Injuns over in the Territory, for a couple of weeks or two." Having turned his back on society by refusing to turn his back on Jim, Huck seeks to avoid the terrors of lonesomeness by sticking close to the colored man. Preparing to light out for the Territory at the end of the novel, he seems almost jaunty at the prospect of a reunion there with Jim and Tom Sawyer. We may well wonder, however, if his jauntiness is not simply boyish bravado—or a mask for the author's bewildered sense of loss, growing out of his awareness of the final and terrible truth about his book: which is that *Huckleberry Finn* proposes, in W. H. Auden's words, the incompatibility of love and freedom.

In *Tom Sawyer Abroad*, Twain would try to write *Huckleberry Finn* all over again, with Jim and Huck aloft with Tom Sawyer in a balloon, instead of floating downstream on a raft. And he just couldn't do it. Throughout the book's tiresome length, Huck and the colored freedman are never really together in any meaningful sense. Huck is wrapped up in Tom Sawyer's schemes, while the sorrowing, compassionate figure of the slave in *Huckleberry Finn* is barely recognizable in the minstrel-show darky of the later book. In one of the numerous sequels to *Huckleberry Finn* that Twain obsessively sketched out in his later years, Jim has somehow been caught again, and Huck fantastically plans to free him by changing places with him and blacking his face, as if by making Huck a Negro Twain hoped to bridge the gulf that now separated "son" from "father." But this desperate masquerade also proved to be imaginatively unworkable, and Huck and Jim remained forever separated. It is scarcely necessary to know that in still another contemplated sequel Twain envisioned Huck as a broken, helplessly insane old man in order to sense that at the conclusion of *Huckleberry Finn* Huck's voyage has become, for all his superficial jauntiness, as doomed to defeat as Captain Ahab's, and that in lighting out for the Territory without Jim beside him he flees with "all havens astern."

ERIC SOLOMON

[The Search for Security]†

* * * As in all great novels, the theme of *Huckleberry Finn* supplies the inner structure of the work. A judgment of the validity of the novel's ending depends in large part upon the book's motive; if art is an attempt to cast the raw materials of life into a suitable form, the author's motives, conscious or unconscious, should be taken into consideration.

All the attempts to fit the last section into the basic framework of the novel seem to lack conclusiveness. The attacks and defenses alike have one element in common—the belief that Twain's motive in writing *Huckleberry Finn* was either to show Huck's growth to maturity, to hail the joys of freedom on the river, or to depict the escape from civilization and slavery. All these elements are present and prominent in the novel. If we consider only these themes, we must see the ending of the novel as failure. By approaching *Huckleberry Finn* from another angle, we may comprehend how Twain does supply his book with a thematic unity that explains the apparent flaws of farcical tone in the final quarter of the novel.

That Twain was not usually in search of the formal perfection of orderly plotting and consistent tone in his fiction is obvious. Nevertheless, *Huckleberry Finn*, for all Twain's haphazard approach, does have a consistent theme, a theme that is emphasized throughout the novel and most heavily underlined at Phelps Farm: the novel is about a boy's search to find his identity through a satisfying family life. T. S. Eliot has touched upon this topic in passing: "Huck Finn is alone: there is no more solitary character in fiction. The fact that he has a father only emphasizes his loneliness. . . ."[1] In spite of the author's customary vigorous freedoms with unity of structure, Huck's search for a family gives Twain's novel a unity of dramatic meaning. We may concede the presence

---

† From *College English*, XXII (December 1960), 172–78. By permission of the author and *College English*.

1. T. S. Eliot, "Introduction," *The Adventures of Huckleberry Finn* (London, 1950), p. ix.

of other motives in the book; still, the idea of family is deeply imbedded in the novel's texture, and this theme makes the ending fit the essential aim of *Huckleberry Finn*.

Lies, disguises, hidden identities run through Mark Twain's fiction like an obsession. The plots of *The Prince and the Pauper, Pudd'nhead Wilson, The American Claimant,* "A Double-Barrelled Detective Story," "The Man That Corrupted Hadleyburg," to name but a few, treat the discrepancy between appearance and reality. All these stories deal with perversions of the truth. Impostors substituted for true heirs, the claims of bastard lines, long-standing feuds, willingness to cheat for family honor—indicate how Twain's fiction betrays the author's fascination with the two subjects of lies and families.

In no work does Mark Twain stress lies as heavily as in *Huckleberry Finn*. From the boys' first trick on Jim through Huck's shattering experience when he learns how a cruel lie can hurt even a Negro to the time when Huck discovers that he can't pray a lie, the novel is punctuated by Huck's elaborate disguises and fabrications. An examination of these rich and enthusiastic prevarications reveals Huck's deepest preoccupations. We see that family relationships provide the motivations for these lies.

There are six major deceptions practiced by Huck in the novel (as well as one by Jim who does not tell Huck of his father's death). In five of these lies the boy, to all purposes an orphan and outcast, invents elaborate family patterns for himself. When Huck is seeking information from Judith Loftus, he first identifies himself as Sarah Williams, a girl whose mother is sick and who is on her way to get help from her uncle, Abner Moore. After being discovered in this lie, Huck calls himself George Peters, a run-away apprentice whose parents are dead. But Uncle Abner Moore is retained as the object of the orphan's quest.

Huck makes his next dissimulation[2] to the watchman of a ferry-boat in order to save from drowning the gang on the *Walter Scott*. Again he invents a substantial family for himself, pap and mam and sis and Uncle Hornbeck. Later, to save Jim from the slave hunters, Huck invents another full family—the smallpox-ridden pap, mam, and Mary Ann. Thus, just as in most of Twain's serious fiction, the invention of family relationships is a recurrent situation in *Huckleberry Finn*.

A further pattern is noticeable in these distortions. Huck's inventions show not only families, but families coming to death and

2. The raft passage from *Life on the Mississippi*, originally intended for *Huckleberry Finn*, shows the hero first pretending to be Charles William Allbright—a child supposedly murdered by his father. Caught in this lie, the boy calls himself Aleck James Hopkins and refers to his pap to justify the boy's presence on the raft. See Appendix A, *Adventures of Huckleberry Finn*, edited by Henry Nash Smith (Boston, 1958), pp. 257–258.

destruction. Among the Grangerfords Huck becomes George Jackson and recounts the decimation of a large family on a farm in Arkansaw. First Mary Ann runs off and marries, then Bill goes off to hunt for her, then Tom and Mort die, and finally pap expires. Lying to the two master-prevaricators, the Duke and the Dauphin, Huck invents another full family, this time in Pike County, Missouri. All his relations die except "me and Pa and my brother Ike,"[3] and the last two have recently drowned.

The pattern of Huck's lies is threefold. The lonely Huck, the boy who could not at first join Tom Sawyer's gang because he had no visible family to sign over as hostages, the youth whose only genuine family is an ignorant drunkard of a father, this boy in the first place invents large families for himself, then he brings them to shocking and untimely deaths. Thirdly, these lies are the result of a positive desire in Huck to protect Jim. They are, as it were, moral lies; the immoral lies—such as Huck's trick on Jim after the storm —have no family basis. Villains, like the Duke lie from self-interest, betray Jim, and seek to harm families.

After his pattern of lies is fully established, Huck arrives at last at Phelps Farm. Once again Huck finds himself a family. But there is an important difference in this sixth dissimulation. Huck does not invent this family. It already exists, and the lie is forced upon him by eager Aunt Sally. Yet Huck's becoming Tom Sawyer is a culmination of his dreams, of the subconscious desires that formed the motifs of his earlier inventions. "I went right along, not fixing up any particular plan, but just trusting to Providence to put the right words in my mouth when the time come; for I'd noticed that Providence always did put the right words in my mouth if I left it alone" (220). We see that there is a special quality about the Phelps family, as Huck's narrative stresses the providential aspect of his arrival in their midst. Here is a kindly providence taking care of the wanderer, giving him in the sojourn at Phelps Farm rest from the toil of his hectic adventures. To be sure, Huck's relief at his acceptance is an immature feeling. But we must not forget that Huck is still a boy, no matter how mature, self-reliant, and cynical he may appear in times of stress. The boy who can believe in a circus clown's antics can relish playing the role of Tom.

As Huck acts out his most elaborate deception, indeed, as he pretends to the limits of Tom's vivid imagination, Huck learns that there are times when he cannot tamper with the truth—even to help Jim. The true climax of Huck's moral development comes not when he learns to respect Jim, not when he learns that he can't pray a lie, but when he discovers that the essence of loyalty to the

3. Mark Twain, *The Adventures of Huckleberry Finn* (New York, 1956), p. 126. All subsequent references to this edition will appear in the text.

genuine familial affection displayed by Aunt Sally is to be true to his promise. Huck does not sneak out to search after Jim and Tom, despite the ease with which he could deceive Aunt Sally. "I wouldn't never do nothing to grieve her any more" (283). Huck has learned the nature of responsibility to a family. The Phelps Farm episode is long because it supplies the necessary time for Huck to use the family relationship to work out his attitudes towards truth and deception.

Huck's lies are only one indication that a substantial basis for the novel is the boy's search for a family. In his perceptive essay "Huck and Jim," Kenneth Lynn catches the importance of this theme in *Huckleberry Finn*. Although his indication that the novel is concerned with the entire problem of parenthood is accurate, Lynn seems to push his conclusion too far when he nominates Jim as the father for whom Huck has been searching. Yet the theme and structure of the novel are predicated on the need for family ties. For, as Lynn says, ". . . in Twain loneliness almost without exception takes the form of alienation from the family."[4] We have only to recall the numbers of childless couples and estranged children that fill the pages of the Twain canon to see the truth of the statement. Such a search for a family, of course, is a fundamental fictional theme. Twain was influenced not only by his own interests but also by a tradition of loss and discovery as old as the Homeric epics. American fiction, from Cooper to Stowe, concentrated on broken familial ties; indeed the American dream of success usually commenced with a boy leaving home and mother to make his own way and family in an alien world.

A glance at the position of Huck in the earlier *Tom Sawyer* indicates Huck's role in life. To be sure, he is free, and the boys envy his outcast condition. Huck's prototype, young Sam Clemens' friend Tom Blankenship, was also free: "He was the only really independent person—boy or man—in the community, and by consequence he was tranquilly and continuously happy and was envied by all the rest of us."[5] Clearly Twain draws from his memories of the Hannibal drunkard's son the sense of freedom reflected in the portrait of Huck Finn. But part of Huck's characterization, the loneliness, comes from another source, the author's own view of the darker aspects of life. Where Tom Sawyer can rejoice at his return from a supposed watery grave to the arms of his Aunt Polly, poor Huck Finn finds no one to greet him. When he first hears the word "welcome," "He could not recollect that the closing word had ever been applied to his case before."[6] *Tom Sawyer* ends on a note of

4. Kenneth S. Lynn, "Huck and Jim," *Yale Review* XLVIII, 422 (Spring 1958).
5. Charles Neider, ed., *The Autobiog-* *raphy of Mark Twain* (New York, 1959), p. 203.
6. Mark Twain, *Tom Sawyer* (London, 1956), p. 203.

temporary triumph. A grateful Widow Douglas takes in the home-less boy who had been accustomed to sleep in lofts and empty hogsheads. How real was this adoption? Was it the genuine Huck Finn who found a welcome in the Widow's genteel home or was it her romantic vision of the heroic youth who had saved her from Indian Joe's revenge and who had gained the respectability of $6000? The opening of Huck's own novel shows that he is still lack-ing a proper family.

Huck's attempt to join the gang after he has found a home with the Widow is met by Ben Rogers' retort: " 'Here's Huck Finn, he hain't got no family. What you going to do 'bout him?' " (8). They make an adjustment for Huck, but there is no doubt in the mind of the gang that his is a special case.

The diction and imagery, the references and subplots of the novel emphasize family. The orphan child Moses in the Bulrushers, Sollermun's lack of sympathy for children, the tragedy that strikes the Wilks' slaves when two sons are sold up river to Memphis and the mother down river to New Orleans—such familial relations make up the substance of *Huckleberry Finn*. Jim runs away rather than be sent down river away from his family. Huck strives to understand why a Negro could feel so strongly about his wife and children that he would threaten to steal them out of captivity. The main moments of pathos in the book come when Boggs' orphaned daughter weeps over her father's corpse and when Jim recounts his unintentional cruelty towards his deaf child. Huck's adventures on the shore, like his lies, follow a family pattern. The Grangerfords fight out old family feuds with the Shepherdsons. Faked heirs de-fraud the Wilks family, and Huck protects the orphans. The Duke and the Dauphin stress their descents from the ducal Bridgewaters and the regal Louis XVI. And, of course, Huck escapes from a cramped and over-civilized adoption (despite the widow's humanity, the harsh religiosity of Miss Watson rules the establishment) and a savage, murderous father. He is an orphan in truth by the time he and Jim start their journey, although only Jim knows that Pap is dead.

Each family Huck contacts is a little better than the previous one; still, all the possible family relationships fail for him. Miss Watson's moral rigidity gives way to Pap's moral laxness—and physical repression; the Grangerfords' warmth, respectability, and sentiment disappear in the bloody, destructive feud that wipes out the family; the Wilks girls are idealized and innocent, but Huck cannot find a suitable role in their midst. Finally, Huck meets the Phelps family. Here, at last, he has a role—as Tom, a blood-relative —and in a decent family. The Phelps are sentimental like the Grangerfords, but without their proud sense of honor. Aunt Sally and Uncle Silas are religious like Miss Watson, but without her strictness. The Phelps, to be sure, are not perfect: they are gullible, at times irascible, bigoted in their unthinking cruelty to Negroes. Yet there is no question but that the Phelps and their farm present one of the few favorable portraits of the family institution in Mark Twain's fiction.

Silas is "the innocentest, best old soul I ever see" (227), "a mighty nice old man" (255). Silas Phelps is patterned on Twain's uncle John Quarles. "I have never come across a better man,"[7] said Twain of Quarles. Twain was quite sure that he spent the happiest days of his boyhood on the Quarles farm; here was the good, free life as opposed to the strict household of Judge Clemens. "It was a heavenly place for a boy, that farm of my uncle John's."[8] What more inevitable climax for a novel of search for family than this recreation of the place Twain recalled in association with the lyric joy of his glorious childhood summers? To be sure, Huck spends one-fourth of his adventure at Phelps Farm. Rather than an artistic flaw, the farm is the proper objective correlative for the happy family of Huck's dreams. Here are the kindly, unworldly uncle, the sweet, honest aunt, the children and the dogs that represent what Huck has been searching for.

Note the prose rhythm in Huck's description of the farm:

"A rail fence round a two-acre yard; a stile made out of logs sawed off and upended in steps, like barrels of a different length, to climb over the fence with, and for the women to stand on when they are going to jump onto a horse; some sickly grass-patches in the big yard, but mostly it was bare and smooth, like an old hat with the nap rubbed of; big double log house for the white folks—hewed logs, with the chinks stopped up with mud or mortar, and these mud-stripes been whitewashed some time or another; round-log kitchen, with a big broad, open but roofed passage joining it to the house; log smokehouse back of the kitchen; three little log nigger cabins in a row t'other side of the smokehouse; one little hut all by itself away down against the back fence, and some out-buildings down a piece the other side; ash-hopper and big kettle to bile soap in by the little hut; bench by the kitchen door, with bucket of water and a gourd; hound asleep there in the sun; more hounds asleep round about; about three shade trees away off in a corner; some currant bushes and gooseberry bushes in one place by the fence . . ." (219)

This sentence, surely one of the longest Twain ever wrote, moves on with the flow of unleashed emotion, despite the objectivity and bareness of the description. Here Huck finds peace.

Providence brings him a family. "But if they was joyful, it warn't

7. Dixon Wecter, *Sam Clemens of Hannibal* (Boston, 1952), p. 29.   8. Neider, *The Autobiography*, p. 4.

nothing to what I was; for it was like being born again, I was so glad to find out who I was" (224). This statement, of course, is made in the negative context of Huck's relief at the face-saving discovery that he is supposed to be Tom. Nevertheless, the statement also has a positive meaning. Huck has been on a journey of freedom; he has learned to worship the river-god; he has committed himself to humanity in the person of Jim—and he has found a family. We need not insist that Twain's primary purpose in *Huckleberry Finn* was to find Huck a family. Yet we must note that the last chapters of the book emphasize heavily this theme that is extremely important to the entire novel.

Huck's response to his acceptance by the Phelps' is stated in deeply moving terms. He is indeed born again, as a boy into a family, after his struggles in the man's role of Jim's protector. Certainly, Huck becomes a boy again. After all, he *is* a boy. Twain's interpreters have assumed that Huck is becoming mature; thus the horseplay at Phelps Farm is a reversion. All picaresque novels, however, need not trace the development from innocence to maturity. Since the novel is the work of Mark Twain, who would scarcely place maturity over childhood in the scale of success, we are justified in considering as integral to the development of the book the aura of safety existing at the farm that enables Tom and Huck to play at releasing Jim from bondage.

As in his lies which are pleas for the sympathy owing to a child, at Phelps Farm Huck can rejoice in a boy's freedom from responsibility. The genuine goodness of Uncle Silas and Aunt Sally provides a feeling of security. There is a comfortable frame for the light irony that satirizes Tom's romantic notions. Indeed, this part of the plot fits the structure particularly closely; since Jim actually has been freed by Miss Watson's will, his "escape" is only the formal working-out of the act of freeing a slave. In addition, for the first time Huck acts positively to free Jim, actually stealing him from slavery instead of going along with a *fait accompli*. Thus Huck makes his most distinct commitment to the idea of freedom. Therefore, this ending helps to supply a logical climax to the themes of freedom and individual rights.

Although the farce is still at times forced and awkward, by attending to a reading of the book that sees Huck finding a family, we can understand why Twain concentrates much of his novel at Phelps Farm, why the mood reverts to happy farce, and why such a shift does not destroy the formal perfection of the novel.

One problem remains. Huck seems to repudiate the warmth of the Phelps Family at the close of the book when he plans to set out for the territory ahead of the others. Twain leaves the reader with a pleasing note of ambiguity. Huck can speak lightly of being civilized because he possesses the security that will enable him to escape and then return home—as a boy should, as Tom Sawyer could do in his book when he and Huck hid on Jackson's Island. Now Huck, too, having gained his family, can head "for howling adventures amongst the Injuns, over in the territory, for a couple of weeks or two" (293). In other words, this last phrase indicates that Huck wants to continue his youthful adventures—and then return after a few weeks. This passage, at least, which has long been taken as an indication of Huck's disgust with the Phelps' and civilization, is hardly that. After all, Tom and Jim are supposed to accompany Huck, and surely they will return to civilization.

Yet Huck ends his book with the words, "But I reckon I got to light out for the territory ahead of the rest, because Aunt Sally she's going to adopt me and civilize me, and I can't stand it. I been there before" (293). Again Twain's critics have been inclined to understand Huck's words as a denial of the workability of his relationship with the Phelps' since he evidently equates Aunt Sally with the Widow Douglas. Two points must be taken into consideration, however. While Huck's last remark may seem to find the Widow and Aunt Sally similar, the tone of the book, as revealed in the whole sense of nostalgia evoked by the loving care given to the description of the Phelps establishment, displays Aunt Sally in a far more motherly light. Then we must remember that here, at the very end of the book, Huck resumes his role as boy-author, in a chapter entitled "Nothing More to Write." Essentially Twain reminds us that Huck is now consciously posturing, taking the part of manly adventurer who is more inclined to the free ways of Pap than the civilizing ways of the Widow or Aunt Sally. Huck, it can be submitted, like his creator, is ambivalent. Huck's words as self-conscious author praise freedom from society. His actions as a boy reveal his desire for a home. In similar fashion, Twain was torn between the ideals of rough individualism and genteel respectability.

The theme of the search for security accompanies the more obvious themes of the novel. The boyish ideal of independence within the restraint of family love, the ideal that Mark Twain firmly subscribed to, is attained by Huck through his long stay at Phelps Farm. Huck's story, like Mark Twain's own, tells of the effort to remain a boy despite external conditions that force adulthood.

ALBERT E. STONE, JR.

Huckleberry Finn and the Modes of Escape†

* * *

Not only is *Adventures of Huckleberry Finn* a richer "boy's book" than those written by Twain's contemporaries, highbrow or low, it is also the climax and summation of Mark Twain's own career to 1885. Within the loose and accommodating framework of the picaresque tale he was able to incorporate the astringent social satire of his newspaper pieces, to extend his critique of a money-centered society back in time from the post-Civil War milieu of *The Gilded Age* to the prewar world of his own boyhood, and to carry a third boy through the maturing process of violent immersion in adult affairs. In his young hero Twain created a figure reminiscent of Thomas Jefferson Snodgrass, Jim Wolf, and, strangely enough, of Prince Edward of England. For Jim, Twain drew upon his earlier sketch of the kindly, superstitious Negro, Uncle Dan'l. From *Tom Sawyer* he drafted characters, the first and final movements of the plot of *Huckleberry Finn*, and the inspiration to look again at boyhood as one version of the American success story. Around the whole he wrapped a narrative technique he first discovered in the "Boy's Manuscript."††

Adventures of Huckleberry Finn is not, however, simply an abstract of Twain's career as a novelist. A good deal of its perennial and puzzling appeal may be explained by the author's personal life during the seven years of the book's gestation, by the various traditions of juvenile fiction available to him, and by comparison with earlier works of Twain. Nevertheless, an essential, elusive quality remains. Any honest assessment of "Huck Finn's Autobiography" must confront this mysterious element.

One way to formulate an answer to the enigma of the novel's hold upon the imagination is to accept and explore Lionel Trilling's statement of its genius. "One can read it at ten," Trilling writes, "and then annually ever after, and each year find that it is as fresh as the year before, that it has changed only in becoming somewhat larger."[27] The prime reason for this cumulative growth in

† Chapter 5 (pp. 153–58) of *The Innocent Eye: Childhood in Mark Twain's Imagination*, by Albert E. Stone, Jr. Copyright 1961 by Albert E. Stone, Jr., and the Mark Twain Company. Reprinted by permission of the publishers, Yale University Press.
†† A manuscript dated by DeVoto *ca.*

1870, in which Billy Rogers foreshadows the sentimental yearnings and romantic fantasticality of Tom Sawyer. Published in Bernard DeVoto, *Mark Twain at Work*, Cambridge, 1942 [Editors].
27. Trilling, p. 108. [In *The Liberal Imagination*, 1950 (Editors).]

appreciation is that Huck Finn's Autobiography seeks to satisfy, at the same moment that it incarnates, a deep-seated urge for freedom. In a comprehensive manner, it is consummately an "escape" story. "Huck is forever lighting out," one critic has observed, and in this respect Huck repeats the pattern of most universal books about childhood. Like *Treasure Island, Alice in Wonderland,* and *The Jungle Book,* it answers a perennial human wish to get away, to be totally free of restrictions. Huck Finn's prototype was Mark Twain's model for the free individual. "In *Huckleberry Finn* I have drawn Tom Blankenship exactly as he was," Twain remarks in his *Autobiography.* "He was ignorant, unwashed, insufficiently fed; but he had as good a heart as ever any boy had. His liberties were totally unrestricted. He was the only really independent person—boy or man—in the community . . ."[28] For many youthful readers this dimension of escape—Huck's freedom to run away from it all, from parents, starched collars, regular hours, and spelling books—is the source of their delight in the novel. Clearly, Twain intended this reaction.

But the adventure story for boys which he started writing burgeoned soon into escape literature of a different sort. What commences as flight from a Sunday School "sivilization" turns into a desperate retreat from society itself. The grim events of Huck's journey down the river of experience (Philip Young reminds us that he sees thirteen corpses) reinforce as they broaden this boy's grounds for secession. Each of Huck's symbolic deaths and rebirths—the fake murder in Pap's cabin, the endless aliases, including the ultimate one "Tom Sawyer"—separates him from a world which he and Jim try desperately and in vain not to accept. Lighting out for the "Territory" is Huck's despairing response to loss of freedom in this area, just as "sliding out and sleeping in the woods" answers his anarchic needs at a simpler level.

Still another reading of *Huckleberry Finn* as an escape story will occur to many adult readers, as it has to Philip Young. Right from the early moment where Huck looks down on the sleeping village of St. Petersburg, his imagination seeking out forms of sadness, suffering, and death in the few blinking lights still burning below, Twain's novel records the history of a boy morbidly fascinated by death. "I heard an owl, away off, who-whooing about somebody that was dead, and a whippowill and a dog crying about somebody that was going to die," Huck reports; "and the wind was trying to whisper something to me, and I couldn't make out what it was, and so it made the cold shivers run over me." This theme echoes again and again through Huck's story, sounding with unmistakable in-

28. *Mark Twain's Autobiography* (New York and London, Harper and Brothers, 1924), 2, 174.

sistence at the moment Huck climbs over the stile at Uncle Silas' farm.

> "When I got there it was all still and Sunday-like, and hot and sunshiny—the hands was gone to the fields; and there was them kind of faint dronings of bugs and flies in the air that makes it seem so lonesome and like everybody's dead and gone; and if a breeze fans along and quivers the leaves, it makes you feel mournful, because you feel like its spirits whispering—spirits that's been dead ever so many years—and you always think they're talking about *you*. As a general thing it makes a body wish *he* was dead, too, and done with it all . . .
>
> "I went around and clumb over the back stile by the ash-hopper, and started for the kitchen. When I got a little ways, I heard the dim hum of a spinning-wheel wailing along up and sinking along down again; and then I knowed for certain I wished I was dead— for that *is* the lonesomest sound in the whole world."

In *Tom Sawyer* this melancholy note of eerie mystery was introduced, as in the graveyard scene, simply for authentic superstitious atmosphere. So, too, earlier, in *The Gilded Age*. Here, however, Huck's sensitivity to death and the possibility of dying is of a different order of intensity. One may hesitate to accept Young's explanation of Huck's raft-borne journey down the smooth, silent river as the metaphor of a death-wish. Still, one source of the novel's imaginative vitality is the tension that develops between a vital, discerning, humorous boy and the progressive fixation of that boy's healthy mind upon ghosts, death, and the pleasures of dying. Conceivably, if not the river then the "Territory" is Mark Twain's unconscious synonym for death.

If so, this is further proof that the moment of Huck's arrival at Uncle Silas' stile is the climax and turning point of the novel. Not only does it depict the moment of greatest tension between the living boy and his preoccupation with symbols of death, but it is also the point of Huck's maximum moral awareness. His "yaller dog" conscience has been conquered only a page or two earlier; he is prepared to "go to hell" for Jim. Instead, he is ignominiously reborn as "Tom Sawyer" and submits to the Evasion, thereby surrendering the moral maturity so painfully picked up on the river. Having tried to escape from Miss Watson and from an avaricious, slave-holding society, Huck now tries to escape from his own moral imagination. This reversion to moral naïveté is another of the levels on which *Huckleberry Finn* explores ambiguously the linked themes of freedom and escape.

The key to Huck Finn's relapse into immaturity is Tom Sawyer, for it is to oblige Tom that Huck goes along with the elaborate and degrading stunt of "freeing" Jim. But, as Leo Marx has pointed out, the ethic under which Huck and Jim have lived on the raft makes inevitable this capitulation. When the Duke and Dauphin settle their first quarrel on board the raft, Huck is delighted, "because it would 'a' been a miserable business to have any unfriendliness on the raft; for what you want, above all things, on a raft, is for everybody to be satisfied, and feel right and kind towards the others." This is Huck's creed of social harmony, the fruit of his initiation, and the most sweeping generalization about life he ever comes to. "I hadn't no objections," he says of the con-men masquerading as nobility, " 'long as it would keep peace in the family . . . If I never learnt nothing else out of pap, I learnt that the best way to get along with his kind of people is to let them have their own way." Huck Finn lives by this ethic. It governs his friendships, his lies, his aliases, indeed, all his personal relationships. It is, in fact, at the heart of his appeal as a character.

Where Huck fails is in adapting his creed to the changing conditions of his environment. He applies the ethics of tolerance and appeasement not only to strangers, frauds, and deadbeats but to his friend Tom Sawyer, with whom he cannot be for a moment without assuming the subordinate position. Assenting good-humoredly to the Evasion, with all that it implies about Jim as a human being, seems little different to Huck than letting the two rascals on the raft call themselves Duke and Dauphin. Evidently he does not recognize this involves accepting responsibility for Tom's romantic game of casual cruelty. Though, shortly before, Huck was willing "to go to hell" for Jim's sake, now he cannot see that his moral duty is telling Tom to go to the same place. Hence the appropriateness of Huck's final alias. He has achieved the ultimate ironic escape—out of his own social and moral identity into the protective coloration of "sivilization's" fair-haired boy. "Evasion" is the right name for Huck's final adventure.

These ten chapters of "Huck Finn's Autobiography" are essential to the meaning of Mark Twain's second novel of boyhood. Without the Evasion, Huck's would be quite a different story. With it, his initiation, like Tom Sawyer's, has proved temporary and incomplete. Having Huck relinquish moral acuity under such disenchanting circumstances may seem, as it has to many, a fatal flaw in the tone and structure of Twain's novel. It might, moreover, argue moral blindness on the author's part, the half-hearted escape from a genteel tradition of optimism and happy endings. As the ironic climax to a narrative of adventure and escape, the Evasion pleases one part of a wide audience while it suggests to other, more perceptive, readers what Twain wanted also to make clear: Huck Finn is no hero.

Furthermore, from the perspective of childhood realistically perceived, the conclusion of *Adventures of Huckleberry Finn* has the merit of portraying Huck Finn as immature boys actually were for Twain—kind-hearted and yet given to cruel practical jokes, anarchic yet conditioned to their moral decisions by social experience, free from the trammels of adult life but never really able to light out for the Territory, victors perhaps in all the small skirmishes with grown-ups but defeated in the larger battle, surrendering the moment of moral insight so painfully achieved. Tom Blankenship may have seemed, in his friend's fond recollection, "the only really independent person—boy or man—in the community," but reborn under the fictional alias of Huckleberry Finn, Mark Twain's boy could not escape his natural or his social setting—nor, finally, the limitations of his private moral world. For Huck's innocent eye perceives more than his mind can fully comprehend or his moral sense can retain.

Bibliography

SAMUEL LANGHORNE CLEMENS: AUTOBIOGRAPHICAL COMMENT AND CORRESPONDENCE

Mark Twain's Autobiography, ed. Albert Bigelow Paine, 2 vols., New York, **1924**.
The Autobiography of Mark Twain, ed. Charles Neider, New York, 1959.
Mark Twain in Eruption, ed. Bernard DeVoto, New York, 1940.
Mark Twain's Letters, ar. Albert Bigelow Paine, 2 vols., New York, 1917.
Mark Twain's Notebook, ed. Albert Bigelow Paine, New York, 1935.
Love Letters of Mark Twain, ed. Dixon Wecter, New York, 1946.

SAMUEL LANGHORNE CLEMENS: BIOGRAPHY AND CRITICISM

Adams, Richard P. "Romanticism and the American Renaissance," *American Literature*, XXIII (January, 1952), 419.
Andrews, Kenneth R. *Nook Farm*, Cambridge, 1950.
Asselineau, Roger. *The Literary Reputation of Mark Twain from 1910 to 1950*, Paris, 1954.
Bellamy, Gladys. *Mark Twain as a Literary Artist*, Norman, 1950.
Blair, Walter. *Native American Humor, 1800–1900*, New York, 1937.
Branch, Edgar M. *Literary Apprenticeship of Mark Twain*, Urbana, 1950.
Brashear, Minnie M. *Mark Twain, Son of Missouri*, Chapel Hill, 1934.
Brooks, Van Wyck. *The Ordeal of Mark Twain*, New York, 1920, rev. 1947.
Cummings, Sherwood. "Mark Twain's Social Darwinism," *Huntington Library Quarterly*, XX (February, 1957), 163.
———. "Science and Mark Twain's Theory of Fiction," *Philological Quarterly*, XXXVII (January, 1958), 26.
DeVoto, Bernard. *Mark Twain At Work*, Cambridge, 1942.
———. *Mark Twain's America*, Boston, 1932.
Dreiser, Theodore. "Mark the Double Twain," *English Journal*, XXIV (October, 1935), 615.
Ferguson, DeLancey. *Mark Twain: Man and Legend*, Indianapolis, 1943.
Foner, Philip S. *Mark Twain: Social Critic*, New York, 1958.
Gerber, John C. "The Relation between Point of View and Style in the Works of Mark Twain," *English Institute Essays*, 1958, p. 142.
Hoffman, Daniel G. *Form and Fable in American Fiction*, New York, 1961 (Pt. IV: "Mark Twain").
Howells, William D. *My Mark Twain*, New York, 1910.
Krause, S. L. "Twain's Method and Theory of Composition," *Modern Philology*, LVI (February, 1959), 167.
Lang, Andrew. "The Art of Mark Twain," *Illustrated News of the World*, XCVIII (February 14, 1891), 222 (reprinted in *Mark Twain; Selected Criticism*, ed. Arthur L. Scott, Dallas, 1955).
Leary, Lewis. *Mark Twain*, Pamphlets on American Writers, No. 5, University of Minnesota, 1960.
Lynn, Kenneth. *Mark Twain and Southwestern Humor*, Boston, 1960.
Paine, Albert B. *Mark Twain, A Biography*, 4 vols. in 2, New York, 1935.
Salomon, Roger B. *Twain and the Image of History*, New Haven, 1961.
Scott, Arthur L. *Mark Twain: Selected Criticism*, Dallas, 1955.
Smith, Henry Nash, ed. *Mark Twain of "The Enterprise": Newspaper Articles and Other Documents, 1862–1864*, Berkeley, 1957.
Stone, Albert E., Jr. *The Innocent Eye: Childhood in Mark Twain's Imagination*, New Haven, 1961.
Stovall, Floyd, ed. *Eight American Authors: A Review of Research and Criticism*, New York, 1956.
Twichell, Joseph H. "Mark Twain," *Harper's Magazine*, XCII (May, 1896), 817.
Wagenknecht, Edward. *Mark Twain: The Man and His Work*, New Haven, 1935.

Webster, Samuel C. *Mark Twain, Business Man,* Boston, 1946.
Wecter, Dixon. *Sam Clemens of Hannibal,* Boston, 1952.

HUCKLEBERRY FINN: CRITICISM

Adams, Richard P. "The Unity and Coherence of Huckleberry Finn," *Tulane Studies in English,* VI (1956), 87.
Auden, W. H. "Huck and Oliver," *Listener,* L (October 1, 1953), 540.
Baldanza, Frank. "The Structure of Huckleberry Finn," *American Literature* XXVII (November, 1955), 347.
Beck, Warren. "Huck Finn at Phelps Farm—An Essay in Defense of the Form of Mark Twain's Novel," *Archives des Lettres Modernes,* Nos. 13–15 (June–September, 1958).
Blair, Walter. *Mark Twain and Huck Finn,* Berkeley, 1960.
———. "The French Revolution and Huckleberry Finn," *Modern Philology,* LV (August, 1957), 21.
———. "Why Huck and Jim Went Downstream," *College English,* XVIII (November, 1956), 106.
Blessingame, W. "The Use of the Lie in *Huckleberry Finn* as a Technical Device," *Mark Twain Quarterly,* IX (Winter, 1953), 11.
Branch, Edgar M. "Mark Twain and J. D. Salinger: A Study in Literary Continuity," *American Quarterly,* IX (Summer, 1957), 144.
———. "The Two Provinces: Thematic Form in *Huckleberry Finn,*" *College English,* XI (January, 1950), 188.
Brownell, Frances V. "The Role of Jim in *Huckleberry Finn,*" *Studies in English,* I (1955), 74.
Budd, Louis J. "The Southward Currents under Huck Finn's Raft," *Mississippi Valley Historical Review,* LXVI (September, 1959), 222.
Coxe, James M. "Remarks on the Sad Initiation of Huckleberry Finn," *Sewanee Review,* LXII (Summer, 1954), 389.
Eliot, T. S. "Introduction," *The Adventures of Huckleberry Finn,* London, 1950.
Ferguson, DeLancey. "Huck Finn Aborning," *Colophon,* n.s. III (Spring, 1938), 171.
Fiedler, Leslie. "Come Back to the Raft Ag'in, Huck, Honey," *An End to Innocence,* Boston, 1955.
Frantz, Ray W., Jr. "The Role of Folklore in *Huckleberry Finn,*" *American Literature,* XXVIII (November, 1956), 314.
Gargano, James W. "Disguises in Huckleberry Finn," *University of Kansas City Review,* XXVI (March, 1960), 175.
Gerstenberger, Donna. "Huckleberry Finn and the World's Illusions," *Western Humanities Review,* XIV (Autumn, 1960), 401.
Gibb, Carson. "The Best Authorities," *College English,* XXII (December, 1960), 178.
Gordon, Edward J. "What's Happened to Humor?" *English Journal,* XLVII (March, 1958), 127.
Gullason, T. A. "The 'Fatal' Ending of Huckleberry Finn," *American Literature,* XXIX (March, 1957), 86.
Hoffman, Daniel G. "Jim's Magic: Black or White?" *American Literature,* XXXII (March, 1960), 47.
Hunting, Robert. "Mark Twain's Arkansaw Yahoos," *Modern Language Notes,* LXXIII (April, 1958), 264.
Kaplan, Charles. "Holden and Huck: The Odysseys of Youth," *College English,* XVIII (November, 1956), 76.
Krutch, Joseph W. "Speaking of Books," New York *Times Book Review,* May 23, 1954.
Lane, Lauriat, Jr. "Why Huckleberry Finn Is a Great World Novel," *College English,* XVII (October, 1955), 1.
Lynn, Kenneth S. "Huck and Jim," *Yale Review,* XLVII (Spring, 1958), 421.
Marx, Leo. "Mr. Eliot, Mr. Trilling, and Huckleberry Finn," *American Scholar,* XXII (Autumn, 1953), 423.
———. "The Pilot and the Passenger: Landscape Conventions and the Style of Huckleberry Finn," *American Literature,* XXVIII (May, 1956), 129.
Moore, O. H. "Mark Twain and Don Quixote," *PMLA,* XXXVII (June, 1922), 324.
Moses, W. R. "The Pattern of Evil in Adventures of Huckleberry Finn," *Georgia Review,* XIII (Summer, 1959), 161.
O'Connor, William V. "Why Huckleberry Finn Is Not the Great American Novel," *College English,* XVII (October, 1955), 6.

Ornstein, Robert. "The Ending of Huckleberry Finn," *Modern Language Notes,* LXXIV (December, 1959), 698.

Podhoretz, Norman. "The Literary Adventures of Huck Finn," New York *Times Book Review,* December 6, 1959.

Pritchett, V. S. "Books in General (Huckleberry Finn and the Cruelty of American Humor)" *New Statesman and Nation,* XXII (August 2, 1941), 113.

Remes, Carol. "The Heart of Huckleberry Finn," *Masses and Mainstream,* VIII (November, 1955), 8.

Robinson, E. Arthur. "The Two 'Voices' in Huckleberry Finn," *Modern Language Notes,* LXXV (March, 1960), 204.

Rubenstein, Gilbert M. "The Moral Structure of Huckleberry Finn," *College English,* XVIII (November, 1956), 72.

Schwartz, Edward. *"Huckleberry Finn:* The Inward Thoughts of a Generation," *Mark Twain Quarterly,* IX (Winter, 1952), 11.

Smith, Henry Nash. "Mark Twain's Images of Hannibal," *University of Texas Studies in English,* XXXVI (1958), 3.

Solomon, Eric. *"Huckleberry Finn* Once More," *College English,* XXII (December, 1960), 172.

Stallman, R. W. "Huck Finn Again," *College English,* XVIII (May, 1957), 425.

Stone, Albert E., Jr. "Huckleberry Finn and the Modes of Escape," *The Innocent Eye: Childhood in Mark Twain's Imagination,* New Haven, 1961.

Trilling, Lionel. "Introduction," *The Adventures of Huckleberry Finn,* New York, 1948

Wasiolek, Edward. "The Structure of Make-Believe: *Huckleberry Finn,*" *University of Kansas City Review,* XXIV (December, 1957), 97.

Wells, Arvin R. "Huck Finn and Holden Caulfield: The Situation of the Hero," *Ohio University Review,* II (1960), 31.

Yates, Norris W. "The 'Counter-Conversion' of Huckleberry Finn," *American Literature,* XXXII (March, 1960), 1.